BOOKS BY THOMAS MERTON

Entering the Silence

THE JOURNALS OF THOMAS MERTON / Volume 2: 1941-1952 / Patrick Hart, O.C.S.O., General Editor

Augustine's problems
not have a war
of Bk. VII is Magn
d. Everything that
existence. Corruptio
have gone to the Words
Day was New Haven
ands came from N.H
book was pasted
tile. The glue on the
in the furnistiles

Thomas Merton

Entering the Silence

Becoming a Monk & Writer

EDITED BY JONATHAN MONTALDO

HarperSanFrancisco
An Imprint of HarperCollins*Publishers*

Book design by David Bullen

FIRST HARPERCOLLINS PAPERBACK EDITION PUBLISHED IN 1997

HarperCollins Web Site: http://www.harpercollins.com
HarperCollins®, 🔲®, and HarperSanFrancisco™ are trademarks
of HarperCollins Publishers Inc.

Library of Congress Cataloging-in-Publication Data
Merton, Thomas, 1915–1968.
    Entering the silence : becoming a monk & writer / Thomas Merton ;
  edited by Jonathan Montaldo.
    (The journals of Thomas Merton ; v. 2)
    "1941–1952."
    Includes bibliographical references and index.
    ISBN 0–06–065476–7 (cloth)
    ISBN 0–06–065477–5 (pbk.)
    1. Merton, Thomas, 1915–1968—Diaries. 2. Trappists—United
States—Diaries. I. Montaldo, Jonathan. II. Title. III. Series:
Merton, Thomas, 1915–1968. Journals of Thomas Merton ; v. 2.
BX4705.M542A3   1995
271'.12502—dc20   95-30457

97 98 99 00 RRD(H) 10 9 8 7 6 5 4 3 2 1

Let me keep silence in this world, except in so far as God wills and in the way He wills it. Let me at least disappear into the writing I do. It should mean nothing special to me, nor harm my recollection. The work could be a prayer. . . .

December 14, 1946

Contents

Acknowledgments

Patrick Hart, monk of Gethsemani and General Editor of *The Journals of Thomas Merton*, has long distinguished himself as an editor of important Merton literature. For over thirty years and counting, as Gethsemani's official Merton liaison to "the world," Brother Patrick has served a host of scholars, artists, enthusiasts, and just plain folks. Hart's magnanimity, his joy, and his genuine enthusiasm for the new task and the latest person set before him are ample testaments to a monastic life well lived. My own great debts to Patrick Hart are unrepayable.

I am likewise indebted to the generosity of Robert E. Daggy of the Thomas Merton Center at Bellarmine College; Patrick T. Lawlor and the staff of the Butler Rare Book and Manuscript Library at Columbia University; Brother Joshua Brands at the Abbey of Gethsemani; and the staff of my home library at St. Charles Borromeo Seminary in Philadelphia. Dom M. Laurence Bourget, the archivist at Saint Joseph's Abbey, Spencer, is a Cistercian living treasure. The importance of Dom Laurence's critical reading of the text with an eye to Cistercian personalities, history, and practice cannot be exaggerated.

Dr. Erasmo Leiva-Merikakis graciously transcribed and translated the non-scriptural, foreign language journal entries. Dr. Robert Urekew translated and Chrysogonous Waddell of Gethsemani reviewed the "incunabula in the vault" material. Kati Moore's computer expertise aided the entire project. My partner, Robert Jerome Moore, III, patiently oversaw the four-year transformation of my business office into "the Merton Reading Room." For over twenty years and counting, Robert Moore has never ceased being his brother's keeper.

My own participation in this project has been an unmitigated joy. Thus gladly, with bows of reverence for my collaborators named above, and with love to my family and friends whose names etch my heart, I dedicate my happy work to Cistercians everywhere, past, present, and yet to come.

The Scribe's Introduction

Like a high-rise building being suddenly removed, exposing the multitude of submerged pilings shoring up its weight, the publishing of Thomas Merton's extant, private journals will finally reveal the hidden foundations that undergird the poetry and prose of one of the most significant American Roman Catholics of the twentieth century.

My personal fantasy is that Thomas Merton would not have stipulated in his will an interval of twenty-five years between his death and the publication of his private journals. All seven volumes would have been published shortly after his accidental electrocution on December 10, 1968, in Bangkok, Thailand. Merton's journals would have been accessible – the fantasy continues illogically – before the first memoir by friends who knew him "best" and "when," before the first scholar's biography, the first doctoral dissertation, before the first interpretive incarnation of Merton's visage in bronze, oils, and woven cloth. With his journals having come first, readers would have had access to important primary data *in context* upon which to fashion a solid image of Thomas Merton's message and its meaning. Heart might have spoken more directly to heart.

Some readers of this second volume might well be acquainted with Thomas Merton only by having read the first volume of Merton's journals, *Run to the Mountain*, edited by Patrick Hart. New readers might well be the luckier ones. It *is* a fantasy to hope that those who have been reading Thomas Merton for over fifty years, who have studied the enormous and important secondary literature appearing since his death, could innocently approach these journals with fresh eyes. The good news, even for the red-eyed, is that each of these seven volumes brings forth its treasure of nuance and surprise. Each volume will send not a few back to their cabinets, dusting off their portfolios on Thomas Merton, reexamining the partial categories under which they have filed him.

Thomas Merton was a monk, a gifted teacher, facile in many languages, an intellectual, above all a poet and an artist whose best medium was the written word. Merton's gift was the *immediacy* of his language, his willingness to expose his "I" and to address a "you," his enthusiasm for and his engagement with the person or idea set before him. Thomas Merton never hid himself behind a wall of self-conscious scholarship and academic bric-a-brac. Merton's personal enthusiasm for a wide range of subjects and his aiming for the widest intended audience are principal reasons for the varied chorus of persons who have become and are still becoming his readers.

Thomas Merton's growing influence and the quiet expansion of his audience is phenomenal. Burrowing himself into a most inhospitable vocation for a writer – American Trappist monk – and grounding his cosmopolitan self in a most narrow spot – rural Kentucky – Thomas Merton against odds took up a heart-at-full-throttle conversation with the world. Nearly three decades after his death, most of Merton's books remain in print. His best writing transcends narrow identification with a period. Merton the man is becoming an icon with whom many identify and from whom many find sustenance for their journeys no matter the road – concrete, dirt, or yellow brick – they travel.

These journals conserve both spontaneous and considered reflections. More than diaries of events, more than notes or meditations on his omnivorous reading, Thomas Merton's journals incarnate his probe for a God who could be experienced day by day, wave by wave. Merton believed God's salt infused the sea Merton needed to swim in moment to moment. For Thomas Merton, transcribing his continuous desire to be submerged in God was one way of experiencing God. By immersing himself in an ocean of his own words, Merton waited for the Word of words to surface from their depths. Word after word, line after line, by the continuous spiritual discipline of writing, Thomas Merton made himself God's bait.

This second volume of Thomas Merton's journals convenes three separate journals for the period December 12, 1941, to July 5, 1952: the novitiate journal fragment, a journal-memoir of Dom Frederic Dunne, and the long and important journal Merton initially entitled "The Whale and the Ivy."

The Novitiate Journal, December 1941–April 1942.

On December 10, 1941, after a long journey by train and bus from Saint Bonaventure College in Olean, New York, where he had been teaching for a year and a half, Thomas Merton arrived at the Abbey of Gethsemani. He was formally accepted as a postulant on St. Lucy's Day, December 13.

Merton began a new journal almost immediately by writing a new poem, a farewell to his closest friends from Columbia University – Seymour Freedgood, Bob Gibney, Robert Lax, and Ed Rice. The length and depth of Merton's earliest monastic journal will never be known. On a small card he sent years later to Thérèse Lentfoehr, a poet and friend by correspondence and the first unofficial curator of his manuscripts, Merton wrote: "I found these old copies of poems & some fragments of a novitiate journal long since torn up & so I send them to you, assuming you might be interested." A remnant of fourteen handwritten pages is all that's left of Merton's earliest monastic journal.

A Journal-Memoir: Dom Frederic Dunne, October 1946–August 1948.

As he would hundreds of others, Frederic Arthur Dunne, Gethsemani's first American-born abbot, received Thomas Merton into the monastic life with the injunction that everything must now be surrendered for God Alone. But it was Dunne who suggested – perhaps even ordered – that Merton recommence his literary career so as to publicize and promote Gethsemani's "Americanization" in tandem with another writer at Gethsemani, the ex-Jesuit Raymond Flanagan. Dom Frederic fathered Merton's dual vocations as monk and writer.

In Raymond Flanagan's memoir of Frederic Dunne, *The Less Traveled Road* (1953), Flanagan exposes the temporal and spiritual ecology at Gethsemani under Dunne, that first climate which would influence Thomas Merton's perceptions of his monastic vocation for the rest of his life. When Flanagan died in 1990, Gethsemani's archivist found among his personal effects a notebook with dated entries: Merton's handwritten reflections on his first abbot. Merton had given this journal to Flanagan at the news that Flanagan planned a memoir: "This stuff on Dom Frederic may come in handy if you can use it – and if you can decipher it." As the young monk approves his abbot's "strictest of the strict" interpretation of Trappist regulations at Gethsemani, as the spiritual son basks in his abbot's approval of early writing projects, Merton reveals much more than Dunne and Dunne's Gethsemani as he filters both through his own sensibilities to the written page.

The Whale and the Ivy, December 1946–July 1952.

On October 21, 1946, Merton shipped the manuscript of his autobiography, *The Seven Storey Mountain*, to his literary agent, Naomi Burton. Burton in turn offered the manuscript to Robert Giroux, who had known Merton at Columbia, and who was now an editor at Harcourt, Brace. Giroux quickly accepted Merton's manuscript for publication in a telegram dated December 29, 1946.

The Seven Storey Mountain was Merton's retrospective on his pre-Gethsemani years, a funneling of his pre-Gethsemani journals into a story that climaxed with his religious conversion and the radical continuance of that conversion by his entering the monastery. This retrospective completed, Merton began writing a new journal on December 10, 1946, timed to mark the fifth anniversary of his arrival at Gethsemani's gate. Nothing in the journal establishes that Merton began writing this new journal with a view to eventual publication. Not until a letter to Naomi Burton dated January 14, 1950, does Merton reveal he is typing up his journal for Robert Giroux, which he had tentatively entitled *The Whale and the Ivy*.

Harcourt, Brace published less than half of this journal from 1946 to 1952 as *The Sign of Jonas* (1953), with new commentaries by Merton to introduce each section. The remainder of *The Whale and the Ivy* was never published. The decision as to what would remain unpublished was not essentially Robert Giroux's, nor of the manuscript's monastic censors, who had objected to the very idea of a living Trappist publishing his journal. The gross editorial cuts were Merton's alone. Some sections of this journal he dropped for space considerations, but other omitted passages intimately reveal Merton's servitude to his conflicting desires to be both a good monk and a good writer. He stifled his most intense journalized debates focused on his temptation to leave Gethsemani for other communities that might offer him greater solitude. He did not expose his most personal prayers, especially to Mary, the Mother of God, and an important vow he had made to her.

Merton dedicated *The Sign of Jonas* to *Beatissimae Virgini Mariae Dolorosae*, the Most Blessed Sorrowful Virgin Mary. The experiences that led him to this particular dedication of his first published journals; the depth of Merton's early and real love for solitude; his unfeigned anguishes at finding himself a bad monk (in his own eyes) and a famous writer; and the intimate archaeological digs into his own personality, the findings of which would influence his choices for the remainder of his life; these and other matters of weight will become more clear with this publication of his complete journal, exactly as he wrote it.

The guiding principle of the editorial interventions in these three journals is minimalism. Each emphasis, that is, italics; each ellipsis, that is, . . . ; and each parenthesis in the text is Merton's. In translating and citing scriptural passages, I have used the Rheims-Douay version. In these early journals, Merton used Rheims-Douay when quoting sacred scripture in English. I have appended to the text a daily schedule at Gethsemani during the 1940s and a brief Glossary of Monastic Terms. The names of individual monks are undisguised.

Before I release you to the voice for which you have come, allow me one word of advice. As you can, Reader, doubt everything you believe you already know about Thomas Merton and entrust yourself to his journals with an open heart. As Merton discloses and withdraws himself, as he masters and unmasters his world, as he names and renames himself, remain patiently with the paradoxes and the contradictions, the search for simplicity becoming more and more complex as Merton's spiritual journey unfolds. Artist that he was, though Thomas Merton seems to be speaking only to and for himself, you will soon find yourself embedded in his web of mirrors. The eyes smiling back at you, as you read these journals, will naturally be Thomas Merton's, but often those eyes fathoming your eyes will be your very own.

PART I

The Novitiate Journal

December 1941–April 1942

POEM FOR MY FRIENDS, DEC 12–13

This holy house of God,
(Nazareth, where Christ lived as a boy)
These sheds & cloisters,
The very stones & beams are all befriended
By cleaner sun, by rarer birds, by humbler flowers.

Lost in the tigers' & the lions' wilderness,
More than we fear, we love these holy stones,
These thorns, the phoenix's sweet & spikey tree.

More than we fear, we love the holy desert
Where separate strangers, hid in their disguise,
Have come to meet by night the quiet Christ.

We who have some time wandered in the crowded ruins,
(Farewell, you woebegone, sad towns)
We who have wandered like (the ones I hear) the moaning
        trains,
(Begone, sad towns!)
We'll live it over for you here.

Here are your ruins all rebuilt as fast as you destroyed them
In your unlucky wisdom!
Here in the Holy House of God
And on the Holy Hill
Fields are the friends of plenteous heaven,
While falling starlight feeds, as bright as manna,
All our rough earth with wakeful grace.

And look, the ruins have become Jerusalems,
And the sick cities re-arise like shining Zions.
Jerusalems! These walls & roofs,

These flowers & fragrant sheds!
Our desert's wooden door,
The arches, & the windows, & the tower!

December 18, 1941

Not one word is lost, not one action is lost, not one prayer is lost, not one mis-sung note in choir is lost.

Nothing is lost.

What in the world would be wasted is here all God's, all for love.

I shiver in the night (not now that I have the postulants' white, wool habit) [but] for love – and I never hated less the world, scorned it less or understood it better.

Because nothing is lost – (and therefore everything is in proportion) – every act is seen in its context, and everything in the monastery is significant.

Because everything here is in a harmonious and *totally* significant context (every face is turned to God – every gesture and movement is His). Thus, everything in the world outside is also significant, when brought into relation with this!

How long we wait, with minds as quiet as time,
Like sentries on a tower!
How long we watch, by night, like the astronomers!

O Earth! O Earth! When will we hear you sing,
Arising from our grassy hills?
And say: "The dark is gone, and Day
Laughs like a bridegroom in His tent, the lovely sun!
His tent the sun! His tent the smiling sky!"

How long we wait, with minds as dim as ponds,
While stars swim slowly homeward in the waters of our
west?
O Earth! When will we hear you sing?

How long we listened to your silence in our vineyards,
And heard no bird stir in the rising barley.
The stars go home behind the shaggy trees:
Our minds are grey as rivers.

O Earth, when will you wake in the green wheat,
And all our oaks and Trappist cedars sing:

"Bright land! Lift up your leafy gates!
You Abbey steeple, sing with bells,
For look, our Sun rejoices like a dancer
On the rim of our hills!"

In the blue west, the moon is uttered like the word
"Farewell."

JMJT [Jesus, Mary, Joseph, Thérèse]
Feast of the Epiphany [January 6], 1942

January 9, 1942

How will I ever do this?

Not by any power of my own, but by two things (God may be soon to fill me with such love that my presence in the world will be not my presence but His presence, and I may be forgotten, and all around in the world, evil give place to good): these two things are prayer and penance.

"Child! First love Me with all your desire, and cast out all other loves – for your body, for your name, for your work, for your health, for your own consolation, *for your own idea of Me* – sacrifice everything. Love my will."

"O Lord! How joyful and happy must they be who, when they come to consider their own selves, find in themselves nothing remarkable whatever. Not only do they attract no attention outside themselves, but now they no longer have any desires or selfish interests to attract their own attention. They remark no virtues, they are saddened by no huge sins, they see only their own unremarkable weakness and nothingness, but a nothingness which is filled obscurely, not with themselves but with your love, O God! They are the poor in spirit, who possess within themselves the kingdom of heaven because they are no longer remarkable even to themselves, but in them shines God's light, and they themselves and all who see it glorify you, O God!   JMJT

CANA

"This beginning of miracles did Jesus in Cana of Galilee"

Once when our eyes were clean as noon, our rooms
Filled with the joys of Cana's feast:
For Jesus came, and His disciples, & His mother,
And, after them, the singers
And the men with violins.

Once when our minds were Galilees,
And clear as skies our faces,
Our simple rooms were charmed with sun!

Our thoughts went in and out in whiter coats than God's
      disciples',
In Cana's crowded doors, at Cana's tables.

Nor did we seem to fear the wine would fail:
For, ready in a row to fill with water and a miracle,
We saw our earthen vessels empty.
What wine those humble waterjars foretell!

Wine for the ones who, bended to the dirty earth,
Have feared, since lovely Eden, the sun's fire,
Yet hardly mumble, in their dusty mouths, a prayer.

Wine for old Adam, digging in the briars.

JMJT

January 25, 1942. Conversion of St. Paul
Ne magnitudo revelationum extollat me, datus est mihi stimulus carnis meae, *angelus satanae, qui me colaphizet. Propter quod ter Dominum rogavi ut discederet a me, et dixit mihi Dominus: Sufficit tibi, Paule, gratia mea!* [And lest the greatness of the revelations should puff me up, *there was given me a sting of my flesh,* an angel of Satan, to buffet me. For which thing I thrice besought the Lord, that it might depart from me: And he said to me: My grace is sufficient for thee, Paul (2 Corinthians 12:7–9, Merton adds "Paul")!]

ST. PAUL   ACTS IX 1–22

When I was Saul, and walked among the blazing rocks,
My road was quiet as a trap.
I feared what Word would split high noon with light;
And lock my sight, and drive me mad:

And thus I saw the Voice that struck me dead!

Tie up my life and wind me in my sheets of fear
And lay my reason in a three days' sepulchre,
'Till Jesus shows me Easter in a dream!

When I was Saul, and sat among the cloaks,
My eyes were stones. I saw no sight of heaven
Open to take the spirit of the twisting Stephen.
When I was Saul, and sat among the rocks,
I locked my eyes, my mind I made a tomb,
Sealed with what boulders rolled across my reason!

O Jesus, show me Easter in a dream!
O Cross Damascus, where poor Ananias in some other room,
(Who knows my locks, to let me out!)
Waits for Your word to take his keys, and come!

JMJT

The Woodcutters and the Harvesters

Now all our saws make holy sonnets in our world of timber,
And oaks go off like guns,
And elms come down like cataracts
Pouring their roar into the woods' green well.

Walk to us, Jesus, through this wall of trees
And find us still Your faithful in these airy churches,
Singing this other office with our work of axes.
Still teach your children in the busy forest,
Letting some little sunlight reach us, in our mental shades &
     leafy studies.

And time has grown our country white with grain,
And filled all our regions with the sun.
Walk to us, Jesus, through the walls of wheat,
When our clean scythes go out to cut them down.
Sow some light winds upon the acres of our spirit,
And cool the regions where our prayers are reapers,
And slake us, Heaven, with Your living rivers.

JMJT

February 1, 1942. Septuagesima. Day of Recollection
  *Quomodo vos potestis credere, qui gloriam ab invicem accipitis, et gloriam, quae
  a solo Deo est, non quaeritis.* [*How can you believe*, who receive glory from
  another; and the glory which is from God alone, you do not seek (John
  5:44)?]

As St. Augustine says of the psalter – it goes for the whole Bible – you do not understand it unless you live out its meanings in your own life.

What is the connection between Faith and Humility – for here they are linked very close, in so close a union they are actually identified? You cannot *believe* because you seek glory from one another.

God's good gifts, the best, most perfect gifts, proceeding in our souls, from the Father of lights, are holy and invisible. They come to us quietly, by night, in the holy night of Faith.

He gives His gifts to all, the Holy Father of Lights, our Lord, our Life, in darkness. Not all accept them. Not all, who want to accept them, know how. Not all who try to accept them are humble or patient enough to wait and *see* how to receive the gift so that it remains with them.

We are drunkards and maniacs, we snatch the cup in our wild and feeble and helpless and shaking hands, and the cup falls down and the drink spills and we die of thirst. If we would only keep our hands off the cup, God would give us to drink from it, Himself holding the cup, which we are too sick and weak to take without spilling.

What does it mean?

God gives us Himself – before we have realized what an immense grace is beginning to be within our souls, we snatch it and draw it out into the only light by which we can see it, and it is lost.

We do not believe things ordinarily without witnesses. If we are weak and foolish, we are not sure even of the greatest gifts unless we see that they are approved of and admired by others.

If we think we have come into the possession of something good, we begin at once to display it – and if we think it is good, [sentence incomplete].

The Ointment

This day throw open all your houses, and forever,
And love, not fear, the many poor.
You who have sometimes fed the beggar in his tenement
But kept the mad in Bedlam, you would kill them
If they came too near to your door!

The smilers in the ticket windows, and the sellers at the
        counters,
The tellers in the friendly banks
All save behind their locks and iron shutters
Some holy pennies for a holy beggar.

But how they stare, with eyes like stones, for fear
When Jesus enters at the wealthy lepers' door!

When God was in the leper's house at Bethany,
There was a woman full of sin
Wasted a pound of ointment in a precious jar
In honor of His burying.
When with the lesson of that wasted ointment the whole
house was sweetened
Look how the traps of the pious & the just were all laid bare.
For who came forward to proclaim the waste, but the
betrayer Iscariot,
who took the part of the poor!

We, like St. Magdalen, are poor and have no money.
We have no merits, only our lives, & our sins:
We have no food, but daily take our bread
(When we grow hungry) from the hand of God.
We work in somebody else's vineyard:
We sleep behind the just man's barn.

And look! The same betrayers come & would accuse us:
Because they say we spent the rain like money
And squandered the strong sun & threw away the trees.
We wasted all the olives of another man's garden
In oil of sacrifice for Jesus, teaching at the leper's table.
We took our dawn & broke it like a jar
And sweetened, with that quiet light, a savior's sepulchre.
We took the flowers of this alabaster spring
And the fruits of all our summers,
And threw them away, but not to the poor!
This way we come happy with our empty hands,
And wait with nothing at the gate of heaven.

O we must quickly give away our lives before one night is
over –
And waste our souls on Him at this one supper:
This is the time of his betrayal by the lovers of the poor!

Now will we waste our works, knowing they cannot keep us
hidden.

Put to no use our fruits, nor into barns our harvest.
They'll never end our endless hungers! Let them go!

So we will give away our nights & days.
Waste them in tears & pour away our praises.
Pour them upon our God, before the face of His betrayers
And throw them away for Jesus, to hallow His grave!

JMJT

Good Friday. [April 3, 1942]

Movement of our lives reveals God's will, and we can obey Him or resist Him, but we cannot clearly know what we are doing without the light of much grace. Therefore I pray to You, my God, with every breath give me grace never to refuse you anything you ask, but to be absolutely lost in Your Will's immense obscurity, doing not what my will wants for my own good, but giving myself to You which is really the only possible good, for myself and for all men.

Not to demand that what I do should immediately show some result that I can appreciate; not to want to esteem anything that I do, or do anything because it will make me think I am something; but to only do things for love, and love alone. This is real obscurity, because the values loved by God's infinite love (the love that is so perfect that it is its own object) are absolutely incomprehensible to me.

Therefore to live for love is to live in darkness of the intellect, memory and will.

I don't even need to know precisely what I am doing, except that I am acting for the love of God. To act out of obedience to the rule of this community of men, who were all brought together by God's grace in order to love him, is obviously to act for love, it is to love God and my brothers and the whole world, because by our keeping our Rule the world also is saved.

Jesus, I beg you, let me live for this one thing alone: Your love. Your love is Yourself. You are love.

If I live for love, I will ask no reward, only more love. Your love is infinite: above my understanding how [sentence incomplete].

[Beginning of the sentence missing] conflict and argument within your mind, even less will there be any resistance or turmoil in your life, and you will find peace in listening and not arguing: because, after all, what you want is peace – and even in winning arguments there would be no peace. Besides which, arguments are never won: they are interminable.

Give up everything for God.

You say that, and you don't know what you mean.

In the Cathedral at Louisville, the afternoon I came here, I knew: it meant going by the way you know not, to get what you can't know. Every time you forget that, and every time you think you know where you are going, you are no longer living for God alone, for we only go to Him in darkness of self-denial, by the way we do not know.

The particular temptations I am armed for are not the ones that will be the most important. I come to God by the way I know not – meeting temptations I could not expect and the joys I could not expect because I never knew they existed.

All the most complicated, deep, immense truths are told in the Gospels, but we do not see them because they are all really too simple to be seen. In themselves the greatest truths are simple. Because we take so long, in the circuits of our pride, to come at them, they seem complicated.

Before I believed in Christ, I was incapable of understanding one fiftieth part of the Gospels – I do not say *agree* with them, I say I could not even hope to know what the words were all about. I say I want to give up everything for God. With His grace, perhaps my whole life will be devoted to nothing more than finding out what those words mean.

You give up everything – and are happy. Then you find your happiness rests partly on something you didn't give up because you didn't ever know you had it. You give this up and are happy, but . . . and so on, through higher and purer kinds of renunciation & happiness, to the purest renunciation, God alone, the purest joy. JMJT

The Candlemas Procession

Lumen! The life, the holy light of men!

Look kindly, Jesus, where we come
New Simeons to church, and kindle
Each at your infant sacrifice his own life's candle.

And when Your flame again takes tongues,
Look where the One is multiplied, among us hundreds,
Goes with the humble to console our sinful kindred!

It is for this we come
And kneeling, each receives his flame:

Ad revelationem gentium. [Luke 2:32]
Our lives, like candles, spell this simple symbol.

Weep like my bodily life, sweet toil of bees,
Sweeten the world with your slow sacrifice.
And this shall be my praise
That by my glad expense my Father's will
Burned and consumed me in a parable.

Nor burn we now with brown & smoky flames, but bright
Until our sacrifice is done
(By which not we, but You, are known)
And then returning to our Father one by one
Give back our lives like wise & waxen lights.

JMJT

PART II

A Journal-Memoir:

Dom Frederic Dunne

October 1946–August 1948

Jesus, Mary, Joseph, Bernard, Thérèse

Rev. Father Frederic

Someday someone is going to be able to write a biography of Reverend Father, and it would be useful to put down at random such facts and characteristic traits and actions of his that come to our notice from day to day. Biographies made up entirely of dates and documents and a few letters are very dull and don't give any idea of the person's character, and [character] expresses itself best in these little incidents and passing words so easily forgotten. And if the biography of a Cistercian Abbot is not to be predominately spiritual, what use is it to Cistercians?

Whatever is written here is unconnected and probably it will too often be completely illegible. But someday someone may be able to make use of it.

Reverend Father's character is full of enthusiasm and of good sense at the same time – a fact which is true in most of the saints, and which gives the lie to those who think enthusiasm is essentially imprudent and therefore opposed to wisdom and holiness. The following may or may not illustrate this trait – probably it will not do so very strikingly; but the elements are there nonetheless. I got some scruples because some poetry of ours had been published and some people liked it, and I thought it was wrong for attention to be drawn to any work of ours.

Reverend Father said: "When St. Peter went around Jerusalem and people came out and put their sick where his shadow would fall on them, do you think that was pleasant for him? Yet it was part of his purification." I was very impressed by that thought, that being in the limelight, by God's will, could *purify* a soul of pride. So much for the good sense of Reverend Father: then comes the enthusiasm. I have often seen him enthusiastic, and I think it has always been when he was speaking of God working in men, doing his will through them.

He went on to speak of how God's power was working through St. Peter, and quoted that first miracle: "Silver and gold have I none, but in the

Name of Jesus Christ I say to thee arise . . . etc." [Acts 3:6]. When Reverend Father said this, his whole face lit up and his eyes flashed and you could see that his heart was stirred with a powerful joy and sense of triumph. He had really so deeply penetrated the meaning of this miracle that he had come to share its sense of victory – the victory of Christ in Peter – and all that it implied. Just to hear him speak this sentence was as fruitful as a lone meditation on it!

Reverend Father has a very special love for St. Paul. He is always quoting him in Chapter. His spirituality is essentially Pauline. He once told me that his favorite Epistle was the one to the Hebrews. I suppose that is because it is the one that has the most to say about the Priesthood and Victimhood of Jesus. I think our Reverend Father's spirituality can be summed up as an ideal of Priesthood and Victimhood with Christ. His thought and actions are dominated by desire of love and sacrifice to please God and to make reparation for sin. He frequently speaks of the "outrages" of sinners against God. Consequently the Sacred Heart plays a dominating role in his devotions. Incidentally the most common penance he gives in Chapter is to say the Litany of the Sacred Heart before the Blessed Sacrament – and how often it is to be said "in reparation for the outrages committed against Him in the Sacrament of His love" – or to make reparation for sacrilegious communions – or for fallen priests.

Another thing he so often insists upon in Chapter – attention to the little rules – a delicate conscience that omits nothing that can please God is more important in his eyes than great mortifications and spectacular penances.

At the same time, he is most careful to enforce every detail of penance in the Rule; he cannot stand the idea of a Trappist who compromises with our austerities and seeks his own comfort. He is adamant against all mitigations to the Rule that are not strictly necessary – and even though our modifications in regard to summer clothing are surely necessary, I have heard him say that it wouldn't kill us to wear wool. Since I have been here, he has cut down on the somewhat large cooked portions (e.g. of corn mush) that were sometimes given with collation outside of Lent. Last year we got nothing but the two slices of bread, the coffee and a little stewed apple or raisins – that is as it should be. However, he does give a relief [the indulgence] with mixt in August.

Fr. Prior (Fr. Mauritius [Lans]) told me that once, when Reverend Father went to O.[ur] L.[ady] of the Holy Ghost [Conyers, Georgia] in winter, he left there to come home in the middle of the afternoon, planning to eat something on the train – but the train was late and the dining car was off, so Reverend Father got nothing to eat. He arrived at home and said his Mass about 11 the next day. So he had a 24-hour fast and an all-night train journey – at the age of 70, with all the work he has to do, that is not bad! Nor is it the only time it has happened. He never pays any attention to it. All winter, since he says his Mass at the time of the Conventual Mass, he goes without frustulum – keeps the strict fast of the Order. He is always careful to remind us that frustulum is permitted, or rather, *tolerated*, but for him, he keeps the fast, for that is the real Rule.

He told me of a monastery where they have butter and oatmeal with mixt – and mixt, what we would call mixt – all the year round, or at least in winter (I guess at that house they have frustulum in Lent) and he said he would rather see O. L. of the Holy Ghost burn down than have such relaxations introduced there.

He is very zealous in defending the Cistercian traditions of simplicity, especially in the Liturgy. One feels that he tolerates much of the display that goes with Pontificals to please others who are weaker than he is in this respect. He would like very much to allow no organ voluntaries, which are against our principles but are tolerated on the grounds that the Pontifical High Mass is Roman, not Cistercian. This Advent he made the experiment of having no organ accompaniment in choir according to the Ritual (the *Usages* permit an organ the whole time) and many liked it better that way. He has let the weaker spirits have the organ back, however, as he seems unwilling to do anything that might savor of asserting his own views over others, or laying down the law too much in things that are accidental – or comparatively so.

Reverend Father likes very much the pamphlet on *The Spirit of Simplicity*, put out at the request of the General Chapter.

When he first came here there was no organ. "Nobody," he remarked, "died on account of this." After a while, a lay brother comes who could play the organ. Next year (1946) will be the 50th Anniversary of Reverend Father's simple profession on the Feast of the Immaculate Conception.

He never takes real coffee when it is served on Feast Days.

Some people in the house are too anxious for excuses to serve candy as dessert, and real coffee and butter with mixt – as on national holidays. I was glad we got frustulum and not this elaborate form of mixt this Thanksgiving. When the big celebration was given for his reception of the habit, I was aware that Reverend Father was embarrassed at the lavish decorations, but he was careful not to do anything to let it be known, and he mentioned the fact that everything was beautiful. He was glad of it all on account of the affection it showed. But as far as he was concerned, the real celebration was at the Altar that day.

Reverend Father is full of the sense of the communion created in an especially close manner between himself and his monks, in Christ, when he stands at the altar, at a Pontifical or Abbatial Mass, offering up the Divine Victim for us as our Father and High Priest. He does not talk much, technically, about liturgy – except concrete points of the rubrics – but his liturgical sense is more basic, rooted in this fundamental mystical concept of our oneness in Christ's Sacrifice.

He would like very much, if it were possible, to see the old Cistercian Mass rite re-introduced, although he said to me he feared he would not be able to make the change himself, at his age. Someone at O. L. of the Valley [Rhode Island] seems to think all our liturgical books should be changed, adopting a new translation of the Vulgate – and Reverend Father is very much against this.

He insists very strongly on the importance of our taking advantage of our intervals for prayer and spiritual reading. That was one thing he mentioned in praise of one of our late brother cellarers, Brother Conrad – whenever he had a chance, he would try to get in "a little spiritual reading" even if it was only a couple of minutes.

Father Timothy [Vander Vennet] remarked to us, in the course of a philosophy class, how much Reverend Father seems to enjoy the Lenten reading and indeed he does. At that time he always comes to the Scriptorium and reads with the community; he always seems extremely interested and intent on what he is doing. The last fifteen minutes, as the *Usages* permit, he devotes to prayer in the Church. He likes Father [Frederick William] Faber: other books I remember him recommending to me are: Pseudo-Dionysius, the *Divine Names* – of course all of St. Bernard – Walter (?) on the Psalms (*in Sermon*) and, when I told him about Ruysbroeck (in the French of E. Hello) he was very interested and got the book, which he liked very much.

He told me that he used to write poetry – I have never seen anything. I wonder if he kept it. He wrote several items in the *Catholic Encyclopedia* over Dom Edmond [Obrecht]'s name, including a biographical note on Br. John of Montmirail and some other blessed of our Order.

———

Although Reverend Father never speaks critically of persons, and is not carried away with indignation at abuses he notices outside, he is deeply offended, for instance, at the haste with which so many secular priests say Mass. He told me of a church where he stopped to say Mass, on the way to Rhode Island, where two consecutive "High Masses" were finished while he was saying his own Mass.

In Georgia a neighbor of the monastery, making no bones about explaining that he did not like to be in the vicinity of a monastery, moved out and tried to force us to buy his place at a price convenient to him, with the threat that, if we didn't, he would put up a road-house[1] there. Reverend Father didn't bite. However, we now have the property, and there is no road-house.

When at Conyers, Reverend Father goes into all the stores etc., wearing the Cistercian habit, and nobody minds, he says. He hopes Fr. James [Fox] is doing the same. Georgia being Georgia, that demands a certain amount of courage.

October 26, 1946

In Reverend Father's room today we were speaking about the Feast of Christ the King which is tomorrow – except that we do not yet celebrate it in the Order. He said that, if he went over the head of the Abbot General, etc., to the Cardinal Procurator, he could get the feast for us at once – and then it transpired that it was he who, in this way, got the 50-days indulgence for all who kiss the ring of their Abbot in our Order.

We were also speaking of the troubles that have been besetting the house: and there have been troubles. It was at the beginning of the month, on the Feast of the Guardian Angels [October 2nd], that Reverend Father had a slight stroke. It was at a theological conference and I think nobody even noticed it. He said he got blind and couldn't see anything. Meanwhile some of the conference enthusiasts were carrying on in grand style – in the way that makes me love silence more and more, so that I wish it were absolute.

Then he went to Louisville and saw a doctor who made him go to the hospital at once. That was the next day or the day after. Since then there have been other minor troubles. Reverend Father says he fears for the future of the community – not of course its existence – but the good order of the house. He said, "The devil does not like our new foundation." Also,

---

[1] A house of prostitution.

when I was talking on the subject of offering one's life – should our Lord desire to take it in the ordinary course of things – for fervor and regularity in this community, he said very emphatically that it was a very desirable thing and a laudable intention and added:

"That is my desire for myself" – namely that, if he should be called to the other world, Our Lord should take him as a sacrifice for the spiritual welfare of Gethsemani and our filiations.

Speaking of his work – he works twice as hard as all the rest of the community put together and has been doing so for the last 52 years – he began to accuse himself of all his "omissions" and said, with tears in his eyes, that he was lazy!

As a matter of fact he is now carrying the full burden of all his work and planning the new foundation in spite of his recent collapse and the warnings of the doctors.

November 10, 1946

This morning Reverend Father returned from Utah after exactly one week. He had a cough or a cold or something and said it rained the whole time he was there. When he saw all those "black mountains, rising straight out of the prairies" – a land without horses, farms or trees, he was at first discouraged. But the fierceness of the Mormons and their hatred of the Church had made him determined to make the foundation anyway.

He said, "The whole place (Utah) seems to be possessed by the devil."

He arrived at Salt Lake at five o'clock in the morning and found himself confronted with a great big mural of Brigham Young discovering the Mormon Valley.

"I only passed the Mormon Temple once," he said, "and I could never go inside it. I made the sign of the cross, hoping the place would fall down, but unfortunately it did not." Afterwards he told the Bishop, "I want to see St. Michael and the Cross on top of that place" – St. Michael – to replace the Mormon angel who is supposed to give the Mormons all their information.

He said he had seen many places and so far was more or less in favor of one town near Provo. However he didn't want to tell me too much for fear he would have "nothing left to tell in Chapter" – those Chapter reports of his journeys, which are usually so parsimonious!! But he is really very much moved by the thought of the Mormons, their strange, crazy ideas which they will not thoroughly publish, and above all their hatred of the Church.

If we are to buy a place it must be secretly through intermediaries, or they will do everything to stop us.

There was never more need of prayer! This will be one of the most difficult foundations in the history of the Cistercians.

November 14, 1946

Today I cleaned out St. John's room – partially. It used to be the Prior's room when Dom Frederic was Prior. He had left a lot of his effects in there, and made me burn a whole file of old letters. No one can tell what was in them. He said he had not time to go through them – which is true! A card autographed by Pius X fell out of the pile and that [I] did not burn. He also wanted me to burn carbon copies of what appeared to be all his letters to Dom Edmond on the latter's journeys – but I managed to persuade him to keep them as a record of the events in the house at that time.

December 10, 1946

On Sunday, the Feast of the Immaculate Conception, we celebrated Reverend Father's Jubilee of Simple Profession. It was also Fr. George's Golden Jubilee of Solemn Profession; we had just finished the annual retreat as usual, and also at the High Mass Reverend Father received the Solemn Profession of Fr. Walter [Helmstetter].

Reverend Father acted as if he were going to get away without being publicly feted, but he had wind of the arrangements made by Fr. Prior when he opened a telegram of congratulations from Cardinal Doherty or someone like that.

The celebration was in the Chapter Room after None, where Reverend Father appeared in obedience to Fr. Prior. It started out with a surprisingly good speech by old Frater Joachim who has been in the novitiate for a little over a year. Brother Isidore, who is the Keeper of the Chickens, made a speech that nearly brought the whole three-story building down on top of us. I never heard the like. He was simple enough to be extremely simple, but not without being conscious of the fact that he was very funny. I could see Reverend Father was especially pleased with Frater Joachim's speech and he complimented him on it when he came up in the Chapter of Faults the following day.

Today it is raining. Reverend Father has gone out somewhere, probably to Louisville.

December 14, 1946. Saturday

Last night (Feast of St. Lucy) after we had all gone to bed at 7:20 P.M., Reverend Father called up the infirmary, so I am told, and left instructions for all the sick who could to be down in the Chapter for voting in the morning. I had to leave with the other simple professed but I could guess it was about Utah – something had come up suddenly.

This morning in Chapter he was teaching us that we should desire, like Moses, to see the face of God and ask God to show Himself to us – and that we should give up everything for God as we have promised. That is what I like to hear – and we hear it frequently. Reverend Father often says, if we listen, God will speak to us.

January 12, 1947

Last Tuesday night, January 7th, Reverend Father left for Utah and perhaps by now he has bought the land for the new monastery. He was not sick, like most of the monastery last Monday night, since he does not eat cheese or butter – under doctor's orders.

January 20, 1947

Reverend Father returned from Utah last Wednesday. He had an option on a farm but would not buy it. It was very beautiful, he said. Very poetic. Beautiful mountains. "But you can't sit and look at mountains all day and then take a drink of water for dinner," he said. You can't eat mountains. Only 90 acres were under cultivation and the man had to buy hay for his 28 cows last year. Reverend Father is absolutely against starting a factory which would bring in the spirit of the world – as if we had to enter into competition in business and always be thinking of how to sell things and make money.

February 3, 1947

When Reverend Father was considering his vocation, his spiritual director wanted him to become a Franciscan or a Dominican, and did not want him to come here to be a Trappist. But Reverend Father never had – nor ever has had since – any attraction to any other order or place. This he told me today.

From the way he talks, Reverend Father seems to believe that the truest contemplatives in the house are to be found among some of the old lay brothers – and I agree with him on sight. But he knows the inside of their souls, too.

The other day I saw a photo of Reverend Father in the "disguise" he wears on his expeditions to Utah. A windbreaker and a pair of army pants loaned him by the Bishop of Salt Lake who was a chaplain during the war.

March 3, 1947

Reverend Father leaves again for Utah this week. This morning at the Matutinal Mass he gave the tonsure to 7 clerics and ordained 3 acolytes.

In Utah there are two good prospects. But someone told some nuns that we were coming and they told the school children and the children told their parents, so the thing is no longer a secret in the West!

In Chapter Reverend Father announced the suppression of two of our houses – N.[otre] D.[ame] de Liesse in China – closed by the reds. The religious are expelled. Reverend Father was sending them $100.00 a month since the end of the war. The other house closed down was Mariastern in Jugo-Slavia. They had once had a community of nearly 200, I hear. They have gone to Mariawald in Westphalia.

Reverend Father told us he received tonsure and all the minor orders in one day – in August, 1878, from the Bishop of Nashville. He narrowly escaped getting the subdiaconate the following day. They had no canon law in those days . . . The subdiaconate was Dom Edmond's idea – but he had it too late. The Bishop of Louisville at that time was an invalid.

When Reverend Father was a little boy he nearly drowned once when he was out on a lake in a boat – and also he was nearly shot when he and some other children were playing with a revolver that went off – and just after it had been pointing at him.

He was sacristan when he was still in the novitiate – and has had important offices ever since.

March 17, 1947

Reverend Father came back from Utah for the third time last Monday (the 11th) with a nasty cold. In fact until Friday he had a fever, but that did not prevent him from coming to most of the community exercises.

This morning he finally told us the result of the trip, which was that he had at last decided on a place – out of a choice of two. It has 1800 acres and at least some water.

He said that those who went out there need have no illusions – there would be plenty of hard work and sacrifice. But above all he said he would rather not make the foundation at all, than to have us go out there and be absorbed in material things. The most important thing is to live our Rule and live lives of prayer and sacrifice.

March 2, 1948

About February, 1900, before Reverend Father was ordained, he was dangerously ill and was sent to the hospital in Louisville. His life was in great danger and he was praying for the grace of at least being ordained and saying one Mass.

One of the sisters found him in his prayers and was able to be present at his ordination in Louisville Cathedral as well as at his Abbatial Blessing. Every year since then, in gratitude, she sent a stipend for him to say Mass for his own intention on the anniversary of his recovery.

She died recently but left instructions for the stipend to be sent again this year.

In February Reverend Father sent 18 "CARE" packages to people in distressed areas of Europe. "Who was it for?" he said – "Jesus Christ."

His big worry now is raising money to pay the debts of the two foundations. He has put this in the hands of St. Joseph. Many gifts come in but the bills are bigger than the gifts. He is still unwilling to beg.

When he went to the consecration of the new Bishop of Belleville at the end of January, he had a heart attack in the Cathedral during the ceremonies but got up and left unaided. Archbishop Ritter saw him go and wondered what was wrong, but saw that he got out all right, so thought no more of it. Reverend Father started at once for home but got no further than Louisville where he spent 10 days or so in St. Joseph's Infirmary. On his return, as a gesture to conciliate the doctors, he stayed in bed until 3 for the rest of February, but now in March he is up again at 2 with the community.

May 28, 1948

Reverend Father's mother – Mary [Lois Stenger] came from Zanesville, Ohio – Protestant parents – did not like her marrying a Catholic. Mr. [Hugh] Dunne was a printer and bookbinder in Zanesville – married on Christmas Day 18[61] and left the same day for the Civil War. On his return they moved to Ironton and then South – mostly to get away from her family.

Her death was very holy – she had lost a child, Edward, killed in an accident when he was 3. She was in bed in corner of room – facing 2 windows. She smiled. Mr. Dunne said, "What are you smiling at, Mary?"

She said, "Don't you see the Blessed Mother of God coming, bringing little Eddie with her?" Then she died.

Her confessor said he believed she had never acted against her conscience in her life. As soon as she became convinced that she ought to be a Catholic, she became one – 18 months before her death.

Reverend Father will go to Utah over the F.[east] of the S.[acred] Heart [June 8th].

August 7, 1948 – after Reverend Father's Death [August 4]
He was [in] upstate N.Y. to see foundation property – Worrell gave him a new suit, $73.00 and a new overcoat, said he looked too shabby.

Didn't say a word about this found. to community.

August 12, 1948
The [Abbot] General sent a special visitor evidently to take up particular matters with Reverend Father – probably something to do with the many foundations. Dom Gabriel [Sortais] was here only to bury him and preside over the election of his successor.[2]

Reverend Father's last Chapter – Tuesday morning, August 3rd. He was talking about humility – St. Benedict's 7th chapter – mentioned incidentally that God gives us everything we need for our perfection. The means are all around us – all we have to do is make use of them – for instance – take advantage of the differences between members of same community in order to learn and practice humility. To this he applied St. Bernard's remark to monks of Tre Fontane [Rome], about God placing herbs around in the fields to cure the sicknesses of that locality.

His last Chapter was typical – forceful, fervent, austere, uncompromising, yet tempered by gentleness and sympathy.

That night he had not slept well. Difficulty in breathing – heart pains. Before leaving he asked several earnestly for special prayers. Yet he was looking forward to many things – planned giving minor orders to Frater Hilary after General Chapter – a benefactor had bought him a plane ticket to

[2] Dom Frederic Dunne was succeeded by James Fox, Abbot of Holy Ghost in Georgia.

G.C. – his passport was coming – he planned to attend dedication at Orval [Belgium] and drive to G.C. with Dom Albert.

Took *Exile Ends in Glory* on train with him to Georgia.

Had a long talk with him that afternoon. He said earnestly – wanted me to start planning a book on the spiritual life, "a book to make people love the spiritual life." I asked could I narrow it down to contemplative life and he was pleased.

When he went to the Valley – F. of St. Stephen etc. – around July 16th & ff. – Dom E.[dmund Futterer, Abbot of O. L. of the Valley] told him to stay in bed for night office. Dom F. said, "Our Lord will take care of everything" and was up at one. Refused to take care of himself. Admitted poor sleep – difficulty breathing. Refused companion on journey.

Proud of Gethsemani – and our austerity.

Dom E. explained how he divided his responsibilities. Dom F. said, "too complicated for me!" Actually Dom F.'s life was terrifically complex. Died of overwork. Everything in his own hands.

An old man, who remembered day Dom F. entered monastery as a postulant, could still picture scene (at funeral) – thought of him walking off avenue. "He was a very little boy."

Fr. Odilo asked him, "Reverend Father, is the supernatural real to you?"

"So real I could reach out and touch it with my hand."

He liked especially a certain picture of Our Lady in his room.

Happy over colored retreats, colored postulant – and colored priest who wanted to enter.

His ideas about liturgical movement were in line with Pius XII's encyclical [*Mediator Dei*, 1947]. Did not like "table" altar at Valley. Complete suppression of statues evoked remark, "This is a fine Protestant church."

A man in Conyers – Protestant – said, "Every time I shook hands with him, I felt like I was receiving a benediction."

When the train pulled into Knoxville, Tenn. – conductor got out to walk on platform – somebody came running out – "There's an awful sick man on this train, awful sick!" Went to get Doctor – came in – found R. F. in smoking room alone, sitting up dead.

Fr. James' comment – final total sacrifice – St. John+ [of the Cross] –
nada [nothing]. Anyway – typical American death – died in harness.

He and Dom Pacôme [Gaboury, Abbot of Notre-Dame du Lac, Oka,
Canada] were two of a kind – terrific workers – monasteries pretty much
alike – same sort of pioneer spirit – close friendship. His highest praise for
souls who were "always busy with something," e.g., Brother Gregory who
came in with buckets of strawberries when watching cows in pasture.

In his early days – as novice – fasted a long time and was falling ill before
it occurred to superiors to ask him if he was under 21.

Fr. Cyprian threw a fit in transept near [altar of] SS. Peter and Paul. R. F.
said it was one time he broke silence – surprised – ran over saying, "Can I
help you?" Later told how Fr. Cyprian told him not to ask for crosses – he
had done so and got this epilepsy.

Fr. Leonard was his theology professor. Someone spoke of certain things
as inspired by the Holy Ghost. "Hah!" said Fr. Leonard, "Holy Ghost with
a tail!"

Reverend Father's mother's family in Zanesville – strict Protestants – antagonism one reason why they moved to Ironton, then to Atlanta, then to
Florida

At Jacksonville – picnics down the river in boats – knew a French family
there – some girls – sociable young man, popular.

PART III

The Whale and the Ivy

December 1946–July 1952

December 10, 1946. Advent

It is five years since I came to the monastery. It is the same kind of day, overcast. But now it is raining. I wish I knew how to begin to be grateful to God and to Our Lady for bringing me here.

There was a long interval after afternoon work. It was good to be in the big quiet church. The church is dark, these winter afternoons. I knelt there behind the pillar with distractions and images floating around on the surface of my mind. But, underneath, a growing recollection got hold of me – a sense of obscure love that anchored me in God.

I have been reading Duns Scotus's *Oxoniense III*, distinction 18, on Christ's will and His love. Scotus is really simple once you get through the barricade of distinctions that are so hard to understand. His underlying thought is beautiful, coherent, and he is always working for simplicity, elimination of non-essentials. Sometimes I get a glimpse of the unity that underlies all his discussions and I find it lucid and easy to see and wonderful to contemplate, once I get the whole perspective. And the contemplation of it fills me with love for God and makes me praise Him. Nevertheless, it is sometimes brutally hard to crack through the shell and get into Scotus' thought!

December 13, 1946. Saint Lucy

The years since I entered Gethsemani have gone by like five weeks. It was a fine bright day, not very cold, with little clouds very high up in the sky. Yesterday, although it is Advent and we are not supposed to receive any letters at all, Dom Frederic gave me a letter from Naomi Burton of Curtis Brown, Ltd. I had sent her the manuscript of *The Seven Storey Mountain*. Her letter about it was very good and she is quite sure it will find a publisher. Anyway, my idea – and hers also – is to turn it over to Robert Giroux at Harcourt, Brace.

At work – writing – I am doing a little better. I mean, I am less tied up in it, more peaceful and more detached. Taking one thing at a time and going over it slowly and patiently (if I can ever be said to do *anything* slowly and patiently) and forgetting about the other jobs that have to take their turn. For instance, Jay [James] Laughlin wants two anthologies for New Directions press. I wonder if I will ever be able to do them. If God wills. Meanwhile, for myself, I have only one desire and that is the desire for solitude – to disappear into God, to be submerged in His peace, to be lost in the secret of His Face.

December 14, 1946. Saturday

This afternoon we were working on the road from the old horsebarn to the lower bottom, filling in a deep gully that had washed out all along the road, down to the bottom of the hill. It was another bright, warm day. The new brick horsebarn, under the water tower, where the vineyard used to be, is almost finished. They are clearing ground already for the new garden house. There were some fat turkeys in the pen. Father Joel has already started to put up the crib in the church and that means Christmas is here. The novena begins tomorrow. Tonight at Vespers we sang the *Conditor alme siderum* which has not been heard for a week on account of Our Lady's octave. But what an octave! I keep thinking of the words, *Posuit immaculatam viam meam* [He has made my way spotless], and of the *Alleluia* of the Mass, *Tota pulchra es* [Thou art all fair (Song of Songs 4:7)]. That is what Duns Scotus is singing in heaven.

Lady, Queen of Heaven, pray me into solitude and silence and unity, that all my ways may be immaculate in God. Let me be content with whatever darkness surrounds me, finding Him always by me, in His mercy. Let me keep silence in this world, except in so far as God wills and in the way He wills it. Let me at least disappear into the writing I do. It should mean nothing special to me, nor harm my recollection. The work could be a prayer; its results should not concern me.

December 24, 1946. Christmas Eve

Old Father Alberic [Wulf] preached the sermon in Chapter. He looks very ill. He said it was his last sermon and I wouldn't be at all surprised. It was all about mutual encouragement. I think he must have been very lonely in the infirmary, all these years. He is a kind, and simple and solitary little person. When he appears in the *scriptorium*, he comes slowly along the cloister like a wraith, holding on to the walls, just to be where people are. The other day he showed me a holy picture. I wish I could have done something more for him than just look at the holy picture and smile, and I was ashamed of the thought that my smile perhaps showed the embarrassment I felt over two facts – first that artistically it was a frightful picture and, second, that my looking at it was against the rule of the house. Dom Frederic interprets the rule, that two monks may not read together out of the same book, in the strict sense that no monk may show another monk anything, any writing, any picture, anything one would want to look at . . . This time I think charity came first.

One of the things I liked about his sermon was the ingenuousness and simplicity with which Father Alberic talked about "devotion to our Superiors." That a novice should instinctively make sacrifices for "his dear Father Master." It was not just something he got out of a book. It was in him and part of him and his whole wasted little person proclaimed the meaning of what he said.

One day when I was in Father Abbot's room, complaining that I was not the contemplative or the solitary that I wanted to be, that I made no progress in this house and that I ought to be either a Carthusian or an outright hermit, Dom Frederic casually remarked that there were some men in the house who could come to him and tell him their troubles and go out quite satisfied with whatever answer he gave them. From a certain point of view the solution sounds utterly horrible. And yet it is also quite wonderful. It implies a faith and simplicity without which it is hard to live the contemplative life. We really have to believe in our Superiors. We cannot simply judge them by human standards, taking the things they tell us as opinions that are to be weighed in the balance with our own. I do not know if I shall ever be able to do it. But I need something of that and I hope Jesus will give me the grace for it.

December 29, 1946. Saint Thomas of Canterbury

The four big feast days were wonderful. Plenty of time to pray and no obligation to do anything else. *Paradiso!*

Yesterday in the confessional, Dom Vital [Klinski] said a lot of good things and it would be well not to forget them. So I write them down.

1. First he said that I ought to be very grateful for my attraction to prayer. I ought to cultivate it and seek recollection and remain quiet before the tabernacle.

2. That I ought to pray to understand writers like Ruysbroeck and go on reading him.[1]

---

[1] John Ruusbroec, a fourteenth-century Flemish writer, emphasized the mystery of the Trinity and union with God in "spiritual marriage."

3. To teach contemplation, and especially to let people know, in what I write, that the contemplative life is quite easy and accessible and does not require extraordinary or strange efforts, just the normal generosity required to strive for sanctity.

4. He said I must remember that my desire to become a Carthusian is full of self-love and only some very extraordinary upheaval in my whole life would justify my leaving here for a Charterhouse.

5. To profit from all the crosses Jesus sends me, especially the ones that come in connection with work – delays, accidents to manuscripts, adverse criticism, insults, and so on.

6. To realize what pleasure it gives Jesus when He sees that we recognize the action of his love, doing good to us in all these trials.

7. To read Carthusian writers and make use of anything of value that they say and, if they make me want to pack up and run off to the Charterhouse, I should treat that desire like any other movement of disordered appetite and not get upset about it.

Then, yesterday at dinner, when the reader in the refectory was reading some spectacular stuff by [Jacques Bénigne] Bossuet on Saint Thomas of Canterbury, out of the *Liturgical Year* – (the martyr dies, with his tongue still forming the word *"l'église"* [the church]) – Father Prior handed me a telegram. I had been thinking: "If anything comes to me in the mail, I shall take it as a present from Saint Thomas à Becket." But when I saw the telegram my heart sank into my dinner. The first thought that came to my mind was that the manuscript of *The Seven Storey Mountain* had been lost. Naomi Burton gave it to Harcourt, Brace only a week ago. I knew quite well that publishers always make you wait at least two months before saying anything about your manuscripts. . . .

I waited until after dinner and opened the telegram. It was from Bob Giroux. And it said: "Manuscript accepted. Happy New Year."

January 5, 1947. Vigil of Epiphany

It is grey outside, and snow falls lightly.

This morning Father Abbot announced in Chapter that I had made my petition to be admitted to solemn vows. This was in order that the community might be able to vote on me.

I have been made assistant cantor, which meant moving to the other side of the choir. For some reason that side seems gloomy – perhaps because all the days have been dark days so far. But the chant is better on that side.

Father Edward [Knecht] is the only cantor we follow and we don't all follow him.

January 7, 1947

We had a wild Epiphany. First, the devils were trying to mess me up yesterday afternoon. I could not pray at first, and then a lot of highly suspicious "graces" came along. I had a series of big, spurious lights about becoming a Camaldolese hermit. Finally I went to confession and got straightened out.

Then we went to bed, but not for long. I woke up at nine fifteen with the sudden and vivid awareness that I was sick and that I had to vomit. I ran downstairs and found half a dozen other monks in the same condition. From then until after midnight the whole house was upset. In the dark little cloister, or on the stairways, you would come upon religious shadows, with hoods pulled over their faces, walking with basins in their hands. At first they seemed to have a purpose: to get from the basement to the dormitory with a basin, and go back to sleep. Actually very few were able to get that far without doubling up somewhere on the way. After which they would return to the basement to clean up and start over again. Eventually many just lay on the floor in some convenient corner, expecting either death or the bell to get up and go to choir.

Father Prior went up to the infirmary and got some medicine which we all took. It made us twice as sick. After midnight I managed to get back to the dormitory and stay there. I piled everything in sight on top of my stomach – blankets, extra shirts, cowl, scapular, and so on, thinking by some obscure instinct that, if I could make my stomach nice and warm, I would eventually go to sleep. I did. But by that time the bell rang and we had to go down to choir.

Nobody seems to know what it was. The latest theory traveling around the sign-language grapevine is that Frater Zeno, a novice who was a doctor in the Army Medical Corps during the war, believes that something was wrong with the cheese we had for supper. Father Anthony [Chassagne], who did not eat the cheese, admits that he was not sick, and almost anything will make Father Anthony sick. Meanwhile I have made so many signs about the affair that I am surprised my arms do not ache.

Father Abbot is starting off for Utah to look for land for a new foundation. This morning we had the Chapter of Faults and it was extremely peaceful and charitable. The whole monastery is as happy as Christmas morning.

January 12, 1947

I am fascinated by [Edmond] Martène and [Ursin] Durand's *Voyage Lit-téraire de Deux Bénédictins* [Paris, 1717]. It is the record of their journey around France in the early eighteenth century, collecting material for the *Gallia Christiana*, in the archives of the old monasteries. And there were hundreds of them. Monastic life was, on the whole, rich and vital even in that dead age. There were many scattered reform movements going on, and they were effective enough, within their limitations. But few of them seem to have extended very far and almost all of them have been completely forgotten. Monasticism was a big tree full of dead wood. It needed to be pruned. It was, in fact, all but cut down. Many rich and beautiful customs were lost with the monasteries that the French revolution swept out of existence. Much art, too, I suppose. But when it was all over, I think the monasteries that survived came out richer in the love of God.

January 14, 1947

God's love takes care of everything I do. He guides me in all my work and in my reading, at least until I get greedy and start rushing from page to page. It is really illogical that I should get temptations to run off to another monastery and to another Order. God has put me in a place where I can spend hour after hour, each day, in occupations that are always on the borderline of prayer. There is always a chance to step over the line and enter into simple and contemplative union with God. I get plenty of time alone before the Blessed Sacrament. I have got in the habit of walking up and down under the trees or along the wall of the cemetery in the presence of God. And yet I am such a fool that I can consent to imagine that in some other situation I would quickly advance to a high degree of prayer. If I went anywhere else, I would almost certainly be much worse off than here. And, anyway, I did not come here for myself but for God. God is my order and my cell. He is my religious life and my rule. He has disposed everything in my life in order to draw me inward, where I can see Him and rest in Him. He has put me in this place because He wants me in this place, and if He ever wants to put me anywhere else, He will do so in a way that will leave no doubt as to who is doing it.

January 18, 1947

On Wednesday Father Abbot came back from Utah without a farm.

He may or may not tell us about it on Sunday.

Today the Last Sacraments were given to Father Odo. Being assistant cantor I was close to his cell. I knelt opposite the doorway, but the long line of novices kept passing and passing, between me and the cell, and they were still going by when Reverend Father began the anointing. I did not get more than a glimpse of Father Odo whose face was sunken and drawn and who seemed to be suffering much. His huge body used to shake with an asthmatic cough on the days when he would come down to Chapter in his wheel chair. (On his jubilee he sat with his hand cupped behind his ear during Dom Frederic's speech and, when it was over, he made a sign that he had heard not a word.) The cough used to go on and on. But now he is so weak that he cannot even cough. He received the Sacraments very devoutly, but I did not hear him say anything. If he tried to speak, his voice was too weak to reach me, out in the hall.

He is ending a long monastic life – over fifty years, half of which were spent in France. He used to be Cellarer at Acey, in the Jura.

January 27, 1947

This week I am serving Father Abbot's Mass. He says Mass in the back sacristy, when the Conventual Mass is going on in the church. You can hear the choir, indistinctly, through the two closed doors. On the other side, outside, down the hill at the mill this morning the brothers were filing the teeth of the big buzz-saw. In choir the monks were singing *Justus ut palma florebit* [the Just Man shall flourish like the palm tree (Psalms 91:13)], in the Mass for the Feast of St. John Chrysostom. And outside the saw rang under the grating file. The sounds of prayer and of distant work mingle well. There, on the altar, in the midst of these various discrete sounds of homage, in the midst of the order ruled by love for Him, the Lord of all things said nothing, but filled the room with peace.

After dinner the day turned into spring. It was one of those warm winter days which, in Kentucky, suddenly turn into blinding cold. But as long as it was warm, the garden was like Eden and I walked there reading Ruysbroeck.

Later in the afternoon Dom Frederic placed in my hands one of the most beautiful books I have ever seen. It is an album of pictures of one of our ancient Abbeys, in Provence – Sénanque is its name. Both the photographs and the layout are wonderful. I was very happy.

Cistercian architecture explains many things about our rule and life. A church like Sénanque is born of prayer and is a prayer. Its simplicity and its energy tell us what our prayer should be. It simply says what Saint Benedict already told us: that we must pray to God "with all humility and purity of devotion . . . not in many words but in purity of heart and in the compunction of tears [The Rule of St. Benedict (cited as RB) 52:4]." The churches of our Fathers expressed their humility and their silence. There was nothing superfluous about either the office of our Fathers or their architecture, nothing useless in their private prayer. They did not waste words with God or with men and in their buildings they did not waste anything either. They did not use up stone and time in an appeal to sentimental taste or in reverence to some false, arbitrary criterion of piety in art. They knew a good building would praise God better than a bad one, even if the bad one were covered all over with official symbols of praise. Their churches were built around the psalms. Their cloisters were like the chant in our gradual and in our old antiphoner. Their buildings were a fit setting for the *Consuetudines* of Saint Stephen.[2] A perfection so pure and so vital, springing directly from a religious Rule and way of life, argues a spiritual fruitfulness deeper than we can appreciate today. And I think it is a fruitfulness that belongs to the cenobitic life as such. The simplicity of Sénanque or Fontenay could only house a community of cenobites. A monastery of hermits is necessarily so clumsy that it can only be an architectural monster. However, I agree that one hermitage for one hermit stands a good chance of being beautiful!

February 1, 1947

Tomorrow is Septuagesima. Tonight we sang the last *alleluia*. When it is sung again, I shall be on the eve of my solemn vows.

Today, at work in the woods, I nearly cut off both my legs. The ax kept glancing off the felled pine tree I was supposed to be trimming. It flew at my knees like a fierce, bright-beaked bird and my guardian angel had a busy afternoon fencing with the blade to keep me on my two feet. The woods were wonderful.

Another postulant arrived: the fourth in two days. The problem of where all these people are going to sleep is becoming acute.

February 8, 1947

The other day Reverend Father announced in Chapter that I would make my solemn vows on the Feast of Saint Joseph. I thought perhaps it might not be until Easter, but the sooner the better.

---

[2] An early collection of primitive General Chapter statutes by Saint Stephen Harding, third Abbot of Cîteaux.

And now it is really cold, for the first time this winter. The other night the holy water was frozen in the fonts of our dormitory cells when we went up to go to bed. But by the time we got up at two o'clock, it had started to melt, because of the presence of so many monks in one room with all the windows closed.

February 17, 1947. Shrove Tuesday
The Forty Hours ended today.

Yesterday morning I made my will. You always make a will before solemn vows, getting rid of everything, as if you were about to die. It sounds more dramatic than it really is. As a matter of fact, as soon as I had renounced all earthly things, I was called into Father Abbot's room and he presented me with a contract with Harcourt, Brace for the publication of _The Seven Storey Mountain_. So, after making my will, I put my living signature on this contract. The royalties of the dead author will go to the monastery. Meanwhile, I spent the afternoon writing business letters and making all kinds of mistakes.

This morning, before the Blessed Sacrament, it seemed to me that these vows will mean the renunciation of the pure contemplative life. If Jesus wants me to be here at Gethsemani, as my Superiors insist He does _(Qui vos audit me audit)_ [He that heareth you, heareth me (Luke 10:16)], then perhaps He does not want me to be a pure contemplative after all. I suppose it all depends what you mean by a pure contemplative.

I soon came to the conclusion that I could not think straight about the problem anyway. Perhaps this is not the most perfect vocation in the Church, _per se_. Well, what about it? It seems to be _my_ vocation. That is the thing that matters. What is the use of having some other vocation that is better in itself but is not our own vocation? But how can it be my vocation if I have such a strong desire for some other vocation? Don't ask me. Our Lord wants that sacrifice. How do I know? I don't know. That is what I am told. Do I have to believe them? I do not have to, I suppose. But something tells me there is no other way for me. My conscience is on the side of my Superiors and, anyway, when I have a moment of lucid thought on the subject, experience reminds me that these feelings will go away just as they have gone away before. No doubt they will come back again and go away again many times before I get used to forgetting them.

I was thurifer at the Solemn Abbatial Mass of reposition. On top of all my other troubles, I could not get a decent fire going. The grains of incense we use are so large and so coarse that, as soon as they are put on top of the charcoal, they melt into a solid mass that gives off no smoke and only puts out the fire. I was working and blowing on the charcoal all through the Canon and got my hands covered with coal and, when it was all over, I forgot to empty out the censer and put it away.

February 20, 1947. Lent

I went and talked over the whole business of my vocation again with Father Abbot and he assured me once again, patiently, that everything was quite all right and that this was where I belonged. In my bones I know that he is quite right and that I am a fool. And yet, on the surface, everything seems to be all wrong. As usual, I am making too much fuss about it. *Concupierunt concupiscentiam in deserto . . . Numquid poterit [Deus] parare mensam populo suo?* [They coveted their desire in the desert (Psalms 105:14) . . . Can God furnish a table for his people (Psalms 77:19)?]

February 28, 1947

This is the second day of a three-day retreat before I receive the last of the Minor Orders – that of acolyte. I had been expecting it since last December. I was ordained exorcist on the Feast of Saint Michael and All Angels last September, lector on the Feast of Saint Dominic in August, porter on the Feast of Saint Paul in June. I was tonsured last Easter Monday. The rite of ordination of acolytes in the Pontifical is full of appeals for light and of promises of it. The order elevates me to the steps of the altar, reflecting on the blood and water that flowed from the side of Christ on the cross as I minister part of the matter for the Eucharist of Christ's Blood. More than anything else, more than ever before, I beg You, my God, to kindle in my heart the love of Christ and teach me how to give myself to You in union with His Sacrifice. It will not be the first time I have reflected on the marvelous prayer the priest says when mingling a drop of water with the wine in the chalice.[3] But I want that prayer to symbolize all that I live for. I want my whole life to be an expression of those words and of that rite.

March 1, 1947. First Ember Saturday in Lent

Last night it snowed again and there is a fairly thick blanket of snow on the ground and on the trees. The sky looks like lead and seems to promise

[3] "O God, who in a wonderful manner didst create and ennoble human nature, and still more wonderfully hast renewed it; grant that by the mystery of this water and wine, we may be made partakers of His divinity who vouchsafed to become partaker of our humanity, Jesus Christ Thy Son, our Lord, who liveth and reigneth with Thee in the unity of the Holy Ghost, one God, world without end. Amen."

more. It is about as dark as my own mind. I see nothing. I understand nothing. I am sorry for complaining and making a disturbance. All I want is to please God and to do His will.

fr M. Louis OCR[4]

Gethsemani. March 9, 1947

I write this in obedience to Dom Vital [Klinski], in spite of my own personal disinclination for it. Still, it doesn't make much difference one way or the other *per se*, so it is enough to have it decided by someone else who has the power to decide. If it is tedious to keep a journal, it is more tedious to keep wondering whether or not I should give the thing up. It does not seem that anything I write here is, by its own nature, going to give much glory to God. But anyway, it is somewhat disinfected by the circumstance mentioned. So there is no more need to apologize to God or to myself about it.

So it is three days before I go on retreat before making solemn vows. They brought down from the attic the suitcase with the clothes I brought here when I came. The stuff is in our dormitory cell for me to check it over, which took about one and a half minutes. The suitcase still looks shiny and new and has a Cuba Mail Line blue and white label on it, and it still has a new smell which I remember being impressed by in a hotel in Florida . . . It is almost impossible to believe that that was seven years ago. But what is more impossible is to believe that I ever wore those clothes. I do not believe in myself as a layman. I was never meant to be one, and that is good to know.

The only question I have ever asked about this vocation is whether I don't belong with the Carthusians, because of the greater solitude, strictness(?), isolation and silence. However, I have been told to drop all that – at least until after I am ordained priest, which I will try to do . . . Anyway, God knows where He wants me and there is no doubt about the coming vows. They are all I desire.

By them I mean to get rid of everything I can get rid of by that kind of an act, so as to dispose myself for getting rid of all the other attachments that are harder to shake off because even vows cannot shake them.

Solitude – not to pay any attention to what goes on in the community – the accidents of community life that don't concern me – differences of opinion, other people's ideas of the spiritual life – the kind of organ music

---

4 Merton here recommences his journal on the first page of a new notebook. No handwritten journals have been found for the entries dated December 10 through March 1, 1947.

that some people like: all that is meaningless. My only job is not to be occupied with such things.

Too much activity. I got permission to ask Reverend Father for permission to give up writing verse. It is a terrific nuisance, and it keeps my mind on myself and on images and ideas. It is a big smokescreen, and chokes the only thing that matters, which is the simple contemplation of God without useless acts. That is the thing I am made for – made for Eden, and I insist on laboring in the briars. Yet it is very difficult to keep from being that kind of fool. It is one of the hardest things I know – to keep myself from doing what is hard and unrewarding and which deprives me of what is easy and full of reward.

It is full of immediate reward – peace and eternal reward. It pleases God much more than all my own work, this step-by-step stuff, full of noise and sweat.

That light is the light of Christ. *Lumen Christi.* The light that shines in darkness and the darkness comprehends it not.

Incidentally I can see how the desire to get more of that in a Carthusian cell can be, for me here and now, an obstacle to contemplation. It is a pleasure and an activity which keep me from being empty. And it is definitely one of the works at which I should not be working. And to leave all that to God will be an act of greater faith, more pleasing to Him. I know I shall see the fruits of it, if I am faithful to it, so, Mary, help me! *Regina Solitudinis, adjuva me, Domina!* [Lady, Queen of Solitude, help me!]

March 10, 1947

Tomorrow I begin the retreat. Yesterday I read a couple of chapters of *The Cloud of Unknowing.* Every time I pick up anything like that – including especially St. John of the Cross, I feel like the three wise men when they came out of Jerusalem and once more saw the star. *Gavisi sunt gaudio magno valde* [They rejoiced with exceedingly great joy (Matthew 2:10)]. They were once more delivered from questions and uncertitude and could see their road straight ahead. In this case it is not even a question of seeing a road – it is simpler than that: it is seeing that, whenever you want to stop traveling, your journey will be already done.

The only difficulty is if you are mixed up in something that makes activity unavoidable – prescribes it practically all the time.

I have felt the same way very definitely several times in reading parts of books – struck forcibly, overwhelmingly with the completely convincing sense that what is said there is the thing God wants of me.

Since being in the monastery I have been hit that way by St. Theresa's *Way of Perfection*, chapter on distractions, etc. in the prayer of quiet, in the novitiate. [Pierre van der Meer de Walcheren's] *Le Paradis Blanc* about the Carthusians at La Val Sainte – the middle section called "Un Chartreux parle." Also the article on "Chartreux" in the *Dictionnaire de Spiritualité* [Tome II. Paris, 1937, 705–76]. Also four years ago on the feast of St. Joseph, in the novitiate – all that part of the third stanza of *The Living Flame*, where St. John of the Cross talks about the "deep caverns". The same way, in a different mode and degree, with Duns Scotus' 49th Distinction of the 4th Book of the Oxoniense, on beatitude, and parts of St. Bonaventure about desire. Then, too, in my second year in the novitiate, I was very struck by [Marie Michel] Philipon's book on Elizabeth of the Trinity, her prayer [*La Doctrine Spirituelle de Soeur Elisabeth de la Trinité*, 1947].

It would be much better and simpler if I could find out for sure if I am called to lead that kind of a life here, where it sometimes seems to be impossible. Yet is that partly my own imagination?

Ruysbroeck, St. Theresa, St. John of the Cross, Elizabeth of the Trinity – perhaps they did not have the opportunities for quiet and seclusion we have. I say *opportunities* – perhaps we do not take them. But they could always get away and be completely alone and pray.

Still, I find that really I can manage to get plenty of physical solitude even here, in Church, in the cemetery. However it is useless to be speculating about all that, it only creates confusion. God will fix things.

One of my big intentions to ask Jesus at profession is that He make us contemplatives in this house and in this Order. Surely we *can* be! Lord, please show me how. It is more than simply *doing things* with an intention to please You – the Sisters of the Good Shepherd can do that – in fact they all must. Teach us the way to perfect simplicity and emptiness of all created solicitudes, of all things that are not Yourself. But anyway, send us the Carthusians and other orders to this country, where they are needed, and where You desire them, Oh my God! You see what a barren and desolate place this world is – send us saints!

March 11, 1947

In Chapter in the martyrology – after the announcement of St. Gregory's day tomorrow (*Apostolus Anglorum* [Apostle of the English] it said) – came the commemoration of a St. Peter, martyr at Nicomedia who, having been scourged, had his wounds filled with salt and vinegar and was roasted on a gridiron.

Following that, I made the promise of obedience.

Fr. Prior received it, since Reverend Father is on his way back home from Utah, where, it is hoped, he has bought the land for the new monastery of Our Lady of the Most Holy Trinity, where it may be that I will be carrying out this obedience *usque ad mortem* [until death].

We had to use a special formula: *Pater, promitto Rev. Domno Frederico Dunne et successoribus ejus legitimis in praesentia tua obedientiam* etc. [Father, in your presence I promise obedience to Reverend Lord Frederic Dunne and his legitimate successors etc.] When I said the part about the successors, I thought of the unlimited possibilities that phrase might mean – I don't mean specific persons in this community, but just in general!

Anyway, my intention is to give myself entirely and without compromise to whatever work God wants to do in my soul, but that work is nevertheless in a certain sense already defined by a *contemplative* [underlined twice] vocation. By that it seems to me that God has signified a certain path, a certain goal, and I am to keep that in view: that is where obedience must tend according to God's signified will. That means total renunciation of the business, ambitions, honors, activities of the world – a bare minimum of concern with temporal necessities . . . However, no matter what a legitimate superior might command me, I have promised to do. So, to a certain extent, that involves the sacrifice even of contemplation. But it seems to me this has a limit, namely sacrifice of contemplation *for a time*, under certain circumstances, but never the sacrifice of *a whole contemplative vocation as such* unless God makes it inevitable by sheer force – and even in persecution I will be all the more bound to seek solitude and recollection. Queen of Heaven, guard me in my vows! However, the important thing is to live for God and not for contemplation. The reason is obvious: because a contemplative is not one who lives for contemplation, but one who lives for *God alone.*

And that is one thing I need to get good and straight. If I am too concerned with *my progress* in sanctity, in contemplation, then I am very definitely dividing my love and my energies between God and something that is less than Him.

That is why it is best to take this obedience business as literally and as universally as possible because as soon as it is divided with conditions and solicitudes, there is no longer any possibility of being a true contemplative, because a contemplative is undivided.

However, if you get too much active work, you can always ask your superiors to have pity on you.

March 12, 1947. Feast of St. Gregory the Great

What I wrote yesterday is ambiguous because it assumes that the Rule of St. Benedict is ordered to a life of pure contemplation which, as matter of fact, it is not. In fact the Fathers would have said the monastic life, as regulated by St. Benedict, was *active* in so far as it involved labor, practice of virtues, works of asceticism, active glorification of God in the Office, etc., not to mention some education implied for the children in the monastery.

Nevertheless work in the fields helps contemplation. Yesterday we were out in the middle bottom spreading manure in the grey mud, but I was so happy I was ready to laugh out loud. I suppose it was mostly the natural relief at getting away from a typewriter.

And then, even when I am not writing, I get distracted at prayer – anything will distract me. My mind is too active. Everything I do, reading, study, writing, etc., simply must be done in such a way that it is prayer and preparation for prayer. That means first of all not doing it to satisfy my voracious appetite to know, to enjoy, to achieve things, to get tangible results and taste the immediate reward of my own efforts because, if that is what leads me, everything turns to ashes as soon as I touch it.

I am disgusted when I read all this because it is a waste of time. Between every line I see the truth that accuses me and will not leave me alone: that I have not given myself entirely to God, that I am trying to hold something in reserve for myself, and that my nature and the devil are working to keep me from seeing what it is in time for profession – and the way they keep me from seeing it is to urge my mind on to more and more activity and false zeal to try and discover it by myself when only grace can tell me.

St. Gregory, you have helped me so much before – help me now. Lead me in God's ways which are beyond all ways. Teach me to advance by withdrawing from all the paths of progress in the world and becoming nothing. Help me to get away from myself.

March 13, 1947

This is the day when the collect of the ferial Mass mentions SS. Cosmas and Damian, my old friends, because the station is at their Church [in Rome], and it is fourteen years, an incredible length of time, since I used to go and look at the big mosaic there . . . that was in Lent, 1933. Christ knew where He was leading me.

I am not in the monastery for the scenery or for beautiful architecture (there is nothing very beautiful about Gethsemani) or for anything else but to learn of Christ in His school. *Ut ab ipsius numquam magisterio discedentes, in eius doctrinam usque ad mortem perseverent.* [So that never departing from His guidance, but persevering in His teaching in the monastery until death (RB, Prologue:50).] And He teaches by removing, first of all, our natural light, our human vision and understanding of things. I will travel to You, Lord, through a thousand blind alleys. You want to bring me to You through stone walls.

One of the hardest things to swallow is that God even teaches us goodness and truth by confronting us with evil and falsity. But the way He teaches us is not by the evil or the lie, but by the grace He gives us at the same time to react against it and to turn to His hidden Truth:

Noli vinci a malo sed vince in bono malum. [Be not overcome by evil, but overcome evil by good (Romans 12:21).] The faults, imperfections and weaknesses of people who are supposed to be holy! I have not been allowed to retain much of an illusion about the universal perfection of the house where I am going to make vows! But it is ceasing to disturb me. How sweet it is to forget all that stuff and to realize that it is none of my business to worry about the apparent faults of others outside of the simple means prescribed by the *Usages.* How many burdens there are that you don't really have to carry! In fact you sin by carrying them, and you give God much glory by dropping them! And so there is no need to make any decision about so many seeming imperfections in a community.

St. John of the Cross' *Cautions* are my food for this retreat and there couldn't be anything better as a preparation for vows. Also, I realize more and more that the great works of St. John of the Cross are not entirely comprehensible unless one also knows the *Cautions, Maxims, Letters,* and anecdotes about his life. For instance what he says about directors in *The Living Flame* must be qualified by what he says on Superiors in the *Cautions.*

Yesterday, walking home from the lake, was wonderful. You do not get a clear perspective of Cistercian life if you do not see your abbey from the fields on the way home from work.

March 16. Laetare Sunday. Day of Recollection

Today in the Night Office Moses went into the "interior of the desert" – *in interiora deserta,* and in the Gospel of the Mass Christ was with the 5,000 in the desert where He fed them by miracle [John 16:1–15] and then, when they wanted to make Him king, He fled "into the mountain, Himself alone," another "interior desert." All this is what strikes me and cries out to my heart. All I can do is seek to enter into the "desert" within me, and beg Him to lead me further into the "interior of the desert." I do not see the way, and I cannot. I beg that the vows I am to make three days from now may mean that. But when I saw Reverend Father yesterday he would not give me permission to stop writing poetry altogether. In fact I went in to see him and started in at once trying to introduce the subject of avoiding too much activity and remaining in solitude and being a contemplative and, before I could get fairly started, he began blocking me all along the line.

So at any rate one thing is perfectly clear. Reverend Father is set on my writing books. He says "it must be a prayer," and "must help prayer." But so far as I can see, it isn't and doesn't. However, *qui vos audit me audit*. [He that heareth you, heareth me (Luke 10:16).] I am going to make vows in the middle of this dilemma. To please God, I must write books, and writing books makes it extremely difficult, if not impossible, for me to be anything like a contemplative. Making vows in a contemplative order to lead the active life. I suppose this demands many qualifications that I am too dumb and too blind to have thought through or seen. For instance, God's ability to write straight with crooked lines. Also there is the important consideration that this conflict may be an artificial creation produced by my own subconscious mind, and my real aim is to get rid of the cross of community life, which is my real repugnance, and which my conscience clearly tells me is precisely the cross God wants me to die on!

He will lead me. I beg Him to break my dumb will between now and Wednesday so that I can give myself entirely to Him. But I have no illusion of being able to do so by virtue of my own non-existent generosity. His Spirit must do the work in me or it will never be done at all. And his Spirit must arm my will against itself and move it to work and remove all of its own obstructions.

St. Joseph, for whom I have no sensible devotion, but who has helped me much and in whose power I believe and trust, help me now! That is why God has given my profession to be on your day.

For a long time I have been praying St. Benedict to send us a regular Visitation, and now the Abbot General is due to land in New York on the 20th, the day after my profession, and the day before the feast of St. Benedict. Which all encourages me in putting all my other desires before God and trusting Him more and more.

March 17, 1947

All through the retreat I had not been struck by anything Fr. Amadeus said at all until yesterday evening and this morning, when he started talking about the Holy Ghost, and that has struck me with great force. Or rather one point he has repeated – for I was half-asleep for part of the rest. But the point is this: it is the Holy Ghost that will transform me, sanctify me. Nothing new about that and nothing extraordinary. It is just that I have suddenly *realized* it with a clarity which I never had before. And how much the work needs to be done. My own natural powers are helpless. I can do nothing about it. The work of my own intellect depresses me by its arid futility. It gets me nowhere. But I do not need to want to get myself anywhere. If I wait upon the Holy Ghost with desire, this great gift Who is God will be given to me. And it is like a kind of an awakening, a sort of intimation of all that may happen the day after tomorrow – what tremendous possibilities! What may begin to appear before that altar!

Meanwhile I will do everything I can to remain empty.

My only desire is to give myself completely to the action of this infinite love Who is God, Who demands to transform me into Himself secretly, darkly, in simplicity, in a way that has no drama about it and is infinitely beyond everything spectacular and astonishing, so is its significance and its power.

March 18, 1947

Reverend Father could hardly get to his room from the refectory last night. I saw him walking very slowly, next to the wall of the corridor, but I could not figure out who it was (it was in the dark corridor of the guest house.) He may be too ill to receive our professions tomorrow. About that, I will not even make a pious speech. God knows very well that I desire with my whole heart to make profession and make it tomorrow, but if I have to wait until some other time, I am perfectly satisfied with His will. It is much more important that Reverend Father conserve every ounce of strength that is life to him: everything important for the house is coming to a head at this moment. The Abbot General should arrive for the visitation next week. The deal for land in Utah for the new foundation is just about to be closed – Reverend Father has his private counsel in his room now, after Sext. And on top of all that, Fr. Alberic is dying up in the infirmary. The fact that two people would like to make solemn profession is of minor importance in the middle of all this.

And yet it is the biggest thing in my life, apart from Baptism – and apart from the Priesthood, if God should grant me such a grace!

It would astonish me, this fact that I am on the point of making solemn, perpetual vows in a Trappist monastery, if I were the same person I was ten years ago. But I am not really the same person in any but the most superficial sense. If I were, I could not be doing such a thing.

The Holy Ghost, Who is Love living in me, is the One Who brought this about, and Who is preparing far more surprising things in the future, if I will let Him act.

There is nothing else worth living for: only this infinitely peaceful love Who is beyond words, beyond emotion, beyond intelligence. Cradle me, Holy Spirit, in your dark silver cloud and protect me against the heat of my own speech, my own judgments, my own vision. Ward off the sickness of consolation and desire, of fear and grief that spring from desire. I will give You my will for You to cleanse and rinse of all this clay.

Tomorrow, or whenever it is, having commended to You all the needs and intentions of everybody in the world and in the Church, and of contemplatives and of my friends and all whom I have ever known, I want to give myself to You without solicitude, without fear or desire, not seeking words or silence, work or rest, light or darkness, company or solitude. For I know I will possess all things if I am empty of all things, and only You can at once empty me of all things and fill me with Yourself, the Life of all that lives and the Being in Whom everything exists.

And this will be my solitude, to be separated from myself so far as to be able to love You alone, and love You so much that I no longer realize I am loving anything. For such a realization implies a consciousness of a self separated from You. And I no longer desire to be myself, but to find myself transformed in You, so that there is no more "myself" but only Yourself. And that is when I will be what You have willed to make me from all eternity: not myself, but Love. And thus will be fulfilled in me, as You will it to be fulfilled, Your reason for the creation of the world and of me in it.

March 20, 1947

The stamp of genuineness of all the many graces of yesterday is principally this one: the sense of deep union in charity, in Christ, with those who are now forever my fathers and brothers, the family of my profession. And all this in spite of their shortcomings and my own, which still remain as obvious as ever. But such things simply don't matter. They will undoubtedly feel as if they mattered once again, but I think I will be taking it in a different spirit.

This community loves St. Joseph, and he was good to us. There were some crosses – it was an exceedingly long and busy morning – but everybody was happy and united in the Holy Spirit. So it was one of those tremendously edifying days that come from time to time when we are allowed a glimpse of what God is trying to do in this house and in all religious communities.

For the rest of my religious life I want with God's help to dispose myself for His work in me, to which I am now totally consecrated, by learning to put into effect the *Cautions* and *Counsels* of St. John of the Cross. There is definitely a life's work there, but it means clearing away a tremendous amount of obstacles. It seems that this is the most effective, detailed, concrete, simple and practical set of rules of procedure I have ever seen. They even go into more fundamental detail than St. Benedict's chapter "De Zelo Bono" [RB 72: "The Good Zeal of Monks"] to which they are a kind of a complement although they may *seem* cold and negative.

When I made simple profession I had no idea of the work the Holy Spirit wants to do in souls, although I had read so much about it. And I was far from realizing how necessary it is to give up my own desires in *everything* [underlined twice]. The truth is I sought – and still seek – my own pleasure and profit in everything, as it were instinctively. I hope I am not doing so in this – I began to write against a feeling of repugnance, I mean just now, this page. I remember how, after simple profession, I was working and studying our Order ostensibly under obedience, but really very much intoxicated with the sweetness of the taste I could draw out of some things here and there. This inevitably led to temptations *against* the vocation when the sweetness wore off.

March 23, 1947[5]

Fr. Alberic finally died last night after a long illness. He had had TB for years, but what caused his death was heart trouble. Rev. Father gave him the Last Sacraments when we were all in bed, although he had received Extreme Unction a couple of months ago shortly after his feast day.

He is now lying in the Chapter Room and looks most contented, thoroughly satisfied with everything. His death was very peaceful. You can tell. As far as I know, he was a very saintly little man. Very quiet and unobtrusive – for the last couple of years you did not see much of him, but he would come down and shuffle slowly along the cloister like a little white shadow. He liked to be with the community when he could – although he

[5] This entry for March 23, 1947, appears in Merton's journal memoir on Frederic Dunne under the title "Other Monks of Gethsemani." The entry on Alberic Wulf is the only entry under this title.

had been practically isolated for years. He and I had a sort of a pact about saying prayers for one another – I would offer communions for him and he would give me a commemoration in his Mass. Once he even gave me a whole Mass, which fell to his own choice.

He was censor, and censored our poems, etc. He wrote the *Compendium [of the History of the Cistercian Order]* about which he was very humble. He had a great love for the *Cisterziënser Chronik* and I suppose he was the only one in the house who had read most of it. He also wrote our *Necrology*[6] we have been reading in the refectory for the last three or four years. In fact, he used to rewrite and make changes all the time. He was in love with the Order and the history of the Order. He had studied [Leopold] Janauschek's *Origines Cistercienses [Tomus I* (Wien, 1877)] from cover to cover.

For several years he had been retreat master for seculars, and professor – I guess for a long time.

He was very charitable and fairly radiated innocence and simplicity everywhere he went. He had grown more and more childlike as he grew older, and had an extremely simple and perfect faith in his superiors. He was very fond of St. Francis de Sales and St. Anselm and often offered to preach and fill in, when there was an emergency, for a conference, etc. He studied at Fribourg under Mandonnet, I believe – came here before the first World War on a *transitus* from some other order.

I don't suppose he'll be very long in Purgatory! In fact he was simple enough to get out of it altogether, perhaps with the mercy of the Christ he loved.

March 25, 1947. Feast of the Annunciation

Yesterday it was a grey, muggy day and we were sweating in our winter robes and this morning outside it is trying to snow.

The particular grace of the Annunciation for me this year is a small material cross of pain. O.K. Glad to have you, pain. Pains are very good things to pry a man loose from his attachments in the spiritual life because if you get a good one, you know that you will probably be too knocked out to draw any pleasure or sensible consolation out of your prayers and reading and the Office and so on. Everything will demand an effort. Even if I spit some blood, that does not mean anything in particular. The thing to do is to go ahead and do as much of the common routine of things as one can, and I am sorry I went and sat down on the bench of the infirm during

---

[6] Short biographical notices of the deceased members of the community.

the morning meditation before I really needed to. The children of Israel didn't get into the promised land because they refused to believe everything God told them about trusting Him in the wilderness.

Fr. Alberic died Saturday night and was buried yesterday. And yesterday Frater Edwin, who is a big strong monk, fell over in the scriptorium after Sext and they heard his confession, as he sat at his desk, before carting him off to the infirmary, where as far as I know he is all right.

The Abbot General is due to arrive this afternoon.

We have got to let God do His will in us. His Spirit must work in us and not our own. But since original sin, we always tend to work against Him when we work under our own direction. Therefore His Spirit will seem at times to be our enemy, that is, the enemy of our flesh. *Qui spiritu Dei aguntur carnem suam crucifixerunt.* [Those who are moved by the spirit of God have crucified their flesh (Galatians 5:25).] Go ahead and suffer. The safe way is pain, weariness, darkness, helplessness. *Beati qui lugent.* [Blessed are those who mourn (Matthew 2:5).] It is the hard way that is the easiest. I wish I would never grieve You, Christ, by refusing the things that are for my good and that come to me from Your love. I beg You today, teach me to accept Your best gifts, so that You may live in me according to Your Father's will! And it occurs to me: after all, what strength was there in Mary? She was nothing but a little girl in a village. What could she do? What did she know? But because she was the handmaid of the Lord, she did and suffered more than all the rest of the world put together.

The snow has stopped and there is a bright sky full of clouds, chased by a wind that lashes the building and sounds cold. I have not been out in it yet. Queen of Heaven, I love you.

Thursday, March 27, 1947

Snow has been falling steadily ever since last night or early this morning. I first noticed it after the Night Office and by now there is more of it on the ground than I have ever seen in Kentucky. It must be close to a foot deep. The arrival of the Abbot General [Dom Dominique Nogues] on Tuesday at about 1:30 in the afternoon was quite impressive. It was cold and there were flurries of snow between bursts of sun. We stood around in a lot of wind while he was getting into a robe and cowl in the Gatehouse. Then he came out with a mitre on and looking as though he meant business.

Opening the Visitation he said: "I believe you have a good abbot, but in any case we'll know in a few days."

This morning I served his Mass, and afterward I handed him his cowl the wrong way and he got it on inside out, but he wasn't upset at all. In fact I can see that he is not the kind of man to get excited over trifles, or to get carried away by anybody's monkey business. It is six years, or five and a bit, since we have had a Visitation. This is the first since I am in the house and I pray to God that it will be a good one.

For my own part, I guess my pains are tied up with the Visitation. Tuesday evening I was so knocked out I had to go to see the infirmarian and now I am more or less on relief,[7] that is, until dinner I am on it less, or not at all. Don't know whether I am supposed to be, but anyway I have been taking things slow and the pains are better, so fasting doesn't really matter. Fr. Vincent de Paul, the novice who came in from the Army Medical Corps, gave me an examination, but found no TB or heart trouble. Maybe it is something like pleuresy. Whatever it is, it is a gift from God and its main value is to remind me how detached I am *not*. Wouldn't it be nice to be a saint and never be distracted by my stupid body and its woes? But I suppose very few of the saints were that way, and so I thank God for my own weakness and the knowledge that I can still get concerned about myself. If you can't be a contemplative when you are sick, or you think you are, when are you ever going to be one? I don't believe in a contemplation that only comes along when you are in health, although St. Thomas somewhere says that health is necessary for contemplation. Someday I'll have to look it up and see just what he means by it.

However, since my profession I don't feel like reading anything except Scripture and St. John of the Cross.

March 30, 1947. Palm Sunday
The visitation is in full swing. If I had kept my resolution about following the *Cautions* of St. John of the Cross and "not seeing" anything that goes on in the community, I would not have found out by signs which of the monks were closeted with the General for two hours or more and I would not have been tempted to get impatient at the foolishness of human beings. It seems to me to be very silly for contemplatives to take their own opinions so seriously when contemplatives are supposed to be beyond opinions . . . Having expressed this opinion, I now proceed.

[7] At Gethsemani the "indulgence," another more nourishing dish at meals, was called the "relief."

I still think the General, who seems to be as wide as he is high, and has a big, determined Daumier countenance under his black calotte, I still think he can handle anything that Gethsemani has to offer, but it is bound to wear him down. He plans to finish the scrutiny[8] and then officiate at everything for the last three days of Holy Week, giving our own Reverend Father a rest.

Dom Benoît [Morvan] of Notre Dame du Phare in Japan came with the Reverend General as his secretary. I went up to see him to ask a few questions about Mother Berchmans and it ended up by a general conversation on everything concerning the Order and the interior life. It was a serious enough conversation to warrant its being as long as it turned out to be.

From what he said I am confirmed in my impression that a new spirit is gradually replacing the old "Trappist" spirit: the old, intense, narrow and rather frigid emphasis on works of mortification with practically nothing else in view except a good crown in the other world and the salvation of some souls in this.

There are definitely real contemplative vocations in Our Order (I am talking about infused contemplation, not "composition of place" and "application of the senses."[9] And at least at Cîteaux they are finding the right kind of encouragement. There Dom Godefroid [Bélorgey]'s Chapters in the morning generally have something in them to keep souls directed to contemplative prayer. This is good. One thing that struck me about Dom Godefroid's book [*Pratique de l'oraison mentale* (Paris, 1945–46)] of which I read bits of the second volume on mystical prayer was that it seemed rather light and thin. But at least it is *something*.

But, oh God! Give us the generosity that will enable You to lead us into the depths. Empty us of our dumb and groping natural tastes and deliver us from the menace of a silly and superficial mysticism, a sort of frivolous and cheap playing with the sweetness of quiet and simplicity and rest. We need to be stripped and emptied, humbled too, as Dom Benoît insisted. If pride goes, the rest will be easy: all that is cheap will go out with pride. Yet it is pride to want to be stripped and emptied in the grand manner with thunder and lightning. Disappearing into the ordinary ways is the simplest and most effective.

He said we have very few contemplative vocations in Japan.

---

[8] Appointments with each individual monk.

[9] Methods of meditation taught by St. Ignatius Loyola in his classic, *The Spiritual Exercises.*

Also a monk of Thymadeuc, who went to the Chartreuse to try it out, came home after ten days saying the people didn't seem to be very serious about their life, but the scenery was pretty. But an ex-Carthusian has settled down happily at Cîteaux. About all this I make no sweeping conclusions. Since profession I have not been bothered in the least by that affair and there is no point in even thinking about it.

Dom Benoît did not think writing verse would do me any harm and would do others good – the common teaching of theologians around here! I wonder what the General will say.

April 1, 1947

Yesterday, Monday in Holy Week, I spoke to the General in the scrutiny and now I see that I was unfair in feeling critical about the ones who stayed in there two hours or so because I was in there an hour before I realized it, and had a very good time, too. Most of what I had to say about the house I wrote down on paper and gave to him, and then we talked about everything else under the sun. However a lot of things transpired which needed to come out.

For one thing the General is pleased with the notion of my writing poems, although he said he didn't understand them. And he told me very emphatically, in fact it was the most emphatic thing he said and the only thing that really sounded like an official pronouncement, that it was good and even necessary for me to go on writing. He said specialists were needed in the Order – writers, liturgists, canonists, etc. And if I had been trained along a certain line, I should by all means use my craft and anyway it was a matter of obedience. So that settles that, as far as I can see, until I get into different circumstances, if I ever do. In other words it should be clear by now that it is God's will for me to write and write poems and write everything else I am told.

However Dom Dominique also said that writing and specialized learning were not for the Order as a whole, which is evident.

He said he did not think Joseph Cassant[10] would ever be canonized – there was nothing to warrant it. There are hundreds like him in the Order and hundreds like Mother Berchmans and Marie Bernarde de Lambilly, whose life was printed by his monastery of Thymadeuc. He told me a lot of

---

[10] A nineteenth-century monk of Sainte-Marie du Désert. Despite having no natural gifts, he lived the Trappist life with a holiness evident to those who lived with him.

funny stories and a long involved tale of Charles de Foucauld's nephew who was five years or so at Thymadeuc and whose mother used to send Dom Dominique three bottles of Pommard every year. The nephew of Charles de Foucauld ended up teaching at Laval, Quebec, and was finally killed in the war. Dom Dominique said he didn't think [Charles] de Foucauld would be canonized either because *après tout il faisait tout ce qu'il voulait* [after all he did everything he wanted]! He thought it was foolish to hide anything in the life of anyone like Joseph Cassant, i.e., his being sent home for a month or two when he was ill, and I think so too, so if I write it, I will know what to do.

He told me to go on publishing under the name of Thomas Merton.

He said sanctity in this Order was a matter of allowing yourself to be formed through obedience and he also said our vow of conversion of manners amounted to the same as vowing to do what is more perfect all the time, which is saying a great deal.

Talking about Italy he said that there were very few Trappist vocations there. Frattocchie is full of Frenchmen. Tre Fontane is practically empty. Fossanova, however, wanted to enter the Order, he said. They are so far still with the Common Observance and empty. Dom Alexis Presse, who left Tamié because the Order wasn't strict enough for him, is in an old Cistercian monastery that is some sixty kilometers from Thymadeuc – I don't know which house it is – but anyway he is not doing well.

About Gethsemani one of things he said was that the questions we asked of the Definitors in Rome made them laugh because we could easily find the answers in our books, and he said we didn't do things according to the books around here. In other words, we don't know our *Usages* and *Ceremonial*, etc. Today he made us stop making a useless bow we had all been making on entering Church in the procession after dinner.

He doesn't seem to take the attitude that we have more lunatics here than anywhere else, and by now he knows the community thoroughly well. Of course he knew who to look out for before he even got here.

I will be very interested to see how the Visitation Card reads. I expect to be working on it the day after tomorrow, translating it with Dom Benoît. Dom Dominique told me to go ahead and modify whatever I liked. I declined with thanks. He told me some other jokes, too, some of which I did not quite understand, like one about the mother of Guy de Fontgalland, who is another one who isn't going to get canonized either. And then he said why didn't I write some poems in French? I told him to write poetry you had to read some and there was not time for that, and he made no difficulties whatever about agreeing.

He said there were several ways of ruining a Cistercian monastery and some of them were: to admit too many postulants to the choir who did not have enough education (i.e., who had not finished humanities); to admit too many priests of the kind who had more or less been asked to leave their dioceses; or, to admit too many people from other Orders. Practically all our postulants seem to fall into groups one and three, and we have too many who crack up under the strain of trying to mix their studies and our life. If you have learned to read and digest things before you come, however, the thing is a snap.

This Holy Week is not for me but for God. I enter it as His servant, His minister, to perform public functions for His glory, a voice for His Mystical Body. I will take for myself whatever He wants me to have, but ask nothing. I want to give it all to Him.

April 3, 1947. Holy Thursday

I began translating the Visitation Card yesterday and it is a very solid and even an inspiring document. Dom Dominique certainly knows how to handle it and I was especially interested in a page he had crossed out and in the way he changed it with the result that the meaning was at the same time more serene and more profound. He had eliminated things that were very good in themselves, but which might have seemed to stigmatize individuals. Yet when it was all done, he had everything in. There were a lot of things I did not expect, but which I was very glad to see. The whole card is marked by a spirit of counsel and charity. And anyway in general it concludes that we have a good, fervent community: our faults are only minor ones, and we must expect defects of character in certain individuals.

So I am impressed and edified at this glimpse of how the Holy Ghost works in the machinery of a religious Order and how peacefully and smoothly he produces His effects. There is a world of difference at this moment between the atmosphere in the house and that which prevailed last October, for example. And no one could put a finger on where and how it all took place. But the answer is to be found in the graces of Lent, Holy Week and the Visitation. Also, I repeat what I observed on the day of my solemn profession, that what a grace for me overflowed and had its visible effects in everyone else, or, at least, in the community at large.

Dom Benoît preached in Chapter about the Mystical Body and it was very much to the point. It was one of those sermons in which familiar ideas strike you as discoveries, yet the theme, our oneness by reason of the Eucharist, was something that was haunting me around the time of the Feast of the Little Flower [Thérèse of Lisieux] in 1943. It appears to be one of her truths anyway. Dom Benoît referred to her first Communion and her sense of increased union with her mother who had died. And again, I am all in admiration at the way the Holy Ghost teaches people – little girls, children – people who don't know anything . . .

It seems to me more and more that I must give up all desire for lights and consolations in prayer and for all other satisfactions. That means not so much getting all in a lather about penance and trying to kill myself with a lot of spectacular mortifications, but simply to go on doing normal and regular things *without any attempt to satisfy my own appetites in them.* The crucial point in all this is Holy Communion and I suppose this is a good day to think about it. I have been getting upset and worried when things interfered with my thanksgiving. Dom Vital told me to receive [Communion] at the second round, when I was serving second round Masses, and, as a result, I had to go straight from the altar to Lauds and, as soon as I get in choir, I am drowned in distractions. Impossible for me to make any kind of thanksgiving – or rather to make my normal kind which consists in simply trying to let myself be absorbed in silence and darkness and peace which are pervaded with a restful and intangible but very real sense of the presence and nearness of God, of union with Him. None of that in choir – only torture. I suppose that was precisely what God wants to detach me from, and I have realized that and obeyed Dom Vital in believing in it, but with no natural attraction!!

Today I am Thurifer. I made my thanksgiving stripping the altars. That is the acknowledgment Christ wants of me, and therefore it is what I want. And all summer I am going to want those things, and for the rest of my life. Not to read for myself, not to work for myself, not to pray for my own pleasure.

And to give up these stupid irritations at my own failings and those of others, and take things patiently in the charity of Christ, not like a fake martyr, but accepting the imperfections of this world in humility and peace, to show my love for Him, my trust in Him. To do otherwise is to show that I still want to rely on some strength, some perfection of my own, something that is in men and in the world around me. And if *that* is the reason why we want the monastery to be perfect, Jesus will never allow it to become so. For it has to be perfect not for the satisfaction of those who live here, but only for His glory.

April 4, 1947. Good Friday

I had a pious thought but I won't put it down.

Outside it rains. The best place to be this afternoon was in Church. It rained hard and you could hear it beating all over the long roof.

I had a thought about the psalter but I won't put that down either.

The thoughts that come to me are stupid.

I and Fr. Tarcisius helped Father Prior dismantle the baldachin that was used in the processions with the Blessed Sacrament and then I unhooked something and it fell to the floor with a loud bang, and Mr. Hogan, the fat lawyer from Cincinnati, was kneeling/sitting there at the bench, but I guess he didn't jump. Which reminds me that the gent whose feet I washed at the Mandatum in the cloister yesterday didn't need the dollar I placed in his hands.

Father Prior could not have found two more impractical monks to help him take apart a baldachin than me and Fr. Tarcisius, but I felt very proud that I was chosen: it made me feel efficient.

And yesterday, when I was thurifer, I got a sore knee and got the bows and genuflections all mixed up and Father Edmund was deacon and he and I were running around the sanctuary incensing first one abbot then another (there are four in the house including Dom Vital), and when he suddenly remembered he had forgotten Dom Vital, he started praying in an audible whisper.

I am knocked out but I can't think of any valid reason why I should want to be otherwise. There is not much use making long speeches to Christ, especially on Good Friday. A pain is a good enough prayer and it is a better one, if you only sit still under it, than an interior picnic. Pains are prayers in proportion as you shut up about them, and love God with them.

But why do I talk as if I really had something?

Yesterday the General told me we ought to desire infused contemplation and repeated that living our life simply and without fuss was the way to dispose ourselves for it. It is good to have this from someone who comes to the monastery with credentials from the Holy Ghost written, so to speak, all over him.

April 5, 1947. Holy Saturday

The Visitation was just closed in Chapter and everybody seems well satis-fied with everything. All smiling and happy and content. That is how the Holy Ghost works. He would work the same even, I think, if there were se-rious things to correct, but there is certainly nothing seriously wrong here.

One of the results of the Visitation is that I must go looking for a new confessor. The Masters of Novices have been forbidden to hear confes-sions as it keeps them too busy. We nearly didn't get to go to Communion today as we had been doing the last two or three years, like the seculars. The General reproved it as contrary to the Order's customs, but allowed us all to go today since we had been counting on it.

April 6, 1947. Easter Sunday

I have been deliberately holding myself back so as not to let myself desire to get too worked up by the Liturgy – to avoid an overflow of sensible con-solation. I know very well that some people – the ones who write the "arty" books about the Liturgy – would be incensed, but it has had good effects. Underneath a certain indifference and even callousness towards the *Al-leluias* there is a deep interior peace that has not been shaken by the neces-sity of a certain amount of running around on errands demanded by obedience.

First there is this upset about the confessors. Nobody is quite sure how things are to turn out, but apparently I can stay with Dom Vital for a while. I'd rather not change, if possible, because he is better able to manage me than anyone I have hit so far, and he has the virtue of telling you your faults point blank without a lot of evasions.

Then I had to talk to Father Francis on some business for the General about our incunabula and manuscripts. And there was a lot of other things, too. But really I didn't get upset by any of it and this grace is attributable to detachment from sensible consolations to do with the Feast, I think.

So for my own part I think it is not necessary to make any special effort to follow the Liturgy by preparations and advanced reading and meditation and what not. Follow the Office and the Rule intelligently and with de-tachment and the thing will take care of itself. We do not always have to be prodding and goading and stirring ourselves up with affections and ideas once we have got well into the rhythm of this life and live it with recollec-tion, and keep in the presence of God. The liturgy takes care of us almost automatically. It ought to be second nature to a professed monk, and it doesn't take any special effort of thought for me to remind myself that

Lent is over. Everything is so different from what it was three days ago that we are in a new world, a completely new atmosphere. To be too self-conscious about it would only be harmful for me. Others can work out their own solutions. Mine is to keep myself and my tastes and feelings and desires and affections and ideas out of the picture, out of God's way, and let Him work on the deep level where these things cannot penetrate.

But the big thing is to do all this not for myself, but for God, for His love, to please Him. Actually, this is in the Liturgy itself. *Quae sursum sunt sapite, non quae supra terram.* [Mind the things that are above, not the things that are on earth (Colossians 3:2).] Good Friday, Holy Saturday, Easter week are all tremendous expressions of what St. John of the Cross was teaching, especially the *Exultet*, which is, in a sense, the key to the whole business.

Our efforts to love God by purifying our hearts for Him, as it were, refresh and rejoice Him. I thought of that on Good Friday. His *"Sitio"* [thirst on the Cross] is for the purity of our hearts, the emptiness of our hearts, that His joy, His freedom, His perfection of health and life may fill them. He thirsts to do us good, and we prevent Him by our selfishness. It is unselfishness, detachment, that procure us our greatest good which is the *amor amicitiae* [the love of friendship], the love of God for Himself alone, because He alone is good. And that love is the *vinculum perfectionis* [bond of perfection], the bond that unites us to Him. In fact by that love we are drawn into union with Him by the same bond that unites Him to Himself, the Holy Spirit.

And we love God as He loves Himself, with His own love.

Dom Benoît told us a lot of wonderful things in Chapter about the Order. Elizabeth of the Trinity worked what seems to be a first-class miracle on the Prior of Cîteaux with a practically instantaneous cure of TB of the bones that had been declared hopeless. At Bellefontaine there is a monk seventy years old or so who just made profession. He had been dean of a Catholic university, entered the Order after the death of his wife, and the sermon at his profession was preached by his grandson. Dom Vital Lehodey is still alive – ninety years old – very holy, talks about the Child Jesus all the time and says Mass in a chair, reads Lives of the Saints all day and can't talk about material things. Brother Francis, an oblate at Aiguebelle, was a big business man, led a worldly life, no faith. One night he walked into a hotel and was surprised to see a young nun there. When he mentioned this to the clerk, the clerk laughed and said he was mistaken.

How could he be seeing nuns in a hotel? A few days later in the house of a friend he saw a picture of the Little Flower and recognized his nun. So eventually he ended up in Aiguebelle. The Little Flower does a lot of recruiting for La Trappe. My vocation is not without her influence. Pray for me, Thérèse, to be a true child of God, to love God alone, to belong entirely to Him, to give Him joy and glory forever.

April 15, 1947

So it is the 15th. This afternoon I had to write some business letters and dated them the 18th. Yesterday we celebrated the transferred feast of St. Ambrose and today, that of Blessed Juliana. Dom Vital is holding on to some of his penitents for the time being but, in obedience to Reverend Father, I changed to Father Anthony [Chassagne]. Yesterday he gave me for my penance, to say three times, the secret for the Mass of Low Sunday, and I noticed for the first time how beautiful it is.[11]

However I am inclined to be not exultant about some things. First of all, it would be so simple if only the clear and definite suggestions of the Visitation Card were put into practice at once and without equivocation. But no. Perhaps there are good reasons, but the only ones that have reached me seem to be quibbles, except the one about not changing the confessors until the new foundation leaves, in a couple of months or so. And that is sensible enough.

But I ask myself: how far can it be said to be God's will for me to worry about the application of the Visitation Card? There is nothing I can do about it. Until there is some clear obligation on my part to do or say something, I can only act as if I had forgotten all about it and saw nothing. God does not want anyone ever to get upset about anything.

And there is no point in acting as if other houses and other Orders all kept all their rules perfectly and had no one in them with any faults.

Once again I renounce my vain desire for a contemplative paradise on earth. This is to be my Paradise, a paradise of pleasure not for me, but for the Heart of Christ, by my renouncing all these fool ideas, and accepting difficulties and human imperfections in myself and in everybody else. That is the only way to the one true solitude which is within my own heart.

---

[11] "Receive, we beseech Thee, O Lord, the gifts of thy exulting Church, and grant that she to whom Thou hast given cause for so great joy, may obtain also the fruit of perpetual gladness. Through our Lord."

Regnum Dei intra vos est. [For lo, the kingdom of God is within you (Luke 17:21).] The way to enter there is by love. *Christus non sibi placuit.* [For Christ did not please himself (Romans 15:3).]

April 16, 1947. Wednesday

A big day. Fr. George [Couillard] celebrated his sixtieth anniversary in religion. He shuffled out to the high altar in the beautiful new white vestments presented last fall by Fr. Anthony's friends at his solemn profession, climbed the steps lifted on either side by the deacon and subdeacon, and sang the Votive Mass of the Immaculate Conception with great emotion and some little incoherence, but with all his heart. He is very happy, full of energy, and kept a better Lent than I did, fasting the whole time without even the indulgence which I had for the last ten days, and he got up at two every morning with the rest of us.

As for me, at last I got a cross I can understand and embrace with joy. The Censor at the Valley, Father Gabriel [O'Connell], flung back *The Seven Storey Mountain*, refusing his *nihil obstat* with caustic remarks about my style, suggesting that I was not yet capable of writing such a book "with his present literary equipment," and suggesting that I take a correspondence course in grammar. He also objected to my frankness about my past. Since the General is going to be at the Valley for their visitation (he is now on the way there from New Melleray [Iowa]) and, since Reverend Father is going there too, I sent back the ms. with a lot of questions. I am afraid I got a bit sarcastic in the three pages of single-spaced, self-defense I wrote. So tomorrow I will write a note and apologize.

However, I have no desire to claim any "rights" or to make a fuss because, thank God, I can see clearly that Christ is working here for His own interests and I am more glad of it than I can say. It is a consolation to me, and it would be a consolation, too, if the whole thing were to be thrown in an ash-can, because I would know it was God's will and that's all I want.

Sometimes I have a great desire to drop all writing, but today I can see that my way to sanctification lies in learning how to write under all the strange conditions imposed by Cistercian life, and in writing carefully and well for the glory of God, denying myself, and checking my haste to get into print.

It will do me good to stop and choose words, to think, re-read and correct. I have done a lot of re-writing in the present book about the Order, and I am glad, though it has slowed everything down. Then I am once again correcting the Mother Berchmans ms., typed by novices for me.[12] All the rest is still mouldering with the diocesan censors. And all this is the will and work of Christ. They are His books and I am His monk. He knows what He is doing. In the end it will all be for His glory and I, from being a wild and lazy and vain and self-centered, third-rate poet, will become a saint, and He will live in me and in the things I write and men will give Him glory and love Him. I am very happy.

April 20, 1947. Good Shepherd Sunday. Day of Recollection

If I were to make any resolutions, it would be the same old ones – no need to make them – they have been made. No need to reflect on them – it doesn't take much concentration to see how I keep them. I struggle along. It is useless to break your head over the same old details week after week and year after year, pruning the same ten twigs off the top of the tree. Get at the *root:* union with God. On these days drop everything and hide in yourself to find Him in the silence where He is hidden with you, and listen to what He has to say.

Cistercians should not have to make the same kind of days of recollection as Jesuits or Christian Brothers, or business men.

What a lot of things since last month's day of recollection which seems like a year ago. I keep thinking of solemn profession and every time it comes to my mind I am more profoundly happy. There is only one thing to live for: love. There is only one unhappiness: not to love God. That is what pains me on these days of recollection, to see my own soul so full of movement and shadows and vanities, cross-currents of dry wind, stirring up the dust and rubbish of desire. I don't expect to avoid this humiliation in my life, but when will I become cleaner, more simple, more loving: *tu Domine, usquequo* [but you, O Lord, how long (Habakkuk 1:2; Psalms 12:1)]? I can't give up writing, and everywhere I turn I find the stuff I write is sticking to me like fly-paper, and the gramophone inside me is playing that same old tune "Admiration, admiration – You are my ideal – you are the one, original cloistered genius, the tonsured wonder of the Western world."

It is not comforting to be such a confounded ape. It would be silly to console yourself that others are probably the same. So then God does not get pure love, perfect adoration from anyone on earth, even in monasteries? It is all this dusty, shopworn business, second-hand, all marked up with

---

[12] The "book about the Order" was later published as *The Waters of Siloe*, and the Mother Berchmans manuscript as *Exile Ends in Glory*.

fingerprints. *Miserere mei, Domine. Peccatum meum contra me est semper.*
[Have mercy on me, O God. My sin is always before me (Psalms 50:3, 5).]
   (Oh, shut up! This is an exercise, too!)
   This week I am on the schola with Fr. Mauritius, Fr. Walter, Fr. Xystus.
It is probably the last time all four of us will even sing together, unless we
all get sent to Utah. We sang for all we were worth. At Benediction *O Filii
et Filiae* and *Hortus Conclusus*. St. Anselm, pray for us.

April 23, 1947. Roman Calendar: The Solemnity of St. Joseph
Our typewriter is broken again.
   I was working on Dom Urban Guillet and Fr. Joseph Dunand. It is easy
to sit back and judge the errors of other people, but nevertheless the story
of the first Trappists in Kentucky gives me the creeps. They wanted to
teach school. They wanted to be missionaries. They couldn't make up their
minds about where to settle; they got themselves in debt simply by being
foolish and reckless. They traveled around, dragging with them their
"schools" – teachers and students – and traveling meant the most fantastic
hardships. The monks died off like flies, living the Val Sainte regime in pioneer America. And through it all you get this feeling, as Fr. Badin said of
Dom Urban, that these superiors were following their own ideas and personal enthusiasms rather than the Holy Spirit, and they wouldn't take advice from anybody. I suppose they had learned all that from Dom
Augustin.[13]
   This is one of the big dangers in Cistercian life – our sheer energy gets
away with us. We think that anything that costs us is God's will. If we want
something, we easily persuade ourselves that God wants it as soon as it requires a little suffering to get it. From this fallacy of making a fetish out of
difficulties for their own sakes, we get into the most fantastic positions, and
use ourselves up, not for God but for ourselves. And we think we have
done great things for God just because we are worn out. The devil has
been having an easy time of it with Trappists ever since de Rancé.[14]
   It is a big danger in my own life. I grouse and complain about the work I
have to do. Secretly I am in it as deep as Dom Urban was in his crazy Third
Order and his Indian school. Reverend Father, who is another one, accepts

---

[13] Merton was doing research for *The Waters of Siloe*. Guillet and Dunand were early Cistercian
pioneers in America; Dom Augustin is Louis Henri de Lestrange, who sent the first Trappists
to America in 1803.
[14] Jean-Armand le Bouthillier de Rancé, the Abbot of La Trappe (1663–1700) in France, made
his community the model for what would eventually be called the Trappist Reform.

all the wild projects I propose to him and then I say "It is obedience, God wills it," and I go ahead and write a piece of junk like the thing I did on St. Lutgarde last year. I had to look at it again today. It is a crime to waste time with that stupid and heavy stuff. It looks learned but it is not. It will never do any good to the simple who won't be able to read it, and those who know something will know enough not to bother with it.

As for the poems: now I am kidding myself that I am an apostle. Still, I guess I can't avoid it. Everyone tells me I must go on. But God keep me from throwing myself away on such nonsense. What is the use of writing the same silly poem over and over again, which is all that I do. I think the things I wrote at St. Bona's [St. Bonaventure's College] were better than what I have written here: they were sharper and stronger and full of economy and went straight to the point without unnecessary rhetoric.

Another big vice of Trappist writers: long-windedness. We go in for interminable, abstract discussions, sermons and lectures. I noticed that with Father Raymond's stuff and everybody said it about *The Seven Storey Mountain*, from Naomi Burton to Father Gabriel.

It comes from laziness and a kind of hypnotism of ourselves by our own ideas.

And then that devouring itch to get into print which makes you override everything.

April 25, 1947. Feast of St. Mark

Litany today after Prime. The weather has been very bad – cold and rainy – and we haven't planted much of anything yet. I talk as if I knew what was going on on the farm, but all I know is what I hear in Chapter.

The infinite God has to compete for possession of my mind with the notion of a beautiful typewriter with French accents on it.

Last night I dreamt that six Carthusians came to Gethsemani to become Trappists. I was just at the point of discovering what had impelled them to do such a thing when I woke up.

When we preach practice sermons in class, the other clerics write down their opinions and Father Anthony gives the preacher the result, anonymous excerpts. The other day I preached a sermon. The comments were interesting. I was praised for avoiding "his usual heavy philosophy." Another said I was in general "too scholastic." I was blamed for being too much like a classroom lecturer. I was worse: I felt myself getting into the chatty tone of a ham radio announcer. It embarrassed me to no end, but I couldn't shake myself out of it. I got into some critical discussion as to whether or not St. Bernard taught the doctrine of the Mystical Body and somebody did not like that.

It had never occurred to me to wonder about most of these things.

In general the monks, myself included, cannot stand controversy, argument, polemics, weighty analysis. It oppresses one beyond measure when someone begins to talk about that sort of thing in sermons and conferences. The business of fighting to establish one opinion with its foot firmly placed on the neck of another: it fills the whole community with silent dejection. Also sermons full of dark allusions and veiled attacks on abuses in the community are intolerable, even when the abuses, minor ones, exist.

I realize more and more the futility of criticism, even true and just. What we need is encouragement, positive and clear direction. Sermons need to show us how to get united with one another, to overcome evil with good.

However all this does not apply to the correction of faults *by superiors*, for that fills a real need and gives everybody peace.

April 26, 1947. Saturday

Today I managed to get out to work. We were clearing stumps out of a field they want to plant with oats, newly cleared land next to St. Edmund's field. We cut down all the trees there the winter before last. It was a nice day for a change and all the hills are beginning to be clouded with green, our spring having finally arrived. And here and there in the green wash that covers the woods you see a little cloud of pink, where there is a wild peach tree, or whatever kind of tree it is that has those blossoms. I wish it would be a wild peach tree – the idea is attractive.

In the refectory we finished the reading of *St. Paul, Apostle and Martyr*, and now we have a brochure on the dedication of the Cathedral of Salt Lake City in 1936.

And as for me, oh my God, I don't care about anything; all I know is that I want to love You. I want my will to disappear in Your will. I want to be one spirit with You. I want to become all Your desires and thoughts. I want to live in the middle of Your Trinity and praise You with the flames of Your own praise. Oh my God, knowing all this, why do You leave me alone in my selfishness and in my vanity and pride, instead of drawing me into the midst of Your love? My God, do not delay any longer to make me a saint and to make me One with You, and do not delay to live in me. And if it requires sacrifice, You will give me the courage to make all sacrifices. And You will consume me in Your own immense love. So do not be afraid of my weakness, oh God, because You can do everything. I believe in Your love above all things. I have forgotten everything else (that is, I want to). I live for Your love if You will only make me live so.

And until You make me a saint, I am at least going to try and act as if I were one.

April 27, 1947. Third Sunday after Easter

Modicum et non videbitis me . . . mundus autem gaudebit . . . sed tristitia vestra vertetur in gaudium . . . et gaudium vestrum nemo tollet a vobis. [A little while and you shall not see me (John 16:17) . . . but the world shall rejoice (John 16:20) . . . but your sorrow shall be turned into joy (John 16:20) . . . and your joy no man shall take from you (John 16:22).] The Gospel rings in my ears. This day's Gospel always does.

I think there are plenty of crosses on their way to me, and I am glad. Maybe within five years I shall be dead. But I am not a prophet. Wherever the cross is, I know I am on the right track. So today I am on the right track.

There are plenty of active works you don't need to burden yourself with: all the material and spiritual functions in the monastery which are none of your business and above all your own health. How free you can become if you stop worrying about things that don't concern you! The first thing for a contemplative is to mind his own business, and all care of yourself, physically, materially, is no longer your business. It is in the hands of somebody else – God.

April 28, 1947

On and off since Easter I have been playing a dandy new game called insomnia. It goes like this. You lie down in bed and listen to everybody else snoring without, however, going to sleep yourself. But the fun doesn't really begin until you get up and try to keep awake in choir, or walk around the monastery bumping into the walls. Actually, of course, it is a fine form of contemplation, if you try to use it, which consists in taking it as it comes without fuss or uproar.

I got a letter from a Father Humphrey [Pawsey, a Carthusian] at Parkminster, it was about some work, a letter from a Charterhouse . . . at the end he asked us for a copy of our *Spiritual Directory*, which made me laugh a little. I suppose he is sitting in his cell thinking about the Cistercians the way I am here thinking about the Carthusians. Tomorrow is the Feast of St. Robert [of Molesme, a Cistercian founder]. All I have got to do is love God. And everything else is a waste of time.

April 29, 1947. St. Robert

I read a little pamphlet from Parkminster on the contemplative, his place in the Church (not *La Vie Contemplative—Son rôle apostolique*). It was good but thin in spots. The historical argument that all the early monastic orders were considered as purely contemplative is weak because of equivocation in the term "contemplative." However, the Montreuil pamphlet is excellent. I do not cease to admire its solidity. Even this little, twenty-nine page thing from Parkminster seemed to insist that *infused contemplation* was the end of a contemplative vocation.

The Carthusians are so clear on that point – and we are *not*. They also sent us *Umbratilem*[15] in Latin and English.

Fr. Bartholomew preached in Chapter and it was good. All about [John of the Cross'] the Night of the Senses. The only intelligent sermon on that kind of a topic I have heard here. Many can preach on trials in general and on abandonment – those things are thoroughly understood. But trials in connection with progress in prayer are not so well understood.

The little dogwood tree planted in the garden is in full-bloom and after evening meditation a humming bird got caught in the cloister, very scared of the monks going to supper. The candles are burning by the relic of St. Robert's finger-bone. In the refectory they began reading the life of some mystic whose name I could not catch. And now I will study something on St. Paul to the Hebrews, Chapter XII.

April 30, 1947

We had a moral theology exam and then my chest was x-rayed, and the mystic in the refectory turns out to be Venerable Maria Celeste Crostarosa. I had never heard of her but the book sounds very good and will help us a lot, except that it will probably make Fr. Raymond sore. He gets excited when books are read in which God says to souls, "Give up creatures and love Me alone, You are nothing and I am everything, etc."

May 2, 1947

Tomorrow is the Feast of the Finding of the Holy Cross.

Today I got two new jobs, continuing Fr. Alberic's work by revising the *Compendium of the History of the Order*, and rewriting the *Postulant's Guide* again. That gives me no less than *twelve* jobs in various stages of

---

[15] Pius XI's 1924 encyclical on the contemplative life.

completion, not counting the books written by outsiders that I am remotely in charge of getting printed for the Order or the house.

I have found myself a very good cross. Question: just because a cross is a cross, is it the one God wants for you? Just because a thing is a nuisance, is it therefore the best thing for you? Is it an act of virtue to sit down and let yourself be snowed under by activities that threaten to ruin your contemplative life? I am called to be a contemplative. But I am not living as a contemplative . . . Ergo, what am I doing in the room over there? Piling up fuel for my Purgatory? Just because it is obedience, does that make it all meritorious? Pleasing to God? I wonder. I don't ask these questions in a spirit of rebellion: I would really like to know.

So much of this stuff is simply useless. It would be bad enough to break your head in writing good books, but this stuffy and useless material . . . I don't mean Fr. Alberic's *Compendium*. And yet, did that work contribute anything to his sanctification? I wonder.

It seems to me that it would be a much cleaner and healthier thing to break off with all this business and bury myself in solitude, absolute poverty, hiddenness, nothingness, to love God alone, giving up all these activities and all this racket of writing. I know I shall never do that altogether. I believe God wants me to write *something*, but to be always up to my neck in censors and contracts and royalties and letters all around the world and reviews and correspondence with my dear readers . . . I don't know.

I put it all in Your hands, my God. I don't demand any quick answer, but please, You settle all this for me in Your own time.

May 4, 1947. Day of Recollection

All day I have waited for You with my faculties still bleeding the poison of their suppressed activity. And I have waited for Your silence and Your peace to staunch and cleanse them, oh my Lord.

You will heal me when You will, because I have trusted in You.

I will not wound myself anymore with the details with which I have surrounded myself like thorns – a penance which You do not desire of me.

You have made my soul for Your peace and Your silence, and it is wounded with confusion and noise of my sins and my desires.

Is there a theological fault in these desires, this interior activity which I cannot help, these continual ideas for books and writing, this continual grasping for intellectual satisfactions and aesthetic joys – the avidity which is my crucifixion?

That is not the question. It is all disordered. It chokes grace, dries it up. Stifles prayer. It wounds, darkens, dirties, lacerates my soul.

But I am made for Your peace, and You will not despise my longing to love You alone in the holiness of Your silence. Oh my Lord, You will not leave me forever in this sorrow, because I have trusted in You, and I wait upon Your holy will in peace and without complaints for Your glory.

I am content that these pages show me to be what I am: noisy, full of the racket of imperfections and passions and the wide open wounds left by sin, full of faults and envies and miseries and full of my own intolerable emptiness.

Domine Deus meus in te confido, non confundar in aeternum. [Lord my God, in you I trust. Let me not be put to shame forever (Psalms 29:13; 117:28).]

May 5, 1947

This was a day of grace.

After None, when I finished doing the Stations of the Cross, Fr. Anthony, my new confessor, called me into the confessional to tell me he thought I ought to be resolved never to willingly entertain any thought or desire of going and being a Carthusian or anything else. He reminded me that neither Reverend Father nor the General would ever give me permission to go. He said the best thing was to forget it all and leave the whole thing entirely in the hands of God, as a challenge to Him as it were, that if He wanted me anywhere else, He would have to pick me up and put me there, get my Superiors to send me there. That would be a blind and heroic act of faith and confidence in God. All this is substantially what Dom Vital told me also.

And it is the right line of thought.

God brought me here, and I simply cannot be thinking of going anywhere else without putting myself in opposition to His will – barring the case where the spiritual life would become impossible here – and this is a fervent community so that does not arise.

The only thing to do is to believe Him blindly, and I know in the marrow of my bones that is what He wants, that I should put myself entirely in His hands and trust Him to make me a contemplative, even though my own natural judgment tells me everything seems to be against it. *Because my own judgment is darkness in the sight of God.* That is all there is to it.

And this is the obstacle that has been robbing me of my peace.

Gethsemani – the place and the community, *locus et fratres* – is the spring where I am to drink the waters of life, and if I look somewhere else, it is to a broken cistern as far as I am concerned because, no matter how excellent it may be in itself, *it is not God's will for me.*

As soon as I acquiesced completely in this decision, which I did at once, peace came back to my soul, although I feel that God does not trust Himself to me completely – He knows what is in me. But He knows that I want to rest in His will and love His will alone. I believe in His love.

And I am sorry and ashamed at the way I trust my own darkness more than His own infinite light. How I am captured by pictures and words and sentences, by paper and by talk and by writing! It is healthy and sobering to realize what an animal I am in all this business about cells and contemplation, which is only spiritual in appearance and on the surface. Actually, what I am following is that old, warm, sensible glow in the solar plexus, the *animalis homo* [animal man] who has no knowledge of the things of the Spirit.

Tomorrow on the Feast of St. John boiled in oil I will renew my profession in a special way after Communion and make it with all the simplicity I can, reserving nothing to myself – none of this loop-hole business. And Our Lady will help me to keep it. There is nothing for it but to let God manage my life. How can I be a contemplative if I am going to decide everything for myself as if I were omniscient? God leaves such people to their own darkness. But I will put myself in the arms of His will and rest forever in His light, in the darkness of faith which is true light, and not in the light of human judgment, which is darkness.

The Owensboro [Kentucky] priests are here on retreat and Fr. Sylvester just made me a sign that he and I were appointed.

May 7, 1947

The censorship trouble on *The Seven Storey Mountain* has all been smoothed out beautifully as far as Father Gabriel is concerned. And for my own part, now that he has given the *nihil obstat,* I am glad to take advantage of all his other observations because the book needs much cutting, and besides that, he has caught a lot of errors and lazy writing.

Reverend Father has gone to Utah. Msgr. Giroux, who was doing most of the work for us out there, has died, and his funeral is tomorrow.

May 10, 1947

Tomorrow the Rogation Days begin. I thought of asking for the publication of the stuff I write, but I got into such a big business distraction at High Mass that I gave it all up in disgust. All I ask is the Holy Spirit, that

I may have Him to love God with, to love God *caste, sancte, ardenter* [chastely, holily, ardently] – for the sake of loving Him and for nothing else. Love will be my beatitude – in darkness, on the Cross.

Ascension Day, my favorite feast, all year round I think of those antiphons – *Vado parare vobis locum* [I go to prepare a place for you (John 14:2).] – and my heart burns within me with joy.

I am to make a private retreat from Ascension to Pentecost to ask for recollection and to empty my heart to receive the Holy Ghost.

One thing to thank God for, I am not reading so much. I did myself harm that way last year, as I now realize.

In the refectory I am very impressed by Ven. Mary Celeste Crostarosa and the things she had to suffer for the love of God and for His work. That is the way Orders are founded, and that is the way God makes saints.

Her fervent community – how it broke up into dissensions and flamed with blinded zeal until they even expelled her from it for refusing to take a vow to follow a director who could not understand her – and nobody else but him. Thank God I have never run across anyone like that! And I thank God that I have a saint for a director now.

May 14, 1947. Vigil of the Ascension

Last night there were thunderstorms, but today how beautiful! The sky is absolutely clean and cool. The leaves on the big hickory tree by the cemetery are small and the flowers fill the branches with fringes of green lace. I hear the engine turning down at the mill, it is so quiet. Only that and the birds singing. I read some St. Bernard [of Clairvaux] on the Mystical Marriage. The tenth chapter of *De Diligendo Deo [On the Love of God]* and the last sermons *In Cantica [On the Song of Songs]* bring St. Bernard and St. John of the Cross into line together. When they reach their goal, they are together in their way of looking at things: we are made for the mystical marriage, it fulfills our nature. While lifting us above nature, it consists in nothing but pure love, union of wills with God, a union from which all self-hood, *proprium* [self-will] is excluded, in which the natural functions of the senses and other faculties are annihilated, that is, *sublimated* by being drawn into perfect harmony with God's will and under the immediate direction of His Spirit, so that we are no longer concerned with them, and even our senses praise God spontaneously by every act of their own in the natural order. We have no longer the first movements of sin . . . *Quando veniam et apparebo ante faciem Dei!* [When shall I come and appear before the face of God (Psalms 41:3)!]

The same old distractions, and worse still!! my mind full of business and vanity.

However yesterday, the anniversary of Fatima, I signed the contract for *Figures for an Apocalypse* with New Directions and heard that Commonweal got the *imprimatur* [ecclesiastical approval] on an article on Poetry and the Contemplative Life, which I rather wanted to get back from them, but they want to print it.[16] In Chapter Reverend Father told us that Our Lady of Liesse, China, had definitely been taken over by the Reds, monks expelled, some imprisoned.

Today I begin a private retreat until Pentecost.

Same troubles, same desires, same intentions – to get empty, to recover silence and interior solitude, to get away from noise and business. And to-morrow is Ascension: after living with us on earth Jesus takes us to live with Him in heaven. *Conversatio nostra in caelis.* [But our conversation is in heaven (Philippians 3:20).] The grace of the Ascension: to be taken up into the heaven of our own souls, the *apex mentis* [the mind's highest point], the point of immediate contact with God, in silence, in darkness, peace. To live through all trials and exterior disturbances with the *tranquillitas Deus tranquillans omnia* [the tranquil God who makes all things tranquil – St. Bernard], but I know my own helplessness. God, be with me on Your day and forever.

I got a letter from Dom Benoît – to love God's will when it seems to contradict all my ideals. The Reverend General says I can write all the slang I like.

May 17, 1947

It is the anniversary of the canonization of the Little Flower, as I am re-minded by the Little Flower calendar with a pious thought for each day in French in the scriptorium. I do not feel very much as if I were on retreat. But Ascension day was fine – full of recollection. I thank God for that much time to pray.

The inviolability of one's spiritual sanctuary, the center of one's soul de-pends on secrecy, the intellectual counterpart of purity of intention. If we find God in the center of our souls, and would remain there with Him, we must bring no one else in with us, on any pretext whatever, however chari-table. The best way to be charitable to your neighbor is to love God in

---

[16] Published in *The Commonweal*, 46.12 (July 4, 1947).

silence and solitude and isolation – unless you are ordered or obliged to perform some special external act for others.

And if we would remain with God in the center of our souls, we must never hope to bring Him out to others, as we find Him there, because it cannot be done. He cannot be communicated by anyone except Himself. It would be presumption to be too eager to preach Him as we find Him within ourselves. And the best way to preach Him is to remain with Him in silence. He will communicate Himself to others by virtue of the merit of such a prayer.

If we strain ourselves to *see* God in others with our eyes and our imagination and our mind, or even strive too hard to *see* Him by faith (which does not see but is dark), the devil will take advantage of it to show us their faults. But if we strive to *love* them for God's sake, no matter what their faults might be, we will soon see good in them. But we can arrive at Him much more quickly if we go directly to Him than if we try to find Him through the outward appearances of a human creature in which there are many faults.

The best way to see God actually in another human being is to see Him in His will in so far as that will is manifested to us by or through that person.

May 20, 1947

Liberum est cor quod non tenet in aliquo amore nisi Dei. [That heart is free which is held by no love other than the love of God.] (St. Bonaventure)

Art and Asceticism. The artist must be free, otherwise he will be dominated by his material instead of dominating it. Hence even in the natural order art demands and imposes a certain asceticism. Religious ascetics have something to learn from the natural asceticism of the artist – it is *unselfconscious*, organic, integrated in his art so that it runs small risk of becoming an end in itself.

But artists have something to gain from religious asceticism. It raises them above their subjects and their material, but above their art itself – they can control it.

Asceticism may involve the sacrifice of art, OR, the happiest consummation for the artist as such: his art might be integrated into an organic whole, a body of spiritual praise of God the Creator.

A magazine called *The Tiger's Eye* wants to give me $96.00 for a poem! I don't think St. Benedict would want me to take that much. However, it is not for me to decide, since by a peculiar irony the vow of poverty prohibits one from *refusing* money which comes to the community, not to ourselves. O.K., if that is what the books believe!

Yesterday I was tempted to get irritated and upset because of the lack of all visible, sensible fruit from this private retreat I have been trying to make, but I realize that it is not without some fruit if I have pleased God, and if I have tried to please Him, which I have, He is satisfied. After all it is for Him that I am making the thing, not for myself.

Snowed under with even more work. I am to do an edition of St. John of the Cross' *Dark Night* for New Directions, and I can't get out of the anthology of religious verse he [James Laughlin] wants me to do, although I have been trying to argue my way out of it for two years. Sometime I will have to finish that liturgical anthology, too.

I wish I had the sense to avoid so many plans. They get accepted and then I have to take the consequences.

Someone dedicated a poem to me and it was printed in *Commonweal* and I feel slightly sick with embarrassment. If I were really humble, I would be able to take it better. What difference does it make? Fr. Odilo [Champagne] just made a sign that he was sick of the retreat conferences he has written for the seculars and I am sick of writing poetry. But that is no reason either for writing or not writing.

A fancy architect's picture of the temporary building for the Utah monastery is on display in the Scriptorium and everybody is astonished at its slickness. It is a very 20th century looking affair and, as such, it is more Cistercian by its simplicity than the permanent place will probably be.

Last week the locust trees spilled all the fragments of their white flowers over the ground until the place looked like a picture by Seurat.

From Parkminster came three volumes of *Méditations Cartusiennes*. I did not think I would find anything in them, but I find them very good, along the same lines as our *Spiritual Directory*. Some good thoughts about the Holy Ghost, the companion of the solitary.

What do I look for tomorrow? Light? No. It is safer to travel in darkness. What I need is the grace to cease making any kind of a fuss over anything: travel in darkness and do God's will. He will get me through the obstacles. I will never reach Him by my own efforts, my own wisdom. I give up all my plans, as if I had any in the first place. Forget what other people do, their virtues and their faults are none of my business. Be guided by obedience even if it seems to lead to the ruin of my aspirations. Easier to write it than to do it. I wonder if I mean it, too, to go on in this hopeless muddle of writing and activities and contacts with the world, and trust that *that* can bring me to God? Yes, that is what I have got to do.

It seems like going around in a circle and saying the same thing over and over again, but it is something that haunts me, and I can't seem to settle it.

If God wants me to stay here, as He apparently does – in fact it is morally certain – it means the renunciation of any hope of the pure contemplative life. Or at least my desire for what I *think* is the contemplative life will have to go.

Father Anthony practically told me that in the confessional.

I am destined for the frustration and denial of every natural and even supernatural desire I may have in this life. That is to be my purgatory. All that has got to die. And I suppose the biggest and strongest desire I have is this one of being a contemplative with a capital "C" according to the books.

The work I do does not mix with contemplation – not pure contemplation.

O.K. *Fiat.* I am leading the active life. Forget about the question. Try to pray and get the amount of contemplation that people in the active life get . . .

I feel in my bones that I will never have any peace until I kiss everything goodbye, even my highest ideals and aspirations. God only tolerates one desire where He is – that of perfectly doing His will and of being annihilated for His glory.

If you know it, *beati eritis si feceritis ei.* [Blessed will you be if you do it for him.][17]

This thing will die hard. If I can make a little less fuss about it in the future, I will be satisfied, God will be glorified.

Holy Spirit, fill me with Your simplicity and teach me to avoid getting myself into useless works by my own blind and impetuous will which Reverend Father always approves. Teach me to ignore the plans and ideas that come to me for new work to be done – or to write them down, as obedience wants me to – and then, I hope, forget them.

I believe there is a way of working where You will do the work and I will rest in You. And after all, St. John of the Cross did not lead a purely

[17] Perhaps a gloss on Luke 6:22–23: *Beati eritis, cum vos oderint homines* . . . (Blessed will you be when men revile you . . .).

contemplative life, and yet he was a pure contemplative because he had risen above everything.

That is the only solution and it is beyond my power.

Another present I really need from the Holy Ghost is a real and supernatural union with my Superiors, not just a cheerful politeness, but confidence in God working through them, for my good, for deeper faith.

(Evening) Well, I have had the grace to see that my desires for contemplation, for union with God, are mostly natural. And if they are, there is not much merit in them, and they have no claim to be pleasing to Him. How can I expect Him to grant them? For they are supernatural in their object but natural in their principle, which is my own will, and I can no more expect to be sanctified by them than the devils were sanctified by the inordinate and selfish desire for beatitude in which they desired the vision of God *for the sake of their own excellence* and were therefore thrown into hell. Therefore, oh my God, I give up these desires, that is, I give up this attachment to peace, the delight and sweetness of contemplation and of Your love and of Your presence, and I give myself to You to love Your will and Your honor alone.

For I know that, if you want me to renounce the manner of my desiring You, it is only in order that I may surely possess You and come to union with You.

And I will try with Your grace from now on to make no more fuss about "being a contemplative," about acquiring that perfection for myself. Instead I will seek only You, not contemplation and not perfection, but You alone.

And then maybe I will be able to do the simple things You would have me do, and do them well, and with a perfect and pure intention in all peace and silence and obscurity, concealed even from my own self and safe from my own poisonous esteem.

And I suppose that is the fruit of the retreat. *Deo Gratias et Mariae.* [Thanks be to God and Mary.]

May 26, 1947. Whitmonday

During the meridienne Father Prior slipped a note in our cell saying that some would be going out to make hay after None, in spite of the holiday, to take advantage of the good weather. So we changed, but Reverend Father canceled it. But it is a beautiful day. When I was at school in Oakham, Whitmonday was the only day of the year we were allowed to ride bicycles.

Father Anthony gave me a book on Cardinal Newman to read, or rather, told me I should get it from the library. I am interested to see how far we are – I am especially – from Newman and all he stood for socially. I feel like a savage. But I certainly have more to do with the 12th century than I have with him. He is completely alien to me – his speech, his attitudes, everything. That is one reason why it is interesting. I would never have picked it on my own initiative.

Plenty of time to pray and get recollected – for once! It is the only thing to strive for – peace, interior solitude, union with God. Without that everything is noise and confusion and barren futility. Take advantage of every opportunity our life can offer to be alone with God, otherwise you will be to blame for all your misery.

The things you don't have to worry about – reforms in the community that you cannot make and therefore do not have to worry about – the faults of others that you cannot correct – if they *are* faults – why burden yourself with all these things? *Martha, Martha sollicita es* . . . [Martha, Martha, thou art busy . . . (Luke 10:41).]

And I can organize the work better so that I am more unified in what I have to do.

May 29, 1947

Father Gabriel sent back the rest of the ms. of *The Seven Storey Mountain* and I am going over it again. And I got an air-mail letter from Laughlin (New Directions), who seems to be on his way here. Today it is cold again and grey and rainy.

I am trying to tone down *The Seven Storey Mountain* as much as I can. It is hard to see the thing in the light of all the different audiences it might reach – people in the world, men riding on the Long Island railroad, monks in Irish monasteries, nuns in English convents, my relatives, Jews, reds, priests . . . and the people Father Gabriel is afraid to offend.

I leave it all in the hands of God, and I give myself more and more to His guidance. *Spiritus tuus bonus deducet me in viam rectam.* [Thy good spirit shall lead me on a straight path (Psalms 142:10).] I am not so much in darkness this week. Thank God for it. It is good to feel oneself drawn by Him and locked in the kind persuasion of His guidance, and to feel the cleanness of His close presence and the peace of His love, and to walk with Him alone and to be with Him.

May 31, 1947. Ember Saturday

Today at Mass we sang the beautiful Communion antiphon, *Spiritus ubi vult spirat* [The Spirit blows where it wills] with its four *alleluias* that mark the end of Paschal time. *Nescis unde veniat, aut quo vadat* . . . [Thou knowest not whence he cometh nor whither he goeth . . . (John 3:8).] And I don't know where Paschal time has gone either. We have not yet had any real summer, which makes it all the more strange.

It is bright sun and cool. The catbirds sing with crazy versatility above my head. A lot of the religious have upset stomachs or something, but so far I am all right. Fasting is easy in nice weather.

Father Prior has read the second carbon of *The Seven Storey Mountain* and says he likes it very much. And he does not want me to cut too much. He does not agree with Father Gabriel.

He began talking to me about his own vocation, how he discovered the Little Flower when he read *The Story of a Soul* in the seminary. And how that was his introduction to the interior life. That situation has been reproduced a hundred times in our order and our generation, I am sure.

Father Anthony now has the ms. too, and in the confessional he began telling me something of his life, and I was astonished to find so much sorrow and suffering in his background. His place in God's plan seems clear in relation to his family among other things. Just as mine is clear in relation to my friends. People are very definitely in this monastery because of certain groups with which they were once connected – for the good of certain people who need grace in a particular way.

However, I will never attach too much importance to any *exterior* influence I may seem to have on any people or any group. I may appear to be an apostle to the intellectuals, but my writing means very little. And by itself it means nothing. I refuse to be misled by any kind of a mirage about any alleged success of what I write. Those things are too easily exaggerated, and even when they are true, they always mean less than they seem to.

One thing occurs to me: how foolish it would be to base your whole life, to base important decisions, *merely* on a feeling of interior peace, or on a vague sense of oneness with God, considered as an experience. Calvinists and pantheists and all the other religions there are have this in common with us: that those who take the thing seriously sometimes get this interior peace and even a strong sense of union with God, or immersion in God, or what you will. That sense can be purely natural and aesthetic. As such it is probably not a genuine experimental knowledge of God, but only an experience of our own spirituality, a withdrawal from exterior things into our own selves, which enable us to taste the peace of our own spiritual nature. Perhaps in ourselves we then see God imaged, as He is, in a *natural* way. Hence the possibility of a relatively high contemplation in the natural order alone. St. Bonaventure and St. Augustine have things to say that are concerned with this.

It is important, therefore, not to seek any mere experience, and not to stop at the aesthetic sense of anything. The enjoyment of no matter what should never be the term of our efforts or of our desires. Rather the annihilation of enjoyment and desire in a faith and love which exceed experience. Scripture says *inquirat pacem, et sequatur eam* [Let him seek peace and pursue it (1 Peter 3:11)], but that is the true peace which comes from perfect union with God's will, which is the guarantee of infused knowledge and love of Him present in our souls in a mystical way *ad eum veniemus et mansionem apud eum faciemus* [And we will come to him, and will make an abode with him (John 14:23)].

Seek only God's will – the Kingdom of God and His Justice – and peace and all the rest will be added to you.

In a sense my vocation troubles vanish before this thought: I am perhaps not here because this life in itself is the one most perfectly adapted to all my own aptitudes, but I am here because it is where God wants me to be for some reason best known to Him. For the rest it doesn't concern me what Order is best for me *in se*. All that matters is union with God. And as for my aptitudes, whatever that might mean, they are God's. They belong to Him to do with as He wills. Besides, since I don't even know what my aptitudes are, I had better leave the whole thing to Him. I know what my *appetites* are, but appetites and aptitudes are very different things.

June 8, 1947. Sunday within the Octave of Corpus Christi
As far as my feelings are concerned – continued disgust with everything – I simply have to hold on to myself and wait until I get somewhere by myself and find some peace in God. In choir, in the community, in the refectory, everything that should normally give pleasure to the senses and so on simply gives me pain. And what would normally be a small annoyance – the organ playing, the defects of our choir – becomes a torture. All this is God's love for me, and from the bottom of my heart I thank Him. All I beg Him is not to let me think – much less say – anything that would offend Him and interfere with the action of His wise love, trying to purify my heart.

All the thoughts that come to mind about how nice things *might* be are futile and barren, and it would be crazy for me to try and entertain them even if I could. But they also only give me a pain. In fact, it seems to give me a pain to think about anything, to desire anything.

For instance it occurs to me sometimes to lament the fact that most of the sermons and conferences and most of the reading we hear are on the level where they might be useful to seculars, but to contemplatives they are a bore. But even if St. Bernard or St. John of the Cross were preaching to us, I would probably be just as disgusted.

So all I have to do is wear my hairshirt and try not to twist and scratch more than I can help.

Apparently Laughlin will be here this week. I hope I don't say anything that will scandalize him, and I am going to pray to God earnestly to put a guard on my tongue and, in fact, to do my talking for me.

The whole place is swimming in honeysuckle – the smell nauseates me! *Deo Gratias.*

Corpus Christi went off better than usual, that is to say I got our design finished in plenty of time and without flying into a rage. But that business of breaking your neck to make those mosaics of flowers seems to me to be an irregularity. It gets the whole community steamed up so that it is impossible to pray. Everybody is sweating and nature is pounding away on all twelve cylinders. It is enough to choke the special graces of the Feast right out of us, but I think God gets in a little work obliquely by the suffering it causes most of us.

From Fr. Mary William [Guillaume Moal], the ex-Prior of Notre Dame de Consolation, I understand that none of that elaborate fuss takes place at Thymadeuc, one of the most regular houses in the Order. They just scatter a few flowers on the cloister pavement before the procession, and that is that. That is what the *Usages* prescribe.

However, all this fuss and display is God's will for *me* – part of my cross, part of His Love. I still have to trust Him blindly to make me a contemplative, to lead me to peace through all these wars, and to the end of my journey through all these blind alleys.

The other day by accident I discovered how St. Hugh had been ordered to make a vow that he would never enter the Carthusians. That is one of the few things that has given me any comfort. Otherwise, the only thing that helps is to get by myself before the Blessed Sacrament or out in the cemetery and shut up and empty my mind and forget everything.

June 13, 1947. Feast of the Sacred Heart

I am bitterly sorry for my childishness in taking seriously the tiny and microscopic imperfections in the details of life at Gethsemani. If I were a saint, I would not ever be scandalized at big things, if there were any. That is over, or with Christ's grace, I mean it to be.

God is using everything that happens to lead me into solitude. Every creature that enters my life, every instant of my days is designed to touch me with the sense of the world's insufficiency. And that goes for every created thing, including monasteries, including even sensible graces, lights of the mind, ideas, fervor in the will. Everything I touch cauterizes me with a light and healing burn. I can hold on to nothing.

It is useless to get upset over these things that pain me. The pain is the token and pledge of God's love for me. It is the promise of His deep and perfect solitude.

Today I seemed to be very much assured that this solitude is indeed his will for me, and that it is truly He Who is calling me into the desert. Not necessarily a geographical one, but the solitude of His own heart in Which all created joys and lights and satisfactions are annihilated and consumed.

Things that should have satisfied me, but did not.

Laughlin was here for a few hours yesterday and we had a good talk and I like him very much. He is a very sincere person and in a way very pure in heart – in a way.

He is much taken up with D. H. Lawrence, but it is because of a kind of desire to find a sacramental character in nature and human love. With his dispositions he could easily be shown that the answer to his questions is in Christianity, since he even borrows our language to talk about it. We are the only ones who have the true *Sacrament* which orders human love to an eternal and mystical and Divine end, and brings it into direct relation with beatitude, which is what he is asking for.

I prayed Mother Berchmans to get us her picture and Joseph Cassant's printed in good time for the Feast of the Sacred Heart and the prayer was answered. With the usual business that I am getting interiorly, I felt ashamed putting the picture out in the refectory – felt the hopelessness of it. But God will make it fruitful if He wills.

June 14, 1947

Yesterday Fraters Urban and Sylvester made their solemn profession and I think it was the pastor of Frater Sylvester's parish who preached. A very edifying preacher and a holy man, he was talking all about what a contemplative Adam was before the fall, and he cried out so melodiously and his sentences got higher and higher: I thought he was going to get up off the ground and fly away. But he is a saint and maybe that has something to do with Frater Sylvester being a saint, too, which he is. Frater Urban, too, for that matter. They both come from Louisville and at least twenty of Frater Sylvester's relatives descended upon the place, if I understood his signs. Today Frater Urban was ordained subdeacon. The Mass was sung – began at 7:30, and Sext ended just now at 10:00.

At these functions they have been playing as organ voluntary a weird piece of music that reminds me of the stuff you used to hear in movie theaters at the time of the silent movies. It turns out to be the hymn they sing at Fatima. Mother of God, why do you let these things happen?

June 15, 1947. Sunday. Day of Recollection

I am happy that we are once again in the plain, straight-forward, post-pentecostal liturgy. It is so perfect and so simple. Without frills. It means so much more to me than the later feasts – speaks more eloquently and directly.

For myself, instead of complaining about activities, reduce them to the minimum within obedience. Cut out:

1) All writing not strictly necessary, especially letters. And be strict about what is strictly necessary.

2) Things that don't have to be done, let them go. You are a contemplative – no obligation to go out of your way to do extra work.

3) Cut out – unnecessary reading

     unnecessary signs

     unnecessary moving around

     unnecessary thoughts.

Thinking about faults, imperfections, defects, controversies, matters of opinion, big speculative problems – all this unnecessary activity. Drop it.

Empty yourself. Prepare for the Feast of St. John of the Cross, not by a lot of extra prayers, but by training myself to drop useless things from moment to moment all through the day.

Gethsemani is Christ's work. Look at the place in relation to His will, His Kingdom, His Mystical Body – America – the end of the world for that matter. I am here for others, not only for myself. Do His will, for His Love, for all those ends which I cannot see and understand, instead of merely seeking my own pleasure and perfection in prayer, etc.

My big weakness is still too ardent and exclusive a desire to see myself ornamented with special sanctity and high graces of contemplation for myself rather than for the love of God.

Beati mundo corde. Beati pauperes spiritu. [Blessed are the clean of heart (Matthew 5:8). Blessed are the poor in spirit (Matthew 5:3).]

June 19, 1947

For some time, a couple of months, I haven't been able to write a line of verse, although I have tried several times and have had some ideas to work on.

But I think God does not want me to write any more the way I have written before – taking an idea and working it out in cold blood. That means no more historical subjects and no more of this more or less forced stuff. If God gives me something directly and spontaneously about Himself, I will write it. Otherwise I will keep quiet. That means no more volumes of poetry for a long time perhaps, and it may well mean little or no variety, and it might mean complete silence.

However, I see nothing for me to write that is not simply a song about His Love and about contemplation. Everything else bores and fatigues me and dries me up.

And this, as a matter of fact, was the subject of the last poem I wrote, one which will not be in *Figures for an Apocalypse*, but which resembles some of the last ones that are. This conviction came to me quite clearly when I was studying St. John of the Cross' *Spiritual Canticle* today.

It will be a powerful help to the solitude where God wants me to be in emptiness of all things, and I hope it means my withdrawal from the professional poet field, magazines, etc. However, that doesn't matter. I'll write what God gives me, not as a writer, but as a lover of God and for Him alone. Then, if He wants it printed, He can take it and print it.

Clifton Fadiman wrote asking me to write for a new magazine called '47, but that is definitely out. So I'll send him a letter today telling him so.

Mère Léonie wrote from Notre Dame des Anges a good sweet letter. I like her – she must be well past her Jubilee by now.

June 21, 1947. Fourth Sunday after Pentecost

It seems the Mother Berchmans ms. is going to be printed by Bruce and Co., but I will have to cut about 100 pages. It is a vice Cistercian writers have, at least modern ones, to say too much and to ramble and repeat the same thing 30 times over. I noticed that with Fr. Eugene Boylan's book *[This Tremendous Lover]* we are just finishing in the refectory, and Fr. Raymond has the same defect. We talk too much.

The pleasure at the thought the book would be published ended up with the same dead, heavy feeling inside me. I was dirty because of it. It was not pure. However, I find that I can counteract all that by the thought of solitude, the desire of being alone with God alone, the thought that there are people who live for Him alone. Maybe that is a natural pleasure, too, but it is higher and seems to cleanse me of this other stuff contracted in my work and my relations with the world as a writer.

Reading St. Bernard's sermon on *St. John Baptist* ["On the Manner of John's Burning and Shining"]. After the Night Office I got an idea for a poem, or anyway an idea about the relation of contemplatives to the rest of the Church. We are hidden in her womb, but we should be mystics and mystically sense the presence of Christ, and the exultation of our experience will awaken the whole Church and she will begin to sing and preach. But instead of writing the poem, I spent the day in prayer. I only got down a couple of lines and maybe I will leave it at that. Because I can see how writing it will make me love God more, and it may well make me love Him less, especially if I write instead of praying. However I shall see at work tomorrow, which is the Vigil.

And I am convinced this is the right road for me.

For the rest I seek no gain for myself. I leave myself in God's hands to work out my sanctification as He has planned it. In order to arrive at what I cannot understand, I must go by the way I cannot understand. And each time I make up my mind to this, I am more convinced that He will lead me by the way of solitude. Every time I pray, get into my cloud, get recollected, that desire and that conviction deepen. I only need to leave everything absolutely to Him, and go blindly where He leads me.

† Maria.

In the four weeks since Pentecost I have found much valuable help in those little books of *Méditations Cartusiennes* – not that there is anything especially new or exalted in them, but their pages are full of simple and practical ideas about the contemplative life, ideas that apply as well to us as to them. I can always get something off one page or another, and then walk up and down the cemetery at peace and in union with God, and look at the sun going down behind the hills.

June 24, 1947. Feast of St. John the Baptist

Another of the beautiful, cool days we have been having all year. We did not work this afternoon. Plenty time to pray. Recollected, I am myself for a while, and I consider the week days when I am full of business and when I am not myself or my own. Why must I make my head so full of things?

It is the day of my great patron and friend and Protector St. John Baptist. *Vinum et siceram non bibet* [He shall drink no wine nor strong drink (Luke 1:15)]: taste none of the pleasures that flatter and intoxicate nature, our own will, our own vanity, our own desires.

I am tired of being my own Providence, of wanting and seeking things for myself, of making decisions for myself, and yet, quite apart from my own will, I am in this complex of things that seem to stand between me and God.

All I want, Jesus, is more and more to abandon everything to You. The more I go on, the more I realize I don't know where I am going. Lead me and take complete control of me.

Doce me facere voluntatem tuam quia Deus meus es tu. [Teach me to do thy will, for thou art my God (Psalms 142:10).] †JHS

June 29, 1947. Feasts of Sts. Peter and Paul

Yesterday in the confessional one thing was settled that badly needed to be settled: my vocation is contemplative. It is worth fighting for. It should be fought for, and if I really can't achieve it here, I should go somewhere else, unless perhaps it might be a special cross I should take to stay here anyway. But anyway, it is morally certain that God wants me to be a contemplative and to do everything I can to be one. All His action in my regard is directed to that end.

This is so evident. I guess that it is stupid to have made such a fuss.

However, the important thing today was the announcement of those who are to go to Utah for the new foundation. Reverend Father talked all around the subject and everybody knew what he was trying to get at, and it looked as though he would never get there. Finally, when he started to talk about a washout on the R.R. line to Georgia, I thought he had altogether given up the idea of telling us.

So for the moment I don't go to Utah. When he got to Fr. Anselm, I began to shiver in our shoes, but he jumped right over a whole bunch of us to Fr. Xystus. Later he came back and inserted Fr. Sylvester who was very close to me – he came in May, 1942, and just made profession the other day.

It is a very well picked group, but in a way it leaves Gethsemani short of competent officers. Very hard to get a new sub-prior and undermaster of novices. At least as long as Fr. Odilo is giving retreats.

Fr. Anselm just went by and said he would pray that I should be sent out there, but I told him not to pray too hard. Yet I think this foundation might well turn into one of the finest houses in the Order. It has every chance of being much better than Georgia. And in a way the mountains attract me from a natural point of view, but all that is stupid. However, no one knows who may get sent where. Surprises always happen and in two months I might be out there with the rest of them. That is for God to decide. I am indifferent. All I want is His will, for all He wants is to unite me to Himself.

They are to go a week from tomorrow – July 7th.

Today very hot and damp weather. I have never sweated so much in my life. I spent the meridienne in a pool of sweat. This morning I was thurifer. This afternoon I settled down and was able to pray a little, but the whole house is a little excited. It is a clean excitement, however, and the Holy Spirit is working in us. Great spirit of deep joy everywhere. Those who are going are wonderful. Most of them feel it, but they are all happy and full of love for God. You can see it shining in their faces and it is terrifically edifying. Some of them are taking it a little hard, naturally, but always in union with God. I was surprised to see Fr. Robert [McGann, Merton's novice master] go. He is a pillar of the house and without him Reverend Father won't be able to find anything in the files. Very surprised to see Fr. Bartholomew chosen, since he has bad health. Maybe they are counting on the mountains to fix him up.

Anyway, God bless that new house and make them contemplatives, and don't let them start any industries and get too deep in secular retreats. †JHS

July 2, 1947. The Visitation

Blessed Mother of God, you have visited me today. You have done some of your work, and there has entered a little health, a little light, into my life. For it is to you I owe the moment of clarity and of strength and conviction I have had today.

After Chapter – therefore after Communion – being struck by the weakness of an apparently strong community and the danger that may face us in the future, for once it actually seemed clear to me that God wants the sacrifice of everything I have precisely for this Gethsemani. I am to throw myself away for Gethsemani. I am to face the danger of losing everything that I hold most high, renouncing my ideals of solitude and contemplation to work in distracting tasks that I shall hate in order that others may become in some measure contemplatives, in order that they may have what I so much desire.

In other words I am to renounce the special consolations of contemplation in order to give them indirectly to others. It is the kind of thing that bears God's sign and seal upon it. And although I am afraid and full of rebellion, my heart burns in my side and I am driven almost in spite of myself to offer myself for this.

It is certain that Gethsemani is God's work. Who shall ever be able to say how much depends and has depended in the past on the prayers and suffering of the men of this house? I am convinced that the fate of America is tied up with the fate of Gethsemani and her foundations. This obscure unit is tremendously important to the whole Church of God.

Can I love God and love the Church if I despise Gethsemani? That is precisely what the devil wants me to do. The house is in danger all the time, internally and externally, precisely because it is so important. And we in our weakness and blindness are in the thick of this tremendous spiritual battle. I was aware of that when I made my decision to come here. That is a clear element in my vocation. It is quite true that God can move me to some other battle front whenever He chooses, but He must make the change, not I myself.

July 6, 1947. Feast of the Precious Blood

Right after the Feast of Our Lady last Wednesday, I landed head first in another big interior struggle. First it looked to me as if the prescriptions of the Visitation Card were being ignored with a sort of callous indifference – one big rash judgment on my part. The second thing was complete darkness and confusion about the whole purpose of my life – what am I heading for – where am I going? The answer to that one is: I don't need to know. All these troubles come from mistrusting the love of God. *Vanum est vobis ante lucem surgere.* [It is vain for you to rise before the light (Psalms 126:2).] Shall I start asking myself all those same old questions all over again? God knows what He wants to do with me. Rest in His tremendous love. *Sapientia = sapor boni* [Wisdom = the taste of the good] – to know the savor and sweetness of God's love expressed from moment to moment to moment in all the contacts between Him and our soul – from outside in events, in His signified will and will of good pleasure, from within myself by the flow of His actual graces. Rest in that union. It will feed you, fill you with life. There is nothing else you need. He will show you the way to increase it and, if necessary, He will lead you into perfect solitude in His own good time. Leave it all to Him. Live in the present.

"*Parata sunt omnia . . .*" ["All things are ready . . ."] we sang at Benediction. The ones going to Utah have got all their effects tied up in cardboard boxes, most of which are marked "whiskey." Tomorrow night they leave, only nobody knows just how or when because Reverend Father has not yet worked up the courage to tell us. When the Mormons see all those boxes and the "whiskey" signs, life in Utah will become very interesting.

Today it is raining again and there is danger we will lose the wheat crop.

Working over the Mother Berchmans ms. again, I am disappointed especially in the first chapters. Don't ask me if it will do any good. That is in the hands of God.

For about an hour and a half this afternoon I just shut up and forgot everything and stayed with God, first outside the Church, then inside it, and all my troubles vanished until Vespers. Distractions get terrific as soon as I start to sing. If that gives glory to God, it is all I want. I mean that all I want is to glorify Him by standing there in confusion trying to do His will.

July 9, 1947. *Octave of the Visitation*

So the night before last our Fathers left us. The monastery seems very empty, although we are still so full. Most of the best ones went. Yesterday there were only three to go out to the common work of the professed choir religious (but still 30-odd novices at least).

This foundation is a great grace both for those who went and for those who have stayed. Yesterday you could feel the effects: the monastery was full of peace and tranquility and moral health and all disturbances seem to have vanished. Incidentally, I am sure that all the internal upsets I have been going through were principally purifications to make ready for these great graces.

They all received the blessing after canonical Compline, thirty-three of them bowing at the presbytery step. It was terribly striking. Of course so many that went were close to me, we had been through the novitiate together, and so many younger than I. There was Frater Sylvester, next to me in choir for a long time, Xystus, Cornelius, Theophilus, Innocent and then some novices. Then, too, on these occasions you suddenly see how holy your brothers really are! I think this is an even better group than those who went to Georgia. However I keep saying to myself: *neminem novi secundum carnem* [I don't know any of them personally] and remembering over and over St. John of the Cross' advice not to think about the good points or the bad points of anybody. I belong to God alone, and this is all helping me to belong to Him more. Or at least I feel that it *can* help.

But I am certainly not completely detached from persons by any means. Well, I did not expect to be. I don't mind *feeling* a little pain at the idea I may never see them again on earth. I am tempted to envy them: I think of those fine mountains I have in my imagination.

Dear Christ, what a poor thing I am! Deliver me from my imagination and my dumb desires and tastes, my likes and dislikes! Sanctify me by them!

We all went to the gate about 7:30 after an early Compline. It was getting dark. People were milling around in silence but with the rustle of clothing and quiet laughter. They were all embracing one another and shaking hands and it sounded like wind in leaves. Reverend Father was in a hurry to cut it short and his car started off first, but the others didn't get away at once. I left before it was all over and came back alone towards the house and walked in to the tremendous, beautiful silence of Gethsemani, silence you could almost feel! Clean, holy quiet!

Underneath it all deep peace has stayed with me ever since, but I don't sleep. I offered that for the travelers and God took it. They are still on the train. I pray that they may get a little rest on the train. They have only chairs to sleep in. Three days locked in one car. God bless them: it ought to be a fine foundation.

There is already talk of a third foundation, an offer in Pennsylvania.

Only God can do it. Whom could we send as superior?

†JHS. MARIA.

July 16, 1947. Feast of St. Stephen Harding

On top of all this year's rain we just had a tremendous storm during Vespers. The mill bottom was turned into a lake and the creek is trying to make a noise like Niagara. A moment ago every path was a torrent and [there] were a hundred rivers coming down all the hillsides. The ducks are very happy. The novitiate garden is swamped but the water is gradually getting out. Water flooded the tailor shop when the area ways were swamped. There will surely be no wheat left by this time, but apparently there isn't much corn planted in the bottoms or it would all be gone.

A Benedictine Abbot from no one knows where spoke to us in Chapter this morning.

July 20, 1947

Today, as far as I know, St. Louis de Montfort, is canonized.

Lately without reading him or thinking about him in any special way I have been giving myself more fully to the love of Our Lady, abandoning myself more and more completely to the graces she has obtained for me from God and to her direction of my life by that grace in all things that are happening.[18]

The Feast of Our Lady of Mount Carmel on the 17th was a great day. Since then I have felt like a different person. Much more consciously and peacefully united with God's will. I am more completely determined to abandon all care for my own interests into His hands through Our Lady, even and especially my highest spiritual interests. I am no longer taking care of my own progress and my own sanctity because it is hopeless. I leave it to Mary's direction, to the Living Christ within me, acting in me, controlling all that I do for His love. It is true, for the moment at least, He seems to have a much fuller control.

On the 17th (Mount Carmel) I also got the corrected galley proof for *Figures for an Apocalypse*, and I had a fine letter from Laughlin who has all of sudden discovered prayer.

Many graces are coming to us because of this new foundation. They have had a lot of hardships and sacrifices out there. None of the splendid things they thought they were going to have were there. The "quonsets" will not be ready until "October" – that means next April, maybe! They have three army huts and, when they arrived there the other day, only *one* was on the property. They lived at least one or two days on dry bread, as far as I know, and for awhile they had the altars fixed up in the dormitory and were doing everything there. They had no toilets until the Feast of St. Stephen Harding, if then, and not all of those who went out there are in wonderful health either. I pray for them and trust to God to take care of all their needs. I still believe it will be a fine monastery.

The other day Reverend Father was talking to me about another offer of land, this time in the Adirondacks (N.Y.). It sounds good, but I hope I didn't scare him by saying we would be crowded out with visitors, which may or may not be true.

[18] In his *The True Devotion to the Blessed Virgin Mary* (1842), Louis Marie Grignion de Montfort exposes his "secret" of achieving union with Christ through devotion to the Mother of God. That Merton has taken this "secret" seriously is evident in his prayers to Mary throughout this journal.

A few drops of rain just started spattering on the leaves and stopped again. The sky is grey. Birds sing. Far away a bob-white exults briefly out there in the fields where our wheat crop is rotting.

What are you going to do with us next year, Lord, in our three monasteries? What are we going to bear? Sorry. I shouldn't have asked. You will take care of us.

I shouldn't be asking either about what is happening to *The Seven Storey Mountain* – for months I hear no word from Bob Giroux. Day after tomorrow is St. Mary Magdalen to whom I pray since she is one of the few people who ever had any sense *optimam partem elegit* [she has chosen the best part (Luke 10:42)]. I saw a fancy picture of her, a woodcut, in one of the forty-five volumes of Denis the Carthusian (of which we have 38). I like Denis more and more now that I am getting to know him better. His thoughts on contemplation, especially on the *merit* of works we perform with the *joy* of perfect love, and on the supreme merit of the *joys* and peace of fruition in contemplation, appeal to me strongly as an antidote to the heresy that whatever is hard is *per se* meritorious, or, whatever satisfies us is suspicious. Same old failure to make distinctions. What satisfies our sensible nature, *concedo* [I concede the point]. Our rational nature on its own level, *concedo*, our supernatural capacity for God by charity, *nego* [I deny such satisfactions are suspicious]. To him that hath more will be given. The greatest joys in this life, the joys that spring from loving God perfectly, are the source of the greatest merit and earn us the highest joys in heaven. We merit joy in heaven by joy on earth, but we cannot arrive at the joy of pure love without perfect and unreserved sacrifice. Ordinarily the sacrifice should be hard, long, difficult. *Per accidens* [by accident], if you give all in one easy throw, you will earn just as much. All that matters is to give *everything* and the quicker the better. Fighting, struggling, rebelling and delaying make it harder, *but not more meritorious*. On the contrary, less. So it is fruitless to multiply difficulties and delays. Give everything and give it in the quickest possible way. All that matters is the gift. That is what pleases God, atones for sin, converts the world, and leads us into the joys of heaven even here on earth. St. Mary Magdalen, you know what I need!

July 27, 1947. Ninth Sunday after Pentecost
Today is the fifth anniversary of John Paul's[19] first Communion here. It was a Monday, not a Sunday.

[19] Merton's brother.

Since Fr. Innocent went to Utah, I have been reading to the seculars at their meals on the week-end retreats. It disrupts things a little but I am glad to do it. If I didn't, someone else would have to. God loves all these good people and so do I. I am glad to read to them.

It came to me, the idea to spend the time between now and the Assumption in a sort of general and peaceful remote preparation for death, according to St. Benedict's *mortem cotidie ante oculos suspectam habere* [To keep death daily before one's eyes (RB 4:47)]. My only practice, my only devotion, is to empty myself and get rid of superfluities, and try to let my mind and imagination get quiet, and so I shall do this in view of death. In fact the thought of death might make it easier. But if God doesn't want it to be easier, His will be done.

How simple it would be if Our Lady would just come down and take me up to heaven! Then all imperfections and weaknesses would be at an end. But I guess I have to earn it!!

August 3, 1947. Sunday

A big retreat. I am not only reading but helping with the dishes, so it turns out to be work. O.K. Everybody has had summer colds, including me. This week there was trouble in choir. I had to fight against feelings of utter disgust at the way things were going. I don't think anyone was morally to blame, but it certainly was not the way a choir should chant. We simply can't hold any tone. I don't know what can be done about it. The most depressing thing is that those who *can* hold the tone have all been choked off and silenced for the sake of unity, so you just have to let the tone fall to the floor and take it as a cross. And it certainly is a cross, too. But in any case my voice is gone with this cold, so I just struggle along and try to get the office said, at least.

It must be a real burden to be head cantor!

But all this is God's love for us. If we loved our poverty more, we would take it a lot better. I want to strive with intellectual and spiritual possessions, but that is not the way to union with God, nor the way to sanctity and perfection of love. *Blessed are the poor in spirit* is to be without talents, or to lose them, or have them frustrated; to be without distinctions, without colors or decorations, without special abilities, or to have them ignored and denied. That can be one way to sanctity, if you accept your emptiness with burning love and gratitude and wait for God to fill you. And when He does, you will get all the rest thrown in with His wisdom. *Venerunt autem mihi omnia bona pariter cum illa.* [Now all good things came to me together with her Wisdom and innumerable riches through her hands (Wisdom 7:11).]

We all have summer colds and there is trouble in choir.[20] [Even when we do not have colds, there is trouble in choir. We are always flat. The most depressing thing is that, those who *can* hit the right pitch have all been scolded and ordered to keep quiet for the sake of "unity." I admit that the chant is less exasperating, to some extent, when we are all flat in the same way, instead of being partly flat and partly on the right pitch.

I suppose that one reason why I still get upset about the choir is that I think I can get rid of my passions by analyzing them. As soon as we start to sing, we start to have trouble. And as soon as we have trouble, my temper begins to burn. So then I reflect on my temper, as if there were something left for me to learn. The more I reflect on my impatience, the madder I get. Obviously, what I need to do is to forget my temper instead of contemplating it. The guilty feeling that I ought *not* to be impatient is all the more exasperating when I stand there musing on how impatient I actually am.

I could do with a little poverty of spirit. I would not get mad at the bad singing if I were not attached to the sound of my own voice. To be without talents, to lose them or to have them frustrated – to be without distinction, without special abilities, or to have them ignored and denied: all that can help a man to be a saint, if he has the sense to accept it with love and gratitude and love his emptiness and wait for God to come and fill him with gifts beyond comprehension.

It is useless to sit back and wait for your passions to die down of their own accord. We have to overcome the feelings that lead our wills into imperfection and sin. However, you can't expect to be without any feelings whatever. A choir that is flat is flat, and if you keep hearing the pitch pipe blow, you cannot help suffering from the fact that the choir is always flat. If they would only throw that pitch pipe into the creek, we could all get used to our flat voices and let it go at that. The only answer to the problem is to overcome evil with good. The chant may be terrible: but that is only an occasion for the ones who realize it is terrible to give God glory by their patience and meekness and humility. As for the ones who do not seem to know about it: well, they have no problem.]

---

[20] The Gethsemani archives hold a typed manuscript on loan from the family of Mrs. Ann Skakel. This "Skakel manuscript" is almost a final draft of the material that was to eventually appear as *The Sign of Jonas*. The following four bracketed paragraphs are a variant on Merton's journal entry for August 3 from this manuscript.

News from Utah. Fr. Xystus filled a notebook with writing and it is being read in the refectory. They are having a hard time but everything sounds very good. They have plenty to suffer, too, so it will be a good foundation. They sent some pictures Frater Sylvester took, but the first batch didn't show much, but the mountains look wonderful. Reverend Father said Mrs. Priest collared him on the station platform in Ogden and asked after me. I wonder what she was doing out there, or whether she came from there in the first place and I had forgotten. I must write to Douglaston to the family – I haven't written for ages. Let it go until Assumption.

Practically finished a special booklet on our life for the centenary *[Gethsemani Magnificat]*. Laughlin wants to do the layouts before going to Europe in October.

We are getting the hot weather we missed all summer.

I think we tend to sit back and wait for our passions to die down of their own accord. That is why I still feel disturbance about things, upset in choir, etc. Not that it is in the will, but I act as if there were some point in studying my upset emotions, my repugnances, my feelings of rebellion. Why bother to consider them? That is the first mistake which brings them that much closer to the will and to consent. I know myself well enough without reflecting on what I already knew before it happened!

Not to be attached to peace in such a way as to be disturbed by the prospect of losing it, but strive for peace by active humility and obedience and renunciation of my will in order to please God – keep empty. It is essential to our vocation and therefore a duty.

Denis the Carthusian on this very good.

August 8, 1947. Friday

Hot, sticky weather. Prickly heat. Red lumps all over your neck and shoulders. Everything clammy. *Paenitentiam agite.* [Do penance.] Better than a hairshirt.

And don't make a fuss about the small things one suffers in this life, as if they amounted to something. The Cross improves prayer immensely, united to God, His presence more vividly sensible. It is good to suffer these things and enter into the glory of His love.

Yesterday old Fr. George was knocked out. I suppose the heat had something to do with it. We gave him Extreme Unction in the middle of the afternoon work. All the time I thought it was Fr. Odo until it was all over and the religious cleared his room, and I saw it was Fr. George on the bed and not Fr. Odo. He had been all right (relatively) up until None.

Bob Giroux wrote from Harcourt Brace with the changes he wanted made on *The Seven Storey Mountain* ms., and the letter never reached me. I wrote to Naomi Burton to find out what was up; he will write it over again. Things are going just as I expected. The book will not be out until next spring. All this is to merit some graces for the people who read it, and proves that God is interested in the thing and that it is His work.

Laughlin sent poems of Patrice de la Tour du Pin.

A fine letter from Dom Thomas d'Aquin [Gondal] of Tamié about the spirituality of our Order. We *are* getting a contemplative spirit. Study of our XII century Fathers has helped since the reunion. He says he has noticed a considerable change in twenty-five years. The biggest obstacle: *activism* – material, intellectual, *spiritual.*

The latter consisting in being in *too much of a hurry* and trying to arrive at union with God by one's own efforts, without suffering, without carrying any cross or denying oneself. *Verb[a] sap[ientiae].* [Words of wisdom.]

In our Order he said a lot depends on willingness to sacrifice oneself to serve the community.

August 14, 1947. Vigil of the Assumption

Heat. But it is not so bad on an empty stomach. The air sings with the din of locusts. Laughlin sent me by a kind of accident Dylan Thomas' poems to show me the type to be used on *Cistercian Contemplatives*. I was glad to see Thomas' poems. He is some writer. His integrity makes me blush. We who say we love God, why are we not as careful to be perfect in our art as we say we want to be in our love, when the people who are perhaps less perfect in their love can be so scrupulous about avoiding mediocrity when they write! So much careless writing by Catholics. Msgr. Sheen in a big hurry to go on the air,[21] writes some English that is much poorer than it looks. And as for me, God forgive me. At least the censors spot some of it, but then they often hit the wrong thing. They can be champions of indifferent writing, too.

Imperfections the punishment of the vice of being in too great a hurry to go to press. Self-love defeating its own ends.

Tomorrow's Gospel. *Martha, Martha, sollicita es . . . Maria optimam partem elegit.* [Martha, Martha you are busy. Mary has chosen the better part

---

[21] Fulton Sheen was on the faculty of Catholic University from 1926 to 1950. Thereafter, as a Bishop, he distinguished himself as a preacher on his television shows, "The Catholic Hour" and "Life Is Worth Living."

(Luke 10:41–42).]. Sometimes I catch myself drumming with my fingers on a book or a table! That is the worst yet. I suppose the retreats have got me doing that. Then, dissipation in the refectory, kidding around with Fr. Odilo, my neighbor, who preaches all day to the guests.

And so tomorrow we stars of the active life will celebrate Mary's contemplation. So much activity in the spirituality of St. Bernard! Pure contemplation only for the weak. I don't know, maybe that is common teaching. But I still prefer St. John of the Cross. "If any should have aught of this degree of solitary love, great wrong would be done to it and to the Church if even for a brief space one should endeavor to busy it in active or outward affairs of however great moment."

Anyway I am weak. I suppose I am given these activities as a punishment for not realizing how weak I am.

Anselme Dimier's *La Sombre Trappe* [Paris, 1946] creates the impression it proposes to want to dispel: that the old school Trappists were very macabre. Perhaps that is the idea of the book: they were gloomy. We Cistercians are joyful. But it can be carried too far. There was plenty of the Cistercian spirit at La Trappe: you can get it from the introduction to [Casimir] Gaillardin's history [*Les Trappistes*. Paris, 1844]. They were not different from us except in accidentals, but some of the accidentals are important for their repercussions on the interior life.

I still pray Our Lady to keep me in that cloud where I belong.

There I go drumming with my fingers again . . .

August 15, 1947. The Assumption of Our Lady

I just learned that Dom T. Verner Moore, the Benedictine who gave us the retreat two years ago, became a Carthusian in Spain. The dog! When I went to him with my problem, he told me "Oh no, you don't want to be a Carthusian!"

Also our Frater Romuald, the Chinese postulant, novice rather, he went to Parkminster to be a Carthusian there.

It is like having something stuck into my heart.

Blessed Lady! What am I waiting for? Is it that I just haven't the courage to do it or what? Am I afraid of having to argue about it? What is the matter anyway? Of course I am obeying my directors . . . Dearest Mother, help me now. Do I really belong here? Do I really belong up to my neck in all this work and activity? Isn't it true that I am a fish out of water here? Please help me. It might well be your desire to make me a Carthusian. I only want to do what pleases God, but show me the way. Show me what is pleasing to

Him. Tell me what to do. Lead me into solitude. Take me wherever I belong. I'm going to try and collar Fr. Anthony somewhere and ask him – poor man! But what am I going to do, let my heart burn a hole in me?

I wanted to sit down and write letters, but how can I? Well, I'll try.

August 17, 1947. Sunday. Day of Recollection

Fr. Anthony said, in substance, "wait and see."

I suppose a lot depends on whether the Carthusians come to this country. I don't see myself going to Europe to try and be a contemplative in that nest of dynamite.

Our life – I mean the Cistercians – _Usque ad exhalationem spiritus discedant._ [Let them keep going until the exhalation of their last breath.] That is what we are all doing today – sweating.

Fr. George is a perfect example of a Cistercian according to the language of the _Exordium Parvum._[22] Last week or the week before, whenever it was, we gave him the last sacraments. Friday he was up for the Feast and even came to choir. You can't keep him out of the community. The Rule is everything, all the business of going here at this time and there at that time, no matter if your legs are falling off, sanctity seems sometimes to boil down to that in a Cistercian monastery.

I don't want to seem critical, but at any rate I think my own vocation means a great deal more than that. I simply can't see this business of following a lot of communal observances as if they were ends in themselves. They are not. They are ordered to _charity_ or they are nothing. However, I suppose that for a Cistercian the measure of your love for God is your love for the community life, for the Rule, for the observances.

In a sense that is true of every Order. And that is perfectly right.

Yet it seems to me that, if I had received the Last Sacraments, I would want above all to be alone with God. To me contemplation means solitude and the need to be alone and in silence burns me up from day to day. Does that mean that the community life is a cross I am trying to escape? No. I haven't anything against the community life and no difficulty in accepting it as a cross, or in realizing that there is profit in it, but it all seems so _inadequate,_ so much of a blank to me.

Maybe that is as it should be. God wants me to be purified. He wants the life to seem a blank, to get my self-love out of the picture.

---

[22] The primitive account of the foundations of Cîteaux in 1098.

But the fact remains: I spend the day doing things and going from one activity to another and wondering when do I get to be alone and in silence with God? The intervals help, and sometimes it works out in choir, even on a day like today when everything is vile with sweat.

But I have put the whole thing in God's hands, according to Fr. Anthony's directions. Jesus will make everything clear in His own time.

Frankly my feeling at the moment is this:

I think Our Lord will lead me into solitude, to the Carthusians perhaps. I believe this desire comes from Him and therefore that He intends to fulfill it, but in His own time and in His own way. My own part is to keep quiet and wait and attend to Him, trust in Him, rest in His presence, as if the cloud in which I find Him obscurely were to be the vehicle, the ship that is to take me there. Desire nothing more than this contact with Him in obscurity, ask no questions, do not try to rush Him or urge Him on, have no opinions, choose no way of my own, be with Him and let Him do the rest. This is the solution that gives me peace. May Our Lady bring it all to fruition for Her Son's glory!

August 20, 1947. Feast of St. Bernard

This afternoon Fr. Anthony called me into the confessional without any initiative of my own and, without my saying anything about it, he finally asked me point blank if I had made up my mind to go off to the Carthusians.

I told him, if they came to this country and, if he approved, I would ask about it.

He said he didn't approve, but didn't disapprove either, and told me that I was free as far as he was concerned to write the General any time and ask his permission.

Even if the General refused, and if I still didn't get peace, I could still write to the Congregation [of Religious in Rome], he said.

So there the matter stands. I haven't made any decisions because, as far as I can see, it would be silly to think of going to Europe, outside of some very special circumstances. Anyway, that still doesn't tell me what is God's will. And I don't just want to do what is *licit* [legally correct] for me to do. I want to do fully what is God's desire, whether it be to stay here or go to the Carthusians. Frankly, I don't know what God wants of me. So much seems in favor of my staying here: it is simpler and all my superiors want it that way, obviously. But then the life seems so much of a blank for me personally, although I am not without peace, and I can pray when I get a chance. Yet there seem to be so many limitations to opportunities for a real, intimate union with God. But when do we rest in Him by love and contemplation? Yes, I admit, by peculiar circumstances I have even more chance than some others. I make some of the study period (morning work) a prayer, contemplation, and it is sweet to be united with Our Lord without fuss or words out under the trees and feel the penetrating goodness of His Presence.

All I can do is seek His Face, His Presence more and more, and rest in Him all I can and He will guide me. I would never go anywhere unless I were far more certain than I am now. I will cling to Him blindly and He will tell me what to do.

One thing: I can cease this silly, small-minded criticism of the Order and the house. It doesn't do any good in any respect to any one, especially to me. Faults are not my business except in Chapter. I am not here to reform the place.

I guess St. Bernard was working on me: before the Blessed Sacrament I was getting lights on the value of our life and its crosses, but there was too much emotion in it.

After Night Office I stood in the door by the kitchen and looked at the stars and the sky paling out behind Rohan's knob, and the barns and the water tower. How fierce and efficient that tank makes this place look – geared for battle.

My God, lock me in Your will, imprison me in Your Love and Your Wisdom, and draw me to Yourself. I will never do anything when the strongest reason for doing it is only my own satisfaction. I want Your will and Your love. I give myself blindly to You. I trust in You. Do You really want me in solitude? Then lead me there, and purify the way of all my own will and of my own desires. I trust in You blindly and I will keep close to You whatever the darkness, whatever the fears may be. Lead me to do all things in Your own time and Your own way.

You know all that is in my soul, all that is to be done there. Do it in Your own way. Draw me to You, Oh my God. Fill me with the Pure Love of You alone. Make me never go aside from the way of Your Love. Show me clearly that way and never let me depart from it and that will be enough. I leave everything in Your hands. You will guide me without error and without danger, and I will love You all the way. I will belong to You. I will not be afraid of anything for I shall remain in Your hands and never leave You.

Oculi mei semper ad Dominum. Per tuas semitas duc nos quo tendimus, ad lucem quam inhabitas. [My eyes are always toward the Lord. By your paths lead us to the place toward which we strive: to the light which you inhabit. (Merton's construction after Psalms 24:1–5, 15.)]

I trust in Our Lady for all this. She will never let me go wrong.

†

August 24, 1947. Feast of the Most Pure Heart of Mary

One day things look one way and then they look another. I suppose it is the result of emotion and natural passions. Today I was once again able to see the value of staying at Gethsemani, not for myself, but for others. I wonder how much self-flattery there is in that! On the other hand, God definitely has a work He wants to do in this Order. We do not know our own Order, we do not know ourselves, or I would better understand what it is all about. But all the fluctuation back and forth means nothing.

The fact remains, it *might* be a good thing for me to go to the Carthusians, but is it God's will? In any case there is nothing to be done about it now. At the moment I can't see anything except to wait until they found a house in this country.

Yesterday for a moment Fr. Anthony was in favor of applying at once for permission (to the General) to get it over with. He is more or less resigned to the idea. He even said that, if I tried a European Charterhouse and didn't like it, I should not come back here, but go to one of our best houses in Europe – Tamié, for instance.

God has brought me to America. I am through with Europe, I hope!

But Fr. Anthony told me a startling thing: the General apparently asked several people here if I would make a good *definitor!!* I am very happy that he should think I might have enough sense to be useful – but of all jobs – I'd probably end up by starting a schism in the Order, and it would drive me crazy. If I thought there was any real danger of such a job (it would be a long way off!), I would pack up and go to a Charterhouse tomorrow. But there is no such danger.

The publication of *The Seven Storey Mountain* may change a lot of things.

I was talking to Fr. Prior about my trouble. He didn't try to deny that the house was over-active. Of course we are practically feeding our houses in Georgia and Utah. Then the crazy situation of so many novices and so few professed priests!

Fr. Romuald left before he knew whether or not the Charterhouse in England would take him. He is in Chicago or somewhere trying to raise money to pay his passage to England. That made me think quite a bit. It looks like the devil's work.

Besides, Fr. Prior heard from Dom Verner Moore, when he was here, that Parkminster is not up to the standard of Gethsemani, at least that was what he thought. That was why he became a Carthusian in Spain. He thought a little of coming here.

When I read the pamphlet *Cistercian Contemplatives* I just wrote, I convert myself all over again with the rosy picture I have painted of our life.

It came back from the New York censor in record time. I seem to be getting on well with Fr. Fearns. I think he is a good censor because he is so nice to our books. This one took less than two weeks. Laughlin is busy on layouts. And Bob Giroux is busy getting *The Seven Storey Mountain* ready for press. I haven't heard anything new about Mother Berchmans or St. Lutgarde.

In the midst of all this I think of the Pure Heart of Mary. *Nihil iniquitatis in eam incurrit.* [No iniquity entered into her.] And what is my heart full of? Myself and business. When I get pepped up about the progress of the work, I think I am doing wonders for the Order and I ought to stay. Then I realize how stupid that is, and begin thinking once again of the quiet little cell where I imagine I would belong to God alone. Or would I just be locked up with all the same work and not even able to escape it for a few minutes in the church or outdoors??

Tomorrow is the feast of my patron who had to run a whole county and started a couple of crusades! Maybe St. Louis will sympathize and make me a true solitary. But perhaps I am on the right track. Everything hurts me. I want to turn away from everything, lose everything, throw away the world, shake off time, lose all things that are trying to grow on to me like barnacles. Of course I can't do it. There is only one Who can do it for me, and He is making me suffer in order to open the way for the love that is the means by which He intends to do that work.

My God, how much there is to be done! What a burden of junk to be burned!

August 31, 1947. St. Joseph Calasanctius and the Fourteenth Sunday after Pentecost
Brings us to the end of another August which we will never see again. It was hot and stuffy all day, but though it didn't rain, now after Vespers the air is cooler and the sky has brushed up to look like September. O frightening and beautiful month with St. Giles standing in your door to be the patron of those who are afraid! Today Job came back in the Night Office,

too, and soon we will fight the fields of corn – or *they* will. I haven't been out to work for three months. I planned to try and go last week but was snowed under with all the things on that desk in St. John's room.

We have the biggest retreat of the year – some say 82 are in it. One of them is an old man with a magnificent beard and big curling mustache. I saw him here before. He is one of the wonders of Kentucky.

I feel more and more isolated from the rest of the community.

I thought for a moment, and with nostalgia, of the old days when I got so much consolation out of the Cistercian Fathers and the history of the Golden Age of the Order – the bright fall days four years ago when I opened Migne [*Patrologia Latina*] and found St. Ailred [of Rievaulx]. But God has taken all the joy out of what was then a brave new world. However, I am reading now William of St. Thierry's *Expositio Altera in Cantica* [*Second Commentary on the Song of Songs*] with profit, but with no special savor of any Cistercianism about it. I mean I don't see the stones of any monastery or see the cloister where he wrote or hear the bells of Signy.

Troubles in choir have done everything to take all joy out of the chant for me, too. God doesn't want me to sing for the sake of the wonderful music which He has allowed to be so largely destroyed all around me.

My God, thank You for stripping me of these things, thank You for not stopping, but going on from day to day without interruption doing this work that hurts me in my soul. But thank you also for peace and for Your presence: they alone make it bearable.

Bring me soon to the day of union with You, when I will love You purely for Yourself alone and not know or see myself at all except in You. Make me so like You that I am lost in You and there is only one self between us. Hasten the day, oh my God, and make me strong enough to take the purification it requires.

Working in secular dining room, in the strong smell of soup and pie. I read some Claudel when there was a lull, waiting for more stuff to come from the kitchen. And I liked him, especially a prose-poem about rain.

Somebody ought to write a book full of things like that. Maybe I ought to. Maybe I ought to shut up.

September 7, 1947

Nativitas est hodie . . . [Today is the Birth . . .] 7th tone. *Cum jucunditate nativitatem Beatae Mariae celebremus.* [Let us celebrate with gladness the birth of Blessed Mary.] Lady, to you God has given the mission of bringing us to union, *ut per unam feminam reformemur ad Sapientiam* [so that through one woman we may be reformed unto wisdom (St. Bernard. Sermo 85, *super Cantica*)]. Through you I can come to solitude to be alone with God. *Coeli fenestra facta es.* [You have been made the window of heaven.]

Manifestations of human affection give me pain. Everything but to be alone and to be absorbed in the presence of God, like a cloud of purifying darkness, translucent and full of rest, anything but this gives me pain. Words give me pain. Song hurts me. Writing troubles me. Reading puts me into the cloud. Sometimes it envelopes me in choir and hides me from all.

The brothers came out for Benediction with the new torches as if they had burning hearts upon poles.

And a priest in Washington state wrote to me about the article in *Commonweal* about the foundation in Utah, which article I have not seen, but I signed the check with one of those mechanical pencils that a novice has been twice proclaimed for having and using.

This Father Reinhold said the monks in Utah ought to do some decent printing in winter, when they can't go out, and rescue us from the frightful stuff that is put out. I had been thinking the same and I wrote to agree with him, and then I took up some other points and sent the letter off. After that I wished I had it back because I felt as if it were full of heresy.

About the same article, it inspired the editor of a thing called *The Marianist* at Dayton, Ohio to ask me for articles for them. Reverend Father has not yet said what I am to do. And last week I had to write one for a new magazine without much of a budget called *Integrity*.

Between me and the shadow, gnats dance in the sun. It is cooler. It is September.

This afternoon I was content looking at the low green wall of the woods and listening to the silence: content, not for the sake of the scene or the silence, but because of God. I don't think as much of Guigo I's *Meditations* as I once thought I might. Very lapidary, but not on an interesting enough level. Why was he apparently writing for seculars? Or was he? I'd better read them some more before I can say.

Paul Claudel's verse bores me but his poetic prose about the Orient is wonderful. I have never read anything as good in its species as *Novembre, La Pluie, Le Cocotier*, etc. Patrice de la Tour du Pin writes too much: it is too glib. I don't like it and I don't like his way of talking about Christ. It is too silly.

I heard a car in the distance. Soon I will wash my neck and go read Fulton Sheen to the retreatants. Somebody told me 70 more photographs were coming from Utah.

That is how everything stands, Mother of God, after the First Vespers of your Nativity in the year 1947. *Dona nobis pacem.* [Give us peace.] Keep us in your heart until next year and the year after until we die in peace, disposed in the four corners of America in new foundations, none of us bishops, me writing less for magazines and being more silent, and myself perhaps you know where, in a cell, all alone with you and God. His will is my cell. His love is my solitude. *Dona nobis pacem.*

September 12, 1947

I am working in the vault cataloging incunabula, ancient mss., etc.[23] These are a few notes on things I have run across.

An edition of St. Bernard's *Epistola de Perfectione Vitae. Si plene vis consequi quod intendis: duo sunt tibi necessaria. Primum est ut subtrahas te ab omnibus transitoriis: ut nihil de eis cures ac si non essent. Secundum ut ita des te Deo ut nihil dicas vel facias: nisi quod credideris sibi firmiter placere.* etc. [If you wish fully to obtain what you are intending, two things are necessary for you. First, that you withdraw yourself from all things transitory, so that you care nothing about them, as though they were not. Second, that you so give yourself to God that you say or do nothing save what you firmly believe is pleasing to him. etc.] Is this St. Bernard's? It occupies 3 leaves (6 pp.) followed by Gerard of Zutphen.

De Reformatione Virium Animae [The Reform of the Soul's Powers] looks very interesting. Purity of heart, interior peace – points to St. John of the Cross. Date given for this: Barcelona, 1510. 2 woodcuts – lactation of St. Bernard – the Annunciation.

So many editions of *De Modo Bene Vivendi [On Living the Good Life]* – not St. Bernard's at all [by Thomas of Froidmont, † after 1225]. One (Paris, 1621) dedicated to Denis de Largentier [the abbot reformer of Clairvaux, † 1624]. Attributed to St. Bernard, *Speculum Divini Amoris* in verse – Köln Quentell – 1505. Beautiful printing. Lament of Our Lady at the foot of the Cross.

---

[23] On September 12, 14, and 18, 1947, Merton took extensive notes on the incunabula and manuscripts purchased by Dom Edmond Obrecht and kept in a protective vault – in which Merton finally begins to enjoy solitude at Gethsemani. Since 1974, over one hundred of these manuscripts have been placed on loan by the Abbey of Gethsemani at the Institute of Cistercian Studies, Western Michigan University at Kalamazoo.

En nos amara dividit mors, nimis ius natura? / Heu quid mihi accidit nunc [?] mansura . . . [Lo, bitter death divides us, nature is indeed a law . . . / Alas, what is happening to me, who am I to remain . . .] Basis – a dialogue between two monks. Our Lord and Our Lady enter into it. Looks interesting.

Nicholas "Salyceti" of Bongart [Baumgarten] (Alsace) – *Liber Meditationum . . . qui Anthidotarius Animae [The Book of Antidotes for the Soul]* (he was a doctor) dicitur. At the end – Impressum Venetijs – AD. Inc MCCCCCJI *[sic]* viij Kal. Martij. P. 71 gives the prayer St. Bernard was supposed to be saying before Crucifix when it reached down and embraced him. It is verse – but not printed as such.

Salve mundi salutare	[Hail, Salvation of the world.
Salve salve Jesu care	Hail, hail, dear Jesus.
Cruci tuae me aptare	You know why I desire
Vellem vere tu scis quare	To fix myself to your cross.
Da mihi tuam copiam	Give me your abundance.
Ac si praesens sis accedo	I come as if you were present,
Immo te praesentem credo	Indeed I believe you present.
O quem nudum hic te cerno	O, I prostrate myself before you
Ecce tibi me prosterno	Whom I see naked before me.
Sis facilis ad veniam	Be quick to forgive me.
. . .	. . .
Grates tantae caritati	Grateful for such great love,
Nos agamus vulnerati	Wounded as we are, we thank you.
O amator pectorum	O lover of hearts,
Reparator confractorum	Healer of the broken,
O dulcis pater pauperum	O sweet father of the poor.
Quidquid est in me confractum	Whatever in me is broken
Dissipatum aut distractum	Unfocused or distracted
Dulcis Jesu totum sana	Heal it totally sweet Jesus.
Tu restaura tu complana	Restore and pacify me
Tam pio medicamine	With your loving medicine.
. . .	. . .
Salve Jesus rex sanctorum	Hail, Jesus, king of the saints,
Spes votiva peccatorum	Desired hope of us sinners.
In ligno tamquam reus	Like a criminal on a cross
Pendens homo verus deus	You hang, true man, true god
Caducis nutans genibus	With bent and bruised knees.
. . .	. . .

Sanguis tuus abundanter	Abundantly your blood poured out,
Fusus fluit incessanter	Flows incessantly for us,
Totus lotus in cruore	You are all awash in blood,
Stans in maximo dolore	Steeped in utter pain,
Praecinctus vili tegmine	Clothed with a vile rag.
O majestas infinita	O infinite majesty,
O egestas inaudita	O unheard of poverty,
Quis pro tanta caritate	Who is it truly seeks you,
Quaerit te in veritate	Impelled by your great love
Dans sanguinem pro sanguine	To give back blood for blood?
Quid sum tibi responsurus	What can I ever say to you,
Actu vilis corde durus	I who am vile and hard of heart?
Quid rependam amatori	How can I repay such a lover
Qui eligit pro me mori	Who chooses to die for me
Ne dupla morte moriar	To prevent my double death?
. . .	. . .
Manus sanctae vos avete	Hail, holy hands of yours
Rosis novis adimplete	Bleeding, looking like new roses
Hos ad ramos dure junctae	Hands nailed fast to the wood,
Et crudeli ferro punctae	Pierced by cruel iron,
Tot guttis decurrentibus	So many drops of blood flowing.
. . .	. . .
In hac cruce sic extensus	As you are stretched out on this cross,
In te meos trahe sensus	Draw my senses to you, make
Meum posse velle scire	My powers, my will, my understanding
Cruci tuae fac servire	Serve your cross.
Te meis apta brachiis	Shape your arms to my embrace.
In tam lata charitate	Into such lavish love
Trahe me in veritate	Draw me in truth.
Propter tuam crucem almam	By your nourishing cross
Trahe me ad crucis palmam	Lead me to the cross' victory.
Dans finem meis vitiis	Put an end to my sins.
. . .	. . .
Salve Salus mea Deus	Hail, my Salvation, my God,
Iesu dulcis amor meus	Sweet Jesus, my love
Salve pectus reverendum	Hail, loving bosom,
. . .	. . .
Amoris domicilium	Dwelling place of love.

Ave thronus trinitatis	Hail, Trinity's throne,
Arca lata caritatis	Ark of wide love,
Firmamentum infirmis	Strength to us who are weak,
Pax et pausa fatigatis	Peace and rest to the tired,
Humilium triclinium	Couch for the lowly.
Jesu dulcis pastor pie	Sweet Jesus, loving shepherd,
Fili Dei et Mariae	Son of God and Son of Mary,
Largo fonte tui cordis	With your heart's flowing fountain
Foeditatem meae sordis	The stench of my filth
Benigne precor dilue	Kindly wash away, I beg you.
. . .	. . .
Dulce Iesu Christi pectus	Sweet bosom of Jesus Christ,
Tuo fiam dono rectus	May I be made right by your gift.
Absolutus a peccatis	Freed from my sins,
Ardens igne caritatis	Burning with the fire of love
Ut semper te recogitem	So that I always think about you.
. . .	. . .
Summi regis cor aveto	Hail, heart of the highest king.
Te saluto corde laeto	My happy heart greets you.
Te complecti me delectat	To embrace you pleases me
Et hoc cor meum affectat	Your heart deeply stirs my own,
Ut ad te loquar animes	Inspires me to speak to you.
. . .	. . .
O mors illa quam amara	O death, how bitter you are.
Quam immitis quam avara	How unkind, how greedy.
Quae per cellam introivit	You violated the chamber
In qua vita mundi vivit	Where the world's life lives,
Te mordens cor dulcissimum	Devouring you, sweetest heart.]

St. Bernard – *In Cantica* – Lyon 1588. Dedicated to Claude Aquaviva, S.J. Another *De Modo Viviendi* – badly printed specimen at Constance, 1599. German so simple even I can read it.

A much older edition of Salicet's *Anthidotarius* – Strasbourg, 1490. Capitals drawn in color. An owner pasted a picture of the Crucifixion on the title page. May have something under it. Popularity of this book due to fervent devotion to Humanity of Jesus. Beautiful devotions.

Diurnale Cist., Paris, 1580. After Psalter, "Jubilus de Nomine Jesu." The whole *Jesu Dulcis memoria*. Blank pages left at beginning and end and prayers inserted in ms. – mostly commemorations. For instance, one for Our Lord's Passion on Fridays. Long responsory, "Tenebrae factae sunt . . ." ["It became dark . . ."] from St. John's Passion.

Rituale of the Feuillants. Starts out with Scripture quotes on the value of observing sacred ceremonies. *"eo quod obedierit Abraham . . . Caeremoniasque servaverit."* [because Abraham obeyed and kept my statutes. (Genesis 26:5)] Levit. V, Deut. IV, Deut. X, etc. Conc. Trid. Sess. VII. Can 13, Sess. XXII. Cap 5. Tradition – among others St. Thomas' *Contra Gentiles*. III. 119. St. Peter Damian – end of *Lib.[er] Dom[inus] Vobiscum*.

Not allowed to lean on armrests when standing in stalls facing altar – they had cuspidors in choir. This volume entirely liturgical. Comes from Feuillant mon. of the Guardian Angels in Paris – crest on cover. Mass – Roman rite, it seems. Did not read all.

Manuale – 2nd Vol. In Appendix. Notation for chant – mostly not Cistercian. V.G. in Solemn Profession:

L'Alphabet Virginal de l'Ordre de Cîteaux contenant toutes les grâces et faveurs que la Ste Vierge a fait à ce St Ordre by a Minim P. Jacques Harel. Dedicated to Madame Elizabet de Chabons, Prieure. . . de N.D. de Grâces à Tulins (OC.)

à Grenoble chez R. Phillipes et P. Dubois Imprimeurs et Librairie près des RR. PP. Jésuites. (1677). Mostly saints – arranged in alphabetical order, but after Bl. Abond [Abundus of Huy] comes *Afflighem* ("Affligement"), the salutation by the Statue of our Lady to St. Bernard.

P. 194. Detailed life of Dame Emerentiane – first prioress of N.D. de Grâces, out of place due to a printer's error. *Considerez quel modèle vous avez vu de vos propres yeux* . . . [Consider the model you have before your eyes . . .] He doesn't give date but the monastery was apparently just founded. Look up in Janauschek.

Many articles on the Saints begin *"Cet illustre mignon de la Ste Vierge . . ."* ["This precious illustration of the Holy Virgin . . ."]

Processionarius, Marnef, Paris, 1510. Belonged to Chiaravalle, Milan. Beautiful woodcut of the Purification.

Missale. The first published Missal – done at Bongart (Pomarius) by Nicholas Salicet in 1486. First page – before gathering a. (gathering of 10 leaves each).

Mandate of John (de Cirey) of Cîteaux ordering the impression. Initial letters, blue and red, hand printed. Calendar. Instructions in general on Credo, Gloria, etc., when sung.

Ms. of St. Bernard *In Cantica* done during his own lifetime at Parc (OSB?) Louvain. One of the most beautiful mss. I have ever seen. Parchment – caroline-gothic hand – easy to read. Beautiful initials in red-green, red & blue. A wonderful gold and green Q at beginning of VIIth Serm. After Serm XX the writing gets much smaller – different hand.

Ms. of St. Bernard's Sermons, XIVth century. Italian vellum. Contains a life of St. Hugh the Carthusian. & the last sermon was a portrait of St. Bernard as the initial letter "I." *Inter Babiloniam et Jerusalem nulla pax est sed guerra continua . . .* [Between Babylon and Jerusalem there is no peace, but continual war . . .]

September 14, 1947. Feast of Holy Name of Mary. Day of Recollection

The *Usages* say it is winter. The weather obligingly got a little cooler so that the sky is clear enough to suggest autumn. This week I am servant of the Refectory because there is no laymen's retreat. The priests of the Archdiocese are here during the week and they do their own reading.

The Archbishop was here and Reverend Father asked him about all those books of ours (Fr. Raymond's, too) he is supposed to have been censoring for the last year, and he just smiled and said nothing.

But it is a day of Recollection.

More objectivity in my spiritual life. Asked St. Francis for it, some of his concentration on Christ!

The Feast of his Stigmatization coincides for us with the transferred Feast of the Exaltation of the Holy Cross this year (no it doesn't!!). Read some of that marvelous VIIth Chapter of St. Bonaventure's *Itinerarium* – Christ on the cross the only entrance, the *via* [way], the *ostium* [door] to pure contemplation.

His poverty coincides, for me, with solitude.

La Soledad! [Our Lady of Solitude] I remembered her. Bishop Davis of San Juan, P.R., was here and happened into the vault and looked at some of the books, and it suddenly occurred to me to ask him about the devotion to La Soledad, which I remembered since Camagüey [Cuba], 1940. He said he would get one of his priests to dig up something for me. But even if he should forget, something has reawakened me.

Tomorrow in the Roman calendar, Our Lady of Sorrows.

La Soledad! My whole interior life is summed up in you.

No need to talk about it, live it to console you. Empty myself of all things to be poor and desolate with you. Look for you in your almost impenetrable solitude. Your loneliness is all my friendship, your desolation becomes my life.

La Soledad! I give you myself, my desires, my thoughts, my life.

I am the orphan given to you in exchange for your Christ in His Passion – and to have me instead of Him is being infinitely worse than alone – yet you have desired this solitude in order to love me in it and bring me, in it, to the perfect likeness of Jesus by your love, by your sorrow, by your solitude.

O Lady, your terrifying sorrows should frighten us more than anything. They are frightful beyond comprehension, and yet I dare to love you most in your loneliness, in your absolute dereliction, even though I am the cause of it and cannot assuage it. But I dare to love you because you have suffered this in order that I may love you, and you want me to love you mutely and helplessly in your solitude.

Haec requies mea in saeculum saeculi. [This is my rest for ever and ever (Psalms 131:14)], to seek to console you by having Christ living in me, for He is my love for you.

He is the one who burns my heart for you, Soledad!

AVE MARIA!

12th century Cistercian antiphonal & *Hymnarium*. With ms. notes by an Italian bibliophile Carlo Trivulzio. When Dom Edmond bought it, it was the oldest musical ms. in the country. Begins with Proprium Sanctorum – Feast of St. Stephen. A wonderful initial "H"

(*Hesterna die Dominus natus est in terris [ut Stephanus nasceretur in coelis]*) [Yesterday the Lord was born on earth that Stephen might be born in heaven], (first responsory). No 4-line staff, only one line. Antiphon, for instance:

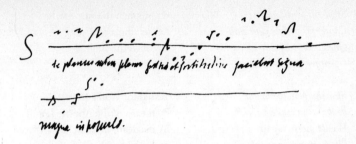

a top and bottom line faintly indicated in pencil. After Feast of Holy Innocents – St. Agnes. Then Purification – giving the Circumcision antiphons there for lst time.

Many of the small initial letters of individual responsories are decorated
with red and gold squares, thus

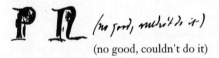

(no good, couldn't do it)

At the Annunciation the alleluias proper to Paschal time are written in
the margins. Then follows *Commune Sanctorum* – then St. Mark.

In margin – around April – notes of St. Robert, Communion of St.
Hugh, St. Peter Martyr, *ergo* written long before introduction of St.
Robert's feast – gives him a responsory, *"Iste Sanctus . . ."*

Feast of St. Bernard inserted – different vellum – different hand – *ergo*
written before June, 1174, date of his canonization.

After *Proprium* – comes *Commune Sanctorum*.

Office of dead – a beautiful black, green, gold and red "C" for the *Clemen-
tissime*. Then the different tones of the "Venite" of Ps. 94 – all recognizable.

Follows *Tonale* – with a few technical notes on how to raise the tone –
and not mix the plagals and authentics. Can't follow the thought or the ab-
breviations. Perhaps these are merely "St. Bernard's" notes as in Mabillon
at the end, showing tones for lessons. Gives *"Domne, jube, benedicere"*
["Lord Abbot, grant your blessing"] instead of *Jube, Domne, [benedicere]*.

Same volume a *Hymnarium* – much later handwriting.

One for St. Stephen – same tone as the hymn *Avete solitudinis* [Hail,
dwellers in solitude] – all Sts. of Order now.

Stephani primi martyris	Of Stephen the first martyr
Cantemus novum canticum	Let us sing a new song
Quod dulce sit psallentibus	Sweet to the singers
Opem ferat credentibus.	May it aid believers.
...	...
Sic enim per Apostolum	Tested for God's glory
Probatus in laudem Dei	By means of the Apostle [Paul].
Vexilla morte rapuit	By his death he snatched victory
Ut praeferretur omnibus.	And marched before us all.
...	...
O praeferenda gloria	O way-opening glory,
O beata victoria	O happy victory
Ut mereretur Stephanus	That Stephen merited
Ut sequeretur Dominum.	Following the Lord.

This is my own notation:

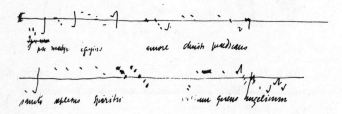

Ille levatis oculis	Stephen raised his eyes,
Vidit Patrem cum Filio	Saw the Father with the Son,
Monstrans in coelis vivere	Showing that he lived in heaven
Quem plebs quaerebat perdere.	Even as the mob sought to destroy him.
Iudaei magis seviunt	The Jews rage the more
Saxis comprehensis manibus	Stones clenched in their hands,
Currebant ut occiderent	They hastened to kill him
Sacratum Christi militem.	Who was Christ's holy soldier.
Ille paratus verticem	Stephen, preparing his head,
Gaudens suscepit lapides	Joyfully received the stones.
Rogans pro eis Dominum	Asking the Lord to forgive them,
Gaudens tradidit spiritum.	Rejoicing he gave up his spirit.

Follows St. John Evangelist – a hymn same tone as we have now for St. Mary Magdalen: *Amore Christi Saucia [Wounded by the love of Christ].*

Amore Christi nobilis	Noble in the love of Christ
Et filius tonitrui	And Son of Thunder,
Archana Ioannes Dei	John revealed God's mysteries
Fatu revelavit sacro	With sacred utterance.
Captis solebat piscibus	After catching his fish
Patris senectam pascere	And seeing to his father,
Turbante dum natat salo	He safely swam an angry sea,
Immobilis fide stetit	And stood steadfast in faith.
Hamnum profundo merserat	He sank the hook into the deep
Piscatus est Verbum Dei	And fished out the Word of God.
Iactavit undis retia	He threw his net into the waves
Vitam levavit omnium	And brought out the Life of all.
Piscis bonus pia est fides	The good fish is the devout faith,
Mundi supernatans salem	Swimming above the world's waves,
Subnixa Christi pectore	Floating on Christ's breast,
Sancto locata Spiritu	Buoyed there by the Holy Spirit.

Saint Bernard, *In Cantica.* Printed by the Brothers of the Common Life in Rostock, 1481. Inside the binding is written *"Pertinet ad Cartusienses in Herbipoli"* ["This belongs to the Carthusians of Würzburg"]. A rarity – one of the few copies of this incunabulum bound with table of contents.

Maybe it was one of the Carthusians of Würzburg that spilled something all over the first folio. Before the *Commentary In Cantica* – the *Librum de Corona Beatae Mariae Virginis* by ?? – inferior and later print. The first folio of *In Cantica* very beautiful but rather rough hand painted initial. The Carthusians (!) put lines and notes in margins. For instance, underlined *Disce Christiane a Christo quomodo diligas Christum* [Learn, O Christian, from Christ how you are to love Christ] (Ser. XX). And in margins – *Disce amare dulciter, prudenter, fortiter* [Learn to love gently, wisely and courageously].

The Serm. XXI – there is a red hand in the margins pointing to the words: *Ergo cum te tepore, accedia vel taedio affici sentis, noli propterea diffidere aut desistere studio spirituali.* [Therefore, when you feel yourself to be affected with torpor, sloth or boredom, do not on that account lose confidence or desist from (your) spiritual pursuit.]

Serm. XXIII – inspired a lot of marginal notes. All down one folio the different "cellars" [of mystical contemplation] are listed. In the passage on nuptial contemplation what is marked is not *Tranquillus Deus tranquillat omnia*, etc. [The Tranquil God making everything tranquil, etc.], but *Clare ibi agnoscitur misericordia Domini ab aeterno et usque in aeternum super timentes eum* [Clearly there it is acknowledged that the mercy of the Lord is from everlasting and for all ages for those who fear him].

Serm. XXX – At *Tu quoque si propriam deseras voluntatem* . . . [You also, if you abandon your own will . . .] A note, *Nota usque ad finem sermonis* [Take note until the end of the sermon] – this includes the famous passage about *observatores ciborum, neglectores morum.* [Fastidious about food, neglectful of behavior.] Almost no marks until the later sermons – then some by a different hand. Picks out a passage on ingratitude in Ser. 51 – one or two symbols noted – after that no more notes. After the Colophon (clearly states printed by Brothers of the Common Life) there is a globe surmounted by a † – Carthusian trademark. Dom Edmond paid $750.00 for this book.

18th Century – a nice piece of litigation – a Cistercian was trying to hold on to a Benedictine priory on the grounds that the Cistercians were Benedictines and could therefore hold benefices reserved to the O.S.B. But that question arose – is a Cistercian different from a Benedictine? Why? How? The discussion gets nowhere that interests me.

A German translation of the Cistercian menology printed at Prague in 1730, when opened smelled horrible. Frontispiece – a lot of fat and rather inane saints sitting around on clouds.

Wonderful initial letters in a XIIth century ms. of St. Bernard's sermons – all very regular – one color – foliage motifs.

Vida y Virtudes de la Prodigiosa Doña Antonia Jacinta de Navarra y de la Cueva, Salamanca, 1678, by Dom Juan de Saracho, O.C. 600 pp. 2 columns! *Lib, Cap 31, n 2*, p. 140. [*Life and Virtues of the Extraordinary Lady Antonia Jacinta de Navarra y de la Cueva.* Book II, chapter 31, number 2, page 140.]

Interesting passage:

Perdiendo los sentidos halléme toda cercada de Dios; y el alma como conocía estava cercada de todo su bien, no parecía cabía en sí. Mas paréceme que su Majestad la llegó a sí de modo que en breve rato me perdí de vista. Lo que aquí goza el alma Dios obra en ella, holgárame mucho poderlo entender . . .

Suele ser esto unas veces más obscuro que otras porque algunas parece que me anego en un abismo y que perdiéndome de vista; y este perder de vista . . . es porque no puedo alcançar a entender lo que allí passa, ni [si] Dios obra en mi alma; sólo sé que quando salgo, es enriquecida de infinitos bienes. Otras veces que comulgo me haze luego perder los sentidos y comiença el alma sentir está junto a su Criador en quien está todo su bien y su remedio . . . , y esto no es con discursos sino que él mismo se trae este conocimiento consigo; que allí no se haze nada de mi parte.

Algunas vezes de esto parece que se está abrasando el alma en fuego de amor y que compadeciéndose de ella su Majestad la allega tanto a sí que la haze una misma cosa, y ella queda descansando como en proprio centro; conociendo que sólo el amor y caridad de Dios podía subir su baxeza a tan alto estado.

[My senses became suspended and I found myself wholly surrounded by God; and the soul, since it knew itself surrounded by all it treasured, seemed to flow out of itself. But it seems to me that His Majesty brought it to himself in such a way that in a short time I had lost sight of myself. Everything the soul enjoys in this state is effected in it by God, and I would greatly like to understand how this occurs . . .

At times all of this happens in a darker manner than at other times. On some occasions it seems that I drown in an abyss and lose sight of myself; and, if I lose myself from sight, . . . it is because I cannot attain an understanding of what is happening with me, nor of how God is working in my soul; I only know that, when I come out of it, I have been enriched with infinite goods. At other times, when I receive communion, the act at once suspends my senses, and the soul begins to feel that it is together with its Creator, in whom is all its good and remedy . . . , and this does not come about through any words or reasonings, but he himself brings this knowledge with him. In all of this, I myself do nothing at all for my part.

Sometimes during this experience it seems that the soul is aflame with the fire of love, and that His Majesty has pity on it and brings it so close to himself that he makes it to be but one thing [with himself], and it remains in repose as in its own center, knowing clearly that only God's love and charity could elevate its lowliness to such a high state.]

As a rule she is more like St. Gertrude than St. John of the †.

Ordinaire de Cîteaux – Amb. [Ambroise] Girault, 1534. French translation of *Usages*. For some unknown reason a print of St. Bruno is bound in as frontispiece. In his hand he holds a Crucifix with our Lord crucified *on a palm tree!* Around the outside of the medallion in which the saint appears, the engraver has drawn a decorative festoon of fish and lobsters – a reference to the Carthusian diet?

Here, too, in the *Ordinaire – Domne, jube, benedicere.*

Things in folio *Antiphonaries* – one dated 1544 – done at Herkenrode – chant degenerate, decorations elaborate, messy and vulgar, many colors.

Cistercian Processional – on flyleaf – "*à l'usage Bernard l'évéque* [n.b.], 1744."

September 18, 1947

So many "*Flores ex operibus S. Bernardi,*" – "*Bernardus Floretus*" etc. ["Flowers *(Florilegia)* from the works of St. Bernard."] Look them up in Janauschek [*Bibliographia Bernardina* (Vienna, 1891)] some time! No wonder people lost a true perspective on St. Bernard, reading him in this dismembered condition. Yesterday another letter from Fr. Reinhold. He had written before concerning the *Commonweal* article, suggesting that they start a printing press at our Utah foundation. Answering him, I took up his point about St. Bernard being responsible for so much bad taste – the trouble is St. Bernard's *posterity* – in his own Order, too: the Cistercians of the 15th and 16th centuries – and after!

This particular ms. "Flores S. B^{di}" – about 14th century – is neat – little blue and red initials.

Ends with a quote on our Lady that savors of an Immaculate Conception controversy.

An ms. of Cistercian Constitutions and Statutes – beginning XV century – full of ugly and facetious drawings out of place in certain capital letters. Other letters – spiky like holly or going off in meaningless lines and flourishes.

A book of beautifully printed "Opuscula S. Bernardi" ... (Modena, 1451), was owned by a certain Cassilo Tötagano, who seems by his markings to have been a man of prayer. Many interesting passages printed out in *De Cognitione hominis [On the Knowledge of Man],* (not by St. B.) made me want to read it all.

One of the prettiest pieces of printing in the little book, *Speculum de honestate vitae,* said that this first book of "St. Bernard" (??) printed by Ulrich Tell – Cologne – undated, perhaps 1464.

Typical sentence – *Sit tibi ergo Christus in corde et numquam imago crucifixi ab animo tuo recedat. Hic tibi sit cibus et potus, dulcedo tua et refectio tua, consolacio tua mel tuum et desiderium.* [Therefore let Christ be in your heart, and never let the image of the Crucified depart from your soul. Let this be unto you food and drink, your sweetness and your refreshment, your consolation, your honey and desire. (This little work appears in PL 184:1167–1172 under the title *Formula Honestae Vitae*.)]

Wonderful printing also – *De Planctu B. Mariae [On the Lament of Blessed Mary]* – 1474, Cologne.

A volume of Sermons of St. Bernard printed in Venice, 1495 (Janauschec. 181). Frontispiece – fine woodcut of St. Bernard and 10 monks. He is preaching to them in chapter. Under a crucifix on the wall is written *"Silentium"* ["Silence"]. The monks are dressed more like Carthusians than modern Cistercians.

In 1659 for the 500th anniversary of St. Bernard's death, the Cistercians of Baudeloo (Gand [=Ghent])?? got out a frightful volume, *S. Bernardi vitae medulla [The Marrow (or Pith) of the Life of St. Bernard]* with some awful illustrations in which St. Bernard looks like some kind of a doll. The execution is very slick. There is a portrait of the then Abbot of Baudeloo, a most unattractive personality.

Dom Edmond paid £175 for a little Spanish incunabulum of St. Bernard – *Meditationes* (i.e., *de Conditione Humanae conditionis) [sic Meditations* (i.e., *on the Human Condition)]* – not even by the Saint. 38 pp. Original price was £250 (£175 then equal to $852.25). 5 copies exist, one in NY at the Hispanic Society of America.

Nearly as bad – a life of St. Bernard in engravings by one G. B. Göz – court painter to one of the H.[oly] R.[oman] Emperors.

Gallus – OC. Abbot of Königsaal in Bohemia. (15th cent.) touches on questions of Mystical Theology in the 3rd Distinctio of his *Dialogus Malogranatum*.

September 21, 1947. Sunday. Feast of St. Matthew

Yesterday Fr. Leonard and Fr. Arnold were ordained to the priesthood. They have sat with us for a year and a half in the Laybrother's Scriptorium while Fr. Anthony expounded to us [Aloysius] Sabetti's *Moral Theology* and [Adolphe] Tanquerey's *Dogma*.

The whole ordination Mass was sung. I think the Archbishop got tired. While the three *ordinandi* (Fr. Urban was for the diaconate) were lying flat on their faces, and the choir was chanting the Litany of the Saints, a bird, maybe a catbird, came and sat in the middle of the sanctuary on the red carpet and chirped somewhat. After a while it flew right over the altar and perched in the open window.

I was thurifer and built the fire for the Gospel too early and so I built another one with the result that I had the biggest fire I ever built in my life.

This morning they sang their first Masses. Neither one is a great singer. Fr. Leonard, shyly making the sign of the cross over the chalice, stiffly as if he had a sore arm. He turned around to the people and said *Orate Fratres* ["Pray, brethren, that my sacrifice and yours may be acceptable to God our Father"] very humbly. It is an astonishing thing to see a new priest make his first consecration and realize what is going on!

Yesterday after dinner we all went to Chapter and the Archbishop presented a medal *Pro Ecclesia et Pontifice* [For the Church and the Pope] to Captain Kinnarney, who has a detective bureau and gives a lot of money to the monastery. Reverend Father made a speech in which it was by no means clear what was taking place. Then the Archbishop made a speech in which everything was plain. After that the Captain made a speech and burst into tears as usual. The Archbishop said to him "You are almost weeping," and he said, "Well, I can't help it!"

He has got some sort of idea that we are good monks. Maybe we are, but not what *he* thinks!

He was happy. Reverend Father was happy. And for my part I felt a little embarrassed and wanted to run away to the Carthusians.

In the Refectory we have a book about Our Lady of Fatima. It seems to me, if what it said is on the level, the social situation in Portugal is a moral miracle. It gives me hope for France. And Our Lady is the best one to ask for help, yet how they have ignored her – look at LaSalette and Lourdes. They'll go to Lourdes for favors . . .

I have given up getting upset about anything. And I thank God's love for the things that hurt me and make me upset. Fr. Anthony gives the key of St. John's room, where we work, to a religious who is a bit of a busybody, and all our business is lying around in there. He goes in there any time of the day, and the thought gives me the creeps. But in the deep end of my soul I am glad that Our Lord is cutting away my attachment to that little private element in my life – keeping me poor. I have no proprietorship then, nothing exclusive. That's what I must grow to be, a thing without walls and defenses, without any private security of my own. All that is "mine" is everybody's and they can kick it around as they like.

With my whole heart I want all the things in community life that burn and purify me of all my selfishness, of that in me that excludes others and shuts them out. I give myself to those flames with all desire, that the walls of my false solitude may be destroyed and that the false sanctuary inside me may be reduced to ashes, because it is a temple of an idol. I cannot be a solitary until my heart has been laid open to the four winds and has been trampled on by the whole world. And I can never have privacy with God until all natural privacy has been destroyed. If I ever become a true solitary, in the physical sense (which God grant!), the flames that burn down my false solitude will have to become more and more furious, and the obscure pains that eat out the very roots of my heart will have to become a hundred times sharper, that I may belong even more to the whole world and to Christ's whole Church and to every soul in it by my annihilation and selflessness.

That's a way of devotion to La Soledad, the solitude of Calvary, the solitude of a target in a shooting range.

I make a novena to the Little Flower to get grace to be altogether abandoned to the action of the Holy Ghost.

Wednesday, September 24, 1947

It is the "feast" of Mother Berchmans. For my own part I think of my filthiness and my sins. It is one of those days when you feel scabby, *quoniam iniquitatem meam ego cognosco et peccatum meum contra me est semper* [for I know my iniquity, and my sin is always before me (Psalms 50:5)]. However I am glad of it because it makes penance a delight. You look around for things to kill this leprous image which was your idol and has been discovered.

Spiritual virginity! To be unstained by any selfish desire – a mind and will clean of every interested motive and of every created concern – to live for God alone.

Reading about the Carmelites in the *Dictionnaire de Spiritualité*, found a remark contrasting their concept of poverty with the Franciscan one. Exactly the idea that struck me the other day. I mean that I realized that in my own interior life poverty is a function of solitude, of "nakedness," detachment, isolation even from creature activity. I wish I were poor. But I am not even rich. I sit in my pawnshop of second-rate emotions and ideas, and oh how they make me want to vomit sometimes.

Did I say Fr. Anthony told me to read the Carmelites a lot, as if it were a message from the Holy Spirit? I do. The other day I tried to change St. John of the Cross for something else and couldn't *find* anything else! Yet I am not at all tempted to become a Carmelite. They may have an ideal of pure contemplation, but it is only a theory. Maybe the nuns are better off.

I wish I had been more attentive to the psalter yesterday, but I was waiting outside Reverend Father's room and everybody made signs and I lost the psalms. God forgive me. Still – going to Reverend Father is always a grace: he is abbot and Jesus does not deceive us when He promises to act in our Superiors. *Qui vos audit me audit.* [Who heareth you, heareth me.]

September 25, 1947

Yesterday being the Feast of Mother Berchmans, I did not omit to put in a word for the manuscript about which I had heard nothing for a couple of months. In the afternoon our little Mother came through very smoothly and simply with the answer. I spotted a letter from Bruce by "accident" in the pile on Reverend Father's desk, and he opened it and found a check for advance royalties and a contract. So I took the contract down to the office and executed it with witnesses (Frs. Hilary and Urban) and a seal and everything and sent it right back, with my heart all full of gratitude and love for Mother Berchmans. However, I don't need sensible favors to love her and all the souls in heaven. How beautiful it was saying the psalter all alone and looking at the hills in the cool morning shadows behind the Church! If I could always say the psalms *sapienter* [wisely], but it is a favor and gift of God. At least I can get where things are quiet! But what a difference, and the psalms stay with you all day afterwards. *Fiat cor meum immaculatum in justificationibus tuis, ut non confundar* . . . [Let my heart be undefiled in thy justifications, that I may not be confounded . . . (Psalms 118:80).] *Bonum mihi lex oris tui super millia auri et argenti* . . . [The law of your mouth is good to me, above thousands of gold and silver . . . (Psalms 118:72).] *Revela oculos meos et considerabo mirabilia in lege tua* . . . [Open thou my eyes: and I will consider the wondrous things of thy law . . . (Psalms 118:18).] *Montes in circuitu ejus* . . . [Mountains are round about it [Jerusalem] . . . (Psalms 124:2).] And this morning I was especially struck by the line *Voluntatem timentium se faciet; et deprecationem eorum exaudiet, et salvos faciet eos.* [He will do the will of them who fear him: and he will hear their prayer and save them (Psalms 144:19).] God will do our will because our will is to love Him more and more. He will give us Himself, His own love to love Him with!

My heart burns in my side when I write about contemplation in an article or anywhere . . . and I want to cast fire on the earth. That is all right. Perhaps it is from God. And that doesn't mean I have to multiply useless works – on the contrary!

However, my big struggle is to empty myself of useless projects, useless ideas, and not burden myself with still more than I have got at the same time continuing to complain.

Fr. Reinhold wanted me to do some Latin translations (from the new text of the Psalms) and, wanting to refuse, I gave him a partial list of what I have to do, and when I saw it on paper, I was staggered by it. Have I chosen all that myself? God has a lot to do with it. Circumstances have crowded four books into the press at one time. I tried to get out of the *Collectanea* article I should start today, but Reverend Father wants me to go on with it.

I don't feel these articles for *Commonweal* are useless, and they may make a book. In fact they are more to the point than monastic history. I do think the Joseph Cassant book would be a waste of time, but that is on the shelf anyway.

The one thing I want to be writing (*Waters of Siloe* – one-half finished) is lying there, and every time I reach out to touch it, something else comes up.

And if Father Raymond wants his typewriter (ours is being fixed), I will be altogether in the soup.

Soledad, I love you.

September 28, 1947. Day of Recollection

On the 24th, Mother Berchmans' feast, they had a meeting at Bruce and Co. and bought our manuscript on St. Lutgarde[24] so Mother Berchmans did very well by us poor Trappist writers.

A sudden secular retreat was sprung on us this weekend, right after all the priests of the diocese got finished. I read to them about our Lady of Fatima. Trouble is they ask me questions and sometimes I go and answer them.

This week I am Servant of the Church.

I made a futile effort to find the notes I was writing these days last year. I don't need to find them. What I wrote then was the same as I am writing now. And yet somehow I know that my interior life is deeper, and I have more peace, and I am nearer to God and under His control. Don't ask me how I got that way because I don't know. Of course Solemn Profession had a lot to do with it, and all the other graces, I could make a long list. What I mean is don't ask me how I applied those graces, how I used them – I don't know. But somehow with God's help they have not been fruitless.

(After First Vespers of St. Michael and all Angels.)

Why don't you finally do something about emptying your memory and imagination: people, places, things, books, ideas for work – forget them, they are unimportant. They are not your vocation. Only when obedience demands it, think about them. And it really takes very little thought outside the time of work. It *should*, I mean.

Keep practicing this blackout of people, places, things.

[24] *What Are These Wounds?*

October 12, 1947. Sunday

Last Sunday was the Feast of the Holy Rosary and very beautiful. Today it is the same. All the hills and woods are red and brown and copper and the sky is clear with one or two very small clouds. And a buzzard comes by and investigates me, but I am not dead yet. This landscape is getting so saturated with my prayers and psalms and the books I read that it is becoming incomparably rich for me. Today again I was walking out there in the cemetery reciting the 118th Psalm and the Gradual Psalms – the last time 'round of this year's psalter.

Everybody has colds and I got a little pain from trying to force my voice in choir when I didn't have any voice. So I went and sat down, which seemed right at the moment, but now I think the Holy Ghost would rather have me stand in choir until they drag me out by the feet. After all, how can I be happy and have any real peace if I am not denying myself and doing penance?

We are in the octave of St. Bruno, we Carthusians. *My* Father, St. Bruno. *Your* Father, St. Bernard.

But anyway, St. Bruno has helped me. Much more sense of God working in me, purifying and pacifying and settling things in order.

What is the use of all my lamentations about not being a contemplative if I don't take advantage of all the opportunities I get for prayer? I suppose I take the opportunities but in the wrong way. How much time do I waste looking for something to *read* about contemplation instead of shutting up and emptying my mind and leaving the inner door open to God to enter from the inside, the outer door being barred and all the blinds down?

Maybe it's not the Carthusians: their cells are too fancy. And La Grande Chartreuse with all those chapels and forty square kilometers of roofs! I feel too much like a big shot at Gethsemani: what would it be in such a palace? That is not for me. A little Charterhouse would be different. La Vendana – is that the name of one? If I want to be a Carthusian, it is to be one the way St. Bruno was, except I'd probably die in a week.

I don't care: God is guiding me. He wants me in solitude, in poverty and alone with Him. Every time the smoke clears, the first thing I am conscious of is the Holy Ghost saying, "No, this way! Be quiet! Get off in a corner and forget things and set your house at rest and wait."

Then some new job lands on me and it is generally my fault.

This writing business is not forever, or, all right, if I should write (I can see that), not so much in a business way.

The article for *Collectanea* is turning into a book.[25] Already sixty pages. If they print it at all, it will be serialized for a couple of years! It is very hard. But I am learning something about Transforming Union. In a way you can't really learn these things (outside of experience!) until you try to put them down on paper. Then you learn at least what the problems are because you see where you get stuck, or condemned or something.

Somebody told me Jürgensmeier was condemned by Rome.[26] I thought, "What has that to do with me?" Contemplatives should be on a level of obscurity where those things don't even penetrate. Somebody else keeps the book from getting to them, and that is sufficient.

Are the little children going around telling one another "Jürgensmeier was condemned"?

It was the Abbot General and his definitory who told Charles de Foucauld that he had a special vocation and paid his passage to Palestine. Reading the little book on the Grande Chartreuse, I got a devotion to Notre Dame de Casalibus. These devotions fuse into one big one which is: simplicity, strip yourself of all images and memories and clothe your naked freedom in the silence of God.

October 16, 1947

Universal disgust. Last October's edition of *Collectanea* with a review of *A Man in the Divided Sea* got here. The monks of Chimay were very fulsome. They said I was everything and had the makings of a great poet. And I am fed up because it isn't true. But it doesn't really disturb me, nor will it make me write any poetry I realize to be bad, write it under the illusion that I am a poet and am therefore obliged to write poetry.

Laughlin sent Patrice de la Tour du Pin's *Dedicated Life and Poetry* [which appeared as part of *La Somme de Poésie*, 1946]. At first sight, seeing the titles, "Solitude," "Virginity," I began to feel enthusiastic. Now the thing depresses me: the clever and obscure language, the context that I don't know or understand, and the vague impression that he has simply taken the terms of the contemplative life and watered them down and degenerated them to suit the experiences of a poet. All this makes me feel sad.

[25] "The Transforming Union in St. Bernard and St. John of the Cross" was published in five issues of the *Collectanea Ordinis Cisterciensium Reformatorum* (April and July 1948, January and October 1949, and January 1950).

[26] Merton possibly refers here to Friedrich Jürgensmeier (1888–1946), who wrote *The Mystical Body of Christ as the Basic Principle of Spiritual Life*. He was never, however, censured by Rome.

But what do I care? It is good not to be interested in what is no more my business, and it would be a mistake to write the article I thought of writing.

Two or three times already Dr. Greenwell has come and given us all injections to prevent us from getting colds. Now we all have filthy colds. The choir can't sing. Everything is awful. And so today Dr. Greenwell came again to give us injections. It was right in the middle of dinner. We all got up and ran coughing and snorting to the infirmary to take the needle and I offered it up for Fr. Alberic because, before he died, he used to sit there and wipe your arm with alky before the Doctor stuck you.

We have had extra work all week and I went out the other morning to pick apples. And I broke the branch of one of the trees. But now I am again writing *The Waters of Siloe*, and I ask myself why: what is the point of such a book? Why do I write the stupid things I write, since it is more or less up to me what I write?

Maybe if I pay attention to Patrice de la Tour du Pin, I will find out how I ought to conduct myself in this matter. So long as I don't end up writing the way he does. Now I will put everything away and meditate for three seconds on the Carthusian meditations.

It is evening. Hot and stuffy. Goodbye, goodbye, goodbye.

"What if this present were the world's last night?"

† Maria!

October 19, 1947. Sunday

I was looking at the chant of the old long offertory *Vir erat in terra Hus* [There was a man in the land of Hus (Job 1:1)] which we have today and which [Dom Prosper] Guéranger [of Solesmes] talks about. The additions (suppressed in the 13th century or whenever it was) are somewhat operatic but very effective.

One thing about the eremitical life, it is hard. St. Peter Damian is always talking about conversion from the free and easy life of monasteries to the "narrow way" of the hermitage. Charles de Foucauld's life was hard and he looked knocked out by it.

And then I think of how easy things are for me, the soft straw mattress, nice warm clothes, cooking done for you, plenty to eat, relatively speaking, and no bother about where it is coming from . . .

Anyway I am pretty sure I could never lead the life the first Camaldolese led, fasting four or five times a week on bread and water and reciting two psalters a day besides their Office, and going barefoot all winter in the Appennines!

I have tried again to read Patrice de la Tour du Pin and sometimes find him very antipathetic. All that stuff is not for me. Keep away from poets!

Suddenly a beautiful yellow rose bush at the edge of the cemetery has filled with flowers and they stand like something very precious in the late slanting sun before me as I write. The evening is very quiet. I can't hear Fr. Amadeus shouting at the retreatants in the Novitiate Chapel anymore, so maybe the conference is over. I suppose one of those postulants is going to get the habit.

The crosses in the cemetery are all absolutely motionless. And yet it is as though I had been expecting them to speak.

God is here with me, in my heart.

October 25, 1947

It is the feast of St. Bernard Calvo with commemoration of Sts. Crispin and Crispinian and, being Saturday, we had the Votive Mass of Our Lady and, after Communion for about thirty seconds, I suddenly knew what St. Bernard talks about and St. John of the Cross talks about when they say "Pure Love."

How different from resting in God's peace within you. You don't rest because you no longer are. All rest, all those functions and modes of being in which you realize your own existence, no matter how absorbed in peace you may be, are laborious and drab and arduous and heave and savor of the slavery of Egypt compared to this emptiness and freedom into whose door I entered for that half-minute, which was enough for a lifetime, because it was a new life altogether. There is nothing with which to compare it. You could call it nothingness, but it is an infinitely fruitful freedom to lack all things and to lack yourself in the fresh air of that happiness which seems to be above all modes of being.

What can I say about it? Don't let me build any more walls around it, or I will shut myself out.

When will You come back? Tomorrow on the Feast of Christ the King?

It seems to me I should never desire anything but this pure love of You which is You loving Yourself, not only in my soul, but in all my faculties so that they are empty and lost and finished and done with and nothing is left but liberty.

Right after that, to fall back into a state where my own existence, the very act of being, seems coarse and laborious and miserable and cheap and vile by comparison with the purity of that love – all sweetness and all other rest is unbearable compared with this activity that is beyond all modes and all being.

October 26, 1947. Feast of Christ the King

That was only for a half a minute. *Heu recidere in mea compellor!* [Alas, I am forced to fall back into myself!] To suffer the indignity of being a member of the human race. It feels like an indignity. No doubt I could argue that it is a privilege, but all argument gives me a headache.

The only thing that gave me any relief today was when I looked in *The Cloud of Unknowing* for a moment at the chapter on the "lump" theory of the interior life (c. 36?), in other words, vague intuitions left without analysis – "sin" – "God" – all I can do today.

I have been spending more time praying in Church or just staying there with the Blessed Sacrament or in the Chapel of Our Lady of Victories. The best thing I can do. Better than wasting time in books I don't need to read.

Correcting page proofs on *Figures for an Apocalypse*, I am disgusted with the verse I have been writing. Reverend Father gave me permission not to write any more "if it is a burden," but he wants to "reach souls." I won't be in a hurry to write, but I don't seem to have permission just flatly to drop the whole thing. Last night at *Salve* what I felt was this: "Lady, if you want this dubious talent returned, I gladly give it back!!"

By accident the other day I found out where Dom Alexis Presse has been these last ten years since his secession from the Order. He went all alone to the ruins of an old Cistercian monastery in Brittany, Boquen, not even a road to it, and lived there as a hermit until he could start rebuilding the place. The Bishop is for him, and the French Government gave him 1,000,000 francs. He has rebuilt half of the monastery, starting with the library. The rumor is that it is more an experiment in archaeology than in the contemplative life. I am not attracted to it – it is the Rule and even the *Consuetudines* to the letter, a rigid imitation of the 12th century Cîteaux, which was not rigid, and therefore cannot be rigidly imitated.

For my own part, any misery I have today comes from not being united to God's will for me here and now, and here and now it is Gethsemani and all that goes with it. If He will ever take me anywhere else, that is up to Him. I want His will, on earth as it is in heaven, that is, myself completely identified in it, lost in it. When that happens I will be all but *glorified* in it: only a mortal body can stand between such a one and glory. To be identified (not just psychologically united) with His will is to be full of heaven, swimming in joy and love and completely out of oneself, the final, total escape from all limitations! But that means more than performing acts, carrying out commands, accepting troubles. Yet those are the means to the end. I have got to be patient and humble enough to use those means. I asked Reverend Father if any monks of our Order had managed to get permission to be hermits in this present age and to my surprise he said yes.

The Fr. Frederic before him was a hermit out here somewhere. He wanted silence and, as soon as he got in a hermitage, all the people went to him to talk about their troubles and ask his advice. Then, under Fr. Benedict Dupont, Bro. Dominic's elder brother, Brother John Walter went off to the mountains in the diocese of Covington for eight months and came back looking very sheepish. I couldn't get just in what this sheepishness consisted except that he had shaved. Maybe the hill-billies shaved him and tarred and feathered him, too . . .

There is still one living at Oka, but no longer as a hermit. One day he came in and started to tell Dom Pacôme how to run the monastery, so Dom Pacôme sent the prior out to set fire to his hut. That was the end of his hermit days. He came back to the monastery but didn't speak to the Abbot for months. Maybe he hasn't spoken to him yet for all I know.

November 1, 1947. All Saints Day

Made a resolution to try and write legibly.

Feast days always upset me a little. I have a hang-over from the wild coffee we had at Mixt and from the long choir. Great functions. Three simple professions and Frater Samuel made solemn profession with everything on hand except the newsreels. There was a somewhat aged monsignor to preach, or rather read, the sermon and in an unguarded glance I saw the balcony full of nuns and the outlines of ladies' hats against the Assumption window.

I have got so that I don't register most of what is going on in these big elaborate functions. I get inside and pray and let the lights and organ do what they will outside my sanctuary.

Last week came the first issue of the fancy new magazine *Tiger's Eye* with one of my less bad poems on the first page. At first I was a bit dizzy at the elaborate and expensive get-up of the thing and was filled with enthusiasm for writing, whereas I had been on the point of dropping poetry more or less for good. But now the old disgust has come back. And the enthusiasm has gone the way of its kind leaving nothing but a bad taste in my mind.

The best inspiration I have had was to spend more time in prayer. As a result, a deeper and more active desire. I won't say fewer distractions, but I seem to come out of them easier, and I have been getting help along those lines. Times when I suddenly get very recollected without realizing how.

I thought of doing some drawings. If that was a temptation, I shall find out when I start. Anyway no one has told me not to.

But the Saints in heaven: they are the ones! They have got rid of all confusions. They have their solitude which is full of company and without disturbance.

November 6, 1947

Here I come with blackberry seeds in my teeth to write down in great haste my beautiful thoughts. That having been done, I may go and bury myself in darkness in the Chapel of our Lady of Victories. Hers are the victories and mine are the defeats.

Sunday I went to get my eyes examined. There was a lot of rushing around during the High Mass. The oculists were trying to set up their instruments in St. Gabriel's room. They put drops in my eyes and they must have put drops in my mind too, because I was in a cloud of stupidity for the rest of the day.

Then my eyes cleared and I finished the galleys of Mother Berchmans. After that, when I wanted to go back to *Waters of Siloe*, which I have been trying to write all year, there came upon me a great scourge of God which is the official souvenir for the Centenary. I tried to get out of it and give it to someone who would be able to turn out just the sort of spectacular job that would delight everybody because it would be a replica of everything that had ever been done before, with ribbons on it and small bells. But Reverend Father insists I must do it and I am punished in the choir with a mind full of layouts that everybody will detest. And the funny thing is that it is what God wants of me – to take the knife in this particular wound – and offer my pride on this particularly silly altar. So I forget that it costs anything and run with love in His ways *inenarrabili dilectionis dulcedine* [with the ineffable sweetness of love], and all complaints shall be as music and their atrocious advice shall be as honey for the love of my sweet God.

The last two days or so I have been reading Deodat de Basly [*Les deux grandes écoles catholiques de B. Duns Scot et de S. Thomas* (Paris, 1906)] and not sure whether I like it, and I was going to toss him away, but the texts from Scotus in the footnotes prevented me. Even if he is an enthusiast and gets too excited and as shrill as Fr. [Frederic William] Faber in spots [*Growth in Holiness*, 1854], yet I like him for the sake of the Scotus. And God comes and dwells in me there in the sun, and I look at the woods and everything obscurely begins to sing with a vivid silence, with the deep energy of absorption His love brings.

It is Our Lady who is working in me in these days, trying to awaken things in me, bring out new worlds to light, draw me into her Christ Who is the center of all. And she does this when I go to her chapel as I have been going, and I know her love. For the first time I have tasted her love as distinct from Christ's and God's and have sapience [deep knowledge] of it (without desserts on my part) as distinct.

Sorry for the fancy language. And now, goodbye.

November 10, 1947. Sunday

Office of Dedication because of the Feast, Dedication of the Lateran, the basilica where for the first time the picture of the Savior painted on a wall appeared to the Roman people. That impressed me in the Second Nocturn – the Church's idea of the dignity of art and its function. My own memories of Rome teach me to appreciate that statement!

Also today I remember the Feast of Elizabeth of the Trinity whose book, or rather Fr. Philipon's, we still read in Chapter.

Above all yesterday, the 8th, was the Feast of Duns Scotus. He brought me, again, graces, and big ones.

For the first time I really saw into something of the import of the Mystery of the Holy Trinity in lines from the *4th* C.[hapter] of the Prologue of the *Oxoniense*, on the end of theology. How is the knowledge of the Trinity practical, i.e. how does it serve to further our love, our union by love with God? *Voluntatem ignorantem Trinitatem contingit errare in amando vel desiderando finem, desiderando frui una Persona sola . . . Essentiale est ratio terminandi actum amandi ut propter quam, SED PERSONAE TERMINANT UT QUAE AMANTUR!* [A will ignorant of the Trinity errs, either in loving or in desiring (its) goal, by desiring to enjoy only one Person (of the Trinity) . . . The reason is essential for accomplishing the act of loving: the act is done because of reason. BUT THE TERM IS THE PERSONS THEMSELVES WHO ARE LOVED!]

To me that was the revelation of new heavens and a new earth although I had read it before without being especially struck by it.

The mystery of the Trinity, considered from a purely speculative point of view, is to me, at least as a *viator* [wayfarer], cold and somewhat dull. It tends to degenerate into feeble metaphors that exasperate my soul instead of feeding it.

Even Elizabeth's preoccupation with the indwelling means far less, until I know this note that the Three Persons are the term of the act of love in concrete, the term of our actual fruition in their Trinity, and not alone or precisely in their unity.

In other words, the deep meaning of the mystery is something that can only finally be indicated, like everything else in God, by LOVE. Love is the explanation and the clue and the key. It is a key that still unlocks little or nothing to the mind, but it lets our own souls into a new and deeper contact with the inner life of God, though in darkness.

And as far as seeing goes, I am more helpless even than before.

I was drunk with that all afternoon yesterday and, when I came to Vespers, blinded by that light, two movements of my own imperfection – the kind of little impatiences that always harass me in choir these days – appeared to me in something of their true light, and I saw how they soiled or wounded my soul, but I saw it in sorrow and in peace and in helplessness that could only seek relief in waiting on the goodness and mercy of God.

The diversity and variety of things and words and experiences wounds and tires me.

I would like to say something more about the Holy Trinity and my tongue is tied, and merely to utter a word or two that sounded like the academic stuff I have just said would burn me with shame.

Today also I thought about St. Leonard of Port Maurice – off my usual track! – and his fight to get the doctrine of the Immaculate Conception defined one hundred years before it was.

It seems to me that that definition was a turning point in the modern history of the Church.

The world has been put into the hands of our Immaculate Lady and she is our hope in the terrible days we live in.

Perhaps another turning point will come when her prayers at last obtain the definition of the other great Scotist doctrine with which her Immaculate Conception is so intimately connected: the Absolute Primacy of Christ.

At first sight these things seem abstract and trifling, but they are of tremendous importance because the salvation of the world depends on what people know and believe about God and the economy of salvation. Christ's Kingdom will not come until the universal Church declares just how much His Kingship really means and that has not yet been done, even by *Quas Primas.*

November 10, 1947

Tomorrow Feast of St. Martin. I have no difficulty thinking up things to ask him for.

To discover the Trinity is to discover a deeper solitude. Then love holds your heart in its strength and keeps it away from exterior things. You do not have to try to ignore or hate material things since they affect you little.

Our Lady has my life in control. She is teaching me and leading me. She has got me to start reading Scripture according to the Liturgy: following the books prescribed for the Night Office of the *Proprium de Tempore* [Proper of the Season of Church Feasts], to try and read the whole Bible in that way in a year as our Fathers did in all the monastic orders.

Rather than ask St. Martin in writing to pray for me, I run to Church to Our Lady of Victories who owns me.

November 13, 1947. Feast of All Saints of the Order

Oh you Cistercian saints, I feel like a step-child in your order today. But the truth is I would feel like an orphan, a step-child, an exile anywhere. I have no place on earth. Only in heaven. So I ought to be grateful for the many things that remind me of it.

Today began the conferences on St. Bernard's *De Gratia et Libero Arbitrio [On Grace and Free Will]*, Father Anthony's project. Less dull than the ones on Tanquerey's "Dogma." Then in choir they have moved the organ console right into the middle of the lower row of stalls on the Abbot's side to see if the organist can keep up with the choir, which he couldn't evidently in the transept.

People are busy with ideas for the Centenary and, like a fool, I had to stick my nose in it. It would serve me right if I got some terrible job as a result. But I wanted at least to make this suggestion that we do some praying and keep the *Usages* in their entirety, although I admit we almost do even now.

November 15, 1947. Dedication of the Church

Weather or something gave me a headache and what not. Yesterday and this morning I thought I was getting flu or something, but now it seems as though I am not.

Even when I can't think straight, God straightens me out when I manage to get a few minutes or a half an hour alone in the church. And it is good to go and pray even when you feel washed out: the mere sacrifice makes you feel better, and it is comforting to feel in the marrow of your bones: "Even if I feel rotten, I don't want anything but God in His solitude."

I was acolyte at the Pontifical Mass and, having so little to do, I could pray, and before I knew it the whole thing was over.

After dinner for a moment I glance at pictures of The Cloisters (the ones they shipped to New York in Fort Tryon Park) and they looked good. They suggest nothing of a former life I might have led if I once existed in the world.

Tomorrow – nine years since my Baptism. Nine years ago this fall my happiest days were in those cloisters. I have half forgotten the rest, but sometimes in choir details of my sins suddenly come back at me and I am astounded at the things I was capable of doing without hesitation or sense of indignity!

With the things God has done in me by His grace, isn't it strange that I should even crease my forehead with a half-conscious anxiety that He might fail to make me the saint He created me to be, that He came on earth for me to be?

If I read books, read Scotus, it is partly to be able to think and say something half-way accurate about the infinite goodness and mercy of this God Who is so close to us, in Whose Son we are predestined, who love Him and are known by Him from eternity as loving Him.

The Abbot General wrote me a very complimentary note which I got the other day about the article on Transforming Union in St. Bernard which I sent to the definitors for *Collectanea*. It upset me a little to be commended by someone so important and in such a friendly way, when everything tells me I ought to be hiding in some hole.

November 16, 1947. St. Edmund

So I am nine years old in the faith.

The chief thing that struck me today before the Blessed Sacrament: I have my fingers too much in the running of my own life.

I put myself into God's hands, and take myself out again to readjust everything to suit my own judgment. On that condition I abandon myself to Him . . .

Consequence? *Quaesivimus bona et ecce turbatio. Diximus Pax! Pax! et non est Pax!* [We seek the good and behold we find disturbance. We say "Peace! Peace! and there is no Peace! (Merton's Latin construction.)]

Jesus, I put myself in Your hands. I rest in Your wisdom that has arranged all things for me. I promise to stop jumping out of Your arms to try and walk on my own feet, forgetting that I am no longer on the ground or near it!

Now at last let me begin to live by faith. *Quaerite primum regnum Dei.* [Seek ye, therefore, first the kingdom of God (Matthew 6:33).] Why do I mistrust Your goodness, mistrust everyone but myself, meet every new event on the defensive, squared off against everybody from my Superiors on down?

Dear Lord, I am not living like a monk, like a contemplative, because the first essential is missing. I only say I trust You, but really my actions prove that I am afraid of You and only trust myself.

Not any more, Jesus. Take my life into Your hands and do what You want with it. I give myself to Your love and mean to keep giving myself to Your Love, neither refusing nor objecting to the painful things nor the pleasant things You have arranged for me. And You have arranged everything for me, and it is *all* love, it is all good, it is all nourishment and strength and health for me.

I want the good things You have provided for me. I want the gifts of Your love. I want the blessings of Your tender care, especially the ones that seem hard, that seem to burn and lacerate my nature; they are the best. They are the ones I most need.

I want the simple and easy way You have laid open before my feet to travel on. But I renounce the hard and bitter way of my own self-will, which seems to promise joy but is always full of hardship and unrest.

If you allow people to praise me, I shall not worry. If you allow them to blame me, I shall worry less. If You send me work, I shall embrace it in joy and it will be rest to me because it is Your will, and if you send me rest, I will rest in You.

Only save me, guide me, protect me, give me Your light to know my own self-will, save me from my own energies and my poisonous urge to act, to change, to move, to unsettle everything, to rearrange everything that You have ordained.

I love You, my Savior. Let me rest in Your will and be silent and then the light of your joy will always warm my life, and its fire will burn in my heart and shine for Your glory, which is all I desire to live for. Amen.

November 18, 1947

Reverend Father started off for Utah again last night. Just before he left he gave me a letter from Mother Paula Williamson in Boston saying she had started on the Sister Gabriella book and also that Dom Wilfred Upson, O.S.B. from Prinknash Abbey was on his way to America. I can't quite place him, but I think he was the one who started Caldey as an Anglican monastery. After the Cistercians took that over, he entered the Church as a Benedictine. Anyway she wants him to come here. I was bothered wondering for a moment, "What if I kissed his ring and then he turned out to be still an Anglican?"

Our Lady of the Valley is supposed to be making a foundation. They are trying to get land, of all places, in New Mexico. They will have to raise goats because, as I understand it, goats are all that can be raised in New Mexico, but the view ought to be pretty. The place is 7,000 feet up.

Today it rains and I put on a winter shirt and so forth before the Night Office, although it is not yet desperately cold. The robes and scapulars have not yet been given out, let alone cowls. And, as usual, no night cowls.

Today there reached me the first issue of one of those so-called "little magazines" – published that is by "intellectuals" – and this one comes from the University of Louisville. How these things swarm! And they are all alike; I didn't read the stories. What is best in them all, in some respects, is the criticism. But on the whole they have a somewhat ugly atmosphere unless they are really superlatively well done. And my only conclusion on seeing this one was that the tide was getting altogether too high, and is lapping at the front steps of the monastery. "You shall know that it is very near, even at the doors."

November 20, 1947. Eve of the Presentation

No feast of Our Lady is of minor importance. St. Pius V tried to abolish tomorrow's and didn't succeed. Sixtus V reestablished it. I wonder what the Franciscans have in it. But anyway I have received much help from her, especially in the last month or so since I have been praying more and praying in her chapel. Now I really know – *nunc scio vere* – that she is the one charged by God with leading us forward in the unitive life.

Even my contacts with the outside have their advantages. To see how seriously men take things and yet how little their seriousness profits them. Their tragedy makes our mediocrity all the more terrible. But Gethsemani is not all mediocrity by any means. Still, we tend to get self-satisfied.

Another thing, I finally realize the truth that people like St. Thomas and St. Bonaventure and Duns Scotus should have told me long ago, that theological wisdom, or the labor of trying to acquire it, far from necessarily and *per se* standing in the way of infused wisdom, makes us thirst for it and prepares us in some way for it, at least by making our desires burn higher and more intensely.

Once again I am busy with Scotus. He always shows me the way to great heights by showing me Christ and Our Lady in a light in which nobody else manages to see them, a light that shows the reality of their greatness in a way no one else has done. Read Scotus and then look at a crucifix and you begin to *see something* you never saw before.

November 23, 1947. Sunday

Tomorrow is the Feast of St. John of the Cross and is not kept in our Order.

On the Feast of the Presentation, after a half serious remark I made, Fr. Prior (Reverend Father being away in Utah for solemn professions at Huntsville) called in Fr. Raymond to talk with this famous Fr. Hugo, one of Lacouture's gang, who was in the guest house for a day. It would take a long time to put down the few confused ideas I have about those people.

I know Fr. Odilo is very excited about them and seems to have learnt most of their book by heart. I have looked at one page of Lacouture and two pages of their Fr. Mooney, O.F.M. (now exiled in Egypt) and heard Fr. Killduff's retreat here four years ago, and it all struck me as the most obvious stuff you could look for. All they say is that you have to mortify yourself to be a Christian which ought to be evident to a child who has had a few lessons in Catechism.

However, it appears that they get specific and enter into certain practical details which offend scores of respectable priests and religious. In other words, instead of just saying that Christians in general must do penance in general, it seems they say you priests specifically must give up so much smoking and drinking specifically, and don't stuff yourselves with so much food and dessert. This makes everybody sorrowful because they really like cigarettes, pie, etc. So they say "Where's the sin in smoking cigarettes . . . ?" And there, so it seems, the trouble begins because *per se* there is no sin in smoking or drinking or eating a lot of pie, provided you don't deliberately choke yourself to death on the quantity of pie . . .

Well anyway, Father Raymond used to get upset when words evidently borrowed boldly from Lacouture came forth from Fr. Odilo in his sermons and conferences. But the other day he went and had a big talk with that Fr. Hugo and now understands and likes them better and maybe in a month or so he will be getting into the same kind of trouble. But anyway he called me into Fr. Prior's room and we had a talk about it. And I wonder if I did wrong not to mind my own business, but I feel as if it was O.K. Anyway we shall see.

Two letters from Holy Trinity read in refectory full of good news. Everything seems to be fine there – all the monks happy and working hard and keeping the Rule and reading and praying with six inches of snow on the roof over their heads and Fr. Denis stoking a hot air heating system. They are in barracks until spring because the men supposed to be building the quonset monastery went deer hunting.

And also I seem to have found a lay-out man for the Centenary Souvenir in Brother Giles [Naughton], the baker, who has time to do things like that while he waits for the dough to rise. It means more conversation with Fr. Prior. And Fr. Hilary had me in there to discuss the pronunciation of some antique language in a life of St. Thomas More printed a hundred and fifteen years ago in Philadelphia, now being read in the refectory.

And I guess that's all except why am I not a solitary, or did I say that before somewhere? Maybe if I never get to be one, it will be as a punishment for having talked about it so much.

Through all this business, in a year I feel as if I have grown. And that is good. St. John of the Cross, keep me from illusions! Take away all the things that keep the Holy Spirit from leading me swiftly to perfect union with God – there is so much coarseness in me. *Riga quod est aridum, fove quod est frigidum.* [Water what is dry, heat what is cold.][27]

I know Whom to trust in this work.

Reading the Prophet Osee reminded me how much I need the retreat that is supposed to come next week.

November 27, 1947. Thanksgiving Day

The other day on the Feast of St. John of the Cross I got a good letter from Mark Van Doren and he said he liked a poem I sent him, written at the end of last month, so that gave me some human encouragement. Then there was a letter from *another* one of those little magazines, this one from Cornell. They had got hold of a poem I wrote in August from Laughlin, so I let them keep it, although it was a poor one.

For the rest I kept that feast very badly, sitting in Fr. Prior's room talking to Fr. Linus and Bro. Giles about that Souvenir for the Centenary. The whole conference was unnecessary. However it wasn't my idea.

Today, Thanksgiving, I give thanks for all the crosses and other blessings of this year. The crosses don't amount to much, but perhaps the blessings do. Fr. Anthony got to talking with impassioned emphasis in Theology class about the great importance of the literal sense of Scripture, and I dare say he is right except that his stress seemed to throw the Fathers, and the *interesting* senses of Scripture, out the window. So it depressed me. How-

[27] From Stephen Langton's *Veni, Sancte Spiritus.* Sequence, Feast of Pentecost.

ever, looking at a chapter of *Osee*, I realized I don't know the literal meaning or any other meaning of it. If that means I have to read these heavy German commentators, who tell you what the prepositions look like in Greek and Hebrew . . . I give up altogether. St. Bernard said the Jews could keep the literal meaning. "The letter killeth." Still you have to know enough of it to go *through* it to what really matters.

Do you mean to say that the *literal* sense is what we have to look for in the Old Testament? It would make strange food for spiritual reading.

And then this Fr. Motherway, S.J. is coming, no doubt to put us through the Spiritual Exercises of St. Ignatius again.

All I need now is a course in mathematics and everything will be perfect.

Five years ago it was Fr. Menth, the Redemptorist. Then Fr. Killduff, who some say is dead, a Carmelite. Then a Jesuit from Cincinnati. Then Dom Verner Moore, who told me not to become a Carthusian and became one himself. Then Fr. Bandey, the Redemptorist, and I feel as if I had forgotten somebody but apparently I have not.

I can always argue that it is the one God wants me to listen to. *Benedictus qui venit in nomine Domini.* [Blessed is he who comes in the name of the Lord (Matthew 23:39 with variations in Psalms 117:26 and Matthew 21:9).]

November 30, 1947. First Sunday in Advent

The Advent liturgy is wonderful for a retreat: *Ecce rex [tuus] venit.* [Behold thy king will come (Zechariah 9:9).] *Vias tuas Domine demonstra mihi, semitas tuas edoce me.* [Shew, O Lord, thy ways to me, and teach me thy paths (Psalms 24:4–5).] *Ad te Domine levavi animam meam.* [To thee, O Lord, I have lifted up my soul (Psalms 24:1).] *Ostende faciem tuam et salvi erimus.* [Shew thy face, and we shall be saved (Psalms 79:9).]

And now the retreat master spoke of Moses saying to God "Show me Thy face." I was very much moved because that is what I desire with my whole heart.

So as usual, although I looked forward to the retreat with repugnance and misgivings, it is going very well. He is a terrific preacher, or he was after Matutinal Mass today. I have never heard anybody do really well in that hour after dinner!

I am holding myself more or less passive and not jumping at everything the first day. What God wants of me will crystallize out, and there are things I need badly to find out, but I know I cannot find them out by pushing and pulling.

The big objectives are the ones I keep in sight, as the preacher brings them out.

To find out God's will.

To get rid of obstacles to God's will.

The Jesuit *tantum-quantum:* using creatures in so far as they help me to give glory to God, etc.

The day before the retreat began, two volumes of the Wisques translation (French) of Ruysbroeck arrived [*Oeuvres de Ruysbroeck l'Admirable*, 6 volumes (Brussels and Paris, 1912–1938)]. Father Kothen in Belgium sent them. I had been trying to get them for more than two years. Everybody said it was impossible. So that is a great grace. Ruysbroeck's feast is the day after tomorrow. So I expect great things from him in this retreat.

The important thing – find out what God really wills for me – perfect union with His will – give Him everything without reservations.

December 4, 1947. Feast of St. Peter Chrysologus

Things are slowly crystallizing out, and without much strife on my own part. The big thing: I am getting a clearer moral certitude that what I ought to have known all along to be God's will really *is* God's will. And a clearer view of the thing that remains for me to do: consecration to the work He demands of me through this Rule, this situation, my superiors, my brothers.

Peeling off layers of self-deception. This year I have allowed the following scales of blindness to form over my conscience:

1. Criticism of Superiors – indignation at the way the Visitation Card was interpreted on points like the hearing of confessions by Masters of Novices (still goes on, but in the Great Silence). None of my business.

2. Obedience – very imperfect in my motives, largely natural, willing enough to do the things I agree with: interior rebellion at decisions that seem to me imperfect or unwise. Deciding in my mind how the house and the Order ought to be run . . .

December 5, 1947

3. Running my own life – a certain spirit of independence – I have somehow acquired a notion that I can pick and choose in the kind of advice that my superiors and directors give me. Take what suits me and leave what doesn't, so that I have unconsciously put myself into a dangerous position of thinking it would be quite all right for me to leave here and go to the Carthusians against the advice of everybody, merely

getting a *transitus* [legal permission to transfer to another Order] from the Congregation. Under the present circumstances that is a grave mistake, although it would be *licit* [legal], and might, in other circumstances, be even worth considering.

4. As a result of this I have come to give too large a place to my own desires and attractions thinking that, because I *prefer* the Carthusian life and *prefer* solitude, that therefore that is God's will for me in spite of the fact that everybody advises me against it. Thank God I have not gone so far as to explicitly accept that position in my own mind.

5. I was getting to the point where I was at peace, to some extent, with my own will in this matter, and even consoled myself in moments of difficulties (especially in community life) with the complacent feeling that I might possibly walk out to go to the Carthusians . . .

6. This even threatened to vitiate the one good thing I *can* do to be a contemplative here – seek all the solitude and prayer allowed by our Rule and *Usages*.

7. Even though I seem to be on my guard against vanity and a spirit of business and ambition in the work I have to do, they have got the better of me without my realizing it.

December 6, 1947. Saturday. Vigil of Immaculate Conception (anticipated)

Most Blessed Mother of God, Mary, Immaculate Virgin, through whom all grace is sent to us by Christ our Lord and Redeemer, at the ending of our retreat which you have given us by His grace to make this year, I desire to offer you the fruits of that grace in these decisions and hopes and resolutions for the glory of Christ my King.

I give you my will, my judgment, my desires. I renounce all things into your hands. I sacrifice for your love and Christ's glory any desire I have to become a Carthusian or a hermit unless circumstances are so completely changed in my life that I have a *clear* indication that such a change is God's will and not my own.

I believe that I can give Christ more glory by sacrificing my attraction and renouncing the desires of my own will for physical solitude and quiet in order to take the unanimous advice of my Directors and superiors, even though that advice does not appeal to my nature in any way. I believe that it is God's will for me to remain here and that He has brought me here for His own purposes, for my own sanctity and joy and for the peace and glory of His Church and the salvation of the world and that the greatest obstacle to these ends is my own will. I believe that, by sacrificing even what seems to be a way to higher perfection and contemplation, I am giving greater pleasure to the Heart of Christ, My King and Savior, and serving the interests of His Kingdom.

I believe that my desires count for nothing and have no value whatever for God or for myself unless they coincide with His all-perfect will.

For the Love of Christ and for the salvation of souls I offer myself to be led and directed in all things by the directors and superiors placed over me by the Providence of God. As an act of special homage to your Immaculate Conception, I offer myself to *seek sanctity and contemplation in the way marked out by the Rule of St. Benedict and the Usages and traditions of the Cistercian Order in conformity with their present interpretation by the united Congregation of our reform called the Cistercians of the Strict Observance,* and to seek no other way of perfection unless you clearly show me that it is God's will.

For that purpose I promise to obey my superiors without criticism, believing that their commands and wishes are part of God's work, not for my own sanctification, but for the good of this Order and of the Church. I promise not to defend myself against the offices that may someday be imposed on me in community life, but to go where God sends me and do whatever His Holy Spirit signifies to me to be His desire through the ordinary channels. And I promise not to defend myself interiorly against encroachments on my egoistic sense of privacy, but to seek a sincere and true interior solitude by giving up my own will and living for God's will alone. Let His will be my only delight. His good-pleasure my only consolation on this earth, and I shall look for nothing else, but be satisfied with one thing alone – the consciousness that I have done what was pleasing to Him and that I have sought union with His will alone.

In all this I trust in the power of Your prayers, Most Blessed Mother of God, and abandon myself entirely to Your wisdom and Your protection and Your loving guidance and care. Amen.

December 14, 1947. Gaudete Sunday

Dom Benoît Morvan and Dom Marie Joseph [Marquis] of Bricquebec are here on their way to the Far East with a Fr. André who is chaplain of the nuns, I suppose, in Japan.

Before I forget I shall try to put down some of the things said in a very good conversation I had with Dom Marie Joseph who was formed by Dom Vital Lehodey.

The most important thing: his complete lack of disturbance or anxiety over the fact that another war is coming. True, he did not want to leave

France for fear he might not get back, but the General told him to go. But looking at the situation below the surface, what he sees is tremendously hopeful.

A magnificent, though small, elite is being formed in France through all these providential trials. These storms are allowed by God to shake the Church like a tree. All the rotten wood is falling out of the tree. France is fifty years ahead of us in that however. The fervor and generosity of seculars, men in Catholic action and some in the active ministry in France, puts Trappists to shame.

The Trappists are able to weather economic storms much better than others on their big farms.

At Bricquebec they have formed a study group, going deep into the Cistercian Fathers, producing for instance excellent conferences on William of St. Thierry. He is very pleased with [Etienne] Gilson's *Mystical Theology of St. Bernard* [London, 1940], valuable for us. Agreed that it was strange that it had taken a secular to discover St. Bernard before the Cistercians themselves got around to it.

About our Order: the generation immediately following the fusion of congregations overemphasized the necessary concern with the letter of the Rule at the expense of our Cistercian spirit. He attributes to Dom Vital Lehodey more than any one man the spiritual revival of the Order.

He says the Order has been leading a spiritual life that is cut up into fragments, i.e. devotions, separate emphases on diverse virtues. What do we need with a special month of Mary or a feast of Christ the King? Modern devotions are all right for people who haven't an integral faith and need something to hang on to. But for us, our whole *Rule* is devotion to Christ the King, *Christo vero Regi militaturus*. [*Ad te ergo nunc mihi sermo dirigitur, quisquis abrenuntians propriis voluntatibus, Domino Christo vero regi militaturus, oboedientiae fortissima atque praeclara arma sumis.* To you, therefore, my words are now addressed, whoever you are, that, renouncing your own will, you do take up the strong and bright weapons of obedience, in order to fight for the Lord Christ, our true King (RB Prologue:3).]

He doesn't like Fr. Bernard of La Trappe's statues, says he had done a huge one for an outdoor monument of thanksgiving. *Trop de mièvrerie* ["too much affectation"]. Orval church is good, an enlargement of Fontenay. Sénanque is inhabited by one or two monks who are nothing more than caretakers. Up until recently Cistercians of the Common Observance have been saying the old Cistercian Mass in Spain.

Twenty-five out of fifty men from Bricquebec are mobilized. Now that they are back, he keeps them *au courant* of events, reading Catholic books on social situation, etc. in refectory. Does not believe in monks being shut up in a box and concentrating on themselves and not realizing their vital connection with the rest of the Church and their function in her struggles.

Other orders have special functions. Our vocation is to live to the full a perfect life, the secret of which is a complete gift of ourselves to God and not just following a collection of ascetic practices. Also we are above all priests, that is, a Cistercian priest is in a sense more a priest than any other. Preaching does not make a priest: it is the giving of oneself that God may express Himself in us.

We are free intellectual beings and yet God uses our freedom and our intellects as His instruments when we give ourselves entirely to Him, completely strip ourselves of self following the spirit of our Rule.

Dom [Lambert] Baudoin, O.S.B., preached a retreat at Bricquebec. He had studied monasteries at Monte Cassino, Mount Athos, etc., and knew everything backwards. Complimented us on our closeness to St. Benedict. Dom Marie Joseph complained of the artificially jammed Lenten morning schedule. Dom Baudoin answered: "The Pharisees would have liked it fine." Dom Marie Joseph says it is much more important and more perfect for monks to sing Vespers in the evening where it belongs, and eat whenever it is convenient, than to throw the whole day into confusion with Vespers before noon in order to "fast until after Vespers."

The souls that do so much harm and bring wars upon the world are those exteriorly perfect, austere men, absolutely punctual and regular in all their actions, but who blow up as soon as you touch their pride; and their anger is far worse and far more easily aroused than that of pagans and "sinners".

Tremendous intellectual activity of Dominicans and Jesuits – Éditions du Cerf – a dozen Friars in a big business building with twenty or thirty secretaries putting out books. He is very friendly with them; also, very fond of Dom Etienne Chenevière of La Trappe, a former Franciscan who loves poverty in their original spirit – talks of Christ with tears – was in prison camp throughout the war.

Dom Vital told him, when he was a novice, "If you ever hear any commentary on the Rule that is not in accordance with the Gospel, forget it, it is false."

Our Rule is the Gospel. He will not explain the Rule to his monks like this: one day Holy Obedience, the next day Holy Poverty, etc. He will make his *exposé* of the Rule a commentary *on Scripture*.

Scripture is not something that is given us to help us understand theology. On the contrary, St. Thomas, Duns Scotus, should lead us to Scripture in which we make an immediate, vital contact with Christ. On this point he was very good.

He said he had thrown over thirty bad statues out of monasteries under his jurisdiction.

Benedictine life is perfectly simple – it is the Gospel pure and simple – it liberates us from ourselves by enabling us to give ourselves entirely to God.

He told me about a Jewish woman, a doctor, one of three survivors out of 3,000 interned in a famous concentration camp. Then she was a member of a powerful Communist cell that formed among the prisoners. On her release she realized she wanted more than this. Eventually he baptized her. She made a pilgrimage to Lourdes on foot. She wanted to go and be a doctor in China, but he made her give that up.

Dom Vital Lehodey is ninety on the 17th of this month, next Wednesday.

Yesterday was the 6th anniversary of my entrance into the community. I have been getting many graces during the last week or so.

During the retreat was read in the refectory the story of how the Reds burned Our Lady of Consolation and imprisoned the monks, subjecting them to such treatment that twelve died in two and a half or three months. It had a powerful effect on everybody.

Another thing Dom Marie Joseph said: too many religious live in a completely unreal world, and that has been true of me to the extent that I have let myself get tied up in these illusions about another vocation under the present circumstances. *In se* the idea may be O.K., but I have allowed it to become quite the opposite.

I give myself completely to God – He draws me more and more to that. I cannot know what lies ahead for me, for us, but more and more I realize God wants me to put myself in His hands, and let Him take me through the things that are to come, and I must learn to trust Him without fear, or questions, or hesitation or withdrawal.

December 16, 1947. Tuesday in Ember Week

Upstairs in the infirmary old Brother Gregory lies dying, most of the time unconscious, so he does not hear the guns beyond our hills tuning up for the next war. They are more concentrated than ever in their noise.

Reverend Father took the two visiting Abbots to Georgia.

Today I finished dummying *Cistercian Contemplatives*. It will be nicely printed. Maybe we will get a folder for postulants printed in California. The Archbishop is still holding on to the stuff we sent him to censor a year and a half ago. Pictures of St. Lutgarde came from Belgium. Fr. Kothen raised them for me, but I don't think there is any use to them. Yesterday I did some drawings. We are working on Vol. II of Tanquerey in Theology class. Frater Urban will be ordained priest this Saturday and I have two years more to go. It looks like an infinite distance and it seems almost impossible that I should ever get there. The closer I get, the further away it seems to be.

Reading Duns Scotus' *Reportationes* III on the Incarnation.

Yesterday *Lord Weary's Castle* by Robert Lowell came and it is terrific. Harcourt Brace sent it after I had begged all around the town. But Lowell is a *poet*. I'd like to write an article about him. You could compare "The Quaker Graveyard" with Hopkins' "Wreck of the Deutschland," and Lowell is in some ways better than Hopkins. Though he is not as deep spiritually, he is sometimes more of a poet. The poems I liked less were the ones "After Valéry," "After Rilke," etc. He has his roots in New England. He couldn't write that way if he were an immigrant. He can call Boston "my city." But there is nothing of the bad New England, Dutchland farms, about him. And he makes a little bit go a long way: the man in Dante who was rolled away by the torrent and two angels fought with billhooks for his soul. He makes no false steps. He is a better poet than Dylan Thomas because he is Catholic and grown up and not drunk. I thank God for this good poet who is really great and I pray for him to write more. I'd like to write to him but I guess it would be smarter if I didn't.

December 18, 1947

Yesterday, which was Ember Wednesday and a fast day, Brother Gregory died, and all the Abbots came back from Georgia, and I was thurifer for the funeral which I found out just before Lauds. Not knowing whether we would bring the body down right after Chapter, I went to check the thurible and found no thurible there. It was in the work-room where a Brother novice was cleaning it and the chains were all tangled up in a knot. Fortunately they didn't bring the body down after Chapter and anyway at that time I was serving Dom Marie Joseph's Mass.

Then I was on to watch by the body during dinner from 12:00 to 12:30, and those who were to relieve us sauntered in late with full bellies, belching politely, and we rushed off to the refectory in such a state that we nearly went straight through the wall instead of around by the door, for after all it was a black fast. And so on all day.

Today I looked at the *Usages* and discovered some of the mistakes we made at the funeral.

I am going over the page proofs of Mother Berchmans. I have read that book over and over again until I almost know it by heart, and it is not a good book. Bob Giroux wrote and said galleys on *The Seven Storey Mountain* would be due in January.

And today it was very beautiful, warmish with the sun out and little neat clouds very high up in the sky and the brown dirt piled high on top of Brother Gregory, who turns out to have been Swiss. And one day here a bull got playful and tossed him over a stone wall and that was why he always limped.

I asked Reverend Father what made Brother so saintly and he said "he was always working, never idle. When he was out tending the cows in the pasture he would come back with a bucket of blackberries. He couldn't be idle." I might have known what kind of an answer I would get! Well, I hope it makes *me* a saint, too. But that doesn't mean I won't take advantage of the minutes I get to pray. Thank God I still get quite a few of them. Now for instance . . .

December 21, 1947. Fourth Sunday in Advent

Yesterday Fr. Urban was ordained priest. I was candle-bearer and got a close view of everything. My own time is two years away and it seems like two hundred. What struck me? St. John Baptist's prominence in the Liturgy of the Day. The amount of oil the Archbishop put on his hands. When the priests came into the sanctuary to put their hands on the head of the *ordinatus*, I suddenly saw Fr. Kemper, S.J., who preached the retreat three or four years ago, and remembered how he asked, "Do you know Jack Snyder?" when I went to see him privately. That was Fr. Urban and he was then just about to get the tonsure. I remembered how five and one-half years ago when Fr. Urban came first to the monastery, I was appointed his guardian angel. It was in Paschal time and that day I didn't get to sleep during the meridienne because I was so nervous, fearing I would forget to give him a book for the antiphon of the Little Office.

But what else struck me about the ceremony? Above all the Introit, *"Ostende nobis faciem tuam . . ."* ["Show us your face . . ."] and then so much *Servus Dei Israel* [Israel, Servant of God] in the prophecies. And no *Sancte Ludovice* [St. Louis] in the Roman Litany of the Saints.

There was a lot of work but everything went off without a hitch, except once they forgot to give the Archbishop his crozier and he started muttering *"Baculus! Baculus!"* [The stick! The stick!]

Then in the afternoon I saw Dom Marie Joseph again but didn't get around to asking the questions I intended. Again he talked about our mission as Cistercians in the Church – our *témoignage* [witness] – bear witness, give glory to God by being full of God.

He told me something of the recent history of Bricquebec, Dom Vital [Lehodey]'s "failure," humanly speaking. How after his resignation the house went to pieces: two abbots killed in auto accidents within a few months; the house under a superior *ad nutum* from Thymadeuc – Dom Marie Joseph was then in Japan, hurriedly recalled.

At one point during the war they were down to eighteen in the community and had a tremendous job of work to keep everything going. But the formation it gave the men was perfect. On that foundation he can build something big.

Yet with the old monks *rien à faire* [nothing to be done] – can't get them to understand. He is working mostly with the young ones. They are the ones studying Cistercian literature and spirituality – one young professed two years on St. Ailred – getting books and manuscripts from everywhere – but the interesting thing is he is not exceptionally gifted, only a normal young monk with average brains and talents. That is what is encouraging.

He says his secretary is very fond of Picasso, and is himself an artist.

The Church at Bricquebec was remodeled by an architect, a converted Communist. And Dom Marie Joseph said he would be ready to found a Cistercian monastery in Soviet Russia at the drop of a hat.

Likes Léon Bloy but thinks he was mistaken about Mélanie in the La Salette affair. Gave *The Woman Who Was Poor* to novices to read, ones who had been in the war. Likes Bloy above all because he understands suffering.

Dom Marie Joseph himself had a "terrible time" for ten years in the monastery, trying to adjust himself to a stuffy atmosphere of old-fashioned "Trappist" spirituality with a big emphasis on "sin, sin, sin." God does not want us to be all the time plaguing ourselves about counting up sins. We should concentrate on loving Him. So he said. And he said it did him a tremendous amount of good when he got out and was sent to Japan and saw how people suffered and saw the mountains and trees and sea, etc.

Last time he said, and this time too, one must go ahead and develop on one's own if the atmosphere of the house is too stereotyped, naturally didn't mean be independent or disobedient, but follow one's attractions, read, study, develop an interior life.

He told me I must work for _excellence_ not for publication, try to write only the very best I can and not be in a hurry to publish, that I should have the guidance of the best theologian I can find, someone who can tell me with full certainty, "Do this. Do that. Write this, do not write that."

Told me to realize I am working in union with others scattered through the Order. Always to aim high. Love and study our Fathers.

December 25, 1947. Christmas Morning

After Chapter, when I was hearing Masses, Fr. Prior sent me and Frater Samuel in to the refectory to help distribute the mail so that everyone would get his letters and cards at mixt. The place was already full of monks sorting them out. The ones who have come recently got a lot and the ones who have been here a long time got only one or two. Brother Owen's mail was all from Ireland, and Brother Raphael had one or two from Germany, and Brother Valentine got almost nothing from Italy, but Brother Alexander, the gatekeeper, got a whole lot. We hid Fr. Anthony's mail under his cup and under his napkin, and Fr. Lambert got a big pile as usual, but the one who got the most was Frater Alberic, a novice priest who just came a few months ago. And I got four cards and a letter from Granny.

Outside the window of the Scriptorium is a monstrous, big heating system, living under a shed with a high tin smokestack: it looks like an ancient locomotive all ready to run away. The brother novices worked day and night to fix it up in time for Christmas because the old heating plant is finished, and this new one pumps hot water through a window by pipes that are wrapped up in tar paper or something. And steam curls around our window pane.

I like it when the Brothers serve the Midnight Mass, and last night old Brother Albert (who got very few letters) was one of the acolytes, and he came running up the altar steps in white beard, holding his right arm extended full length with the wine cruet in his hand, his other arm swinging with nothing in the hand, and the 2nd M.C. after him with the water cruets.

Humble George, the negro pilgrim, is here again, and after the Consecration at the Mass of the Aurora, he raised his arm in the air and made three big signs of the cross in the air towards the altar.

Last night all I could think of was to give my will entirely to God and desire no light or consolation, but only His will. I chanted the psalms of

Lauds thinking how the only thing that matters is the glory of God, and nothing else in the world is of any importance whatever.

Outside the fields are full of hard frost, and I am reader in the refectory, and it was cold in bed and I thought *Praesepe non abhorruit / Foeno jacere pertulit / Parvoque lacte pastus est / Per quem nec ales esurit.* ["He did not despise the manger / Nor did He refuse to sleep in straw / And He who does not permit the smallest bird to go hungry / Was Himself nourished with a little milk." (Hymn for Lauds, Christmas morning.)] And then I went to sleep and dreamt that I was knocking on the door of Reverend Father's room, and I heard jazz coming from inside, and I looked in and there were many old ladies in white sitting on his desk. And he ordered me to go to Finland and attend a convention in memory of the scientist Pasteur, and I reached the convention by an escalator and, as a result of my attending this convention, I was late for mixt and didn't get the food that was coming to me.

When some unknown person (I didn't look) started playing the organ after Communion, it sounded like drinking songs or "The Sidewalks of New York," and I began to be tempted to become a Carthusian again, but I said the only thing that matters is the will of God and His glory and I am resolved to suffer all things, even that.

And Father Anthony says he got a letter from Dom Anselme Le Bail which is more than I ever got, though I wrote to him over a year ago.

But one of the best things about yesterday was that I had a long time to read Duns Scotus on the Incarnation, and didn't get roped in to decorating any trees. The choir novitiate is bulging with greenery: it is a forest. They have two Christmas trees in the hallway just inside the door, and no one knows how many when you get around the corner. And the laybrother monks' windows are full of paper icicles, and I don't dare imagine what is inside.

Gloria in excelsis Deo! [Glory to God in the highest!]

All that matters is the glory of God and that Jesus Christ is the Word of God and is very God of very God and the glory of the Father.

December 28, 1947. Holy Innocents

The Child Jesus in the crib tells me this: The reason 12th century Cistercian architecture was what it was was not that the Cistercians tried to start a new technique, but our Order was built and grew up an organic whole, out of the basic and all-consuming desire for a perfectly pure love of God, for the possession of Him, perfect union with Him.

The reason why we can't reproduce that is that we approach the problem from an angle from which it cannot be solved: how to make beautiful monasteries, how to reproduce the style of the 12th century . . .

If we had a spirituality, a desire for God as deep as theirs, we would never need to go in search of a style, still less of digging one out of the past.

You will say: Trappist monasteries, or at least poor ones as Gethsemani was, were built to be poor. That is true, but they did not grow out of a desire for the possession of God by pure love, a desire that was aware to the possibilities of experience latent in pure love, mystical, infused love. Fontenay reflects all that. I admit that all the monks were not mystics. And St. Bernard sent Achard of Clairvaux to *look at churches*, the poorest and simplest that were being built. Nevertheless, a clean kind of mysticism was in the air of the age: it purified the hearts of men and that was reflected in what the monks built.

All right, some Trappists desired God: *all* of them, but in a different, more fragmentary way. Their eyes were fixed more on penance, practices, disparate *means*, not so much on the *end*.

Fr. Odilo was talking about our Church decorations for feasts, called the sanctuary a "sacred grove" and said he expected to see a couple of druids come out of the bushes at any moment . . .

Anyway, the Cistercians of the 12th century built their own monasteries. However, so do we. But we gave the Georgia business to an architect for the *plans*, and the place is going to look like the worst lunatic asylum or penitentiary in the country.

At Gethsemani the best buildings are the Hog-house and the new horse-barn.

I have to dig to find out things about the spirit of our Order, but it is all there, and when I strike water, it is the water of life all right. I am glad to realize it again. It is what God wants of me, I know.

At the same time I am fully prepared (I hope to be, I mean) to see all my ideals, even all the *true* ideals of our Order and spirit frustrated and destroyed in favor of all kinds of abominations, if God so wills it, for my crucifixion. I mean all the external *expression* of these ideals, for the expression is only accidental, beautiful *execution* of the Chant; a clean, simple sanctuary without rubbish and bushes; the real Rule; the balance of a real Cistercian life: all of this is not essential, but it is certainly integral to our spirituality. I can be prepared to see it all sacrificed in order that God may make the one essential thing: pure love of Him growing in my heart. That is the thing that will make me a Cistercian.

As a result of this Christmas I can say without partisanship or sectarianism or any sort of "old school" spirit that I am glad to be a Cistercian monk and I feel the true life of the Order, the life the Holy Spirit has destined for me and given me by my profession, I feel that true life in my veins. God knows I have suffered for it and I must suffer more because I shall not be a Cistercian for the "atmosphere" or for the cowl or for the name, still less for the sake of speeches and conventions and pamphlets and the rest, but I shall have in me that love which God has decreed Cistercian monks and they alone should give Him.

Penance, yes, that is a most important factor, *formula perfectae poenitentiae* ["the form of perfect penance"] said the *Exordium Magnum*. And St. Bernard's Third Christmas Sermon, which I read in the refectory the other day, leaves no illusions. The return to our ideal means a thirst for poverty, fasting, labor, hardship, but again the *means*, the *exercises*, the *expressions* are accidental. The substance is what matters: God, to possess Him in an emptiness, in pure love, absolutely selfless love; to taste and know His joy by giving up everything and loving even ourselves for Him alone.

I know St. Thomas à Becket will pray for me tomorrow and obtain for me growth in this life, in this vocation. And my limbs will grow spiritually to something like the strength of the columns of Pontigny!

Our Lady knows something about all this because our spirit is above all from her.

December 31, 1947. St. Sylvester

It is the last day of the year. I wrote to Granny in New Zealand. Tomorrow all the jobs in the monastery are to be changed, I suppose, as usual, and everybody is making signs that Fr. Odilo will be Prior. I hope (I doubt) I will be fortunate enough to be nothing.

Twice I have had to spend an hour or so talking with Brother Giles about layouts on the Centenary Souvenir, but thank heaven he is someone who knows what it is all about. The way he talks, we ought to be using what little talent there is in art in the monastery. He wants to start a good printing press here, and so many other things seem to point to that.

From Switzerland the nuns of La Fille Dieu sent Reverend Father a wonderful new book in commemoration of the canonization of St. Nicholas de

Flue last Ascension Day. I have never seen such magnificent layouts, and the photographs themselves are wonderful. The pictures are not merely grouped: they are orchestrated. I have never seen such smart work, such variations, spacing, bleed-outs, etc. And the type job is also fine. It occurred to me that this was a magnificent way to pay homage to a saint! The text is very simple, mostly documents, especially homilies and allocutions of Pius XII. And everything throws into relief the sanctity of Klaus von Flue and his message.

Stripped of all the stupid decorative accidents of showy piety and invested in this kind of a medium, the sanctity of that 15th century soldier and peasant and hermit and peacemaker comes home to you with an impact that is literally tremendous. I have been praying to him all day and all night, so to speak, and I can't get him or the book out of my mind!

That is what we ought to be doing! That is the way we ought to be preaching! The fresh air and the actuality of the things! How the supernatural Order – miracles and all – slides into that context and takes possession of these modern forms and media so easily, so smoothly! It is exhilarating beyond measure to realize how fully religion and praise of God belong in a modern idiom!!

I hope this will sink in to me and I can be doing the same.

I feel I have grown up this year . . .

Pope Pius XII said he thought there were more heroes and saints in the Church now than ever before and I believe it. I believe we are going to begin to bear tremendous fruit.

And maybe I shall be glad to die for it!

January 1, 1948

Father Odilo is Prior and I am Sub-cantor and a lot of other things have happened. Today Dick Fitzgerald, whom I knew at Bona's and who was ordained two years ago, came here on retreat and I spoke to him for a while. He is running a minor seminary in Erie, PA., and he says one of my best students, Red MacDonald, was killed in the war. I pray for him, but I think God will have not made much difficulty letting him into heaven. He was a good, simple man.

Fr. Nivard seems to be happy to be bell-ringer. Fr. Hilary takes cod-liver oil like me.

Today was a warm windy day with a lot of blue and grey clouds flying over the woods, and the sky full of different shades of color from slate to the white of milk, and all this was communicated to the hills, so that I realize that there is more color in the winter than in the summer in this part of Kentucky. But the real seasons for color are spring and autumn. And today I have begun the year badly by running around all day, but I suppose in a way I had to.

Nisi Dominus aedificaverit domum . . . [Unless the Lord build the house . . . (Psalms 126:1).] Useless to hope that, by being sub-cantor, I can do anything wonderful for this choir. But God can keep us from going to pieces. I'll make a novena to St. Bernard about it, and study the *Méthode de Chant*.

January 4, 1948. Day of Recollection

I just read some of the notes I wrote in the journal a year ago (end of 1946) and I am wondering what I thought I was talking about. The first thing that impresses me is that practically all I wrote about myself and my trials was stupid because I was trying to express what I thought I *ought* to think, and not for any especially good reason, rather than what I actually did think. I couldn't very well know what I meant when I hardly meant it at all, and I couldn't mean it either if I didn't know what it was . . .

However, it was correct to say that that vocation business was an illusion and it was right that I should let my superiors judge. What was wrong was that I made such a fuss about it, and the reason I did so may have been a subconscious desire to satisfy myself by making other people worry about me. And also to have something of the natural pleasure that was refused me by at least kicking up a lot of smoke in my imagination.

The only thing that could settle it was grace, and thank God it seems to have done so. But if God wants me to go through it all again, all right. I'll take it again.

What was painfully artificial in that diary was that I was trying so much to write it like every other pious diary that was ever written: "I resolve this" – "I pray that." Well, I am very slow to learn what is useless in my life! I keep thinking that I have to conform to a lot of artificial standards, things external and fragmentary that tend to keep my interior life on the surface, where it is easily scattered and blown away.

Now I ask myself this: what did you mean by all that talk of giving up everything, giving up your own ideas in everything, living for God alone, letting your superiors do *all* your thinking for you, etc.? These things are very general. What precisely do they *mean*? What good will it do you to fling that kind of talk around without having any idea what it is all about? Do you think it will make you a saint to say these things without understanding them, just because others have said them? Maybe the saints knew what they were talking about, but I confess that I didn't last year. Perhaps I am better off now.

Giving up everything for God doesn't mean that you just give up *existing*. It is not that easy. It means living and thinking and suffering and loving for Him in the way determined by His will. Giving up your freedom for God doesn't mean that you cease to be free and never have to make any more choices. It means using your freedom for God and making choices for Him until He Himself lifts you above the level of choices momentarily and gives you a higher freedom which is above responsibilities and action, but which unfortunately doesn't last and never depends on you.

"Let your superiors think for you." Do you think you will ever find a superior who will do *even a small proportion of your thinking for you?* What is the matter with you – are you crazy? To let the abbot think for you means that you have to go to work and think along the lines laid down by the Rule and by the labor of faith bring your mind into line with a lot of judgments that seem, at first sight, to be absurd. But it does not mean that you blindly swallow everything your superiors say about the spiritual life and theology and art and everything else. He *expects* you to have different ideas on certain things. You are, in fact, given a job in which you are supposed to do something of the superior's thinking for him. That applies to everyone who has any kind of a job in the house.

The cellarer does not let the abbot do all of his thinking. On the contrary, he is there to do the abbot's thinking about most of the details of the material side of the life. The abbot makes the big, general decisions and approves whatever else is of moment, but the cellarer has to do the *thinking!!!* He does it along broad lines laid out by his superior, that is all.

And so with me in the writing I do! In fact, Reverend Father leaves more and more to my own judgment, subject always to his approval. And I was writing down stuff in the journal about getting all my thinking done by somebody else. It's about time I woke up and started to be myself and be what God intended me to be.

Before Christmas I got a letter from *The Messenger of the Sacred Heart*, of all things, asking for an article on contemplation and the priesthood. Father Anthony told me to refuse. That much thinking I managed to get done for me by somebody else! O.K. Yesterday Fr. Lynch came back at me again for an article for his *Messenger*. He said he was trying to turn the magazine upside down and make it intelligent. I don't know what all the old ladies will say when they discover he is trying to rob them of the confectionery they have been getting out of the *Messenger* for the last 100 years! But Fr. Anthony said I could write the article. I would do anything to help clean the mush out of the devotion to the Sacred Heart. It is a job that needs doing almost as badly as anything else in the universe!

Today in Chapter Fr. Leonard gave a good solid conference and I am glad.

And by some kind of a miracle the choir has been going well for the last few days, but I say to myself, "Wait!" And it gets cold again now, rain and sleet. But the Child Jesus smiles very much in His crib. We couldn't get near it for several days because the floor was full of varnish.

January 6, 1948. Epiphany

St. Joseph was moved over to the other side of the ox to make room for one of the Kings. Fr. Benjamin, who is in charge of the crib, has got a couple of sheep looking at the camel with mild surprise. Fr. Stephen preached a very nervous sermon, but this evening he was happy and made me a sign that the hills were beautiful, which they were and are. I read some of Baldwin Thomas on the line *Vivus est sermo Dei et efficax* . . . [The word of God is alive and efficacious . . .], and I still think he is good and even original to some extent, although Dom David Knowles despises his writing. The question is, how much did he write as a Cistercian? But it doesn't matter: it is all in the Cistercian tradition. He gave me as clear a schema of the relations of faith and understanding as I have found with the distinction between *two* understandings, one of which is *"auditus"* [listening], the *beginning* of faith, and the other its consummation.

> *Verbum Dei* [Word of God] *(in corde audientis)* [in the heart of the hearer]
> *intellectus (auditus)* ➝ *fides* ➝ *amor* ➝ *Intellectus* [intellect (hearing) ➝ faith ➝ love ➝ knowledge]
> *Sermo Dei vivus et efficax* . . . [the word of God is alive and efficacious]

In the library I looked at some notes on the architecture of Vaux de Cernay and saw a picture of St. Theobald's crozier, the only good looking one I have ever seen. The figures in the crook represented the coronation of Our Lady. 13th century. He was a friend of St. Louis.

January 11, 1948

The General's circular letter was read in the refectory today and it was very good. His letters are austere and he always talks as if it took an effort to keep the Order from slipping into relaxation. I can see where it does. One point he made: the reason why health is bad in some houses is that so many unhealthy subjects are accepted. This was against the argument, "Our health is so bad the present generation cannot stand the Rule." Nevertheless, I have seen Frater Damian, who was a terrifically muscular and powerful man when he came, worn down to a ghost of what he was and now he is confined to the infirmary – couldn't even come down to make solemn profession. He wasn't an unhealthy subject when he made his simple vows!

The General also said we should blame ourselves more than others for the fact that there is no peace in the world. Are we living up to our obligations? There are people here who get very annoyed when you make that kind of statement. Personally, I don't know. I think we are trying, at least here, to be good Cistercians, and if we miss the point here and there, it is largely through ignorance. However, there are one or two who don't conceal the fact that they want things easy and comfortable, and they are so intent about it that I can see what the General means. There is always an element in an order like ours, when it is as big as it is now, that will not shrink from a definite and concentrated campaign to soften the life in every way: less prayer, less work, more food, less silence, recreation, etc. I can't figure out why they came here in the first place.

There is a rumor (confirmed in the Circular) that there was rather an argument about that at the General Chapter.

He also said that ours was the true mysticism – contemplation and penance – contrasted with the false mysticisms of Class and Race floating around outside.

Talking to Reverend Father today I learned something that might develop into a third foundation. I had known for some time that Clare Boothe Luce wanted us to take a place of hers in South Carolina. Now she is so anxious to get rid of it she may give it to us. Wants us (characteristically enough!) to grow some kind of fancy flowers there. It is forty miles from the biggest city in South Carolina (Charleston?), has woods on the property and buildings to live in. Then another offer in Louisiana eighty miles from Mississippi. I said both of them would be very hot and he said no hotter than Georgia. That is hot enough.

My voice is gone and I have those pains in the chest again, but it makes no difference. God can do anything with my life and my body and all that I have, anything He pleases. I see no matter whether I am healthy or sick, dead or alive, so long as it is His will. And I *mean* it more than before. Since solemn profession this indifference has become more real. I belong to God for the world's peace, and I want to throw away the desires and preferences of my body and my senses and my own self: be content to feel pain and incapacity and even attachment, so long as my will is His.

January 17, 1948. Feast of St. Anthony

Yesterday it looked like snow. Today there is deep snow, and the sun is out, and the cedars full of snow stand up against a bright blue sky and the white hills are in a sort of haze and the abbey buildings are golden. That is the way Gethsemani looks in the winter and Fr. Linus' box of Kodachromes is full of just such pictures.

I stood in the door of the Little Cloister a minute ago and thought about the new foundation from the Valley in New Mexico on a dude ranch outside of Santa Fe. And the wealth of our snow and our sun and the wealth of our relative in New Mexico made me feel prosperous.

But yesterday, when I was reading Scotus in the cemetery, or rather thinking about Scotus, I thought how the silence you find in yourself, when you enter in and rest in God, is always the same and always new even though it is unchanging. For that silence is true life, and even though your body moves around (as mine did vigorously, being cold), your soul stays in the same place, resting in its life Who is God, now in winter just as it did before in summer, without any apparent difference, as if nothing had changed at all and the passage of seasons had only been an illusion.

January 21, 1948. Feast of St. Agnes

For the first time since the beginning of December, I went out to work to let some fresh air into my stuffy head and let a few phantasms fly away into the trees. We broke rock down on the road to the lower bottom, outside the enclosure, past the old horse barn. Fr. Anselme Dimier sent me an article of his on Cistercian architecture and we got a book on the convent of Notre Dame de Bonneval perched high up on the side of a hill in the Aveyron – very impressive. Fr. Guillaume Möal, the ex-prior of Our Lady of Consolation who was here last year, wrote from Thymadeuc. He found a tremendous deepening of interior life in the house on his return after eight or nine years.

St. Agnes brought me graces and my mind was emptied and quieter than it has been with all my business! Underneath it all there is a deeper and deeper peace and a deeper indifference to the small surface troubles that come along in choir, etc. How good it was to be out working with my brothers! And I felt this even about those who ordinarily rub me the wrong way! How good it is to have a rule in which simplicity and poverty and hardship play so large a part so that you can give yourself up to God by it!

Finished page proofs for *Cistercian Contemplatives* and sent them back yesterday.

January 25. Septuagesima

. . . *in qua deponitur canticum Domini "alleluia"* [. . . in which the song to the Lord, "alleluia," is set aside]

It is the season of tracts, and I am trying to see that we don't drag too much in singing them: they can be very stimulating if they are properly sung.

Deep snow. It snowed for a day or so and since then it has been freezing all day so there is a lot of it, clean and blue and mostly undisturbed. I walked in the cemetery in work boots and read the book about Bonneval Abbey and looked over the wall where the entrance to the woodshed was all messed up with deep-bitten caterpillar tracks in the snow. The hills are very beautiful. The other day wind was blowing clouds of dry snow off the roof of the church and the eaves steamed with it as if with white smoke.

Yesterday, during Conventual Mass (Votive *De Beata V.[irgine]*), Fr. Samuel rushed in in Scapular (from Reverend Father) and called out Fr. Prior (Odilo) and he got Fr. Sub-prior and Frater Linus and later got some more, and when someone else came running in for an extinguisher, we knew there was a fire. It was at the Introit. Then we sang the *Kyrie* with much feeling but in confusion. I knew it was somewhere in the direction of the Guest House and had visions of all our notes and work and material and manuscripts going up in flames, but I stayed in choir and offered them all to God if He wanted them. However, at the Offertory, I did go out and take a quick look, and everything was O.K. It was in the gate house and was under control. I saw them clambering around on the roof – thick snow flying – some smoke coming out of a hole they had made by knocking over one of those little cupolas. And so they got it out, and Frater Benjamin came to Theology class with his hand bandaged, and Frater Linus didn't come at all.

After that we had our heads shaved.

Today with the Gospel of the workers in the vineyard I think about heaven, as the liturgy means us to, and with St. Paul's epistle about chastising yourself I think about the Lent that is to come, and think about my pain, and put everything in the hands of God to arrange everything according to His love without any need for fuss on my part.

In the refectory we are reading the Baroness [Catherine de Hueck Do-herty]'s book *Friendship House*, and it is the best thing we have had in more than a year. What an impression it makes to hear something that has gen-uine *life* in it, and not the same old conventual stuff – cool and tame.

Bob Giroux sent me Harcourt Brace's new catalog with a blurb about *The Seven Storey Mountain* in it and I felt that it was just as silly as all the other books in the world.

Catalogs from Catholic bookstores in this country are full of the most indifferent stuff imaginable – how poor we are in books! Yet whenever I see what is coming out in Europe, I get all excited, and then we try to order them and nothing ever comes. I am still wondering by what kind of a mir-acle I've got the Wisques edition of Ruysbroeck! Now I am after the new book on *Cistercian Architecture* that came out in Paris during the war [Mar-cel Aubert. *L'architecture cistercienne en France*, 2 volumes, 1947]. For a long time I have been waiting for some of Dom [Jean Marie] Déchanet's new things on William of St. Thierry – asked Dom Gabriel Sortais to or-der them, but I guess he was too busy. I am now trying to rope in the ar-chitecture one through Fr. Anselme Dimier in whose article I found out about it.

January 26, 1948. Feast of St. Alberic

Proofs on *The Seven Storey Mountain* came, and there is a lot of it, and still 8,000 words to cut, but that won't be hard. I'll cut more. Cutting is not merely something you have to do to save money for the publisher. It is part of the making of the book and just as much a part of it as writing the thing, especially with me. There is this whole mass of stuff, this big, frowsy, di-sheveled tree that has to be pruned into some kind of order and fruitful-ness. St. Paul, help me out, sharpen all my scissors! As usual with the fast writing, there was an awful lot of mediocrity and bad stuff. I am glad the thing waited long enough for my eyes to clear a little.

In the refectory *Friendship House* is really very good. Today a long inter-lude by Mary Jerdo and one of the best parts of the book, and I feel like writing to her and above all I feel like writing to the Baroness.

I bet it will snow tonight.

Yes, there are too many speeches in the *Mountain*. How dead they are. And all the speeches in this thing, too. I wonder why? Why do monks get the idea they have to preach sermons all the time to everybody else and if nobody else will listen, they still preach to themselves? Dull, dead sermons that God has no use for! And it has taken me six years to find out about it: and all the time the publishers are right in wanting to cut. The only trouble is Bob Giroux didn't cut nearly enough. But he did cut one job I liked. However, let it go.

My God, I pray better to you by breathing and walking than by talking, just as in choir I sing best when I am thinking about something else, or better still, praying.

We do not know how to do things well. We concentrate so much that we get ourselves mixed up and we make so many dumb plans that God can't do anything with us.

Last night I prayed to Our Lady to give me some sense of realities and now I'll go and do it again: pray her the same prayer. And as soon as I have written it, it is already done. Nothing is necessary but to be with her for love's sake alone.

January 27, 1948

Zero weather today for St. Amadeus, and yesterday for St. Paul, and the day before: many days a lot of zero weather, and the snow stays clean and dry and somebody made a lot of false deer-tracks in it under the trees of the garden.

The proofs of *The Seven Storey Mountain* are not as bad as they might be. In fact, as far as printing goes, they are wonderful. I haven't found a misprint in 50 galleys, but some shark they have there has made all kinds of corrections of *my* faults, especially commas in the wrong places. On the whole I feel that is the way I really ought to write.

God defend me from the stuffy academic language and from the pious jargon I fell into in so many parts of *Mother Berchmans* on the theory that, since I was a monk, I *had* to write that way. NO! That is NOT the way to write! It does NO good.

On the other hand, it is chastening to see myself, I mean myself and not just my writing, in print. At times I sound nasty even to myself. My own bursts of indignation surprise me. They seem petulant and even weak. I think many of my tirades are the fruit of something wrong with me and not with the world, and I don't know how to fix it. But I need to stop shouting that way.

They are varnishing the floor of the Church, now they are past the *jubé*, and doing all the area from there to the end of the Church, I mean the seculars' end. So the big life-sized statue of Our Lady from the choir of the infirm, the one that looks like a prim movie star and makes Brother Leo gasp so, she has moved into the room where we work and she overshadows all the proofreading I do. She needs to.

January 28, 1948

I saw a postcard of the Pecos Valley in New Mexico where the new foundation of Our Lady of Guadalupe is starting and it seems to be a wonderful place for a monastery. The postcard was full of green, but even if it is only half that green, it is still much more than a desert.

Lately I am wondering if resignation to so much work and too much technical theology (Scotus) is deadening my interior life without my realizing it. It is something I am always afraid of. And next to prayer, what do writing and big ideas in theology matter? They are only useful if they help that union in myself and in others, for that is all they are good for. Day after tomorrow I am thirty-three years old.

February 1, 1948

Well, things happen. God rearranges our affairs in ways that take us by surprise.

Thursday Reverend Father went off to Belleview, Illinois for the consecration of the new bishop. Thursday night, as I was on my way to the dormitory, Father Odilo stopped and told me to get Fr. Alfred's bedding and take it to the infirmary. Fr. Alfred had been getting thinner and thinner until now he is nothing more than a skeleton, and besides he had a bad foot and was dragging himself around the community literally half-dead. The other day Fr. Nivard was making him signs that he ought to *eat*. But I guess he couldn't eat any longer. Thursday night he was standing in that infirmary cell and I threw down his bedclothes and made him a sign to have a good rest. But for the last couple of days he had been looking as if simple signs just didn't sink in. Anyway, he made me, as best he could, his elaborately polite sign for "Thanks" and I went away. Friday Reverend Father sent a message that he wasn't coming home. Saturday Fr. Alfred got the Last Sacraments. As soon as he had hit the bed, he had folded up altogether. Saturday afternoon we knew Reverend Father had had a stroke somewhere. Saturday night we learned he was in the hospital in Louisville.

This morning when we came down to choir, someone made a sign that Fr. Alfred was dead.

They brought him down at the first bell for Prime. The whitest corpse I ever saw. Very emaciated, like a rake with a cowl draped on it. People are trying to say he starved himself to death, but that can't be done. Reverend Father never allowed inordinate fasting. Something was probably wrong with him that made it hard, if not impossible, for him to eat. He was a funny fellow anyway: very good, very quiet, rather slow, painstakingly holy. When he came up for profession, there were a lot of doubts as to whether he was able to lead our life. And I certainly don't think he had the strength. But anyway all I can see in it is the mercy of God Who brought the good man into heaven quickly and without fuss. He was five months professed. He would have had a long, hard life of it as a monk. People would be impatient at his slowness. But he had a very good heart. He was in our theology class.

February 5, 1948

It is hard to believe that this time last week Fr. Alfred was walking around the community for better or for worse, and now the red pile of dirt on top of his grave is already beginning to settle and sink, and I am half through a psalter for him.

And yet in this last week *seven* postulants have entered the community. Nor do I doubt that our holy little brother had something to do with it. He was a good man, and he is with God, or at least well on the way to his rest by now.

Fr. Cantor proclaimed me for not being authoritative enough about making everybody on our side observe the pauses in the psalmody, so for a couple of days I rushed around with signs saying "observe the pauses" and "don't precipitate," and the novices giggled and it didn't do much good. I stuck the sign in front of one of them and he jumped as if he had been shot.

Yesterday I finished the galleys of *The Seven Storey Mountain* and sent them off in an old envelope that will probably break open and spill them all over the New York Post Office.

Today I am so disgusted with technical questions in dogma (not in class so much as in my own reading) that I could find no sense in anything except St. John of the Cross. I can stand just so much, and then all the ideas and concepts and problems land on me and kill me. And I begin once more to look around for the living God.

Now that these proofs are finished, perhaps I can get back to some kind of sensible way of working, because I have been too steamed up for the past six months or nine. And it has done me harm. The depths of my soul react against it. Something inside me moves to heave all this weight off and thrust it away and get myself some peace.

February 8, 1948. Quinquagesima. Forty Hours

Yesterday I suddenly realized something that had been obscurely bothering me for some time. But at last it has caught up with me. Here I am supposed to be preparing for the priesthood and not only do I have no clear notion of what the priesthood is all about, but I don't even know if I have any desire to be a priest.

Of course there is this: I want what is God's will in it. And since people are telling me that that is what I am here for, and since it is what being a monk originally meant implicitly, then I want it, sure. And the other thing is, if I am *not* a priest, there is nothing left.

And so it is in this more or less negative way that I know I want to be a priest: without it, my life points to nothing but emptiness and confusion. But if I have to say what my life looks like *with* the priesthood in it: it is still a mystery. I can't figure it out.

I suppose the trouble is I can't imagine what it would mean precisely for me to come walking out of the sacristy in one of those comic chasubles, carrying a chalice. But I can't imagine any better what it would mean for me to go out and try to say Mass in decent vestments and at a decent altar either. So it is not the decorations that puzzle me.

Today as acolyte I watched the three priests on the altar. I could see that they were serious and they seemed to have some idea what it was all about and that comforted me. But then I thought of the books about the priesthood in our common box and said to myself: if I try to get at it through those channels, I'm finished. The atmosphere with which the ordinary level of meditations surrounds the priesthood confuses and distresses me beyond measure.

But during the Litany, when we sang *Sancte Laurenti . . . Sancte Augustine . . .* I got some comfort because I knew they knew what it was all about in that age.

Above all at the *Pax Domini*, I looked at Our Lord and *He* definitely knows what it is all about, and that is the important thing.

Maybe I'll die or go to the crazy house before I get ordained. We've got two deacons in the crazy house, no, three. And another permanently in the infirmary with epilepsy. But during the Forty Hours I'll make that my intention and ask for some understanding of the priesthood and the courage to go through with whatever God wants.

Perhaps I am afraid of being absorbed in the public anonymity of the priest, of becoming one of those masks behind whom Christ hides and acts. I think of so many priests I know in their strange, sensitive isolation, innocent, hearty men, decent and unoriginal and generally unperplexed, too; but all of them lost in a public privacy. They are Christ's property and everybody's property. And besides all that, they have their own characteristics, too, characteristics under which I don't recognize myself. And I fear they will be disappointed if I don't act and think in all things the way they think Cardinal Newman must have acted and thought, or Gerard Manley Hopkins for that matter.

And the funny thing is that it is completely irrelevant that I am different from them in the same way that everybody is different from everybody else.

So, if I am going to be a priest, the last thing I should be wondering about is who or what I am.

Lord, is it all right if I come and pray to you feeling more like a Communist than anything else? If there is anything the matter, please fix it or let me know what to do. And keep me out of trouble. And if I am alive this time next year, let me be somehow closer to you and more in the clear. I think the only solution will come from Christ in the Blessed Sacrament. I don't expect it right now from books or people. But because those answers come from the places from which you don't expect them, I suppose that is where this one will come from, too.

Monday. February 10, 1948. Still XL Hours [Forty Hours]

I suppose that business yesterday was some kind of a shadow.

Anyway, yesterday Reverend Father turned up in Chapter (he was back Saturday) and received the simple profession of Frater Pius whose other name was Francis Anthony Thomas Mazzarella. The initials spell FAT, but he is thin. He came here on the feast of Lucy, same day as I only four years later, so I prayed for him a lot.

Tuesday. February 11, 1948. Shrove Tuesday

As invitator I had the pleasure of announcing Ash Wednesday in Chapter. *Dies cinerum et initium Sacratissimae Quadragesimae.* [The day of ashes and the beginning of the Most Holy Season of Lent.] As an ordinary monk I had the pleasure of eating the usual Shrove Tuesday portion of butter while Fr. Paulinus read to us *The Story of a Family*, all about the Little Flower.

The XL Hours are over, and all of us have had our turn watching before the Blessed Sacrament except the novice who overslept and accused himself in humiliating language suggested by Dom Vital (I suppose) in the refectory before dinner.

Jesus was very good to us, more than we knew. He stays there with all those candles all around Him and we don't begin to realize what particular graces He is giving us. But anyway, right at the end of everything, after the Litany and *Tantum Ergo*, just before the blessing, He surprised me right in the middle of a distraction by an assurance that cleared up all my trouble so that I don't worry about it anymore. So I'm going to be a priest and there is nothing more to worry about.

How peculiar it is that we should be able for a moment to forget how much Christ loves us and how infinitely powerful is His love for us. If we were simple, He would show His love in ways we would apprehend, but we cannot prevent Him from expressing His love anyway, and in every kind of language, in every kind of way. All day long and all night He loves us and tells us about it and surrounds us with affection and care, the affection of a God and of a Father and of a Brother and of a Lover. *Quam bonus est Dominus quaerentibus se.* [*Quaerentibus autem Dominum non deerit omne bonum:* But they that seek the Lord shall not be deprived of any good (Psalms 33:11).]

Everybody is happy in the monastery and ready for Lent. The snow is not off the ground. I mean the same snow that has been there three weeks or a month. It is always cold, more consistently so than I have seen it so far in Kentucky.

But it is nice that God makes us cheerful at the beginning of Lent. I always remember it being that way. *Cum gaudio sancto* [with holy joy]. I mean I remember it being that way *here.* The Ash Wednesday liturgy is serious and our Lenten time-table is now completely unbalanced by the crazy compromise which puts Vespers before noon in order that we should fast until after Vespers . . . But anyway these mornings in Lent are gay.

After dinner I walked around the cemetery with the second volume of St. Bernard. I am tired carrying the XIVth volume of Duns Scotus. This Lent I'll make a change. I thought of reading Dom Gone's *À L'École de Saint Benoît.* Incidentally, I am glad Pope Pius XII took some of the Benedictines to task for being too exclusively highbrow about the Liturgy. That is aimed at my old bugbear, Dom Theodore Wesseling, among others, I surmise. Still, my friend Fr. Reinhold might come in for his share, and so might I in some of my off moments. Though I am not very liturgical.

Still, I had a burst of enthusiasm for articulation in choir – got tired of this Kentucky Latin. It is no more natural to me than any other kind, so I thought I would get a little Gallic, at least. That is closer to Rome.

And so, dear Mother, I love you with this Lent and I offer it with joy to your Son for the World's Peace. *In Nomine Domini.* [In the Name of the Lord]. Amen.

Tomorrow St. Stephen of Granmont, to whom I have devotion, is concealed under the liturgy of Lent. Lent does me good. When I fast, I haven't the energy to get dissipated. And my mind seems to have no inclination to grasp disputed points in theology. There is much less turbulence in me and more silence and I have no desire to think in terms that would lead to any kind of a dispute about anything.

But, on the other hand, I read Ruysbroeck with joy, all about immediate contact with God, "meeting" Him in the unity of our Spirit – our natural and supernatural union with Him – how He wants us to dwell with Him "above all gifts, graces and virtues". The concept has been fascinating me for a year.

And this afternoon the writing job turned out to be healthy. I am at last come back to *Waters of Siloe* and am writing steadily on it. Today, with pictures of Sénanque and Fontenay and other places (Silvacane, Thoronet, Hauterive, etc.) before me, I was thinking and writing about our cloisters in the 12th century, and the work was meditation and prayer and benefited me immensely.

Today in the refectory I got two portions of rice instead of one rice and soup. My neighbors did nothing about it, so without scruple I attacked them both. Out of shame I left about a quarter of one of them. But, as I ate, I felt very Franciscan, applying the principle "eat what is set before you."

This morning we sang the Solemn Office of the Dead transferred from January 31. I was invitator and had a lot of singing to do and I still don't know if I performed the ceremonies correctly. I never watched to see what the other invitators did, and wasn't sure whether I should have been facing the altar, or facing in choir, singing my verses of the Responsories. I faced the altar.

Then, at the third responsory, Fr. Cantor faced in choir.

Tomorrow, if there is a Chapter of Faults, they will forget to proclaim me. Or is there a procession already?

I was thinking of drawing up some suggestions about a less insane Lenten time-table than we have now, and sending it to the General. Just look as the mess we are in: Terce and Sext jammed together at seven, which is about the *Second* Hour. None at eight, before the Third Hour; Vespers before noon! And people have the audacity to write books saying that, if St. Bernard came back to earth, he would be perfectly at home in one of our monasteries.

And that gives the lie to what I said about not being interested in disputable questions. I guess I had better go and pray.

February 14, 1948. Saturday

Tomorrow is the first Sunday of Lent. I feel indescribable, well, describable, but anyway *deep joy* at the antiphon *Ecce nunc tempus acceptabile, ecce nunc dies salutis!* [Behold now is the acceptable time: behold the day of salvation (2 Corinthians 6:2)!] Lent is a time of happiness. The Liturgy is full of cries of confidence, and our spiritual battle is joy because it is joy to serve God by denying yourself.

The greatest joy in life is to give up yourself altogether for the honor and glory of God, to know you belong to Him entirely, that your will is owned, possessed by His love.

Anything that tends to that end, any sacrifice, therefore, brings joy and happiness, even though it may be bitter to the flesh. However, there is nothing especially bitter about our fast. I am glad to be able to take at least what our present Rule offers.

First Sunday in Lent, [February 15], 1948

I just came from covering the statues in Church. St. Paul's hand with a forefinger pointing upwards is still sticking out from behind the purple screen I put in front of him, but I had to hurry because Dom Vital was going to confession right next to the pedestal.

On the way through the cloister there was a strong, merry smell of potatoes, and the windows were open to let in the beautiful air. Yesterday morning, when it was snowing (again), I asked Our Lord for some nice weather and in about two hours it cleared up and became very nice and the sun melted the snow and there was a blue sky. And today it is even nicer, so I sat outside writing a poem and then reading the life of St. Guerric by Fr. Beller, who was the village priest of Arcis-le-Ponsart, which is over the hill from Igny.

So there, that is what I have been doing.

And all day long it was good to be glorifying God with psalms, from the Invitatory on down.

This morning the Lenten books were given out and I was terrified that I would get that thing with the horrible purple cover called *The Heliotropium*

[Jeremias Drexelius's seventeenth-century *Turning to HIM*, or, *Conformity of the human will to the divine*] and I also told Father Anthony I was afraid of getting yet a third volume of [Alphonso] Rodriguez [the sixteenth-century Jesuit's *Practice of Perfection and Christian Virtues*, 3 volumes]. (I had the other two the last two years.) So, when I was handing out the Lenten books, I came to Fr. Anthony and his book was Rodriguez (I don't know which volume). And I put a book with a light blue cover at our own empty place and then, on the other side of me I gave Fr. Athanasius *The Heliotropium*. Fr. Nivard got *The Heliotropium*, too. So you see I had a narrow escape. But do not be alarmed. I would gladly suffer even that for the sake of Lent. What I *did* get was Terence Connolly's translation of St. Bernard's *De Diligendo Deo [On the Love of God]*, and I could hardly have done better from a natural point of view (my own taste) and a supernatural as well (find out more about the love of God).

And then, when I got down to the end of the line, I came to Brother Isidore and he was asleep. I had to wake him up to give him his book. And last of all Brother Leo was either asleep or in ecstasy, but when I gave him his book, he jumped up and made his bow standing and actually gasped with effusive joy, for joy is prescribed in the *Usages* though not necessarily external. And Brother Gabriel received his book with his eyes tight shut to show he wasn't looking.

So that is how it was with the Lenten books. And this has been one of the most beautiful days I ever saw in my life because of the goodness and mercy of Christ. If it is this way when we do penance, what is it going to be like in heaven?

But the reasons these consolations are without smoke and bitterness and leave no bad aftertaste is this: I have tried to do what Ruysbroeck said somewhere and *accept* consolations with joy and thanksgiving, entering in to find God within myself, bearing to Him my praise and thanksgiving. In that way abandonment and praise of God are a more real joy than the consolations themselves, and so there is less impurity in them. It is more clean and more innocent and therefore in all things there is more joy. So that now I am beginning to understand that God wants us to rejoice and be glad in all things by loving and thanking Him for them and by them and through them and that in this way we use all creatures for the praise and glory of God.

When I was more afraid of consolations, it was because I was afraid they might upset me, and my fear was a lack of trust in God. My attempt to refuse them was full of human misgivings and suspicion because I thought, implicitly, that I could keep my heart pure by an act of my own will.

But now I see that it is more perfect to accept all that God sends, not only the bad but even the good as well, with joy and satisfaction and abandonment, that He may have glory, to make all things a reason for entering into the peace that is in the midst of myself, to bring Him praises and thanksgiving and glory to His Name, without the pressure of exuberance and passions, but in tranquility of heart and a joy that is serene.

O Love! How good it is to know Your name! †

Saturday [February 21, 1948] in Ember Week of Lent

I am confined to the Scriptorium. Outside it has begun to snow, small flakes blowing parallel to the ground, and I have that pain again. This time I think it is rheumatism rather than pleurisy.

Yesterday, over the one portion we got for dinner, Fr. Alphonsus prayed lugubriously and I saw the expression of one novice as we sat down. With his eyebrows raised and his forehead puckered, he gazed at his bowl of potatoes with perplexity and disdain, but at the same time with intense hunger: "Is this what they expect me to eat?"

But anyway, fasting and pain and all, it is good and satisfying to love God and to rise above all these things with joy because that is what He wants of us. And I thought, too, it no longer matters that I can't complain to anybody about anything, because I have no desire to complain and no desire for attention or relief. I went to the infirmary to see about it some weeks ago and the doctor said all *he* could do for me was give me some pills to take away the pain. So I have a little bottle marked "pain pills." It is blue. It is almost half full of big pills, none of which I have yet taken.

The Lenten Book *(De Diligendo Deo)* is, from the point of view of my own interest and alertness to its value, the best I have had so far.

Sometimes when I fast, my imagination gets a little rowdy. Or I begin composing sermons to convert all the people in the world. But generally my mind is nice and quiet and I don't think about anything much until I get started on the book. And the book *(Waters of Siloe)* is going better because, doing one thing at a time, I think about it all the time and consequently have ideas in my dumb head when it comes time to go to work.

Also I have discovered there is no law forbidding me to read over the poems I have written and make changes. Lent helps me to make cuts. When my stomach is empty, I can see more easily where the poem is too full. So I have pulled the stuffing out of some of the new ones, which is what I should have done with *Figures for an Apocalypse*, but it is too late now.

The New York censors like *The Seven Storey Mountain*, and I like the New York censors.

This week I don't think de Rancé was as bad as people sometimes say. Reading the *Exordium Magnum*, I find those old monks and the Trappists do not differ so much!

February 22, 1948. Second Sunday of Lent

Gospel of the Transfiguration. I always think of the *nubes lucida* [shining cloud] as a symbol of the Gift of Understanding. Then, every time we sang an antiphon, it seemed to be about the Three Tabernacles: *Unum tibi et unum Moysi et unum Heliae.* [One for you, (Lord), one for Moses, and one for Elias (Luke 9:33).] A laybrother novice received the habit, and somebody took an old broom and cleared a path in the snow from the little cloister to Fr. Alfred's grave. I walked out there a bit. We have had a lot of winter this year.

Today it is six years since I received the habit of novice and not until today did I realize that I had received the habit on Washington's birthday. Fr. Hilary, he knows all these things, made me a sign it was the secular big day of the president who chopped the wood.

One of the things I shouldn't have been doing was thinking about the Thomists and Molinists (not deliberately, I hope) when I was ostensibly hearing the Mass of the first round at Our Lady of Victories. By the time I came to the Scriptorium, I thought I had worked out a wonderful, simple solution that did away with both *praemotio physica* and *scientia media*[28] and gave full play both to human freedom and the universal causality of God. However, at the moment I am no longer sure. Tomorrow or the day after I will probably realize what the hitch is.

Humble George is here again. He goes around praying with a medal in his mouth, and the other day he was kneeling in church with a book, and had a rosary around his neck and the cross of the rosary in his mouth. I think Humble George needs a little spiritual direction.

Maybe it will help me to do something about distractions if I restrain my famished appetite for the things that distract me – new books about the Order, my own work in print, etc. I don't expect to be without distractions: they are my cross. I suffer them with love in the sense that I am resigned to

---

[28] *Praemotio physica* refers to the Thomist belief that God physically affects the free will of the elect so that they will cooperate with grace. *Scientia media* refers to the Molinist belief that human beings are both determined by God's infallible foreknowledge and yet free to choose, in some way, to cooperate with grace.

the drab business of remembering to sink below them when I can, and keep with the God Who holds my will in His darkness. But I have given up expecting to overcome distractions by a method. I just have to love, and love blindly, and deepen the union that is there in spite of everything, and not break it up by fighting the air.

Anyway, today I didn't look at the copy of *Epoch*, a new magazine just out at Cornell, which Reverend Father gave me. Maybe I ought to be ashamed of myself, when the other monks never see a magazine, but since I'm in the business, I don't see any point raising a howl about it. I was fretting all last year and it was a waste of time and thought. And all the perplexities I left on paper about it are stone *dead*. They mean nothing. I thought I was trying to please God with all that fuss, but God isn't pleased with fuss and racket.

And today it suddenly dawned on me: I am a *monk*, a Cistercian monk, under solemn vows, on the way to being a priest. It is almost unbelievable! I belong to this Order, this austere Order with a rule that has such a terrific reputation, and with its long history, and with its twelfth century, and I am part of all that. It is fantastic.

But that wasn't the way I felt last year.

I looked at the new history by Jean Berthold Mahan [*L'Ordre cistercien et son gouvernement, des origines au milieu du XIIIe siècle* (1098–1265). Paris, 1945], who was killed fighting in Italy in 1944. It is very business like and looks tremendously solid. I felt flattered that this extremely capable historian belonged to my own generation (born in 1911 in Paris). And also it struck me: these people with their minds and their appetite for structure and solidity, they find things that satisfy them in twelfth century Cîteaux. [Etienne] Gilson, too. Henri Pirenne, too. And when I see Cîteaux as they saw it, I begin to find out something else about the way God's love works in the world.

February 29, 1948

Well, God teaches us things all the time.

The day before yesterday, Friday, when we were sitting down again to that one portion (potatoes and sauerkraut), there was a lot of fuss in the refectory – Fr. Prior hurrying in and out and getting strong men to come and help him in some mysterious emergency.

Later I learned by picturesque signs that Frater Damian had gone out of his head in the infirmary and started running around the monastery, making an outcry. So I assumed they had him taken away that afternoon. But the next day I saw that the strong men in the house were not in choir. Eight of them, no less, were absent at one time or another, and later all at once, and most of them were sitting on Frater Damian trying to keep him on the floor. This time it was in the hotel, where he was definitely waiting to be taken somewhere where somebody would be able to help him instead of just sitting on his arms and legs.

Frater Damian came here five years ago during the annual retreat. And just after that there was a day of recollection or a sermon or something in which Fr. James told some horror stories about desecrations of the Blessed Sacrament, and I remember thinking at the time: what will this man with the curly hair and blue serge shirt get into him with all this? He looked very serious, rather tough and not too brainy. But he turned out to be a nice quiet sort of a fellow with a sense of humor. Very strong – got all the hard work. Then this year, just the day before going on retreat for solemn profession, he was sent to bed with TB – that was, rather, last year, just at the end of December. He was also just about to begin theology and would have been tonsured with Frater Hilary in January. He had a hemorrhage back in August some time, but had been around the house as usual, on relief no more.

Two months in the infirmary finished him apparently.

Reasons people give for the trouble: Fr. Anthony said he was reading too much of St. John of the Cross without understanding it. Fr. Odilo hedged and said, "Why do you look for some mysterious reason?" Fr. Abbot said, "Evidently he must have been a nervous individual." I never noticed any nervousness about him. He was slow and stolid. All I know is, after his profession (not in the novitiate though) he started to yell in his sleep: "Jesus" or "St. Michael." Fr. Linus made a sign "The devil is behind it."

So Fr. Odilo told me how it was trying to hold him down. Sometimes he would fight and shout "No more rule for me." Then he would break down and sob and say, "I tried so hard to love God and it didn't work." Fr. Gerard gave him a shot and he calmed down.

Then two detectives came to put handcuffs, and he had a lucid moment and looked at the handcuffs, and you could see he realized what had happened.

That part of it must have been simply terrible.

So there's the story: very strong man, used to be a sailor, as far as I could tell a good monk, very serious, very much good will – fasted a lot, no frustulum in winter until last year. But they say he keeled over and fainted at work once or twice even in the novitiate.

And now I hope he is in a place where he will be treated nicely and not just kept in a cage. And I think of myself waking up some fine day with a pair of handcuffs on me . . .

Still, that is his particular vocation and his way to heaven. It is a hard and dreary one. But God knows what He is doing . . .

I have been reading about de Rancé and this connects up with that. That old Trappist business of trying to starve and beat your way to sanctity and [of] assuming that your own efforts and energy are practically everything – beating your head against a brick wall at the end of a dead end in order to fulfill some particular negative ideal . . .

Our Cistercian Fathers and St. Benedict knew better. So did the Little Flower. So did our Lord.

I don't know any universal solution of the problem of why monks go crazy, except yesterday it was such a beautiful day I walked under the trees and looked at the sunny hills and listened to the quiet sunlight and kicked the gravel with my feet and said, "What is there to go crazy about anyway?" We have a wonderful vocation. Christ has brought us here to live: to live and breathe and be happy under His gaze, to play in His sight like children, while He takes care of us – to sing and fast and pray and (for me) to write books and to love all the time. It's not an effort; there is nothing to get excited about. Sure, I am distracted, I am vain, I am full of dumb books, and I get into interior arguments about the chant, so what? He knows I don't want to get into all that stuff, and He loves me.

I am happy that I can at least want to love God. Perhaps that is all I've got, but it is already all that is essential. And He will take care of the rest.

How sweet it is to trust Him, to leave everything to Him – fasting, contemplation, writing, the Rule, my health – and for my own part just to go ahead from moment to moment stumbling over my own feet half the time, but simply existing to give glory to God. And I find out that I believe this more this year than I did last, when I was so upset by problems of my own making.

Some people are worried about the community, and sometimes I am tempted to be also. But no, we are in God's hands and He is doing a tremendous work in us and for us, and one day we shall see the fruits. But before that, I don't ask what we may have to go through. JHS.

March 4, 1948

Dominus pugnabit pro vobis, et vos tacebitis. [The Lord will fight for you and you shall hold your peace (Exodus 14:14).]

The book of *Exodus* is very graphic and very exciting. I am reading it. The plagues piling up on Pharaoh are like our Lent – plagues piling up on our enemy who nevertheless will not let us go.

God in His love, to do me good, sent back that insomnia. Sunday night I got two hours' sleep and Monday I was staggering around in a fog. With trembling hands I took down Dom Vital Lehodey's immortal volume on abandonment, *Le Saint Abandon.* Also I read the chapter in the *Spiritual Directory,* or, at least, *began* the chapter on infirmities. I am too attached to my sleep. My body loves sleep, my soul well-being. I want to be able to keep awake and work well and get pleasure out of reading and prayer – that is why I fear to lose my sleep. But what does it matter to God what pleasure I get out of reading and prayer? Am I reading to please myself or to find Him?

But if I am reading to find Him, and He gives me a better way to find Him by suffering sleeplessness, by accepting His will, why should I complain?

But I don't complain. I am glad. Anyway last night I slept O.K., and today I know sleep is a gift of God.

Yesterday I discovered that there were marvelous poets in the 12th century. I never knew it except by vague hearsay. But for the first time I read Marbod of Rennes and he is wonderful. Such skill! What he can do with meters and rhymes. He is very slick and very sure of himself and his poetry is above all *alive.* It is just as much a living medium as classical Latin and somehow younger than classical Latin. Plenty of delicacy and energy at the same time. Serious in such a way that he is as stimulating as if he were being funny, and his poems make you dance and laugh and make you very happy. What a good way to talk to our Lady:

> *Producens Dominum lucis vitaeque Datorem*
> [You bring forth the Lord, Giver of light and life.]

or:

> *O Sancta virgo virginum! quae genuisti Dominum*
> *Triumphatorem Zabuli, reparatorem saeculi*
> . . .
> *Jam mihi multa vulnera inflicta sunt, O Domina!*
> *Quae nisi tu curaveris sunt mihi causa funeris.*
> [O Holy Virgin of virgins! You gave birth to the Lord,
> Victor over Zabulon, the restorer of the world.
> . . .
> Already many wounds have been inflicted on me, O Lady!
> Unless you heal them, they will be my death.]

To say nothing of a very sharp piece of writing about the city of Rennes. In my mind I think already of an article on "Five Medieval Latin Poets" I would write, say for this new *Hudson Review*, and at once my Lent begins to spoil.

Who would be the five? Marbod, Hildebert, Walter of Châtillon, Abelard, I don't know.

But I sent a poem to *The Hudson Review* anyway. That was ten days ago.

Cistercian Contemplatives is on the way from New York in boxes in a freight train. I hope.

A Dominican Tertiary in Erie writes to me about the contemplative life. She knows Dom Verner Moore and says he is now called Pablo Maria at the Charterhouse in Burgos. And if I will write a leaflet on contemplation, Sister Madeleva may get it printed.

March 4, 1948.[29] *(St. Peter of Castelnau)*

St. Peter of Castelnau is submerged in Lent and only his long, learned collect, devised by the Cistercians of the common observance, sticks out above the surface. But I am glad. For today was the Gospel of the Samaritan woman and I thought how much there is in it [John 4:4–42]. Above all I thought how the Gospels take people as they are. Jesus does not start out with people as they are not, or with a world in which nobody gets tired. It is a world of wells and roads and fields and small towns and individual people each one with his own story. Some are happy and some are mixed-up and all of them are willing to come out and take a look at a prophet on the chance that He could straighten them out.

Nos adoramus quod scimus. [We adore what we know.] I wonder if William of St. Thierry quotes that. He ought to. The passage in his *Speculum Fidei [The Mirror of Faith]* I just read, about how faith penetrates the sacraments of visible things and seizes the *res sacramenti* [the matter of the sacrament] by the understanding which is a gift – an experience – *sensus amoris illuminatus* [the sense illuminated by love] – all this fits in with that Gospel and could be a commentary on it.

But the day is very bright. There was already some sun slanting into the cloister by the kitchen door when we went around the corner with the penitential psalms in procession.

By mistake, I left our bookmark in *Deuteronomy* instead of *Exodus*, but what I found was very fine, so I take it to myself.

[29] Merton repeats the date as March 4th.

Omnis locus quem calcaverit pes vester erit. [Every place that your foot shall tread upon shall be yours (Deuteronomy 11:24)] (and I think of St. Bernard's application of that text). *Vos enim transibitis Jordanem . . . Ad locum quem elegerit Dominus Deus vester . . . venietis et offeretis in illo holocausta et comedetis ibi in conspectu Domini Dei vestri . . . Non facietis ibi quae nos hic facimus hodie singuli quod sibi rectum videtur; neque enim usque in praesens tempus venistis ad requiem et possessionem quam Dominus Deus vester daturus est vobis (Deut. 11, end–12 beginning.) . . . ut requiescatis a cunctis hostibus et absque ullo timore habitetis in loco quem elegerit Dominus Deus vester ut sit nomen ejus in eo.* [You will cross the Jordan . . . You will come to the place which the Lord your God will choose . . . you will offer holocausts there and you will eat there in the sight of the Lord your God . . . You will not do there what we do here today, each man what appears right to him. Nor until the present time did you come to the repose and the possessions which the Lord your God will give to you . . . that you may rest from all your enemies and without any fear you may dwell in the place that the Lord your God will have chosen, that his name may be there (Deuteronomy 11:31–32; 12:1–11).]

Full of sermon on the interior life.

Exodus to me is all about contemplation. The Epistle today – the people who did not trust God, but wanted consolation in the desert. "Hey! Give us a drink!"

But bring me with joy, God, across Thy Jordan. I am sorry I forget my desires and burn with other desires to complete my work, to get books distributed to people. But above all there is only one desire, to find the promised land and the freedom of a pure love that is without concern for anything but love, that is without concern for anything but the purity of God, for His will, His glory. Peace above language, not in some esoteric *state*, but in the living reality of a love that is contemplation and act, and clings to God and embraces all the world in Him, in peace, in unity.

During the theology class, when we were fussing about predestination, I was called up to the infirmary to get another x-ray of my chest. Since the picture won't show anything of the God Who dwells within me, I can't say I am very much interested in it. He is the One Who knows precisely what He wants to do with me for my good, and I am not going to waste time insisting on any preferences or even formulating them, for I have only one preference which is Himself, His love.

In the infirmary Fr. George was sitting in a wheel chair making disciplines[30] and strings were all tangled up. And Fr. Maurus, who has become
extremely fat, was sorting out a lot of old postcards – Paris, Belgium,
Palestine – left over from the globe trotting days of Dom Edmund. They
are destined for the flames. I saw one or two of the Grande Chartreuse.
One showed a narrow little library and another a refectory with cloths on
the table, and another showed some snow. And later Reverend Father
showed me a picture of the new buildings at Thymadeuc which are phe-
nomenally ugly.

On the whole the day was very gay. First Friday in March and tomorrow
also the First Saturday. And if there is anything wrong with my chest, I offer it up for peace in the world and no war.

March 7, 1948. Laetare Sunday. Day of Recollection
Ego sum via et veritas et vita. Nemo venit ad Patrem nisi per me. [I am the way
and the truth and the life. No man cometh to the Father, but by me (John
14:6).]

*Sicut ergo accepistis Jesum Christum Dominum, in ipso ambulate . . . abun-
dantes in illo in gratiarum actione.* [As therefore you have received Jesus
Christ, the Lord, walk ye in Him . . . abounding in him in thanksgiving
(Colossians 2:6–7).]

*Videte ne quis vos decipiat per philosophiam et inanem fallaciam secundum
traditionem hominum.* [Beware lest any man impose upon you by philosophy and vain fallacy, according to the tradition of men (Colossians 2:8).]

Omnis spiritus qui solvit Jesum ex Deo non est. [And every spirit, that dis-
solveth Jesus, is not of God (1 John 4:3).]

Qui videt me videt et Patrem. [He that seeth me, seeth the Father also
(John 14:9).]

St. Bonaventure: *per contemplationem ingredi non potest Jerusalem supernam
nisi per sanguinem Agni tamquam per portam.* [He cannot proceed through
contemplation to the heavenly Jerusalem unless he goes through the blood
of the Lamb as through a gate.] *Omnis qui audivit a Patre et didicit venit ad
me.* [Every one that hath heard of the Father, and hath learned, cometh to
me (John 6:45).]

Lord Jesus Christ, true God and true Man, in Whom the fullness of God
dwells and is manifested to men, the man who tries to be a contemplative

---

[30] Small whips of knotted cord used to beat one's back for the space of a "Miserere" (Psalm 50)
as an exercise of penance on Fridays of the year, outside Paschal Time, and other Major
Feasts.

without You is dead. The man who enters into an interior darkness in which You cannot be found enters into the gate of hell. The man who enters into a silence in which Your voice cannot be heard enters into the antechamber of the devil. The man who willingly goes where You cannot be seen by him is crazy.

But I will not fear the darkness where, though I desire You, my desire cannot seem to find You. Because, if I desire You, I have already found You, and if I love You, You are with me. And if I cry out to You, You have already heard my voice.

Savior of the World, fill me with faith, fill my heart with desire, deliver my mind from all the illusions of the devil and enlighten my soul with Your discretion. Anoint my will with the grace of the Holy Spirit and bring me, through Your Cross and by the power of Your Blood, to the heaven of Your love for Your Father and for all men, that I may dwell with You where my life is hidden in You in God forever, one with Him through You in the unity of His Spirit. Amen.

It never fails. As soon as a Day of Recollection comes along and I start examining myself, I get upset and start pushing myself around and asking: what is it all about, anyway? I think one of the favorite sports of Trappist monks is mentally beating the air.

For myself: keep at least one area clear and clean always, one department of yourself that you never write about or talk about except in the confessional. Most of these problems come up merely because I have started to consider them in relation to paper or people. If I belong in the Carthusians, how could I write it down so that people would understand?

In that way something that is not a problem tends to become a problem right away. And I get myself mixed up in what is unreal, and I think it is a question I am obliged to answer, when it is not even a question that I need to consider.

Figures for an Apocalypse came in yesterday. A child's garden of bad verses. I should have pulled out a lot of weeds before I let that stuff get in print, but the damage is done now. May God have mercy on me. The reviewers won't. I hope this time Reverend Father will let me look at the reviews – I might learn something.

This Lent I have been very active, I mean in the intervals, taking notes on Ruysbroeck, etc. But I think it has done me good.

The only thing that worries me is: do I let myself get satisfied with work and reading, etc., and is my peace merely natural? Fr. Anthony says the stuff is God's will, which I suppose it is. However, I am not raising a lot of questions about it.

The Archbishop doesn't want to ordain me subdeacon until December, taking the *exeunte tertio anno* [having completed the third year of theological studies] of the Code very literally. But I can hear the voice of Fr. Amadeus preaching a retreat conference in the infirmary chapel to Frater Amandus, who is six months ahead of me, and is to be ordained subdeacon this Saturday.

March 11, 1948

Yesterday, Wednesday of the 4th week in Lent – was the anniversary of my solemn profession as far as the Lenten liturgy is concerned. I had never realized what an important day it is. Trying to discover why there was a prophecy, I found out that the catechumens in the old days went through half the Baptism ceremonies, exorcism, etc., and the Mass is full of all that.

Cum sanctificatus fuero in vobis, congregabo vos de universis terris et effundam super vos aquam mundam et mundabimini ab omnibus inquinamentis vestris et dabo vobis Spiritum novum. [When I shall be sanctified in you before their eyes. For I will take you from among the Gentiles, and I will gather you together out of all the countries; and will bring you into your own land. And I will pour upon you clean water, and you shall be cleansed from your filthiness, and I will cleanse you from idols. And I will give you a new heart (Ezekiel 36:23–25).]

Dabo vobis cor novum et spiritum novum ponam in medio vestri . . . et eritis mihi in populum et ego ero vobis in Deum. [And I will give you a new heart, and put a new spirit within you . . . and you shall be my people, and I will be your God (Ezekiel 36:26, 28).]

Et habitabitis in terra quam dedi patribus vestris. (Ezekiel 36 and Introit). [And you shall dwell in the land which I gave to your fathers (Ezekiel 36:28).]

Lavamini, mundi estote . . . si fuerint peccata vestra ut coccinum, quasi nix dealbabuntur (Isaias 1). [Wash yourselves, be clean . . . if your sins be as scarlet, they shall be made as white as snow (Isaiah 1:16, 18).]

And finally the Gospel of the man born blind [John 9:1–12] . . .

In the afternoon it was warm and like spring and buds are showing on the willow in the yard, and I took Ruysbroeck out and stood by the cemetery wall and heard the sharp notes of a spring bird coming from over by the sheep barn and thought of the infinite fruition hiding within me that I cannot get to, ever, by myself, but only through Christ. But it isn't warm anymore today, for it rained in the night and then froze. But the bird was still there today and so was a caterpillar that came out too soon.

Anyway, yesterday afternoon I thought I was going to finish *Waters of Siloe,* but the dentist came and I sat in the infirmary for three quarters of an hour, and he tore a tooth out of Fr. Raymond with much hacking and cracking because the thing broke. And Fr. Raymond kept making remarks like "Get a derrick! . . . Get a bulldozer!" Afterwards I gave him some pills Fr. Gerard gave me, marked "pain pills," and I have still not asked the permission I presumed. For myself I got away without a scar.

Then *Cistercian Contemplatives* arrived and it looks very decent, in fact it looks good, but some of the pictures are very weak. The printing is beautiful. Weiss is the type, and the italic is good. However I didn't finish *Waters of Siloe* yesterday, or today either.

I am afraid to try to get a copy of *Cistercian Contemplatives* for the common box because I am becoming aware that a lot of my brethren are not happy with me and my talk about contemplation.

Before dinner I was brooding about it and thinking: "The people in the world are so eager to hear about contemplation and monks hate it. What is the matter?" But it is not true, I hope, that most monks hate it. A few are very disturbed by expressions like "infused contemplation." Such language literally makes them so nervous, they suffer acutely. I wonder what is behind it: maybe they strained themselves at prayer and never got over it.

Now I am beginning to wonder if I hadn't better keep quiet around the monastery and just preach "the ordinary way" so as not to upset anybody.

From the comments on a "meditation" I had to give in class (with great repugnance), I find that others are also terribly sensitive to slang, so I'll have to stop that, too.

All I know is that it doesn't matter whether these objections are reasonable or not. I will do everything I can to keep from hurting people. Sympathy and kindness are almost the most important things in this life, and sometimes the most neglected.

March 12, 1948. Feast of St. Gregory

This morning early, Fr. Gilbert left the monastery and I suppose the Order with an indult of secularization to look around and find somewhere for himself. I was very surprised. Found out when the monks were making signs about it downstairs after the Scripture conference we had this morning. I first noticed something was up when Fr. Walter, the next one ahead of me, had moved his work things up one hook in the long line of hooks arranged in order of seniority.

Yesterday Gilbert wrote me a note asking for a copy of the dumb meditation on St. Gregory. I had said something about contemplatives who returned to the active life . . . I suppose God slipped that in for him. He didn't come down to the Little Office and I had to go out of choir during the first nocturn. I was surprised to find him washing up at his leisure about 3:15, when the brothers were coming down after their discipline. Then Fr. Anthony, whose Mass I was serving at the second round, came in late and I wondered if it was something to do with Gilbert, his penitent, but couldn't imagine what.

Poor Gilbert was always the problem-child of the monastery: plenty of brains and talent and extremely active – lots of imagination and too much emotion. Came here very young, from an orphanage I think, precocious as he could be – turned the novitiate upside down and had Fr. Master and everybody else wondering how to handle him. When I was a novice, they thought he had developed TB. He was strong for particular affections, always throwing himself at someone or other until lately. With Fr. Anthony directing him, he was much more peaceful, but I think he did well to go, unless he gets himself into some mess outside.

But I write this down to remember the point I touched on from the *Moralia* [of St. Gregory] which was very applicable to him, only I didn't develop it. St. Gregory said that there are men who try to be contemplatives when it is not their vocation. You can tell by the way everything about their life becomes complicated and upset. They do not find peace, but only turmoil in trying to live an entirely inward life. For them the thing to do is to pluck out the eye of contemplation that scandalizes them and enter into eternal life with one eye, i.e. action. From that you can conclude that the normal thing is to have both eyes, contemplation and action. *Per se* everyone is called to both, *per accidens* [through circumstances] it is better to give up one or the other to *some extent.*

Anyway I pray for him and I am sorry I wasn't nicer to him when I had a chance to be. I was always a bit short with him and now I am sorry. It is not right to make people suffer because their temperament, which they can't help, doesn't agree with your own. At the moment, for the first time in my life, I feel extremely fond of him now that he has gone.

March 14, 1948. Passion Sunday

I don't know what a diesel tractor is doing out on Sunday, but I can hear it over the wall. However I have got my hands too full to get up and look. It is the first time this year it had really been warm enough to sit outside. After dinner I sat here in the sun and read T. S. Eliot's *Four Quartets*, or rather *East Coker* and part of *The Dry Salvages*. Eight years ago, when we were at the cottage at Olean, Nancy Flagg had *East Coker* in ms., for it was still not published, and we all said we didn't like it. But today I like it quite a bit except I paused a bit at the archaic English, but there were only two or three lines of that. I was surprised at so much St. John of the Cross and do not immediately see how it fits in. And in the second section I was brought up short by the "That was a way of putting it" and the other self-conscious section. Maybe I'll see the point later. But the beginning is fine and the rhymed sections are very beautiful, as beautiful as anything that has been written in English for fifty years or more.

> Thunder rolled by the rolling stars
> Simulates triumphal cars
> Deployed in constellated wars
> Scorpion fights against the sun
> Until the sun and moon go down
> Comets weep and leonids fly
> Hunt the heavens and the plains
> Whirled in a vortex that shall bring
> The world to that destructive fire
> Which burns before the ice-cap reigns.

I think this book is the best of Eliot. Also I admire Eliot's chastity. He is not afraid to be prosaic, rather than write bad verse. But when he is very prosaic, he is weak. However, a word like "grimpen" can liven up the prose. Then when he comes to the part:

> Do not let me hear
> Of the wisdom of old men but rather of their folly,

it becomes poetry again.

> The wounded surgeon plies the steel
> That questions the distempered part.

It may be the best of the whole thing, not only beautiful but sharp and deep and precise and poignant. It makes a good contrast with the cosmic bit about the triumphal cars in heaven. Here everything that was thereby big, vast, universal, is brought down to the pointed, the moral and the human. The heavens are indifferent, but here are real wounds in a real moral order. A real death.

I have no longer any questions about Eliot being a great and important poet and a most stimulating one. And a religious one.

> The chill ascends from feet to knees
> The fever sings in mental wires . . .

(And I think of Dylan Thomas: "The pleasure bird sings in the hot wires," but it is the same fever.)

I have got to be sharp and precise like Eliot – or else quit.

March 15, 1948

When I had begun to write all that yesterday, Fr. Placid, who is retreat master this year, called me in to Fr. Prior because somebody was up in the guest house all full of Marx and Freud and Kant and wanted to argue. But the conversation got off on the world situation and many strange things: how in Italy there is going to be an election and the Pope has issued a bull that it is a mortal sin to vote the Communist ticket. And if the Reds get in, it is all up with the Vatican. And America has got the draft board together again, which I thought they had done long ago anyway.

March 16, 1948

So, going into Passion week, my mind is in tune with the Liturgy and with Jeremias. At Communion it is Christ in the garden Who prays in me. I don't feel like writing anymore.

The Easter moon is up, thin and pale. Last night much rain, and the building leaks. There are puddles in the cloister, but not big ones, and drops off the window above me land on my head in choir. Mark Van Doren wrote a beautiful letter about *Figures for an Apocalypse*, full of sympathy for the problem of poetry vs. contemplation. At the beginning of the year he wrote another with the same sympathy for the problem of solitude.

They are painting the dormitory and we all shift around from cell to cell as the paint comes after us. The brown paint they put on the floor is like the stuff you see on the decks of tug boats, and when you go to bed it smells like going on board a tramp steamer.

I am reading over *Waters of Siloe* and can't tell whether or not it is dull.

Today in the Epistle an angel took up Habakkuk by the top of the head and carried him to Babylon, that the dinner he had prepared for the harvesters might be given to Daniel in the Lion's den. And when they took Daniel out of the den and threw in his accusers instead, the lions ate them up quick [Daniel 14:33–42]. But in Jeremias I read how the bones of kings and priests are to be taken and scattered from their tombs and laid bare to the moon and stars that they had worshiped.

"They shall cast out the bones of the kings of Judah and the bones of the princes thereof and the bones of the priests and the bones of the prophets . . . out of their graves. And they shall spread them abroad to the sun and the moon and all the host of heaven whom they have loved and whom they have served and after whom they have walked and whom they have sought and adored: they shall not be gathered and they shall not be buried. They shall be as dung upon the face of the earth." viii, 2.

"Woe is me for my soul hath fainted because of them that are slain." iv, 31.

March 19, 1948. St. Joseph

I spend the anniversary of my solemn profession in the infirmary, a piece of great kindness on the part of St. Joseph as I am beginning to realize. It has all the earmarks of a plot arranged for no other purpose than to give me a little consolation on this feast and make it a *very* happy one.

As soon as I get into a cell by myself I am a different person! Prayer becomes what it ought to be. Everything is very quiet. The door is closed but I have the window open. It is warm – grey clouds fly – all night and all day the frogs sing. Reverend Father sold all the ducks (Fr. Peter kept proclaiming Bro. Isidore and Bro. Cyril because the ducks quacked all night), and it is an improvement.

This is the way I happened to come to the infirmary.

Tuesday I got a cold. It was warm and damp and, when I walked into the church to pray in the afternoon interval before work, something got in my throat and I have been coughing a lot. That night in the dormitory was no fun nor was the one after. The paint made me feel ill. I coughed a lot. Lungs full of green slime. Finally, yesterday morning, Thursday, I came up to Fr. Gerard and found out I had a slight temperature, 99 or so. However it got worse. Yesterday was full of penance. I tried to finish going over the ms. of *Waters of Siloe*, but finally left it in a good enough condition to be sent off, though not completely gone over. Reverend Father sent me up to the infirmary again towards the end of the afternoon work, and since by that time the thermometer was up to 101, they put me to bed in the room marked St. Gertrude.

I was in this same room six years ago today with the same thing, "flu." It is the one Brother Hugh died in. However, it does not look as though I am going to stay long.

As I came up the steps the thought came to me that maybe I might be fortunate enough to develop pneumonia and even die. How nice it would be to celebrate Easter in heaven! However, I have too much penance left to do on earth, and I don't want to get out of it necessarily.

But even with your eyes aching and your head spinning, how good it is to be alone, in silence. How close God is in this room! The presence of people around me is always something that divides my attention between the world and God: well, not always either. At meditation or after Communion in church, I generally don't know that anyone else is there. But in the intervals people moving about are a distraction.

To have nothing to do but abandon yourself to God and love God! It is the greatest of luxuries. Silence and solitude are the supreme luxuries of life!

Anyway, I woke up about the time the bell was ringing for Lauds. I was soaked in sweat and that meant most of the fever was gone. I lay awake and listened to the frogs.

How this silence keeps claiming you for itself! As soon as you start anything, it says, "Come back for a moment! Pray! Be quiet! Rest in your God!"

Plenty of time! Plenty of time! No manuscripts, no typewriter, no rushing back and forth to church, no Scriptorium, no breaking your neck to get things done before the next thing happens!

I went down to Chapter because Reverend Father wants you to go to Chapter if your temperature is less than 100. Mine was. Fr. Amadeus preached vehemently on the sufferings of St. Joseph, his mental sufferings when he discovered that Mary was with child. I should not have made funny faces when he said Abraham was born 1,959 years after the creation of the world, nor can I figure out why he imagines that this event should be commemorated next year, 1949. But he says things like that; they come into his head and he says them.

Then I came back to the cell. On the table were bread and butter and a can of barley coffee, and before I said the *Largitor* [Prayer before eating], Fr. Gerard came in with the bottle of Mass wine in which much was left because Fr. Odo could not say Mass. And he said, "This is a *feast* day," and poured out half a tumbler of wine. He was not aware of any anniversary of mine, but it was then that I realized what was going on, and that St. Joseph had arranged all this as a way of giving me some manifestations of God's love, and that I might have joy.

So I drank the wine and it was good and it gave me back my appetite. For last night butter was hateful and I could not eat it.

Then I moved the table to the window and ate looking out of the window as the Carthusians do. The clouds flew, and the huts of the ducks were empty and the frogs sang in the beautiful green pond.

And it was a very happy feast day. Now I shall say Sext.

Now it is evening. The frogs still sing. After the showers of rain around dinner time, the sky cleared. All afternoon I sat on the bed rediscovering the meaning of contemplation, rediscovering God, rediscovering myself, and the Office and Scripture and everything.

It has been one of the most wonderful days I have ever known in my life, and yet I am not attached to that part of it either. My pleasure or the contentment I may have got out of silence and solitude and freedom from all care does not matter. But I know that is the way I ought to be *living*: with my mind and senses silent, contacts with the world of business and war and community troubles severed – not solicitous for anything high or low or far or near – not pushing myself around with my own fancies or desires or projects – and not letting myself get hurried off my feet by the excessive current of natural activity that flows through Gethsemani with full force.

Once again the question arises: is it possible to be quiet in an atmosphere like the one in this house? Should I move somewhere where I can find solitude and silence and peace to be alone with God in this pure tranquility that is impossible for a Cistercian?

Fr. Anthony came up in the evening. He said if I wanted to be a Carthusian, he would never oppose me. On the other hand, Europe is out of the question.

But there is no hurry. No need to be solicitous or anxious about that any more than anything else. God is hidden within me. I find Him by hiding in the silence in which He is concealed. All things that are not means to purify my heart and give it tranquility in His will are useless. But if I follow Him, He will lead me to His peace.

Tomorrow I go back downstairs to the community and the dormitory full of paint. And I hope it will be with a mind able to say "No" to all cares and anxieties and ambitions and ventures and images and things that have no profit for union with God in darkness above the level of change and desire and delight and sorrow and greatness and littleness and life and death and everything else that is not God alone.

I go to say Matins of Our Lady of Sorrows.

March 20, 1948. Our Lady of Sorrows

I feel as if I were in a hotel in Cuba. The landscape has something of the grey-green-yellow nondescript color that belongs to Cuba. And the air is full of the sound of birds and water frogs and tree frogs and crows, too. As for those frogs, as I lay awake last night for several hours listening to them, I began to get a bit bored with their lyricism. They are inexhaustible and ring those same bicycle bells all day and all night. I began to think: don't they ever *do* anything, don't they ever stop to eat? Then when I was just about to fall asleep, they all stopped for 30 seconds and the silence was so astonishing that I woke up.

I woke up when the bell rang for the Night Office at 2:00, and got up at 3:30, but it turns out that I stay up here for today.

After Communion I found myself asking Our Lady that, if it were God's will, I might be in a Charterhouse by next Easter.

Then, as I was eating mixt, Fr. Gerard came in with what was left of the Mass wine and said, "There is nothing that so strengthens a man as a drink of wine." It tastes like very dry sherry. I suppose there is worse wine in the world. However, it tasted a little like medicine to me today.

Fr. Anthony is definitely upset about the community. Reverend Father has overworked himself against the advice and even the polite orders of everyone from the General on down and has lost touch with things. The house is full of nervousness and unrest. People are overworked and overstrained and the novitiate is allowed to fill with all manner of fish. Fr. Anthony is having a hard time reconciling himself to the fact that Reverend Father wants insufficiently endowed characters to become priests.

March 21, 1948. Palm Sunday

Palm Sunday on the Feast of St. Benedict, 850 years to the day from the foundation of Cîteaux, for some time I got away from the frogs. Now I am back with them. The landscape is nice. White fluffy clouds, late afternoon sky. Brother Cyril feeds the chickens. And for a wonder the frogs are all quiet.

During the High Mass I kept thinking of the Christ Who is crucified in His Body, His enemies armed against Him in Europe, and His voice singing in our church in Kentucky: *Deus, Deus meus, respice in me, ut quid dereliquisti me* . . . [God, my God, look upon me, why have you forsaken me . . . (Psalms 21:1).]

Unbelievably peaceful here! I think of the church, the way it was at the end of Benediction, and of Fr. John Baptist setting the monstrance back on the altar, and all the brothers and monks getting up off their knuckles on the floor, and some sunlight coming in on the nearby varnished floor. And I thought: we are still at peace.

March 22, 1948. Monday in Holy Week

Reverend Father in Chapter told (again) about how Blessed Henry Suso looked out the window and saw a dog shaking and tearing an old rag and got an interior illumination, that that was the way he himself was to be treated, and he applied it to us and said that is the way *we* ought to expect to be treated. Only he didn't say it as directly as that.

Right after that he suddenly got the community to vote on the proposal of accepting an offer of a place in South Carolina for a new foundation. He first announced it on the Feast of St. Joseph, last Friday, saying he would tell us more about it and get a vote after Easter.

The vote is only a preliminary, a "feeler." Eight black votes came of it, including one from me.

The offer is a 7,000 acre place thirty-eight miles from Charleston, South Carolina, a gift from Henry Luce or Clare Boothe Luce. It is on a mile-wide estuary of some river. Reverend Father isn't very good at names. It is twenty-five miles or so from the sea. Luce used it to go duck hunting and the forest is full of game. But we don't hunt. The ground will grow at least potatoes, but from all indications it must be pretty poor.

My reasons for a black vote are, first, we haven't had any real thought about the thing, we don't know about it, and the procedure doesn't seem to me to be very regular. I am not so sure we have any authority from higher superiors. Secondly, I don't think we are *capable* of making a third foundation, even if we wait until 1950, which I'll bet we won't. The house is practically drained of good men already. Who will be superiors there – and here? We are expanding beyond our limits. It would make much more sense if we stayed at home and weeded out some of the useless plants we have planted in our garden and cleaned up Gethsemani and tried to make a first-rate community of ourselves and stopped admitting everyone that walks in the front door.

However, I know it is the Cistercian tradition to refuse no one who "really seeks God." But the General's Visitation Card is explicit enough on the matter of taking useless subjects.

Then I think the climate there will be not only extremely hard, but unhealthy. I remember what it was like sitting on the estuary of the Rapahannock in Virginia. Of course, rich people build themselves a palace of pleasure in places that are intolerable, so it must be all right, at least in winter.

Still, it doesn't matter who objects, as the thing is going through anyway.

Saturday I sent the ms. of *Waters of Siloe* to Naomi Burton and another to Fr. Gabriel at the Valley. Fr. George was making disciplines, and I got him to bless the ms., which he did. It is a wonder it didn't explode. I said some strong things about the spirit of de Rancé and La Trappe.

Holy Week – well, there goes the bell ringer to ring his bell.

What I was going to say about Holy Week is the obedience of Christ. If this foundation goes through – and it almost certainly will – the ones who get sent will have their martyrdom mapped out for them. They will have their chance to become saints.

Yet I still wish we could plan monasteries as Edens of contemplation rather than hells of heat and activity. Perhaps it is the prudence of the world that makes me have such thoughts. Utah is fine. It seems to me that we should pick places where we can really live our rule well. However, now we are broke and can't choose. But I don't think we need another foundation.

Anyway, some of us will have a very good chance to imitate the obedience of Christ, dumb as a lamb before the shearers.

March 24, 1948. Wednesday in Holy Week

In the last two days I have been depressed and unhappy. I suppose it is the after-effects of 'flu, and the devil trying to upset me about the South Carolina foundation. Lately the more I think about it, the more it seems to me to add up to seven thousand acres of fever and snakes. But that cannot be true. Millionaires don't build houses in swamps. And evidently it is a splendid house with very fancy gardens.

Really, it is easy to see the point of the foundation. Reverend Father says it would be a sin to refuse such an offer, and he is clearly right. If it costs a sacrifice to try and make a monastery out of it, so much the better. I'll offer up my anguish as part of Holy Week, in union with Christ in His garden and His agony. And, in any case, I am not surprised at my own weakness and my own crazy imagination. Both of them have been giving me the same kind of work-out for thirty-three years. So I'll accept them as they are and let God's grace carry me through all things that may come. I want His will to be done perfectly in me. If my nature and emotions get upset, so much the better. It will remind me of who I am and Who He is and will make me rely on Him and not on myself.

I had the same trouble about Utah. I got the idea we might have to dig our own coal, and then began to see myself buried in a mine two thousand feet under the earth, with the last mouthful of air giving out, and the monks feebly hacking at the rocks with pick-axes a mile away from the right place . . . And now I am in South Carolina: damp moss hangs from the trees, you can barely see ten feet through the miasmas of the swamp. Nearby I recognize the tree on which the local citizens lynched four of the other monks. All around me the water moccasins slither through the grass, and I wonder if I can't get a pair of high leather boots to keep the snakes from biting me on the legs. Is that moss on the branch of that tree, or is it another snake?

Tomorrow is Holy Thursday. I expect Easter with more than the holy joy St. Benedict recommends. Maybe the risen Christ will give back to my mind some kind of a healthy life and take away the spooks. But it is terrible: I think of what is happening to the Church in the whole world and turn pale to the soles of my feet. *Infirma mundi elegit Deus.* [The foolish things of the world hath God chosen (1 Corinthians 1:27).] I think of the way our monks in China were scourged to death by the Reds: men as weak as I with my feelings, my fears, my sufferings, my sensitivity.

Well, anyway, the sun is shining. It is a nice day. I'll leave the rest to God.

March 25, 1948. Holy Thursday

The cloud has lifted.

One of the big graces of Holy Week came by surprise yesterday. External graces almost always do come that way, I mean the big ones, by surprise. Three books which I think must have been ordered for us by Dom Marie-Joseph arrived from Éditions du Cerf. One by Louis Bouyer, *Le Mystère Pascal* [Paris, 1945], was precisely what I most needed and I began reading it before Vespers yesterday.

It reminds me in a good, direct way of the fundaments of the whole Christian life and teaches me, as I ought to have realized but never did, just how important a place Holy Thursday holds in Christianity. Before, I had always been a little uncomfortable, trying to place it, and I suppose, like so many others of our age, I thought I understood the Mystery of the Eucharist better where it is really *less* relevant: separated from its most vital and active context and isolated in the feast of Corpus Christi.

An understanding of the real meaning of the Easter liturgy, the Paschal Sacrifice and resurrection of Christ, is the key to all my troubles, especially interior ones about the life and the priesthood.

Today I want to go to this great Mass with my mind clearer of all kinds of preoccupations – not that I am especially attached to the typical wrong emphases that obscure the real meaning of the liturgy – but to abandon any tendency to hold on to a complex of human rubbish and let Christ teach me in this "action" in which time and everything in it and all reality is elevated and transformed.

Then too, I will discover what I need to know about the priesthood and my vocation as a priest. It is *not enough* to consider the Blessed Sacrament as a static object – a Person if you like – but a mere static presence locked up in the Tabernacle and waiting for "visits," so as to receive and give personal consolation. The center of all spiritual life is Christ in His Mass, Christ our Pasch who is slain and "dieth now no more," *iam non moritur,* but "draws all things to Himself," *omnia traham ad meipsum,* that we, baptized in His death, crucifying our flesh and its desires, may live His life with a life hidden in Christ in God. And the heart of all life is not merely in the static presence of the Blessed Sacrament, although Christ is truly living in our tabernacles, but above all in the *action* of the Mass that is the center of all contemplation, an action in which the Christian family is gathered around Christ and in which Christ in His Body glorifies His Father. A sacrament of living unity in which the Love Who is God unites men to God and men to one another in Christ. When the Mass discovers its meaning, then devotion to the Blessed Sacrament reserved in the Tabernacle acquires its own true meaning also and begins to live. But then also the whole interior life is unified and vitalized and every department of it flows with life. In fact, "departments" and "sections" of one's life cease to exist in isolation and everything functions together.

History and the terrible things that are happening and will happen in our time, all the events planned by Christ's love, all things fuse and become transformed in this hour, this "mystery of faith" which our century is trying to rediscover.

I go to that altar offering Christ a sorry world to give to His Father in Thanksgiving, [a world] transformed into His own human life by our union with Him and His union with us in His Sacrifice and our Sacrifice which is His Pasch.

O God, give peace to Your world. Give strength to the hearts of men. Raise us up from death in Christ. Give us to eat His immortality and His glory. Give us to drink the wine of His Kingdom.

March 28, 1948. Easter Sunday

> *Post transitum maris rubri*
> *Christo canamus principi.*
> [Having crossed the Red Sea
> Let us sing to Christ our prince.]

When we sang the *Benedicamus Domino* with two alleluias at the end of Lauds, it seemed to me as if only three days had passed since we sang it the Saturday before Septuagesima, two months ago.

All the Easter *alleluia* antiphons come back to me with rich associations of the happiest days in my life – the seven Paschal seasons that I have had in the monastery – this being the seventh now beginning: the Sabbatical.

All the apple trees came out in blossom Good Friday. It rained and got colder, but today is very bright with a pure, pure sky. The willow is full of green. Things are all in bud.

And in my heart, the deepest peace, Christ's clarity, lucid and quiet and ever-present as eternity. On these big feasts you come out on top of a plateau in the spiritual life to get a new view of everything. Especially Easter. Easter is like what it will be entering eternity, when you suddenly, peacefully, clearly recognize all your mistakes as well as all that you did well: everything falls into place.

Sanctity! That is, of course, the thing. And you have a long way to go. And you have been deceived and mixed up in a tangle of illusory problems. The state of the house, for instance – the advisability of the new foundation – mistrusting Reverend Father – attaching too much importance to the inevitable failures and mistakes of men, including your own.

All these mistakes and failures and stupidities and cross-purposes and imperfections enter into God's plan for your sanctification. Why do you strain yourself in your efforts to keep everything going in a way that pleases your human prudence: fearing sickness, fearing sleeplessness, worrying about your work, worrying about the monastery, devising plans to improve the regular life of the house? All these things are good in themselves, but not one of them demands the kind of preoccupation you give it. It is true that we are provincial and do not have all the perfection of the Cistercian Spirit, and we should desire that perfection and work for it. But it is wrong to get upset at the obstacles and delays. All that enters into God's plan for your sanctification, for the perfection of His risen life in you.

Quae sursum sunt sapite non quae super terram. [Mind the things that are above, not the things that are on the earth (Colossians 3:2).]

What a mistake to judge your community at all! It is the community God has chosen and planned for your sanctification and His glory. You must work to improve it for His glory. But if you fail, do not despair and think everything is wasted. Does God's glory depend on the success of your ideas? Does your sanctity consist in bringing everybody around to see things the way you see them? And anyway, is Gethsemani as bad as you think, as bad as it looks to you on the days when you have not slept? Even if it were, it would be good *for you*. It would be the situation God's love had prepared for you, for your perfection, for His glory, for the peace of the world.

And yet, not only today but for several months, I have loved my brothers very much. I have great affection for them and I thank God for it, and I desire their sanctification as I desire my own.

In the library I looked at that marvelous book *The Faces of the Saints* [by Wilhelm Schamoni, London, 1948], pictures as near as possible genuine portraits – contemporary – of saints. The Patristic ones from mosaics were some of the most beautiful. St. Catherine of Siena, too, and another I have forgotten. More modern ones – some of the death-masks frighten me. St. Vincent de Paul looks very real, very much of a Gascon peasant and tough as he can be. Terrific energy in the man's face, fiery black eyes and a mouth like a bear trap. The one that most astonished me was St. Francis de Sales. He was ponderous and unlike anything I would have imagined. On the other hand, after the book we had about St. Clement Hofbauer last winter in the refectory, his heavy German face did not surprise me one bit.

One that most impressed me, St. Benedict Joseph Labre. One that scared me least, John Bosco. Also St. Catherine of Genoa looked nice and normal for a mystic, and Louise de Marillac was a French housewife in her picture. St. Mary Magdalen de' Pazzi looked a little like my mother. St. Aloysius Gonzaga was too beautiful. St. Theresa was funny, a plump little Spanish lady, like an innkeeper's wife in that picture, with all due respect.

But I love her. St. John of the Cross I knew: looks surprisingly unascetic. The saint's face that is most really to me the face of a saint is the child's face of St. Francis of Assisi with big, astonished eyes looking out from that over-ample hood – the famous thirteenth century portrait.

Some saints I had never heard of I wanted to love as soon as I saw their pictures, but I have already forgotten their names.

But all of them had faces that had suffered: some more, some less, some very intensely.

Last year I was very supercilious about the Easter liturgy. This year I have followed the Holy Week liturgy consciously and more intelligently, without extra fuss or anything, but immensely helped and stimulated by the Bouyer book. It has done me an immense amount of good. Yet, both this year and last, much peace. Easter grace.

This year, however, I think it is deeper and more powerful and much more serene. Not troubled by any shadow of anything, not for lack of occasion, but the grace of these days seems to have taken much more completely hold of me than ever before. And it came from being more immersed in the liturgy. I take back most of what I said last year.

One very sad thing: a plane crashed in our woods yesterday afternoon about two o'clock. Six people all killed, terribly mangled, bodies cut to pieces and then burned – a woman's hand up in a tree – two children in the wreck. They were going somewhere for Easter, just getting near Louisville. What a terrible Easter for some family, or two families! I hope the reason God let them crash here at this time was to give them a part in our prayers.

All day at the Collect I thought about them and hoped they had found mercy with God.

April 4, 1948. Low Sunday. Day of Recollection

We prayed for fair weather for our planting and lo, today was the fairest I ever saw. Clear sky and warm sun and when you came out of church and looked through the open cloister windows, you saw the pale green flowers on the maples in the *préau* and all the shrubs in flower, too.

During the week they lighted the orchard heaters to fight the frost and the farm looked like a valley in hell until dawn, when they put them out again, and the pipes smoked as the sun rose on the hoar-fields, and the monastery smelled faintly of gasoline.

Fr. Edward got a bad throat and I was cantor for three days. The first day I was unprepared and made a lot of mistakes. I had not realized that some of the Easter Week Masses were difficult. I knew all the *alleluias* because I had practiced them before.

Tomorrow: the Annunciation, transferred. After that, St. Benedict.

Lambs bleat under the cedars by the sheep barn and the other day we looked at all the little pigs running around on the hillsides and charging upon the teats of their huge mothers.

Last Monday, when I had prayed hard at Communion for the community, Reverend Father announced in Chapter that, in the future no one would be admitted to profession unless he could get past an examination by a psychiatrist. That is a big improvement. This kind of life is not good for neurotics. They might keep their balance outside, but here they crack up. It is remarkable how many of them break down just before getting to the priesthood. God has weeded out His vocations where men failed to do it for Him. I pray that He won't pull me out of His garden because now I am beginning to see how all the glory we can give Him is in the Mass.

I am writing a leaflet on contemplation with a Dominican Tertiary in Erie which she says she can get Sister Madeleva to print. Already it is more than a leaflet. I go slow and rewrite. Today, instead of writing about contemplation, I *had* some of it and it was good to rest and stop fussing and tugging at my wits for useless ideas.

More nourishment and strength in one hour of obscurity than in ten weeks of typewriting and reading and thinking. Nevertheless, every day love corners me somewhere and surrounds me with peace without my having to look very far or very hard or do anything special. God is Who He is and therefore my life needs nothing else but Him.

April 7, 1948. St. Joachim

All our prayers for dry weather were not answered as fast as we thought for it has been raining cats and dogs for two days. Yesterday with hailstones hitting the windows like a war, I finished the pamphlet on contemplation and today Fr. Anthony as censor made me signs that he was not pleased with it *at all*. So in a minute I go to confession to find out what is wrong. Over the two feast days, St. Benedict and the Annunciation, both transferred, I got practically no sleep, three hours and no meridiennes. On St. Benedict's day Fr. Edward's voice went off again and I had to take over the choir.

For some reason *Commonweal* wants me to review [Francisco De] Osuna's *Third Spiritual Alphabet*, which appeared four hundred years ago. But the Newman Bookshop has reprinted the translation.

Tonight was the first time in six years I have been here that we sang the hymn for St. Joachim. Usually his Vespers are eclipsed by St. Joseph and St. Benedict. I discovered only after Vespers that I had never seen the thing before. Time came for me to give it out and I wondered, "What do all those black marks on the red lines mean?" So I gave it out wrong and went and fell on my face under the sanctuary lamp and offered up *The Magnificat* in thanksgiving.

April 8, 1948

Everything is all mixed up. Now it is the Feast of St. Ambrose.

Yesterday I read some of the first issue of *The Hudson Review.* It is in many ways impressive. In the first place it is thick. It starts out with something by R. D. Blackmur which I haven't time to read. But above all their manifesto is good, although in very heavy language. They are looking for discipline and consciously striving after formal perfection. They are not just a place where malcontents can gather and let off steam and air their experiences. I think it is very healthy in principle and perhaps that is why I have felt a lot like praying for them, even before seeing the thing.

"The Summer Campaign" is a terrifying war story in this first issue of HR. I read it. Everything unidentified. You don't know *who* the people are, what side they are on, in what country they are fighting, but at the same time the features of the living and dead are described in vivid detail. All the physical violence is in sharp outline with the appropriate colors, at least the fundamental ones. It is a very extraordinary piece of writing and says all that needs to be said, in this indirect way, about the complete inhumanity of war.

Laughlin writes that they (the U.S. – and I don't mean "we") have discovered an atomic cloud that will sweep over cities in the wind and silently wipe everything out. Laughlin wants to know if this is the wrath of God. I'll tell him what I think. What enrages me most is that apparently no Catholic moralist seems to have anything much to *say* about all this. Perhaps that is one of the reasons why the wars are getting to be as bad as they are now.

What Father Anthony did not like about the leaflet was the assertion that mystical contemplation was for everybody and was an integral part in Christian perfection, but he told me that I could hold it and he didn't want me to delete a word of it, and I won't if I can help it, except to make clearer what I mean. Because if contemplation – experimental knowledge of God – is given with the perfection of love for God that empties a man of all other affections, then it is certainly integral to Christian perfection. As a matter of fact, it is given to plenty of people who do not attain that perfection on earth.

But anyway the thing I can't understand is how anyone can live for two days in a place like this without desiring mystical union with God. What else is there to live for here or anywhere? His will? But to be united with Him in contemplation is a more perfect union with His will. In fact, to say you love His will *without* desiring union of love with Him, knowledge of Him, is to contradict yourself. Because that is His will: "That they may be one in us." Jesus told us that, if we did His will, He and His Father and His Spirit would come and dwell in us, that eternal life was to know Him and His Father. If we say we *don't* want that union, or want it to remain a secret from ourselves, what are we driving at anyway? How can we want His will perfectly if we have no interest in the perfect union of wills which is the end of the whole spiritual life, of all love and all obedience?

April 11, 1948. Good Shepherd Sunday
Jesus, the "Shepherd and Bishop" of our souls, gave me many graces appropriate to this day. *Ego cognosco eas et cognoscunt me meae.* [I know mine, and mine know me (John 10:14).] "My sheep hear my voice." I read over St. John of the Cross' *Cautions*, which were the things I had in mind to keep when I made solemn profession, and I saw to my dismay how much I had forgotten them.

How occupied I am with what goes on in the community, preoccupied with the personnel of the house, the faults of character, physical deficiencies of the monks, the weaknesses of the choir, the way we lead our life, etc. Preoccupied with all these details I still let them upset me instead of handling all that with supernatural peace and indifference. I am still so much more occupied with created things than with God their Creator.

I let my mind fill with all the little irrelevancies about Reverend Father's character, and his age, and his way of doing things. How weak and human my obedience is: always considering the way things affect me in my own personal tastes and judgments.

I went to Fr. Placid in the confessional and he told me I was too restless and that what I was looking for (union with God) was right in front of my nose and I couldn't see it. Also there was no earthly reason why any amount of work should prevent my union with God, provided it is His will.

And all that is true. My mind is scattered among things, not because of my work, but because I am not detached and I do not attend first of all to God. On the other hand, I do not attend to Him because I am so absorbed in all these objects and events. I have to wait on His grace. But how stubborn and slow my nature is. And how I keep confusing myself and complicating things for myself by useless twisting and turning.

What I need most of all is the grace to really accept God as He gives Himself to me in every situation. "He came unto His own and His own received Him not."

Good Shepherd, You have a wild and crazy sheep in love with thorns and brambles. But please don't get tired of looking for me! I know You won't. For You have found me. All I have to do is stay found.

April 25, 1948. St. Mark

Everything went well in Italy, and Dom Eugène of Aiguebelle was here and gave us an extremely interesting talk, so everybody feels happier.

However, since we had the Litanies today, I prayed more for peace and for our Order, that we should be simple and keep everything straight.

The two volumes of Marcel Aubert on Cistercian architecture in France finally arrived. Fr. Anselme Dimier got them for us, and it is a wonderful book. Then I sent *The Spirit of Simplicity* off to the printer. The *imprimatur* didn't come from Louisville after some sixteen months of waiting, so Reverend Father sent it to Cincinnati and got an *imprimatur* in a few weeks.

Thursday I went out and got a big blister on the palm of my hand digging mud out of a ditch along the west side of the upper bottom, and everything was beautiful. The spring is in its first stages of transformation. All the trees are full of small leaves just beginning to unfold and work themselves out into something. There are flowers in the ditches and along the edges of the woods and in the woods, too, I suppose, but I haven't been there.

The more selfish you are, the more involved life becomes. As usual I have to check my appetite for books and work and keep close to God in prayer, which is what He wants.

April 27, 1948

Tomorrow is the commemoration of St. Vital and, after that, St. Robert's feast. Today we had the Votive Office of St. Bernard. I went to see Reverend Father before Mass and he surprised me by saying it was likely we would make still a fourth foundation in Adams County, Ohio, wherever that might be. At any rate it is in the archdiocese of Cincinnati.

Incidentally, the South Carolina foundation is now definite. The land has been accepted. I got a glimpse of some huge photographs of the house which are in a portfolio leaning against the wall in Reverend Father's chapel. It is a fancy, modernistic place, very clean and full of that stall furniture which the monks probably won't be able to use. There is a swimming pool and I believe there is also a bar. But not for us.

In a scatter-brained moment of enthusiasm ten days ago or so, I tried to get Reverend Father to send Clare Boothe Luce a book about Charles de Foucauld on the grounds that she might get excited about it and promote it into a movie, which is a thought I have been cherishing in secret for, oh, maybe a year.

Anyway the colony for South Carolina will leave – provisionally this is the date – in the fall of 1949. A lot of things can happen between now and then, but the smoke in my imagination has cleared. Naturally I will go wherever I am sent. What other thing would make sense for a monk? I think we ought to plan small foundations from now on, monasteries that would themselves found houses as soon as they go over sixty or seventy men in them.

April 28, 1948

When Dom Eugène was here, I heard for the first time of the apparitions of Our Lady at Tre Fontane and at Bonate. At the moment in the refectory Fr. Edward is trying to read a translation written by Fr. Odo of an account of the Tre Fontane apparition. It is all on bits of brown wrapping paper and Fr. Odo's hand must be getting very shaky because there are a lot of long pauses in the reading. Reverend Father knew about it all a long time ago, but wouldn't let the news get around in the community.

Before that we had a good book by a young Jesuit called Fr. McCorry, S.J. The book had for its title *Most Worthy of All Praise*. So was the book. It was sensible and good and it was addressed to nuns. I am glad I am not the chaplain of a convent.

Second set of galleys of *Seven Storey Mountain* – up to about the middle. This thing is going very slow. It looks better with cuts and I cut some more, but not much.

I am too full all the time. Worse than last year, except that I am no longer worrying about the problem of vocation, since that is useless. It is a great improvement to be able to rest in the elementary conviction that God really is directing my life to His own ends without my being able to see how He is getting me anywhere except into a hole. Yet, once in a while, I can see where it makes sense.

Nevertheless for my own part, I have got to be much more *supple* than I have been. How stiff I am: I am a piece of wood in the spiritual life. So much inertia, stupidity. I am so gross in my distractions and attachments. My head is full of work, or else I grind in anguish over some silly repugnance like the flatness of the choir. In all this God is leading me and God is working with me, and even my grossness somehow can fit into His plan.

The only relief – simple awareness of His love, the rest and joy communicated by His presence, when He allows my mind to relax and perceive it. How well I know that it can only be His gift!

Well, I am content to have a mountain of labor ahead of me in the interior life, just to keep myself free for God. I am content to be a beginner, and nothing at all. It is so good at least to be inside a monastery, to be before the Tabernacle, to be chanting in a choir of monks, and to be called to be a saint, even though I am so far from it.

It seems to me the most absurd thing in the world is to be upset because I am weak and distracted and blind and constantly make mistakes! What else do I expect! Does God love me any less because I can't make myself a saint by my own power and in my own way? He loves me more because I am so clumsy and helpless without Him. Underneath what I am He sees me as I will one day be by His pure gift and that pleases Him, and, therefore, it pleases me, and I attend to His great love which is my joy.

People misunderstand and dislike the things I write. Not many, but some do. And Fr. Anthony is definitely suspicious of me now. He tells me so. I don't mind.

I will never argue with a censor. I don't have to. I can say all God wants me to say in the right area where no controversy enters at all. I don't care about difficult technical questions and would rather avoid them. The Holy Ghost did not bring me here to break my head over problems of terminology and language.

May 2, 1948. Day of Recollection
No more than last year or the year before that or the year before do I succeed in entering into a less complicated way of life. Still tangled up in my

own nature to an extent that would terrify me, if I were able to realize it. The wonder is that I should expect anything else.

Be content to be blind and helpless. My first trouble is [that] I insist on wanting to *see*. I want to have everything in the interior life tapped and under my own control. Fundamentally it is a desire to be a contemplative without depending on God. Too close to the sin of Lucifer to be comfortable!

Oh God, teach me to be satisfied with my own helplessness in the spiritual life. Teach me to be content with Your grace that comes to me in darkness and works things I cannot see. Teach me to be happy that I can depend on You. That should be enough for an eternity of joy. That by itself ought to be infinitely greater than any joy my own intellectual appetite could desire.

My interior activity must begin gradually to die down. (But it tends to *increase!*)

All the useless twisting and turning of my nature, analyzing the faults of the community and the choir, and figuring out what is wrong with everything and what *could* be right; comparing our life to the 12th century with what we have today, trying to figure some way to make a break and get into solitude: with all these things I have lost time and made myself suffer and I have ruined the work of God in my soul.

And I still get mad when I have to go on [perform] ceremonies in the sanctuary because I don't like to run around in an alb carrying a candle. It is my punishment, I mean the repugnance is my punishment, for imagining that I had outgrown the childish imperfections that people have. Well, I haven't. But I won't make it worse by lamentations.

A long, long way to go, a long time to be patient and humble *sub potenti manu Dei* [under the powerful hand of God], hoping God will help me to be quiet and stop thinking about the things that are without profit, all this interior activity that is my daily torture when my whole soul longs to rest in God and cannot. *Circuibunt civitatem sicut canes.* [They sniff around the city like dogs.]

It is useless to complain in the confessional. Fr. Anthony has decided to be firm and tell me that my desire for solitude and contemplation is selfish, and that I must resign myself to a life of hard work. I only partly believe him. I know that there is too much nature in my desires for peace and fruition of God – sure. That is evident. That is why I have to toil so much, to get it out of me.

On the other hand, this business of being condemned to the active life of practices and meditations that satisfy so many people: it doesn't even upset me because I know that I don't have to suffer that. So the only one I can look to for any help is God, and not by trying to make Him hurry either.

Wind and sun. Cat-bird bickering in a bush. Ringing bells and blowing whistles and then squawking in a lamentable fashion. Trees are all clothed and benches are out and a new summer has begun.

May 4, 1948

I am interested in that magazine, *The Catholic C.O.* *[The Catholic Conscientious Objector]*, which Larsson sends me. I don't entirely understand what they are driving at, or rather what is the basis of the things they claim. For in that they are not very clear. And yet it seems to me more and more that nowadays a Christian ought to be something very close to an *absolute pacifist*.

Of course they can treat the whole question with a sublime disdain for all the stupid niceties of moral theology that people argue about, and perhaps they are lucky. Will anybody listen to them?

What is this Christian anarchism? Robert Ludlow says he is a Christian anarchist. No organized state. That is a hot one, but secretly I am attracted to that sort of thing. Tell it to the hierarchy. Tell it to St. Peter, for that matter: *[Servi,] subdite estote . . . [in omni timore dominis, non tantum bonis et modestis, sed] etiam dyscolis.]* [Servants, be subject to your masters with all fear; not only to the good and gentle, but also to the forward (1 Peter 2:18).] – obey the King. I don't think there can *be* such a thing as a Christian anarchist, but I *do* know that *justis non est lex posita* [the law is not made for the just man (1 Timothy 1:9)], and *ubi autem Spiritus Domini ibi libertas.* [And where the Spirit of the Lord is, there is liberty (2 Corinthians 3:17).] Anarchy is a waste of time and a way of getting many headaches.

May 6, 1948. Ascension

Usually this is my feast, the most beautiful of the year. It rained all day, but that made no difference.

Yesterday Fr. Anthony and I went out and blessed the fields, starting with the wheat and oats and coming around by St. Bernard's field and Aidan Nally's and across to the bottoms. Out in the calf pasture we blessed some calves who came running up and took a very active interest in everything.

Then we blessed pigs, who showed some interest at first. The sheep showed no concern and the chickens ran away as soon as we approached. The rabbits stayed quiet until we threw holy water at them and then they all jumped.

But today was beautiful. It seems to me I have been foolish not to let God run my life entirely. Why do I want to will anything or seek anything for myself? Why should I get so concerned about things like absolute perfection in chant and architecture and liturgy and all the rest – the Cistercian life – in such a way as to get upset when I can't make everything perfect just by willing it to be the way I want it to be? I should know these things and seek what is best, but with detachment, and only because God wills it and in the way He wills it, leaving the results to Him.

Trust your Superiors, and realize how much God is working in your soul and how much more He will work, if you stay quiet and don't try to plan your own life with elaborate devices to avoid the crosses God may or may not have prepared for you – like being cantor or philosophy professor in some miserable foundation. Today Reverend Father was exposing to me a simply horrible plan to begin the buildings in South Carolina with the monks and secular retreatants all huddled together in one wing. I don't think anyone will be able to talk him out of it.

Yet Brother Giles made me a sign to pray that his new plans for a slick, shiny monastery à la Frank Lloyd Wright would not make Reverend Father faint.

May 13, 1948. Octave of the Ascension

The chief thing that has been going on lately is this. Fr. Anthony seems to have got fed up with the stuff I write. In any case he has been giving me a lot of criticism on that and things in general. He has a way of seeming to be more sharp than he really means, but anyway I suppose he was building up to it for a long time before he started to talk.

I have always felt in him a suppressed hostility to my notions of contemplation and my aspirations in that sense. But he has never said anything overtly to oppose them.

Anyway, he told me that perhaps I might question the notion that I had some mission to teach contemplation to the Church in America. I more than question such a notion: I don't want any part of it. As if I didn't have enough headaches without having a big, capital "M" mission like that.

He tells me to remember I am a convert and not get into fights "in the family," "even about contemplation," things like that.

It is all O.K. I am glad to get something like that because it helps me to pray by helping me to be less occupied with things that have no real importance by cutting down on preoccupations that grow up without one's knowing it.

[I] was servant of the refectory this week. Pentecost will be in a few days. I looked into [Matthias Joseph] Scheeben's *Mysteries of Christianity* [St. Louis, 1946] and found some good pages on the Mission of the Holy Ghost. Also in St. Bonaventure and St. Thomas.

One of the Owensboro priests on retreat is supposed to have made some records of the choir singing the Conventual Mass (of the Octave) today. Waste of wax.

May 17, 1948. Whit-Monday
A beautiful Pentecost.

Returning to the fundamentals of the spiritual life: the supreme dominion of God, existing for Him, realizing that He is everything, and that my life has no other reason than to proclaim that fact. What other possible importance can life have than to belong entirely to Him Whose will is life, and to belong to Whom is to live most perfectly, if we only give Him everything. For He is the life of everything that He entirely possesses. Therefore, I give Him my freedom.

What liberty there would be in desiring nothing for myself! Once everything is God's, life becomes easy and simple. Thus the importance of humility in the contemplative life, to empty oneself of all the irrelevant desires and preoccupations that get in the way of God's love for us.

The only misery in life is to *be* something in your own eyes. As soon as you cease to worry about your spurious importance and remember that God is all-important, life becomes a joy. And how easy contemplation becomes when all that matters is your own poverty in the presence of God. For if contemplation depends on our poverty, it seems to me we can all infallibly be contemplatives, if only we know how to use the poverty which is the only thing we have plenty of. To descend into the depths of our own poverty and helplessness: how can we help finding God when we get there?

The reason for this jive was Saturday Fr. Anthony told me I was too immersed in the Middle Ages and too much of a pedant. He said I was to read some modern book. Glad of a chance to get away from my own choice and tastes, I obeyed him for the sake of the sacrifice. But providentially Dom Godefroid Bélorgey's new book, *L'Humilité Bénédictine* [Paris, 1948], came in at that moment. It is on the whole very good. So I started it and with the grace of the Holy Ghost the familiar ideas of Dom Anselme le Bail struck me in a new way and opened up new depths and let some fresh air into my prayer and delivered me from myself, and so, I have a lot to be grateful for: a recollected weekend, peaceful and free!

O God, do not let me take away from You the time that belongs to You in contemplation.

May 22, 1948. Ember Saturday

A tremendous, bright sky. I let the warm sun shine on my back. The hills were wonderful. All the green of green things is clean and dark and fresh and the sun is so high on the elliptic that the shadows of things are right under them. Under my feet is the richness of all the new crushed lime-stone, or whatever it is that has been put on all the paths in the garden.

Mr. Bruning, a little old man from Cincinnati, who is supposed to be printing *The Spirit of Simplicity*, was down here and we had some consulta-tions and fingered paper samples. I pray for the pictures of Fontenay to hurry up and come from France.

(The clock strikes eleven. How clean the bell sounds in this quiet air!)

O God, I am happy to be in Your house! *Dilexi decorem domus tuae.* [I have loved the beauty of thy house (Psalms 25:8).] *Unam petii a Domino, hanc requiram, ut inhabitem in domo Domini omnibus diebus vitae meae.* [One thing I have asked of the Lord, this will I seek after; that I may dwell in the house of the Lord, all the days of my life (Psalms 26:4).] I am reading the Aubert book on *Cistercian Architecture*, and it is fine. I think of those monasteries. I am trying to figure out whether or not a village church Fa-ther and I looked at near Lexos was Beaulieu abbey (Tarn et Garonne).

I think that the church at Valmagne must have been big for that part of the country. I think of how they ran the river through Clairvaux and Sé-nanque, and how they put the Dormitory at Fontfroide in an unusual place so that the jakes would be out over the stream. I like the name of Vauluisant and the site of Valcroissant (in the Alps of the Drome), and something fascinates me about Flaran. At Clairvaux St. Bernard's secretary worked in a cell under the dormitory stairs. The brothers had their own re-fectory next to the *Cellarium*. The guests had their own chapel. Fontenay must have been more influential than we think because the church at Kirk-stall in Yorkshire was a copy of it.

Yet Royaumont and Ourscamp do not impress me. They were too fancy. I like L'Escale Dieu in the Pyrenees and I think of the founders of Bonne-font-en-Comminges who had a hard time. They were all slow in building, from fifty to a hundred years in finishing the abbeys usually, and so during the twelfth century our saints all developed in half-finished monasteries.

Silvacane is another one that intrigues me – down in the Rhone estuary.

I wonder whether to believe the story that the monks of Leoncel moved out to a grange in a lower altitude, a warmer valley, in winter time?

I am second servant of the Refectory, and soon I will have to say None and go and put out the soup.

Someone said the hay was all in: I hoped to get out and help pitch some of the first crop. But also I'd like to get busy on an article on St. John of the Cross, with reference to those in _Horizon_.

May 27, 1948. Corpus Christi

This is the first time I have been here that Corpus Christi has not been a work day both morning and afternoon, although it is a Feast of Sermon Major and ordinarily such days are kept as full holidays in the _Usages_ and in other houses of the Order.

However the other day in Chapter Reverend Father told us that Frater Romuald, the Chinese novice who left last summer to go to the Carthusians, had been rejected by them and was wandering around England.

So after that I went and saw him and made, as humbly as I could, the suggestion that fewer of us would be tempted to go to the Carthusians if we got the time for prayer allowed by our _Usages_ on feasts of Sermon and even some feasts of two Masses. I have never seen a feast of Two Masses kept as a half-holiday here. We almost always work on the afternoon of a Feast of Sermon Minor and generally on the Feasts of Sermon Major in summer. Reverend Father said he was afraid some of the monks didn't know how to use their intervals. That of course is the reason behind it all. But since those religious are a diminishing minority, he decided at least to let us have the Feasts of Sermon Major for a start.

So today, although there was the usual rush to make elaborate mosaics of flowers all over the floor of the cloisters, we had time to get our wits together and read and think and pray in the afternoon after clearing up the flowers again, which took about half an hour.

We finished Night Office at 4:20. I got busy on our design: a crown for Christ the King at the door of the refectory, and had the essentials established in sawdust and cedar-greens about 4:45. Fr. Odilo let me at the flowers and we were well under way by Prime. The whole thing was finished by about 8:00. I notice that Fr. John, a veteran, and Fr. Anthony who has no patience with this elaborate business, finished their design in much less time, not having put a grain of anything on the floor before Prime, since they were saying Mass.

That would have left me about an hour and a quarter to get recollected and sink into the reality of the Feast. However, it is a feast of sacrifice – *memoriale passionis Domini* [memorial of the Lord's passion]. The rest of the time was spent running around trying to allay the confusion surrounding the more wildly elaborate efforts, jobs that could scarcely be finished in a full work day by any two religious alone!

In other houses of the Order they are content to do what the *Usages* prescribe: scatter a few flowers on the pavement and then go pray. However, this is a respectable Gethsemani custom, and customs of the house are God's will, and I think most of the monks would rather do that than pray: to them it represents great love of God. For me then, it remains to conform myself to them and keep quiet and not upset them by trying to make things better for those of my own bent. After all, it is Reverend Father's spirituality, too: active, sacrificial, ascetic. O.K. All I need to do is keep in union with him and I please God.

May 30, 1948. Day of Recollection

I just upset the whole house by spilling half a bottle of ink on our cowl and then running to Reverend Father for ink eradicator, which didn't work, and then trying to get another cowl from somewhere. Fr. Placid had one because he preaches to the guests, and he lent it to me. It was in the room where he is making a shiny model of the new monastery in Utah to dazzle all the guests that come for the Centenary.

Fr. Raymond lent me [Giovanni] Papini's new book, *The Letters of Pope Celestine VI* [New York, 1948], and although it is a bit scatterbrained in parts and a little out of line here and there, it is full of things that need to be said, which it says, things that comfort and encourage me and make me glad and help me.

So far the strongest parts I have read are those about priests, monks and theologians.

That we are narrow, small, mediocre, stuffy, restricted. That we tend to lose contact with life and to lose the feel of vital issues, the sense of real needs. The bookishness of religious, occupied with accidentals, people perishing from spiritual starvation and theologians rehashing a lot of sterile technicalities that nourish no one. All these things I feel, and he is not just talking to make a noise. However, there is a lot more rhetoric than substance in much of it, and I also tend to wonder if the real Popes, in their real encyclicals, have not said the same things more effectively and without so much bombast. The recent document from the Congregation, correcting and penalizing religious who get into connivance, was by no means tame, and there is nothing in Papini to measure up to the sanctions it fulminated.

Dom Vital Lehodey died on Ascension Day. His death notice came in a few days ago.

In Dom Godefroid's book on humility I find out a lot about the real life and spirit of our Order, the life that breathes richly in our French monasteries and also here to some extent. It is not the sort of thing Papini is condemning either. It is genuine. That is the direction in which I have to tend. Giving up my own will as a *hilaris dator* [cheerful giver], desiring obedience, and hurrying for the *bonum oboedientiae* [the good of obedience]: thirst for God's will to be done. He will keep our houses full of fresh air and see that we won't get stuffy and stupid and smug. But what a danger it is nevertheless. The disease of monasteries.

I have a hard time trying to imagine what it is going to mean for me to become a priest. Sometimes I am terrified at the thought of being incorporated into a caste full of spiritual limitations and rigidity, but that is not what the priesthood really is, although some people make it look that way. Ultimately the only solution to that problem is obedience. I go ahead under obedience. If my superiors want me to be a priest, it is at least safe. God wants it and He will do me good by it, although it might contain an unimaginable death.

Sometimes I want to run away and be a tramp and hang around on the roads without anything, like Humble George or Benedict Joseph Labre.

On the whole it is a blind business, but simpler than it sounds. And faith does not merely . . . .

June 6, 1948

Third Sunday after Pentecost – we are in the plain post-pentecostal liturgy and that always makes me happy. I have been reading the *Book of Kings* and understand that the life of the twelfth century monks was by no means dull. Those books fulfill all the instincts to which movies appeal much better than the movies themselves. And, like St. Theresa, I like David *et omnis mansuetudinis ejus* [and all his meekness].

But I am always talking about what I like and what I don't like.

That is because I have never changed and that is why my life still consists of likes and dislikes. Still it is just as well to be simple about it and not try to act as if I had the interior life of an angel. Yet I can see where I need to let God open certain doors for me to pass out into His darkness and liberty. I am sure He will not reproach me for liking the *Books of Kings* because they do not constitute an attachment and I don't read them much because I like them, or make the fact that I like them the all-important thing about them.

On the other hand, the importance I seem to want to give prayer in my life is rather of that kind. It is an attachment to my own progress and consolation. It is because I really desire prayer and sanctity, rather than God alone, that I do not advance towards God.

Over and over again I have read St. John of the Cross and seemed to understand him and yet the most elementary notions he teaches have failed to sink into my life. But all right, they gradually will. And that fact, I mean my blindness, is part of the poverty I want to love for the glory of God. And not act as if I could somehow possess the secret of some knowledge or some technique for arriving at the possession of God.

I rest in my poverty. My prayer is helpless and I am glad. The only thing that upsets me is the futility of interior acts destined to produce lights and affections that only torture me because they are not God.

I tell Him I do not care if He does not want me to be a priest. I leave that to Him.

And about books, the ones I write, let Him take care of them. I am not obliged to think about all that, except when the proofs come.

They gave me some kind of an award for being a poet, and it made me unhappy. But I want to be nice about it for the sake of those who wanted to be good to me in that way.

I wouldn't mind being recognized as a poet if I really were a *poet*.

But it gives me comfort to read poets who are poets. Eliot's *Little Gidding* and Robert Lowell.

. . . the flies, the flies of Babylon.

June 13, 1948. Fourth Sunday after Pentecost

O my God, I have loved myself in all things and I have not loved you. I have worked hard at the chant in the vain hope that our choir would sing beautifully, but it was for my own pleasure more than for Your glory. I have eaten many books, trying to find out the spirit of the Order, and it was all for my own satisfaction. And yet it wasn't: in a way it was for You since all my superiors have wanted me to do it, and I thought that affected my intention. But still, what was my desire?

Because of my greed for books and writing, I have always complicated my life and I have made useless complaints and lamentations, but the same hunger has always got me over and over again into the same trouble, and I have loved myself and not You.

I have acted as if I could come to You by some superior knowledge. I have tried to discover and possess some secret that would put peace and all the pleasures of contemplation in my power so that I could enjoy them whenever I liked.

But You have not given me any such secret, except the very public one, which is Your Cross. This I have pretended to accept, and I have rejected it, looking for spiritual comfort and pleasure and feeling dejection at everything that did not please my intellect and my tastes and fulfill my own desires in all things, in spiritual doctrine, and in the usages of religion and the life of the Order and penances and everything else. That was why I wanted to go to the Carthusians, because I thought that, once I got myself in a cell, I would be guaranteed to be drowned in consolations and I would have all day to write and think besides, and nobody would interfere with my spiritual pleasures.

My God, in all these things I am sinning and I am a useless monk. I am not living like a monk because I am living for myself and not for You.

But, O my God, look down on me and have mercy on me, and teach me how to live and to seek everything that is laborious and without pleasure and without consolation and without brilliance and without grandeur for Your love. And if my cowardice gets me too mixed up, at least let me be obedient and humble so that my superiors and my Rule might form me, and the Cistercian life might make me a monk and be lived in me, through the grace of Your Holy Spirit and through the merits of Christ our Lord.

In the refectory Fr. Raymond reads the account of Clare Boothe Luce's conversion, which was in *McCall's* magazine. Her daughter who was killed in the accident is buried on the South Carolina plantation she has given us.

Reverend Father says there is another offer of a place – free – he doesn't say where, but I think it is Maryland. He can't take it now, and I think he is scared. We are in debt and there is a begging campaign going on, and when he went to Utah two weeks ago, he had another heart attack.

It is quiet. The birds sing and I hear the rams and the lambs, and it is the Feast of St. Anthony of Padua. I write (during the week) *Seeds of Contemplation*, and doing it I work more peacefully, even if the work, to which I am attached, is interrupted by many errands.

A good letter from Fr. Gregory at Mount St. Bernard about writing a book on the English Cistercians. I wanted them to try it, and we would print it, chancing we are not all bankrupt and in jail before it is finished.

Retreats in full swing. A negro postulant for the laybrothers – looks good, but today I was scared the place was getting him down. He was all hunched up at the *Asperges*.

June 16, 1948

Yesterday morning I woke up about one with the conviction that I had been singing the *Veni Creator Spiritus* ["Come, Creator Spirit"] very loudly in my sleep.

Then in the refectory were read Clare Boothe Luce's reactions to Freud in her articles on her conversion. It was rather curious to hear all that being read to an audience of monks, including Freud's notion of the symbolism of church steeples. They mostly laughed heartily. On the whole I think it will do Trappists no harm to have heard about Freud, although the little there was probably won't have much of an effect on them one way or the other, except to give them the complacent notion that psychoanalysis is much more crazy than it actually is.

Personally I have always felt that a little clearer understanding of the subconscious mind would help a lot of priests to be good spiritual directors.

June 20, 1948. Fifth Sunday after Pentecost

Fr. Cletus thought up a way of fixing up arm-rest writing desks on the benches under the trees, so here I sit at one and write and maybe it will be more legible . . .

So just when we were finishing Clare Boothe Luce's articles about her conversion, in the refectory, and the catty letters from Protestant ladies which they aroused, I got a letter from Bob Giroux at Harcourt Brace saying Clare Boothe Luce had been reading page proofs of *The Seven Storey Mountain* and liked them and, in fact, Henry Luce had swiped one set of proofs and her secretary had had to call up Harcourt Brace for another.

The book has been accepted by the Catholic Book Club for August. The date assigned for publication is August 12th, Feast of St. Clare, the day on which with so many prayers I finished *The Journal of My Escape from the Nazis* seven years ago.

When I look at the way things have finally built up to this book, I cannot help getting a little understanding of what God has been doing all this time. It has been cooking for nine years, since I wrote *The Labyrinth* at

Olean, and then couldn't sell it to Farrar and Rinehart, or Macmillan, or Harcourt Brace, nor could Naomi Burton sell it to Modern Age, or Atlantic, or Little Brown, or the other people she tried.

And even then the thing isn't finished. There are parts badly written, but on the whole, it is the book in which I have tried to put something, although I scarcely began. The English edition is planned for next spring. And it is beautifully printed. Bob has done a fine job. So on the whole I see now how God has taken the thing, and how He had built up to it in His own time, how He prepared the Bob Giroux-Naomi Burton combination that has really *made* the book, and how He brought F. X. Connolly in on it. All this was completely beyond my control. I didn't even know what was going on, and now it is about to be launched.

It has been growing so long that I can no longer be diffident or scared.

Since I belong to God and my life belongs to Him and my book is His, and He is managing them all for His glory, I only have to take what comes, and do the small part that will be allotted to me: reading the letters of people who will hate me for having been converted and for having written about it, and those of people who will perhaps be pleased. It seems to me there can be great possibilities in all this and that God has woven my crazy existence and even my mistakes and my sins into His plan for a new society, *omnia cooperantur in bonum* [all things work together unto good (Romans 8:28)]. So, if I get lynched, I'll offer that up for the glory of God and for the souls He will save by all this.

Because now I see what it is all leading up to: to the happiness and the peace and the salvation of many people I have never known. And there is no greater joy than to be drawn into union with God's great love for the souls of men, of Himself in them, and cooperate with Him in drawing them into His joy.

But the best thing of all is that Bob Giroux or somebody did an index to *The Seven Storey Mountain:* the most peculiar collection of names you ever saw. Starts off with Abbot, Father and goes on to Advent; Adler, Alfred; Ellington, Duke; or Fields, W. C.; but Smith, Pete is followed by Smith, Robert Paul, and there is Bob O'Brien, the plumber at the Olean House and Pierrot the teamster at Saint Antonin, and the Privats at Murst, and Brother Fabian, who went to Georgia, and Mary Jerdo, and Helen Freedgood, and Burton, Jinny and Flagg, Nancy and Wells, Peggy. (Peggy wrote to me from Hollywood the other day. I can't figure out if she is acting or only writing or both at once.)

I was fascinated. The index is beautiful. It is like the gathering of all the people I have known at a banquet to celebrate the publication of the Book, and it is like a pledge that they will all belong to me somehow as trophies in heaven, or I will belong to some of *them* as a trophy.

Blake, William; Francis of Assisi, Saint; Bonaventure, Saint; Aquinas, St. Thomas; Bernard, Saint. I think that index is a partial, optimistic preview of the General Judgment with the four Marx Brothers among the sheep.

So God is very good. *Sanctus in omnibus operibus suis.* [Holy in all His works.] Though the natural pleasure of success sickens me a little, and I get smoke in my eyes from thinking about how the book will look, still, I have to take all that on the chin and stay as tranquil and detached as God's grace will grant me to do.

About Gethsemani, what is more worth desiring than to be perfect in obedience? In the last weeks God has been working on me a lot and His grace has been softening up that interior toughness, and I am getting a kind of hunger to do things for Reverend Father, for God through him, and listen to his way of looking at things. I want to give up all the reserves of independence in me, all the last lines of defense. I don't want to possess anything more, and how crazy it would be when God Himself is hurrying me to my end faster than I could ever conceive or plan it, hurrying me most when I seem to be going backwards.

But how a man can lose time in a monastery trying to live by some other spirit than that of his own Order and trying to travel in two directions at the same time by trying to harmonize obedience and his own silly will!

June 24, 1948. Feast of Saint John Baptist

The heat has got us and we change our torn shirts and hang them out in the sun for the sweat to dry out of them, and we sleep in work blouses. Since the floor was painted, I ended up with a cell next to a window.

This is a great and happy feast. Yesterday, the Vigil was beautiful and to-day, the Feast is beautiful. God talks in the trees. There is a wind, so that it is cool to sit outside. This morning at four o'clock in the clean dawn sky there were some special clouds in the west over the woods, with a very perfect and delicate pink, against deep blue. And a hawk was wheeling over the trees.

We pushed the psalms a little in the Night Office, or rather I did, and the Head Cantor let me get away with it. The organist put up the tone a little and for once the office was bright and lively and the angelus rang at five to four instead of about five or ten after!

So God also gave me the spiritual joy of the feast, and there was time to pray, and Reverend Father is keeping his promise about letting us keep the feasts of the Holy Days instead of working.

And the Epistle moves me – *Servus meus es tu Israel – posui te ut sagittam electam* [Thou art my servant, Israel – I have made you as a chosen arrow (Isaiah 49:2)] – and the Kings and Princes shall rise up and adore God. And I think we need another Saint John Baptist to come in the spirit and power of Elias. Last week I was reading about Elias in the third *Book of Kings*, how he hid his head and covered his face when he heard God speak to him in a small voice.

Deep tranquility. But I am not poor. When I read the beginning of *The Ascent of Mount Carmel*, I realize that my spiritual life hasn't even begun.

> *Para venir a saberlo todo,*
> *No quieras saber algo en nada . . .*
> *Para veni a serlo todo,*
> *No quieras ser algo en nada . . .*
> *Para venir a lo que no gustas*
> *Has de ir por lo que no gustas . . .*
> [In order to arrive at knowing the All
> Desire to know nothing in anything . . .
> In order to arrive at being All
> Desire to be nothing in anything. . . .
> In order to come to that for which you have no taste
> You must go by the way of that for which you have no taste. . . .]

And that I should speak against myself and desire everybody else to do so? Sure, if it's a *joke*, all right! But seriously?

Still, what can I do but remain tranquil and resigned and keep my soul in silence, and recognize this truth, and wait upon God's will, and not confuse my inner life with too much reading and too many choices and too many desires and too many problems.

Every minute life begins all over again. Amen.

July 2, 1948. Feast of the Visitation
How beautiful it was last evening, the Vigil, with a long interval after colla-tion. Since it was a fast day, we weren't long in the refectory in the evening,

got out early and the sun was higher than it usually is in that interval, and I saw the country in a light that we usually do not see. The low-slanting rays picked out the foliage of the trees and high-lighted a new wheatfield against the dark curtain of woods on the knobs that were in shadow. It was very beautiful. Deep peace. Sheep on the slopes behind the sheep barn. The new trellises in the novitiate garden leaning and sagging. A cardinal singing suddenly in the walnut tree, and piles of fragrant logs all around the woodshed, waiting to be cut in bad weather.

I looked at all this in great tranquility, with my soul and spirit quiet. For me landscape seems to be important for contemplation . . . anyway, I have no scruples about loving it.

Didn't St. John of the Cross hide himself in a room up in a church tower where there was one small window through which he could look out at the country?

Anyway, on the Feast of Saints Peter and Paul the first copy of *Exile Ends in Glory* arrived. So much was cut (and wisely so!) that it is a thinner book than I had expected.

So now it has its final shape. It has taken its place as something finished. I think of it no longer as a pile of paper waiting to be born, but as a thin grey book with a pale green jacket that is simple enough not to be disturbing (but I don't know what the Japanese nuns will say when they see the picture of that Shinto gateway in front of Our Lady of the Angels!) Then they got the captions on a picture mixed up. Said the convent in Japan was the one at Laval. That will mean writing more letters.

This too I am able to take quietly. There is certainly nothing to get excited about except the faults which are numerous enough to make me try to practice the sixth degree of humility. *Omni vilitate vel extremitate contentus sit monachus* . . . [Let the monk be content with all that is base and with privations in everything (RB 7:48).] Well, Dom Benoît told me, *Il faut goûter les humiliations* [You must have a taste for humiliations]. I am smacking my lips over the second chapter of *Exile*. It is one of the worst pieces of cheese that has ever been served in our refectory or any other.

Anyway, it is being read in the refectory. Fr. Raymond made me signs about how the sweat runs down his ribs when *his* books are read in the refectory. I prayed a lot to Our Lady and find I don't mind it so much. When the reader gives the stuff a peculiar interpretation, I feel that the book is still getting better treatment than it deserves. However, I was surprised and comforted when everybody was happy over the first few pages.

Brother Gabriel and Brother Dominic are painting the outside frames of the church windows. The other day I was kneeling in church praying on the presbytery step. Up in the St. Benedict window St. Benedict sat making that gesture to St. Scholastica. His crozier and miter lay on the floor among those Bavarian flowerpots. Then underneath all that, in two open spaces, side by side, Brother Gabriel and Brother Dominic – just their faces, beards and straw hats – busy painting the frames very fast, trying to finish something before the end of work.

Benedictine tranquility. *Pax.* [Peace.] That's what I think about. I have more of it perhaps because I am less mixed up in peculiar tensions of desire and pride that come from fighting the will of God in an obscure way, under the pretext of a greater good.

There is only one way to peace: be reconciled that of yourself you are what you are, and it might not be especially magnificent, what you are! God has His own plan for making something else of you, and it is a plan which you are mostly too dumb to understand.

A letter from Dom Thomas d'Aquin at Tamié says our monastery of El Latroun in Palestine has been destroyed. Didn't say how. Are they fighting in Palestine?

Anyway the monks are living in the cellars. In the Scriptorium is a picture of a statue of Our Lady with flowers on her head. It says the flowers, real flowers, stay fresh all the time by miracle and that the whole thing is somewhere in England, but I didn't see where because there were too many monks in front of the picture.

July 11, 1948. Eighth Sunday after Pentecost

All day it has been dark and hot and wet. Sweat rolls down your back in church. It is a day of Recollection. What was I thinking about? The false joy I take in created things – people, books, my own work.

Last Wednesday the 7th – anniversary of the departure of the Utah colony last year – I went to Reverend Father just before the afternoon work to see if I couldn't go out into the fields. But he handed me the first copy of *The Seven Storey Mountain* and told me to look it over. It is a good job of printing, and I skipped through it with the general feeling that it is, with *Thirty Poems*, the only respectable book I have written. And if I had never published anything but the *Mountain* and *Thirty Poems*, I would feel a whole lot cleaner. *Exile* continues to be read in the refectory and people in general seem to accept it all right. Nevertheless, there are parts of it that make my stomach turn somersaults. Where did I get all that pious rhetoric? That was the way I thought a monk was supposed to write, just after I had made simple profession.

Thursday Reverend Father went away to make the Visitation at the Valley and Father Prior (Odilo) says he is also going to take a look at some land that is being offered us for a foundation in the Adirondacks. I heard something of this before and at the time the proposition sounded a little queer.

About *The Seven Storey Mountain*, two Book Clubs and the Catholic Literary Foundation in Milwaukee have already guaranteed the sale of fourteen thousand copies. The second printing is already under way.

And I tell myself, "Look out! Maybe this business is going to turn your whole life upside down for true!"

I caught myself thinking, "If they make it into a movie, will Gary Cooper be the hero?" Or maybe there is no Gary Cooper anymore. But anyway that is the kind of folly I have to look out for now. I am reduced to that. I don't dare listen too closely for fear I might hear Dom Benedict[31] roll over in his tomb. But I pray to him to help me be very simple and tranquil and quiet in all this, which is God's will and is for Gethsemani. Here is the book I couldn't make a go of ten years ago. Now it is a success just when I am at Gethsemani and Gethsemani most needs the money . . .

Yet the business of being poisoned in spite of yourself by the pleasure you take in your own work! You say you don't want it, and it gets into your blood anyway. You don't taste the dish, but the smell of it goes to your head and corrupts you. You get drunk by sniffing the cork of the bottle.

There are compensations: the opposition of Fr. Anthony to me and all I do. He seems to be developing a real repugnance for everything I write, if not everything I *am*. And yet he swallows it down until it breaks out in some gesture or some remark. It all began with that contemplation pamphlet last Easter, and no one knows what has become of *that* [underlined twice].

I have no special difficulty in seeing that the greatest good for me lies in taking this with a big whoop of joy, and *liking* it as much as I can, and not worrying about the fact that I can't like it altogether. And above all not to be a Pharisee about it, or make a martyr out of myself, or get smug about it all and take complacency in somebody else's suffering just because I can barricade myself behind those books and kid myself that I am a success . . .

---

[31] Dom Benedict Berger was the second abbot of Gethsemani.

Oh God of peace, *tranquillus Deus tranquillans omnia* [the tranquil God making all things tranquil], empty my heart and keep me free and let me live in Your will!

July 18, 1948. Ninth Sunday after Pentecost

Very hot. The birds sing and the monks sweat and about 3:15, when I had just changed all our clothes for the fourth time today and hung out the wet ones to dry, I stood in the doorway of the grand parlor and looked at a huge pile of Kentucky cumulus cloud out beyond Mount Olivet – with a buzzard lazily planing back and forth over the sheep pasture, very high and black against the white mountain of cloud. Blue shadows on the cloud.

Yesterday, when we had the Feast of Our Lady of Mount Carmel, Our Lady made me happy in many different ways. At prayer – aware of God's purity surrounding my own imperfection with purity and peace. Yet helpless to get myself out of the way so that there could be nothing left but His purity. No other solution but to wait in love and humility and love my imperfection. Fr. Urban, in a very good sermon for our founder Saint Stephen on the 16th, told of the Little Flower being glad on her deathbed, not only that she could be judged as imperfect, but that it actually was true. That struck me very deeply.

All my desires draw me more and more in that direction. To be little, to be nothing, to rejoice in your imperfections, to be glad that you are not worthy of attention, that you are of no account in the universe. This is the only liberation, the only way to true solitude.

As long as I continue to take myself seriously, how can I be saint, a contemplative? As long as I continue to bother about myself, what happiness is possible in life? For the self that I bother about doesn't really exist and never will and never did, except in my own imagination.

Sometimes the desire or thought of being something great makes me physically sick. All greatness is abhorrent – considered as greatness, as an ornament to myself, not as glory given to God in me and through me. Even the desire of great graces of prayer, contemplation, sanctity, repels me when the graces are considered as something apart from God, created accidents decorating my own contingent being.

Yesterday morning, Our Lady's Day, after we had had our heads shaved, and I was trying to study theology out under the trees by the Little

Flower's statue (which Brother Gabriel has just repainted in the wrong colors) Frater Hilary came running out from Father Prior and gave me a big book. It was Denis the Carthusian, Volume 41, one of those we didn't have, and the one containing his *De Contemplatione*. I nearly got up and flew around the trees. A long time ago I began painful negotiations with the Carthusians at Parkminster to get at least this volume, but I had given them up as a bad job. But Our Lady brought it along yesterday as a mark of her love and to remind me that she is my guide in the interior life.

Meanwhile, Father Peter, the professional mystic up in the infirmary, has been deluging me with letters on the mystical life – in connection with *Exile Ends in Glory*. He has got Mother Berchmans all figured out! Knows just where she entered spiritual betrothal and everything. He told me flatly she was a mystic before the mystical business even began. Then he told me all about the mystical life of our late Frater Alfred, who died this year on my birthday. He explained to me that Frater Alfred was not really stupid and slow as everyone thought, but that he had the ligatures and was far advanced in union, living in a perpetual trance.

Then he turned on me with, "Son, are you in the mystical way? I don't think so – you act too much on impulse," and he went on to tell me all about the mortification of the passions, assuring me that I was still an animal and that, before I could ever live by faith, I would have to jack myself up to the level of reason. Then he gave me a bird's eye view of the mystical life which he thinks I should nevertheless aspire to.

His letters are very picturesque. He doesn't like the Jesuits and [Augustin] Poulain and [Francesco de] Suárez and he calls them "the self-worshipers" and the "outfit-worshipers." He adds that all our superiors are incompetent and nobody knows anything about mysticism, only about how to make cheese, etc., etc.

Life is so complicated when you get mixed up with other people!

Here come great slate-colored clouds. I hope there will be a storm and my animal will cool off. For the glory of God. *Vivat Crux!* [Long live the Cross!]

July 25, 1948. Feast of Saint James

Yesterday Fr. Timothy finished reading *Exile Ends in Glory* in the refectory and then read a report of a revelation about the end of the world to that Capuchin in Italy who has the stigmata. I have seen it before – Reverend Father had shown it to me. One thing that struck me: everything is going to smell terrible. Also Our Lord said the elect shouldn't go looking out the window, when things start to happen, or be too curious about what happens to the others. But the important angle: praying and suffering for others. Although *Exile* is not a good book, as I have written it, nevertheless it did me good to write it and hear it read. Only after it was all over did I realize that there is a great deal in that Mother Berchmans. Terrific fortitude.

Last Monday Naomi Burton wrote that Harcourt Brace had accepted *Waters of Siloe* for printing next spring, and gave the terms of the contract in outline. So I stay in the Scriptorium and re-read the letter a couple of times while outside the window rain came pouring down in torrents. It rained on and off all week, but yesterday was fine and I got permission to go out to the common work and develop a few blisters. We cleared ground for a new road between the sheep-barn and the highway on the other side of the creek, and it was hot grubbing out cedars and hacking at their roots.

Today in Chapter Reverend Father said Dom Gabriel Sortais, the Vicar General, was coming here next month to make a regular Visitation and that made me very happy. It seemed like the answer to many prayers for Gethsemani. It is the first time in 100 years we have had Visitations in two consecutive years, according to the *Carta Caritatis!* At the Communion of the High Mass, before I ran off as servant of the church to put out the Sanctus candles, a thought struck me which I had known before, but it suddenly struck me deeply. It is this: the desire to love God, the desire for perfect union with God means nothing at all and is without any value or merit whatever in the sight of God unless it is inspired and guided by grace and in conformity with God's will. Someone will say: all desires for union with God are inspired by grace. That is not true. The devils desire to possess God. There is a natural desire for heaven, for the fruition of God, in us. There is a natural desire for contemplation which may never get to be explicit in most men, but it exists. All this is without merit or value. Our desire for God must come from God and be guided by His will before it means anything in the supernatural order.

So it is not sufficient to rush into church with a desire of contemplation or to do a lot of good works and acts of virtue with a desire of sanctity. In everything the supreme good, which includes everything, is God's will. Without it, contemplation and virtue are nothing – at least to a Christian. The first movement in all prayer, together with faith in His Presence, ought to be the *desire* to know His will and to abandon oneself entirely to all His dispositions and desires.

Without that, the desire of contemplation will only lead you to beat your head against a blank wall. But with it – peace. And contemplation has already begun.

August 4, 1948. Feast of St. Dominic. Wednesday

Reverend Father is dead.

This morning when we came down to choir he was not there. I had forgotten all about his leaving for Georgia. When he did not show up all through the Night Office, I began to worry and pray for him, and I was praying as much for him as for Dom Dominique whose feast it was. At Prime there was a lot of confusion and running around, and in Chapter Father Odilo told us that Reverend Father had died on the train last night before they got to Knoxville, Tennessee.

Yesterday afternoon I had a long talk with Reverend Father about work and books and so on. It was very pleasant and cheerful, and he was exhorting me to write something to make people love the spiritual life. He was glad about the Sheed and Ward job.

He has had a lot to suffer in the last two years. And he has done a tremendous amount of work. The house is sad. He will come back from Knoxville embalmed and in an ambulance sometime tonight and the funeral isn't supposed to be until Monday.

Meanwhile, Dom Columban Tewes, Abbot of Achel, showed up here today and so did Humble George. Dom Columban was in choir for Vespers and the choir behaved better than usual and wore a calotte [skull cap] and kept his head on one side, and he in the *Pater Noster* softened all the endings, so you couldn't hear them at all.

This afternoon I tried hard for the third time to rewrite the second chapter of *Waters of Siloe*.

Laughlin sent three books on St. John of the Cross from Paris.

I keep thinking about Reverend Father. I suppose he is in purgatory. But I nevertheless feel that he is very close to me and will remain so all the rest of my days. I trust a lot in his help. His sympathy was deep and real all the time he was alive. I don't know who was ever kinder to me. His patience with this community was wonderful. He had a lot of crosses, even in the last few days. He felt them very much. He was sensitive to the way people felt about him and he was very hurt when people couldn't get together with him in things.

People are making signs that the election will be hot. I think it will at least be strange. There won't be a wide choice. So much depends on it.

I can't think much about it any more. I keep contact with God by the touch of a sort of interior hollowness and that counts as my prayer for Reverend Father and for this house.

August 13, 1948

I have never been so busy in my life. But also very much at peace.

About the things said by various abbots who are here or have been here:

Dom Columban of Achel – I saw pictures of the new monastery at Achel – a beautiful job, on the whole, and very good adaptation of modern methods to Cistercian style. Huge brick arches in the Scriptorium – very effective. Indirect lighting in the cloister. He and his companion thought our chant a bit rough. In Chapter today Dom Columban, speaking in French, made the point that it was not the strictness with which we kept the Rule that counted, but the *love* with which we kept it: his logic being, I suppose, that, generally, strictness will be proportionate to love. But it is not necessarily so always. So he added that it is possible for a monastery to be very observant of the Rule and yet to have very little interior life, if the observance is based on imperfect motives.

Yesterday I had to go in to Louisville. It was the first time I was out of the monastery in seven years. I had to go in to act as interpreter for Dom Gabriel Sortais, who was called in to the Good Shepherd convent because their Mother General from Anger was there and wanted him to talk to the community and hear her confession. The Sisters received us in a cool sort of library with a lot of armchairs and carpets. The place was cool because all around the buildings were big shade trees and, on the whole, the convent is a pleasant one and very big. Big police dog, a laundry, and what not. So he told them in French to love their vocations, and I translated it into English and I think they were happy. One Sister held the black hat I had been wearing in her hand while I drank a glass of ginger ale and ate a cookie. We went in in Senator Dawson's car and we both dressed in black suits, although there was no real reason, as far as I could see, why we shouldn't have gone in our habits.

August 14, 1948. Vigil of the Assumption

Going into Louisville the other day I wasn't struck by anything particular. Although I felt completely alienated from everything in the world and all its activity, I did not necessarily feel out of sympathy with the people who were walking around. On the whole they seemed to me more real than they ever had before, and more worth sympathizing with. Without any

conscious effort being necessary, I went without remarking anyone, including women, except two. One wild-looking jane in a black dress with much
lipstick – I thought of her all of a sudden when I was taking the discipline
yesterday morning and hoped she didn't happen to be in the way of need-
ing some vicarious penance.

The country was all color. Clouds. Corn in the bottom lands. Red rocks.
A lot of rolling land and more hills between here and Bardstown than I realized. I had the impression of having remembered much on my first journey, when I came to the monastery seven years ago, and now I realize I had
forgotten practically everything.

It was nice saying the Office in the car and saying the *Gloria Patri* while
looking at the woods and fields.

But Louisville was boring. Anyway, the whole thing was obedience. It
meant losing a day's work. We were back at seven, ate eggs in the guest
house, and I was on time for the *Salve*.

When I got to bed, I remembered I had forgotten to say the Nocturn of
the Dead in the car: I got my seasons mixed up. So about 8:45 I got up
again and went down to church and said the Nocturn kneeling by Saints
Peter and Paul's altar where the light wouldn't be seen. It was the wrong
Nocturn, too.

I ought to put down some of the things Dom Gabriel has been saying.

To me and in Chapter, too, he said some sensible things about electing
abbots. For instance, never to elect a difficult character. They simply dis-
courage the whole community. The absolutely essential qualities for an abbot are fatherly kindness and firmness and common sense. Also he needs
learning, interior life, tact . . . etc. etc.

The list of "postulable" candidates is never to be ignored, but it is only
there in case there is no one really suitable among the "eligible" candidates.[32] He told me Dom Edmund Futterer of the Valley would under no
circumstances accept the job, if he were elected, which would be extremely
unlikely anyway, and Dom Edmund told me the same thing himself before
the funeral of Dom Frederic Monday.

Dom Gabriel said he thought it was essential for Cistercians to have opportunities for solitude and that he has places in the garden, etc., at Belle-

---

[32] "Postulable" candidates are capable monks who do not meet all the requirements of the Cistercian Constitutions to be elected abbot, that is, required age or sufficient time in solemn
vows. "Eligible" candidates are those monks who meet all of the constitutional requirements
for abbatial election.

fontaine where you can meditate and read in peace, out of sight of every-one else. I certainly agree with him on that.

He told me of the work they have been doing on the Church at Melleray. They have uncovered the original twelfth century work, very simple and pure, the ordinary sort of work the simplest stone masons of this district would have done. There is no vaulting – a wooden ceiling XIVth or XVth century. He thinks the original ceiling was plain wood and cross-beams.

Somewhere in the Order is a nun who learned how to be a dentist and takes care of the Sisters' teeth. And monks do dental work in some of the monasteries in Canada, he said.

Gethsemani is definitely austere as far as diet goes. The house is simple and poor. The food is evidently better at Bellefontaine. Dom Herman Joseph Smets said Abbots ought not to be afraid to give all the food allowed by the Rule, and make it palatable. At Bellefontaine they get extra potatoes every meal; they rate as "bread," and this is permitted. At Aigue-belle, where they do poorly with potatoes, they order a couple of carloads of potatoes each year from Brittany. However, he says he hadn't eaten any rice since 1939 until he got some in Canada.

Dom Gabriel gave a very funny account of the dinner in the guest house (here) with all the Bishops after the funeral, Monday. Everything was on the table and the Bishops were left to help themselves, boarding house style. He said he found it very shocking, but I said it was that way every-where. One Bishop reached out and grabbed two oranges and handed one to him saying, *"Pour vous."* ["For you."] Then he got into an account of a fantastic luncheon party in the Park Avenue apartment of one Whitney Warren, who designed Grand Central Station. But that was before the war.

August 20, 1948. Feast of St. Bernard. Friday

Monday a telegram arrived from the Abbot General saying Dom Gabriel was to make the Visitation here in spite of the fact there is no superior. In other words, the General really *wants* a visitation. The whole thing is prov-idential. In fact, everything that has been going on in the past month wears the mark of a special Providence for us. I don't think there is anyone in the monastery who imagines Reverend Father could have found a better time to die. The Visitation is going to require some things that would have hurt his feelings very much, but they seem to be necessary.

Tuesday, Wednesday and Thursday were taken up with the scrutiny. I did a lot of interpreting. One of the things that struck me was that the

Seniors in the house didn't seem to realize that there was anything wrong, except perhaps the Chapter of Faults could be a little quieter.

The Visitor has some very big question marks in his mind about the South Carolina foundation, about the expenses in Georgia, which are simply terrific, about our secular retreats, about our sublime recklessness in accepting postulants, no matter how scrawny they are or how little education they have or how many aunts and uncles in the crazy house. But that has been a big issue since the last Visitation.

Dom Gabriel was talking about some of the people who tried to be postulants at Bellefontaine. An American who ran after the novice master with a pitchfork and wrote *à mort le Père Maître* ["Death to the Novice Master"] all over the dormitory. A negro from Haiti called Fritzy, who showed up one morning in a tuxedo, registered as guide to the Cathedral in Port-au-Prince, did no work, went to the Dominicans at Angers and got a job as a gardener. While working in the Friars' garden, he started throwing kisses at a maid in one of the houses that overlooked the place . . . Then a man who was in prison for manslaughter wrote to Bellefontaine asking permission to enter . . .

Dom Gabriel told me not to let myself get roped into any magazine as a *collaborateur*, i.e., not to get my name on the mast-head as a staff writer, and be slow to accept work. They are all commercial. They ruin you. Told me to refuse book-reviews except in exceptional cases.

He told me not to worry about suffering in choir – told me how the cantors suffer at Solesmes! Told me to think of Jesus going up to Jerusalem with all the pilgrims roaring psalms out of their dirty throats. He is an artist, but he says he has at last progressed to the point where he can live in a room like the one they have given him in the guest house without putting all the statues and pictures of the Little Flower in a closet. He says at Solesmes, where they are good in art too, it took three years to get rid of a statue of St. Benedict in a magician's robe with moons and stars all over it. Then he told me of the forty-eight statues of saints in the church of the Trappists at Mistassini. His description of Canadian Trappists rushing out to work, and Canadian monasteries shaking with machinery, is very funny. He caught one brother trying out a new bulldozer during the reading before Compline. He couldn't wait until the next morning. (This was in Canada.)

I don't know whether or not my health is funny. I suppose it is O.K., but I might as well be ready for anything.

August 22, 1948. Sunday

It is the Octave of the Assumption – Feast, I suppose, of the Immaculate Heart of Mary outside. The Visitation was closed in Chapter. Being secretary I read the Visitation Card which I had translated and typed yesterday afternoon. It was a long session in Chapter – finished at 8:30. There were many observations made, and reference to the past Visitation Card not being sufficiently well kept. That had upset the house a little. As Dom Gabriel pointed out, it was largely a matter of misinterpretation.

Tomorrow is the abbatial election. A table in Chapter with pens, papers and chairs with backs to them looks very official. It does not have the cloth prescribed by the *Usages*. This afternoon Scrutators were elected and I turned out to be one of them. Fr. Edmund, one of the others, just made me a sign that he had a box of matches and there is a stove in Chapter to burn the ballots, not, however, to keep the electors warm, since it is August, and they will probably be warm enough for other reasons.

Some expect Dom James to be elected on the first ballot. He arrived today with Fr. Ephrem and Fr. Mary from Georgia as witnesses. Fr. Mary sat in choir as though he were in heaven. Afterwards I gave him a good hug and he made me a sign that the work was hard in Georgia and that he had liked *Exile Ends in Glory*, which was read in the refectory there. Well, he looks holier than ever. I was glad to see him and Fr. Ephrem, too, but Fr. Ephrem had to look twice at me before he remembered who I was, if he did so then.

Tomorrow we choose the one who is to lead us for a certain time to God, to make saints of us. I got time to think about it and to remind myself of the vow I will renew when he is installed – that is to be tomorrow also. And what it means. I read over St. John of the Cross' remarks about obedience in the *Cautelas*, and all I want is to carry them out, to let God guide me by the one He is choosing. I am not, I think, voting on any natural motive – food and what not. Writing doesn't enter into it. Our Lady will manage everything. I don't expect the house to be any more perfect this time next year than it is now. But still, perhaps it will be so anyway. I pray God to make us much more united than we are. That is what we need. It has been growing on us, I admit.

August 25, 1948. Feast of Saint Louis

The election lasted from 7:45 to 12:25 – and this included confirmation and installation of Dom James who, of course, was elected. It is easy to see from this end of the affair that he was the Holy Ghost's candidate – in more senses than one. When we were in there, a photographer's bulb went off outside. A newspaper man had got into the garden and took a shot of the smoke coming out of the stove-pipe where we were burning the ballots. Dom Gabriel made some observations on this fact. They were not kind. The whole thing got to be quite impressive after a while. When the voting was over, the result was announced in Latin at the Chapter door, the doors of the church, and the monastery gate. The cloister was unlocked and the novices, young professed, and laybrothers came in. Captain Kinnarney strayed into the cloister and sat on a bench and we went in disorder to church singing the *Te Deum*. Then everyone went back to the Chapter Room and the ones who hadn't voted sat there in silence and waited, rather confused, for the long business of installation, while all the professed made their promise of obedience to Dom James.

It was very moving. Big room packed with people, all silent. A long file of monks moving up to Dom James' throne. The scrutators' table in a big mess and most of the chairs empty except where Father Anthony sat writing furiously, being notary. It was far past dinner time and we had not even sung Terce and Sext. (These were recited after Meridienne with None.) Every once in a while I had to run some kind of errand for Dom Gabriel.

When it was all over we had an abbot. And a holy one too. Now it is very consoling to go into choir and have our own abbot beginning things again. Dom James is quiet and humble.

That afternoon, when he was in Louisville at the Archbishop's, I got a check for nine hundred dollars on *The Seven Storey Mountain*, so I gave it to him the next morning and he told me to go on writing. Today the contract for *Waters of Siloe* came in and also a letter from Dom Humphrey Pawsey at Parkminster asking me if I thought I could help him place an article on the Carthusians to arouse some interest in an American foundation. So today I am very happy. It is a good feast, but for supernatural reasons also. *Magnificat anima mea Dominum!* [My soul doth magnify the Lord (Luke 1:46)!]

September 6, 1948. Sixteenth Sunday after Pentecost

Reverend Father, Dom James, flew to the General Chapter last week. He is supposed to be in Paris now.

For the last few days I was worrying about vocation, complaining to Fr. Anthony in the confessional that everything is in confusion here, although that is not exactly true. Still there are abuses which many people don't seem to see. Fr. Anthony told me I simply had to make the best of it. I was grousing that I would make some spiritual progress if only I were in a well-organized community (meaning, of course, a Charterhouse). He told me that I had to learn to get along for myself – which, as a matter of fact, is more or less what I have been doing – had to do – ever since coming here. That was what Dom Marie Joseph told me also. It is true. I only waste time worrying about defects of the community even when they are real. Meanwhile the defects get smaller and, anyway, I pay less and less attention. I have plenty of peace. I wouldn't find it easy to say I was absolutely convinced I belong here, but I don't know where else I belong either.

I have a terrific undefined longing to give everything to God, and a constant feeling that I am not doing so here – or not now.

Really though, I can't see what God wants of me. So far it seems to be this. But this writing business has become a chaos of correspondence, and that is certainly not our vocation.

However, I have to be content that I am more or less up against a blank wall interiorly. As soon as I ask too many questions about it, I suffer. But if I keep still, I have peace.

To make a *Rule* the whole meaning of my existence is not enough. To make an Order, a spiritual tradition, the center of my life is not enough. Contemplation is not enough. By itself it is not enough of an ideal. The complete gift of myself to Christ – transformation – total simplicity and poverty – they are some of the things I need. In other words, I need to get *rid* of everything. Here I am compelled to keep my hands full. And if I write, I am bound to live submerged in books.

Theology has been a great trial. So inadequate! We have been sifting the dry ashes of what the text book considers to be a fitting treatment of Our Lady! I gave up in despair and read De Montfort.

One good thing. Evelyn Waugh sent me a fine book to help me to write better, *The Reader over Your Shoulder* by Robert Graves and Alan Hodges. They seem to think that the time for experimental prose writing is now spent and that we are heading for clear, logical prose that can be rapidly read. I have a definite hunger for clarity and order in my writing – not necessary for conventions of grammar. Anyway it helps me see my faults and has ascetic implications as well.

For I have been thinking that monks are sometimes very sloppy thinkers. One of Gethsemani's biggest failings is a deplorable lack of logic.

September 7, 1948. Vigil of Our Lady's Nativity

In Dom David Knowles' new book (*Religious Orders in England* [volume 1 of 3, Cambridge, 1948]) I found a few fine sentences on St. Francis and they got me all up in the air about poverty. Still, with the grace of God I might be able to do something about it, because it doesn't seem to be much use in going on as I am now. Today we were cleaning out that room and I got rid of a lot of things I don't really need. And it occurred to me also that perhaps when Dom James comes back, I would try again to get out of so much writing and try to live more simply – and go out to work in the fields, which has been practically impossible for two years. There is no sense in all this activity and pressure, all the elaborate reading I do, all my fussing with architecture and poetry and all the rest of it. That is not what I am here for. And yet I am stopped dead unless God helps me, unless Our Lady wills to do something for me and delivers me and lets me be little and hidden and poor.

However, it is all in the hands of my superiors. I can't do anything but leave it up to them.

September 9, 1948

Since reading those lines about St. Francis I am haunted. The idea of that poverty does not leave me. I have been shedding books and getting rid of things, as if that amounted to anything. I talked to Fr. Anthony about it, but got no satisfaction out of it, which was good, because I ought to have known that human satisfaction was what I was unconsciously looking for. In all my talking and most of my writing it is the same. However, I am beginning to be convinced that something can be done about this. This would be a very good time to throw away everything. I am pursued everywhere by the feeling that, if I made some sort of an effort at the right moment, I could throw everything overboard and be free – and have my poverty. It is a kind of conviction that God does want to give people – me too – grace to avoid all those lives in which you accumulate honors and burdens and bury yourself under jobs. I don't know how it is going to be done. Maybe the answer will be that I will get sent to stew in South Carolina, where the snakes will pursue me through those hot mists and branches full of moss. It will be like St. John of the Cross in prison in Toledo. The very thought of that place on the Cooper River gives me the creeps.

The laybrother novices with pneumatic drills and sledge hammers are pounding and battering the foundations of this wing under the Scriptorium to make a hole big enough to get a new heating plant into the cellar. What with the machinery the place sounds and smells like New York. In fact, this place is so mechanized with tractors and bulldozers and lawn-mowers as big as tanks that it is the noisiest part of Kentucky. Very fine for contemplation.

September 12, 1948. Feast of Our Lady's Name

Since it is a day of recollection – the first since somewhere in July – I sup-pose I ought to write about the state of my soul, if my soul can be said to have a state.

But I don't see why I should say the same old thing over and over again, and perhaps not even in a new way. So the chant is a penance – so we don't keep the *Usages* with the *finesse* and dignity with which they are kept in France – so we are a bunch of hicks. If I can accept the fact that my voca-tion seems to be, at least for the present, precisely this, I may practice some of the interior poverty I say I am so crazy about. I can think of no better place to learn poverty of spirit than in our choir in which there is positively nothing to please the senses.

Ironically, yesterday Clare Boothe Luce sent two volumes of records of the monks of Solesmes singing everything I like best. She is also sending a record player, but that has not yet come. So I have only read the red labels of the records. They are as red as claret and they all say the chant is di-rected by Dom [Pierre] Gajard of Solesmes. (Dom Frederic was afraid to let us hear the singing of Solesmes for fear the astonishment of hearing real Gregorian chant might make us all proud.)

In the refectory we are reading Fr. Bruno [de Jésus Marie]'s *Life of St. John of the Cross* and today it was all *todo y nada* [all and nothing] – to be at-tached to absolutely nothing, it said. Two contraries cannot coexist in one subject. He that loves a creature becomes as low as that creature, subjects himself to it. I had been making resolutions about Gregorian chant. I don't think I love it as an end in itself. Still, by the treatment I am going through now, Our Lord evidently wants to make sure.

I love music. I love architecture. I love poetry. I love nice pictures of Our Lady.

Today they slipped some fancy coffee on us at mixt and I drank it by mis-take and knelt before the Tabernacle with my mind full of visions of how we could easily build a very beautiful, simple, white monastery with long windows and a low belfry, very simple and clean, on the edge of the Cooper River . . .

O.K. O.K. I am glad to go without all that. I promise to keep quiet about it – until I burst.

That is what I need to do more and more – shut up about all that: architecture, Spirit of the Order, contemplation, liturgy, chant – be simple and poor or you will never have any peace. Take what is atrocious without complaint, unless you are in some way officially bound to complain. Otherwise keep still, until the Visitation gives you another chance. But if everything really gets awful . . . ?

Two contraries cannot co-exist in the same subject!

> *Para venir a gustarlo Todo / no quieras tener gusto en nada. / Para venir a lo que no gustas / has de ir por lo que no gustas.* [To arrive at having a taste for everything / seek to have a taste for nothing. / To come to that point where you have no taste / you must go by that way for which you have no taste.]

We are still overwhelmed with seculars. The other day I was trying to read Theology on a bench under the trees, and Fr. Benedict came by with some visitors. I heard a rattle of machinery and one secular priest had just taken my picture with a big newspaperman's camera. While he was changing the film, a Franciscan sneaked up with a little miniature camera and took another one. *O Beata Solitudo!* [O Blessed Solitude!]

September 13, 1948. Monday

It is the last day of the summer season. Tomorrow the fasts of the Order begin with shorter work and longer intervals. I have been breaking my neck in the last week to clean everything up in the hope of going out to work at least three times a week. *Seeds of Contemplation* is finally off to the printer and *Waters of Siloe* is being more definitively edited. In the last two months I do not seem to have done anything but write letters and run around in circles. The Visitation, election and all the rest that has happened account for this.

Evelyn Waugh wanted to edit the English edition of *The Seven Storey Mountain* and has apparently already done so. I am glad. I trust him more than anyone else on a job like that. Also, it seems he is going to do a feature for *Life* on the Church in America. The idea seems to be that there is a great Catholic revival in this country and that the future of the Church depends on *us*.

That is all news to me. If we are supposed to be reviving, where are our saints? Who keeps the fasts of the Church? Who does any penance?

Where is the poverty of religious? And what about our comfortable, well-fed, easy-going priesthood? What about the stuffiness that pervades the whole self-satisfied atmosphere of American Catholicism? When we have had something to suffer, we might do something for the world.

I am starting all over again with the business of getting out citizenship papers.

September 20, 1948. Monday

The last two Ember Days were like great feasts. Friday was in fact a feast, the Stigmatization of St. Francis, and I sat with my empty stomach and prayed behind the church while the wind moved the trees, and nobody in the world was in sight, and clouds crossed the sky with motion that was imperceptible, and those red wasps clambered all over one another on the wall of the church.

I don't know what this business is that they go in for every autumn under the eaves of the side chapels, but every once in a while a gust of wind would blow a bunch of them off into the bushes and they would struggle back up the wall and start all over again.

Day and night I think about St. Francis and about poverty as I re-read the seventh chapter of St. Bonaventure's *Itinerarium*. That same day, Friday, a letter came from Frank Sheed about that book he wants me to do. I had written asking him if he wanted me to stress the ascetic aspect of the contemplative life as a *preparation* for infused prayer, and he said no, that he wanted me to stress infused prayer. After that I realized that I was trying to be either (a) lazy, or (b) conciliatory to Father Anthony, who doesn't like me to "preach contemplation," and to the others around the house who might get upset by it.

It still strikes me as rather peculiar that in a contemplative order one should have to make so many gestures of hesitation and apology before saying anything about contemplation.

The best thing of all is that at last I can get out to work. The Tricenary has begun. Saturday, after we got our faces shaved with electric shavers, we went out and picked up apples in the orchard, walking around bent double under the low branches like the woman in the day's Gospel. Today we shoveled dirt into ditches that the rain washed out of the sheep pasture, and out of the corner of my eye I could see there was an awful lot of corn waiting to be cut in the bottoms.

I know why I will never write anything about prayer in a Journal, because anything you write, even a Journal, is at least implicitly somebody else's business. When I say prayer, I mean what happens to me in the first person singular.

In the novitiate they practice the Gradual for the Feast of St. Matthew, very loud.

September 26, 1948. Nineteenth Sunday after Pentecost

Love carries me around. Love sails me around the house. Love, love, love lifts me around the cloister. I walk two steps on the ground and four steps in the air. It is love. It is consolation. I don't care if it is consolation. I am not attached to consolation. I love God. Love carries me all around. I don't care for anything but love, love, love. I don't want to *do* anything but love. And when the bell rings, it is like pulling teeth to make myself shift because of that love, love, love, secret love, hidden love, obscure love, down inside me and outside me, where I won't talk about, where I don't care to talk about. Anyway, I don't have the time or the energy to discuss such matters. I have only time for eternity, which is to say for love, love, love. Maybe St. Theresa would like to have me snap out of it, but it is pure, I tell you; I am not attached to it (I hope) and it is love and it gives me soft punches all the time in the center of my heart. Love is pushing me around the monastery, love is kicking me all around like a gong. I tell you, love is the only thing that makes it possible for me to continue to tick.

That was the way it was up in the apple trees yesterday morning with all that blue sky. The bulls in their pens were rumbling like old men, and I thought it was Father Sub-Prior starting to sing under his breath. I say that, not because Father Sub-Prior is old, but because he happened to be near, hidden by leaves.

But, O love, why can't you leave me alone? – which is a rhetorical question meaning: for heaven's sakes don't.

That was the way it was after Communion, and in Chapter I couldn't even laugh at Father Prior's witticisms in commenting on the Rule, O love, and that was the way it was going into the refectory and hearing about the death of St. John of the Cross, who dies of love rather than epilepsy, and that is the way it is writing this, too. I feel all clean inside because I am full of You, O God, and You are love, love, Love!

Cease! Cease! Bowl me off to church!

October 3, 1948. Feast of the Holy Rosary and St. Thérèse

That was the way it was all week. In choir the less I worried about the singing, the more I was possessed by love. There is a lesson in that about being poor. You have got to be all the time cooperating with love in this house, and love sets a fast pace even at the beginning and, if you don't keep up, you'll get dropped. And yet, any speed is too slow for love – and no speed is too fast for you if you will only let love drag you off your feet – after that you will have to sail the whole way. But our instinct is to get off and start walking . . .

I want to be poor. I want to be solitary. I had a tough time after Communion and I think I was twisting and turning too much, as usual. This business burns me. *Aruit tamquam testa virtus mea.* [My strength is dried up like a potsherd (Psalms 21:16).] I am all dried up with desire and I can only think of one thing – staying in the fire that burns me.

Buildings – chant – phooey. All right for rich guys.

Dom James put flossy books about Orval in all the Scriptoriums and the flossiest of all was in ours. I looked at it and the buildings are gorgeous, but I wouldn't be seen dead living in such a place. I'd be afraid to proclaim anybody in that Chapter Room. The Sacristy looks like the circular bar on the Promenade Deck of the *Conte di Savoia* which is probably long since at the bottom of the ocean.

Yet all the liturgical stuff is beautifully done – a bit too fancy for our traditions. It is not the lines of Orval or the conception that is out of place, but the scale on which it is done. The monks have to polish floors all day and all night.

The most interesting thing Reverend Father told me after getting back from Cîteaux Wednesday was that he addressed this model community in his French, and was a terrific success. My guess is that it was his personality that went over rather than his message or his language. His message, however, was the usual one: *Tout pour Jésus, tout par Marie, toujours avec un sourire.* [All for Jesus, all through Mary, always with a smile.] Did I already say he has a rubber stamp with that on it, for okaying things? Well anyway, one of the monks came in and nearly kissed his feet afterwards and said, "What a wonderful message," and wrote him a little poem about "always with a smile," in French though. And the poem was on pretty blue paper with a drawing of a smiling saint, which was clever but a bit on the cute side. All the religious are in rapture.

The one who did it turns out to be Fr. Robert, who wrote me a beautiful letter about *Cistercian Contemplatives* on behalf of Dom Godefroid. He was saying Cîteaux wasn't as gay as it was five years ago when he came there. I guess that disease is universal and I have been going around *toujours avec un sourire* and it is mostly up my sleeve.

Father Paulinus is reader in the refectory and he has transformed an ordinary, pious book about the lady who got the Pope to institute the Feast of Christ the King – he has transformed it into something incredible. His reading makes all the syntax completely surrealistic. He inserts periods in the middle of sentences and reads unrelated thoughts as if they were tied together, and the whole thing seems to be moving under water. It makes the book most interesting. Like seeing the life of a saint from an upside down diving-bell.

October 10, 1948. Sunday

Sooner or later the world must burn, and all things in it – all the books, the cloister together with the brothel, Fra Angelico together with the Lucky Strike ads, which I haven't seen for seven years because I don't remember seeing one in Louisville. Sooner or later it will all be consumed by fire and nobody will be left, for by that time the last man in the universe will have discovered the bomb capable of destroying the universe and will have been unable to resist the temptation to throw the thing and get it over with.

And here I sit writing a diary.

But love laughs at the end of the world because love is the door to eternity, and he who loves is playing on the doorstep of eternity, and before anything can happen, love will have drawn him over the sill and closed the door and he won't bother about the world burning because he will know nothing but love.

I am coming to the conclusion that it is an advantage that our choir is so terrible, because since I have been forced to admit my absolute incapacity to do anything about it and have abandoned myself to God, I have been assailed by love in every hour of the Office. So what do I care if God wants me to glorify Him by loving Him in patience and peace through all that cacophony? Who cares about sounds, when there is Love to keep you busy and tie you up in the cloud? If God wants glory from our singing, He will know how to get it fast enough.

Today for the first time we tried a schola of eight, singing the whole Mass, and I can see where it would one day help a great deal. That was one of the ideas Reverend Father brought back from Cîteaux.

In Chapter he told us about how it was at Lisieux and La Grande Trappe and Port du Salut, where they run a power station. At La Trappe our Father Bernard, the sculptor, has discovered a system for making plaques of pious subjects, four at a time, all different sizes: the notion made me quiver.

But sooner or later the world must burn – and *The Seven Storey Mountain*[33] and *Figures for an Apocalypse*, and all the nasty pictures I did for *Jester*. I have several times thought how at the Last Day people will see my most shameful sins, and it occurs to me that I am likely to be one of the ten most abjectly humiliated sinners in the history of the world, but it will be my joy, and it will fill me with love, and I will fly like an arrow to take a back seat, very far in the back, when the last shall be first. Perhaps if Saint Francis will pray for me, and Saint John of the Cross, and Saint Mary Magdalen, I'll slide down off my high horse now and begin being the last and least in everything, but not out of injured vanity as I was in the eight-cylinder schola we had, that sang so fast *vir erat in terra Hus nomine Job* [there was a man in the land of Hus whose name was Job (Job 1:1)].

It is a toss up whether I should ask Reverend Father to give me another and fatter book to fill, for we have been talking about my writing less. In fact, I have begun to tell him all about the Carthusians and everything, and he says he doesn't see why things can't be fixed up right here. I looked at Frater Alfred's grave this afternoon and thought, "Boy, he's lucky."

But *nos qui vivimus benedicimus Domino* [we that live bless the Lord (Psalms 113:18)] by love, love, love, in the cloister and in the choir and out there in the presence of the forest and the hills, where all the colors are changing, and under the steeple whose topmost cross has been painted with yellow traffic paint by Brother Gabriel, who swung up there for days in the sky with his patron holding on to him. He upset a bucket of paint and I could see it flying upside down on the end of a rope, and the paint turned to spray before it was half way down, and a spot fell on our psalter, and there were little yellow spots all over the stones and the bushes of the cemetery where today I saw a hawk.

LAUS DEO TRINO ET MARIAE. [Praise to the Triune God and Mary.] That is the end of another book.

PERSONAL NOTES III. THE WHALE AND THE IVY.

October 15, 1948. Feast of St. Theresa

The fire of love for the souls of men loved by God consumes you like the fire of God's love, and it is the same love. It burns you up with a hunger for the supernatural happiness first of people that you know, then of people you have barely heard of, and finally of everybody.

[33] *The Seven Storey Mountain* was officially published on October 4th, six days before this entry.

This fire consumes you with a desire that is not directed immediately to action but to God. And in the swift, peaceful burning tide of that desire you are carried to prayer rather than to action, or rather, action seems to follow along with prayer and with desire, as if of its own accord. You do not think much of what you are to do and write and say for souls: you are carried away to God by hunger and desire. And this hunger is exactly the same as the hunger for your own personal union with God, but now it includes someone else, and it is for God's own sake above all, though you do not reason and separate.

Here is a great hunger, and it has a direct reference to persons, to individuals, rather than to abstract groups. Or, if it is for groups, it is for groups concretized in a typical representative who is individual, real.

In this hunger there is pain and emptiness and there is joy and it is irresistible, and somehow it is full of the strong assurance that God wants to hear all your prayers.

Sometimes you get the feeling that, when you are carried away by this desire of love for souls, God is beginning to pour out everything upon you, to deluge you with all that you need, to overwhelm you with spiritual or even temporal favors, because you are no longer paying attention to your own needs, but are absorbed in the torment of desire for the happiness of *that* soul – *that* soul – or *that* other one. Always individual and concrete.

It does not always have to be that way. You can lose sight of them all in God and pray for them as well or better perhaps, but it is still a sweet thing to be swept with the flames of this hunger and thirst for souls and, with a strange, mysterious sense of *power*, to obtain tremendous riches of joy for them from God. It makes you want to sing, and songs come up from your heart and half smother you with joy. At the same time there is anguish as if your heart would burst, giving birth to the whole world. *Rugiebam a gemitu cordis mei.* [I roared with the groaning of my heart (Psalms 37:9).]

St. Theresa of Avila, ask our God to consume us with this passionate love, and fill the world with rivers of the fire of salvation – *fluvius igneus rapidusque egrediebatur a facie Dei!* [A swift stream of fire issued forth before the face of God (Daniel 7:10)!]

October 17, 1948. XXII Sunday after Pentecost

It is getting near the end of the world, at least in the liturgy. *Si iniquitates observaveris . . .* [If you observe iniquity . . .] 3rd tone. St. Hilary in the night office says that the best way to handle the problem of rendering unto

Caesar the things that are Caesar's is to have absolutely nothing of the things that are Caesar's and then he will have no claim on you.

This morning we sang the *Te Deum* faster, but not, as I think, better. Anyway, the Angelus rang before 4:15. It is probably the first time it has done that after an ordinary Sunday office since I have been here.

October 19, 1948

This morning I got the idea that perhaps I ought to be reading something about the subdiaconate, since my ordination is coming up soon. So instead of getting off somewhere quietly and praying, I wasted almost the whole morning interval in the Scriptorium dipping into Ruysbroeck and books like that, and [Gerald] Ellard's *Christian Life and Worship*, not to mention the index to Migne *P.[atrologia] L.[atina]*. I couldn't get settled on anything. I have less and less desire to read anything about anything – all I need is a book about prayer – or a Bible – something that can give me one sentence as a spring board for contemplation. Maybe it would be better *per se* if I had a lot of thoughts about the subdiaconate. But for the moment this peaceful union seems to be God's will.

Fr. Anthony went to Georgia with Reverend Father for the Abbatial election at Conyers. Classes started again, but not ours. This morning I finished some rewriting on *Waters of Siloe*, and this afternoon I was wondering what to do about it when a telegram from Harcourt Brace said to send it there instead of waiting for them to send the ms. here. That is the way it is in this business of working for God. Sometimes you wait for months and nothing happens. Then His time comes and things begin to click so fast, they make you dizzy.

This morning before work I was thinking, "I will be lucky if I get finished this week." Laughlin is supposed to come next week and I won't get much work done – not writing. We will, I hope, get a lot of things talked about and settle them that way.

October 31, 1948. Vigil of All Saints

Floribus ejus nec rosae nec lilia desunt [Her (the Church's) flowers lack neither the roses (of martyrdom) nor the lilies (of virginity)] – and in a way the Feast of All Saints is a little sad, because I think: how many of them would have been much greater and simpler saints if the Holy Ghost had been free to make them what He wanted them to be. Many were, no doubt, pious robots and many were terrible to get along with. But all that has ended up by contributing something to their beauty.

It is not the beauty of the saints' own glory that matters, but the beauty of their glory in so far as it is the crown of Christ their King.

Beautiful stuff in a Letter of St. John of the Cross to the Nuns of Beas (Carta V) [Letter 5, vol. 3]:

Veremos las riquezas ganadas en el amor puro y sendas de la vida eternal y los pasos hermosos que dan en Cristo, cuyos deleite y corona son sus esposas: cosa digna de no andar por el suelo rodando, sino de ser tornada en las manos de los ángeles y serafines, y con reverencia y aprecio la pongan en la cabeza de un señor. [We shall see what wealth you have gained in pure love and in the paths of eternal life and what excellent progress you are making in Christ, Whose brides are His delight and crown: and a crown deserves not merely to be sent rolling along the floor, but to be taken by the angels and seraphim in their hands and set with reverence and esteem on the head of their Lord.]

Nobody ever writes us Trappists a letter like that.

Monachorumque omnium [and (the feast) of all monks] . . . the ones who copied that antiphonary from Gorimond in our vault. The ones that lived in the deserts of Egypt, of Taberna and Scete, and the ones in the deserts of the Carmelites, and the ones who prayed at Notre Dame de Casalibus, and the ones who lived at Sénanque or Vauluisant or Bonport, or the ones who started Clairvaux or were formed at Bonnevaux by St. Hugh . . .

And the pure of heart like Ida of Louvain.

And the poor in spirit like the first followers of St. Francis.

As I knelt to pray before writing this, I smelled the smell of the volumes on the shelves here – Denis the Carthusian and Duns Scotus. I am more likely to read the former than the latter. I am finished with subtleties.

It is very hard for me to read anything. I spent the whole afternoon in the cubby hole where it says *sepultura fratrum* [the brothers' graves] and watched the rain falling on the cemetery and burned with the love of God in silence and joy. Part of the time I held a book in my hand, but I couldn't read more than a few lines.

Yet I am deluged with books. Dom Moore, who is Dom Pablo Maria at Miraflores, got another Carthusian novice to get me the Burgos edition of St. John of the Cross, and that came, in red and green half-leather, utterly splendid. It makes St. John's room look like a palace. The novice's name is Conde de Puerto Hermoso.

Then Mother Paula Williamson sent me a life of Marie Victoire Thérèse Couderc, who started the Cenacle, and was pushed around quite a lot, and has a face something like Madame Privat.[34] She came from down there somewhere in the Cévennes.

And the nuns at Laval lent me some manuscripts dealing with the history of their house and with a lot of nuns whose feast is tomorrow, and I can't seem to get into any of it.

This week was busy. First Laughlin came down, then the place was full of priests of the Byzantine-Slavonic rite who, when encouraged to sing, ended up by singing two Masses a day and Benediction, and the last night they were here, they were still singing when Dom James left the Church after sprinkling everybody with holy water.

The Eastern rite – we got a good look at it this time – is in many ways impressive. More than ours, in fact. I like seeing Priest, Deacon and Subdeacon all praying together at the altar with their hands up in the air like the *orantes* [praying figures] in the Catacombs. I like the way they give the kiss of peace at the Offertory instead of just before Communion. It is more theological. "But when thou goest to present thy gift, if thou remember that thy brother has anything against thee . . . etc." Three priests coconsecrating also make the Mass more striking. Their Mass gives you a much greater sense of the reality of the Mystical Body. There is much more vital a participation between celebrants and people. It is a more contemplative Mass. I didn't bother to follow it with any of the leaflets that are floating around, but I like the wonderful triumphant thing they sing right after Communion. I like the Blessing of the People with the Chalice after Communion, and I like the "entries" or processions, especially the one at the Offertory. They make things so clear. As for pronouncing the words of Consecration out loud or, in fact, singing them while everyone answers "Amen" – that is splendid. I wish we did that. It make much more sense. Our Liturgy is too private. And yet I admit that all the polyphonic music got so lush that it sickened me a little, and at the last great Mass I was deliberately paying no attention to the singing or the movements of the ministers, but simply uniting myself interiorly with the Sacrifice and trying to keep empty and at peace, without being dragged around by emotions.

For hours and days afterwards the monks have been going around holding their heads with polyphonic Ruthenian music chasing itself round

---

[34] Mme. Privat tended Merton as a boy in France when he was ill.

and round in their memories. Last night one of them was singing their "Alleluia, Alleluia" in his sleep.

Laughlin came and liked the Greek rite and took some poems I was not altogether ready to let go. He read a life of Charles de Foucauld, and had with him something by a Jewish mystic[35] which Rexroth had lent him. He brought proofs of *Seeds of Contemplation*, and said he was going to vote for Norman Thomas in the presidential election, as a gesture of despair.

He said Munich was terrible – I mean the bombing had been awful. He said that the people outside seem to have an obscene hunger for violence and death – a craving to be destroyed. That was what Christopher Hollis said, too, in *Horizon*. But I think, on the other hand, of all the happy letters from our monasteries in France and all the good Catholic writing that is being done. He said, "Well, the monasteries are in the country." Our Order, yes.

His mother has a farm called Big Springs about fifty miles from Pittsburg in the mountains, and he said, if he inherited it, he couldn't think of anything he would rather do with it than give it to the Carthusians.

I got permission to take him for a walk outside the enclosure, as if we were just going to stand on the hill behind Nally's and look at the view, but in the end we went all the way out to the top of the knobs, behind the lake. I did not know they were so steep. We seemed to be high and looking right down on the monastery, although we couldn't see it much because of the trees. We sat on the top where there was a fine view across the valley and he told me Robert Lowell was leaving the Church . . .

When we were climbing down again, I stopped in the middle of a very steep place and explained to him about Theresa Neumann, how she never ate. When we got back to the monastery, there was a letter from Sister [Mary] Madeleva about the leaflet I wrote on Contemplation and I am glad that is going to be settled.

We sat in the garden and one of the Byzantine-Slavonic priests walked around and around reading *Cistercian Contemplatives* with his forehead all puckered up. Maybe he is the one who, as Reverend Father told us, wants to become a Trappist.

In the refectory we read [Theodore Maynard's] *Mystic in Motley*, but it was just interrupted and replaced by a translation of *Quas Primas*, the encyclical on Christ the King, today being the Feast of Christ the King. And

[35] Martin Buber.

the more I think about it, the more I believe that, if we ask Him, He will give us peace – and that He is preparing great things for us, but in His own way – *per crucem* [through the Cross].

November 9, 1948

It is the feast of Elizabeth of the Trinity.

I used to think it would be a good thing to die young and quickly, but now I am beginning to think a long life with much labor and suffering for God would be the greater grace. However *in concreto* [concretely] the greater grace for each individual is the one God wills for him. If God wills you to die suddenly, that is a greater grace for you than any other death, because it is the one He has chosen, by His love, with all the circumstances of your life and His glory in view.

It is beautiful to see God working in souls. I thought the letters about *The Seven Storey Mountain* were going to be a penance. In a way they are. And yet they are all very beautiful and spiritual and filled with the love of God. People write with great simplicity to me as though it were the most natural thing in the world, and I feel as if I had known them for a long time and I wish I could answer them. To most of them I send a printed card. But it is beautiful to see how genuine people really are. They are not bitter or twisted or warped the way one might suppose. The ones who *are* at any rate haven't been writing to me.

But it is beautiful to see God's grace working in a soul. The most beautiful thing about it is to see how the desires of the soul inspired by God so fit in and harmonize with grace that holy things seem *natural* to the soul, seem to be part of its very self. That is what God wants to create in us – that marvelously simple spontaneity in which His life becomes perfectly ours and our life His, and it seems absolutely inborn in us to act as His children, and to have His light shining in our eyes.

Dear God, I love you so much. Please make Your light shine in souls. Fill them with your love, and make them act in You and for You and express Your love unconsciously in every thought and every act of their lives *in laudem gloriae gratiae tuae, amen* [in praise of the glory of your grace, amen].

November 14, 1948. Sunday. Day of Recollection

Tomorrow is the Feast of the Dedication of the Church. I am Servant of the Church this week and went around lighting the candles on the anointed walls, reaching over the heads of the choir with a flaming taper on the end of a long pole. As I lit the one under Our Lady's window, the choir was reciting *Nisi Dominus aedificaverit domum* [Unless the Lord build the house (Psalms 126:1)], and I asked Our Lady to bless this house and all of us with her peace. But then Benediction was terrible – a mix-up in the singing. But I am resigned. It was so mixed up that it would be hard to say just whose fault it was, but really, if we are going to sing *in toto corde* [with whole heart], we ought to practice it. We started out too high. Then the choir did not sing the parts assigned for the choir . . . etc., etc.

We have found out who is the new Abbot in Georgia. They elected Fr. Robert McGann, my novice master, and theirs, too, for a long time – at the moment novice master in Utah. And Reverend Father and Fr. Anthony leave for Utah tomorrow, to hold the election there. And Reverend Father said, "Fr. Robert isn't eligible any more, so he can be the other witness."

Day of Recollection: somebody has got to take the chant and office seriously. I am so scared of being made cantor that I have been holding back and trying to stay in the background, out of a humility that is utterly false. Also, it does no good for people to pass over me – it only makes me feel smug. For me it takes more humility to do a real job of work in choir than to keep out of the picture. May God guide me. If I try to yell, I get flat. If I don't yell, I'm not heard. If I do yell, nobody follows me anyway. It is useless to try to keep up the tone, yet on a rough guess that that is what the cantor wants me to do, I try to keep up the tone.

Before I can do what is expected of me in this choir, I must have all the simplicity of a dove and the prudence of a serpent – and some courage. Sometimes the burden of continuing to sing against what seems to be simply inhuman obstacles gets to be so heavy that I am ready to run right out of the Church. At least I hope God will keep me from doing that.

Still, I realize that, when He wills, everything will suddenly get to be O.K.

Evelyn Waugh is supposed to be on his way here. Two telegrams from Harcourt Brace said so, and several phone calls from *Time* said so. *Time* called all the way from New York to get J. Edward Hagan, the painter in New Haven, to hold his car in readiness to drive Waugh to the airport when he leaves here. And Hagan said, "Gee, that man must own the whole of New York." But none of the telegrams or telephone calls have said when Waugh is going to come.

November 24, 1948. Feast of St. John of the Cross
Et praeparavit Dominus piscem grandem ut deglutiret Jonam. [Now the Lord prepared a great fish to swallow up Jonas (Jonah 2:1).]

It is the feast of St. John of the Cross and during the morning interval I sat in the choir of the infirm – not that I was sick – and looked all the way down the empty nave at the angel right up in the top of Our Lady's window and listened to the silence of the graces obtained for me by St. John entering the center of my soul.

When Fr. Anthony was away in Utah, he left us some work to do on the Gifts of the Holy Ghost, and so I took this opportunity to use the red half of the ribbon on the rebuilt Remington Clare Boothe Luce gave us, and I typed some notes on John of St. Thomas' *De Donis [Concerning the Gifts of the Holy Spirit]*.

St. John of the Cross was, I think, guided eminently by the Gift of Counsel, which should be very strong in all who are called to teach contemplation. In fact, Counsel shows us the best means for arriving at contemplation and for staying there, and I think it is ordered to exterior action in so far as that action can ultimately contribute to contemplation, at least in heaven. Or, to put it another way, Counsel orders external action in such a way that it interferes as little as possible with the contemplative life. St. John of the Cross' notes on direction, on when to give up meditation, and on the "three blind guides" *(Living Flame)* show you the Gift of Counsel at work. Counsel says, *venite seorsum [in desertum locum] et requiescite pusillum* [Come ye apart into a desert place, and rest a while (Mark 6:31)].

November 30, 1948. Feast of St. Andrew. Tuesday

It is already Advent. In the last minutes before the retreat the novices are practicing some sweet polyphony for the small centenary celebration we are supposed to be holding on December 21st. Bishop Cotton is alleged to be going to say the Matutinal Mass, and Archbishop Floersh is to sing the High Mass, but nothing has been said about anyone being ordained subdeacon by either of them.

I am terrified that Archbishop Floersh might want to talk to me – and will thus discover that I know no theology.

Evelyn Waugh arrived Saturday night after everyone was in bed and left Sunday at noon in a storm of rain. I expected him to be taller and more dashing: but he was very nice and friendly.

The first thing he did was to reproach me with the fact that the house was so hot. He said it made the book all wrong. The laybrother novices have got that huge boiler working now, and that is the cause of all the trouble. We are still in summer clothing and yet I sweat in choir.

E. Waugh said Hollywood was very dull. He expected great jewels and thought everything would surely be done with parades of elephants, but found that the people were just business men doing their business and that there was not entertainment anywhere except in the cemetery which, he said, he visited every day.

He offered to send us books but said that [Graham Greene's] *The Heart of the Matter* and [Waugh's own] *The Loved One* were not proper material for our refectory.

The lady on *Time, Life* and *Fortune*, who arranged his itinerary for him, routed him from Cincinnati to Louisville via Washington, D.C.

He said he was doing America the way Americans did Europe. He was on the way to New Orleans where there were pressing invitations for him to accept the hospitality of the Archbishop, and he energetically refused.

Also he said he couldn't read any poetry written since [Alfred Lord] Tennyson, and when I talked about pious art, he said that at any rate the pious art that is going out of fashion now is far better than that which is coming in – saints fixed up "like motor mascots." He thought the house had character and that it looked Irish. I said perhaps that was on account of the weather, but he said it was on account of the pointed windows of the novitiate.

At his home in Gloucestershire he says he has a painting of a Trappist by [Francesco de] Zurbarán, on the stairway. I argued that it must be a Carthusian, but we settled for "Cistercian." Privately I still think it is a Carthusian. Anyway the monk's name was Jiménez.

Waugh is doing an article for *Life* on the Church in America and he kept repeating that it would "necessarily be superficial." He is very careful about trying to do things well, if possible, and so he wants to prepare everyone in case this cannot be done marvelously well. He saw some "charming negro nuns" in Baltimore, and saw Dorothy Day, and was at Grailville. I forgot to ask him what he was going to see in New Orleans. Maybe the Leper Colony down there.

Also Dr. Law was talking to a group of monks – mostly confessors and novice masters – Fr. Vincent de Paul and I being the only non-priests. The talks were about psychiatry and ended in a general discussion as to whether the average novice could read St. John of the Cross with profit or even without harm. I don't know the answer. Right now they are singing and singing and singing, and they have already begun to decorate the place for Christmas.

December 1, 1948. On Retreat

Tonight we will sing the commemoration of little St. Bibiana who stands in the doorway of the new liturgical year. She always meets you there. She is quiet and unobtrusive and generally has nothing to say. Her prayer is in the antiphonary and you notice it at the end of the old season, with a picture of an angel under it holding, I think, a scroll, saying *Deo Gratias*. The *Deo Gratias* is for the old season, but St. Bibiana belongs to the new.

I can judge retreats I make by the quality of what I write about them in the journal, and I must say the quality of none of my notes is very high, especially when I am on retreat and pushing and pulling at myself to find out what is wrong. But what I mean to say is, when my investigations look silly on paper, then they *are* silly in fact. If my questions and examinations really had some point, they would also, I think, be interesting – at least to me. I am the one they are supposed to concern.

Here goes.

During the past year, temptations to become a Carthusian have more or less subsided, at least for the time being. It seems to me they began to subside the precise moment when, on retreat last year, I opened an envelope from France which had a 13th century picture of St. Louis in it, from Fr. Anselme Dimier at Tamié. Dom Marie Joseph helped and Dom Gabriel helped and I am ashamed to say the success of *The Seven Storey Mountain* helped, and Dom James got me to declare formally I didn't intend to run off and be a Carthusian before he would let me be a subdeacon. I told him I didn't intend to do that right now and never would do it unless he would let me.

So this year that is not what I am being asked to give up.

What is God asking? Last night the retreat master (Fr. Cletus Mulloy, a Passionist) dropped some such phrase as "more generous cloistered service" or "more generosity in my life of cloistered service" or "more generosity in my cloistered life of service." I am holding back with both hands on the reins against the possibility of being shoved into jobs that will take all my time and upset me and in which I will get worn out and be a spectacular – or unspectacular – failure. All this is not willed on my part – it is subconscious or half-conscious. So I'll have to exorcise it by a more complete obedience and renunciation and get ready to take it on the chin if I have to be cantor. Hardly anything could make the choir worse. I suppose one of the first things I need to do is to stop brooding over how bad it is.

Then take a deep breath and trust in God to pull you through. *Os meum aperui et adtraxi spiritum quia mandata tua desiderabam.* [I opened my mouth and panted: because I longed for thy commandments (Psalms 118:131).]

December 2, 1948. On Retreat

Today, unless I am mistaken, is the feast of Bl. John Ruysbroeck – or would be if he had one. The morning sky behind the new horsebarn was as splendid as his writing. A thousand small high clouds went flying majestically like ice-floes, all golden and crimson and saffron, with clean blue and aquamarine behind them, and shades of orange and red and mauve down by the surface of the land where the hills are just visible in a pearl haze and the ground was steel-white with frost – every blade of grass as stiff as wire.

In my interior life there is a small area of raw and inflamed and infected thought and emotion, and it concerns the choir and the head cantor. The pitch-pipe blows and the cantor comes in a quarter-tone below the pipe and the choir comes in a quarter-tone below him and we all start singing together like a bunch of rusty machines. This week I am sub-invitator, and so my pride is involved. I give out the psalms on what I think is the right note which is supposed, these days, to be "f♯." In ten seconds we are all singing "f," and then "e," and I, on my side, continue with painstaking refinement to sing what I think is "f♯." Father Raymond's voice can be heard on the other side in a loud, piteous complaint which gets everybody mad, and f-sharp becomes totally unpopular. Then someone else, as a reproach to the Abbot's side, sings e-flat and immediately the novices and the solid contingent of flats on our side picks it up and it goes down to "d", and I relapse into a dignified undertone, sulking with all my might and muttering things that do not assuage my feelings. And that is how it is every day. Sometimes I get so sore, I'm out of breath. Then the head-cantor comes in with his notion that we must stop abruptly every time we come to a bar, and I shudder and enter into a significant hush, which is intended to convey the thought that I cannot possibly cooperate with a sacrilege.

I wonder if Jesus ever gets tired of waiting for me to grow up. I hope not.

The things that strike me most about the subdiaconate all remind me how incomplete and half-baked my notion of my vocation has been even until now. *In ecclesiae ministerio semper mancipatus* [In the ministry of the church always the servant]: that is something that I already am, by virtue of my solemn vows. I am a *public* minister of the Church – I am not merely here for my own sanctification: my vocation implies a special public function in the Church. I am assigned a very definite duty – that of officially praising God for the Church and for the whole of creation, and doing it in public, and doing it as well as I can for those who cannot do it at all. More depends on this than my own soul. The Church militant will be better or worse for the way I do things in choir, and the way I help others do them. To be subcantor in a Cistercian monastery – and worse still, to be cantor – is to hold a position on which tremendous issues depend. The very notion of such a thing makes me shiver and moan. I hope that patience and control of one's temper can contribute something to all this and make up for what we don't give by singing.

If the choir is a cross – it is still not enough to say, "Oh well, it is a cross," and fix a smile on your face and try to bear it. You also have to make some attempt to *improve* things – and do them well.

Generally this is not much fun.

I have been very poor in liturgical sense.

Now I am to be appointed to work in the sanctuary – to bring up the paten and chalice and the matter for sacrifice – to stand at the altar with the priest and deacon, as the link between the people and the ministers, connecting the people's sacrifice with Christ's.

The Mystical Body comes into the Rite of Ordination very explicitly. The *Pontifical* is careful to point out that the ministry of the subdeacon does not extend merely to formalities and rites concerning inanimate things – vessels, linen. The altar is the living Christ and the linens are the members of His Mystical Body. Bringing their gifts to unite them with Him on the Cross, I am dressing Christ in His members and clothing His sacrifice in the glory of a saved Church. *Attendite quale ministerium vobis tradetur.* [Be aware of what kind of ministry has been given to you.]

So I think that is why, at this precise moment, God has caused me to start getting so many letters from people who want prayers. I'll take all those people up to the altar of God who rejoiceth my youth.

Et ideo si usque nunc fuisti tarde ad Ecclesiam. [And so, if up to now you have been late for Church.] That means not only late in point of time, but indifferent to the liturgy. The very first time I was appointed to anything in the novitiate – torch-bearer on the Feast of the Epiphany, 1942, three weeks after I arrived – I made a gesture of protest. "Too soon! What do I know about all that stuff." I have never been good at ceremonies. Sometimes I have gone through them with positive irritation. *Si usque nunc tarde . . .*

Dr. Law thinks the best treatment for neurotics in our life is to keep giving them something to do in the community. Psycho-therapy for a hermit: put him in the sanctuary, give him a maniple and tunic and appoint him to some function and let him sing. Fr. Thomas Plassman says all this comes after the Litany to remind you what you are getting into – you take your place in line with those you have been invoking, and *do* something in the Mystical Body.

December 4, 1948. On Retreat

The only sign so far that there is any fruit for me in this retreat is that I am recapturing a great respect and love for the *Usages*, the common life, subjection, in obedience, to a Superior. I think it is very important that a retreat should help a Cistercian to recover *a taste* for *The Spiritual Directory*, if he has lost it a little – recover a little unction in his relations with his community – his brothers – if he has lost that. Apart from this – the retreat has been a long string of temptations which have not, however, affected my underlying peace. And I just had a very good, though somewhat extra-curricular, talk with Reverend Father.

Key words jump out at me from p. 31 of the French Directory: *La vie en commun assouplit le caractère*. [The common life softens the character.] I had just been talking to Reverend Father about someone in the community who thinks he has the ligature. I was thinking about the freedom and ease and suppleness of the spirit that makes the true contemplative. For us, the way to that goes right through the cloister and the community. Lower down on the same page I read, *C'est vraiment la maison du Seigneur, il la remplit de sa présence et de son action, la vie divine y découle toutes parts.* [This is truly the house of the Lord, He fills it with His presence and His action, here the divine life overflows on all sides.]

Dieu caché dans nos supérieurs à peu près comme au Tabernacle, nous instruit par leur bouche. [Hiding in our superiors, somewhat as in the Tabernacle, God instructs us through their mouth.]

The atmosphere of contemplation is the atmosphere of happy humility that pervades the Rule of St. Benedict, and especially Chapter VII. It is *not* an atmosphere of conflict and strain in which everyone is trying to get away from everybody else, and trying to get out of monastic or liturgical duties, but striving in all things *ut nemo contristetur in domo Dei* [that no one be sad in the house of God].

Also read Dom Lehodey's introductory letter in the General Chapter report on means to increase the interior life (1922) – importance of detachment, especially humility, of knowing how to use every incident of the Cistercian life as a means to detachment and love – sanctify all our exercises by a deep spirit of faith.

Nos voeux et nos règles sont pour nous le plus sûr moyen de sanctification. [Our vows and our rules are for us the best means of sanctification.]

Il ne faut rien négliger, rien ajouter, rien n'omettre non plus dans nos saintes règles. [Where our holy rules are concerned, we must neglect nothing, add nothing, and omit nothing.] Use these rules for what? To separate us from the world and unite us to God. *Plus un religieux met de ferveur à arracher ses facultés au souvenir des choses d'ici bas pour les fixer dans les choses supérieures, plus son âme deviendra pure, plus intense sa vie intérieure, et plus cette âme sera pure et dégagée plus la grâce y agira puissamment.* [The more fervor a religious invests in wrenching his faculties away from the memory of the things of earth in order to attach them to the higher things, the purer his soul will become and the more intense his interior life; and, the more pure and detached this soul becomes, the more powerfully will grace work within it.]

He also refers to the beautiful passage in the Directory where the monastery is described as a *Schola Divini Servitii* [a School of Divine Service], and he shows how Christ directs and teaches us through the Rule and our Superiors.

In all this there is nothing exteriorly very exciting, and it has taken me seven years to really notice and appreciate it. However, it takes the Rule and the Common Life to untie all the knots of worry and trouble and unquiet that gather in your head when you are living on your own.

December 6, 1948. On Retreat

The sun is coming up between the garage and the hog-house. The duck pond is nearly dried up. Of course I told you, my dear Osric, that the ducks are long since gone. Yesterday, Feast of St. Francis Xavier, it was so warm that I could sit out there in one of the coves behind the church, holding the *Usages* in my hand, and squinting out through the fine rain at branches of the whitewashed sycamores.

I went to the retreat master yesterday and he sat in that ratty old throne we still use for pontificals and heard my confession. He told me he had read *The Seven Storey Mountain* and liked it. He told me to pray every day for humility. He told me to write books to help, for instance, nuns in mixed orders. And he said I ought to try to write on the contemplative life in the same style as the *Mountain,* if I could. About fan-mail he said I ought to have someone to screen it and sift it out. Dom Frederic used to. Fr. Prior has the mail now, but his tendency is to dump everything in my lap un-opened. One of the first things I must fix is this mail situation. Without working out any solution of my own – put it up to Reverend Father and take the solution given by obedience. Fr. Mulloy also said, concerning poverty, that I ought never to ask for anything without first consulting su-periors – in other words, not so much presuming of permission and mak-ing it O.K. afterwards.

Poverty is another thing in my life that needs fixing very much!

Clare Boothe Luce sent us two volumes of records of Handel's *Messiah*. It arrived all of a sudden Saturday. That seems to me to be on the border-line of what Cistercians can't use. Then Laughlin sent a volume of Lino-type faces for which I had asked. It is so fat, it embarrasses me. Also in that room I have Pound's *Pisan Cantos* and Williams' *Paterson* and copies of *Horizon* and a XIVth century martyrology I forgot to put back in the vault – and the record player and all those records and the new typewriter Clare Boothe Luce sent, and all the Burgos edition of St. John of the Cross and some of the books Sister Thérèse [Lentfoehr] sent.

The mere fact that the room is dirty does not make me poor.

Among the fifteen thousand external graces I have to thank God for in this year have been my meetings – by letter – with so many charming people – Sister Madeleva, Sister Thérèse, and all the other nuns who have been writing here. Almost all the letters I have been getting have been smart and intelligent and holy. All the same there are too many and they ought, in Fa-ther Mulloy's term, to be "screened."

Yesterday Reverend Father announced I was supposed to be ordained sub-deacon on the Feast of St. Thomas the Apostle which is also our hun-dredth anniversary.

I took a good look at the subdeacon at Mass. I never realized what a dif-ference between the subdeacon and the deacon. The subdeacon is really not a glorified acolyte. During all the essential parts of the sacrifice, he is standing down there *in plano* [at the lowest level of the sanctuary] hiding his face behind the humeral veil and saying, "I am excluded from the mys-teries – I am waiting until some menial job needs to be done, some errand between the altar and the credence table." In short, he runs errands for the deacon. On the other hand, he is much more than the Servant of the Church, whose proper place is in choir. The subdeacon is at least vested and localized in the sanctuary, and he has an epistle to sing. On the other hand, the epistle is only one step above a prophecy and, if the Conventual Mass were to be merely sung by the hebdomadary alone, someone would be appointed to go from the choir to sing the epistle, just like a prophecy.

I have never seen that done, but may see it at a new foundation.

Talking about new foundations, the roof leaks at Our Lady of the Trinity and this was one of the thoughts that distracted me this morning during meditation.

December 8, 1948. Feast of the Immaculate Conception

This afternoon the guns over at Fort Knox were making a lot of noise, Lady, and I wondered if it was because I was impatient in choir. However, I asked you for peace last winter and there are saints somewhere asking you for peace this winter, and so I join my prayers to theirs. And tonight, when we renew our vows here, I for my part will certainly be meaning it, even though I may be in a funny mood about something. And the same thing holds good for the *Te Deum* we are going to sing so loud and so off-key.

I would say I give myself to you, I consecrate myself to you, but I have said it before, and now I mean it more than before, only I can't think of a strong word. Lady, I have written too much and I am not as good at words as a writer ought to be, and when I talk to you, the deep things I ought to say simply leave me inarticulate. But anyway, I can say I love you, not by spectacular speeches and gestures, but by being a poor, plain Trappist, obscure and more or less stupid and not notable for anything. Never mind. My turn will come soon, and I will be left in a corner like everybody else.

December 13, 1948. St. Lucy

So I begin my eighth year in the community at Gethsemani.

One of the things that makes me happiest is that, by some miracle, I have been able to get out into the woods a few times this month to the common work. The work has never, as far as I remember, been so far away: more than two miles out, and on the other side of the knobs.

At Achel they complain they have no vocations and make a novena to get some. Today in chapter we voted on some seven professions, maybe nine. Three were to be solemn. We are too easy, taking people in.

What do you think, you dope, after having been a Trappist for seven years? I think – where did the time go? I caught myself thinking: have I changed? Not that it matters. I have and I haven't. I'm balder. Somehow I have more of an interior life, but I'd have a hard time trying to say how.

But I know some of the things that account for it: solemn profession – theology – the trials I have had with people here and there concerning writing, singing, contemplation. What graces all these little crosses have been. They have been always the very best thing in our life here. It seems they are so small. They do their work. They are coming in greater abundance now. How God works on your soul by these obscure and unremarkable sufferings that cleanse and drain your wounds. I am glad of every cross I have had and thank God in advance for all those that are to come. Other graces – minor orders – the writing job, to some extent – all the books, hours of prayer – and God has taught me to find myself more in Him or lose myself more: it comes to the same thing. And I am tremendously glad of the prayers of the people who have read *The Seven Storey Mountain* and glad to pray for them.

December 14, 1948

I am richer, now that I am poor, than I ever was when I was bourgeois with a well-to-do grandfather. Today we got 1,000 copies of the pamphlet I wrote on Contemplation last spring. Sister Madeleva printed it for us out of the sheer kindness of her heart. I had scarcely finished looking at that when a check for $1350.00 came in from Curtis Brown. Harcourt Brace thought it would be nice to advance some royalties as a Christmas present . . .

And the most precious thing I had today was an hour of silence behind the church. It has been warm and damp and the knobs are hidden in mist. It started to rain a little and I came in, but the laybrother novices were practicing part singing in the choir novitiate and were singing better than the choir novices who were practicing Gregorian chant in the professed singing room. By that time I discovered that it wasn't really raining after all and so I escaped to my silence and stood out there all alone, drugged and happy, with a book under my arm.

Tomorrow: revolution. Self-shaving is to be introduced at Gethsemani for the first time in a century. Father Prior is going to give out brushes and safety razors and small bars of ivory soap and (O horror!) mirrors. Father Abbot has received a letter of instructions from Our Lady of the Valley telling all about how to shave. We are supposed to shave twice a week. Such effeminacy! All the electric shavers are to be, perhaps, sold. We shall rake and hack at our own miserable chins. In the end this is going to be more penitential – but faster. We don't have to sit around waiting our turn.

Apparently this is what they do in Europe. Dom Gabriel was shocked to see us so hairy.

I am invitator and I sing, *Tota pulchra es, Maria* [You are wholly beautiful, Mary].

Elevare elevare consurge Jerusalem! [Arise, arise, stand up, O Jerusalem (Isaiah 51:17)!] Who cares about royalties? *Solve vincula colli tui captiva filia Sion.* [Loose the bonds from off thy neck, O captive daughters of Sion (Isaiah 52:2).]

Berliner and Lanigan sent us an Advent house – you open a window each day and lo! a picture symbolizing one of the "O" antiphons. Tomorrow is Ember Wednesday – O happy fast! – and the Great "O's" begin Friday.

December 19, 1948. 4th Sunday of Advent
O Radix Jesse! [O Root of Jesse!]

I was kneeling in Reverend Father's room while a stream of people kept coming in and out. One of the people was Fr. Prior with a program for the centenary celebrations on Tuesday and I realized how kind God's Providence had been in getting me ordained subdeacon on that day. *Omnia cooperantur in bonum iis qui diligunt Deum.* [To them that love God, all things work together unto good (Romans 8:28).] There was once a passing thought of getting me ordained in September, but first Fr. Anthony was against it, and then Reverend Father died and things conspired to make this the only sensible time, and as a result I am dispensed from any part in the singing and charades or whatever is coming off to celebrate our founding. I will just sit still and fast and be smug and wait to receive the *tunica jucunditatis* [the garment of rejoicing].

Everett Hogan is going to bring a stove all the way over from New Haven to fry (he says) some fish and it will be so unusual that everybody will probably get sick and I remember the last big banquet (Dom Frederic's Jubilee in the Order – 1944). I was reader in the refectory and ice cream set aside for me melted and I didn't eat the fish and I couldn't sleep during the meridienne either because I thought I had insulted the Archbishop.

Today (it is colder) I walked about in the cemetery learning the prayers you say when vesting for the Conventual Mass. *Da Domine virtutem manibus meis ad abstergendum omnem maculam.* [O Lord, give power to my hands to cleanse away every stain.]

I write out on little yellow cards all the rules for what the subdeacon must do in all the different kinds of Masses and keep them in the top left pocket of our robe, over my heart, to show that I am disposed to love the liturgy above everything. And I have put (or tried to put) everything out of my mind except being a subdeacon.

[Pius] Parsch says the subdeacon sings the Epistle facing the altar because the altar represents Christ and the Office of subdeacon is like that of St. John the Baptist.

December 20, 1948. Vigil of St. Thomas

Today Fr. Amandus and I had a day of recollection before ordination – our regular retreat having been accounted as the annual one.

Going up to the infirmary chapel for two short conferences somehow made a deep impression on me. The little chapel has filled up with associations attached to all the retreats I have made since receiving the habit nearly seven years ago. And what is more, the three happy days last Lent, when I was up there listening to the frogs, all came back with a rush. I looked at the primitive perspective in Fr. Odo's decorations, and read the curious letters that spelled out *Joseph Filii Dei nutritie* [Joseph, foster-father of the son of God], and the melody of St. Joseph's litany began to play over and over again in my mind.

And Father Amadeus was the same old Father Amadeus, but he made a deep impression, too. After the last conference I stayed alone in the chapel and let everything sink in, and steeped my heart in the great warmth flowing out of the Tabernacle.

In the cemetery I looked up at the sky and thought of the great sea of graces that was flowing down on Gethsemani as her hundredth year is ending. All the crosses stood up and spoke to me for fair this time. It was as if the earth were shaking under my feet and as if the jubilant dead were just about to sit up and sing.

And I got some taste of how much there is to be glad for in the world because of Gethsemani. Not that I am looking for any such taste any more: only how to serve God better and belong more completely to Him.

Fr. Amadeus was speaking of the need for a concrete spiritual ideal. What strikes me is the need of something absolutely concrete and definite – poverty, humility: not something abstract, off in the heavens, but here, at Gethsemani. Not for other people first, but for myself first. To make it a real ideal you work for, not just one you occasionally think and preach about. To ask God somehow to make me the quietest and meekest and most unobtrusive man in the whole house, the *poorest* man, the one with nothing. I am right at the other end of the pole from all that – but in the circumstances God has given me to work with, there are still graces – and all the Fathers of Gethsemani, whom I love, will all pray for me.

Fr. Euthymius who was, I think, the first sub-prior; Fr. Theotine who was, as I believe, the cantor; Fr. Timothy who did the fancy woodwork; those who ran away once or twice and came back; Brother Theodoret to whom I prayed one cold St. Thomas day when I was feeling sad in the woods – and later Brother Simon the shoemaker who gave me the Holy Ghost poem – all will pray for me.

There are little blue flowers on the grave of Brother Conrad, the cellarer, who used to run all around the fields swinging his arms to the great scandal of many.

December 25, 1948. Christmas Day

Yesterday the first snow of the winter fell and last night before the Midnight Mass someone made me a furtive sign that it was snowing again. And so this morning is very beautiful, not because there is much snow, for it is as thin as sugar on the porridge of the monks under twenty-one who can't fast, and the grey grass comes through it everywhere. Nor is it beautiful because the sky is bright, for the sky is dark. But it is beautiful because of Christmas.

Last night at the Midnight Mass I went on for the first time as subdeacon. The thing that most struck me – in fact it amazed me: I felt as if I had been wearing a maniple and tunic all my life, and it seemed to me as if I had grown up in the sanctuary and never done anything else but minister at the altar and sing the Epistle, as if I belonged there and always had belonged there and as if anything unrelated to this were strange and difficult. Not that I didn't make mistakes. I chased the acolyte away, thinking Reverend Father would not use any water at the ablutions because of the three Masses, but would only wash out the chalice and ciborium with wine. I suppose he could have put his fingers in the little glass of water that was there, but since the M.C. emptied it for him to pour the wine in from the chalice . . . well, anyway, he wanted water for the ablutions.

I felt somehow that I was giving the *Pax* with a new kind of authority, as if a special power to spread Christ's peace all over the world had now been vested in me. Standing there with the paten in front of my face, the only unfamiliar thing was that my thumb got tired. I thought of St. Augustine and the Mystical Body. It seems to me subdiaconate ought to take me back to the Fathers, who had such a perfect sense of what the liturgy is all about, who knew how to make it contemplation because they saw themselves praising God in the One Christ. For now I am much more a *part of the*

Mass than ever before. I am much more closely identified with the Host Who is broken on the altar. I am a member, that is an instrument, a limb He uses in explicit reference to His Mass and His worship of the Father.

And the *tunica jucunditatis* is the first garment of any kind about which I have consciously realized, from the first moment of putting it on, that it *belonged on my shoulders* and that *I was born for it.*

(Father Amadeus walks through the scriptorium smiling and making gestures and bumping into the desks. The brothers sing vociferously in the singing room because today we are to have another show in Chapter.)

In bed I was singing over and over to myself *Exivit per clausam portam.* [He came out through the closed door.] I mean the second time we went to bed. I served Father Anthony's Mass at Our Lady's Altar (Immaculate Heart) in the Brother's choir and he had on the white chasuble which was part of the set his friends gave him when he made solemn profession: one of the few decent vestments. (Father Michael had another good chasuble at the High Altar for his private Masses – that sort of ivory affair with a Byzantine looking figure of Our Lady and the four evangelists). Anyway, on the back of Fr. Anthony's chasuble was written *Mater humilitatis* [Mother of humility] in blue, and after the Consecration I looked at Our Lord and got a terrific desire for His humility. I am humble after a fashion, but when people cross me up, although I give in, I am interiorly too sardonic and tough about it, and I resist, and try to get even by being secretly contemptuous. But Christmas is given us to make us love the kind of humility that is *love* and embraces contradiction and difficulties and all the rest with joy. Maybe He will give me some of his joy in being in the crib. How can I say I love Him until I like what He likes? So in the end I was thinking of St. Francis and his spirit. That made three saints I thought of and invoked especially in this night. In between St. Augustine and St. Francis came St. John of the Cross – at the Matutinal Mass.

Christmas makes me think for some reason of our Fathers of 12th century Cîteaux. The landscape is Cistercian, for one thing – bare and covered with white – austere and simple. And yet there is all this innocence, the mixture of austerity and childhood joy . . . I looked up in the *Nomasticon* [*Cisterciense,* "Digest of Cistercian Laws and Ordinances," 1664, revised 1892 by Hugues Séjalon] what our Fathers used to do. How there was a fire in the callefactorium but they could sit in the cloister and read, and they didn't go back to bed. I wonder what time they got up? Then I started looking for the Homily from Origen prescribed for the 3rd nocturn of Christmas Eve, but it isn't in the half-baked Latin version of Migne's *P. L.* we have in the Common Box . . .

And then I think of Blessed Richard and the monks who went to live under the trees in Skelldale (Fountains) on St. Stephen's Day. And I think of how St. Bernard loved the Christmas martyrology, and how he told the monks not to be fooled by people who wanted them to make the life soft and comfortable: austerity as part of the temper of Christmas, but austerity overwhelmed by liberty and joy. I can't think of anything better to give Jesus than the humility of the Rule – *quippe quibus nec voluntates nec corpora habent in sua potestate.* [The Rule actually reads: *quippe quibus nec corpora sua nec voluntates licet habere in propria potestate* (since they are permitted to have neither body nor will in their own power RB 33:4).] And to be very glad and satisfied at all the occasions for giving up my judgment – which is only a burden anyway – except too, that there are times when it is humility to use your judgment.

In fact, the whole problem is this: it would be relatively easy just to give up your mind and will and be a block of stone. But when you have to keep using your head and making decisions according to the Rule and for the glory of God – and go on doing so with measure and love and proportion when you are crossed up and sat on – to accept the obstacles and yet go on *doing* God's will, *too*, besides suffering what He *permits*, when the two tend to be contradictory. I might be wrong, but it seems to me this is enormously difficult and demands a kind of genius for humility, which I certainly haven't got. But it is in Our Lady's hands.

I wonder how Christmas was at Tintern in 1248, at Clairvaux in 1148, at Cîteaux in 1108? How was it at Bellevaux and Rosières and Châtillon, at Bonport, at all the places where there were saints: Villers, Heisterbach, Tamié, Bonnevaux, Poblet, Santes Creus, Heiligenthal, Ter Doest, Rievaulx, Fossanova . . .

Later.

I dug up the *Omelia Origenis* [Homily of Origen] in the vault after dinner: found it in a Breviary printed at Strasbourg in 1494 by order of Jean Petit. It is pretty much the same as the Homily of St. Jerome we now have, but I like the Origen better for the sake of the following passage (iii Lesson): *Mater inquit ejus Mater immaculata Mater incorrupta mater intacta mater ejus: cujus ejus? Mater Dei unigeniti Domini et Regis omnium plasmatorum et creatoris cunctorum. Illius qui in excelsis est sine Matre et in terris est sine Patre. Nisi qui in coelis per suam deitatem in sinu est Patris et in terris per suam corporis susceptionem in sinu est Matris.* [His Mother, his Immaculate Mother, his uncorrupted Mother, his intact Mother: of whom is this "his"? The Mother of the only-begotten Son of God, who is Lord and King of all creatures and the Creator of all this. Of him who in heaven has no Mother and on earth has no Father. In heaven, by his divinity, he is in the bosom of his Father, and on earth, by his taking on a body, he is in the bosom of his Mother.]

(ivth lesson) *O magnae admirationis gratia, o inenarrablilis suavitatis gloria, o inestimabile magnumque sacramentum – Ipsa eademque virgo, ipsa et mater Domini, ipsa Genitrix, ipsa ejus ancilla plasmatis ejus ipsa quem genuit.* [O the grace of this great marvel! O the glory of this unspeakable sweetness! O priceless and great mystery! – One and the same Virgin is the Mother of the Lord and the God-bearer, and she is the handmaid of him whom she had formed and had given birth to.]

December 27, 1948. Feast of St. John

This is one of the first moments I have had to concentrate on anything sensible for three days. Or, in case that is an exaggeration, which it is, the first in [incomplete sentence].

The 1494 Breviary again.

Two homilies by St. Bede in the 3rd Nocturn.

A beautiful oration for the end of Matins, Christmas Night.

Deus qui hanc sacratissimam noctem veri luminis fecisti illustratione clarescere, da quaesumus ut cujus lucis mysteria in terra cognovimus ejus quoque gaudiis in coelo perfruamur. [O God, who has made this most sacred night to shine with the splendor of the true Light: grant, we beseech you, that we may delight in heaven in the joys of Him the mysteries of whose light we have known on earth.]

At Lauds – the Collect is the one we have now for all hours . . . *Concede quaesumus omnipotens Deus ut nos Unigeniti tui nova per carnem nativitas liberet,* etc. [Grant, we beseech you, almighty God, that your only-begotten Son's new birth in the flesh may deliver us, etc.], same as Tierce. At Sext – the collect is the wonderful prayer – *Deus qui humanae substantiae dignitatem [et] mirabiliter condidisti et mirabilius reformasti . . .* [O God, who in a wonderful manner did create and ennoble human nature, and still more wonderfully has renewed it . . .] – which is now in the Ordinary of the Mass at the Offertory.

At None – Collect: *Da nobis quaesumus Domine Deus ut qui nativitatem Domini nostri Jesu Christi nos frequentare gaudemus, dignis conversationibus ad ejus mereamur pertinere consortium.* [Grant, we beseech you, Lord God, that we, who rejoice in celebrating the birth of Our Lord Jesus Christ, may, by our praiseworthy life, attain to fellowship with him.]

Various different collects for St. Stephen. Proper hymns for St. Stephen and St. John.

One of the biggest graces of this or any Christmas – Sister Thérèse at Marquette sent me a first class relic of the Little Flower and Reverend Father told me I could keep it and wear it. I have it over my heart and it gives me great comfort. I have no doubt that now my whole life is going to be completely transformed and that at last I shall do something to please our dearest Lord. Here I have this seed of miracles resting at the center of my physical life. It fills me with deep recollection. Here what was once part of her now is, her soul's gaze will still be fixed, and she will be offering me all day to God. She will sing with me and penetrate my prayer and lead me along in contemplation and protect me. I think she has been sent to me, not because I am worthy or have done anything good that might seem to deserve it, but because I have perhaps been going backwards, or am in danger of doing so fast, and she has been sent to keep pushing me forward as well as to remind me of the pact I once made with her and to remind me to stop all this monkey business and begin to behave.

Another reason – the whole place has been, I don't say a turmoil, as if this community were upset and didn't like it, but the old order has been giving place to the new in a great hurry. To begin with, they have played the whole of Handel's *Messiah* over the refectory loudspeaker system. At first the reader would get up and start something; then the music would burst in – loud and strange. After that they got it fixed up so that the stuff sounded quite good. Then later, Isobel Baillie came on and it sounded fine. So on Christmas Day – or was it St. Stephen's? – the Huddersfield Choral Society was chugging away with "All we like sheep have gone astray" and the monks were happily eating candy and popcorn, and I was making signs across the refectory and scandalizing the novices. And the singing about the sheep going astray was so graphic that I was afraid Brother Jerome, our shepherd, would get nervous and lose his appetite. On the other hand Isobel Baillie, the soprano, was so lovely I nearly started to fly. It made me feel very tender and happy, and helped me to pray.

I think it helped many to pray and they are mostly happy about it. As for what the Abbot General would say, that is another matter.

January 7, 1949

It is a new year and the Epiphany is already passed. Pictures of the quonset church at the Utah monastery – very spacious, shiny floor, lots of light – have everyone in admiration. I notice their sanctuary is more regular than ours – with a *gradus altaris* [altar step] according to the Ritual, not like ours.

When Dom Robert was here, he advised me to pray that I would not be made cantor. I did and now I am not even assistant sub-cantor. I have reached my ambition of being nothing whatever in choir and it gives me a certain amount of peace. I don't mind the bad singing now that I am not responsible for it. I can spend the office praying instead of fretting. The job I got this year is Assistant Master of Ceremonies, which is just what I need. I couldn't have been given the job at a better time – just getting ready for the priesthood. It keeps me in the sanctuary and I am forced to learn all the ceremonies, at least the salient ones from the Deacon on down. It all started yesterday when, besides the Pontifical, we had the blessing of a monastic crown, a minor order (Fr. Hilary became an exorcist), and Brother Dominic, to celebrate his Golden Jubilee of simple profession, renewed his vows, this time in Church. He is the first brother to have gone through the profession ceremony in Church according to the statutes of last year's General Chapter. He spoke in Chapter but I'll get that down later.

Fr. Placid, now cellarer, kicked me out of St. John's room, painted it up in one day, and threw out all the rubbish, and now it is a very efficient place rattling with the noise of business, with three or four brothers in there all the time. Meanwhile, of course, I am out. He wanted to send me up to room 14 on the third floor of the hotel, but I balked at that – people would be after me for autographs as soon as they found out. I ended up in the rare book vault. *Omnia cooperantur in bonum eis qui diligunt Deum* [Romans 8:28]. The place has two steel doors and is as nearly soundproof as any corner of this noisy Trappist monastery. I have permission to take some of my intervals in there to work on the manuscripts, and Dom James said with a spark of encouragement, "Maybe this is the solution to your vocation problem" i.e., the Carthusians. That has ceased to be a problem, but the vault is nice and quiet and when I went from there to second Vespers of the Epiphany with the folios of a XVth century manuscript – all about the presence of God and the mysteries of Christ – fresh in my mind, the office was better than it had been for months, and love, love, love burned in my heart. Still does. Waves of it come and go. I swim on the waves. It is beautiful. How quiet it is in the vault. I open a top window and you see nothing but a little square of blue Kentucky sky and then sun streams in on the bindings of the codices and the big quartos and the little duodecimos and everything is silence and you are steeped in the presence of God until it makes you numb. And in the refectory they were reading about St. Augustine . . . and it nearly made me cry.

January 8, 1949

Today, Sunday within the Octave of the Epiphany, is the first day of recollection for 1949. When I came here seven years ago, I knew I would have crosses, but I never expected that one of the biggest would be mail. I am getting something like seven to ten letters a day, and I am praying to Our Lord to make them stop before it gets any worse. One lady told me she had wanted to write, but decided not to, and then she read an article in *Cosmopolitan* which said, "If you like a book, sit down and write a letter to the author." Whoever wrote that article ought to be shot.

I had some cards printed at the print shop and they all went. The first batch said I had received the letters and read them with deep appreciation, but the second batch now just says thanks for the letter because I hope to work out a plan by which most of them will not be given to me. But then that only means it is a nuisance for somebody else. Besides, I feel like a heel, not wanting to read all the letters, most of which are very kind and sensible and full of Christ's charity and, as a whole, they manifest such a thirst for God and for prayer that they make me feel good about the world outside.

Not that the world outside is, physically, any more lovely than it ever was. Wednesday, the Vigil of the Epiphany, Reverend Father and Fr. Odilo and Fr. Raymond and I were all driven in to Louisville by Senator Dawson who is a kind of official chauffeur for the monks although I don't see why a brother couldn't drive us just as well, and leave him in peace.

Fr. Raymond had to go to the hospital and it turns out he has cancer. Fr. Odilo and I were making application for citizenship, vulgarly known as first papers. It is the second time for both of us. Our first papers lapsed while we were busy with the pursuit of perfection in the novitiate and then the idea came back to us both simultaneously last summer. We are still busy, of course, with the pursuit of perfection. That was what Fr. Idesbald's speech in Chapter was about this morning.

Louisville was dull as usual. The only good thing about the trip was that we stayed two hours in the Cathedral waiting for Reverend Father to finish his business. It is the first time in years – since the novitiate – that I have had a chance to pray two hours at a stretch. And then we fasted all day. Got back to the monastery at 4 and gobbled the warmed-up bowl of macaroni they had saved for us, and rushed in to first Vespers of the Epiphany just as the invitator (a novice) was having a nervous breakdown over the first antiphon, *Ante luciferum genitus* [Begotten before the daystar].

In winter the stripped landscape of Nelson county looks terribly poor. The houses of our neighbors between here and Bardstown are pretty miserable. We are the ones who are supposed to be poor. Well, I am thinking of the people in a shanty next to the Brandeis plant, on Brook Street, Louisville. We had to wait there while Reverend Father was getting some tractor parts. The woman who lives in this place was standing out in front of it, shivering in some kind of rag, while a suspicious looking, anonymous truck unloaded some bootleg coal in her yard. I wondered if she had been warm yet this winter. And I thought of Gethsemani, where we are all steamed up and get our meals, such as they are, when meal time comes around, and where I live locked up in that room with incunabula and manuscripts that you wouldn't find in the house of a millionaire! Can't I ever escape from being something comfortable and prosperous and smug? The world is terrible, people are falling to pieces and starving to death and freezing and going to hell with despair, and here I sit with a silver spoon in my mouth and write books and everybody sends me fan mail telling me how wonderful I am for giving up so *much*. And what, I'd like to ask them, have I given up anyway except headaches and responsibilities?

Next time I start sulking because the chant is not so good in choir, I had better remember the people who live up the road. The funny thing is, though, they could all be monks if they wanted to. But they don't. I suppose, somehow, even to them, the Trappist life looks hard!

(Evening, after supper.) I just read the Gospel of the Purification (I am taking St. Luke to meditate on in this interval for a month, and it is so beautiful that I am all lighted up with lights inside and there is a feast in my heart).

And I hear the antiphons being sung already. Also, I think of St. Ailred, who comes the day after. And I think of Adam of Perseigne's *Mariale* [treatises in praise of Mary] and of digging up blackberries in the calf pasture when I was a novice, and praying to Our Lady and St. Ailred. The Purification is one of my favorite feasts. But it is poignant, because it means the Christmas cycle is over.

How beautiful the Mass of today: Jesus has manifested Himself to the whole world in His Epiphany and so now the Church sings, *Servite Domino in laetitia* [Serve the Lord in gladness] and Christ goes back to Nazareth with His Foster Father and His Virgin Mother *et erat subditus eis* [and he was subject to them (Luke 2:51)].

January 12, 1949

It is the anniversary of St. Ailred's death when he went to heaven singing "Christ . . . Christ" in English because he liked it in English.

Perhaps one of the functions of a contemplative is to help other people, by word or merely by example, to become aware of how much they are capable of loving God – or perhaps already love Him without knowing it.

Christ recognizes Himself when the souls that possess His likeness in them by charity recognize one another by some actual expression of His love in one another, and begin to praise Him and thank Him and move one another to greater love by His joy.

It is a great thing when Christ, hidden in souls – and perhaps forced by the world to keep in hiding – manifests Himself unexpectedly by an unplanned expression of His presence, and souls light up on all sides with recognition of Him and discover Him in themselves when they did not even imagine He could be there.

His one Image is in us all, and we discover Him by discovering the likeness of His Image in one another. This does not destroy the differences between us, but all these accidentals cease to have much meaning when we find that we are really one in His love. And it is great praise of Him when people rejoice at finding Him in one another – not by effort, not by mere blind acts of faith, but by the experience of a charity illuminated, perhaps, by wisdom – for it is "sapience" and fruition of God's reflection in the joy which is His mirror in souls.

January 14, 1949

I read these words in St. Luke and they greatly comforted me: *Perambulabat autem magis sermo de illo; et conveniebant turbae multae ut audirent et curarentur ab infirmitatibus suis. Ipse autem secedebat in desertum et orabat.* [Merton underlines twice.] [But the fame of him went abroad the more: and great multitudes came together to hear, and to be healed of their infirmities. *And he retired into the desert and prayed* (Luke 5:15–16).]

And that is the best thing to do about fan mail.

January 17, 1949. Feast of St. Anthony
Schedule for the time being:

Feasts MM [of Blessed Mother] & Holidays

    Hear 1 Mass.
    Before Prime.   Work on Liturgical mss. in vault.
    After Chapter.   (Asst. M.C. – work in sanctuary, etc.)
    After Work.   [blank]
    After Dinner.   Read on Order – modern mss. from Laval

Retraite des Supérieurs, 1913, etc.

    After None.   In vault – Cistercian mss. (S. Bernard)
    After Vespers.   Pray in Church.
    After Supper.   Gospel – then pray in Church.
    (Collation)

Ordinary Days

    Communion
    After Chapter. Cistercian Theology (William of St. Thierry,
        De Natura et Dignitate Amoris [On the Nature and Dignity of Love])
    After 1st Bell.   Mass – pray in Church.
    After Work.   Scripture (now [am reading] Ephesians)
    After Dinner.   Spiritual Reading – prayer – outside (now *Le Moine dans
        L'Eglise du XIème*)
    After Work.   Read a little *Cloud of Unknowing*, then go pray in church.
    After Supper.   Gospels – then pray in Church

January 22, 1949. Third Sunday after Epiphany
So I sit down to figure out an article in *The Thomist* which has gone to the great trouble of refuting something I must have said somewhere about contemplation.[36] I am very flattered at being refuted by learned men. It almost makes me feel as if my opinions were important – almost, but not quite.

However, what does he say?

[36] In the journal entries for January 22 and 24, and for the first part of January 26, Merton refutes an article by John Fearn, O.P., "States of Life" in *The Thomist* 12, no. 1 (January 1949): 1–16). Fearn's article is a refutation of Merton's article "Active and Contemplative Orders" in *The Commonweal* 47, no. 8 (December 5, 1947): 192–96).

First, I have not clearly distinguished between the contemplative *life* and the contemplative *state*. So, here comes St. Thomas' doctrine first of all: the division of active and contemplative – divides the intellectual life of man into two kinds, depending on what is chiefly intended by that life – contemplation of truth or external activity. This distinction is sufficient in the abstract. In the concrete, every life is a combination. But a man's principal intention will still be centered on one or the other. (This is good – tapped as one of my mistakes in that A.[ctive] C.[ontemplative] article.)

Evaluate them all to three priorities:

A. priority of nature – contemplative life lst – makes men happier. St. Thomas' eight reasons.

B. priority of merit – contemplative life lst: *per se* contemplative life directly concerned with charity – root of merit. (*per accidens* active life can be more meritorious.)

C. priority of *generation* – active life (practice of virtues). Now, religious *state* [underlined twice]. He admits that the "states" are dedicated to the works of the active or contemplative "lives" and, therefore, understanding of the two *lives* is essential for understanding states.

State = condition of stability dependent on permanent personal obligation. State of perfection (all religious Orders) primary interest to cling to God and enjoy union with Him; practice counsels to remove impediments to this – assumes counsels as obligations.

(i.e. more or less external and legal definition – a man can be a saint and not be in this "*state* of perfection," i.e., not a religious.)

> *Active* state – a) purely active b) derived from *fullness of contemplation*
> *Contemplative* state – c
> b & c preferable by virtue of their *works* to a.

So far, O.K. The part about Thomas Merton is cockeyed. He got it all distorted. He thinks I am trying to reshuffle St. Thomas' technical distinctions into different exterior categories when all I am saying is that in *practice* every Christian is called to close union with God and to share with others the fruits of that union one way or another – certainly not all by being teachers!!! God forbid!

However, I suppose I was really pretending to analyze St. Thomas in order to put this across in a way that resulted in misinterpretation.

He winds up by stating what I wanted to state, but in such a way that it loses all its punch: that those engaged in "works flowing from the fullness of contemplation" ought to be contemplatives. He nowhere in the article says what he or St. Thomas mean by contemplation. And in effect his conclusion is that the Dominicans, etc., ought to be supplied with good vocations to make sure that they will make an impression on the non-Catholic intelligentsia.

January 24, 1949

This *Thomist* article – points against me:

1. "The sequence of thought is rather perplexing." p.g. *concedo* [I concede].

2. I am supposed to argue "that all religious and all lay people do (or at least should) in some sense arrive at this peak of mystical life the author (me) considers he has reconciled the contrariety . . ." but g. and 188 a. b. *do – nego prorsus* [I absolutely disagree].

3. He concludes that there is only one vocation – yes, to *perfection:* but not technically one "vocation" in the juridical sense.

4. and that degrees and varieties in perfection of religious vocations depend on *the perfection of divine union and not on the means the Order has at its disposal for teaching and preaching.*

His point of view – which is correct in its own way – is that St. Thomas was not attempting "a concrete evaluation of religious orders based on the spirituality of their actual members, *but on an objective analysis of the nature of these institutes . . .*" That this is St. Thomas' view – *concedo.*

That I was confusing the issue in taking the *concrete, factual* view based on individual sanctity – *concedo.* It made me miss the target, but it does not affect the truth of the statement I was really trying to prove. This is simply that, since the works of the preaching orders are "by their very nature derived from *the fullness of contemplation,*" *a certain fullness or perfection of contemplation* is required for the institute to carry out its function. Whether that fullness implies infused contemplation (and hence an obligation of the members of such an institute to lead lives *tending* to infused contemplation) I did not say and neither did Fr. F[earn]., but it is important someone should have taken it up. Also, in saying that the dignity of the preaching orders springs not from the *fact* [underlines twice] that they preach, but the fact that preaching is supposed to be derived from the fullness of contemplation. It is thus the *contemplative* element, and not the active element, that gives the works of this life their superior dignity.

However, if he had taken the trouble to wipe his glasses, he would have seen that I was basing my own interpretation of the mixed vocations as taken in the concrete on *St. Bonaventure* who does take it so in the text I quoted. He says the term "mixed" orders is not exact.

5. *"It is absolutely false to conclude that there is only one type of religious and one vocation."* In the juridical sense, *concedo.* That was not my intention. I was speaking of the general vocation of all Christians to perfect charity and even to the contemplative *life* (not contemplative *state*) in some degree, and perhaps even to share the fruits of contemplation (but not in the strict, technical sense of preaching and teaching).

6. "Degrees and varieties of religious vocation (i.e. vocation in the objective sense of state) do most certainly depend upon the works to which the various institutions are ordained." *Concedo.* But here is the point I hold on to: works flowing from the fullness of contemplation *ipso facto* imply a certain fullness of contemplation. Even taking vocation in the sense of a juridical state this is true. To be obliged by vow to do works that flow from the fullness of contemplation is to be obliged in some sense to tend to contemplation. In such an institute there must be some place for works of the contemplative life. Hence "mixed" orders is not an inaccurate term after all. *Qui vult finem vult media ad finem. Nemo dat quod non habet.* [Whoever wants a goal also wants the means to attain that goal. No one gives what he does not have.]

7. *"In St. Thomas the degree of union with God has nothing to do with this problem."* The concrete union of individual with God – *concedo.* But this institute must by its nature supply a reservoir upon which teachers and preachers are to draw. In other words, it must, by statute, favor union with God and works of the contemplative life.

8. I do not attempt to prove the Cistercians are a mixed order!!!!

9. *"An ecstasy is not a work of the active life."* *Concedo prorsus.* [I absolutely agree.]

January 26, 1949. Feast of St. Alberic

When all that has been said, I am very glad they wrote that article because it has been an immense help to me. Yesterday I read St. Thomas' explanation of what he means by a "state" – that it is not a matter of external and accidental things, like poverty or riches, dignity or the rest, but rather a permanent disposition of a man in accordance with some mode proper to his nature, here by virtue of an obligation – *quod pertinet ad rationem libertatis vel servitutis. Ad statum requiritur immobilitas in eo quod pertinet ad conditionem personae* [what pertains to the reason for freedom or servitude. For a "state" to exist there is required an immobility in what pertains to the condition of the person]. (Summa Th. II-II, Q. 183, a.l.)

In Q. 184, a.4., he explains in what sense he is taking the word state here.

Not – with regard to man's interior dispositions (v.g. a *state* of prayer) *spiritualis status in homine per comparationem ad judicium divinum* [a spiritual state in man by comparison to the divine judgment].

But – his exterior condition in relation to the rest of the Church – *secundum ea quae exterius aguntur accipitur spiritualis status in homine per comparationem ad Ecclesiam* [according to those things which are done externally, a spiritual state is accepted in man by comparison to the Church].

And he concludes: *Sic nunc de statibus loquimur prout sc. ex diversitate statuum quaedam Ecclesiae pulchritudo consurgit.* [We are now speaking of states in this manner because from the diversity of states there emerges a certain beauty of the Church.]

To see by this, with finality and certitude, just what St. Thomas was talking about, and how I had been wrong, was a great relief and brought much light. And far from obstructing my ideas, it helps me to see my own way much more clearly. I see how I can arrive at a more correct theological argument for the primacy of contemplation even in the mixed life. Also, I cannot do better than base everything I write ultimately on St. Thomas. In the first place, I don't understand Scotus and, even if I did, he does not carry enough weight as an authority. I have never been able to use him for anything anyway, and it seems to me the time I spent walking around the cemetery with the big black Vivés edition [1891] of the *Oxoniense* under my arm was largely wasted, although he does say some marvelous things about love. St. Thomas, on the other hand, is so clear and he has the whole Church behind him. The things that do not appeal to me immediately here and there will probably show up in their true light if I study the questions in relation to one another and to the whole *Summa* instead of simply plucking out isolated texts, and pulling them to pieces like daisies, "he loves me, he loves me not."

Anyway, one of the big graces of yesterday was seeing in a flash how much there is in the plan of the *Summa*, how much more the parts mean in relation to that whole. Never having seen this before, I had never before really known anything about St. Thomas or the *Summa*, except isolated pieces of information. I had resolved not to do anything about *The Thomist* article saying, *Mihi vindictam [ego retribuam] dicit Dominus* ["Revenge is mine, I will repay, saith the Lord" (Romans 12:9)], and maybe this is His revenge – to give me a little understanding and the conviction of how much lies hidden in St. Thomas for me. *Pulsate et aperietur vobis.* [Knock, and it shall be opened for you (Matthew 7:7).] It is as if the *Summa* were some kind of Sacrament, working *ex opere operato* [solely by its own power]! Incidentally the Thomist position on the mode of causality of the Sacraments seems to me (without any investigation of the other views) to be the only one acceptable. That is, it makes an immediate appeal.

Lately I have been hearing so much about apostates it makes me sweat. Someone sent the monastery pictures from a Georgia paper of a priest undergoing a civil marriage ceremony. Then a priest in England, ex-Anglican, supposed to be a very brilliant writer, goes back to Anglicanism. Says the dogma of the Church is "too rigid". Then that Franciscan in Colorado who was running all the hospitals. Picture of him in *Time* in a sports shirt holding up some sort of scientific specimen with a pair of tweezers.

Plans are underway for building a group of little cells outside the Little Cloister – including one for me and one for Fr. Raymond to write in. The joys of the vault are not to go on indefinitely. About the vault – I made a resolution never to go in there under the pretense that I was a displaced Carthusian. I always think of it this way – I mean in the intervals: here I am going to study these Cistercian manuscripts: our Liturgy, our Theology, our history, first for myself to find out more about our spirit, then for the whole Order, because, after all, I am supposed to be a member of this informal Historical Commission centered at Aiguebelle, where they are writing the history of the Order. Obviously the reason why they put me on there was in order to make sure there would be someone at Gethsemani writing to answer questions and get microfilms and so on. No one here knows what is in those codices. The only one who ever did know was Dom Edmond and he has been dead fourteen years. But I pray fervently for his soul out of gratitude for that room full of vellum.

It seems to me there is a lot of grace connected with our old Liturgy and the study of it brings unction, especially when you have such handwriting before you as the script of that Morimond Antiphonary and the hymnal of Morimond in Italy, where I found the old hymn for the Feasts of Our Lady, melody and all, *Mysterium Ecclesiae.*

January 29, 1949
A good thing that happened to me on the Feast of St. Paul is that the block in my mind about the chant in choir suddenly slipped out of place and I got

free again and could pray along without worrying about the flat tone or criticizing the cantor under my breath.

Reverend Father is supposed to get home from Utah today. He has been gone for about two weeks: the reason was that Dom Robert's abbatial blessing took place in Atlanta on the 18th and Dom Maurice [Lans] was blessed a week ago in Utah. Last night in Chapter Fr. Prior (i.e., Father Anthony) read us a very funny letter from Reverend Father describing Dom Robert trying to get to bed in the pullman berth on the way from Georgia to Utah. Then Clare Luce wrote a big long letter from Jamaica and I was two days trying to answer it, tearing up two attempts before I finally got down to business. When I say Jamaica I mean B.W.I. and not Jamaica, Long Island.

I am supposed to be studying up the immensely complicated functions of the 2nd Master of Ceremonies on Candlemas Day. Being between the hammer and the anvil I never simply get a candle and hold on to it. No. People suddenly rush up and give me candles which I have to pass on to someone else. If they refuse, I use my authority and mutter, "*Take* it! . . . or else! . . ." and then scuttle behind the pillars and drag out the little book to find out what I really ought to have done.

Father Anthony in Chapter talked about Blessed Guerric and St. Amadeus and quoted Gerard Manley Hopkins at least twice.

After Chapter it was trying to snow: but we have had practically nothing resembling cold weather all winter. In Utah it is supposed to have been the worst winter in 15 years. So there! It just goes to show you never can say anything sensible about the weather.

Last week I was busy writing copy for *Cistercian Magnificat*, which is to be the Centenary book, and it seems to be turning out beautifully, not through any fault of mine, but because of the photographers and Wayne Jackson's layouts. Really the book is five hundred times better than I ever dared hope for, and all because by a providential "accident" I happened to mention that we needed a good layout man when Angaus was in Reverend Father's room and he went and got Mr. Jackson, who got Terrell Dickey and Dickey, Sr., who took all the pictures.

But the Purification is a beautiful feast. Here I sit and look at the big snowflakes flying around the window like feathers and my heart grows warm within me at the thought of those lights. *Lumen ad revelationem gentium.* [A Light for the revelation to the peoples.] Candlemas is to me a feast of inexpressible joy – joy in the lights of the Holy Ghost that lead men to God, as Simeon was led to the Temple *in Spiritu* at exactly the right time.

And God disposes us in the Church, bearing the lights of our proper vocations, in the procession. St. Bernard's sermons are beautiful above measure on this feast although they are very simple. He seems to say, by the way, that the Purification was the only Feast on which the Cistercians had a procession in his time. The Feuillants started the procession with the Abbot singing out *Procedamus in pace!* [Let us proceed in peace!]

I was reading in the *Rituel Propre de Cîteaux* that at Cîteaux they read nothing but St. Bernard at the reading before Compline for "many centuries" – the reading lasted *un demi-quart d'heure* [half a quarter-hour] and was varied by the *Exordium Magnum* during the Octave of St. Stephen Harding. Incidentally our Fathers also had an octave for the Purification.

(Evening.) Dom Robert and Reverend Father got here and Reverend Father's room had been cleaned up. The huge black desks and bookcases that were a mountain of darkness in the middle of the place have gone and the floor and new chairs are pale, and the desk is clean-cut and low, and the whole place is so shiny it looks as if it were made of glass.

For my own part, this evening I was thinking, "Maybe I am finished as a writer." Far from disturbing me, it made me glad. Nothing seems so foolish as to go on writing merely because people expect you to write. Not that I have nothing to say, but fame makes me inarticulate. And Clare Luce was saying the same thing, more or less, about herself in her letter. Anyway I certainly find it extremely difficult to believe in myself as a poet.

On the other hand I am haunted by beautiful thoughts – solitude, obscurity, emptiness, *munditia cordis* [cleanness of heart], a virgin spirit. That my spirit, which has been raped by everything stupid, could again become virginal spirit in the clean, simple darkness of pure faith, with no more half-lighted shadows between myself and God and no more desires biting my spirit like a bed of thorns!

Theology? Do I have to be tough about it, like a Dominican? That is not our spirit. No question, of course, but that I must know it if I am to *write* it. But do I have to write it in the first place? If I have to, all right. I'll take time, because I see no more reasons for hurrying and a million reasons for taking time – if I *get* [underlined twice] time.

It was supposed to be a penance for St. Joseph of Cupertino to be locked up in a little obscure convent in the hills where nobody knew he could fly . . .

January 30, 1949

Tomorrow is my 34th birthday. I was brought into the world for prayer – to pray and to love God, and everything else is accidental. Writing is accidental. If I were not such an idiot it would be criminal the way I can sometimes get interested in things that are not prayer. How is it possible that I should be able to work for two hours at a time in the vault without dropping everything and forgetting about the book and simply loving God – instead of just asking Him to help me write or turning half my will to Him, occasionally, for nothing but a moment. I must be nuts.

January 31, 1949

Anyway, that was what I thought yesterday afternoon (Sunday), when I got a silent hour and a half in the vault, and opened a couple of codices of St. Bernard's Septuagesima sermons, and then remembered God and forgot about the sermons.

Dom Robert sang a Pontifical High Mass and we had no green vestments for all those people, so we used "gold" which usually stands for white, but if you used your imagination, they might have been green vestments.

Today, after the night office, we were discovered to be deep in snow. For that matter the holy water was frozen in the dormitory cells last night when we went up. In a minute we have the Pontifical Requiem – Solemn Anniversary for the Superiors of the Order, which means Dom Frederic and very likely also Dom Benoît.

Since it is my birthday, a missionary in the Philippines wrote to say he would offer His Mass for me today. And a charming family – a mother and her children on Long Island – wrote and said they were receiving Communion for me today and "lots of other times, too."

February 1, 1949

Deus quem innocentes martyres non loquendo sed moriendo confessi sunt . . . [O God, whom the martyred innocents confessed, not by speaking but by dying . . .]

I was thinking of that all during collation. It is our vocation. It is our innocence to die without argument. People ask me advice. I suppose I shouldn't give it. I feel terrible when I do – not because they will think I am a fool, but because they might go ahead and take it.

(Fr. Osee goes by and signals, "you write too much – take a rest, take a rest.")

It was utterly beautiful out there in the snow this afternoon. Everything was blue. Plenty of snow in the branches of the cedars but it was melting fast in the sun. Before Vespers the shoulders of the hills were brown. But it was beautifully quiet except for a moment I could hear what might have been bombers, but not bombs or guns.

Why do I desire things that are not God?

Inside me, I quickly come to the barrier, the limit of what I am, beyond which I cannot go by myself. It is such a narrow limit and yet for years I thought it was the universe. Now I see it is nothing. Shall I go on being content with this restriction? If I never become anything but a writer, that is what it will amount to – sitting on my own desert island which is not much bigger than an English penny. Desire always what is beyond and all around you, you poor sap! Want to progress and escape and expand and be emptied and vanish into God.

How quickly my limits accuse me of my nothingness and I cannot go beyond. I pause and reflect and reflection makes it more final. Then I forget to reflect anymore and by surprise I make a little escape, at least to the threshold, and love moves in darkness just enough to tell a man that there is freedom.

Now – Gospels! Gospels! *Percussus sum ut foenum et aruit cor meum quia oblitus sum comedere panem meum!* [I am smitten as grass, and my heart is withered: because I forgot to eat my bread (Psalms 101:5)!]

February 2, 1949. Purification

The feast was beautiful. The only thing I did that was really bad was to waltz away with the bookstand with the book on it while the candles were being distributed, not realizing that the book would be needed afterwards, and Fr. Timothy reproached the Sacristan, Fr. Francis, for this misdeed.

In the refectory was read a short life of St. Benedict Joseph Labre who is definitely one of my favorites. The only way he could find solitude was by being the most despised person in a crowd – going so low that everybody ignored him, although he had to work to keep himself there: refusing friendship, practically never speaking, insisting on treating everyone who treated him kindly as a benefactor, not as a friend.

There is something in my nature that makes me dream of being a tramp, but from what I know of my experiences of being one, sanctity does not lie that way for me. I was always strictly a tourist, even when I traveled on foot or hitched rides. And a respectable one, too, in the pejorative sense of the word respectable. Even as a Trappist I am respectable, though not conventional. I have no fleas either because I don't *like* fleas, and I guess I'm not the kind that becomes sanctified by lice, although one never can tell what the future holds in store.

I wonder if, after all, sanctity for me is tied up with that vault full of manuscripts, and writing, and poetry and Gregorian chant and Liturgy. It seems absurd for a man to be sanctified by something he naturally likes.

The answer is of course simple. I have made my vows according to a certain rule which does not, *per se*, involve fleas, but on which my sanctity does depend. The essence of that Rule is obedience and prayer – the renunciation of your own will, community life, undivided and uncompromising love and adoration and praise of God.

Stop asking yourself questions that have no meaning. Or if they *have*, you'll find out when you need to – find out both the questions and the answers.

February 3, 1949. St. Ailred

The High Mass was quite beautiful – first the organ went dead, and that made the sanctuary (where I am subdeacon for the week) quite peaceful. Then on the altar were a few pink blossoms from those strange bushes in the *preáu* that have bloomed on and off all winter. They bloomed at Christmas too, but then the flowers were so aenemic that they were greenish white – and they stayed on the altar for a couple of weeks, until the Epiphany. If I were a Carmelite nun – or any kind of nun for that matter – I'd think those flowers were a miracle. The other night the thermometer was somewhere near zero. There was still snow on the ground today. I went over to the woods for the first time this year. Not a chance during January. We were in the woods at the foot of the biggest knob, trimming the crests of trees that must have been felled two years ago because the wild grape vines were growing all over them.

This morning there arrived unexpectedly a little book from Parkminster: their anthology of prayers and devotions to the Sacred Heart from the ancient Carthusian writers – beautiful, ornate, High Medieval affective prayers, the kind of thing that sprung up all over the Low Countries and Germany in the 14th and 15th centuries. Like our own [Nicholas] Salicet, in his *Anthidotarius Animi.*

Mother Lutgarde Henery, late Abbess of Laval, certainly had a vocation to be abbess. She took the habit with her own name, Céline, and when profession came along, her superiors changed her name to Lutgarde so that she would be abbess with the name of a Cistercian saint. She prayed God not to let her get elected next abbess of Laval and was spared. But Mother Antoinette was a cripple who had to be waited on by three or four laysisters and couldn't do anything, so Mother Lutgarde was finally elected abbess unanimously and stayed that way for over forty years.

Pictures of the convent at Rivet were posted – the nuns from Blagnac moved there.

The affair rigged up behind the apse of the church to throw a light through Our Lady's window at the *Salve* stands outlined against the sunset like a gallows, but I am glad those blue bulbs around the statue are no longer used. I hope they will be taken down so that they can't be used at Pontifical Masses either. The window looks nice at *Salve* and the first time the new stunt was tried it made Brother Leo gasp with mystical love.

February 7, 1949

Dom Benoît finally died of his cancer after all, died on January 31st, a week ago today, when we had the commemoration of all the Superiors *hoc anno defunctorum* [who died this year]. And the day before yesterday Fr. Raymond came back from the hospital in Louisville with ten inches of his intestine gone – and apparently rid of cancer and all its effects. He looks better than he did a month ago and might never have been ill at all. Gets up at 3, comes to choir, is in community refectory. However he is still "under observation."

Poor little Dom Benoît – he was a saint. He loved and understood contemplation, and practiced it. He was steeped in the spirituality of Elizabeth of the Trinity, a quiet, cheerful little man – Breton I suppose. He originally came from Thymadeuc and volunteered for the Far East like so many others from there. He never had good health. He looked like some of the more sprightly engravings of de Rancé. The first time I saw him, Dom Frederic was taking him around the house and he stuck his head in the door of the laybrothers' chapter room where we were having theology class, and I remember his round eyes and his exclamation, "O! So many! . . . So many students!" I suppose there were seven or eight of us.

He always gave me good advice and told me to pray for humility and *goûter les humiliations* [develop a taste for humiliations]. I can't say that I get very many to "taste."

When he came here the first time, he had a beard, one of the last monks in the Order who still wore one, but I suppose the Abbot General was the one who made him shave it off because when he came back with Dom

Marie Joseph, he didn't have a beard any more. He wanted me to read [Dom Vital] Lehodey's *Saint Abandon* – I have never completely done that yet. I hope he will pray in heaven for me to love Jesus with very great simplicity.

February 9, 1949

I had written to the Dominicans at St. Maximin, La Sainte Baume, for a book they put out about their place. Henry de Segogne recommended it as a model of its kind. The Prior wrote and said it was already out of print and reprinting was too expensive, but he sent a little folder about the place and some postcards.

I can think of no better place for a monastery than over the tomb of St. Mary Magdalen. The Trappists had it for a while, under Dom Augustin [de Lestranges], but it was a thirteenth century Dominican foundation. The cloister seems huge. I had also asked them about the Camaldolese at Roquebrune (Var) and they told me that two years ago the hermits packed up and went home to Italy and that now Roquebrune was a Discalced Carmelite "desert" and this made me happy. I did not know they really had "deserts" to go to for contemplation anymore. It is very comforting to know that they have. I wish *we* had. Well, there's the vault and the far end of the cemetery . . .

My work has been tied up in knots for two months – more. I am trying to write *The Cloud and the Fire*[37] which is a book about contemplation and the theology of contemplation at that. The theology of contemplation does not mix well with fan mail. Also it is difficult. It is certainly impossible to write such a book with a lot of other concerns on your mind. For instance, at the end of January the printers gave me the dummy for the centenary book and I was busy for two weeks writing captions and finishing the copy for *that*.

It takes a tremendous effort of will to get back to *The Cloud and the Fire* and I am usually helpless when I try to move that typewriter and get something on paper.

I have a huge mass of half digested notes, all mixed up, and I can't find my way around in them. My ideas are not fixed and clear. I have been trusting more or less to see them work themselves out on paper as I type, and have in any case made up my mind to regard the whole first draft of this book simply as preliminary notes. On the other hand, when I rewrite any-

[37] Eventually published as *The Ascent to Truth*.

thing, I entirely revolutionize it, sometimes with no improvement at all, because I only lose the freshness of the original and am just as prolix over again, but in a different and duller way. It is hopeless for me to write without the heat of some new ideas.

Into the middle of all this came [Antonin] Sertillanges' *La Vie Intellectuelle* [Paris, 1944] which might have what I need to cheer me up and keep me organized. I have glanced at it here and there and it has on me the effect that Dale Carnegie's "How to Stop Worrying and Start Living" might have on a despondent salesman.

Definitely, I have simply got to make time for this book and get at it and finish it, patiently, and not let myself be eaten up by fan mail or other chores that do not really count – always expecting what comes directly by obedience and there is a fair amount of that. When I say fan mail I am wrong, too – that is not the problem: but letters that need to be answered out of charity or monastery business . . . Like the monk at Aiguebelle who wants a map of North America with all our monasteries and all those of the Common Observance marked on it.

February 13, 1949. Septuagesima. Day of Recollection

Last night we threw away the *Alleluia*, very loudly too. Today we got the *massa damnata* [St. Augustine's predestined "damned multitude"] in the second nocturn and purple vestments at Mass and we all made a lot of mistakes. In chapter we heard about what happened to Cardinal Mindszenty in Hungary. Standing at the foot of the altar with humeral veil wrapped around the paten and up in front of my face, I realized that it was I who was in prison in Hungary, and that that was the reason why I was standing there at the moment, because what is done to Christ is done to me: what Christ suffers I suffer and what I do in Christ's name Christ does, and this Mass is part of Christ's crucifixion in Hungary and Christ's triumph over anti-Christ. And at the consecration I thought how much of me is still like the Apostles before the Crucifixion, who only understood glorious victories and didn't believe in suffering or defeat.

Cardinal Mindszenty's face with huge eyes popping out of his head is posted by the door, next to a polite, comfortable picture of what he looked like before the Reds got after him with the needle.

I feel as if in the past month everything has been physically pushing me forward. After Communion it was as if God's urging was in a sense rushing me off my spiritual feet – telling me to go and desire, desire breaking open the huge hole in my heart and hustling me away from selfish prayers to succeed in writing and trying to tumble me over the edge. And I know I couldn't grab anything and couldn't fly either, but I consented to stop asking for what was useless and to desire God in the presence of a blank, knowing with certainty that I had been framed and that it was very good.

When harsh voices came from the choir, pushing and pulling in the Tract, one end of the crew ahead of the other, it suddenly occurred to me that this was the singing voice of Cardinal Mindszenty, and it pierced my heart and nearly made me weep.

As usual on Days of Recollection, I got to thinking about myself – after all, that is what one is *told* to do and it is accounted a virtue, and thus I raise a lot of fake issues and chase a lot of wild geese. But I am getting older, and I don't chase them very far. I just let them honk. (Maybe there'll be real ones in South Carolina.)

Anyway, a man soon gets to the point where no amount of thinking will help him to know himself any better. One can develop a habit of thinking about himself in such a way as to miss the point with a consistent, subconscious accuracy that almost looks like a genius for evasion.

Now – about *La Vie Intellectuelle* – it would be a nice feat to prove that it is *not* diametrically opposed to St. John of the Cross. I bet no one can do it. Maybe Jacques Maritain can see how the two can be reconciled.

Yesterday I got to the part where he says that solicitude for one's health is a virtue of the intellectual. I took to laughing, perhaps immoderately at sentences like this: *Un travail manuel doux et distrayant serait également précieux à l'esprit et au corps. Soignez votre alimentation. Observez-vous en matière de sommeil comme au sujet de la nourriture; trouvez la mesure qui vous convient et faites-en l'objet d'une résolution ferme. Il n'y a pas ici de loi commune.* [A light and distracting form of manual work would be equally valuable to soul and to body. Watch your diet. Find out what you need in the way of food and sleep and make this the object of a firm resolution. This is not a matter that falls under common law.] No. Definitely not. I wonder how the Abbé de Rancé would like that book. He and Sertillanges are now capable of discussing it without undue heat in heaven, for Sertillanges died last year on the feast of St. Anne, as suddenly as Dom Frederic, and a week or so before him. Dom Frederic wouldn't have agreed with this book any more than de Rancé – or St. Bernard either.

It is all *true*. The monks in the Common Observance know that. But it is not our vocation, I suppose. You'd go crazy trying to practice that here.

There is a wonderful passage beginning, *Au sortir du travail l'homme est comme un blessé, il a besoin d'enveloppement et de calme: qu'on n'aille pas le violenter; qu'on le détende et qu'on l'encourage; qu'on s'intéresse à ce qu'il fait* . . . [The man who comes away from his work is like one who has been wounded. He needs to be cared for in a calm atmosphere: do not treat him with violence! Help him to relax. Give him some encouragement! Show some interest in the things he does . . .] (p. 59).

John of the Cross getting out of that jail in Toledo, scrambling down a wall in the middle of the night and following a dog through the weeds and rubble on the river bank . . . *Au sortir du travail l'homme est comme un blessé.* Well, he had in his pocket the manuscript of *The Spiritual Canticle* and *The Dark Night*, and he was certainly *comme un blessé.*

On the other hand there could be a way of being humble and following Sertillanges, and nobody can say whether Mabillon was not a greater saint than de Rancé.[38] But I have long since given up the idea that working with the kind of intellectual steam prescribed by Sertillanges for his Dominicans would be any vocation of mine.

It seems to me that what I am made for is not speculation but silence and emptiness, to wait in darkness and receive the Word of God entirely in His Oneness and not broken up into all His shadows. But the truth is there is room for both. In what proportions is there room for them in my life? That'll work itself out in practice.

An intellectual here – old Fr. Alberic, how many years in the infirmary? – took what he got – paid for every page of his *Compendium* very dearly, a careful censor and a good old man. On the whole that was his way to sanctity. Could be mine.

In any case, the life of a Christian has meaning and value only to the extent that it conforms to the life of Jesus. But Jesus lived in poverty and hardship and died on the Cross. And all our lives are offered with His to God in the Mass, if we are true Christians. This can be fulfilled in any vocation, and Sertillanges shows the particular way in which it is fulfilled in the life of an intellectual, which he describes as "consecrated" and which he doesn't need to tell me has crosses and an asceticism all its own.

---

[38] Jean Mabillon (1632–1707), the great Benedictine Maurist scholar, wrote *Traité des études monastiques* (1691) in response to de Rancé's denunciation of monks engaged in scholarship, like Mabillon and his Maurist community.

There exists in our Order a kind of contempt for intellectuals, and to live an intellectual life is regarded as a weakness, a *defection*. Nevertheless, there was a letter I got from Fr. Edmund [Mikkers], the librarian of Achel, complaining discreetly of the lack of intellectuality in our Order. He thinks if we knew how to read, we'd be better contemplatives.

February 15, 1949

I had been worrying and bothering for two months about being unable to get anywhere with this new book, *The Cloud and the Fire*. There were some forty pages of it, written mostly in blood, since the end of the retreat. And they were terrible. Great confusion. Too long-winded, involved, badly written, badly thought out and with great torture, too. Finally it has come to seem obvious that God does not want the book and that He has simply blocked it by not giving me the strength, the sense or the time to write it.

Yesterday, when I had to do a prefatory note for *Waters of Siloe*, it went like a breeze and I had six pages done in an hour and a half and time to spare to write Bob Giroux before the end of work. And besides that I had taken time out to read a long letter from Laughlin and another from Sister Thérèse.

I had been thinking of tearing up *The Cloud and the Fire* for a long time. I haven't done that exactly, but I have simply stuffed it into an envelope, plans and all, and reconsidered what it was I was supposed to start.

Sheed and Ward had asked for an expansion of *Cistercian Contemplatives* into a book with emphasis on infused contemplation, and we had agreed on no history, and also they were not keen on too much about monastic observances. Why did I have to be such a fool as to try something elaborate and almost completely different from what was asked for?

So I'll start again. Only today I had to write letters and sign a hundred colophon sheets for the deluxe edition of *Seeds of Contemplation*, and when I was half way through, I began to feel very foolish, because I am probably the first writer of a spiritual book who has signed one hundred copies of a *De Luxe* boxed edition in cold blood. My original idea was to get a specially beautiful book and the signing came in when Laughlin took it up.

However, about *The Cloud and the Fire*, I have in mind something that needs to be done some day: the dogmatic essentials of mystical theology based on tradition, and delivered in the context and atmosphere of Scripture and the Liturgy. In other words a mystical theology that is not a mere catalog of "experiences," many of them outside the range of the ordinary economy of the Gifts, but a book that drinks contemplation *de fontibus Sal-*

vatoris [from the wellspring of the Savior] and exploits all the mysticism there is in the Liturgy and in revelation: an *objective* mysticism, integrated with the common intellectual heritage of the Church as a whole and yet with its full subjective application to the experience of the actual or potential mystic, the concrete and individual contemplative. The contemplation of the Mystical Body in all its members.

Reverend Father thought it was a good idea to work towards it and to take it step by step, getting the various parts up as magazine articles first of all. *Et det mihi Deus vitam aeternam.* [And may God grant me eternal life.] Amen.

February 20, 1949

More pages in Sertillanges that made me laugh – the ones about getting up in the middle of the night to scribble down the ideas that come to you. I'd hate to put down any of the notions that occur to *me* when I wake up in the middle of the night. Sertillanges is definitely not my tempo, and yet he has very good stuff about organizing one's work. Reflecting on my own position – I have exactly the two hours minimum a day which he calls a minimum. These I have, I mean, for writing. I have other time for reading and prayer. In those two hours I have to take care also of correspondence, duties of charity (reading mss.) or obedience, proofs, contracts, photos for illustrations, talk to the printer on occasion, and order books, and resist the temptation to read catalogs and scraps of magazines . . . it is a wonder I turn out anything at all. Yet with Our Lady's help the book, now changed and called *The School of the Spirit* goes quite smoothly. I have to simply sit down at the typewriter with what I want to say planned out. That is the *sine qua non* – even if I write something completely different, as I did today.

Boy! It is hot in this Scriptorium. Praise be to God.

It was like summer or late spring out behind the church. I stood in the sun with the Holy Ghost and thought of the first time I came here, on retreat, that Holy Saturday, when the sun was warm and I made the mistake of arguing with those fellows from Notre Dame instead of keeping silence and loving God.

My complaints about the world in the *Mountain* and in some poems are perhaps a weakness. Not that there is not plenty to complain about, but my reaction is too natural. It is impure. The world I am sore at on paper is really a figment. The business is a psychological game I have been playing since I was ten. And yet there is plenty to be disgusted with in the world.

February 21, 1949

All last year a periodical has been coming in from France – *La Maison-Dieu*. Perhaps it was Dom Marie Joseph who gave us the subscription that has now run out. Anyway it was ignored by everyone. I think most of the copies were thrown away unopened. I have the very last one, the only one I have looked at, and it is very good indeed.

It comes from the Éditions du Cerf – Father Bouyer and that crowd. It is a magazine dealing with proposals to revive the Christian Apostolate, to bring to life a vivid and deep and universal form of preaching and teaching that will make people Christians inside and out and not just in one department of their persons and on one day of the week.

Anyway, in this issue especially on preaching I find a very good article by Bouyer, *"Prédication et Mystère,"* in which I am glad to see that he takes a crack at deformations in spirituality *provenant très spécialement de certaines formes de cette culture cléricale dont les produits les plus exquis sont la philosophie de Barbedette et la théologie de Tanquerey . . .* [deriving most particularly from certain forms of that clerical culture whose most exquisite products are the philosophy of Barbedette and the theology of Tanquerey . . .] Tanquerey is our present master in Dogma. So it feels good to read a sentence like that.

Also it makes me happy to see someone insist that the ordinary person might be expected to understand the parables without having them exegeted after the fashion of the modern German scripture scholars.

February 24, 1949. St. Mathias

On St. Mathias' day we had two meals, which is rare. But it is not yet Lent.

Last night I read some more of that Bouyer article on preaching and it is tremendous. The preacher is not an apologist, not a professor, not a lecturer: he is a *kērux*, a herald, an instrument announcing the salvation that God has decreed for men who accept it. The reaction of the Church to this is a thunder of apocalyptic *Alleluias*. The whole history of the world since Jesus ascended to His Father is simply marking time until the Gospel gets announced to all nations. Then the final purification and . . . *Parousia!* [The Second Coming of Christ.]

Isaac de l'Etoile thought his monastery was at the ends of the earth because it was on an island in the Atlantic off the coast of France. All the same the monks must have felt pretty desolate, with nothing beyond them but grey sea. To this situation he applied the Quinquagesima text, *"Ecce ascendimus Jerosolymam."* ["Behold, we go up to Jerusalem."]

February 27, 1949. Quinquagesima. Forty Hours

Reverend Father read to us in chapter a letter from Fr. Cletus Molloy, the Passionist who preached our retreat. He is in Brazil – or *was* in Brazil when he wrote the letter. He says the spiritual life of Catholics there is terrible. I don't see how the Church can get by for much longer without a terrific persecution on this side of the Atlantic. Of course they already had one in Mexico.

My own vocation to the priesthood has relation to the way all the other priests and religious in North and South America are living – the way the priests in France are living, the Ruthenian priests in concentration camps, the Jugo Slavs like the two jubilarians from Mariastern who are in prison, among others.

Some of us lead lives that cry out to heaven for vengeance and persecution and others suffer the persecution. And – *in medio* [in the meantime] – I write books.

I have given up wondering what lies ahead for Gethsemani and for myself – I mean I have given up doing it consciously although some time this morning I was speculating, in a fierce distraction, as to how long one would remain conscious if he were being martyred by having a pole driven into his head. Nice thoughts!

This week I am subdeacon again. Going around the big dirty house and sprinkling the cloisters and dormitories and other offices with holy water at Tierce, I was very happy to be a subdeacon. Coming down from the lay-brothers' dormitory, I caught a shaft of sun coming through the window and God was with me in the huge empty building – everyone being in Church. However, in the refectory Brother Alexius was working and Fr. Vincent the infirmarian was eating his mixt, because there was a very short interval. Chapter finished at 8 and Tierce began about 9, and there was a long line at the visit of the sick. The reason I know that is that I whipped up there with a note for a psalter. We have to recite the psalter for Father Odo because Father Odo is dead.

He died on Friday afternoon just before a theology conference. He had been ill in the infirmary for years, anointed several times. They think they got him again just as he was going. His heart finally gave out. He had been sitting up saying rosaries all the night before because he couldn't sleep and he said Mass, sitting down, at 2 A.M. All morning he was painting pictures of Our Lady and the Sacred Heart of Jesus, and after dinner he had a crisis and died.

He was guest-master when Dom James arrived, about 1925. I suppose Dom Edmond gave him the job to let him learn some English. I put down in *The Seven Storey Mountain* what he said to me in the confessional when I was a postulant, namely that many souls depended on my staying here. Several people have written to me since the book came out saying, "Father Odo was right."

After High Mass and Sext I suddenly remembered that last year on the first day of the 40 hours I was being beaten up by violent feelings of repugnance for the thought of being a priest – disgust, fear, misgivings. Mixed in with all that, I remembered, was the question whether I would be alive *this* year and whether I would be a subdeacon. Well, I was subdeacon at the Mass, and knew more or less what to do and did it, and what is more I realized I am much better off for knowing and doing things. Major Orders are definitely one of the great graces of my life. I have had very much peace since subdeaconship – feel a greater interior *solidity* which comes from serving God in the sanctuary, in the Liturgy, in closer contact with the immensely powerful action of Christ's Sacrifice. This power in me comes from a closer union with the whole Mystical Body. It comes from being united in sacrifice with a Body that is sacrificed along with Christ its head.

The difference between the person who stood there as subdeacon this year and looked over the top of the paten at Christ on the Cross, and the acolyte who stood between the pillars last year, gnawing his heart with fears and strange questions, is very great indeed.

All the same, the wheel may well go 'round and bring back more questions. But it will still be different. I believe some theologians teach that subdeaconship confers a sacramental character. I am convinced, from experience, that it does.

Deaconship is slated for the Feast of St. Joseph. St. Joseph is my great friend. I have never been sensibly attracted to devotion to him as I am to St. John Baptist, St. Francis, St. John of the Cross, St. Augustine, St. Mary Magdalen, who gave me a jolt in the litany today, St. Agnes, St. Theresa, St. Bernard.

March 5, 1949. First Saturday

Three long chapters in *Exodus* tell how Aaron was to be ordained priest. Then a chapter on the Sabbath – contemplation. Immediately after that is recorded Aaron's first known act as priest: he made the people a golden calf and had the heralds blow their trumpets and announce a feast for the idol and the people sat down to eat and drink and arose to play. Chapter XXXII is a tremendous chapter for deacons. The sons of Levi are introduced, declaring themselves against the naked people standing among the victims offered to the idol.

Aaron: "I put gold in the fire and this calf came out . . ."

March 6, 1949. First Sunday of Lent

Yesterday *Seeds of Contemplation* arrived and it is very handsome. The best job of printing that has ever been done on any book by me. I can hardly keep my hands off it. Laughlin says the burlap effect we have on the cover is really a material they are using now on the walls of night clubs. Well, it is the Christian technique: sanctify the *saturnalia* and *lupercalia* [Roman festivals] with Christian liturgy . . . Turn them into Christian feasts.

Every book that comes out under my name is a new problem. To begin with every one brings with it an immense examination of conscience.

Every book I write is a mirror of my own character and conscience. I always open the final printed job with a faint hope of finding myself agreeable, and I never do.

So there is nothing to be proud of in this one either.

It is clever and difficult to follow, not so much because I am deep as because I don't know how to punctuate and my line of thought is clumsy and tortuous. It lacks warmth and human affection. I find in myself an underlying pride and contempt for other men that I had thought was all gone, and it is still there, as bad as ever. I don't see how the book will ever do any good. It will antagonize people, or else make them go around acting superior and stepping on everybody.

Laughlin tells me a book club is taking it and advertising it as a "streamlined *Imitation of Christ*." God forgive me. It is more like Swift than Thomas à Kempis.

The Passion and Precious Blood of Christ are too little in the book – only hinted at here and there. Therefore the book is cold and cerebral. What is the good of trying to teach people to love God without preaching through those wounds? The reason I do not do so is because I am still selfish. I find myself thinking about what we ought to get for dinner in Lent; about how to distribute signed complimentary copies of the *deluxe* edition of this book. I should never have gone into such a thing as a boxed special edition. I must be nuts.

Ever since the death of Fr. Odo and the Forty Hours my mind has been overactive and I didn't finally get back to resting in God in silence until this afternoon when I got into the vault for an hour and a half and once more became a rational being. All week I had been underwater with the whole world swimming between me and God like a fleet of large fish.

Sister James, in Malden, sent me her book on Emily Dickinson and I am happy to dip into it and find one person in the world – Emily – with my own aspirations though in a different way. I wish I had Emily's good sense.

March 12, 1949. Feast of St. Gregory

Tomorrow I go on retreat for the diaconate.

Big pain in the back. Also I have a cold. It would be flu if I were not so full of cod-liver oil. Also Fr. Prior badgered me into taking the *frustulum* this year and it helps to take the edge off a cold. Finally I have big red vitamin pills that go with the *frustulum*.

The Lenten schedule has changed and this is a big relief. It makes much more sense now with an hour's reading or more after Chapter and with Vespers in the evening where it belongs.

We gave Fr. George Extreme Unction. I don't believe it was on the Feast of St. Thomas, but I cannot remember when it actually was. Anyway, he came down to Church, and sat in his wheel chair up there in front of the Prior's High Mass stall, and I could hear him say, *"Credo,"* before he received Viaticum. It was after dinner.

That morning when we came down at 2 A.M. he was sitting on the steps of the Scriptorium and, when Fr. Prior tried to persuade him to go back to the infirmary, he made some complaint about his Mass ticket. He is so old that he doesn't get things straight anymore. But the central idea in his mind is that he wants to say Mass, and he is worried about certain real or imaginary obstacles to this. Anyway, he is still saying Mass practically every morning, sitting down.

March 14, 1949. On Retreat

In Leviticus – *Iste est sermo quem praecepit Dominus, facite et apparebit vobis gloria ejus.* [This is the word which the Lord hath commanded: do it, and His glory will appear to you (Leviticus 9:6).]

If that is true of the sacrifices of the Old Law, it is much truer still of our Liturgy.

Yesterday in Chapter Reverend Father said something about solemn vows being more of a gift to God than the priesthood, as if in vows we gave something, but in the priesthood we only received. It is true that at ordination – priest or deacon – you get much more than you give. But at the same time I think that, when you are ordained, you are still giving more to God than at solemn profession. One might object that at profession you give God everything and so you cannot give Him any more. But the mode of the gift is more perfect because it is more limited. You give yourself *to the Mass* and to the Sacraments and to the people.

A monk under solemn vows can still be concerned first of all with his own perfection, his own sanctity – in other words he can confine himself to seeking his own spiritual advantage. The priest cannot put himself first in any way whatever: Christ is always first. A priest does not exist merely for his own sanctification, but for the Sacrifice of Christ and for the Gospel, for the people, for the world. This implies his own perfection, but the perfection of a priest consists essentially in His offering of Christ's sacrifice perfectly for himself and for the Church. He no longer belongs to himself whereas a monk can very well belong to himself in a legitimate way and be concerned exclusively with his own progress, leaving the salvation of the world on a secondary plane.

A priest must not put the salvation of souls above his own soul. There is no question of a choice like that. But he has to put God and the Mass before everything. He has the whole Church on his conscience, and he not only gives up his will in order to possess the virtue of obedience, he gives up his will in order to become an instrument for the salvation of the world and the pure glory of God.

This afternoon we were out sawing up a lot of cedars that have been felled behind the wall on the east side of the enclosure. I came back in at three on account of the retreat and paused in the cow's gate to pray and came home slowly enough, looking at the big hole in the hill that leads into the new boiler room under the Scriptorium.

I took the *Spiritual Directory* and read the chapter on "Employments" *(Les Emplois)* because in point of fact that is what the priesthood means in a Trappist monastery: employments, jobs, business. It is a good, sensible chapter. Don't desire them too much, don't fear them too much. And St. Francis de Sales' principle: "Ask for nothing, refuse nothing."

There was a slight shakeup in the house today because Fr. Cellarer (Placid) needed to be relieved of his job as Master of Laybrothers. This shift occasioned many others, as usual. New Sacristan, because the Sacristan became Fr. Master. New refectorian because the refectorian became the sacristan. New bookkeeper. And so on all the way down to the shoemaker's apprentice.

The sun was warm. I stood by the wall and watched the lambs, which I noticed quite by surprise. Little black-legged things, jumping like toys on the green grass. I thought, "Feed my lambs." There is certainly something very touching about lambs, until they find their way into a holy picture and become very unpleasant, at least to me.

Aiguebelle wrote and gave me a chore for the history commission – telling them exactly what is in those documents in our archives about the abbeys of Theuley, Bithaine, Rosières, etc. We have some 18th century transcriptions of their cartularies. Today I did Theuley in summary fashion. It was founded by a gent called the Lord of Malregard who went to Purgatory – as his name would have led anyone to expect – and appeared to a pious person with the injunction that his four sons had better build a monastery to get him out quick.

What impresses me is the fact that in the 18th century the monks suddenly got very interested in their history and copied out all the records just in time, before the revolution came along to burn down their houses and make a bonfire out of all those deeds of gift. By that time I don't think the monasteries were entitled to all the land they had accumulated and had long since ceased to work for themselves!

March 15, 1949. On Retreat

The first thing about the diaconate is that it is *big*. The more I think about it the more I realize that it is a *major* Order. You are supposed to be the strength of the Church. You receive the Holy Spirit *ad robur* [for strength], not only for yourself, but to support the whole Church. You have got to fight the armies of the devil. The devil has his agents in the world – a body of his own armed members. And they are armed against people like me, who want peace. Because it is a crime to look for peace in God, and to seek it in the depths of your soul where God is found. A man who gives himself to God is likely to be destroyed by a world that hates everyone who loves God's law, God's will. Fundamentally, that is what they hate: God's will. They cannot destroy Him, but they can destroy the bodies of those who are the instruments of His will and the voices of His Gospel.

But You, oh my God, shut not the mouths of them that sing to thee.

I cannot write about martyrdom. I fear it and I do not understand it. And I was afraid the retreat would get around to that, and it did. That is why the Holy Spirit is given *ad robur* in this Sacrament. He is the Spirit of the martyrs.

It is not that the Spirit of God is waiting to get everybody killed. He has His will for each one. For each one it means the highest liberty. *Ubi Spiritus Domini ibi libertas.* [Where the Spirit of the Lord is, there is liberty (2 Corinthians 3:17).] It does not seem to me that His will for me is a martyrdom of blood. But perhaps I only say that because I am afraid. Anyway, I do not ask one thing or another, only strength.

This life for me has never been a martyrdom. Sometimes I am ashamed that it has not. It makes me feel a little funny. I am supposed to be suffering. Well, I've had a pain in the back and shoulder. And a cold. So what? Fr. Prior makes me take the *frustulum*. So it is God's will for me to have breakfast. Round and round the mulberry bush.

Sufficient unto the day is the evil thereof – and the grace thereof. By now I ought to be getting enough sense not to care what happens tomorrow, after the way God has guided me and tended me so far. Is he going to stop taking care of me now that I want to love Him more? *Not a sparrow falls to the ground . . .*

What I need from the diaconate – to realize that I can lack nothing. *Dominum regit me, et nihil mihi deerit: in loco pascuae ibi me collocavit.* [The Lord ruleth me: and I shall want nothing. He hath set me in a place of pasture (Psalms 22:1–2).] To trust Him – I wonder if I have ever really done that? What is the good of a priest who does not trust God, and who has no practical belief in His power. [You] say a lot of things about His power and then trust yourself rather than Him! We are no better an advertisement for religion that the Communists who hate it.

Pius XII said the Church needs witnesses rather than apologists.

Why should I be afraid of suffering martyrdom? I am already suffering it. My body is being killed in Hungary and Yugoslavia and China and it was killed before in Mexico and Spain and Germany. And in France a hundred and fifty years ago and in England and Ireland and Scandinavia before that. I am always being killed.

Making the Stations of the Cross, at each station, when Jesus fell under the Cross, and when He was stripped and nailed to the Cross, that is happening to me now because it happened to Him then and to Him in Hungary and Yugoslavia and the rest. *Quoniam propter te mortificamur tota die.* [Because for thy sake we are killed all the day long (Psalms 43:22).]

To be solid and sane about my Christianity. To become supremely unselfish. To become Christ's voice in the world. To announce His salvation, the acceptable year of the Lord. To build the walls of the Temple of Jerusalem in a world that has been destroyed. And may Our Lady of the Apocalypse gain me the Spirit of God *ad robur.* This, I think, is essentially in order to preach Christ in the teeth of persecution.

March 15, 1949

Yesterday afternoon, when Fr. Amadeus was preaching to us about the Holy Ghost in the infirmary chapel, Fr. George came bursting in, made the sign of "Thank you" three or four times, and departed. Last night he came down and wandered around the monastery.

Reverend Father, who used to be infirmarian, says that sometimes, when they are near death, they get this urge to travel.

There was a Brother Mary up there who used to be gate keeper. He was dying. He had a wooden leg and a cane. He used to take his cane and go clumping around instead of staying in bed. They hid his wooden leg. He found it behind the door, and put it on and got going. They hid it again in a closet where he couldn't find it. He lay in bed waving his hand and making signs, "The cane! The cane!"

There was another Brother who was dying. It was summer, very hot. He was in bed with very few clothes on. They found him walking out of the infirmary with nothing on him but a shirt. "Where are you going?" they asked him. "Nebraska!" he said. Nebraska is where he used to live.

This retreat and this ordination might well make a very profound change in my whole life. I believe that I shall come much more intimately under the direction of the Holy Ghost. In fact I shall certainly do so if I clean my soul out and prepare myself well for the sacramental graces of the Order. The character of the diaconate in my soul will mean a tremendous amount. Another degree of isolation from the world, in Christ. But in leaving the world behind, I am finding the whole Christ.

Today I felt something of the warmth of life that binds all the hierarchy together in the Sacred Heart. The life that is in the Church, the vitality that organizes and disposes all things – as it is stated in the Preface in the ordination ceremony. Fr. Amadeus was talking about that well this afternoon. And Jesus in the Tabernacle was talking about it, too. I am no longer afraid of the priesthood now. I know that it is not a caste, it is a family of brothers bound together by a love that is as strong as death and above anything on earth and is simple and perfect because it is the love Christ gave to His Apostles after His Resurrection and at the Ascension. If I am ordained priest on Ascension Day this year, I shall consider it the most tremendous and happy accident of grace, something full of the richest fruits and special, with magnificent promise.

Our Lady is helping me, and I shall trust entirely to her. I am soberer in this joy than I have ever been in my life. It is a sincere and frugal happiness, with a promise of strong fulfillment in glory to God and selflessness and gift of myself to Him.

March 16, 1949

If I lived to be five thousand years old and took the discipline every day, I could never deserve to be a deacon or a priest, and when I think of the obstacles that might come up out of my past, and perhaps even start a row that would stop my ordination, I am not surprised or upset. For if God has planned it that way, it will be for the good of the Church and for His glory.

Meanwhile the Church, whom I asked for faith at my Baptism, is now asking an Archbishop to ordain me deacon. The Church – who is no myth or figure of speech – asks for me to be made one of her hierarchy of Bishops, priests and ministers to do Christ's work in the world. The Church has singled me out and selected me to stand at the Altar in the Mystery of Faith in which God reveals the depths of His will to men, and effects what He has eternally decreed for their salvation.

Since I began this retreat, my attitude toward the artillery that I can hear practicing all day at Fort Knox has changed considerably. For seven years it had given me a feeling of uneasiness in the pit of my stomach. Now I realize the Church's mission in the world. It makes no difference essentially whether the world be at war or at peace because the Church is going to emerge victorious anyway. The Kingdom of Christ is being established, and the crimes and stupidity of men and devils, instead of hindering our progress, is only pushing us forward – and doing so sometimes a lot faster than our bodies would like. Yet it is no contradiction to pray for peace, as the whole Church does, for peace is the will of God and peace depends on union with His will, war being the fruit of its violation.

I shall be able to say *Dominus Vobiscum.* [The Lord be with you.] and lay open something of the mystery of God to men. I am already standing between Him and them, a mediator in Christ. I shall have the Gospels as my special heritage. Please God that I may understand the power that will be in my hands and use it.

I shall be permitted to touch God in the Holy Eucharist and take the Sacred Host in my fingers, *comministri et cooperatores corporis Domini* [fellow ministers and workers of the Body of the Lord]. I shall be a minister of the sacrament of Baptism (I wish I might some day use that power.) A six-day retreat isn't enough to begin to penetrate these things and I have been going around in a fog of amazement, very happy, in spite of what the devil wanted to do to me a lot of times. It is all for God's glory, whose power is made perfect in infirmity. *Munda cor meum ac labia mea, omnipotens Deus!* [Almighty God, cleanse my heart and my lips!]

March 20, 1949. Third Sunday Lent

Yesterday Fr. Amandus and I went out to the ordination in albs so starched that they rustled like canvas and stuck out all around us like hoop-skirts.

I don't think I have ever seen a day like yesterday, and I am still dazzled by a dazzle that comes at me from all sides and from a source that I am not used to and which I can't spot at all, not in the way I could spot the contemplation that I am by now used to.

The first thing that happened was that, kneeling in the sanctuary after ordination and during Mass, I realized clearly that I ought to stop writing poetry and be definite about it too. I went to Reverend Father afterwards and he said all right. And I have recovered a great deal of interior liberty by that one thing. In the afternoon I tore up all the rough notes for a poem. They had been lying around for a few days.

So after ordination in this respect and others I felt for the first time in my life like a more practical person. All of a sudden I seemed to know just what to do about everything that is on my mind at the moment.

Today I was on as deacon at Benediction. The new sense of practicality did not extend to the ceremonies. I was in a fog but very happy. All I could think about was picking up the Host. I was afraid the whole Church might come down on my head because of what I used to be – as if that were not forgotten!

But God scarcely weighs anything at all.

Though containing more than the universe, He was so light that I nearly fell off the altar. He communicated all that lightness to my own spirit and when I came down I was so happy I had a hard time to keep myself from laughing out loud.

March 21, 1949. St. Benedict

Yesterday and the day before I felt as if I had found a new center. Something I could not grasp or understand, but nothing else in the world seemed worth trying to grasp or understand either. The miracle of three days in which to be quiet has made all the graces of the diaconate sink deep into my soul. Today – two hours in the vault practically. The tentative Lenten schedule gives us all that between dinner and Vespers.

Am supposed to be getting up some notes on some 18th century copies of old documents on monasteries in the archdiocese of Besançon for the C.H.O.C.[39] Did a little, then tried to go on to St. Bernard, but in the end couldn't do anything but sit still and be dazzled.

The other day a French baroness was down here to see the place. I spoke to her. She came with gilt-edged recommendations from Dom Godefroid at Cîteaux. She was born in America, married a Baron Gourgaud left over from the "nobility" of Napoleon's creation. Her picture was painted at least once by Matisse and at least twice by Marie Laurencin and one of these pictures included a spaniel. She lives in a chateau at Orly where she puts honey in her eyes to improve her vision. If anyone wants to see her he must send a telegram because her servants don't answer telephones. She is a serious convert to the faith.

Visiting her for about twenty minutes was not a distraction except on the surface. It turns out that the diaconate seems to carry with it a two-edged grace for being sociable and recollected at the same time. One is at once more united to people and more isolated in God.

That is why I feel as if I had a new center, outside the orbit of my old yearning for pure solitude. And yet I desire solitude just as much, perhaps more, but in a different way which I cannot explain yet and which does not altogether exclude doing things and being with people. And yet I have been given swift feet for getting away from people and sociability when they catch up with me. It is a nice combination. In the last three days I have lived right. My energies have been running smoothly. I have had plenty to do – washing dishes Sunday morning, then beating it to Church at the first bell to uncover the altar and put out the chalice – and today getting everything ready for the Pontifical and chasing the brothers all around the Church.

I think I am beginning to understand something about the 15th chapter of St. Luke – the lost sheep, the lost drachma, the Prodigal Son. Our dearest Lord is showing that He means everything about the fatted calf and the rejoicing to be taken literally and that He means to pour out every kind of happiness in rivers upon those who ran away from His mercy but could not escape it.

39 *Commission de l'Histoire de l'Ordre Cistercien.*

March 27, 1949. Laetare Sunday

Since the diaconate Our Lady has taken possession of my heart. Maybe after all *She* is the big grace of the diaconate. She was given to me with the book of the Gospels which, like her, gives Christ to the world. I wonder what I have been doing all my life not resting in her heart which is the Heart of all simplicity. All life, outside her perfect union with God, is too complicated.

To think, Blessed Lady, to think that you should love me so much and that you should be the first one to tell me about giving my soul to you and losing myself in your simplicity! But if you had waited for me to discover it by myself, you would have had to wait a long time.

I am your deacon, your own special and personal deacon, your hand-and-foot deacon, and what made me want to laugh in the middle of the Gospel this morning was the fact that you were doing the singing and I was just resting and loving and sailing along.

Because you told me that, if I gave you my soul, it would become your soul. After all, if I give you a book, it becomes *your* book, and if I give you a picture, it becomes your picture. So if I give you a soul – my soul – it ceases to be mine and becomes *yours* [underlined twice] and you are the one who uses it and moves it. And believe me, dearest Lady, that is all I want. Because everything that is yours is perfectly united to God in pure simplicity.

So the quickest way to be perfectly united to God is to give my soul to you.

April 2, 1949. Saturday before Passion Sunday

We sang the *Vexilla Regis* and I thought – with a certain deep satisfaction messed up by confusion on the surface – that I am probably going to be separated from all this writing to which I am attached in spite of my complaint about it.

Not a chance to do anything on the Sheed and Ward book before I went on retreat for diaconate three weeks ago. The last week or two I have been trying to clean up the galley proofs of *Waters of Siloe*. Then four crates of Migne's Greek and Latin Fathers came in from a bookseller in Melun and I had to break them all open and see just what we got. I was surprised to find so many of the Latin Fathers practically brand new. Physically the Greek set was a little ratty, but I was happy to see St. Gregory of Nyssa whom we don't have here. The rest are for the South Carolina foundation.

Faults and imperfections grow out of me like weeds. Their leaves are waving all over me. They grow out of my hands like tobacco. And still I am not unhappy. I ought to be satisfied with life, since I am so far from pleasing God. Fr. Anthony, quoting St. Bernard, says, *O optanda infirmitas (id est – libenter gloriabor in infirmitatibus meis).* [O longed-for infirmity (that is – I shall gladly glory in my infirmities).]

It is God who wants me, no doubt, to have pleasure in work and in prayer. But it must be more referred to Him from whom it comes. The way to purify it is perhaps not to reject it, but to pour it all back into its source. Inhale and exhale – don't just breathe in and try to pretend your own lungs are the universe.

The question of motives – not merely to think I have faith, because a book sells. The formal motive of faith is not best-sellers, or the way you feel or whether the singing sounds good in choir. Faith does not rest on anything that is in me or in the world either. It rests on God Whom nobody on earth has ever seen.

April 3, 1949. Passion Sunday. Day of Recollection

When I sing the Gospel I am searched and penetrated by the light of what I sing, for the words of God are a two-edged sword piercing you to the division of the soul and the spirit. There are words of Christ which, when I sing them, I cannot sing them as one with Him because they are not true, coming from me. For instance, one day last week – *Ego non judico quemquam* [I judge not any man (John 8:15)]. I sang those words for Him, but for myself I had to add, "I judge everybody and laugh at everybody and think the whole monastery with everybody in it is a joke." It is not the healthiest condition to be in – to have to be divided against yourself when you sing the words that are meant to be as true of you as of the Head of your body!

I am trying laboriously to comb the unkindness out of *Waters of Siloe.* What a disease! To see what is wrong with everything! – and not to see the faults in my own books until after they are set up in type.

I wish I had in me, I mean permeating all my soul like oil in a fabric, that kindness of Christ which I sang in last week's Gospels – when He raised from death the son of the widow of Naim and Lazarus.

The sorrow of Martha did not make Him weep, but the tears of Mary made His own tears spring up and overflow from His eyes. And that is how much he prefers contemplatives, because they are closer to Him.

Today, according to the desires of the Holy Father, all the priests said Mass twice and we sang two conventual Masses. The first was an abbatial, after Prime. I was deacon and sang the wrong *Bendicamus Domino,* and afterwards, when I prostrated and got the signal to get up off my face, half the community thought it was time to go to Chapter and bowed and got ready to move.

Grey day. Apple blossoms on this side of the barn, but not yet on the other side.

To be led and moved by the love of God: indifferent to everything except that. This is the source of the only true joy. *Laetabor ego super eloquia tua sicut qui invenit spolia multa.* [I shall rejoice at thy words, as one that hath found great spoils (Psalms 118:162).] There is no sense in seeking or desiring anything but His will. But when you have found that, you have found everything, not because His will is just arbitrary and you love it blindly for its own sake. But His will is the expression of His wisdom and His infinite truth and it springs from truth and brings us all truth, and catches us up into itself, and sweeps us away with the inexorable tide of truth. To have His will in your heart and in your mind and in your love is to have sanctity and happiness. It is the foundation of all vision. Without it, even what you know to be true is no use to your soul because you are divided from the truth and armed against it.

April 5, 1949. St. Juliana

Yesterday was a landmark in the history of Gethsemani.

In the Chapter room, before the assembled community, and scrutinized by the portraits of Dom Eutropius, Dom Edmond, and most of all Dom Benedict, Robert Speaight gave us some readings from *Murder in the Cathedral.* That was our "reading before compline" last night. It ended at about quarter to seven and we got to bed late. The first time Gethsemani stayed up to go to the theater.

It was very good. Obviously.

But what was best about it was that I felt the community was responding to it far better than the New York audience in which I sat and saw *Murder in the Cathedral* twelve years ago or whenever it was. Here there was plenty of laughter at the apologies of the four knights. The last time I saw the thing I was the only one laughing and thought I was going to get thrown out by the ushers for being so indiscreet as to laugh at a play which, to judge by the programs, was obviously high art.

There were many who were deeply moved by the whole thing. I think the chorus about hell went over big. Even Dom Benedict's picture liked that. The Christmas sermon was beautiful and I had the feeling that it was more fully appreciated – because it is so simple.

The thing that struck me was the thought "saints are not made by accident," "martyrs are not made by men's choice but by God's," and that after all was the echo of what Dom Frederic used to say so much in that same chapter room, *Non vos me elegistis, sed ego elegi vos* [You have not chosen me, but I have chosen you (John 15:16)].

It all began when Reverend Father came in to the vault in the middle of the afternoon work asking if we had a copy of *Murder in the Cathedral* in the house. Then he took me in to talk to Speaight, and since he is a member of Hollis and Carter, who are publishing the London edition of the *Mountain*, I gave him the fancy set of galleys of *Waters of Siloe* which was sent for the General when he comes here.

Speaight said that half the people he knew had at one time or another tried to become Carthusians. One of them had been sent away after having been told kindly, "We never kept anyone so long with such a bad voice as you have!"

About the way the community received *Murder* he was very pleased. He said the first night of the play in New York was the closest he ever got to Purgatory.

He goes all over England telling people how the last time he was here, Fr. Augustine, who heard his confession, told him that, to inspire himself with high ideals, he ought to think of the illustrious English Catholics Hollis and Lunn. The first two to whom he told the story seem to have been his friends Hollis and Lunn.

He said the statue of Our Lady on the facade of the Portiuncula at Assisi is supposed to move her head quite frequently and thousands of people go to see it. Graham Greene went to see it and remained lying with his head on the ground to make certain that any movement he saw was not on *his* part. Sure enough her head moved.

Then he told me all about Mrs. MacIssacs on a farm in Ontario. She has the stigmata on Fridays.

He said Gethsemani had a good atmosphere and approved of the smell in the corridor under the guest house – a smell which Dom Gabriel described as horrible – and which to me has always been completely indifferent.

Speaight wanted me to write a book about St. Bernard. In fact he suggested it without my having had time to bring it to mind. But his suggestion was just what I had been thinking about for months now.

He said T. S. Eliot regards every poem as a temptation and resists it for years. Amen.

April 6, 1949

Yesterday a short but beautiful letter came from Dom Porion, the Procurator General of the Carthusians in Rome. I had written to him, at the suggestion of Jacques Maritain, telling him that a copy of *The Seven Storey Mountain* was on the way. Maritain thought he would like it and also told me to send copies to Paul Philippe at the Angelicum and to Monsignor Montini.[40] He also told me to mention to Dom Porion an idea I had taken up in a letter to Dom Humphrey Pawsey at Parkminster about a foundation in this country. However, Reverend Father forbade me to mention it. I spoke of the vocations we were getting however.

His letter was very beautiful. It spoke directly about the possibility of a foundation which, he said, was unlikely. But he said he was going to bring it up at the next General Chapter, but that the idea would probably not be accepted. Then he said how little chance there was of finding really genuine Carthusian vocations in this country. Said how difficult it was to find people who could live purely for God alone in solitude, occupied with nothing but Him.

The way it was put was so concrete and well-stated that I saw at once very clearly how literally the contemplative vocation is taken by the Carthusians and how loosely and improperly it is taken in our Order. I wonder if there are four or two or even one in this community who could qualify as Carthusians. Probably not even one – including myself. Those who, as I know, have leanings in that direction, are all very active or else unqualified in some other way.

Really the letter tore me to pieces, and yet it made me happy.

Of course it reminded me of my longing for solitude, interior purity, perfect silence, a life for God alone. I haven't prayed in months as I have been praying since I read that letter: not praying to be anywhere but here (except of course in heaven), but burning up with the desire of God and with shame at my unmitigated interior activity and the futility of so much that I do.

And yet since the diaconate I have a new attitude. Although it half kills me, I find myself accepting the idea that I do not have a purely contemplative vocation. I say "accept." I do not *believe* [underlined twice] it. It is utterly impossible for me to believe any such thing: everything in me cries out for solitude and for God alone. Yet I find myself admitting that perhaps I don't know what that really means, and that I am too low on the spiritual

[40] Montini would become Pope Paul VI.

scale of things to grasp it, and that I am somehow excluded from it by God's love. The feeling is absolutely terrible – the power of an attraction that seems to draw the whole life out of me, to tear out the roots of my soul – and then the blank wall against which I stop: they will never let me leave here, perhaps the Carthusians would never receive me, and I would not dare to go for fear of offending God and wounding His love.

And yet in the middle of all this is not unrest or rebellion but happiness and peace, and I rejoice in it, because, blindly, something in the middle of me grabs on to the one reality that remains accessible to me – but this is the supreme reality of all – the love of God.

Somehow I have to give up this thing that I love above everything else on earth *because the love of God is greater.* It seems like a contradiction be-cause what I have to give up is, in the last analysis, what I am convinced is the most perfect way I could love and serve God! But that is *per se. Per accidens* there is something greater: to renounce the purest and greatest of all vocations simply because it is not the one God has chosen for me – accept something far less, in which it seems likely that my highest personal ideals will be altogether frustrated, purely because of His love, His will. He who loves me prefers it this way, and to accept His love is to send up to Him the incense of the purest prayer, the sweetest praise, without pleasure for my-self – and yet in the end it is a supreme joy! *Adoremus Dominum qui nos re-demit per crucem.* [Let us adore the Lord who has redeemed us through the cross.] It is the beginning of my priesthood and my union with His sacri-fice, the joy and the victory which is Calvary.

April 14, 1949. Good Friday

First, I must copy out some words from Dom Porion's letter, or rather from his first letter. A second came, saying the book had reached him, and it was written in some clinic where he had just been operated on for "an ul-cer." Anyway, here is what was in the first letter among other things. He wrote in English.

"Most people find their balance in doing, in creating something, mere contemplative life requires a special grace – and a special fidelity. It re-quires a ripeness too, a maturity of soul which is not often to be met (with) in converts." (He was not aiming this at me since when he wrote that he didn't know I was a convert.) "This seems to result at least from the exper-iments we have made. But to contemplate in the first meaning of the word – to look directly at God and to keep quiet – calm and purity being at once the condition and consequence of the vision – this indeed seems to me the true life, the life everlasting we are made for. The modern world seems to fly passionately from that ideal: but I am convinced that mankind in the end will find again the way of contemplation – nature and surnature, in their deepest, lead to this divine joy."

There are also a lot of good things in [Johannes] Tauler whom I like very much – when he is explained by notes like Fr. Hugeny's [*Sermons de Tauler*, 3 volumes, Paris, 1927–35].

This morning the psalter was wonderful except that perhaps I was a bit too much concerned as to how much I personally was getting out of it. Still I had the feeling that I was getting a lot out of it anyway. I don't mean "lights or spectacles," but a deep unitive awareness of God and a sapience that came up out of the midst of me in waves, under the impulsion of the psalms. I keep seeing the psalter as a compendium and a summary of the whole spiritual life, with everything packed into it, everything.

One thing did strike me *in individuo* [with personal meaning for me]. It was the line, *Ponite corda vestra in virtute ejus*. [Set your hearts on her (Sion's) strength (Psalms 47:14)], and the application that occurred to me was "put your hearts in the power of Our Lady, unite them with her influence and let your hearts ride in the stream of her will," and I said the rest of the psalter in her power, *in virtute ejus*.

Fr. Edward lost his voice and wrote me a note last night to replace him as "Evangelist" in the St. John Passion. The only direction he gave was "in all movements you are in the middle." Got all muddled up on the movements, but it went well otherwise, and when it came to the lines, "Woman, behold thy son," I suddenly realized that *I* was John the Evangelist at that moment. And I "beheld my Mother."

This afternoon I tried to be as quiet as I could for two hours in the vault and came out with the conclusion that writing is something very low and insignificant, and that I, who seem to have become inseparable from writing, am also low and insignificant.

Holy Saturday. [April 15, 1949]

The Night Office of this day is bewildering. The confusion of sorrow and joy is so complex that you never know where you are. The responsories might have been composed by James Joyce. All the associations of terms and symbols are thrown into confusion. One responsory starts out with *Jerusalem* . . . and you are all set to be glad, and you are told to mourn. Then in the end, speculatively, you find that you are saved. This is the product of the historical circumstances through which the Holy Saturday liturgy has passed.

But there is no confusion about the *Exultet*. Well, I am supposed to sing it today. I am going to sing the whole of theology. It is marvelous. The *Exultet* is real liturgy, except perhaps it is too speculative. But, really, the Deacon who sings that and does the things the rubrics say is teaching all theology, and the people who hear it are learning all theology, and the Holy Ghost, who operates what is signified, throws light in darkness upon the whole meaning of Christianity, on the Mass, on Good Friday and Easter, the center of everything.

Saturday before Low Sunday. [April 23, 1949]

Well, I sang the *Exultet* and stuck the four red grains of incense into the paschal candle in the form of a cross and afterwards sang the *Ite Missa est* [Go, the Mass is finished] with two *Alleluias* and both on Holy Saturday and Easter Day, when I was also deacon, I slipped on the red carpet which lay too loosely on the altar steps and nearly broke my neck.

And now the week has passed and the two *Alleluias* after every *Ite missa est* and *Bendicamus Domino* are finished, and I sang the Epistles from the Acts and from St. Peter and especially the one about the eunuch of Candace who was riding in his chariot reading Isaias, which he did not understand.

On Sunday and Monday afternoons I prayed in the vault and came out feeling as if I had been pierced and baptized, and with new knowledge about prayer and I hope new humility, as if I had also passed some milestone and gone down lower, or if you prefer, up higher or at least out of myself.

How much I need to go out of myself!

On Monday morning it was announced in chapter that the Archbishop would really be coming here on the 26th, that is Ascension Day, to ordain me and Fr. Amandus to the priesthood and make four subdeacons into the bargain.

Today Fr. Timothy was trying to teach us how to say Mass. I put my hand on the altar, there, one of those altars in the back sacristy. I stood there while he talked. I kissed the altar, genuflected with my hands on the altar. I turned around and made the movement you make with your hands when you say *Dominus Vobiscum*. I held the paten up on my fingers with an imaginary host and said the *Suscipe sancte Pater* [Receive, Holy Father]. Afterwards I thought how the union of ceremonies and words in the Mass is the simplest and deepest and most fundamental and also the easiest and most perfectly satisfactory way of adoring God that could be imagined – even from our own subjective point of view, and apart from all that is in it *in se*.

So I think very much of Our Lady of Cobre and the question I once asked her.[41]

April 29, 1949. Feast of St. Robert

It is extremely difficult to write theology well. The main reason why I can't write it is that I don't know it. I don't know precisely what I mean to say, and therefore when I start to write, I find that I am working out a theory as I go. And I get into the most terrible confusion, saying things which I try to explain – to myself more than to anyone else – and rambling off the track of the plan I had arranged.

I wonder how many plans I have made for this book, *The School of the Spirit*? Perhaps six – including the ones I made for it when it was called *The Cloud and the Fire*. So I sit at the typewriter with my fingers all wound up in a cat's cradle of strings, overwhelmed with the sense of my own stupidity and surrounded by not one but many literary dilemmas.

I am supposed now to be working on the book three afternoons a week and try at all costs to get something down on paper, terrified that if I merely stop and read and organize notes, I will go around in circles forever and ever. This business of "getting my notes together" is something that can go on absolutely interminably, because there exists an almost unlimited number of combinations in which you can arrange the statements you have jotted down so carefully on some eight hundred pages of various notebooks.

All that undigested material is utterly terrifying and fascinating at the same time. Sometimes I try to "meditate" on this monster which I call "my notes." (I should say "our" notes, but skip it.) But the statements standing out of context and in my own crazy handwriting do not have the meaning and unction they had in Migne or St. John of the Cross or wherever I first read them . . .

They seem to divide and slacken my mind and leave my spirit in a vague state of perturbation at the thought that I have eaten the Fathers and produced nothing but this unhappy web.

But when I tell myself, "I am no writer, I am finished," instead of being upset I am filled with a sense of peace and of relief, perhaps because I al-

---

[41] "There you are, Caridad del Cobre! It is you that I have come to see; you will ask Christ to make me His priest, and I will give you my heart, Lady: and if you will obtain for me this priesthood, I will remember you at my first Mass in such a way that the Mass will be for you and offered through your hands in gratitude to the Holy Trinity, Who has used your love to win me this great grace." From *The Seven Storey Mountain*, 282 ff.

ready taste, by anticipation, the joy of my deliverance. On the other hand, if I am not delivered from writing by failure, perhaps I might go on and even succeed at this thing, but by the power of the Holy Ghost, which would be an even greater deliverance. But whatever happens, success or failure, I have given up worrying. I just wonder about the business on paper on the assumption that it might mean something to me if I should ever re-read all this at another season.

Nor is saying Mass as easy as I expected. I practiced it again today, this time alone, in the back sacristy at the Altar of Our Lady of Lourdes. It is all right up to the "consecration" and would be all right after it too, if you did not have to be so careful about your fingers. Your thumb and forefinger of each hand are only for picking up and breaking the Host. You use the other fingers on everything else. But I find myself uncovering the chalice, taking off the paten with those forefingers and thumbs, and touching the Host and purifying the paten with all the other fingers. In fact, the moment you have "consecrated" everything gets in the way. Then the dry host is hard to swallow too.

I am glad I am doing all this before ordination. If I waited until afterward, it would complicate life no end.

St. John of the Cross at his first Mass asked God for the favor of suffering for Him and dying abandoned as an outcast of men. I asked myself what it was I was going to ask of God at my first Mass, and I think it is not that. If I did ask that, it would be an act of insincerity in me because it is not what grace usually seems to move me to, and it would I think be only a piece of natural vanity, at least in my present dispositions. What does God want me to ask Him? He will tell me, and when I find out, He will also give me what I ask. And no doubt the best thing in the world I could do about it would be to tell no one and do one greater thing than all the worthies did.

May Day, 1949. SS. Philip and James. Day of Recollection
The air is full of apostasies: perhaps no fuller than usual, but under Dom James we hear all about them. In the refectory today we are reading an article by Fr. E. Boyd Barrett, a Jesuit who went out and came back. It is interesting. At the same time in Boston there is a big fuss about Fr. Leonard Feeney, who wrote that book *Fish on Friday* and a lot of others which I used to see on the shelves of the Catholic Book Club in New York. I remember also the fragments of information I have heard about Dom

David Knowles who is a much subtler and more poignant case. After all, there are passages in those two big books of his which are as good as anything that has been written recently about the religious life. I can see how he felt about so many things – the Carthusians, St. Francis' poverty. Really, here is a man who has perhaps understood and appreciated some of the finest things about monastic and religious life much better than the minds with whom he might have come in conflict. Speaight told me Dom David Knowles and some others at Downside were trying to get away from all that stuffy semi-active atmosphere and get back to something like real asceticism. But their idea was opposed and then squelched. It must have been terribly hard. So hard, in fact, that some of them broke under it. But look where he is now: a Don at Peterhouse – no Mass – no monastic life *at all* – no contemplation at all. It is very easy to shrug and say "disobedient – no solid foundation to his interior life, etc., etc.," but I can see Boyd Barrett's point, too. How crude and seemingly unjust the positions of their opponents can be. Yet it is the *only* position, if it is really backed by all the higher superiors . . . How do these things turn out in the end? How many of the saints have been condemned or silenced in their own time, but the experience is that the saints did not run away . . .

And now people – following a strange sort of logic – assuming that all writers are proud and are therefore potential apostates, seem to think that probably I will be one of the next. *Cras tibi.* [Tomorrow you.] Of course the rumor has already gone around in some places that both Fr. Raymond and I had left Gethsemani. The "scandal" about Raymond even got to Parkminster, and Dom Humphrey asked me (two years ago) if it were true.

As soon as a religious writes a book and gets it published, the rumor starts traveling around: "he has left the monastery, you know!" It began with me as soon as I had published *Thirty Poems*.

Nevertheless, it is true: *Hodie tibi* – maybe *cras mihi*. [Today for you – maybe tomorrow for me.] But not because I am a *writer*. I am proud and I am defectible because I am an ordinary human being. Plenty of people have left this monastery – I don't say apostasized – who were not writers, and there were a lot more apostasies, real ones, in the old days when the monks could hardly write their own names.

Still, in the end, the problem remains: this terrible business of giving up everything, even a *religious ideal*, even what seems to you to be the highest perfection, in order to obey someone who might be objectively wrong, but who nevertheless has the right to be obeyed. *The highest perfection can be to abandon perfection out of obedience* – giving up your own judgment even in what is objectively best and noblest. Thank God, sin is excluded from all this! At least you can't be made to do *that!* But some things can look that bad, when a man gets upset and crushed by such a trial. No wonder the Church sometimes looks inhuman to the people outside.

And on top of all that, when it is all over, and your saint has been sat on and his work apparently destroyed, the others will continue in their same obtuse mediocrity, and preach on him from pious books the sentiments of Job's friends! *Diviserunt sibi vestimenta mea . . . consideraverunt et inspexerunt me . . . dinumeraverunt omnia ossa mea . . .* [They parted my garments among them . . . they have looked and stared upon me . . . they have numbered all my bones . . . (Psalms 21:18–19).] They shall look upon the one they have pierced.

Sooner or later some such trial will probably land on me. It is always more than a passive potency: definitely active. How will I ever be able to take it? And yet I have got to, if it comes. Every day I get some idea of what is in myself when I have to swallow my own ideas about chant, the interior life, solitude, the Cistercian vocation, etc., etc. Every day I kill Isaac – my beautiful dream about a silent, solitary, well ordered life of perfect contemplation and perfect monastic observance, with no intrusion from the world, no publicity, no best-selling books, just God and that nice archaic little Carthusian cell!! And I have to make that blind act of faith that God and Our Lady are drawing me – *per crucem* – to something better which I will probably never see this side of heaven.

I am not saying this against Reverend Father. He has suffered a great deal and made something of this sacrifice himself. Which is one of the reasons why he is such a saint.

At the beginning of May, I think: Our Lady is coming gradually to be the *whole* of my interior life. The more I leave everything to her, the simpler everything becomes, and the easier I travel. And this morning I was reading marvelous things in Adam of Perseigne about Mary being "the way." She is that. Through her we come quickly to – everything.

May 5, 1949

Today is the feast of the Saint Sacerdos who was abbot of Huerta and bishop of Sigüenza. The other day I was reminded that Huerta is still a Cistercian Abbey by a letter from Spain, but the letter was from Viaceli and it contained information about another magazine they are starting, again in Spanish. Fr. Anthony wondered whether to subscribe to it for the new monastery in South Carolina of which he will be the superior.

But the reason I started talking about St. Sacerdos was that there is a lot about the priesthood in his Mass, which is *Statuit* from the Common of Confessors Pontiffs. Also the second *Alleluia* verse surprised me by being the melody we have in all the *Alleluias* at Christmas time in the Masses of the great feasts. And here we are in the midst of spring and everything is green and saturated with light, and birds sing, and the air is perfumed with the smell of the burning cedar wood where we have been clearing out the grove in front of the abbey to prepare for the centenary celebration, which is to be on June 1st only and not, thank heaven, on June 1st, 2nd, and 3rd.

The other day I was out there with an axe and there were big fires all down the side of the little hill where the wayside shrine is and the secular cemetery. The flames were angry and high and one delicate sapling, which was left standing in the midst of all the fires, withered and was blasted in the burning air. I watched the shuddering of the leaves in the gusts of that furnace and it made me think of Joan of Arc.

At the Conventual Mass (this week it is my turn to be subdeacon) I have hardly been able to think of anything but Our Lady. Either that, or else I sink down into the depths where God is found alone. But to do that is to be occupied implicitly with her, for she is the way there. Yet I do not say I do all this easily – I am surrounded by distractions and yet drawn into this love of her in spite of them. And I have worried about them, too, thinking of what the Spirit said to the various Churches of Asia in the Apocalypse: "I know thy works, that thou hast the name of being alive, and thou art dead . . ." May the mercy of God deliver me from those words. It is this that makes me run to our dearest Mother.

More and more I abandon anything of my own that might seem to be a "technique" of prayer and throw myself upon her mercy, leaving myself to be moved and guided by her, certain that she alone, by God's dispensation and decree, can help my helplessness.

I wondered much about how to state the fact of a mystical union with her. I still don't know, but I believe it to be very real in the spiritual life. And even, in a certain sense, there might be a way of looking at it that would permit me to say there was nothing greater in the spiritual life. For to be identified with her, to share all her gifts and all her graces, by her own will and the will of God, would be to be identified with the one Soul that can (apart from Christ's own) receive most of God. If my soul becomes hers, I can receive as much of God as she can; whereas if my own soul retains its own narrow limits, I will have much less capacity for loving God.

How true is this? Perhaps I shall write to Père Paul Philippe at the Angelicum and ask him about it. Jacques Maritain told me to send him also the *Mountain* and I did, and he wrote a nice letter.

Our Church is now, by the grace of God and a decree of the Holy See, a minor basilica. I think most of us, including myself, did not know how much of a formal dignity that could be. We are now technically on a level with Lourdes or St. Anne de Beaupré, but I hope we don't start getting pilgrims, although the Holy Father says he likes our retreats. It all makes me feel like being more careful about ceremonies, and I tell myself, "Listen, you're in a minor basilica, slow down! Don't run!"

May 6, 1949

I just came across these lines by D. S. Savage about American poetry in an English magazine, *The Wind and the Rain*, issue of last winter:

"It seems inherently probable that in his isolation from the mass society (reference to reaction against the Whitman-Vachel Lindsay tradition in verse) the American poet, forced back into his interior life, will be led to discover the reality of the individual and the relevance of the metaphysical-religious perspectives which open up when the individual existence, and not the collective being of society, is taken as the central point of reference for the adventure of human experience. *And he may as poet, prophet and seer open a way for the eventual transformation of the quality of American life from within.* Such a transformation will depend upon the reversal of the current of modern life: that is to say upon the subordination of civilization to culture, and of culture to the inner life and destiny of man in relation to the metaphysical absolute. It will be a religious transformation."

May 8, 1949. Third Sunday after Easter

Modicum et non videbitis me [A little while and you shall not see me (John 16:17)] . . . I sang the beautiful Gospel, "Yet a little while and you shall see me no longer, because I go to the Father . . . The world shall rejoice and you shall be sad . . . but your sorrow shall be turned into joy and your joy no one shall take from you."

Which means – yet a little while and it will be Ascension Day.

It seems to me impossible that I should live the next two and a half weeks without keeling over, dying of heart failure, or having the house come down on top of my head. How can I possibly achieve such a wonder as the priesthood? To do the one thing that saves the world and brings health to it and makes you capable of being happy! To continue the Mystery of Christ's Calvary and do all those simple and easy things by which the work of our Redemption is accomplished.

Because the Mass is so easy seems to me to be all the more reason first, for saying it perfectly, and second, for making it your whole life.

I love the prayers that go with the incensation at a solemn Mass – the prayers and the ceremonies. These, too, are so easy and simple and happy! What could be more joyful than swinging the censer full of sweet smoke around the chalice and host and praying that our incense might go up to God and His blessing might come down to us, and that the fire of His everlasting love may burn our hearts!

Incidentally today is St. Michael's apparition by whose intercession the incense is blessed.

Most of my troubles come from a subtle lack of poverty. I mean the troubles at work – the correspondence that keeps me from writing that book. I have wanted to acquire too many things – books especially. Of course it is all "for the monastery" or "for the foundations" and all "blessed by obedience," but in the end it is all my own idea and I am in actual fact exercising the appetites of proprietorship and acquisitiveness even though the acts are legally purified. Hence all these complications – bartering books with the Librarian at Achel and the Librarian at Viaceli and the Librarian at Aiguebelle. Still, some of it is unavoidable. And Dom Déchanet came after me to dig out the variants in our ms. of William of St. Thierry's *Golden Epistle* so that he can identify it by the "family" to which it belongs. He can tell.

From all this flow distractions and bothers of all kinds and it has been sapping my spiritual energy – or trying to – for months. And here I sit resolving to stop it, and the catbird mocks me up there in the cedar tree.

I was reading the ms. from the Archives of Laval all about the Trappistines there and at Ubexy a hundred years ago – simple, fervent and tough. They make me ashamed of myself and my "literary career."

Brother Charles comes up and asks me by signs "when Hundred year big day book come?" And I signal back to him "plenty late, plenty late." He says, "How full pages? Two hundred?" I say, "Yeah." He goes away not sad but not altogether happy.

The General is on his way here *pour une visite sérieuse* [for a serious visit], but I don't know when he will arrive. Reverend Father spoke in Chapter about what a headache the Centenary is going to be, and he has been promising that, once that is over, down will come the iron curtain. I hope we get all the reporters outside *before* it comes down.

I think almost entirely about the ordination and not at all about the Centenary. Once I get those oils on my hands I'll be ready for anything.

May 15, 1949. 4th Sunday after Easter

The sun is rising. All the green trees are full of birds, and their song comes up out of the wet bowers of the orchard. Crows swear pleasantly in the distance, and in the depths of my soul sits God, and between Him, in the depths and the thoughts on the surface, is the veil of an unresolved problem.

What shall I say this problem is? It is not a conflict of ideas. It is not a dilemma. I do not believe it is a question of choice. Is it a psychological fact: any interior problem is a psychological fact. Is it a question that I can resolve? No.

This problem is my own personality in which I do not intend at any time to take an unhealthy interest. But (I speak as one less wise) this problem is my personality, or, if you like, the development of my interior life. I am not perplexed either by what I am or what I am not, but by the mode in which I am tending to become what I really will be.

God makes us ask ourselves questions most often when He intends to resolve them. He gives us needs that He alone can satisfy and awakens capacities that He means to fulfill. Any perplexity is liable to be a spiritual gestation, leading to a new birth and a mystical regeneration.

Here are a few points:

What is the Mass going to do to my interior life?

I am confronted with the fact of my past prayer. Acts, thoughts, desires, words, became inadequate when I was a novice. Resting in God, sleeping, so to speak, in His silence, remaining in His darkness, have fed me and made me grow for seven years. Now that, too, is likely to become inadequate.

The Mass will hold the key to this inadequacy, I hope.

I cannot explain more at the moment, except that Christ the High Priest is awakening in the depths of my soul in silence and majesty, like a giant Who means to run His course.

When practicing the ceremonies of Mass, when standing at the altar as Deacon, I have been more and more impressed by the fact that it would be utterly insufficient for me, as priest, to stand at the altar and say prayers with great personal love and fervor to Christ in the Sacrament before me. I once thought that would be the consummation of all joy – to be united by a bond of love with Christ in the Sacrament of love – to be lost in His presence there as if nothing else matters.

And now – there is much more. Instead of *myself* and *my* Christ and *my* love and *my* prayer, there is the might of a prayer stronger than thunder and milder than the flight of doves rising up from the Priest Who is the center of the soul of every priest, shaking the foundations of the universe and lifting up – me, Host, altar, sanctuary, people, Church, Abbey, forest, cities, continents, seas and worlds to God and plunging every thing into Him.

In the presence of this huge power, my own thoughts and words and affections cannot seem to mean anything! Not that they have no value whatever, but now they are lost and sublimated in a far greater and simpler prayer that is beyond my comprehension.

As I sit here and write this now at the end of the afternoon, the robins are making much noise but not half so much noise as the novices who are full of polyphony for the day of wrath that is to come upon us on the first of June.

Meanwhile the community has been purged by sickness and accidents. The temporary door of the horse barn fell down on Brother Casimir and crushed two vertebrae of his spine, and Fr. Gerard the novice-master is in the hospital with something unidentified, and Fr. Subprior fell down on his head and got knocked out while he was nailing up a partition in the red-house. And maybe there is going to be another accident in the novitiate because Fr. Philip, who is conducting their oratorio, is stamping so hard that I expect him to go through the floor and break his collar-bone among the pots and pans and bottles in Fr. Linus' dark room.

Anyway, there have been some colds in the community and one of the worst was the one that hit me. For two days I slept late – that is until 2:45 and I still have no appetite for food. For that matter I haven't much appetite for anything else either.

Reverend Father told us a sad story in Chapter. Last year we had a curious fat man in the house as a brother oblate. He was called Brother Fidelis. He couldn't seem to get along. I remember the day he came. Dom Vital brought him in to Dom Frederic with two others – that was before the Utah foundation. I remember the fat one seemed in a hurry to get out.

Anyway, he went away. This week a letter came in from some boarding house where he had been living. They wanted to know if we knew anything about him – if he had any family left – etc. He had died in a hospital. It sounded very forlorn. Then another letter came from some religious congregation. They had heard about his death and hoped he had died here. The reason why they worried about him was that he had once been a member of their congregation, and he was a priest. Bro. Clement told me the man had worked a long time in a steel mill. I remember he was teamed up with that other anxious oblate who had been a prison guard and who also went away.

Ave Maria, gratia plena [Hail Mary, full of grace], sing the novices, *gratia plena, Dominus tecum* [full of grace, the Lord is with you]. Lady, take care of poor brother Fidelis and of all of us poor sinners in this valley that is as sad as the novices' Russian opera.

But in the vault everything was clear. The page proofs of *Waters of Siloe* lay neglected on the table, and I expect them to lie that way more or less until after ordination. I come out of myself and look at my books and at letters and am sad, but I return to God and know that my vocation is to be a priest and a contemplative, and that my vocation is PRAYER, and that makes me happy.

Fr. Edmund comes by with his rosary and makes me a sign, "Eleven days."

I had resisted the temptation to count the days, on the grounds that it might be an imperfection – or that it might turn out to be something like David's census. The Epistle of the day – *[in mansuetudine] suscipite insitum Verbum* [with meekness receive the engrafted word (James 1:21)]. And the collect, "that our hearts may be fixed where true joys are." Another beautiful letter came in from Dom Jean-Baptiste Porion. He said he liked the last part of the *Mountain* and that he shared my affection for Blake. That reminds me that the only other Catholic (besides Maritain) that I actually remember impressing me by a really sympathetic interest in non-Catholic mystics is Dom Humphrey, another Carthusian – the one at Parkminster. But someone wrote me a letter criticizing me for belittling oriental mysticism – took exception to remarks about Quakers in the *Mountain* and Sufis in *Seeds*, and said I had treated Blake with patronage. I do not think I did that. As for the Sufis, he is right in spotting me for talking through my hat, saying something I don't really know. I have not read more than fifteen words of any Sufi mystic and I was going on somebody else's authority. I had heard somewhere that you could call Mohammedan mysticism "sensual." It wasn't told to me, I simply heard.

May 23, 1949. Rogation Days

In three days, if I am alive, and if the Archbishop does not fall down and break his leg, I should be a priest. I keep thinking: "I shall say Mass – I shall say Mass." And I remember Our Lady of Cobre, to whose basilica I went nine years ago this May. She has done very well by me, and her love has followed me this far and will take me to God.

I can't read anything but St. John of the Cross. I opened *The Living Flame* at the line *Rompe la tela de este dulce encuentro* [Tear the veil of this sweet encounter]. The priesthood as an encounter of the substance of my soul with the Living God! I do not understand it yet. Perhaps I will know more about it on Thursday. Anyway, that will be my prayer: that more of the curtains may be taken away, and that the servitude of desires that burden my whole life may be diminished, and that I may be liberated and come closer to Him in the Mass – in every Mass I offer. That each Mass may lighten the atmosphere and be a step forward to heaven and to vision. That each Mass may be an enrichment and a liberation to my soul and all those souls who, in the designs of Our Blessed Lady, depend on these Masses to come to holiness and to contemplation, to find liberty and joy.

Apart from Dom [Odo] Casel and Bouyer, most of the writing about the priesthood does not satisfy me, and now I cannot read even them. They seem too technical, and I need not theology but the living God. *Sitivit anima mea* [my soul has thirsted]. The strong living God. I burn with the desire for His peace, His stability, His silence, the power and wisdom of His direct action, liberation from my own heaviness. I carry myself around like a ton weight.

To begin with, I am oppressed with shame. Shame at simply existing outside of God, in my own will. Every judgment, every opinion of my own makes me feel sick with sin. And I obviously can't stop thinking and judging – at least not on my own, without God. And the coarse movements of my mind and will disgust me like filthy deeds which I cannot avoid, as if they were acts of impurity.

They all remind me of two things: that my only hope is to become one with God, that is, to be absorbed in His purity, His infinite unselfishness for which I thirst with my whole being. The poverty, the simplicity of the infinitely rich God. Oh how I hate to be *something!* To be doomed to possess things, a name, a notable personality.

Most books about the priesthood speak of the priest above all as a minister, as a shepherd, who works for souls, saves people. That is good. And yet the mere thought of myself uttering doctrines nauseates me. I don't know what the solution can be. I wish somebody had written about the priest as lost in God – the priest as solitary.

May 24, 1949

The problem of the priesthood for me is among other things a problem of poverty. I know that all priests are not necessarily committed, by their priesthood, to absolute poverty. But for my own part it seems to me that the two are connected. Anyway, we had some intelligent reading about religious poverty in the refectory. Fr. McCorry's new book. He is one of the few good writers one gets to hear in a monastery.

To be a priest means, in my particular case, to have nothing, desire nothing, and be nothing but to belong to Christ. *Mihi [enim] vivere Christus est et mori lucrum.* [For to me, to live is Christ, and to die is gain (Philippians 1:21).] In order to have everything desire to have nothing. Priesthood for a contemplative ought, I think, to mean an unusual degree of emptiness and self-effacement. For St. Benedict it certainly means a greater obedience and submission to Superiors than is demanded of the others.

That we have nothing to do with the active ministry does not necessarily imply superiority over priests outside in the world. On the contrary, it contributes more to our special poverty, making it more complete and more spiritual. It implies the realization that we have practically nothing to give to souls in the way of preaching and guidance and talent and grace. We are shamed of any active apostolate that might conceivably come from us, and we vanish into the Mass – *omnium peripsema usque adhuc* . . . [the offscouring of all even till now . . . (1 Corinthians 4:13).]

And so my poverty in spiritual things, my defects and imperfections, all have their part in this too. I shall go to the altar remembering that St. Paul said God has chosen the weak things of the world: *infirma mundi elegit Deus ut confundat fortia* [the weak things of the world hath God chosen, that he may confound the strong (1 Corinthians 1:27)].

Also: in my prayer and all my interior life, such as it is, I am concerned with the need for a greater and more complete interior silence: an interior secrecy that amounts to not even thinking about myself. Silence about my prayer, about the development of my interior life, is becoming an absolute necessity, so that I am beginning to believe I should stop writing about contemplation altogether except perhaps in the most general terms. It seems to me to be a great indecency for me to pass in the opinion of men as one who thinks he knows something about contemplation. The thing makes me feel as if I needed a bath and a change of clothing.

May 25, 1949. Vigil of the Ascension

In the Martyrology, together with the announcement of the great feast which always makes me so happy, there came also the commemoration of the St. Augustine who re-converted England. After all these centuries I am one of the children of his prayers and apostolic labors and sacrifices. Then there is also St. Philip Neri, who seems at first sight to have little to do with the contemplative priesthood. However, he had the privilege of saying Mass locked up in a room all by himself – and it took him three or four hours. I blush to think of what the authorities of the liturgical movement would think of that.

The liturgy of the vigil is matched by the brilliant weather of the day. Not a shred of cloud anywhere in the deep blue sky. This morning it was rather cool – like September. A thin, thin rind of moon hung high over the bottoms and I almost expected to see fields full of tall ripe corn.

Vocem jucunditatis annuntiate et audiatur, alleluia . . . [Declare it with a voice of joy and make it heard . . . (a gloss on Isaiah 48:20).]

I was very happy to sing the Gospel – the magnificent triumph of Christ which is echoed and expressed in the ordination to the priesthood of a thing like myself that He picked up out of the wreckage of the moral universe and brought into His house. It is He Who looks up to heaven, in my own soul full of weakness and infidelity, and cries out, *Pater venit hora, clarifica Filium tuum, ut Filius tuus clarificet te.* [Father, the hour has come, glorify thy Son, that thy Son may glorify you (John 17:1).] And the context reminds me to whom I belong – *[sicut] dedisti ei potestatem omnis carnis, ut omne quod dedisti ei, det eis vitam aeternam* [As thou hast given him power over all flesh, that he may give life everlasting to all whom thou hast given him (John 17:2)]. My joy is the great power of Christ. And for that, above all, I am glad of my deep moral poverty which is always before me these days, but which does not obsess or upset me because it is all lost in His mercy.

The truth is, I am far from being the monk or the cleric that I ought to be. My life is a great mess and tangle of half-conscious subterfuges to evade grace and duty. I have done all things badly. I have thrown away great opportunities. My infidelity to Christ, instead of making me shudder, drives me on to throw myself all the more blindly on His mercy. How could

I dare to go to the altar and say Mass after the way I have treated my other obligations, at least interiorly, in the past two or three years? After the way I have chanted office with my head full of distraction or criticism or argument or complaint . . . And yet I can go to the altar with confidence and great joy and know that my Mass is going to make a tremendous difference to the happiness and salvation of the world, not only *in spite* of the fact that it is my Mass, but even *because* it is my Mass, that is, because of the special mercy of Christ to those who have nothing of their own to offer, nothing except weakness and misery and sin. And on the feast of my own "Ascension," when by his power I am taken into heaven, I shall sing, *Ego te clarificavi:* I have given You glory!

May 29, 1949. Sunday within the Octave of the Ascension

I could not begin to write about the ordination, about saying Mass, about the *Agape* [love banquet] that lasted three days with all those who came down. Perhaps some day it will come out retrospectively, in fragments.

A sense of the absolutely tremendous work that has been done in me and through me in the last three days, each day bringing its own growth. Ordination, anointing, ordination Mass – then the first low Mass and what followed, finally the Solemn Mass yesterday and the talking in the afternoon out under the trees of the avenue. I am left with the feeling not only that I have been transformed, but that a new world has somehow been brought into being through the labor and happiness of these three most exhausting days, full of sublimity and of things that none of us will understand for a year or two to come.

(I got that far when Fr. Amandus told me we were to go up and bless the sick. The sick are old Fr. George, who was up there leaning over the table thinking or something, and Bro. Casimir in his cast, with a great big grin.)

I wish I could explain something about the gradation that seems to have marked the three days of my festival. Each one seemed to represent some gigantic development that I am powerless to grasp or to explain. In the end I had the impression that all who came to see me were dispersing to the four corners of the universe with hymns and messages and prophecies, speaking with tongues and ready to raise the dead because the fact is for three days we have been full of the Holy Ghost, and the Spirit of God seemed to be taking greater and greater possession of all our souls through the first three Masses of my life, my three greatest graces.

It is all unfamiliar to me. These graces belong to an apostolic order that are beyond my experience. Yet I cannot say, without ingratitude and stupidity, that they were outside my vocation since they were in a sense its crown: I mean the crown of this portion of my history – of the last seven years. I was brought here for this. For this I came into the world.

It seems like the triumphant conclusion of an epoch and the beginning of a new history whose implications are utterly beyond me.

Friday I said that Mass I had promised to our Lady of Cobre. It was the feast of St. Bede, but we don't celebrate that. I had been told one got so mixed up in the rubrics that the first Mass was no fun. I did not find that to be true at all. On the contrary, I felt as if I had been saying Mass all my life, and the liturgical text of the Votive Mass of our dearest Lady in this Season became immensely rich. It was at St. Anne's altar and the church was full of sun (after Chapter) and there was no one else saying Mass nearby so I could really speak it. Then there was a beautiful chalice Dan Walsh brought down, and I had an amice and corporal and purificator and even a finger towel which all came from some colored boys and girls in a Catholic High School in Mobile, Alabama; and I had a cincture given by a Sister in a hospital in St. Louis, and if I had tried to say all the names of all the people I wanted to remember at the *Memento* I would have stood there until dinner time; but I had kept forming intentions for them all days beforehand, so they would all be included when the time came and even then I took time to remember all those that God wanted me explicitly to remember over again at that moment.

So I gave Communion to Nanny and to Dan Walsh and Bob Lax and Ed Rice and Bob Giroux in a jacket that said U.S. Navy, and to Tom Flanagan who came with Ed, and Rod Mudge who came with Dan, and to McCauliffe who wrote here about poetry. But I couldn't give communion to Jay Laughlin or to Seymour or to Elsie, my aunt, who sure wanted to come to communion but couldn't because of the trouble about her marriage. And after the Mass I had plenty of time to make a good thanksgiving by myself at Our Lady of Victories altar and after that I went out and talked, or rather Someone talked through me. It was a marvelous morning under that tree that Fr. Mauritius once marked *Gingko Bilboa*, though all the botanical signs are now gone.

Now I know that I had the whole Church in America praying for me and I am scared and consoled by so much mercy and the sense that I myself have contributed nothing to the whole business, that I have been worked on and worked in, carried upward on the tide of a huge love that has been released in people, somehow, in connection with a book printed over my name, and on this tide millions of us, a whole continent perhaps, is riding into heaven. It makes me truly the child of Our Lady *(Mulier, ecce filius tuus!)* [Woman, behold thy son (John 19:26)!] to whom the greatest mercy was given. When she has produced in me something of her humility there will be no end to what God will pour out upon me, not for myself alone, but for the whole world – even perhaps to make others very great while I remain in my nothingness, and this would be, to me, a great joy.

In a way the experience of these three days has been a reversal and contradiction of everything I was thinking about solitude on retreat: or is it a fulfillment that I do not understand?

June 4, 1949. Vigil of Pentecost

Hot day. Stomach empty. Beautiful cumulus clouds sail over the woods, and everything is quiet.

The Mass is the most wonderful thing that has ever entered into my life. When I am at the altar, I feel that I am at last the person that God has truly intended. About the lucidity and peace of this perfect sacrifice I have nothing coherent to say. But I am very aware of the most special atmosphere of grace in which the priest moves and breathes at that moment – and all day long. True, this grace is something private and inalienable, but it springs also from the social nature of the Mass. The greatest personal gift that can come to anyone is to share in the infinite act by which God's love is poured out upon all men. In this sense the supreme graces of the personal and the social order coincide and become one – and they do this in the priest at Mass, as they do in the soul of Christ and in the Heart of Mary.

What a joy it is to remember the people I pray for at the *Memento*. Once, before I was ordained, I thought it would start a distraction. So far it only intensifies the glowing radiance that fills the depths of my soul.

Yet it is a dark radiance – burning in the depths of a faith without images – all the more radiant because I rejoice that it is dark.

If I had held to my resolution, perhaps I would not have talked so much about what occurred to me and filled my mind after my first Mass last Friday at St. Anne's altar. But that was one of those resolutions that ended up by being swept aside by the Holy Spirit. I suppose we quite often decide on good things which are not good enough because they are only our own ideas. And when God sees fit, He lets us know that He ignores them in favor of what is obviously much better. The change is not to be taken as a basis for generalizations, and I still hold on to my desire to be reserved. So much self-revelation is useless, and, worse still, in revealing what you think you have found you reduce it to a common and tangible level and lose what was best, what was spirit and life in it.

The Centenary celebration on June 1st was well managed and everything was far better than we deserved, and I have to admit, along with everyone else, that I remember it as a pleasant experience, or at least as something not altogether terrible. It seems to have been a day of grace for us and for others. But everyone is glad the affair is over.

It was a bright day, but there was enough of a haze to keep the sun from being too fierce and knocking everybody down. In fact it was just the precise kind of weather I had prayed for.

In the afternoon when we came slowly back from Benediction in the field, chanting the *Pange Lingua* and passing from the crowded world into the cool shadows of the Basilica, all the monks were sunburned flaming red from the backs of their necks to the summits of their tonsured crowns. And thus the door closed behind us, and the Blessed Sacrament passed though our midst under a curious white umbrella, which is assuredly an Italian invention, and we put away our *Laudes Vespertinae*[42] and hoped there would be no more commotion and no more speech. The terrible day was over.

The men from WHAS captured our *Kyrie* and *Gloria* in a little box and took it away to Louisville to play to the people after we had all gone to bed. I wonder if this is or is not a violation of the Statute made by the General Chapter in 1938 forbidding broadcasts. The Fox Movietone men, both of whom were very plump, ran back and forth through the crowd with their newsreel cameras and I wondered if this was a violation of the Statute of the same General Chapter prohibiting the filming of movies in our monasteries. You see, St. Mary's field is *outside* the monastery and outside the enclosure, and for the purposes of this feast, St. Mary's field has been regarded as the wide world which belongs to everybody and where you just can't stop people from broadcasting and making movies.

In the morning, delivered from the job of second Master of Ceremonies, I sat in the press-box and answered questions and saw Monsignor Sheen in the distance standing in front of three or four microphones that did not

---

[42] A Cistercian collection of Gregorian hymns and antiphons used for paraliturgical, devotional services.

work so well at first. But when they got louder, he was discovered to be preaching well about our silence.

And I, a solitary cloistered contemplative, told some seven thousand nuns and other people that I was neither allowed to speak nor to sign autographs and that I could only speak with reporters. Then they made me bless them and their rosaries and let me go, and I stumbled away with the cameras going clickety click on every side. *O beata solitudo!* [O blessed solitude!]

One of the most impressive people I have ever seen is Archbishop Paul Yu-Pin of Nanking, who was here for the Centenary. In fact he spoke in Chapter about China and the contemplative life and Buddhist monasticism – and the reproach that Buddhists fling at us that we are all very fine at building hospitals, but that we have no contemplatives. He spoke of the two million (or was it five million) Buddhist monks and nuns in China. He told of whole mountains covered with monasteries. He described 1,000 Buddhist monks together in a great liturgical service, and then spoke of the immense influence exercised by a Christian contemplative community like Our Lady of Consolation. He by no means dismisses the Buddhist monks as hypocrites or "dreamers."

June 10, 1949. Easter Friday

The Mass becomes more wonderful every day. When I get to the altar it seems as if nothing in the world could possibly trouble me and I sail through everything in a glow of intense peace in which I can grasp nothing particular of the great thing that is going on, but in which I am simply possessed by the action of which I am the dazzled instrument. However, I do not expect this imperturbability to last forever. It is an accident and a grace for which I am thankful and from which I am, I hope, detached.

The big thing in my day used to be Communion: now it is rather the *action* of the Mass, the Sacrifice of which Communion is only a part. The center of balance of my spiritual life has shifted from the half hour when I kneel in the dark by Our Lady of Victories to the ten or fifteen minutes in which the Body and Blood of Christ are on the altar before me and I stand with my hands sketching that cramped little gesture of supplication that we have instead of the wide-flung arms of the *Orantes*.

Yet a certain restraint seems to be the best thing about the Mass in our liturgy. The whole thing is so tremendous that no amount of exuberance will ever get you anywhere in expressing it. To bend down, unnoticed, and kiss the altar at the *Supplices te rogamus* [Humbly we pray you] is a movement that lifts me out of myself and doubles my peace, and saying the *Pater* [Our Father] is like swimming in the heart of the Sun.

For hours after Mass it remains most difficult for me to get interested in anything else, and even reading makes me feel ashamed. Later on in the day, at odd hours, the Mass comes back and seizes me and envelopes me in a moment of recollection that makes me wonder why I am doing whatever I am doing and which only allows things to be bearable in so far as I have been told to do them by the Rule or Father Abbot.

Ipse est pax nostra [He is our peace] – the Mass is peace.

Speaking of peace, the prayers before Communion are beautiful and I love them and yet they embarrass me a little by the contrast with what has gone before because now I am once again speaking for my own poor self – and yet it helps me to remember at that moment that I exist apart from God in the depths of an awful poverty which is nevertheless loved by Him.

I am never allowed to forget that poverty. I wish I knew her beauty as well as St. Francis did, for the external poverty he married was simply the expression of the nothingness which he loved in himself.

This week, the week full of the Holy Ghost, I found out once more something of the joy there is in being nothing and in depending on Our Lady for everything. To have no virtue of your own but to cling by faith to her power, her sanctity and her virtue: this makes all her virtue and sanctity and power our own at every moment, when we most need them and in the way in which we need them. This is the key to the simplest and most sublime and easiest way of the interior life: to have no greatness or holiness or distinction that one can claim as one's own, but to rely entirely on her love and her protection – knowing that she will produce in us, at the right moment, the good thing that God wills us to do: the thought or the movement or the prayer that God asks of us for His glory. From then on the whole spiritual life becomes nothing else but a question of looking at her in confidence and attentively, and faithfully receiving everything she has to give us, at the moment when she gives it, without clinging to it or keeping it as our own, and without reflecting on ourselves but only returning, all the time, to her.

It is hard to think of any greater joy than the certitude that this is one's vocation and that this is all that matters. Such a certitude would be, I am sure, a pledge of the highest sanctity, the greatest contemplation and of an almost unlimited power to bring peace and happiness to the souls of men.

———

Last Saturday the Abbot General, Dom Dominique, opened the Regular Visitation in Chapter in a simple and business-like fashion. Since I am secretary again, I accompanied him when he inspected the Tabernacle and Sacristy, and just finished translating and sealing the visitor's report which we for some reason call the Visitation Card. It is anything but a card – ten pages of foolscap, double-spaced. And as usual I have learned a great deal by the experience.

It is surprising how naive and dumb one can be about obvious things after seven years in religion – or twenty-seven for that matter. I know the theory, I suppose, but there is still all the crassness and obtuseness of a second rate monk in me – and I suppose in some of the others, too. There is always that tendency to judge everything by abstract standards of justice and the ideal instead of in concrete standards of mercy which are those of God and which mark the common sense of the saints.

June 12, 1949. Trinity Sunday

The antiphons are beautiful – I mean their chant rather than the words.

Standing at the new screen door by the secular kitchen (they are putting in screens everywhere now) Brother Basil was making me a lot of signs about how would I like to be Master of Laybrothers.

Talk, talk, talk. I went into Vespers thinking how it would be to preach conferences on humility, manual labor, obedience, to people like old Brother Dominic who came here over fifty years ago and got his thumbs cut off in various accidents and who has been humble and obedient since before I was born.

The other day by chance I mentioned to Dom Dominique that perhaps I would be writing a life of St. Bernard and asked him if he would approve of my going to one of our monasteries in France to get some material. He said he would approve of that and right away began telling me I ought to come and write books in the *Maison Généralice* [Abbot General's Headquarters] in Rome. He explained how I would have a great deal of time to myself and peace and solitude and what not and it sounded very nice. But when I spoke to Reverend Father about it, he said NO several times with considerable emphasis and in a big hurry and went on to explain that "there is nothing so distracting as new scenery." Then the General spoke to him about it and Dom James said, "If I let him (i.e., me) go to Rome, he will never come back." He told him I was likely to become a Carthusian at the drop of a hat, which is still true and perhaps truer than ever. If I had the slightest inkling that it was God's will . . .

However, after that, all talk about Rome became mere academic speculation and it turned out to sound not so wonderful after all, for the General came out with sentences like, "There is no sound except the noise of cars going by in the street outside," and "We can reach out of the window and shake hands with our neighbors," meaning, perhaps, the Benedictines at St. Anselm's, and "The park behind us became the scene of so much immorality that they cut down all the trees and made it into a football field."

One day he happened to mention the Carthusians (before all this came up) and dropped the remark, *Après tout, ce sont eux qui sont les vrais contemplatifs.* [After all, they are the true contemplatives.]

And that brings me to a letter from the Prior of Parkminster to a priest in Lebanon which for some mysterious reason came into my hands via Fr. Prior, for the priest in Lebanon lent it to Fr. Urban, who gave it to Fr. Prior saying I might be interested in it.

Well, I was.

It is dated May 27th. Dom Benedict Wallis says he has just come back from the General Chapter of the Grande Chartreuse.

"Needless to say," he writes, "I raised the question of an American foundation . . . Their opinion remains unchanged. If the Americans want a Charterhouse, let them come over to Parkminster and show that they are fitted for the Carthusian form of life . . ." He advises him not to write to the Grande Chartreuse as "between ourselves, the French are not over keen on Americans, at least some of them . . ." Then he says that there are no professed available for a foundation because two new Charterhouses have been started in Spain in the last year. That made me sit up. Also there is talk of reopening all the old French Charterhouses.

Meanwhile he goes on to say, "Supposing a number of Americans, particularly priests, thought of getting together in a community, they might try to live as closely as possible the Carthusian form of life and eventually be affiliated to the Order." "This," he says, "would mean that one or two of them would need to be first trained in a real Charterhouse."

After reading that I was practically ready to jump on a boat and go.

This thing has now been going on for nearly five years – I mean with this particular intensity, on and off. However, I am now altogether reserved and stoical about it. There is no point in giving myself a fruitless emotional beating by thinking about it one way or the other. I wouldn't be at all surprised, however, if one day this whole thing should unexpectedly pan out in the best possible way. If it does, it will be because I kept quiet and did my best to keep my fingers and my own natural initiative completely out of it.

June 15, 1949

We have been praying for rain, and this has been the *imperata* [special prayer] at Mass. So this morning around the offertory a steady rain began (it has been raining on and off for the last thirty-six hours anyway) and it has gone on pouring down ever since, floods of it in a constant and uninterrupted and very vocal cascade all day long. The land is full of its rumor and all our fields have rivers running through them.

Tomorrow is *Corpus Christi* and there are practically no flowers in the house anywhere.

After None I sat in one of the windows of the Scriptorium, next to a fresh piece of fly-paper that wasn't doing much business, and watched the rain. Out near the big sycamore, where there are usually swine, shorn sheep and lambs were standing in the downpour, about twenty or twenty-five of them I should say. They were all absolutely motionless. Not browsing, not looking about, not considering the slightest change of position. They looked as if they had all been carved out of something. And they were that way for half an hour.

The Mass tomorrow will be a hymn of gratitude for me. Today I said the Votive Mass of the Seven Dolors and I can see that Votive Masses of Our Lady are going to mean a tremendous amount in my life.

June 19, 1949. Sunday within the Octave of Corpus Christi

Heat, flies, lilies and the Blessed Sacrament. I am deacon and forget my genuflections. And the Word of God in His monstrance dries up all desire in me to write or to be anything but a priest.

Christ has come to stand among us and our dust and rugs. We offer him our ceremonies and our shirts cling to our soaked ribs, and I want to look up at the monstrance to ease the heat and the heaviness, but I am conscious of the acolytes standing between the pillars, and it upsets me a little, and anyway I am tongue-tied. During the canon, a fly passed through the flame of a candle and came down giddily on the corporal and began somersaulting around with burned wings just before the consecration of the chalice. But the burnt fly was at the back of the corporal and I didn't dare reach for it. Anyway, after the *Pater*, it got under the Missal and then disappeared altogether.

Since the Visitation we are getting a little more to eat in the refectory, and Dom James, who said last week that he thought he would allow us to go and read in the orchard on Sundays, took it back today because he said the General didn't seem so sure . . .

Last year when I was writing *Seeds of Contemplation*, one Pierre Blanchard was doing an article on *Solitude et Communauté* ["Solitude and Society"] for *La Vie Spirituelle* in which he said more clearly some of the things I was trying to say about Solitude. I was interested in his analytical line-up: Romanticists – Existentialists – Whitehead – St. John of the Cross. It reminded me that solitude is not an exclusively personal preoccupation of my own. It comforted me with the assurance that it is a vitally important preoccupation – a problem which has a Catholic solution – my own (thank heaven!) solution – that solitude and society do not exclude one another, but that solitude is necessary for society. The Christian saint is always in some sense a solitary, interiorly and exteriorly, too, in so far as he can be, and his solitude is not a rebellion against society or a denial of social obligations but the condition upon which his fruitfulness in the world depends. It is in the desert that God forms the men who save the world of their time.

Then there is the false solitude that is the solitude of pride and excludes God and society. Yet I think that this artificial solitude tends to turn itself inside out in the end: it, too, can be a trap door by which a man, pressed by the torture of his own unbearable anguish, suddenly falls through himself into the abyss of peace which is the solitude of true salvation.

I would copy out half that article into this book, but I can't, because I left that issue of *La Vie Spirituelle* with all the others over in the vault.

The Mass each day purifies and baffles me at the same time. This beautiful mixture of happiness and lucidity and inarticulateness fills me with great health from day to day. I am forced to be simple at the altar.

For this I am eternally grateful to our Western liturgy which has a peculiar intensity of its own precisely because it is so straight-faced and noncommittal. There is never an exclamation. There is never an outcry.

But in the middle of this beautiful sobriety the indescribably pure light of God fills you with what can only be described as the innocence of childhood.

Day after day I am more and more aware how little I am my everyday self at the altar: this consciousness of innocence is really a sense of replacement. Another has taken over my identity, and this other is a tremendous infancy. And I stand at the altar – excuse the language, these words should not be extraordinary – but I stand at the altar with my eyes all washed in the light that is eternity, as [if] I am one who is agelessly reborn. I am sorry for this language. There are no words I know of simple enough to describe such a thing, except that every day I am a day old, and at the altar I am the Child Who is God. Yet, when it is all over, I have to say, *Lux in tenebris lucet et tenebrae eam non comprehenderunt* [The light shineth in darkness and the darkness did not comprehend it (John 1:5)], and I have to fall back into my own, in my poor *[voluntas] propria* [self-will] which cannot receive Him altogether, and even have to rejoice at being a shell; well, I have contained some echo of His purity, and it has meant something tremendous for me and for the whole world, so that at my *Memento* of the living, which is very long, I swim in seas of joy that almost heave me off my moorings at the altar.

It is here, by the way, that I am deepest in solitude and at the same time mean something to the rest of the universe. It is really the *only* moment at which I can give anything to the rest of men. And I am the only one who can give it to them, for unless I apply it to them, the special fruit of this Mass will never be theirs.

June 27, 1949. Feast of the Sacred Heart

Today is Monday and yet it is the Feast of the Sacred Heart because the Feast of St. John Baptist came last Friday, and in our Order the Feast of St. John Baptist still has greater dignity than that of the Sacred Heart. We are having work again in the afternoons on all these feasts of Sermon! Dom Frederic's concession last year didn't go on for long. We just don't seem to be able to take the time the Rule gives us for reading and contemplation. We are full of labor-saving machinery and yet they seem to save no labor; or rather, instead of making room for the time the *Usages* allow for reading and prayer, they just make room for more labor on feast days. In Europe the monks would be absolutely forbidden to work on the Feasts of St. Peter and Paul because they are holy days of obligation. Not so in America. The feast is not binding under pain of sin and so we don't keep it. The lay people don't *have* [underlined twice] to hear Mass and so the contemplatives don't have to contemplate.

Yesterday morning (Sunday) I went to Reverend Father and we were talking about solitude, and quite by surprise he gave me permission to go out of the enclosure into the woods by myself.[43] And so I took advantage of it in the afternoon, although there was a wall of black sky beyond the knobs to the west, and you could hear thunder growling all the time in the distance. It was very hot and damp but there was a good wind coming from the direction of the storm.

Anyway, I made Bro. Hugh a sign to come and open the gates right after None, before the Brothers went to Catechism. (Before None, during the meridienne in the dormitory, I dreamed of going out, and in the dream I crossed the field where the platform still remains from the Centenary and walked up toward Aidan Nally's, but before I got to Nally's, in the dream, the wagon road developed sidewalks and I came not to solitude but to Jamaica High School, which we used to pass going up a hill on the way to the movies at Loew's Valencia in the days when I was generally drunk. But when I woke up and really went out, it was nothing at all like the dream.)

First I stopped under an oak tree on top of the hill behind Nally's and sat there looking out at the wide sweep of the valley and the miles of flat woods over toward the straight-line of the horizon where Rohan's knob is.

As soon as I get away from people the Presence of God invades me. And when I am not divided by being with strangers (in a sense anyone I live with will always remain a stranger), I am with Christ.

The wind ran over the bent, brown grasses and moved the shoulders of all the green trees, and I looked at the dark green mass of woods beyond the distillery on those hills down to the south of us and realized that it is when I am with people that I am lonely and when I am alone I am no longer lonely because then I have God and converse with Him (without words) without distraction or interference. Like the man in Ramón Llull who was meditating on the hill, and a stranger came to him and said, "Why are you alone?" And he answered, "You are right in saying I am alone. Before you came I was not alone, but now you are here with me and I am alone indeed."

I thought, if it rains, I will have to go back to the monastery.

---

[43] Merton discloses a quiet and important turning point for his vocation at Gethsemani, at least in these journals, when Dom James gives Merton permission to leave the enclosure and walk deep into the woods alone for the first time. The expansiveness and depth of Merton's prose, as he recalls his walk, marks June 27, 1949, as a day on which Merton's life at Gethsemani breaks out beyond a past mental and physical confinement.

Gethsemani looked beautiful from the hill. It made much more sense in its surroundings. We do not realize our own setting and we ought to: it is important to know where you are put on the face of the earth. Physically, the monastery is in a splendid solitude. There is nothing to complain about from the point of view of geography. One or two houses a mile and a half away and the woods and pastures and bottoms and cornfields and hills for miles and miles. And we huddle together in the midst of it and jostle one another like a subway crowd and deafen ourselves with our own typewriters and tractors . . .

And I thought: if we only knew how to *use* this space and this area of sky and these free woods.

Then the Spirit of God got hold of me and I started through the woods. I used to be afraid of lightning before I came to the monastery. Now there didn't seem to be any particular objection to walking right into the storm although behind me was the big field where two boys were killed by lightning last summer or the one before . . .

I had a vague idea that there was a nice place beyond the field we call Hick's House, although there has been no house there for years. I went to the calf-pasture beyond St. Malachy's field at the foot of the knob where the real woods begin. It is a sort of *cova* where Our Lady might appear. From there we started walking to get to the forest fire we went out to fight on All Saints Day two and a half years ago.

But this place was simply wonderful. It was quiet as the Garden of Eden. I sat on the high bank, under young pines, and looked out over this glen. Right under me was a dry creek, with clean pools lying like glass between the shale pavement of the stream, and the shale was as white and crumpled as sea-biscuit. Down in the glen were the songs of marvelous birds. I saw the gold-orange flame of an oriole in a tree. Orioles are too shy to come near the monastery. There was a cardinal whistling somewhere, but the best song was that of two birds that sounded as wonderfully as nightingales and their song echoed through the wood. I could not tell what they were. I had never heard such birds before. The echo made the place sound more remote and self-contained, more perfectly enclosed, and more like Eden.

And I thought – "Nobody ever comes here!" The marvelous quiet! The sweet scent of the woods – the clean stream, the peace, the inviolate solitude! And to think that no one pays any attention to it. It is there and we despise it, and we never taste anything like it with our fuss and our books and our sign-language and our tractors and our broken-down choir.

One moment of that quiet washed clean the deep, dark inward mirror of my soul and everything inside me was swamped in a prayer that could not be quite pure because there was necessarily so much natural exultation. There was smoke in it, but I had to accept that, and there wasn't much I could do about it because, anyway, I am full of grime.

To say I was happy is to say how far short the prayer was of perfection, but I was consciously and definitely and swimmingly happy, and I wonder how I ever stayed on the ground at all. The black clouds meanwhile piled up over the glen, and I went to where there was a shed, down at the entrance to the wilderness, a shed for the calves to shelter in in cold weather in the fall.

Yet it did not rain.

I looked up at the pines and at the black smoke boiling in the sky and nothing could make that glen less wonderful, less peaceful, less of a house of joy.

When I finally decided it would soon be time for Vespers, I started back for the monastery the long-way round, keeping a screen of woods between me and the house so that I would not hit the road anywhere near where I might be seen from the back of the house where the monks were. I got in just after the first bell for Vespers and only when we were in choir for first Vespers of the Feast of the Sacred Heart did it begin to rain. Even then it did not rain much. On my way home I turned to the storm and saw it was marching northeastward following the line of the knobs, over on the other side of them, following the line of the Green River turnpike that is far over there beyond our property in the woods, going from New Haven to Bardstown.

I don't know what light this all throws on my vocation. I do not understand. Last night in my imperfection, I came out of meditation with a wild scheme for starting a sort of Carmelite Desert out there. I know I'd never be allowed a one-man hermitage, but perhaps one might start a little house for special retreats, where Priors and Guestmasters and what not could escape for a little recollection. Where one could go for a month at a time or even more and get in some real and solid contemplation.

I can imagine no project less likely to meet with the favor of our General Chapter. Such a notion has almost nothing to do with our Order. For us, a retreat means only one thing: a more complete immersion in the community.

That is where the graces are for a Cistercian: in choir with the rest, at the common work, in Chapter, reading with the others.

And what about me? I wonder more and more about the whole business.

Most of the time my mind is in a jam. I make one movement to think about it and everything clogs and I remain helpless and thoughtless and open my hands and wait with my tongue-tied existence hanging on the inscrutable will of God.

One thing I must say: both in the wood and especially on my way back, crossing an open hillock, all that I had tasted in solitude seemed to have a luminously intelligible connection with the Mass. It seemed to be a function or an expression of that morning's offertory and of the next day's – the Feast's. It seemed to be, in my own very personal instance, the very heart of the Feast of Christ's Heart, its clear manifestation to me. It seemed to clarify and express in an ineffable way my identification with Christ in the Mass, and my prayer in the wood was eminently the prayer of a priest, so that I wonder if my eyes have been momentarily opened and if what I have seen is really more than a poetic intuition – really something that could put in a claim to deeper and more directive significance. Could I end up as something of a hermit-priest, of a priest of the woods or the deserts or the hills, devoted to a Mass of pure adoration that would put all nature on my paten in the morning and praise God more explicitly with the birds?

Maybe that too is a dream and a sin.

Back in the refectory one of the novices read to us at supper an article taken from *The American Ecclesiastical Review* on the privileges of a minor basilica. Everyone was laughing himself silly at the description of the half-open parasol and the bell on the end of the pole and the other incidentals which go to make life unusually complicated in a minor basilica. Today we are back in the middle of a book about Russia called *God's Underground*, parts of which I almost believe.

Practical statement: One obvious and simple thing can be said.

For the moment my job in the vault is God's will for me. The solitude that it implies is God's will. The Abbot General said several times, and once even to Dom James in my presence, that the best thing I could possibly be doing is writing books. And he said this required a certain solitude. And he said, "If you go to the Carthusians, you are not as intelligent as you seem to me." In a word, no one could be more clearly and forcefully explicit in his favor of what I am doing now than Dom Dominique was at the

Visitation. Furthermore, he was the one who first gave his approval to the idea of my going to the woods.

What to do? Make every use of these opportunities. They are marvelous. Thank God for them. Use them in line with a *Cistercian* vocation. Use them as sources of a more fervent and intelligent participation in the great work of the Order – the liturgical praise of God. Use them to pray better and love others better. Use them as sources for contemplation that can be shared with the rest of the monastery. The devil wants to cut off all communication to others of any good I might find in solitude and study and prayer. He also wants to cut me off from the sources of grace and vitality that are in the community, *my* [underlined twice] community, to which I am vowed.

One thing that disturbs me unreasonably is that my life has what might appear to be an unusual and eccentric pattern. I don't live like the others in the monastery. (So I argue – ergo, I belong in a Charterhouse. That doesn't follow necessarily. It might later. I don't see why it should.) But I live the life that has been devised for me by Superiors and which everybody with any knowledge of my soul agrees to be just what I need. Sacred Heart, give me the humility to see this and use your graces to be satisfied. Teach me to let *You* [underlined twice] sanctify me, and do not let me spoil it by trying to change all *Your* [underlined twice] plans with my own stupid ideas and feelings.

July 10, 1949

Here I sit surrounded by bees and I write in this book. The bees are happy and therefore they are silent. They are working in the delicate white flowers of the weeds among which I sit. I am on the east side of the house where I am not as cool as I thought I was going to be, and I sit on top of the bank that looks down over the beehives and the pond where the ducks used to be and Rohan's Knob in the distance. And that big wobbly stepladder I nearly fell off, cleaning the Church once, is abandoned out there at one of the cherry trees, and the branches of a little plum tree before me, right by the road, sag with the plums.

In the Chapter Room they are finishing *Seeds of Contemplation*,[44] reading a couple of pages each evening before Compline. It began when I was on retreat for ordination. I do not know what the general feeling about it has

[44] Published in the spring, 1949.

been in the house – as far as I know, it is not unfavorable. Fr. Anthony told me, "Those who think they are intellectuals like it." Once or twice I felt as if everyone were a bit exasperated at passages that were at the same time excessively negative and subtle and obscure.

I am glad the book has been written and read. Surely I have said enough about the business of darkness and about the "experimental contact with God in obscurity" to be able to shut up about it and go on to something else for a change. Otherwise it will just get to be mechanical – grinding out the same old song over and over again. But if it had not been read aloud at me, I might have forgotten how often I had said all those things, and gone on saying them again as if they were discoveries. For I am aware that this often happens in our life. Keeping a journal has taught me that there is not so much new in the interior life as one sometimes thinks. When you re-read your journal you find out that your newest discovery is something you already found out five years ago. Still, it is true that one penetrates deeper and deeper into the same ideas and the same experiences.

As usual, after one of my own books has been read at me, I am left with the wish that I were simpler.

Jay sent me the reviews. There are three kinds of reviews. First the majority – those in which the reviewer merely copies the publisher's blurb on the jacket. Second, those in which he has found out for himself what is in the book, but without thinking about it, so that he registers an emotional reaction, the fruit of some vague impulse, good or bad. It looks like criticism because it is set down in professional language, but is not really so. Finally, those who really have something to say about the book. Such reviews are rare. I am getting the impression that a number of priests are hostile to the book. The terminology is unfamiliar to most of them and some of the statements are, by their standards, careless. One priest wrote a scorching letter which Father Anthony didn't show me.

In any case I'll try to do some revision on the book next month.

Dom Porion sent me a little book he wrote anonymously, *La Sainte Trinité et la Vie Intérieure* [Paris, 1948], and I was charmed by it. It is perfect in its kind. It is really a summary of all dogma, but very simple. It is a contemplative summary and therefore at the extreme opposite to anything that might have been boiled down for students. This is a summary which reveals the simple, all-embracing intuition of the contemplative who sees all theology in the light of his mystical taste of reality in its highest causes. And that is why it is a summary that is more living and more true than most of the more detailed books about the same thing. Its extreme simplicity places it, paradoxically, at the point where opposites meet, for it is very deep and very full and yet at the same time very plain and clear. It has a great deal to say both to the very wise and to those who have no learning because it speaks to what is of God in all of them. I wrote him an enthusiastic letter about it at his Procura [Order's headquarters] outside Rome, at a place called *Tomba di Nerone*, which fascinates and perplexes me. What do the Carthusians want with Nero's tomb? And yet it is appropriate, for Nero and his living progeny are no ones more dead to them.

I have had several dreams of becoming a Carthusian – one that I was on my way to enter a Charterhouse near Strasbourg. Jacques Maritain, I found out later, is in Alsace now and I wrote to him there yesterday.

Saying Mass in the Secular Church these days has been very beautiful. Because of the heat, the front doors are left open, and I stand and speak to Christ on the dark altar and outside the catbirds in the damp trees shout and sing.

I have never sweated so much in my life, even at Gethsemani. The heat has gone unrelieved for some three weeks. No air. Nothing is dry. Water comes out of you as soon as anything – even the air itself – touches your skin, and you kneel in choir with sweat rolling down your ribs and you feel as if you were being smothered by a barber with hot towels, only this barber doesn't leave a hole for you to breathe through.

Out at work the other day we got into some tomato plants that had been overwhelmed by morning glories, and the soil was full of broken bricks. I think it must have been on the site of the old monastery. Anyway we did penance that must have been like the days of Dom Benedict. Tides of sweat coming out of you, blinding your face, making your clothes weigh twice their ordinary weight. And yet somehow it is good and satisfying to suffer these things for the world and do some of the penance we are supposed to do. At night, when we stand in our boiling tunnel and shout our *Salve* at the lighted window, you feel the whole basilica moving with the exultation of the monks and brothers who are dissolving in their own sweat.

In the refectory they finished *God's Underground*, full of terror and beatings and tortures in a Red prison in Prague, and suddenly switched to a namby-pamby Italian biography of Sister Benigna Consolata, "the Little Secretary," whom Jesus called "my joy and my Benjamin." I have here and now got to make some attempt at a resolution to keep my fingers quiet and stop making fun of the virtuous little nun, upsetting the novices who are full of edification from head to foot.

July 11, 1949

We have a new mechanical monster on the place called a D-4 Traxcavator which is enormous and rushes at the earth with a wide open maw and devours everything in sight. It roars terribly, especially when it is hungry. It has been given to the laybrother novices. They feed it every day and you can't hear yourself think in the monastery while the brute is at table. It is yellow and has a face like a drawbridge and is marked all over with signs saying it comes from the Wayne Supply Company in Louisville, but really, as I know from secret information, it was born on a raft in Memphis, Tennessee. There the hippopotamus abounds, which this instrument greatly resembles.

Also we have bought fans. They are exhaust fans. You make a hole in the building and put the fans there and they draw all the hot air out of the dormitory. Nobody knows what happens after that. My guess is that the hot air that went out through the fan is then replaced by the hot air that comes in through the windows. The fans are not yet running because the laybrother novices have not yet made the holes in the building. However, they have begun. They have a scaffold up on the roof of the infirmary and they have been blasting at the gable of that wing with jack-hammers, and two frail novices who are very young were posted down on the ground floor near the doorways with artistic signs which read "Falling Bricks." At first one of them was standing at the precise spot where all the falling bricks would land on his head. He was saying the Rosary in an attitude of perfect abandonment. Afterwards he got a stool and moved inside the cloister and popped the sign in his lap and took to reading the immortal masterpiece of Fr. Garrigou-Lagrange, *Christian Perfection and Contemplation* [According to St. Thomas Aquinas and St. John of the Cross, 1937].

July 17, 1949

Today, in our Order, we celebrate the Feast of Our Lady of Mount Carmel, although to the world it was yesterday. But yesterday was our St. Stephen.

The chief thing that happened to affect the history of my existence was this: I was on as deacon for the Pontifical High Mass. Everything was going along fairly smoothly, although it was a nasty, muggy day. Three doorkeepers were ordained. They were ordained not with the Key of the Church, but with the key of the vault where I work, so that I wondered mightily about the validity of the form of ordination: "Receive charge of these keys and the things which are locked up by them." So! They were ordained to take charge of the manuscripts of St. Bernard and the incunabula and all the old antiphonals, not to mention our typewriter and our voluminous notes and our copies of *The Hudson Review* and *Horizon* and Empson's poems and *Four Quartets* and the Nonesuch Vaughn and the 200,000th copy of *The Seven Storey Mountain* and the page proofs of *Waters of Siloe* which has been announced for October 6th . . .

But that is a digression. Here is the thing that happened.

Time came for the Gospel. I don't remember feeling anything special, except that I was a little on edge as I sometimes am on ceremonies. We got the blessing and lined up to sing the Gospel and the book was open. Things seemed pretty dark. I guess they really were – it was a grey day. The organ gave me too low a tone. While I was wondering whether to raise it or not, I got mixed up with the incensation. Then I raised it, and it was a little too high, higher than I wanted, and the next thing I knew was that I was not able to get my breath. I felt as if I were suffocating. The thought came through my mind, "I'll not be able to finish this." Then I seemed to be choking.

After that, I looked around and I was lying on the floor and people were trying to pick me up. It was a nice soft carpet. I might have landed on it like a feather. I think I remember starting to fall and being completely unable to do anything about it. Anyway, there I was. I was only unconscious for about half a second, as far as I can judge.

At first I was angry, believing that I had been thrown on the ground by the devil. I got up and finished the Gospel and then, when we started to mill around to get in position for the *Credo*, I got lost and started off in some wrong direction and the subdeacon got me straightened out. I was thinking, "Must recite the *Credo* with fervor and attention" in order to rectify this business of lying on the floor. I said what I could remember of the *Credo*, the central thought in my mind being *Christ! Christ!* While I was focusing on Our Lord and trying to get saved from what had thrown me down, the M.C. came and chased me off to the sacristy where a substitute (Fr. Gerard) was wriggling into a lace alb. Fr. Prior was there. By the time we got to the sacristy I had begun to rationalize things more clearly and was in a fit position to explain to everybody that I thought the cause of the fall was some medicine I have had to take to prevent my stomach from getting too upset by cheese.

Well, anyway, I went to the dormitory. Fr. Vincent came along presently with some spirits of ammonia. I wished I had our relic of the Little Flower but, since we are sweating so much, I had taken it out of our clothes and left it in the vault. Got it after. Tried to sleep on and off during the day – under orders from Father Abbot, but didn't succeed. Today I am all right but my stomach feels funny. Anyway, I have been getting pains. So that is that. It made me spend St. Stephen's feast in humility and recollection!

I thought about a lot of things, lying on the straw mattress in there. One of the thoughts was that I am glad to be at Gethsemani and that the way to be a Saint is to give yourself up entirely to your rule and the circumstances in which God has placed you and work out the Secret which is His will.

You don't really clearly know God's will in all its details until you have worked it out in your life – given it expression. Then you know what it is – by doing it. That is happiness, to do His will so well that you find your whole life proclaims, like the heavens, His glory!

July 20, 1949

We are in the Octave of St. Stephen. I have never thought so much about St. Stephen before or prayed so much to him.

The other day – Sunday – on the Feast of Our Lady of Mount Carmel, since I was still a little knocked out, I went and sat at the benches of the infirm during the Matutinal Mass. It was the first time in my life I had seen the Matutinal Mass from that angle and it gave me a new slant on the community and on God's providence. There must be something like one hundred and forty brothers and novices and clerics going to Communion in that long line. Since the line was relatively short when I first came here, and since I was close to the head of it for the last four years of theology, and since I had my eyes shut during my thanksgiving, I never realized what an enormously long line it was. It takes over twenty minutes for the whole business to form and file up to the Epistle corner and get back again in choir . . . At the end of it are a number of great, tall laybrother oblates who used to be paratroopers, "night-jumpers" and what not.

Then I thought how intimately all these vocations were connected with my own vocation and it struck me with greater force than ever before that God certainly didn't bring any of us here without reason – and least of all myself. I saw the poor little handful of priests and I thought of our poverty . . . And the thought that I have wanted to withdraw myself from all this by my own choice began to appall me.

One of the things that has struck me in the last few days is not merely a change of heart or a change of mind about the question of running off to the Carthusians: I am beginning to beat my breast and be sorry and ashamed of things I have entertained in my mind and to see how much strange folly there has been in them.

I do not belong to myself. And the vow of stability isn't something you take just for fun. It doesn't mean just a vague promise not to go wandering around without permission. If I went from here to the Carthusians *merely* because it was my own choice, merely because I preferred to be there rather than here, and because I knew I could get permission to go if I made enough fuss about it – all that might well add up to a mortal sin, if I wasn't careful. Anyway, I don't think it would be the way to please God. I no longer have the right to prefer one place to another. If it became *necessary* to change, for the sake of saving my soul for instance, that would be quite another matter.

I said the Mass of the Seven Dolors again today, out in the Secular Church.

In the afternoon, after praying out under the hickory tree with Tauler tucked under one arm, I went into the vault to work, and prayed before working, and it was hard to get out of the bottom of my sea and come up to the surface to write about St. Ailred. Yet outside in the hot garden some seculars were talking. So, you see, it does not really matter after all if there is something there which is *per se* distracting because, if God wills, what is *per se* distracting might, *per accidens*, not distract or take away anything from your prayer. (I thought of that, too, when there was hammering in Church. There is almost constantly some hammering in Church now because they are enlarging the laybrother's choir to accommodate all those soldiers that are being drawn here, as I think, by the many tractors.)

At the same time I am finding myself forced to admit that my lamentations about my writing job have been foolish. At the moment the writing is the one thing that gives me access to some real silence and solitude. Also I find that it helps me to pray because, when I pause at my work, I find that the mirror inside me is surprisingly clean and deep and serene and God shines there and is immediately found, without hunting, as if He had come close to me while I was writing and I had not observed His coming. And this I think should be the cause of great joy, and to me it is.

The thing that upsets me is answering letters. There God is *not* found, and there I generally do not pray except with difficulty and anguish and outside the depths, in laborious acts and cries for help to heaven. This work I now leave to Saturday afternoons and try to dispatch a week's correspondence in two hours. Surely that ought to be enough.

The community has never been so big as now. I do not know the official figure, but it must be around 185 including one or two in hospitals or non-stabilitated in other monasteries of the Order. Three postulants arrived one day last week and five more on Monday – all these for the choir. One of them stands in the lower stalls in front of me in a very distracting shirt, printed all over with huntsmen and foxhounds in green and brown. What disturbs me especially is that one of the huntsmen on a very fat horse is riding directly through the middle of the pack of hounds at right angles to the apparent direction of the chase. And I say to him, "Where do you think *you're* going?" when my mind ought to be on the psalms.

It is doing me good to write about St. Ailred. The job came upon me as one of those providential "accidents" when Sister Rose of Lima at Seton Hall wrote about the St. Ailred poem ["Rievaulx: St. Ailred"] and said she wanted to translate him, and I got permission to write an introduction which is turning into a book without any effort at all. It is one of those jobs which simply goes on spontaneously, like a breeze, so that I feel like the little Italian Sister whose life was just read in the refectory. And the *School of the Spirit* is on the shelf, though Bob Giroux and Dan Walsh both liked it immensely. I can see where it simply has to wait.

Soon I will go to Chapter and a little novice with a calm and somewhat metallic voice will read a translation from the Hungarian about *Life Everlasting*. He will go peacefully through all those comforting sentences, and again and again the phrase will recur, "life everlasting . . . life everlasting." It fills the Chapter with a happy, evening charm while darkness comes down upon our hills and our frogs and our robins and our wet-grass that was freshly mowed this morning by Fr. Raymond and rained on this afternoon by the rains. *Life Everlasting!*

July 21, 1949

Tomorrow is the Feast of St. Mary Magdalen. We sang *Ardens est cor meum . . . desidero videre Deum meum . . . quaero et non invenio . . .* [My heart is burning . . . I desire to see my God . . . I seek but I don't find . . .]

I have found many good things in Hugeny's Theological Introduction to his translation of Tauler [*Sermons de Tauler,* 3 volumes]. He is especially good on the psychological factors in contemplation and on natural contemplation. I have never read anything so clear and so sensible on the subject. At the center of contemplation is this complete, global comprehension of a truth, not in its details but in its wholeness, not as an abstract matter of speculation, but apprehended in all that appeals to our affective powers so that it is appreciated and prized and savored. This in the natural order alone.

That is what this book in the Chapter room is doing – it is an incantation of familiar sentences, stated in a way that is calculated to carry with it a certain enchantment to a Catholic, to bring back this global and appreciative savor of the whole subject and all its associations, and you get a sort of low degree of contemplation out of it. I suppose many of them think they are acquiring arguments and convictions. Not at all. They are feeling good. The same book would mean practically nothing to someone outside the Church. So many books are like that. I am not sure whether it is a good thing or a bad thing. Contemplation is O.K. But whether or not you can get too much supernatural contemplation, the natural kind can certainly be overdone. As for the really infused kind, it is not up to you to say how much you are going to get anyway.

July 27, 1949

Yesterday on the Feast of St. Anne they put up a wallboard partition across the middle of the monks' scriptorium and gave half the place to the novices to save them from bursting the walls of their novitiate. The old monks are staying down in the part that was left to us, and it is like a Turkish bath, being right over the bake-oven. I am writing this in the library. The younger element moved their desks up here and I have ours jammed up against the shelves full of all German collections of sermons that nobody would think of touching with a twenty foot pole. I write this leaning on the broad window still looking over the *préau* that echoes with robins and locusts, for it is still very hot, and the bell in the tower has just rung seven and the grey buildings are beginning to be in shadows.

A long letter from Sister Marialein, O.P. came from Rosary College. She is the one who was teaching the kids in Mobile, the colored boys and girls who sent me a purificator and an amice and corporal for my first Mass. She is a gay, extroverted little sister who wants to put absolutely everything in her letter. She has the most astounding sources of information. She hears all kinds of things and not all she hears about Gethsemani and me is accurate, but it is close enough to scare me. For instance, she had heard I was in

the Vatican Library studying the history of our Order. I am trying to remember if I told anyone that the General thought of taking me to Rome.
She heard that *Seeds of Contemplation* was read in the refectory and the
reader covered my identity by saying it was by "a Chinese Monk." What
actually happened was Fr. Romanus announced *What Is Contemplation* last
winter as "translated from the Chinese."

I sent the essays of the colored kids – about Trappist life – to Fr.
Sylvester in Utah. She posted the *Life* article about the Utah monastery
and the kids came and looked at it in awe and said, "Our compositions are
there!" [underlined twice].

July 31, 1949

It is the 8th Sunday after Pentecost and the Feast of St. Ignatius Loyola
and the Gospel says, "Give an account of thy stewardship," and I took up
the sapiential books beginning in the middle of *Ecclesiasticus* where I left off
last year.

Give an account of thy stewardship.

The bier, the black open box with long handles in which we carry our
dead out behind the Church and bury them, is parked in the drying room
and I look at it on purpose every time I go by to remind myself of the
happy day when, please God, I will go home. The bier has shirts hanging
on its gunwales and handkerchiefs draped upon its handles.

Today Reverend Father gave official and general permission for the first
time for the professed to go out into the orchard and around the wagon
shed and out behind the old horse barn in their intervals – or rather between None and Vespers on Sunday. Our garden and the cemetery are in-
tolerably crowded and it is hard to get extricated from the other monks.

Anyway, I made a bee line for the little grove of cedars that is behind the
old horse barn and crowded up against the far end of the enclosure wall
and it was nice. By the long time it took me to get completely recollected,
I realized that I have been awfully busy and my mind is terribly active. If I
had to give an account of my stewardship, I would have to fall upon God's
mercy more heavily than ever because it seems to me that, since I became
a great success in the book business, I have been becoming more and more
of a failure in my vocation.

Not that I haven't made efforts to keep my head above water, but in the
spiritual life it is not so hard to drown when you still imagine you are
swimming. Activity is already so strong in my nature, and it is piled on me
by the circumstances of this abbey, but beyond that, my mind goes on

rushing into business, carried away by the sheer power of its own momentum. This morning after Chapter we first had to wash the breakfast dishes, which is fine. I am glad of the merit, and it is a grace to be able to do some such chore rather than my own will. Perhaps I pleased God more by swabbing out those new aluminum coffee tins we have than I would have done sitting outside in the cool shadow of the west transept and desperately hoping to pray. Nevertheless, when the dishes were finished, I lost time window shopping in the last questions of St. Thomas' *Secunda Secundae*.

August 3, 1949

Tomorrow – St. Dominic. We sing a Solemn Requiem for Dom Frederic who died a year ago. I said a requiem Mass today and at the Consecration of the Precious Blood I was thinking how much I owed to Dom Frederic and I was glad I had here a way of repaying him for everything. There are many in the Order and in the world who owed him very much. He died alone on the train to Georgia, and I think it was because he was really a very lonely man. People might not believe that. He had many friends who loved him, yet he was isolated from everybody in a peculiar way, in spite of all his kindness and affability. There was a great deal of Dom Frederic that no one had access to including, perhaps, himself. One reason for this was that he had buried a great amount of suffering inside himself and had forgotten it with the help not only of charity, but also of his activity which, though excessive, was perhaps in his case merciful.

Which leaves me thinking that perhaps objectively he should not have killed himself as he did with overwork: things were perhaps best as they were. It leaves one thinking that all things continually turn out the way they ought to even though it seems they might have been much better.

I have so many more Dominicans praying for me than Franciscans that it is having an effect on my interior life! Tomorrow is a bigger day for me than it would have been without the letters and friendship – how real and warm this friendship is! – of Jacques Maritain and Fr. Paul Philippe, and so many others, not forgetting Dan Walsh. There is Ruth Hallisey, too, the Tertiary through whom I "met" Sister Madeleva and *What Is Contemplation* got printed. Then there are the Fathers at Washington, the ones who run *The Thomist* . . .

Tonight at evening meditation I remained with my eyes open which I do not usually do. The altar was ready for tomorrow's requiem. No flowers or bric-à-brac: plain candles and a bare wooden crucifix, the one we always have in Lent and adore on Good Friday. It was a comfort for me to look at the Crucifix and presently (there had been showers of rain since Vespers began) a shaft of sunlight broke through a window somewhere and fell like gold on the head and arms of Christ on the crucifix, and it was quiet and beautiful in the sanctuary with no one moving and light falling on the crucifix.

The Portiuncula always brings me great blessings – and that is the Franciscan side, which continues to grow also. It was last year I first realized how much there is in Portiuncula Day for those who will take it. If we are granted indulgences, it is because there is so much in the feast, which they represent. They are counters. The feast brings graces of contemplation and spiritual joy, because every church becomes that tiny little church that St. Francis loved above all others and everyone in the world can share the bliss of his sanctity.

God can recollect us quicker [unfinished sentence].

August 4, 1949. St. Dominic

Here I sit under the trees full of locusts, near Dom Frederic's grave, with my feet in the blue limestone gravel, and I think about the spirit of St. Dominic. It is a spirit that has little or nothing to do with ours, but it is impressive and means much more to me today than it did four or five years ago.

I wish I had gone into the study of theology with something more of the mind of St. Dominic. The thing I most lack is the outstanding Dominican characteristic of sharpness, definiteness, precision in theology.

I admit that sometimes this precision is the fruit of an oversimplication, but it is good anyway. The sharp contrast between the Dominican colors – black and white – is a good symbol of the Dominican mind which likes to find clear-cut divisions and separations.

I admire St. Dominic above all for his respect for Scripture, and for his respect for the *study* of Scripture. Scripture was the heart of his contemplation and his preaching. I have often meditated on Scripture, but I have never in my life seriously studied it and this is a lack that I ought to weep for and beat my breast. Now that I am finished with the theology class and have four months or so to go on by myself in Scripture, to fill out the time required by Canon Law, I pray St. Dominic to guide my study of Scripture in these months and for the rest of my life.

In St. Dominic's first Friaries they were brief and quick about the Offices (just the opposite of the 12th century Cistercians) in order to get to their books, and the friars were encouraged to prolong their vigils in study. Study was not precisely the essence of the Dominican vocation, nevertheless, each house was a house of study and the study was to lead to contemplation that would over-flow in preaching. Honorius III, I think, refers explicitly to the Dominican life as essentially contemplative but *without* implying any contradiction between contemplation and activity. In any case, what they studied was *Scripture*. The Bible was their best textbook of theology.

I wish St. Dominic would finally give me an understanding of this problem of contemplation vs. action – clear as the line of the landscapes of Southern France!

The Epistle from St. Timothy *(argue-obsecra-increpa . . .)* [persuade-entreat-rebuke . . .] struck me with great power at the Mass. *Sana doctrina!* [Sound doctrine!] What an ideal! Clean and precise thinking – sweeping the Church's floor clean of the dust of heresy and bad theology. Of course, you have got to be pretty sure of yourself to do that kind of job and I am not called, myself, to be a hammer of heretics. But I need that *sana doctrina* and it will not hurt me at all to realize that everyone who loves Truth is in this world called upon in some measure to *defend* it.

Divinas Scripturas saepius lege: immo numquam de manibus tuis sacra lectio deponatur. Disce quod doceas; obtine eum qui secundum doctrinam est, fidelem sermonem ut possis exhortari in doctrina sacra et contradicentes arguere. [Often read the Holy Scriptures: indeed, let the Bible never be out of your hands. Learn what you are to teach; get a firm grasp on the truths of faith according to Doctrine, in order to exhort men in Sacred Doctrine and refute those who oppose the faith.] St. Jerome, Ep. 52.

The short Prologue of St. Thomas to his *Summa Theologiae* is a very beautiful paragraph containing a whole discipline of study. His three points are that students (beginners, but it applies to all) are impeded from arriving at truth by: 1) the great number of useless questions, arguments and articles, 2) the lack of order in the way doctrine is presented, 3) repetition which produces confusion and boredom.

The Dominicans and Cistercians had this at least in common – that they wanted to get rid of all non-essentials.

August 5, 1949. Our Lady of the Snows

Here are some words of a Jesuit – the theologian Maldonatus – that ought to give all Cistercians something to think about.

"Where shall our morning and evening (theological) work begin if not among the riches of the Bible? I do not regard as theologians those who neglect the Scriptures, spending their time and labor and wasting their strength and their talents in other books . . . After your exercises of piety, *devote an hour to the reading of the New Testament in the morning and an hour in the afternoon to the reading of the Old.* Read the New Testament in Greek and the Old in Hebrew."

This makes me hang my head considerably. Sometimes I get bursts of fervor and make a resolution to give the best of my intervals to Scripture, but I never do, and even as I write this I find myself mentally defending myself against giving up the half hour after None to anything but Tauler or Rolle or John of the Cross. Of course, I have the morning study period and that is a wholesome chunk of the day, but it has been *assigned* to me, not chosen. Then, at any rate, I can get my hour or more of New Testament for the time being, but not, I fear, in Greek.

How little Scripture I read in the Novitiate! I remember walking in the garden on summer mornings and reading Jeremias and also St. Paul, but not very consistently. However, I *did* read the Fathers commenting on Scripture, but more to get the thoughts of the Fathers than anything else. I did read the *Canticle of Canticles* – I remember that – especially the last few paragraphs.

This year I have been going along regularly with the books assigned to the Season by the liturgy and it has done me much good. I went through the books of Kings again and loved them more, and loved David more. Every time I read Kings, David grows in my estimation and Solomon decreases. Now I am in Ecclesiasticus and study the qualities of good women.

If I had only spent the time on Scripture that I wasted on Duns Scotus! Not that the study of Scotus is essentially useless, but I really never got around to understanding more than a tenth of what I read with so much labor. There is much more nourishment for me in Thomas, after all.

I find an interesting passage in St. Thomas' commentary on St. John, Chapter I (Lectio XIV), the place where Jesus turns to Andrew and John who have asked Him where He lives and He says, "Come and see." Thomas interprets this mystically as evidence that we can only come to know Jesus dwelling within us by experience. But I take this experimental knowledge of the presence of God in us to be contemplation. He then says there are four ways of arriving at this experimental knowledge. Two are, as one might expect, by interior quiet and rest, and by the taste of the divine sweetness. But the other two are, first, by the performance of good works, and second, *per operationem devotionis* [by works of devotion]. I don't know precisely what that means but in any case it is an activity. Hence it is easy to see that for St. Thomas there is in practice no contradiction between contemplation and activity. There are characters and situations in which activity can even favor contemplation to some extent. How this checks with the questions in the II, IIae, I don't know. But it is interesting. I have noticed myself sometimes that, when your mind is utterly dead around the house and in Church, you can go out to work and soon find God within you after you have been sweating a little out in the sun. The sacrifice, the obedience and the penance have brought Him there quite quickly. Just how much there might be of nature in this, I don't know, but it is true that obedience and work clear your mind of preoccupations that make conscious union with God impossible: preoccupations of that kind tend to accumulate when you are left to yourself and to your books.

I also find God quite easily sometimes after an hour or half an hour of intense intellectual work. This too gets rid of my other preoccupations and cleans the surface of my inner mirror without my knowing it. But both those experiences of contemplation are of a low and elementary kind. Conceivably, to continue activity beyond this point would only hinder progress to a higher and deeper union – something more fundamental and more real, though perhaps less "felt."

But, for instance, as I write now, with a vacuum cleaner or something going up in the dormitory, and crickets and locusts ringing their bells all over the place, and the traxcavator mumbling in the far distance on the other side of the buildings, God is with me here, with St. Thomas and Scripture, in the peace of Our Lady's summer morning. And much as I love Kentucky, I wish the veils were gone and that I were in heaven.

August 6, 1949. Feast of the Transfiguration

In lumine tuo videbimus lumen . . . Erat lux vera quae illuminat omnem hominem venientem in hunc mundum. [In your light we shall see light . . . That was the true light which enlighteneth every man that cometh into this world (John 1:9).]

I love this feast of light, of Christ *Splendor Patris* [Splendor of the Father]. I love the chant, the sacred texts, the psalms of the feast *(quam dilecta tabernacula tua, Domine virtutum!* [How lovely are thy tabernacles, O Lord of hosts! (Psalms 83:2)] . . . *Eructavit cor meum verbum bonum* [My heart hath uttered a good word (Psalms 44:2)] . . . *Fundamenta ejus in montibus sanctis* [The foundations thereof are in the holy mountains (Psalms 86:1)] . . . [Psalms] 45, 46, 47 all together, and my beloved 103 – *Amictus lumine sicut vestimento* [Clothed with light as with a garment (Psalms 103:2)]), and then the hymns above all, and the Mass – *Candor lucis aeternae et speculum sine macula* [A shining of eternal light, a mirror without blemish].

I can think of no better day to begin praying to Christ to move the Holy Father to write an encyclical about contemplation, the contemplative life, the relations between the contemplative and active lives. It needs to be done.

Yesterday I was burrowing through the copies of *La Vie Spirituelle* to find an article that Dom Robert in Georgia was worrying about. It is by one T. Camelot, a Dominican [*"Action et Contemplation dans la tradition chrétienne"* 327, March 1948], and he works out a disturbing thesis which simply throws Christian tradition out the window on the question of contemplation. He says that there is nothing in the Gospel about the contemplative life and that the whole theory of the contemplative and of contemplation vs. action was developed by the Greek Fathers (e. g. Origen, the first to interpret Martha and Mary in this light) on a basis of neo-platonism. The whole idea is Greek, he says. It is pagan. It is a contamination of genuine Christianity in which action and contemplation are inseparably one in true charity.

Although he goes on to "save" the Christian contemplatives, whitewashing the Desert Fathers and the rest, it seems to me that the thesis is altogether extreme. However, here are some questions that do need to be answered:

1. Is there anything in the Gospels about the contemplative life? What is the value of the Martha-Mary story? It seems to me that the literal sense is plain, and that the superiority of contemplation over action is explicitly stated there. But as St. Thomas himself proves – and the whole life of Jesus shows – the supreme Christian life is one in which one shares the fruits of contemplation with others.

2. I am becoming more and more inclined to feel that there is, in fact, no real opposition between contemplation and activity *when they are properly ordered*. In every Christian life there must be elements of both. But in what proportion the two are united depends on your vocation. When contemplatives write about the problem from their own point of view, from the standpoint of a *contemplative Rule*, they stress the danger of activity *for them*. For a contemplative, a life that is preponderantly active will necessarily be in conflict with his vocation *per se*. But for an active religious this will not be true – a life ordained essentially to action will not hinder contemplation if activity is kept within due bounds.

August 8, 1949

I said the Mass of Sts. Cyriac and the other martyrs, his companions, and prayed particularly for Robert Lowell and Raymond Larsson. Poor Larsson got into an argument with a policeman about the legality of smoking a cigarette on the elevated in New York and the policeman took him to Bellevue and from there they took him to Rockland State Hospital. I hope the holy martyrs will soon get him out again because he is a good poet and lately he has been writing better than ever and doing fine drawings, too.

Yesterday was a day of Recollection. If in the past I have had problems about how not to waste the day of Recollection in useless self-analysis, I no longer have any problem. Scripture and the Blessed Sacrament are all that is necessary to make a day of Recollection supremely rich and deep.

I simply took up Ecclesiasticus where I left off the other day, without looking for anything special, and spent an hour or so on the 32nd chapter, which happened to be what turned up. On the surface it is a prosaic little chapter about table manners. On the surface only! Nothing is prosaic in Scripture if you know how to read it.

The fact that God is speaking ought to be enough to invest everything with an inestimable value. There are meanings within meanings and depths within depths, and I hasten to say that mere irresponsible allegory does not reveal the real meaning and the real depths.

In the 32nd chapter of Ecclesiasticus I found out, for the first time, that Ecclesiasticus is not dull.

It tells you what to do if you are the "ruler of a feast" – it could be applied to the Servant of the Refectory in a Cistercian monastery, to some extent – you see that everyone is in his proper place and you see that they are all served and everyone is taken care of. You sit down and see that the talking progresses pleasantly but wisely, but you do not talk much and you stop talking to listen to the music for "a concert of music in a banquet of wine is as a carbuncle set in gold. As a signet of an emerald in a work of gold, so is the melody of music with pleasant and moderate wine." Then what do the younger guests do? They keep quiet and listen and let themselves be urged and questioned before talking. At the earliest opportunity they get up and go home and then (verses 15–17) they occupy themselves with whatever seems good to them. One is given to understand that they are very happy at home all by themselves doing whatever they like to do.

Under the surface of all this the following things strike me:

1. The Holy Ghost is telling us that we ought to be happy and that happiness is found in moderation and restraint in all the ordinary things of life.

2. Even in the most ordinary things of life the Sacred Books expect people to live, within themselves, quiet and deep interior lives.

3. The business about going home and there doing what pleases you calls to my mind Christ's own words, "When thou wilt pray, withdraw into thy chamber and close the door, etc. [Matthew 6:6]."

4. It seems to me that this has implications that can concern the graces and consolations of prayer – not to be too raffish about grabbing at them.

5. The ordinary pleasures of life, properly used, do not need to interfere with a deep interior wisdom: they can even contribute to it. Balance and moderation in social living can permit and even help us to live interior lives.

6. The wisdom of *Ecclesiasticus* is the balance that should be characteristic above all of people in monasteries. Test a religious rule by the way it reflects the calm and the measure of the sapiential books. It is easy to see that the same Spirit that wrote Ecclesiasticus speaks in St. Benedict.

Merely to set down some of the communicable meanings that can be found in a passage of Scripture is not to exhaust the true meaning or value of that passage. Every world that comes from the mouth of God is nourishment that feeds the soul with eternal life. *Non in solo pane vivit homo sed in omni verbo quod procedit de ore Dei.* [Man liveth not by bread alone, but by every word that proceedeth out of the mouth of God (Matthew 4:4).] Whether Scripture tells of David hiding from Saul in the mountains, and Saul's men surrounding his hiding place like a crown, or whether it tells about Jesus raising up the son of the widow of Nain, or of the prescriptions for the evening sacrifice of incense, or sings the hymn of Deborah, or tells us that Heli, the priest of Silo, thought Anna was drunk when she prayed to have a son; whether it tells us in the *Canticle* that the Spouse has gone down to see if the vineyards are in flower, or shows us the new Jerusalem coming down from God adorned as a bride, or rebukes the incestuous Corinthians, or leads Paul to the river in Macedonia where the women gather and the Holy Spirit opened the heart of Lydia, the seller of dye, to hear the Gospel – everywhere there are doors and windows opened into the same eternity – and the most powerful communication of Scripture is the *insitum verbum* [the engrafted word], the secret and inexpressible seed of contemplation planted in the depths of our soul and awakening it with an immediate and inexpressible contact with the Living Word, that we may adore Him in Spirit and in Truth . . . By the reading of Scripture I am so renewed that all nature seems renewed round me and with me. The sky seems to be more pure, a cooler blue, the trees a deeper green, light is sharper on the outlines of the forest and the hills and the whole world is charged with the glory of God and I feel fire and music in the earth under my feet.

The blessings of my Cistercian vocation are poured out on me in Scripture and I live again in the lineage of Bernard and I see that, if I had been deeper in Scripture, all temptations to run to some other order would have lost their meaning, for contemplation is found in faith, not in geography: you dig for it in Scripture, but cannot find it by crossing the seas.

The concept of *obediential potency* explains the fact that we can have a natural desire for a supernatural vision of God. We naturally desire to see God as He is in Himself, but no such vision can ever be naturally *due* to a created nature. However, we do not really *feel* the intensity of this hunger that is in us, as an inborn capacity, until *grace* makes it a more active potency and we become aware of the yearning and emptiness of what St. John of the Cross calls the "deep caverns of sense" – the yearning to receive the vision of God which can only be impressed upon us immediately by the direct action of God Himself, His own infinite Truth taking the place of all inadequate species and concepts of His essence.

Someone is playing the harmonium in the novitiate: maybe it is Bach or Purcell – I can only hear the undertones for the whole harmony does not reach me through the hot morning and the locusts. Maybe it is only an ordinary hymn which the circumstances make to sound like Scriabin or Ravel.

August 10, 1949. St. Lawrence
Sapientia scribae in tempore vacuitatis et qui minoratur actu sapientiam percipiet (Ecclesiasticus 38:25).

I was very interested in this verse and everything that followed. R[heims]. Douay version translated it: "The wisdom of the scribe cometh by his time of leisure and he that is less in action shall receive wisdom." Even the stuffiest and most timid of commentators admits that this simply means that the wise man *debet vacare ab aliis occupationibus* [ought to leave off other occupations]. *Sapientiae studiosus autem debet omnem laborem in ea inquirenda collocare, quod studium honore ac benedictione divina eximie utilitate pollet.* [The person intent on wisdom ought to dedicate all of his work to pursuing it, because this study far surpasses all usefulness in dignity and divine blessing] ([Joseph] Knabenbauer).

The following verses give wonderful descriptions of farmers ("his whole talk is about the offspring of bulls"), blacksmiths ("sitting by the anvil and considering the iron work. The vapor of the fire wasteth his flesh and he fighteth with the heat of the furnace." "The noise of the hammer is always in his ears."), silversmiths, potters, "Everyone is wise in his own art," "Without these a city is not built." Yet, "they shall not go up into the assembly." "They shall not be found where parables are spoken." "But they shall strengthen the state of the world and their prayer shall be in the work of their craft, and searching the law of the most high." *Deprecatio illorum in operatione artis* [their prayers are for the working of their arts] – this, says Knabenbauer, means that they pray that their work will turn out successfully and do not have a higher end, but it seems to me one could also take it to mean that their work is a prayer: a Benedictine interpretation.

What does Ecclesiasticus mean by wisdom here? Not contemplation, but rather wisdom in the sense of acquired prudence. The context shows it is the "wisdom" of judges and rulers: the kind of thing Solomon asked for. It is still a practical wisdom that is meant. 38:25 can legitimately be applied to the contemplative life in the strict sense without, however, excluding manual labor. All the jobs mentioned are (apparently) incompatible with the constant full-time study of law or theology, but that does not mean they exclude contemplation – if one does not become utterly absorbed in them. And I think how well *deprecatio illorum in operatione artis* can be applied to pious writers. I know the danger!

However, I do not mean to turn this Journal into a Scripture notebook.

Yesterday I was very happy and still am because a letter from Dom Porion arrived. Dom Porion seems to be the one person in the world that I have actually come to have as friend who has an interior life that rings bells inside me and chimes with all my aspirations and echoes in me for days afterward. In every letter of his he comes out with some phrase or sentence that so exactly expresses what I love or think or feel, or what I desire, that it is as if my own soul had spoken it within me. Seeing God in his soul, I am immensely helped to return to my own house and find God there. When someone else who has pretty much your own soul says something about God, it shows you at once that God is much nearer to you than you realized. Seeing your own thought objectified in the mirror of another makes you return with greater profit to your own mirror. Such correspondence, far from being a distraction, is a huge grace. After one sentence in yesterday's letter I was left in an atmosphere of prayer for hours. I will copy it down when I get my hands on the letter, so as to have the exact words. Meanwhile, last evening, I read these words in Ecclesiasticus. They sum up everything:

But be continually with a holy man, whomsoever thou shalt know to observe the fear of God, whose soul is according to thine own soul . . . and establish within thyself a heart of good counsel . . . The soul of a holy man discovereth sometimes true things more than seven watchmen that sit in a high place to watch (Ecl 37:15–18).

August 11, 1949. Feast of the Holy Crown of Thorns

When I was copying that text from Ecclesiasticus yesterday, I skipped some words which I thought might be irrelevant. They are not, however, so I add them:

"Be continually with a holy man . . . whose soul is according to thy own soul *and who, when thou shalt stumble in the dark, will be sorry for thee.*" Which reminds me how much I stumble in the dark and need someone to be sorry for me, although I don't intend to burden poor Dom Porion with all my miseries. They should be evident enough from what I write – the harsh contentiousness of *Seeds of Contemplation,* the ease with which I lay down dogmatic definitions of what is and is not the correct doctrine about contemplation, my vicious descriptions of the faults of other people and my impatient, resentful descriptions of my own!

And yet I am glad that my ferocity is there and that I know about it and that it is being knocked out of me by interior trials, and that I am able to rejoice when I am stepped on or at least a little bit slapped down.

It is a humiliation to me still not to be able to express my ideas calmly and with detachment, especially orally. I almost never speak like a monk of St. Benedict: *leniter, paucis verbis, sine risu, humiliter . . .* etc. [softly, with few words, without making faces, humbly . . . etc. (RB 7:11)].

I talk excitedly, get out of breath, try to ram my opinion down the other man's throat, even interrupt others – from the Abbot General on down – tell people frankly that they are all wet and then discover ten minutes later, on reflection, that I am the one who is all wet! What a curse!

So I groan and rejoice under the heavy burden of my nature and even try to thank God that others see my failings. And I thank Him for their charity towards me, and I beg Him not to let anyone be upset by me – or follow my example.

I tell myself how happy I would be if I were more of a priest! I pray all day to become one of those mild, quiet, patient priests who have little to say because they realize they know so little, yet through the Holy Ghost can talk whenever He pleases! The long-suffering of a true priest! The quietness, sobriety, silence of the true priest: all this based on love.

My own nature is my crown of thorns.

In the Church someone practices the hymn for the Assumption, *O quam glorifica* [O how glorious], one of the most beautiful of the whole year. My heart fills with love at the thought of Our Lady's feast. Singing the *Salve* I am sometimes almost completely crushed by the weight of my own miseries and yet rejoice at the great glory of Our Lady, and somehow rejoice the more because I am so far down in the scale of things and yet she, who is so exalted, really loves me. It is enough to make a man drunk with happiness and paradox!

To my great joy, Fr. Paul Philippe's book, *La Très Sainte Vierge et le Sacerdoce* [Paris, 1947] arrived the day before yesterday: that was the other thing that made me joyful besides Dom Porion's letter. There were four copies of the book and I began it at once. It is short but I have to read slowly. I can't read more than three paragraphs of anything without stopping. If I read fast and go right on, I get confused and my mind simply ceases to grasp anything, and in half an hour I am exhausted and worried, as if I had been roughed up in a dark alley by a gang of robbers.

Books pile up all around me and I can't finish any of them. For months I have been sticking with Tauler. I finally dropped Dom Casel and the liturgical people. Jay Laughlin sent a beautiful picture book of the Abbey of Silos, outside Burgos, in Spain. It was inscribed to Ezra Pound by the Spanish author. I'll have to ask how it got to me. Maybe a mistake, or maybe Pound threw it away in the presence of Laughlin who retrieved it for me. Sister Thérèse sent Dom [John] Chapman's letters, which I am anxious to get into, and a Montfort Father in Quebec sent all the works of St. Louis de Montfort which I want to read right now but can't. Sister Thérèse also sent *Priest Workmen in Germany*, but that'll have to wait. Maybe I can wrangle it into the refectory.

August 12, 1949. St. Clare
I copy out the sentences from Dom Porion's letter, that I spoke of the other day. Speaking of his book on the Holy Trinity – so simple, so deep and so comprehensive, he says:

Il se trouve d'ailleurs naturellement que son climat n'est plus tout à fait le mien.
Je voudrais vivre d'un regard sur Dieu saisissant ce qu'il est dans un pur silence.
Dans la limpidité de ce calme l'homme peut faire à jamais un bienheureux
naufrage. [It turns out, furthermore, that my book's atmosphere is of course
no longer my own. I would like my life to be one of continual looking at
God, seizing what he is in pure silence. In this light-filled serenity a *person*
could forever experience a blessed shipwreck.]

How I sympathize with that sentence! No matter how simple discourse
may be, it is never simple enough. No matter how simple thought may be,
it is never simple enough. No matter how simple love may be, it is never
simple enough. The only thing left is the simplicity of the soul in God, or
better, the simplicity of God.

August 16, 1949

Steamy hot day, the first in the Octave of Our Lady's Assumption. For the
first time it occurred to me to wonder who might be this St. Hyacinth with
the ladylike name. I haven't time to look him up.

Some other time I'll write down a note, *Deo dante* [God giving it], about
how it was in the woods yesterday on Our Lady's feast. Nice as it is to be
out there alone and silent, you miss certain other graces you would get by
going out there with the community at common work.

The rejection of Christ. *His own received Him not* [John 1:10].

The most terrible thing about the rejection of Jesus was that He was rejected by the holy and He was rejected because He was God!

The Pharisees rejected God because He was not a Pharisee.

The Pharisees would have nothing to do with God because God turned
out to be not made in their own image.

"I am come in the name of my Father and you receive me not: if another
shall come in his own name, him you will receive" (John 5:43).

What is implied by the expression "in the name of my Father?" Jesus
came to us having nothing of His own. Not merely did He have nowhere
to rest His head, not only was He poor on earth, but He explains that the
very fact of His divine generation means that He has absolutely nothing of
Himself and yet He is everything. In this same chapter Jesus defended
Himself against the charge of violating the Sabbath by explaining that He
lived in the very heart of the Sabbath, which is the interior life of God,
where "The Father works and I work [John 5:17]" and that "the Son cannot do anything of Himself, but what He seeth the Father doing [John

5:19]." The condition on which Divine life is given to men is that they accept it from Him Who has received everything that He has, and therefore does not come in His own name. The Father has given all judgment to the Son and they who do not receive the Son, by believing in Him Who has nothing of his own, are by that very fact judged. The Father wills that the Son, Who has nothing of His own, should be honored as the Father is honored because, without this honor given to the Son, the Father cannot be honored as He really is. The test of our honor and adoration of God is in our reception of Him Who cannot come to us in His own name.

But those who live for themselves, who live "for their own name," cannot believe in such a God because He contradicts everything they really believe in and live for. They will not go to Him that they may have life because He does not receive glory from men. *Claritatem ab hominibus non accipio* [I receive not glory from men (John 5:41)].

How can you believe, you who receive glory one from another? And the glory which is from God alone you seek not [John 5:44]!

This explains the meaning of the word vain-glory – *vana gloria* – ultimately it implies the love of non-existence because it is the love of what is not and cannot be.

And this is at the root of the rejection of Christ – we cannot believe in Him because we want to believe only in ourselves, and we want to fabricate a basis for that belief by making other men praise us.

Mother of God, save us from this death. Teach us that humility is peace and life. Show us how all our acts and all our thoughts need to be washed in the waters of humility in order that they may be clean and may grow. We cannot believe in Christ unless we have somehow begun to be like Him, and we cannot begin to be like Him until we begin to receive from Him something of the light He has received from His Father. And this light is darkness to the world. It means death to our dead glory. That is why it is the seed of true glory. Glory is vision. It is the vision, not of ourselves, but of God. Hide me in the light of glory! Truth, hide me in thy vision!

August 17, 1949

The sixth chapter of St. John's Gospel was written for me. When Jesus worked the miracle of the loaves and fishes on the hillside outside Tiberias, when He escaped into the mountain Himself alone, walked on water to find the disciples, and afterward first told the people of the mystery of the Eucharist, He saw all His priests and He saw – or sees – me sitting here, writing this, His priest, crushed that I do not understand the greatness of Mass and happy because I do not have to – for in any case it is impossible.

"I am the bread of life [John 6:48]."

A moment ago I knelt at the Church doorstep and looked at the empty sanctuary and Christ in the Tabernacle poured out power into the veins of the whole world.

"That if any man eat of it he may not die [John 6:51]."

Each day a priest should want to say Mass with more fervor. What does that mean? Working up a more intense heat of thought and emotion? God help the man who thinks he can do such a thing and remain half-human. I think it means having a deeper and simpler faith in the power of the Mass, "realizing" (believing) more and more that the Mass is the one great fountain of sanctification to which everything else is subservient.

To realize one's own need, one's own poverty, and weakness, and to realize the power of the Mass. To say Mass more fervently each day will be to say it more simply each day, each day with one less crease in your brow and one less anxiety in your head and one less shadow of fear in your heart. To arrive at this no doubt one may have to say Mass for ten years in the valley of the shadow of death, but for my part I don't see why a priest couldn't say Mass from the beginning with simplicity and joy and go on saying it with more and more simplicity and joy each day. *Servite Domino in laetitia!* [Serve ye the Lord with gladness (Psalms 99:2)!] One reason why we are less fervent than we ought to be is that we cripple our own spirit by taking ourselves too seriously. We expect too much from ourselves when we ought to expect everything from God on Whom we utterly depend.

"Except you eat the flesh of the Son of Man and drink His blood, you shall not have life in you [John 6:53]!" What is easier than to eat and drink, even the bitter wine they give us to consecrate here? What is simpler than this greatest sacrifice by which, nevertheless, we are united with the Word Incarnate and become most fully and truly the sons of God because His Word is our life?

"As the living Father hath sent me and I live by the Father, so he that eateth me the same shall live by me [John 6:57]."

Also this chapter contains the community-solitude problem (v. 15ff.) stated almost violently. Jesus made no compromise with a merely worldly society. Confronted with Kingship, His answer was not even a word – it was reflection and solitude. But He emerged from this solitude to teach men of a "society" that was to be one flesh and one bloodstream with Himself, a mystical union of all men in His Body, where solitude and the common life are realized perfectly both together at the same time.

I am consoled to realize how often Jesus was abrupt in His words and movements. He never bothered to be diplomatic. Yet He was never impatient or impulsive. He did things without hesitation because He was the Truth. *Et sic est omnis qui natus est ex spiritu.* [And so are all who are born from the spirit (John 3:8).]

August 19, 1949

[Louis Claude] Fillion, a Scripture scholar whom I am appointed to read, encourages young priests to study Hebrew, Greek, Aramaic, Itala, Arabic, Syriac, Assyrian, Ethiopian, Coptic, Armenian, Persian, Slavonic, Gothic, and the three main Egyptian dialects, namely Saledic (spoken at Thebes), Fayonnic (spoken at the oasis of Fayonen), and Memphitic (spoken at Memphis). Besides being grounded in oriental archaeology and ethnography, the young priest should also have a smattering of botany, zoology, geology and have more than a nodding acquaintance with the Talmud. Also, he says one might read a few Jewish novels, by way of recreation.

When you have mastered all this, you will be able to elucidate the ivy passage in Jonas, for instance, and you will come to the conclusion that Jonas in Nineveh sat down under a castor oil plant and became attached to its shade.[45]

On the whole, I think St. Theresa's interpretation of Jonas' ivy is more interesting, she didn't know one word of Egyptian either.

Yet, on the other hand, at Mass this morning I was momentarily distracted with a mild fit of compunction at the Little Flower's statement that, if she were a priest, she would learn Hebrew and Greek in order to read the revealed word of God in the original languages.

From Fillion (*The Study of the Bible* [Ireland, 1926], p. 220):

"One day Cardinal Foulon, Archbishop of Lyons, said to me, "Why is the cat, that charming animal, not mentioned in the Bible?" (Is it so charming after all?) – Fillion's comment!

I answered, "Your Eminence, it is mentioned in the Book of Baruch, or to be more exact, in the letter of Jeremias at the end of that book. The prophet shows it walking over the heads and bodies of the Babylonian idols."

---

[45] All of the Book of Jonah, but particularly chapter 4:5-11, is relevant for understanding the scriptural referent when Merton names his journal "The Whale and the Ivy."

So I rush to the book of Baruch (VI 20:21) and find:

"Their faces are black with smoke that is made in the house. Owls and swallows and other birds fly upon their bodies and upon their heads, and cats in like manner."

It is the first time I have read the sixth chapter of Baruch, and it is a wonderful chapter, written by Jeremias to the Jews going to Babylon into captivity, to preserve them against temptations to idolatry.

"For as a scarecrow in a garden of cucumbers keepeth nothing, so all their gods of wood and silver, laid over with gold. They are no better than a white thorn in a garden upon which every bird sitteth . . ."

August 22, 1949. Octave of the Assumption

One of the advantages and disadvantages of having our own inviolable rite, such as it is, is that we do not get the new feasts instituted by the Church, unless we go through a whole system of rescripts and indults and what not. So we do not have the Feast of Our Lady's Immaculate Heart, which is today. However, Fr. Anthony and Brother Basil and Fr. Linus and Bro. Giles all started out for South Carolina during the night office yesterday morning (after saying Mass at 2 A.M. in the infirmary chapel), and today they say Mass – the first Cistercian Mass – at the Mepkin Plantation which is to be the new monastery of the Immaculate Heart. The deeds were signed and the affair was made public (with many errors) in the newspapers and we expect the foundation to be made after the General Chapter and after the annual retreat which, for some reason best known to the retreat master, begins this year a month early, on November 1st.

Anyway, I was very happy saying the Mass of the Octave day this morning at St. Robert's altar with a little side chapel all to myself. I will remember this whole octave as a time of great joy – days in which my body burned and raged with prickly heat and my soul swam with idyllic joy. The really hot weather stopped all of a sudden the evening before St. Bernard's day, but prickly heat tends to be especially sharp when you are cooling off.

On St. Bernard's day[46] I sat up on the hill behind Nally's, not wanting to walk far into the woods because the more time you spend walking, the less you have for prayer. So I looked at the great big sweep of country and that far line of hills that is steeped in spiritual associations for me and at the

---

[46] August 20th.

abbey and the basilica sitting in the carpet of fields, like a reliquary containing all that is most precious in the world, the Body of Christ, His Divinity, the Living God. And I was turning over in my mind some sentences from St. Augustine's commentary on the 118th psalm. They concern the line, *Bonitatem et disciplinam et scientiam doce me* [Teach me goodness and discipline and knowledge (Psalms 118:66)], which he reads as *Suavitatem et eruditionem et scientiam doce me* [Teach me docility and delight and knowledge]. *Suavitatem* – the wisdom that comes from delight in virtue. *Disciplina* – docility – the wisdom that is born of suffering. Here are the lines from Augustine:

Cum quo ergo facit Deus suavitatem: id est cui propitius inspirat boni delectationem; atque ut apertius id explicem, cui donatur a Deo charitas Dei, et propter Deum charitas proximi; profecte instanter orare debet quo tantum sibi augeatur hoc donum, ut non solum pro illo contemnat delectationes caeteras, sed etiam pro illo quaslibet perferat passiones. Ita suavitati salubriter additur disciplina. [The person whom God comes to delight – that is, the one whom He mercifully inspires with the enjoyment of what is good; or, to explain it more plainly: the one to whom God gives the love of God and, for the sake of God, the love of neighbor – that person, I say, should pray ardently that this gift should so be increased in him that he will not only despise all other enjoyments because of it, but that likewise because of it he will prefer sufferings of all kinds. Thus is discipline added to delight with salutary results.]

How true it is that our knowledge and sense and experience of God is so much sharper and cleaner when we are uncomfortable and hot and physically cramped and suffering than when we are cool and at rest. So true it is that it does not depend on us or on our efforts how and when we shall be visited by His special grace! So, though I am always recollected and in God's presence in the woods, at peace and happy with Him, I am in more obscurity sometimes when I am in the hot choir, kneeling before the Blessed Sacrament on a day of recollection with the sweat pouring down my ribs. Usually in Church my mind is paralyzed with distractions, especially during the evening meditation. Yet how often in the last three minutes of that meditation my mind will suddenly be swept clean of images and my heart will sink into deep rest in God and I will be free for that little moment of rest and joy He allows me. I never would have to look at the clock on those days, if I wanted to know that the meditation was nearly over! This week, too, in choir, at the office and at Mass, when I am usually so tortured, there has been great peace and recollection, though mostly a rather dry recollection, [but] still, fruitful and healthy. *Suavitati salubriter additur disciplina.* [Discipline is added to delight with salutary results.] One reason for this is, I think, that with the full approval of Reverend Father and Father Anthony, indeed on the latter's advice, I have altogether stopped trying to battle the choir for decent Gregorian chant. I have lapsed entirely into the background and remain content to follow whatever is going on, without any more of those politely testy exhibitions of zeal which were only upsetting my whole system and making it harder for me to pray.

My friend, the Abbé Fillion, has written a book that is in some ways strange. However, it is very good – especially for someone like myself – to read, under obedience, a book that I would not otherwise have touched with a ten foot pole. Now, although I still think some of his notions are funny, I have conceived a real affection for Fillion because his book has brought so many graces with it.

Whether or not this particular sentence contains a grace, I do not know, but here it is. It has struck me and made me pause. It is something I had never really thought of. I don't know whether it means something to me or not:

"Every priest ought to be as familiar with the geography of the Sacred Books as that of his own country, and with the plan of the city of Jerusalem as that of his own town or the place where he lives" (p. 225).

Since I have a vow of stability, geography has more or less ceased to interest me, except when I think we are going to start a new foundation somewhere.

All I know about Palestine now is what I hear from our monastery of El Latroun, which now seems to have been finally evacuated. So many people in the world think it is ridiculous for Catholics to worry about the Holy Places. I am inarticulate when it comes to trying to think up an explanation of this love that would satisfy a rationalist, but it is a terrible thing to think of all this that we love and which really belongs spiritually to us being destroyed and overrun with armies. It is no new situation. It existed in the time of St. Bernard. And I have never really thought about the mystery of the Holy Land being in the hands of those who have no interest in Christ or who hate His Church. It is a strange and terrible thing that I cannot talk about. I guess Léon Bloy can give me some words on the subject. It was one, I think, on which he was quite vocal.

But it seems to me that a Christian who could have no interest in the Holy Sepulchre or Gethsemani or Bethlehem or Nazareth or the Sea of

Galilee or Capharnaum or Nain or Jacob's well . . . what kind of Christian could he be?

Yet all I know about Jerusalem is what the Jesuits tell us when they preach our annual retreat or what we get from Archbishop Goodier in the refectory. Not now! This month we have been having *Damien the Leper* – another book that does not make the soup and sauerkraut go down any easier!

August 25, 1949. Feast of St. Louis

This morning, after two hours of peaceful meditation and night office, I went to vest for Mass completely unmindful of the indignities that were to be imposed on me for my feast day. I had thought of all that yesterday, and had made a few rudimentary efforts to steel myself for the ordeal, but, by the divine permission, that was all forgotten, so that I was floored by the lace alb and by the vestments, which I cannot describe as I am not sufficiently familiar with the language of dressmakers. It was the evident intention of my brethren that I should say the Mass of St. Louis in oriental splendor. I wormed my way into my horrible decorations and proceeded to the altar palpitating with anxiety. There were, as far as I can remember, at least three carpets in St. Robert's chapel and, since you cannot possibly get three carpets in that small space in any other way, they were piled one on top of the other. Being of different sizes, you could see the elements of the ones underneath sticking out on all sides. I tried to begin Mass with my eyes shut, ignoring the gilt bookstand covered with little bits of red and green glass and the huge chocolate frames of the altar-cards. It did not work. I went through the Mass in unrelieved misery. After the *Gloria* I said, "*Dominus vobiscum,*" and then wondered if I had said the *Gloria*, hoped that I had, and made for the book, saying the prayers in a daze. At the Offertory I got a closer look at the base of the chalice which was a labyrinth of the most intricate carving, and it suddenly occurred to me that I was really saying Mass in a bazaar in Cairo. So I accepted the bitter humiliation in union with the humiliations of St. Louis' imprisonment by the *paynims*, thanked God that no one was physically present at my Mass to see me in my atrocious finery, and went on with interior peace but not without superficial anguish. Finally I flopped down on the kneelers in front of Our Lady of Victories, when it was all over, and, before I knew what had happened, some thirty-five minutes had gone by, and I staggered out of Church dimly aware that perhaps, after all, I had been subjected to some great but painfully incomprehensible grace.

August 26, 1949

My pious Abbé Fillion suggests that, when we are stumped and cannot find out the meaning of a passage of Scripture, we ought to pray to the "sacred author," that is, to whomever it was that served as God's instrument in writing the work. The suggestion appeals to me, for I have a great though confused affection for the writers of the Bible. I feel closer to them than to almost any other writers I know of. Isaias, Job, Moses, David, Matthew, Mark, Luke and John are all part of my life. They are always about me. They look over my shoulder, earnest men, belonging to the facade of a medieval cathedral. I feel that they are very concerned about me and that they want me to understand what God told them to write down, that they have always surrounded me with solicitous prayers, and that they love and protect me.

They are more a part of my world than most of the people actually living in the world. I "see" them sometimes more really than I see the monks I live with. I know well the burnt faces of the Prophets and the Evangelists, transformed by the white-hot dangerous presence of inspiration, for they looked at God as into a furnace and the Seraphim flew down and purified their lips with fire. And I read their books with joy and with holy fear, *cum tremore divino*, and their words become a part of me. They are solemn and dreadful and holy men humbled by the revelation they wrote down. They are my Fathers. They are the "burnt men" in the last line of *The Seven Storey Mountain*.[47] I am more and more possessed by their vision of God's Kingdom, and wonder at the futility of seeking anything else on earth but the truth revealed in them and in tradition – the Church's treasure to which she holds the keys.

I also have great reverence and love for the Patriarchs of the Old Testament – Abraham, Isaac, Jacob, and for the Prophets – Samuel, Elias, Eliseus. When I walk in the cemetery in the cool evening when the sun is going down – (there is almost no sunlight left now in the interval after supper) – I think of Isaac, meditating in the fields at evening, and of Rebecca coming to marry him from a far country, riding on a slick camel bigger than a ship.

August 27, 1949

My soul is united to the soul of Christ in the priestly character impressed upon me, and in the Mass His soul and my soul act together as closely and

---

[47] "That you may become the brother of God and learn to know the Christ of the burnt men."

as inseparably as two rays of light shining together. That is why I am not aware of a foreign "Stranger Presence," but rather it seems to me as if, without ceasing to be who I am, I had become Somebody else, as if I had been raised to a higher and much simpler and cleaner level of being.

August 30, 1949

Last Sunday was the Feast of Our Lady's Most Pure Heart, whose Mass I love well, and the whole day was beautiful. Beautiful, I mean, for me, although the weather was cloudy and it rained in the morning. After Chapter I was on the Kitchen-Refectory squad and spent one hour going around the one hundred and ninety-two places counting out four thin cookies for each Trappist and handing out various very small bon-bons and some stuff that pretended to be candied orange. But I was very happy doing all this, not because of the candy, which nauseates me, but because of God and Our Lady and the Feast Day.

In the afternoon I went out to the old horse barn with the Book of Proverbs and indeed the whole Bible, and I was wandering around in the hayloft, where there is a big gap in the roof. One of the rotting floorboards gave way under me and I nearly fell through. Afterwards I sat and looked out at the hills and the gray clouds and couldn't read anything. When the flies got too bad I wandered across the bare pasture and sat over by the enclosure wall, perched on the edge of a ruined bathtub that has been placed there for the horses to drink out of. A pipe comes through the wall and plenty of water flows into the bathtub from a spring somewhere in the woods, and I couldn't read there either. I just listened to the clean water flowing and looked at the wreckage of the horsebarn on top of the bare knoll in front of me and remained drugged with happiness and with prayer.

Presently the two mares and the two colts came over to see me and to take a drink. The colts looked like children with their big grave eyes, very humble, very stupid and they were tamer than I expected. They came over and nudged me with their soft muzzles and I talked to them for a bit and then Fr. Columban, who was hiding behind some sumacs a hundred paces away, came out to see what was the matter.

Later on I saw other interesting things – for instance a dead possum in a trap and a gold, butter-and-egg butterfly wavering on the dead possum's back. There are many Rhode Island reds over in the southwest corner of the enclosure this year. When I was on retreat for ordination to the priesthood, I galloped to be at work on the roosts we were building for them then.

August 31, 1949

Morning after morning I try to study the 6th chapter of St. John and it is too great. I cannot study it. I simply sit still and try to breathe.

There is a small black lizard with a blue, metallic tail, scampering up the yellow wall of the Church next to the niche where the Little Flower, with a confidential and rather pathetic look in her eyes, offers me a rose. I am glad of the distraction because now I can breathe again and think a little.

It does no good to use big words to talk about Christ. Since I seem to be incapable of talking about Him in the language of a child, I have reached the point where I can scarcely talk about Him at all. All my words fill me with shame.

You cannot say of a chapter in the Gospel, "It is terrific." It is indecent to call the Bible wonderful. It would be indecent, too, to say, "My mother is a wonderful person." So, you cannot praise Christ the way you would praise a human being. You have to fall on your face and cry out for mercy. The only way you can talk about God is to "confess" – *confessio laudis* [confession of praise] – either that or confession of your shame. If Christ is merely interesting to you, or merely admirable – what will become of your miserable soul?

That is why I am more and more thankful for the Office and for the psalms. Their praise of Him is perfect, and God gives it to me to utter as more my own than any language I could think up for myself.

Domine Dominus Noster! Quam admirabile est nomen tuum in universa terra! [Lord our Lord! How admirable is your name throughout the whole world (Psalms 8:1)!]

When I have the whole Church crying out with me, there is some chance of finding peace, in the feeling that God is somehow, after all, receiving praise from my lips.[48]

September 1, 1949

This morning, under a cobalt blue sky, summer having abruptly ended, I am beginning the Book of Job. It is not warm enough to sit for long in the shade of the cedars. The woods are crisply outlined in the sun and the clamor of distant crows is sharp in the air that no longer sizzles with locusts.

---

[48] Pages numbered 113–46 in the original holographic journal have been cut from the journal with a razor blade. Nearly one-sixth of an inch of these pages remain with evidence of writing on both sides of the missing pages. Since the journal entries which follow for the dates September 1 through October 7, 1949 were later published in *The Month* (February 1950): 107–13, the thirty-four pages of journal were probably cut by Merton himself for typing.

And Job moves me deeply. This year more than ever it has a special poignancy.

I now know that all my own poems about the world's suffering have been inadequate: they have not solved anything, they have only camouflaged the problem. And it seems to me that the urge to write a real poem about suffering and sin is only another temptation because, after all, I do not really understand.

Sometimes I feel that I would like to stop writing, precisely as a gesture of defiance. In any case, I hope to stop publishing for a time, for I believe it has now become impossible for me to stop writing altogether. Perhaps I shall continue writing on my deathbed, and even take some asbestos paper with me in order to go on writing in purgatory. Except that I hope Our Lady will arrange some miraculous victory over my sins that will make purgatory unnecessary.

And yet it seems to me that writing, far from being an obstacle to spiritual perfection in my own life, has become one of the conditions on which my perfection will depend. If I am to be a saint – and there is nothing else that I can think of desiring to be – it seems that I must get there by writing books in a Trappist monastery. If I am to be a saint, I have not only to be a monk, which is what all monks must do to become saints, but I must also put down on paper what I have become. It may sound simple, but it is not an easy vocation.

To be as good a monk as I can, and to remain myself, and to write about it: to put myself down on paper, in such a situation, with the most complete simplicity and integrity, masking nothing, confusing no issue: this is very hard, because I am all mixed up in illusions and attachments. These, too, will have to be put down. But without exaggeration, repetition, useless emphasis. No need for breast-beating and lamentation before the eyes of anyone but You, O God, who see the depths of my fatuity. To be frank without being boring. It is a kind of crucifixion. Not a very dramatic or painful one. But it requires so much honesty that it is beyond my nature. It must come somehow from the Holy Ghost.

One of the results of all this could well be a complete and holy transparency: living, praying, and writing in the light of the Holy Spirit, losing myself entirely by becoming public property just as Jesus is public property in the Mass. Perhaps this is an important aspect of my priesthood – my living of my Mass: to become as plain as a Host in the hands of everybody. Perhaps it is this, after all, that is to be my way of solitude. One of the strangest ways so far devised, but it is the way of the Word of God.

Yet, after all, this only teaches me that nothing vital about myself can ever be public property!

September 3, 1949

It is alarming to find out how much one's theology fits the theology of Job's friends! The form of the drama of Job demands that the reader identify himself with Job. Actually most of us are more like Eliphaz or Baldad. We are hardly much closer to God than they were. And, after all, at least one of them was a mystic. Eliphaz started out with a modest enough explanation of Job's suffering, based on mystical experience. I am startled to find that this is the interpretation I myself made of Job eight years ago. It is the explanation I gave to Bob Lax's sister, Gladio, and to Mary Davis, before I came to the monastery.

Numquid homo, Dei comparatione, justificabitur? aut factore suo purior erit vir? "Shall man be justified in comparison with God, or shall a man be more pure than his maker [Job 4:17]?" And the same strain is taken up by Baldad in XXV, 4 *[Numquid justificari potest homo comparatus Deo?]* Then, too, *Beatus homo qui corripitur a Deo* (Job 5:17), "Blessed is the man whom God correcteth" is written on the heart of every Trappist in the first months of his novitiate.

God's purity, says Eliphaz, who knows from experience, causes us anguish and suffering when we come in contact with Him. But it is for our good that He thus purifies us. We should be humble and patient. Which reminds me that Job is a proverbial model of patience when he was anything but patient: at least so his friends thought. But that is only one of the paradoxes of Job. His tempestuous impatience is really a higher form of patience. It is a kind of adoration.

Really, the problem of Job is not so much to find out who has the right answer to the question of suffering. All their answers are more or less correct. But what Job himself demands, and justly, is the *Divine* answer, not to the problem of suffering in general, but to his own personal suffering. In the end, the answer that God gives to Job is simply a concrete statement of what Eliphaz has said in the abstract: "Shall man be compared to God?"

Job wanted the answer and he got it. God Himself was his answer. In the presence of God, Job acknowledged his sufferings to be just and God reproved all the arguments of Job's friends, because they were all insufficient.

Thus the Book of Job does not solve the problem of suffering, in the abstract. It shows us that one man, Job, received a concrete answer to the problem, and that answer was found in God Himself. If we are to have

Job's answer, we must have Job's vision of God. Otherwise, our arguments are only modifications of the arguments of Job's friends. I hasten to say that those arguments should be sufficient for most of us. But they probably would not have been sufficient for Job.

Then there is the fact that Job is a type of Christ. And what argument of men can convince Christ that He ought to be put to death for us? Jesus did not die to prove any argument of ours. His death was not measured by any human standard of justice. The Pharisees who reviled Him and told Him to come down from the Cross were Job's friends, speaking now no longer as personages in a drama, but in their own name and in that of fallen man.

September 10, 1949

Once before I read the Book of Job and got the feeling that I was going to begin living it, as well as reading it. That has happened again.

September 13, 1949

I find consoling lines here and there in Dom Chapman's *Spiritual Letters* [*The Spiritual Letters of Dom John Chapman, OSB*, London, 1935]. For instance: "Humility in oneself is not attractive, though it is attractive in others." I do not know if what is in me is humility. But it is certainly not attractive. Anguish and fear. Nobody likes to be afraid.

There are different kinds of fear. One of the most terrible is the sensation that you are likely to become, at any moment, the protagonist in a Graham Greene novel: the man who tries to be virtuous, and who is in a certain sense holy, and yet who is overwhelmed by sin as if there were a kind of fatality about it.

One sentence of Job is always with me: "Even though He kill me, yet will I trust Him." *Sufficit tibi, Paule, gratia mea.* [My grace is sufficient for you, Paul (2 Corinthians 12:9; Merton adds "Paul").]

Two more sentences from Dom Chapman:

> "Pray as you can and do not try to pray as you can't.
> Take yourself as you find yourself: start from that."

September 14, 1949. Feast of the Exaltation of the Holy Cross

There has been a legal change of seasons, and the monastic fast has begun today. It is cool again, and the leaves of the sycamores are already beginning to turn yellow and brown. We brought down our mattresses and blankets from our dormitory cells and spread them out in the bright September sun. My mind is full of Saint Francis on Mount Alverna.

A moment ago, someone was playing the harmonium in the novitiate. Our psalms sound very wistful and strange on a harmonium: plaintive, sentimental and thin, as if they were filled with an immense nostalgia for the heaven of the books of meditations. It reminded me of the night Father Alberic died, three years ago. I watched by the body in the middle of the night, and then went back to the dormitory and could not get to sleep, even when I stayed to catch up my two hours while the others went down to church for the Night Office. Finally they sang Matins and Lauds of the Dead for Father Alberic, and I could hear the garbled music coming into the dormitory through the back of the organ pipes – that great, big, dusty closet full of muffled chords! The poignancy of that music was very affecting. It seemed to sum up all the sufferings of the long life that was now over. Poor little grey Father Alberic, writing the history of the Order on scraps of paper in the infirmary! All the relief, all the mystery, all the unexpected joy of his meeting with God could be guessed at in those strange harmonies. And so, this morning, the sound of this harmonium in the novitiate (it has begun to play again) chimes in with the last two days of a two weeks' battle, and I feel a wistful and chastened sobriety filling my heart, as if I were one of the eight human survivors of the deluge, watching the world come back to view from the summit of Mount Ararat!

In the tempest I have discovered once again, but this time with a peculiarly piercing sharpness, that I cannot possess created things, I cannot touch them, I cannot get to them. We who are supposed to be Christians know that well enough, abstractly. Or rather, we say we believe it. Actually we have to discover it over and over again. We have to experience this truth with deeper and deeper intensity, as we go on in life. We renounce the pursuit of creatures as ends on certain sacramental occasions. And we return, bit by bit, to our familiarity with them, living as if we had in this world a lasting city. . . .

But creatures remain untouchable, inviolable. If God wants you to suffer a little, He allows you to learn just how inviolable they are. As soon as you try to possess their goodness for its own sake, all that is sweet in them becomes bitter to you, all that is beautiful, ugly. Everything you love sickens you. And, at the same time, your need to love something, somebody, increases a hundred times over. And God, Who is the only one who can be loved for His own sake alone, remains invisible and unimaginable and untouchable, beyond everything else that exists.

You flowers and trees, you hills and streams, you fields, flocks and wild birds, you books, you poems, and you people, I am unutterably alone in the midst of you. The irrational hunger that sometimes gets into the depths of my will, tries to swing my deepest self away from God and direct it to your love. I try to touch you with the deep fire that is in the center of my heart, but I cannot touch you without defiling both you and myself, and I am abashed, solitary and helpless, surrounded by a beauty that can never belong to me.

But this sadness generates within me an unspeakable reverence for the holiness of created things, for they are pure and perfect and they belong to God and they are mirrors of His beauty. He is mirrored in all things like sunlight in clean water: but if I try to drink the light that is in the water, I only shatter the reflection.

And so I live alone and chaste in the midst of the holy beauty of all created things, knowing that nothing I can see or hear or touch will ever belong to me, ashamed of my absurd need to give myself away to any one of them or to all of them. The silly, hopeless passion to give myself away to any beauty eats out my heart. It is an unworthy desire, but I cannot avoid it. It is in the hearts of us all, and we have to bear with it, suffer its demands with patience, until we die and go to heaven where all things will belong to us in their highest causes.

September 15, 1949

If I were more immersed in the Rule of Saint Benedict, I would be a better writer.

If I were more absorbed in the Presence of God, I would be a better writer and would write much less.

There are now over two hundred in the community.

September 17, 1949

Nisi granum frumenti [cadens in terram mortuum fuerit, ipsum solum manet] . . . unless the grain of wheat, falling into the ground, die, itself remaineth alone [John 12:24]. The words are much more poignant in their context. Some gentiles had asked Philip if they might speak to Jesus. This is Our Lord's answer. They cannot come to Him through Philip and Andrew, they cannot even come to Him if they talk to Him, because words will not unite them with Him. They can only come to Him if He dies for them.

Itself remaineth alone. Saint John emphasizes more and more the loneliness, the moral isolation of Christ before His Passion. He is alone from the beginning because He is God and all the rest are men. He is alone because nobody can understand Him. Already in the sixth chapter a whole crowd of disciples has abandoned Him because His doctrine of the Eucharist is so far beyond them. He is isolated by the increasing hatred of the Pharisees, who form a stronger and stronger front against Him, forcing others to separate themselves from Him. He is isolated by His own greatness, which elevates Him further and further above His enemies. Now He is alone among men who either hate Him or do not know how to love Him, because they are unable to know Him as He really is. Yet there are some who want to come to the true knowledge and love of Him. If they want to be with Him, He must pass through death and take them with Him into life.

I am alone in the world with a different loneliness from that of Christ. He was alone because He was everything. I am alone because I am nothing. I am alone in my insufficiency – dependent, helpless, contingent, and never quite sure that I am really leaning on Him upon whom I depend.

Yet to trust in Him means to die, because to trust perfectly in Him you have to give up all trust in anything else. And I am afraid of that death. The only thing I can do about it is to make my fear become part of the death I must die, to live perfectly in Him.

Our souls are baptized in His death. Our souls have passed from death to life. Yesterday at the Communion of the Conventual Mass, my faculties were also baptized in His death, for a short time. Without any work on my own part, and in spite of myself – for I was dull and distracted – I suddenly found myself completely recollected and sunk in Him and protected on all sides by His Presence so that my imagination became incapable of going anywhere and doing anything and my memory was completely sated by darkness. Comfortably locked away in recollection and peace I had the feeling that I couldn't get out if I tried. I was so numb that all the business of movements in choir slowed down to a dream and this went on until after Sext. The dream ebbed out of me when I walked off to our books. The same thing came back at None and Vespers, but not at Compline, and not today either. It was a great and merciful relief because it washed away much of the strain and sorrow of all the interior fighting I have been doing and still have to do.

September 21, 1949

The word "poignant" is taking a very prominent place in my vocabulary these days! That is because there is some power that keeps seizing my heart in its fist and wringing cries out of me (I mean the quiet kind that make themselves heard by twisting within you) and beating me this way and that until I am scarcely able to reel. Day and night I am bullied by the most suspicious of joys. I spend my time wrestling with emotions that seem to be now passion, now anguish, and now the highest religious exaltation.

Fortunately I have much intellectual work, and the books are my best shock-absorbers. But the absorption is not complete, it is only sublimated. The emotion is transferred to a spiritual plane. Every article in *La Vie Spirituelle*, every line of Job or Tobias seems to send me sky high, and I don't come down again for an hour. It is a terrific nuisance.

This morning, consecrating the Precious Blood, I became so overwhelmed that I had doubts (I hope they were negative doubts) whether I had actually said all the words properly and whether the consecration was valid.

But occasionally I get a little rest. Yesterday, for instance, I was able to relax practically all day in a blessed aridity in which things were once again mercifully insipid and distasteful. What a relief to be indifferent to things, after having been pushed around by a crowd of different intoxications, some of which seem to be intensely holy and some of which do not even bother to wear a disguise.

It is not much fun to live the spiritual life with the spiritual equipment of an artist.

Yesterday afternoon in the cornfield I began to feel rather savage about the whole business. I suppose this irritation was the sign that the dry period was reaching its climax and was about to go over again into the awful battle with joy. My soul was cringing and doubling up and subconsciously getting ready for the next tidal wave. At the moment all I had left in my heart was an abyss of self-hatred – waiting for the next appalling sea.

We have a new machine that rushes through the cornfield, raffishly seizing the corn and reducing it instantly to finely minced particles, which it then sprays into a truck that travels along beside it. This apparatus charges through the field doing all the work and the rest of us simply have to cut a few stalks that have blown down and are lying too low for the monster to snatch with its knives. Things have changed greatly in the six years since I was a novice. But since there is much more work, we can do with a few machines.

October 7, 1949

Spiritual joy depends on the cross. Unless we deny ourselves, we will find ourselves in everything and that is misery. As soon as we begin to deny ourselves out of love for God, we begin to find God, at least obscurely. Since God is our joy, our joy is proportioned to our self-denial for the love of

God. I say our self-denial for the love of God because there are people who deny themselves for love of themselves.

It is not complicated to lead the spiritual life. But it is difficult. We are blind, and subject to a thousand illusions. We must expect to be making mistakes almost all the time. We must be content to fail repeatedly and to begin again to try to deny ourselves for the love of God.

It is when we are angry at our own mistakes that we tend most of all to deny ourselves for love of ourselves. We want to shake off the hateful thing that has humbled us. In our rush to escape the humiliation of our own mistakes, we run head first into the opposite error, seeking comfort and compensation. And so we spend our lives running back and forth from one attachment to another.

If that is all our self-denial amounts to, our mistakes will never help us.

The thing to do when you have made a mistake is not to give up doing what you were doing and start something altogether new, but to start over again with the thing you began badly and try, for the love of God, to do it well.

November 16, 1949

Today on the eleventh anniversary of my Baptism, I began teaching theology, an introductory conference lasting an hour and a half, as a start for both my classes – Scripture and Mystical Theology. On Monday I began a series of orientation classes for the novices.

The colony left for South Carolina Monday morning. It was very quiet because they got out while we were chanting the night office at about half-past three. During the morning meditation we could see the non-priests going to Communion at St. Joseph's altar. Twenty-nine left, in all. I saw Fr. Linus and Bro. Basil off with the big-end truck and trailer when I came in from the woods on Sunday afternoon. They looked extremely tough in overalls. Fr. Samuel and Fr. Cletus had left soon after None in their station wagon. The others went in a chartered bus except for some who were on another truck. The foundation has been sensibly planned and there was no excitement – no drama – and, as far as we know, no publicity.

A priest is here with a "Pilgrim Statue" of Our Lady of Fatima. It is one of those super-pretty statues, but I like it without apology, not for art's sake but for Our Lady's sake. Fr. Hilary tapped it all over with his knuckles to see if it was wood or plaster and it sounded (to my relief) like wood. I asked Our Lady for the grace of interior solitude and spiritual virginity. There is nothing to live for but God, and I am still full of the orchestras that drown out His voice.

November 24, 1949. Feast of St. John of the Cross

The other day I read how Ezekiel saw the glory of God – those whales, those wings, those fires flashing and those living creatures running to and fro – going back to Jerusalem from Babylon.

I think I shall write to a Hindu who wrote about Patanjali's yoga, and who is in Simla. I shall ask him to send us some books. A chemist, who has been helping us with some paint jobs, turned out to have been a postulant in a Zen Buddhist monastery in Hawaii and he spoke to the community about it in Chapter.

It was raining and there was a wind. I went out to the wagon shed. You could still see the hills in the distance, not too much rain for that – many black clouds, low and torn, like smoke from a disaster, flying angrily over the wide open ruin of the old horse barn, where I now love to walk alone. On sunny days it does not have this Castle of Otranto look about it. Today I was full of a melody that might have been related to something in Stravinsky's "Firebird" which I have nevertheless forgotten. This was mostly my own and I sang it to God along with the angels. Then the melody went away and I sat on a stone and got into a deeper prayer than at any other time this day.

November 25, 1949. St. Catherine

In the refectory we are reading *Exodus* and I have discovered St. Gregory of Nyssa's *De Vita Moysis* [Life of Moses]. I will probably try to talk about it in the Mystical Theology class. Having trouble organizing material. I refuse to follow any known text. – except I will take [Etienne] Gilson on St. Bernard when I get the preliminaries out of the way. I feel much better mapping out my own approach – from Scripture and the Fathers, Mysticism and Dogma together – blending and culminating in experience.

In Osee (iii, 3) *Dies multos exspectabis me: non fornicaberis et non eris viro, sed et ego exspectabo te.* [Thou shalt wait for me many days; thou shalt not play the harlot; and thou shalt be no man's; and I also will wait for thee.] Long period of emptiness after reconciliation with God. Probation, between heaven and earth. No man's land. The half-light of the cloud.

Fr. Bruno, describing a Carthusian monk somewhere, uses the expression "sacred exhaustion." It amuses me, but I see the point. This from the special number of *Études Carmélitaines* which Msgr. Sheen gave us and which I read each day behind the horse barn. Very good. Also, it has pictures and an article on Kierkegaard.

December 3, 1949

Kenneth Patchen's "For losing her love all would I profane" struck me with great force and after a moment I realized that for me (perhaps not for him) it simply echoes St. John of the Cross' *Por toda la hermosura nunca yo me perderé* [for all the beauty in the world never will I lose myself].

I remember the misty afternoon (late October), when I was out in the woods behind Nally's, walking uphill in the bare washed-out lace where the oak trees were cut down and the stumps and roots are black in the wreckage of shale. And so I sit bewildered by the dialectic of those two similar yet contrary poems, equally good. I wrote this suddenly. The bell rings. I say fifteen decades of the Rosary each day before Our Lady's Feast.

Naomi Burton came here today to try somehow to stop the publishing of the St. Lutgarde book.[49] I wish it could be done away with but it is perhaps too late. Kenneth Patchen is an admirable poet. Laughlin says Patchen is sick. And then Dylan Thomas is drunk.

December 4, 1949. Second Sunday of Advent – Day of Recollection

Last Sunday morning Father George died, after Reverend Father had announced that we would give him Extreme Unction in the afternoon. Fr. William, who is always in the infirmary, anointed him quickly just before he died, and Reverend Father told us about it over the refectory microphone at the end of dinner.

I am hebdomadary, sang Mass this morning at the temporary altar in the front of the presbytery (the new marble one shines in the gloom behind it but the steps leading up to it are not finished.) After Sext went out for a moment to see Naomi at the gate. She came out from Louisville smartly and soberly dressed in a costume I am sure would be approved in any ecclesiastical circles. I gave her a letter from Bruce & Company that was handed to me too late to give her yesterday. They definitely want that lousy book to go through. I am resigned to the total loss of my reputation.

[49] *What Are These Wounds?*

Walking along the fence of the new vineyard after Benediction, I looked at the dim full moon and the bare brown woods on the far side of the bottoms where some neighbor built that little wooden house last summer. It is the only house we can see in that direction or in fact in any other. But what I wanted to say was that I don't think I like to walk in the fields with our clothes smelling of incense.

But behind the horse-barn after dinner I made my thanksgiving. The little clouds were beautiful. The sun on the grass was beautiful. Even the ground seemed alive.

December 6, 1949

Tomorrow is the Vigil of the Immaculate Conception. I am busy most of the time preparing classes – Orientation, Scripture, Mystical Theology. I am still trying to lay foundations for all of them and I make notes on a lot of things that I will probably never talk to them about. There is supposed to be a special group coming to the vault after Benediction on Sundays and Feasts to talk about special points. That means mostly St. John of the Cross, as far as I am concerned. I am going through *The Spiritual Canticle* again in Spanish out behind the horse barn in a little corner behind the cedars where I can sit among the blackberry bushes out of the wind. It is still warm enough to sit out there even in summer clothes. I feel like learning snatches of St. John's Spanish by heart – just snatches. It is inviting and easy. Phrases cling to you without your making half an effort to grasp them.

This evening before Vespers low gray clouds, very dark, all the woods and bottoms looked grim, but there was a brushfire along the road that skirts the ridge of Mount Olivet, and you could see the jagged bloody wound of flames eating its way among the trees, with blue smoke pouring out over the road and the pasture. It was a strange and beautiful background for the Sorrowful Mysteries of the Rosary. I walked along the edge of the dead vineyard and there was a strong wind that blew our summer cowl against the barbed wire and it got torn.

December 7, 1949. Vigil of the Immaculate Conception

One of the many nice things about being hebdomadary is that you get the Scriptorium all to yourself during a good part of the wonderful interval after the Night Office. All the other priests are saying Mass and the young professed are going to Communion. I listen to the clock tick. Downstairs the thermostat has just stopped humming. God is in this room. He is in my heart. So much so that it is difficult to read or write. Nevertheless, I'll get busy on Isaias which is Your word, O my God, and may Your fire grow in me and may I find You in Your beautiful fire. It is very quiet, O my God. Your moon shines on our hills. Your moonlight shines in my wide open soul when everything is silent. *Adolezco, peno y muero.* [I languish, suffer and die.]

December 9, 1949

Here is a passage in Rilke's Journal that I like immensely. It ought to be true of me, but I talk too much – keep the contacts open.

"What's the use of telling anyone that I am changing? If I am changing, then surely I am no longer the person I was and, if I am something else than heretofore, then it is clear that I have no acquaintances. And to strange people, to people who do not know me, I cannot possibly write."

Is the last sentence true of me? No! I write for a hundred thousand people who do not know me, but I am not writing this for them.

Tomorrow it will be eight years since I came to Gethsemani. I somehow feel less clean then I did then when I thought I was throwing my civil identity away.

Last night in the little cloister a disheveled young layman with a lot of black hair, who looked as though he might be one of the neighbors, burst in through the door out of the dark, came up to me as if he knew he ought not to do it, and stretched out his hand to shake hands with me. Then he rushed out the door, pleased but guilty. He seemed to be wearing two raincoats. I had never seem him before. I wondered if he were some stranger who had done this on a bet. But today I saw him in choir with the laybrothers, so he is a postulant. (Later he left.)

(Evening.) It is snowing now. First snow of the winter. We are wearing summer clothes all winter – or at least I am – since the Church is now heated.

Today after dinner I got Fr. Placid, the Cellarer, to discuss amicably and in sign language the possibility of putting more bookshelves in the vault and throwing out the closets full of the vestments we wear on the big feasts for Pontifical High Mass. At present I have the *Vie Spirituelle* lying all over the floor. I also got him to remove two hideous small statues of plaster saints which I found there when I first came. I had tried to stuff them out of sight, but the only place that would contain them had a glass door to it, so you could still see their faces congealed in expressions of the most fatuous piety. Fr. Placid took one saint in each hand, holding them by their heads, and walked off to the guest house convinced that the retreatants would love them. I suppose they will. My guess is that the saints were St. John Eudes and St. Vincent de Paul, but I never had the courage to look and see if their names were on them. Poor saints! Pray for us, holy Saints! May God have mercy on us.

Emotion does a man great injury in this monastic life. You have to be serious and detached and calm all the time. I am still recovering from the emotions of September and October that were, I do not know how, voluntary. Faith is the antidote: cleansing yourself of impressions and feelings and the absurd movements of a half-blind understanding by a clear penetration into the heart of darkness where God is found.

December 10, 1949

I am abashed by the real solitude of Rilke which I admire, knowing, however, it is not for me because I am not like that. But his is a solitude I understand objectively, perhaps not by connaturality at all, but it moves me tremendously. You see, to begin with, he did not *want* it or go looking for it. It found him. Tremendous how he finds himself in the solitude of Christ (David) in the psalms, all of a sudden, there on page 53 of *Malte Laurids Brigge*. Who is the French poet that he quotes there?

Anyway, here is something Rilke himself wrote down. It will make one of these pages good:

"For a while yet I can write all this down and express it. But there will come a day when my hand will be far from me and when I bid it write, it will write words I do not mean. The time of that other interpretation will dawn, when not one word will remain upon another, and all meaning will dissolve like clouds and fall down like rain. Despite my fear, I am yet like one standing before something great . . . This time I shall be written. I am the impression that will change."

No, one does not envy the fear that is another man's private vocation. But I am abashed by that fear and by Rilke and Kafka who are solitaries without, for all that, being my brothers – not my close brothers like the calm and patient and long-suffering men in cowls who live and pray with me here in this busy family – all wearing dirty summer cowls in the middle of winter.

I guess it is the right fictional element that makes this solitude in Rilke's book just intangible: real, but not quite my own. Same too with Kafka.

December 13, 1949. St. Lucy

Eight years since I walked into the novitiate carrying my suitcase with the Cuba Mail Line labels on it, behind Fr. Robert, with the fat boy from Buffalo. Fr. Walter and I were making signs about it tonight.

I am deacon this week. As soon as I stand in front of the open book at the Gospel-stand to sing the Gospel, the memory of that time I passed out in the middle of the Gospel last July comes over me, and I can't breathe and my legs turn to jelly, and it is all I can do to look at the book and keep an ordered series of noises coming out of me. This morning I thought I was going to collapse for sure. A big wave of darkness came up from inside me somewhere, but I shook my head and it went away for a bit. Hope I can finish out the week with its three Ember days. Reverend Father is making me sleep late – until 3 A.M. – tomorrow and the rest of the week.

I am throwing myself too much into this class-work. That is the one thing that is wearing me down. There is no need to try to sweep them off their feet by sheer intensity. "It is pride only – sit still."

A novice sent me a note last night to ask what I thought about St. Louis de Montfort's "true devotion" to Our Lady, and it reminded me that I think a very great deal of it. The fact, to give yourself to Our Lady – but really to give yourself – seems to me to be the most obvious and simplest way to become a saint, because if my mind and my will and my heart and all my thoughts and all my desires become her mind and will and heart and thoughts and desire, obviously they will all be holy. She is *the* [underlined twice] saint and *the* [underlined twice] contemplative.

Objectively, this gift really demands a very perfect and constant faith and it is the quickest way to a detachment that is simple and complete and without contention and without strain. We do not depend so much on our asceticism – we simply put ourselves in her hands and leave everything to her which in practice cannot be done without a relentless interior mortification of thoughts and desires. But under her guidance it is easy and peaceful and sweet and not really much trouble at all.

All I do is renew that gift to her, all the time.

Lax too has discovered Our Lady. He sent me a fine poem about her.

December 15, 1949

The other night I woke up at midnight and began to worry over whether I would be able to get through the Gospel at High Mass. By Chapter the next morning I was so worn out thinking about it and making all kinds of resolutions that I had to ask Reverend Father to let me off being deacon for the rest of the week. Father Sebastian took over. Dom Vital, who is celebrant, upbraided me in sign language. But it was a great relief. I felt much lighter. I am under pressure through my own fault. The Gospel business can be tackled sometime when, by God's grace, I am a little more in the clear.

Nevertheless, working in the woods in the afternoon, I felt lonely and small and humiliated – chopping down dead trees with a feeling that perhaps I was not even a real person any more.

Perhaps the terror that comes over me at the Gospel is a sort of exhibitionism in reverse, induced by the ceremonies and preparations. Prayers, blessings, processions, music: everything concentrates the attention of the world on the deacon who is now going to sing the Gospel. Stand in ceremony and listen to the deacon! And the deacon turns to jelly and wants to run and hide, not because he is modest, but because a terrible judgment rises up against him from within the depths of his soul and says, "You like them to look at *you*, to listen to your voice." So I get terrified of the blasphemy and try to run out of myself and hide somewhere in non-existence where God can't find me with His accusations, His reality, His truth.

Apart from that it was nice working in the woods. The day was very grey and gloomy. We were on Mount Olivet clearing out cedars that had been killed by the brush fires. Through the trees I could see the next-door farm, the one where the Fontgombault monks once were. And I could see the knobs from a new and interesting angle. The *Introit* of the Christmas Midday Mass kept going around and around in my mind because we had practiced it, all together in choir, right after Chapter. So that contributed to keeping me alive.

Otherwise – feelings of fear, dejection, non-existence. Yet it gives me a kind of satisfaction to realize that it is not by contact with any other creature that I can recover the sense that I am real. It is the beginning of a most frightening divorce from the many things with which I have had adulterous weddings! Solitude means being lonely not in a way that pleases you but in a way that frightens you and empties you to the extent that it means being exiled even from yourself.

I suppose my gift to Our Lady has something to do with it.

I must have mixed inks in our well for the ink is turning pale green.

December 17, 1949
Vacío, hambriento, solo, llagado y doliente de amor, suspenso en el aire. [Empty, famished, alone, wounded and pining with love, suspended in the air.]

Walking back from the barns in the warm sun on the muddy road between the orchard and the vegetable garden with *The Spiritual Canticle* under my arm and saying those wonderful words. I found a wonderful place to read and pray, on the top floor of that barn building where the rabbits used to be. Up under the roof is a place reached by various ladders. Some stove pipes and old buckets are there and many of the little boxes in which the novices gather strawberries in the early summer time. There is a chair and there is a beautiful, small rectangular window which faces south over the valley – the outside orchard, St. Joseph's field, the distant line of hills. It is the quietest and most hidden and most isolated place I have found in the whole enclosure – but not necessarily the warmest. However, it was good yesterday with the sun coming into the window. *Vacío, hambriento, solo, llagado y doliente de amor, suspenso en el aire*. Almost all activity makes me ill, but as soon as I am alone and silent and still again, I sink into deep peace, recollection and happiness.

Almost all the time my breathing is hard and my heart is fast. I have a nice, dry little cough, too, but I do not flatter myself with a disease. Nor do I boast of wanting to be left alone, though that is indeed all that I can think of wanting.

However, I have been elevated to a position on the monastery fire department. We are just organizing one. A man was here from Louisville today. Broad, muscular and calm. He told us that fire fighting was serious business, and that our equipment was hopeless, and that in the city they would lock people up for being as careless as we are about fire hazards. After that there was a lot of conversation about fire creeping up on you inside the walls and under the floor.

I heard somebody practicing the Graduals of the big feasts that are to come – Christmas, St. Stephen, St. John, and somehow I thought of all the old monasteries of the Order and of the life our Fathers led. All this has become part of my body of Christmas associations. And I am happy – perfectly happy to be a Cistercian – not a Carmelite or Carthusian or Camaldolese, but a Cistercian – and sit in the top of a barn with more beautiful stove pipes and strawberry boxes and lovelier old junk than a Carthusian ever saw, all alone and *suspenso en el aire*.

December 20, 1949. Vigil of St. Thomas

Rilke's Notebooks have so much power in them that they make me wonder why no one writes like that in monasteries. Not that there have not been better books written in monasteries, or no books more serene. But monks do not seem to be able to write so well – it is as if our professional spirituality sometimes veiled our contact with the naked realities inside us. It is a common failing of religious to lose themselves in a collective, professional personality – to let themselves be cast in a mold. Yet this mold does not seem to do away with what is useless or even unpleasant about some personalities. We cling to our eccentricities and our selfishness, but we do so in a way that is no longer interesting because it is after all mechanical and vulgar.

I have fallen into the great indignity I have written against – I am a contemplative who is ready to collapse from overwork. This, I think, is a sin and the punishment of sin, but now I have got to turn it to good use and be a saint by it somehow.

Teaching wears me out. Like Ezechiel I am in a big hurry to show all my treasures to the Babylonians. Not that the novices and the young monks are Babylonians in their own right – but relative to me and my treasures they might just as well be. And yet what can I show them, or what can I share with them? There is so little one can communicate. I talk my head off and they seem to be listening but, when I ask them questions, I find they have been listening to somebody who wasn't there, to stories I never told them. They have received messages I never intended them to hear. While I talk, they sit there perhaps imagining they like what I say – and all the while they are building up myths of their own upon a few fragments of words that came out of me. I am astonished at their constructions. But in the end I think I am astonished that I am able to say anything at all that passes from me to some other mind in the universe except God's.

The terrible thing is the indignity of thinking such an endeavor is really important. The other day, while the new high altar was being consecrated, I found myself being stripped of one illusion after another. The ceremony took two hours and the choir was only allowed to sit there and watch it as a spectacle. Active participation was not only not encouraged, it was forbidden. I suppose they want the consecration to go off in good order. But anyway there I stood and sat with my eyes closed and wondered why I read so much, why I write so much, why I talk so much, and why I get too excited about the things that only affect the surface of my life. I came here eight years ago and already knew better when I arrived. But for eight years I have obeyed the other law in my members and so I am worn out with activity – exhausting myself with proclaiming that the thing to do is rest. *In omnibus requiem quaesivi . . .* [In all things I sought rest . . .]

December 22, 1949

Yesterday, the Feast of St. Thomas, was, as I think, an important day. It was warm and overclouded and windy but tranquil. I had a kind of sense that the day was building up to some kind of deep decision. A wordless decision, a giving of the depths and substance of myself. There is a conversion of the deep will to God that cannot be effected in words – barely in a gesture or ceremony. There is a conversion of the deep will and a gift of my substance that is too mysterious for liturgy, and too private. It is something to be done in a lucid secrecy that implies first of all the denial of communication to others except perhaps as a neutral thing.

I shall remember the time and place of this liberty and this neutrality which cannot be written down. These clouds low on the horizon, the outcrops of hard yellow rock in the road, the open gate, the perspective of fenceposts leading up the rise to the sky, and the big cedars tumbled and tousled by the wind. Standing on rock. Present. The reality of the present and of solitude divorced from past and future. To be collected and gathered up in clarity and silence and to belong to God and to be nobody else's business. I wish I could recover the liberty of that interior decision which was very simple and which seems to me to have been a kind of blank check and a promise.

To belong to God I have to belong to myself. I have to be alone – at least interiorly alone. This means the constant renewal of a decision. I cannot belong to people. None of me belongs to anybody but God. Absolute loneliness of the imagination, the memory, the will. My love for everybody is equal, neutral and clean. No exclusiveness. Simple and free as the sky because I love everybody and am possessed by nobody, not held, not bound. In order to be not remembered or even wanted, I have to be a person that nobody knows. They can have Thomas Merton. He's dead. Fr. Louis, he's half dead too. For my part my name is that sky, those fenceposts and those cedar trees. I shall not even reflect on whom I am and I shall not say my identity is nobody's business because that implies a truculence I don't intend. It has no meaning.

Now my whole life is this – to keep unencumbered. The wind owns the fields where I walk and I own nothing and am owned by nothing and I shall never even be forgotten because no one will ever discover me. This is to me a source of immense confidence. My Mass this morning was transfigured by this independence.

———

They are pulling down the horse-barn. The traxcavator was tethered to it, in the rain, after dinner. The barn was already half in ruins. And house upon house shall fall. The roof was down in a hoisted heap, spreading its red old wings clumsily over the wreckage of the stables. The other half of the barn was tied to the monster and ready to fall. The stone pillars were already crooked and awry. When I was at work, I could hear the engine roar but did not hear the fall of the old building.

I seek no face. I treasure no experience, no memory. Anything I write down here is only for guidance because of my constant gravitation away from solitude. It will remind me how to go home. Not to be like the man who looked in the glass and straightaway forgot what manner of man he was. But, at the same time, not to be remembering myself lest I come to remember the person I am not.

As I rediscover solitude, prayer in choir becomes difficult again. But the other day – Tuesday at the Night Office – Psalm 54 had tremendous meaning for me. I felt as if I were chanting something I myself had written. It is more my own than any of my own poems. There is nothing I have ever written or could write that expresses so completely the depths of my own soul than these verses:

> *Cor meum conturbatum est in me, et formido mortis cedidit super me.*
> *Timor et tremor venerunt super me, et contexerunt me tenebrae.*
> *Et dixi: Quis dabit mihi pennas sicut columbae et volabo, et*
>   *requiescam?*
> *Ecce elongavi fugiens; et mansi in solitudine.*
> *Exspectabam eum qui salvum me fecit a pusillanimitate spiritus, et*
>   *tempestate.*
> [My heart is troubled within me: and the fear of death is fallen
>   upon me.
> Fear and trembling are come upon me: and darkness hath
>   covered me.
> And I said: who will give me wings like a dove, and I will fly and
>   be at rest?
> Lo, I have gone far off flying away; and I abide in the
>   wilderness.
> I waited for him that hath saved me from pusillanimity of spirit
>   and a storm. (Psalms 54:5–9)]

It is terror that is driving me into solitude. Love has put drops of terror in my veins and they grow cold in me, suddenly, and make me faint with fear because my heart and my imagination wander away from God into their own private idolatry. It is my iniquity that makes me physically faint and turn to jelly because of the contradiction between my nature and my God. So that yesterday, for example, I thought I would fall with the ciborium, distributing Communion to the brothers. But last night in the middle of the night I was awake for an hour and a half and the last line I have quoted there was verified. All five lines are truer of my life than anything I have ever written, and this gives me great confidence in the liturgy. This is the secret of the psalms. Our identity is hidden in them. In them we find ourselves and God. In these fragments he has revealed not only Himself to us but ourselves to Him. *Mittit cristallum suam sicut buccellas.* [He sendeth his hail like morsels (Psalms 147:17).]

December 23, 1949

St. Augustine, of Adam in Eden: *vivebat fruens Deo, ex quo bono erat bonus* [He lived in the joy of God, and by the power of this good he was good himself].

It is very quiet now in the vault where I pause in my work on the *City of God.* I am supposed to be doing a preface for Random House. The work feeds me, strengthens me, knits my powers together in peace and tranquility. The light of God shines to me more serenely through the wide open windows of Augustine than through any other theologian. Augustine is the calmest and clearest light.

Now I listen to the watch ticking on the table. It loses time, but nobody cares. A train whistled out in the valley a moment ago, but now everything is silence except for the faint clanking of ropes against the metal flagpole in the garden, as they move in the wind.

Sunlight on the table. *Bolletino Bibliografico Internazionale* (a book catalog), [Ambroise] Gardeil, *La Structure de l'âme,* on inter-library loan from the Catholic University. Father Bartholomew, all smiles, is shooting the second volume on microfilm and I will soon let him take the first. I liked the passage where Gardeil thought it necessary to defend himself against the charge of having become an Augustinian. The whole first volume is on Augustine. [Fulbert] Cayré's book (*La Contemplation augustinienne*) is here too. Kenneth Patchen's Dark Kingdom. Henry Suso in French. *Le Paradis Blanc* (with pictures of La Val Sainte, the Swiss Charterhouse), Saint John of the Cross, red and green false leather, in Spanish, Tauler, [Henri] De Lubac,

Belière, *Renascence*, Dom Jean Leclercq on Saint Bernard, *Études Carmé-litaines*, Dom Anselme Stolz, and [Jean] Daniélou on Origen, John of Saint Thomas in Raïssa Maritain's translation. Jacques Maritain's *Quatre Essais sur l'esprit dans sa condition charnelle*, and a College Handbook of Composition lent to me by the Infirmarian, which I ought to consult some day.

[Fra] Angelico's *Annunciation* on a postcard Clare Luce sent from Flo-rence, and Giotto's *Flight into Egypt* on a Christmas card from the Poor Clares in New Mexico. The sun shines in a very happy room this morning in which a monk is where he belongs, in silence, with angels, his hand and eye moved by the living God in deep tranquility. The watch ticks: but per-haps there is after all no such thing as time.

> *(Lux mundi Dominus cum potestate venit.)*
> . . . *in anima tota tranquillitas.*
> *Nihil omnino triste, nihil erat inaniter laetum*
> . . . *nulla ex cupiditate vel timore accidebat bonae voluntatis offensio,*
>   *gaudium verum perpetuabatur ex Deo in quem flagrabat*
>   *caritas de corde puro* . . . *De Civitate Dei*, XIV, 26 PL
>   41.434.

> [(The Lord, the Light of the World, cometh with power.)
> . . . in his soul was all tranquility.
> There was nothing at all of sadness in him, nothing of empty
>   joy
> . . . Nothing of cupidity or fear stood in the way of his good
>   will as an obstacle, but his true joy was ever renewed out
>   of the depths of God for Whom he burned with charity
>   in his pure heart . . .]

(Late afternoon.) The quiet of the afternoon is filled with an altogether different tonality. The sun has moved altogether around and the room is darker. It is serious. The hour is more weary. I take time out to pray, and I look at the Angelico picture, feeling like the end of Advent, which is today. *Ecce completa sunt omnia quae dicta sunt per angelum de Virgine Maria* [Behold all things are fulfilled which the angel spoke of about the Virgin Mary] – that was the antiphon after the Benedictus this morning. For about eight minutes I stayed silent and didn't move and listened to the watch and won-dered if perhaps I might not understand something of the work Our Lady is preparing.

It is an hour of tremendous expectation.

I remember my weariness, my fears, my lack of understanding, my dimness, my sin of over-activity. What is she preparing: have I offended her? What is coming up? She loves me. I reject emotion about it. Her love is too tremendously serious for any emotion of which I might be capable. Her love shapes worlds, shapes history, forms an Apocalypse in me and around me: gives birth to the City of God. I am drawn back again into liturgy by a sense of my great need. I look at the serene, severe porch where Angelico's angel speaks to her. Angelico knew how to paint her. She is thin, immeasureably noble, and she does not rise to meet the angel. But I have here what is said to be a relic of her veil. Mother, make me as sincere as the picture. All the way down into my soul, sincere, sincere. Let me have no thought that could not kneel before you in that picture. No image. No shadow. I believe you. I am silent. I will act like the picture. *Ecce completa sunt* [Behold, everything is brought to an end]: it is the end of Advent and the afternoon is vivid with expectancy.

Perhaps I have found an answer to this mysterious thing. It is a certain strange presence of Our Lady, who is here before Jesus is here. That would be the solution suggested in [Jean] Daniélou's article in *Dieu Vivant 10* [*"La Vierge et le temps,"* Dieu Vivant *10*, (1948): 17–34].

She is here, and she has filled the room with something that is uniquely her own, too clean for me to appreciate. She is here, with the tone of her expectancy. There is nothing wrong in writing it, for it is she who makes me write it down.

December 24, 1949. Christmas Eve

Constantes estote, videbitis auxilium Domini super vos. [Persevere, and you shall see the help of God descend upon you.]

Daniélou quoted something from Abbé [Jules] Monchanin – an unpublished document on the sweet and terrible virgins adored in India – dealers of death and of pleasure or of asceticism and wisdom.

But our Lady's virginity – contained the Word of God, the Virginity of God.

She kept all His words in her heart which was therefore immaculate and was established in virginity by marriage to God.

She comes bringing solitude and society, life and death, war and peace, that peace may come out of war and that my solitude may place me somewhere in the history of my society. It is clear to me that solitude is my vocation, not as a flight from the world, but as my place in the world, because for me to find solitude is only to separate myself from all the forces that destroy me and destroy history, in order to be united with the Life and Peace that build the City of God in history and rescue the children of God from hell.

Christ is to be born. He is the hermit Who is the center of history. He has made His solitude the Heart of society – Cross and *Agape*, Sacrifice and recovery, death and love. Virginity is therefore both terrible and necessary. Without it I do not live. Without it no fruitfulness. Tomorrow I am born of a virgin in order to die of virginity and draw all things to Christ.

The best thing for me is a lucid silence that does not even imagine it speaks to anybody. A silence in which I see no interlocutor, frame no message for anyone, formulate no word either for man or paper. There will still be plenty to say when the time comes to write, and what is written will be simpler and more fruitful.

December 27, 1949. Feast of St. John

On Christmas day I walked in the woods and discovered many things I had never known before about the contour of our land – you can see the country from the knobs now because the trees are all bare.

Yesterday Fr. Cellarer lent me the jeep. I did not ask for it, he just lent it to me out of the goodness of his heart, so that I would be able to go over on the far side of the knobs. I had never driven a car before. *Once* [underlined twice] or twice at St. Bonaventure's I took lessons. Fr. Roman tried to teach me to drive a little broken down Chevvie he had. Yesterday I took the Jeep and started off gaily all by myself to the woods. It had been raining heavily. All the roads were deep in mud. It took me some time to discover the front-wheel drive. I skidded into ditches and got out again, I went through creeks, I got stuck in the mud, I bumped into trees and once, when I was on the main road, I stalled trying to get out of the front-wheel drive and ended up sideways in the middle of the road with a car coming down the hill straight at me. Thank heaven I am still alive. At the moment I didn't seem to care if I lived or died. I drove the Jeep madly into the forest in a happy, rosy fog of confusion and delight. We romped over trestles and I sang, "O Mary, I love you," went splashing through puddles a foot deep, rushed madly into the underbrush and backed out again.

Finally I got the thing back to the monastery covered with mud from stem to stern. I stood in choir at Vespers dizzy with the thought, "I have been driving a Jeep."

Father Cellarer just made me a sign that I must never, never, under any circumstances, take the Jeep out again.

This morning at the beginning of Matutinal Mass Reverend Father passed a note around the choir that Brother Owen was dead. He had a heart attack last night and they took him to the hospital this morning about three, and he died a half hour after arriving there. He was about seventy-six years old, but had not been in the monastery much longer than I. He was a novice when I came and I remember he was very ill in the infirmary in Lent, 1942, when I was up there. He was a good, quiet, holy brother.

December 28, 1949. Holy Innocents

We buried Brother Owen this afternoon. It was a beautiful afternoon, as warm as May. The funeral was after None and the procession went out, as usual, through the Chapter room. On the way around the apse of the Church we passed the bench under the first cedar tree. I remember Brother Owen sitting there, all by himself, on the day of his solemn profession. No one came to see him. His family was in Ireland. In fact he was in the country under the wrong kind of visa and was in some technical trouble about it. I believe he was even formally placed "under arrest" (in the monastery of course) by the FBI for a while. Good simple brother! Of all the people in the world to be arrested! Fr. Edward was responsible for him in case he broke jail. He was going about mending clocks and working in the smithy as usual. Nobody knew he was at odds with the G-men. But anyway, I remember him sitting there peacefully that afternoon after his solemn vows. It was one of those summer feast days, like the Assumption.

December 29, 1949. St. Thomas of Canterbury

At collation I was preoccupied with a momentous problem: I happen to know that at horse-races they have what they call a starting-gate. I have seen this in the movies. I remember it as a series of superimposed wires and the whole system flies up into the air with a jerk when the starting bell rings and all the horses dash off down the track. All right. Here is the problem. Eating our bread and raisins I began to wonder what happened to the horses that got too eager and had their noses between the wires when the gate flew up in the air. Must be pretty disconcerting for the horse. Probably make him lose the race. On the other hand, suppose the jockey held the horse too far back in order to help him from getting caught in the gate . . . and so on.

I got around to thinking that I must tell the orientation class that the most important thing in the spiritual life is *balance*. I have told them that already, and I shall tell them again. That balance made me think of Equipoise. I couldn't remember whether "Equipoise" was the name of a famous horse or the name of a famous yacht. I decided on "horse" and then . . . came the problem.

Perhaps we set too little store by light in our interior life here – stress the will to the exclusion of understanding. If we just "will" without being able to judge between right and wrong, perfection and imperfection, we tend to get ourselves into little neurotic alleys in which all spiritual life stagnates and dries up.

So I am thinking of the possibilities of, say, spiritual narcissism in our life. An article in the *Études Carmélitaines* set me on this track. I wonder how much of that there is in my enthusiasm for solitude! Perhaps quite a lot. Yet there is nothing very new in the diagnosis: it is a concept St. Bernard was well aware of, although he didn't know that particular term. Narcissistic solitude as a substitute for the responsibility of living with people. Yet at the other pole is the crass activism that delights in company and noise and movement and escapes the responsibility of living at peace with God. Our whole life must be a dialectic between community and solitude. Both are tremendously important, and our contemplative life subsists in the fruitful antagonism between these two terms.

Which reminds me that yesterday a miraculous catch of books came in from France – J[ulian] Green's *Journal*, H[ans Urs] Von Balthasar on Maximus the Confessor, Roland de Piny's *Journal de Cellule*, [Paul] Claudel on *Ruth and the Apocalypse*, and several other books, and finally *La Mort de Jean Madec*, which sets forth in chapters one and two the antithesis that so concerns me. It looks like a book to recommend to Jay Laughlin for New Directions.

December 30, 1949

Tomorrow is St. Sylvester's and another year is over. I wish I knew what I had done to justify my existence this year – besides collect royalties with which the monastery supports General Motors by buying new trucks. There is only one thing – and that is better than anything else I have done in my life. For six months I have been saying Mass. That one fact is teaching me to live in such a way that I do not care whether I live or die.

Yet there is a sinful way of being prepared to die: to live in the midst of life, at the source of life, and to feel in your heart that cold taste for death that is almost ready to refuse life – the dead rot of *accedia* that eats out your substance with discouragement and fear!

I wonder if there are not hundreds of people in monasteries with that most pitiable of sicknesses. It makes you wish you could get something respectable, with a real pain attached to it, like cancer, or a tumor on the brain.

I like the Augustinian themes in [Brice] Parain's *Mort de Jean Madec* [Paris, 1945] yet I would not know whether it was a good novel. To me it is a good novel. The only other novel I have read in the eight years I have been here is [Graham] Greene's *Heart of the Matter* and I read only half of that. Then I read bits of *The Loved One* and a few pages of *Brideshead Revisited*. Oh, and then *Les Illuminés* about Dom Alexis [Presse] and his secession from the Order's monastery at Boquen. Only read a few pages of that, too.

I like Kenneth Patchen's *Dark Kingdom*, but it does not do anything beyond interesting the surface of my mind. It does not make a deep impression and it cannot because it is only poetry. The only books that move me deeply are the Bible, St. John of the Cross, *The Cloud of Unknowing*, and a few others like that: Tauler, St. Augustine – parts of St. Bernard – St. Gregory of Nyssa.

December 31, 1949

Let us run by patience to the fight proposed to us.

Looking on Jesus, the author and finisher of faith, who, having joy set before Him endured the cross, despising the shame and now sitteth on the right hand of the throne of God.

For think diligently upon Him that endured such opposition from sinners against Himself that you be not wearied, fainting in your minds.

For you have not yet resisted unto blood, striving against sin . . . Persevere under discipline for God dealeth with you as with sons . . .

But if you be without chastisements, whereof all are made partakers, then are you bastards and not sons.

Hebrews, c. 12 [:1–5]

I spent the whole day, morning and afternoon work, trying to reestablish the appearance of order in the vault. It took all that time to clean up the piles of ragged envelopes full of notes and manuscripts, the accumulated books and copies of *La Vie Spirituelle*. I even had one *Life* and two *Atlantic Monthlies* stuffed under one of the closets. The *Life* was the one with Waugh's article on the Church in America and the *Atlantic* was an issue with two of my poems in it. I hadn't looked at them, though, because I hadn't had time and because almost everything with a picture or an advertisement suggesting secular life makes me ill to look at. The whole business finally made a nice bonfire. Turned in some twenty books to the library, sent off a lot of old galley proofs to Sister Thérèse and Fr. [Terrance] Connolly to save myself the trouble of burning them, and finally the place began to look neat. I like to feel that there is something almost ascetic about those two clean tables. I wonder how long it will last. I am hoping that I can start the new year with more discipline in my work and in everything – once again trying to tighten up and simplify things and work more slowly and more thoroughly.

Evelyn Waugh got Burns, of Hollis and Carter, to send me a copy of Ward Fowler's *Modern English Usage* as an incentive to clean up my prose style, if I can be said to possess a prose style. I am resolving to use it. That is one of my New Year's resolutions, along with a return to the Stations of the Cross daily and regularly after Chapter – or sometime – at least once a day.

Before it is too late I want to say that my three Masses Christmas morning were three of the best things that have ever happened in my life. I took plenty of time – perhaps too much time, not realizing that Fr. Pius was waiting to say his three Masses after me at the same (Sacred Heart) altar.

Before we got up at five-thirty, in the lovely sleep that follows Lauds of Christmas morning, I had been dreaming of my Masses. I dreamed I was driving to a new foundation we were to make on the Pacific coast, somewhere in the Northwest. And I was going to say my three Masses in three different Churches in three different towns on the way, and each would be a big step nearer to some inexpressible happiness in union with God. The way I felt about where I was going, in the dream, makes me think of a few dreams I had about going away to be a Carthusian – which is all over now.

January 2, 1950

I have entered the new and holy year with the feeling that I have somehow, secretly, been granted a new life and a new hope – or a return of the old life and hope I used to have. I hope it is something deeper than the spurious exaltation that follows mixt on feast days when we have strong coffee.

Since it has lasted until today, I do not think it is just a result of yesterday's coffee.

The contemplative life becomes awfully thin and drab if you go for several days at a time without thinking explicitly of the Passion of Christ. I do not mean, necessarily, meditation, but at least attending with love and humility to Christ on the Cross. For His Cross is the source of all our life and without it prayer dries up and everything goes dead. When I was in the novitiate I used to make the Way of the Cross regularly every morning after Chapter (at least in winter; after None in summer) and I kept this up too as a young professed. Lately I have been making the Stations only rarely, assuming that my Mass was quite enough, and that for the rest, silent prayer was better. But it turned out that I just wasted time, turned over the pages of a book, sat on my behind. It is better to make the Way of the Cross; and for me it is very simple – a matter of absorption, of letting myself be held.

A saint is not so much a man who realizes that he possesses virtues and sanctity as one who is overwhelmed by the sanctity of God. God is holiness. And therefore things are holy in proportion as they share What He is. All creatures are holy in so far as they share in His being, but men are called to be holy in a far superior way – by somehow sharing His transcendence and rising above the level of everything that is not God.

January 3, 1950

In the natural order, perhaps solitaries are made by severe mothers.

There is a beautiful passage on manual labor in *La Mort de Jean Madec*. It tells me one reason why I like the book so much. I am secretly reading it as a new and more interesting edition of the Cistercian *Spiritual Directory*.

Solitude is not found so much by looking outside the boundaries of your dwelling, as by staying within. Solitude is not something you must hope for in the future. Rather, it is a deepening of the present, and unless you look for it in the present, you will never find it.

The fact that the Holy Father has proclaimed this a Holy Year means that he has turned it over to Our Lady and that she will make her influence felt in many ways that will make us glad and, with her near us, we will run in the ways of God's commandments. I had not planned to speak of her yet in orientation. But I was talking about grace and it would be foolish to talk of grace without talking of her. Instantly the love of her filled the room.

Wide-eyed attention. You could feel the quiet. There was a different sense of peace – deeper than before: the peace of children who are at home and satisfied. And I feel as if I had contracted a new spiritual relationship with them all – novices yesterday, professed today. It is as if we had all discovered something new to love in one another, something more innocent and perfect than any of us had seen before. This year Our Lady will bring a deeper union of charity in the Mystical Body of Christ where those who live by her will be speaking to one another of her love.

January 4, 1950. Octave of the Holy Innocents
The tide of feasts has ebbed. We are left without grace and without any celebration – a comfortable condition. Now we go forward into the new age, walking in simplicity: our hearts are dilated with faith and obedience. The Innocents have saluted us. Last night at the Magnificat, *when we sang their antiphon* [underlined twice], *O Quam Gloriosum* [O how glorious is the Kingdom in which the Innocents rejoice with Christ], I envied them. I would have wept, but I am as dry as a stone. Thank heaven for it. Tears are not for our choir.

There has been no sun in the sky in 1950, but the dark days have been magnificent. The sky has been covered with wonderful black clouds, the horizon has been curtained with sheets of traveling rain. The landscape has been splendidly serious. I love the strength of our woods in this bleak weather. And it *is* bleak weather. Yet there is a warmth in it like the presence of God in aridity of spirit, when He comes closer to us than in consolation.

On Sunday, that is on New Year's Day, I took one of the two raincoats that hang in the grand parlor for the use of the monks, and went out into the woods. Although I had not at first determined to do so, I found myself climbing the steepest of the knobs, which also turned out to be the highest – the pyramid that stands behind the head of the lake, and is second in line when you begin to count from the southwest. Bare woods and driving rain. There was a strong wind. When I reached the top, I found there was something terrible about the landscape. But it was marvelous. The completely unfamiliar aspect of the forest beyond our rampart unnerved me. It was as though I were in another country. I saw the steep hills, covered with black woods and half-buried in the storm that was coming at me from the southwest. And ridges traveled away from this center in unexpected directions. I said, "Now you are indeed alone. Be prepared to fight the devil." But it was not the time of combat. I started down the hill again feeling that perhaps after all I had climbed it uselessly. Half way down, and in a place of comparative shelter, just before the pine trees begin, I found a bower God had prepared for me like Jonas' ivy. It had been designed especially for this moment. There was a tree stump, in an even place. It was dry and a small cedar arched over it, like a green tent, forming an alcove. There I sat in silence and loved the wind in the forest and listened for a good while to God.

After that I quickly found my way into the gully that leads through the heart of the hills to Hanekamp's house. Hanekamp is the hermit who comes down to Mass in the secular church. He used to be a monk here. I saw him Christmas Eve, kneeling at the communion rail in his black beard, and he reminded me – quite unreasonably – of [Bob] Lax. He does not really look like Lax at all. I came home walking over the shelves of shales that form the bed of the creek. Our woods are beautiful. The peace of the woods steals over me when I am at prayer.

January 7, 1950

I wanted to write down an incident that happened New Year's eve, in the afternoon.[50] I was sitting by the ruins of the old horse barn, looking down at the bleak pasture, the cedars, the enclosure wall, the woods and then that little heavenly vista of far hills in the southeast. It was grey. Hunters were in the outside orchard. I saw them going into the woods. White pants and brown pants. They were not very serious hunters because they were talking all the time. Their talk echoed all through the wood. Their dog was far ahead of them, barking and barking. Soon they just stopped in the middle of the road and talked. But the dog ranged from one end of the wood to the other, barking. It was easy to see that the whole hunt was a lie. The dog was after nothing. Neither were the hunters. Suddenly the one with the white pants climbed up on the enclosure wall. He stood on top of it with his gun. It was all an act. "Well, I am standing on the wall. I am preparing to shoot all the rabbits as they go by. My dog will rout them out and they will all come running past this point in the wall in an orderly procession. From my point of vantage I will easily be able to pick them off one by one."

---

[50] A week after this journal entry, in a letter dated January 14, 1950, Merton writes to his agent, Naomi Burton, that he is working on a journal for publication. Thus, at least by the entry dated January 7, 1950, Merton's journals are becoming artifacts of conscious self-presentation for a future audience. Merton begins blurring any line that might have previously existed between his journals as spontaneous diaries of remembrance and as conscious, semi-fictional reconstructions of the self, autobiography as a work of art.

The whole universe knew that, as soon as he fired the gun, he would fall off the wall backwards into the enclosure, perhaps into the dirty old bathtub full of rain water and spring water and green weeds which is placed there as a horsetrough.

Meanwhile I was in an equivocal position. I began to wonder if perhaps I was expected to resent his presence on top of the enclosure wall. Was I supposed to act like a responsible member of society, stand up, wave my arms and shout, "Hey!" and make guttural sounds signifying, "Get down off the wall!" Naturally he knew I could not *talk* to him. But we came to an understanding. I allowed him to gather, by my immobility, that I was invisible. I permitted him, however, to deduce, from the fact that I looked in his direction, that I entertained towards him and the universe he represented an abstract, disembodied, and purely official good will. So there we stayed. He sat on top of the wall, hunting, and I sat on a board reading, meditating on eternal truths, or what you will. I believe I must have had some book or other with me, just as he quite clearly had a gun. Both were simply factors in a disguise. I don't know who he was. I am not quite sure I knew who I was. In neither case did it matter.

Soon the dog came inside the enclosure, through a hole under the wall, and ran about barking and wagging his tail with mongrel optimism. Then the three colts ran from the other end of the pasture to investigate the dog. White pants spoke to his companion, "Call that dog." Then he picked himself up and walked off stiffly, eastward, along the top of the wall. I do not know what became of him. If I had watched, I might have ascertained.

Not a shot was fired. I did not turn a page of the book I had with me. Not a drop of rain fell. Not a bird sang. Ours is a comfortable world, without either science or wisdom.

January 8, 1950

The dialectic between silence and utterance. We have to keep silence for two reasons: for the sake of God and for the sake of speech. These two reasons are really one: because the only reason for speaking is to confess our faith in God and declare his glory.

In practice, a priest lives in silence – or should have much silence in his life – for the sake of his Mass. The Canon of the Mass should emerge from that silence with infinite power and significance. Mass is the only thing we really say. The Office is a preparation for that utterance. Everybody in the universe is tongue-tied except the priest, who is able to speak for them all. Speaking for the people, he also speaks to God. He unites men and God in a few simple sentences that are the words of God. To be exact, he unites men and God in the act of consecration in which he pronounces the Word that is uttered by the Father – he causes the Word to be present in time in a new way, in a new state – incarnate and sacrificed.

We should realize very clearly when to speak and when to keep silent. It is important to speak seven times a day, in praising God. It is above all important to confess Him before men at Mass. Here we must speak and know what we are saying and realize at least some of its implications. Here everything in us, body and soul, must speak and announce our faith and utter the glory of God. Here speech is more important than life and death. Yet it does not have to be loud on earth – only heard in heaven, and somehow signified in time. It must be simply and essentially public.

But it is terribly important to keep silence. When? Almost all the rest of the day. It is essential that priests learn how to silence all their routine declarations of truths that they have not yet troubled to think about. If we said only what we really meant, we would say very little. Yet we have to preach God too. Exactly. Preaching God implies silence. If preaching is not born of silence, it is a waste of time. Writing and teaching must be fed by silence or they are a waste of time.

There are many declarations made only because we think other people are expecting us to make them. The silence of God should teach us when to speak and when not to speak. But we cannot bear the thought of that silence, lest it cost us the trust and respect of men. *Dabitur [enim] vobis in illa hora quid loquamini.* [For it shall be given you in that hour what to speak (Matthew 10:10).]

January 9, 1950

There is a hunger for humiliation that is nothing else but a hunger for admiration turned inside out. It is a sincere desire to be despised, and it is perhaps a desire cherished by those who might be saints. But is it not a desire to be admired by angels? And is it not a desire to be admired by angels *only?* And is it not a desire to despise what men admire? And do we not often despise what men admire in revenge for having to do without it? And is it not even more humiliating to be admired for what men admire than to be despised for what the angels admire?

Reading the sixth chapter of *La Mort de Jean Madec* – where Blaise is summoned before the *conseil de discipline* [disciplinary committee] for having sabotaged all his school work as an experiment in mysticism – I began to tremble and I had to force myself to go on reading. It really frightened me. And that is significant. It was a relief to see the solution and relief, at last, that he settled down to behave. Also the scare reminded me again of Job and his friends. And now it reminds me that perhaps, after all, I am not Job and that the fear of being Job (which is, of course, the desire to be Job) always gets me in trouble.

Why, for instance, do I tremble when I teach? Partly perhaps because I am in love with the monks and novices and want (that is to say fear) to be immolated in their presence. But why should I want to be immolated in the presence of those I rightly love? Because, I suppose, I want to kill what is not right in my love for them – for I am bound to love them without being in love with them. It all throws a very interesting light on the problem of solitude and humility and silence and sacrifice. The solution is in the Mass where all these things are found and where we are all alone together and proclaim God together and are offered to God together and all the rough ways are made plain and the crooked ways are straightened and the hills are leveled and the valleys filled. That is why I am a voice crying in the wilderness, yet not in the wilderness because I am laced flesh and bone into the body of my brethren and. . . .

January 10, 1950

In the Chapter room, each day now for three days, Albert de Quevedo electrifies the monks. He stands somewhere near a microphone, but never talks into it even though he may run all around it. He tells us how we can make a success in the religious life. Sometimes he is very funny. Nobody in the world has ever made the monks burst into such spontaneous explosions of laughter. To sum up his message: he reminds us that we have wills and that we have destinies. That those who fail to work out their destinies fail through fear. For because of fear the vital power that is in them turns against them and devours them instead of fulfilling them.

It is a strange thing that monks should forget that they have wills and how much a will can do with the grace of God. It is also a strange thing that they should forget they have minds, that they have grace, that God loves them, that the service of God is simple and easy. We forget all this because we surround ourselves with the arguments of death – and then die because we have convinced ourselves that we have to. It is true, we must die. But not without having first confessed our faith and confessed it completely and given the full testimony God asks of us, in order to be what He wishes to make of us, and to have eternal life.

January 11, 1950

For the first time in my life I am finding you, O solitude. I can count on the fingers of one hand the few short moments of purity, of neutrality, in which I have found you. Now I know I am coming to the day in which I will be able to live without words, even outside my prayer. For I still need to go out into this no-man's land of language that does not quite join me to other men and which throws a veil over my own solitude. I say, "live without words." By words I mean all the merely human expressions that bind men to one another. I mean the half-helpless and half-wise looks by which they seek one another's thoughts. But I do not abdicate all language. For there is the word of God. This I proclaim and I live to proclaim it. I live to utter the Mass, the Canon that implicitly contains all words, all revelation, and teaches everything. One day I thought I heard thunder all around me when I was saying it, but that was fancy. It is the Canon and at the words of Consecration that all solitudes come to a single focus. There is the City of God gathered together in that one Word spoken in silence. The speech of God is silence. His Word is solitude. Him I will never deny, by His grace! Everything else is fiction, half-hiding the truth it tries to reveal. We are travelers from the half-world of language into solitude and infinity. We are strangers. Paper, I have not in you a lasting city. Yet there is a return from solitude to make manifest His Name to them who have not known it. Then to re-enter solitude and dwell in silence.

January 12, 1950

It is in deep solitude that I find the gentleness with which I can truly love my brothers. The more solitary I am, the more affection I have for them. It is pure affection, and filled with reverence for the solitude of others. Solitude and silence teach me to love my brothers for what they are, not for what they say. Now it is no longer a question of dishonoring them by accepting their fictions, believing in their image of themselves which their weakness obliges them to compose, the wan work of communication. Yet there will, it is true, always remain a dialectic between the words of men and their being. This will tell something about them we would not have realized if the words had not been there.

Blaise est toujours saisi d'une sorte d'épouvante qui dégénère ensuite en pitié lorsqu'il s'aperçoit à nouveau que l'art est tant nécessaire aux hommes. [Blaise is always seized with a kind of panic which afterwards degenerates into pity when he realizes anew that art is so necessary for men.] *J. Madec*, p. 273.

———

La Mort de Jean Madec is a magnificent tract against angelism.

It is a tract on transcendence and immanence. It says that God is above all and yet in all. I thought the theme of purity of heart was in it. Now I find it is indeed the heart of the book. *Madec, le seul homme pur, . . . Madec n'aurait pas eu besoin de la guerre pour être malheureux. Madec n'avait jamais eu besoin de vouloir qu'il y eût la guerre pour ravoir le silence.* (280) *C'est en lui seul que tout pouvait renaître.* ["Madec, the only pure man, . . . Madec never would have needed a war to make him unhappy. Madec never would have needed a war to make him recover silence. (280) It was in him only that everything could come back to life.]

The solution of the problem of language in I Cor. xiii: "If I should speak with the tongues of men and angels . . .

Solitude is not merely a negative relationship. It is not merely the absence of people or of presence with people. True solitude is a participation in the solitariness of God – Who is in all things. Everything is related to God but God is related to nothing. His solitude is not a local absence but a metaphysical transcendence. His solitude is His Being. For us, solitude is not a matter of being something *more* than other men, except by accident: for those who cannot be alone cannot find their true being and they are less than themselves. For us solitude means withdrawal from an artificial and fictional level of being which men, divided by original sin, have fabricated in order to keep peace with concupiscence and death. But by that very fact the solitary finds himself on the level of a more perfect spiritual society – the city of those who have become real enough to confess and glorify God (that is: life), in the teeth of death. Solitude and society are formed and perfected in the Sacrifice of the Mass.

January 18, 1950. Feast of St. Peter's Chair in Rome
Last Saturday, the Feast of St. Hilary, I signed a long term contract with Harcourt Brace for four books – St. Ailred, St. Bernard, *The Cloud and the Fire,*[51] and a book on the Mass. I prayed hard over it for three days, especially at the conventual Mass of the day itself which was a Votive Mass of Our Lady. It is all her doing and her business.

I did not expect this legal act to have the effects it did. I put the thing in the mail, completely reconciled to my position and determined to waste no more time turning around and around like a dog before lying down in the

---

[51] Published as *The Ascent to Truth.*

corner that has been prepared for me by Providence. That means the final renouncement forever of any dream of a Charterhouse or a hermitage. God will prepare for me His own hermitage for my last days, and meanwhile my work is my hermitage because it is *writing* that helps me most of all to be a solitary and a contemplative here at Gethsemani.

But the real reason why the signing of this contract left me in peace, with no more desire to rationalize my fate, was the fact that all my days are now completely ordered to God's work in prayer and teaching and writing. I have no time to be anything but a contemplative or a teacher of the contemplative life. And because I still know so little of my subject, I can no longer afford to waste time dramatizing my approach to it in mental movies or interior controversies. There is nothing left for me but to live fully and completely in the present, praying when I pray, and writing and praying when I write, and worrying about nothing but the wish and the glory of God, finding these as best I can in the sacrament of the moment.

January 20, 1950. Eve of St. Agnes

> O small St. Agnes dressed in gold
> With fire in rainbows round about your face,
> Sing with the seven virgins in my Canon.
> I am your priest,
> My feet upon forget-me-nots.
> Come home, come home, O centuries
> Whose soundless islands ring me from within.
> Whose saints come down this winter morning's iris
> To wait upon our prayers with hyacinths.
> I speak your name with wine upon my lips,
> Drowned in the singing of your lovely catacomb.
> I sink this little frigate in the Blood of peace
> And put my pall upon the cup
> Working our peace, our mystery, who must
> Run down and find you, saint, by St. John's stairs.
> No lines, no globes,
> No compass, no staring fires,
> No candle's cup to swing upon my night's dark ocean,
> where no signals claim us.
> O small St. Agnes dressed in martyrdom
> With fire and water waving in your hair.

January 21, 1950. St. Agnes

I mean to write down the words of responsories that made a deep impression on me at the night office. Meanwhile I probably will not get time.

St. Bernard's Sermon 110, *De Diversis*, which I stumbled on just now by accident when I set out to look for the Sermon for the Fourth Sunday of November, is an interesting commentary on *La Mort de Jean Madec*.

He laments the poverty of man. We are so indigent, we even need words. (Consequence: the more words we need, the greater our poverty.) We need them not only to communicate with others, but also with ourselves. For we are not ourselves. We are divided, exiled from ourselves. We have to communicate with the self from which we are separated. *Nempe cor meum dereliquit me et necesse habeo ad meipsum nempe ad me alterum loqui.* [My heart has indeed forsaken me, and I need to speak to myself as to another self.] Here too, our indigence is proportioned to our division. *Atque id interim tanto amplius quanto minus sum adhuc reversus ad cor . . . unitus mihi ipsi.* [And in the meantime I must do this all the more widely as I am still far from returning to my heart . . . or becoming unified with myself.] (Corollary – if I become silent without finding myself – damnation: atheism. Like Madec's father.) But the solution (as Brice Parain says) is *charity* [underlined twice]. When we shall all unite in one perfect man, the Mystical Body which [Émile] Meersch says St. Bernard neglects. *Opportune igitur linguae interibunt.* [Tongues will become silent at the right time.]

January 23, 1950

Some time ago the editors of *The Month* sent me Egon Wellesz' *Byzantine Music and Hymnography*, with some other books, in partial payment for some pieces of *Elected Silence*[52] they had published. I have not yet attempted to read the book. This morning I persuaded Frater Francis de Sales to play me some of the hymns on the organ in Church. I could not follow the Greek words. But for the rest of the morning I had the flavor of the hymns in my mind. There were surprising movements of sprightliness in them. Their melody dances more than Gregorian. In fact, dancing is not a notion one would connect with Gregorian at all. I would like to hear them sung by a great choir of monks with black beards.

Frater Francis de Sales is a very charming person, one of the novices. He came from another Order where he was in the seminary studying theology. He is an intellectual and a musician, and on his account I asked Jay Laugh-

---

[52] The British version of *The Seven Storey Mountain*.

lin to send down a copy of Rimbaud's *Season in Hell*, for he wanted me to ask for it. Fr. Urban, the novice master, is still trying to decide if he should have it. Frater likes the incunabula and comes in to work on them. He is one of the most comprehensible sign-makers in the monastery. He likes St. Ailred and I am trying to get him completely interested in our Fathers.

January 26, 1950. Feast of St. Alberic

Msgr. Sheen sent us another special edition of the *Études Carmélitaines* and Fr. François de Sainte Marie, who writes and edits Carmelite books at Bruges, sent among other things a book I had been longing for with great desire and which is now out of print, *Les Saints Déserts du Carmel* by F. Benedict Zimmerman. But in this issue of the *Études* are many exciting things, including an article on Hindu mysticism by a Swami, which makes me regret all the rash judgments I ever made of Hindu mysticism. It is surprising how much Yoga has in common with St. Bernard – at least in the psychology of mysticism. Self-knowledge is the first step in the ascent. The problem of liberating our deeper energies from base preoccupations which enfeeble and dissipate them. I have been talking about Sermons 81 and 82 *in Cantica* in the Mystical Theology class as a general view of the psychological situation which Cistercian Mysticism starts out with. Then also in the *Études* is another even more exciting article than the one by the Swami: this time by a Russian Orthodox monk on the Orthodox approach to contemplation. The emphasis on technique, on bodily control, on interior discipline in both Oriental and Orthodox mysticism makes me realize how supremely indifferent we are to techniques. I have never had any method of contemplation. St. Benedict's *"simpliciter intret et oret"* ["he may simply enter (the oratory) and pray" (RB 52:4)]. Yet I find I had discovered all by myself many things they talk about and insist on, especially that Hesychian business about attention concentrated in the "heart" and all energies flowing down uniting there to produce a smooth and effortless absorption that is held in being by God "within our own heart . . ."

January 27, 1950

*Nam gloria nostra haec est, [testimonium conscientiae nostrae] quod in simplici-
tate cordis et in sinceritate Dei, et non in sapientia carnali sed in gratia Dei, con-
versati sumus in hoc mundo [abundantius autem ad vos.]* [For our glory is this, the testimony of our conscience, that in simplicity of heart and sincerity of God, and not in carnal wisdom, but in the grace of God, we have conversed in this world; and more abundantly toward you.] (II Cor. I:12).

The more I read St. Bernard and the Cistercian Fathers, the more I like them. There was a time when I was tempted not to like St. Bernard at all (when the *Sermons in Cantica* were read in the refectory, during my novitiate, I was irritated by the breasts of the Spouse.) I think that now, after eight years and more, I am really beginning to discover the depth of St. Bernard. This is because I have realized that the foundation of his whole doctrine, which is expressed as clearly as anywhere in Letter 18, is that God is Truth and Christ is Truth Incarnate and that salvation and sanctity for us means being true to ourselves and true to Christ and true to God. It is only when this emphasis on truth is forgotten that St. Bernard begins to seem sentimental.

Today, in a moment of trial, I rediscovered Jesus, or perhaps discovered Him for the first time. But then, in a monastery you are always discovering Jesus for the first time. Anyway, I came closer than ever to fully realizing how true it is that our relations with Jesus are something utterly beyond the level of imagination and emotion.

His eyes, which are the eyes of Truth, are fixed upon my heart. Where His glance falls, there is peace: for the light of His Face, which is the Truth, produces truth wherever it shines. *Aequitatem vidit vultus ejus.* [His face has beheld justice.] There too is joy: *adimplebis me laetitia cum vultu tuo.* [You will fill up joy in me with your face.] *Signatum est super nos lumen vultus tui; dedisti laetitiam in corde meo.* [The light of your face is sealed upon us; you have given joy to my heart.] And again, *oculi tui videant aequitates* [may your eyes behold justice]. And he says to those he loves, *firmabo super te oculos meos* [I will fix my eyes upon you]. His eyes are always on us in choir and everywhere and in all times. No grace comes to us from heaven except He looks upon our hearts.

The grace of this gaze of Christ upon my heart transfigured this day like a miracle. It seems to me that I have discovered a freedom that I never knew before in my life and with this freedom a recollection that is no impediment to moderate action. I have felt that the Spirit of God was upon me, and after dinner, walking along the road beyond the orchard by myself under a cobalt blue sky (in which the moon was already visible), I thought that, if I only turned my head a little, I would see a tremendous host of angels in silver armor advancing behind me through the sky, coming at last to sweep the whole world clean. I did not have to mortify this fantasy as it did not arouse my emotions but carried me along on a vivid ocean of peace. And the whole world and the whole sky was filled with wonderful music, as it has often been for me in these days. But sitting alone in the attic of the garden house and looking at the stream shining under the bare willows and at the distant hills, I think I have never been so near to Adam's, my father's, Eden. Our Eden is the Heart of Christ.

January 30, 1950

"Let grace come and let the world pass away. Hosanna to the Son of David."

These words are from the *Didache*. They come from the thanksgiving after Communion. It also says, "Permit the prophets to make thanksgiving as much as they desire."

Let grace come. Jesus, Your Name is on my heart. Your Holy Name is on the tower of my heart.

The Greeks say that interior silence is not perfect unless it is centered upon the Name of Jesus. For they do not love silence for its own sake. Silence for its own sake is only death. Love silence for the sake of the Word. There are surprising affinities in the theology of the Oriental Church with the thoughts in *Jean Madec*. They understand that there is a solitude that is death and a solitude that is life. The solitary who is dead is walled up in his own self. The solitary who lives is eternally delivered from this world and is present to God. *Dum sumus in corpore peregrinamur a Domino . . . audemus autem, et bonam voluntatem habemus magis peregrinari a corpore, et praesentes esse ad Dominum.* [While we are in the body we are absent from the Lord . . . we are confident, I say, and have a good will to be absent from the body, and to be present to the Lord (2 Corinthians 5:6).]

Let grace come and let this world pass away. Jesus living in my exhausted heart.

January 31, 1950

And now I am thirty-five years old. Thirty-five is a nice number. It is the middle of an average life. If I live the other thirty-five years, I hope they will be as happy as this year – 1950 – has so far been.

Hesychasm – is that the English word for it? – has been my latest discovery. I came across it in the *Études Carmélitaines*. It is a discipline, a technique to dispose the mind and body for contemplation. It is, or was, practiced by monks in the Orthodox Church. It is something like Yoga, but not so formal or so detailed. And it centers upon the Name of Jesus (as the Yogis concentrate all their powers upon the Mantra or Name of God) or on words of Scripture. What I like about it is that it reflected the spirituality of the Fathers of the Desert (cf. Cassian's conference on the *Deus in Ad-*

jutorium is not really comprehensible, I think, without reference to the kind of interiorization implied by hesychasm) and of the Greek Fathers. But it also throws light on St. Bernard's sermon on the Holy Name. St. Bernard's prayer must have been something like hesychasm. I thought of that especially this morning at the Offertory of the Conventual Mass. It was a votive Mass of St. Bernard and we sang, *Fasciculus myrrhae dilectus meus mihi; inter ubera mea commorabitur* [A bundle of myrrh is my beloved to me: he shall abide between my breasts (Song of Songs 1:12)], and St. Bernard applies this line to the *memoria Christi*, constant awareness of the Passion.

Hesychasm distinguishes what one might call psychosomatic centers of recollection. I believe this concept can be very practical. Contemplation, whether we like it or not, realize it or not, involves some bodily reactions. No matter how spiritual it may be, it tends to call into play certain big nerve-centers. It even centers around them. Physically speaking I know nothing about it, but I have begun to realize that a contemplation that seems to involve a deep, powerful radiation around or below the solar plexus, can become rather animal eventually in its intoxication, or it can involve us in sensuality and eventually sleep. It is almost always a lazy, lethargic contemplation, and I think it confuses and degrades the higher powers, though in a subtle way. Contemplation, on the other hand, that has its physical "focus" in the summit of the heart, is powerful and clean and long-lived and simple. To have the Name of Jesus focused at that point in living faith can become the secret of a simple and pure and intense recollection that might last for hours and easily merges into infused prayer.

February 1, 1950. St. Ignatius Martyr

Magnificent chapters in Gardeil substantiate my own conclusions arrived at independently concerning this business of "hesychasm." Prescinding from the question of breathing or not breathing, which is purely mechanical and dangerous without direction, I find myself happy with the realization that it is *all important* to enter into yourself and concentrate all the supernatural energies of your soul on God made present to you through the Name of Jesus – or at least God dwelling in you by grace. But to think of His name is the quickest way, perhaps, to enter into His presence.

February 5, 1950. Septuagesima

Beautiful hard frost. The sun was coming up and throwing soft mother-of-pearl high-lights on the frozen pastures of Olivet. And the birds were singing. And I thought of the lessons from *Genesis* in the night office on the creation of the world. Really, I think the thought of creation is neglected in the Septuagesima liturgy. We should see this day as the beginning of the Easter season, not as a sort of "feast of original sin." It is the first chapter in the Church's Theology of the Redemption. It begins sensibly by telling us of the joy for which we were created by God – the joy which Jesus died to restore to us.

I spoke on joy in Chapter – Day of Recollection conference.

It helps me to speak, although I hate speaking. My classes help me very much, too. I have learned more theology in three months of teaching than in four years of studying. But it helps my prayer, too – at least in the sense that it inviscerates the mysteries of our faith more deeply into my soul. It is very important to live your faith by confessing it, and one of the best ways to confess it is to preach it. Yet I abhor preaching as such and would never speak in public except under obedience.

I think the chief reason why we have so little joy is that we take ourselves too seriously. Joy can only be real if it is based on truth, and since the fall of Adam, all man's life is shot through with falsehood and illusion. That is why St. Bernard is right in leading us back to joy by the ways of truth. His start-ing point is the truth of our own insignificance in comparison with God. To penetrate the truth of how utterly unimportant we are is the only thing that can set us free to enjoy true happiness. This morning, before speaking, I felt very strongly the limitations imposed on me by my absurd desire to speak well as if it somehow *mattered*, as if something *important* depended on it! In-stead of simply desiring to speak as best I could in order to please God.

Father Abbot recalled the sentence of the householders in the day's Gospel, "Am I not free to do what I please [Matthew 20:1–16]?" These are God's words. It seems to me that they, too, contain the secret of all joy, be-cause there is no joy without liberty and these words contain the truth that makes us free. To accept them is to enter into the infinite liberty of God. To accept them! Dear God, that I may fully accept them and love them and live them! If everything that pleases You, pleases me, where will there be any sorrow left, or any [indecipherable word], or any captivity?

February 7, 1950. St. Romuald

Today in orientation class I shall try to make all the young professed happy by showing them two wonderful photographs of St. Martin-du-Canigou where St. Romuald was a hermit – or near which he was a hermit.

Reading _Genesis_ again, I am fascinated by mysterious discoveries. What was this fountain that sprung up in the center of the earth and watered it all before man was made and before there was even any rain? (II:6)

Importance of the notion of "Generations" in _Genesis_. The transmission of the totality of life from a common Father to a whole race. All life goes back to God the Father and Creator of all; but the great Patriarchs contained in themselves the pattern of their race's destiny. All this is fulfilled in the "Seed of Abraham," Christ, the New Adam, in Whom we all live to God, in the Holy Ghost. He brings back all things to God. _In ipso condita sunt universa et in ipso omnia constant._ [In Him all things have been made and in Him all things exist.] In Him all things came forth from God.

February 10, 1950. St. Scholastica

I went to the garden house attic, as usual, after dinner. Climbed up the ladder, observing all the hoes and shovels lying on the floor. I made my way through the litter of old stove-pipes and broken strawberry boxes to the chair by the window. On the chair is a sack stained with either paint, creosote, or the blood of something slaughtered. I opened the small window (a pane fell out one day when I let it slam. I can still see the fragments of glass on the red roof of the shed below.)

Today it was wonderful. Clouds, sky overcast, but tall streamers of sunlight coming down in a fan over the bare hills.

Suddenly I became aware of great excitement. The pasture was full of birds – starlings. There was an eagle flying over the woods. The crows were all frightened, and were soaring very high, keeping out of the way. Even more distant still were the buzzards, flying and circling, obscuring everything from a distance. And the starlings filled every hill tree and shone in the light and sang. The eagle attacked a tree full of starlings, but before he was near them, the whole cloud of them left the tree and avoided him and he came nowhere near them. Then he went away and they all alighted on the ground. They were there moving about and singing for about five minutes. Then, like lightning, it happened. I saw a scare go into the cloud of birds, and they opened their wings and began to rise off the ground and in that split second, from behind the house and from over my roof, a hawk came down like a bullet, and shot straight into the middle of the starlings just as they were getting off the ground. They rose into the air and there was a slight scuffle on the ground as the hawk got his talons into the one bird he had nailed.

It was a terrible and yet beautiful thing, that lightning flight, straight as an arrow, that killed the slowest starling.

Then every tree, every field was cleared. I do not know where all the starlings went. Florida, maybe. The crows were still in sight, but over their wood. Their guttural cursing had nothing more to do with this affair. The vultures, lovers of dead things, circled over the bottoms where perhaps there was something dead. The hawk, all alone in the pasture, possessed his prey. He did not fly away with it like a thief. He stayed in the field like a king with the killed bird, and nothing else came near him. He took his time.

I tried to pray, afterward. But the hawk was eating the bird. And I thought of that flight, coming down like a bullet from the sky behind me and over my roof, the sure aim with which he hit this one bird, as though he had picked it out a mile away. For a moment I envied the lords of the Middle Ages, who had their falcons, and I thought of the Arabs with their fast horses, hawking on the desert's edge, and I also understood the terrible fact that some men love war. But in the end I think that hawk is to be studied by saints and contemplatives because he knows his business. I wish I knew my business as well as he does his.

I wonder if my admiration for you gives me an affinity for you, artist! I wonder if there will ever be something connatural between us, between your flight and my heart, stirred in hiding to serve Christ, as you, soldier, serve your nature. And God's love a thousand times more terrible! I am going back to the attic and the shovels and the broken window and the trains in the valley and the prayer of Jesus.

February 11, 1950. Our Lady of Lourdes

I have just finished a week of Masses at Our Lady of Victories, where scholastics receive Communion, and where I always make my thanksgiving, and where John Paul received his first Communion. I once might have thought that it would disturb my own prayer to have to leave the altar and give Communion to others. As if this function made my union with Jesus less perfect because less recollected. I now see what a terrific error that is. I feel as if my Communion were somehow less perfect when I cannot turn and give the Body of Christ to one of my brothers also. There is something a little cold and rigid about Sunday Masses for that reason. The servers all go to Communion at Matutinal Mass. And you are left stranded with no one to share your Mass with you visibly and tangibly. But there is much more exterior beauty and warmth, humanly speaking and spiritually also, when ten or twelve monks approach the altar at the *Agnus Dei* and receive the *Pax* and kneel there waiting for Our Lord to come to them from your hands. There is an inexpressibly sweet and deep joy in giving Communion to your brothers, whom you know and love so well and so completely after years with them in the monastery. I can think of no private satisfaction that could surpass or even approach this sharing.

Father Abbot no longer lets me say Mass in the secular Church. The reasons are obvious. But it used to be a great joy for me to give Communion to a dozen strangers. You feel a profound interest in these faces, these overcoats, the old ones and the young ones. You wonder what their troubles are, their joys and their sorrows. You love them and you want them to be happy and it is very, very good to be able to give them Christ, their freedom, and pray that they might go away to be great saints if they are not that already.

February 12, 1950. Sexagesima

Gardeil is magnificent. He unties all knots – above all the central and Gordian knot of the problem of knowledge and love in contemplation. Pure love perfected and intensified by wisdom is the immediate impression made by the Substance of God on the soul. He is known in this love; He is directly experienced in this effect without the medium of any idea or species, infused or otherwise. Nothing can represent Him as He is.

Can one say that by love the soul receives the very "form" of God? In St. Bernard's language, this form, this divine likeness, is the identity we were made for. Thus we can say, *caritas haec visio, haec similitudo est* [charity is this vision and this likeness]. By love we are at once made like to God and (in mystical love, pure love) we already "see" Him (darkly), that is we have experience of Him as He is in Himself, and wisdom is the *medium quo cognoscitur* [the medium by which He is known]. The soul knows God in this effect, this love, in the same way (analogously) as it knows itself in the consciousness of its own existence and activity. I know God because I am aware of His life in me and the Spirit bears witness to my conscience crying out that God is my Father. Thus by loving we know God in God and through God, for in love the Three Divine Persons are made known to us, sealing our souls, not with a static likeness, but with the impression of their infinite Life. Our souls are sealed with fire. Our souls are sealed with Life. Our souls are sealed with the character of God as the air is full of sunshine. Glory to God in the highest, who has sealed us with His holiness, sealed us all together, brothers in His Christ. Amen. Amen.

February 14, 1950

Abraham and Lot could not live together because they had too many possessions. The whole world was hardly big enough for both of them with all
their tents and all their flocks and all their fighting shepherds. The language
the Vulgate uses for this situation is *Erat [quippe] substantia eorum multa, et
nequibant habitare communiter* [For their substance was great, and they could
not dwell together (Genesis 13:6)]. They could not live in common. They
could not live the common life. Their possessions made it impossible for
them to live as brothers unless they lived apart (*Genesis* 3:8–9). Their riches
imposed on them an imperfect solitude. Lot retired to the paradise that surrounded Sodom, and this was marked for destruction because of great sins.
Genesis is the history of the breaking up of the human race, originally one
man in Adam. But, in this dispersal, the seed of unity is saved.

February 16, 1950

We do not appreciate the writing of a St. Bernard or an Ailred of Rievaulx
because the Scripture references mean little or nothing to us. And since all
that they write is apt to be a tissue of Scripture passages, we miss the point
altogether. We must first possess something of their knowledge of Scripture and have the same *pictures* in our imagination, and something of the
same associations. Ailred's first Palm Sunday Sermon is delightful and full
of meaning, but only on condition that you see Jeremias' two baskets of
figs and know their import, and see the ark coming through the divided
Jordan carried by the Levites and followed by Josue's army, and have in
mind at the same time the expectation of Christ's final triumph and entry
into Jerusalem with all the elect, and the expectation of being one of them.
And your heart must burn with love and faith that sees all Scripture and all
history pointing to this last event which is the fulfillment of everything.

February 21, 1950. Forty Hours

This is the third day of the forty hours. I have been rather dry and a bit
scared. Also I had the flu. Last night at collation the Servant of the Refectory astonished me by bringing me a saucer of badly scrambled eggs (pale
white) with a sign that Fr. Prior had sent them to me. The first time such
an astonishing favor has befallen me in my eight years in the monastery.
Last night in the dormitory I kept waking up when the novices came in and
out after changing guard before the Blessed Sacrament. Between these
awakenings I dreamt in relays of a curious ascetical problem. I dreamt that
Reverend Father was to take a party of religious to Haiti, not for a new

foundation, but just for a trip. In fact I think they were to give a concert in the Cathedral of Port-au-Prince. I had asked permission, on impulse, to go with them: not to sing, but just to see Haiti. The permission had been granted. And now the substance of the dream was this: I kept debating in my mind whether God wanted me to take back my request and just stay home. I dreamt of many factors in the problem and finally asked Reverend Father what I should do and he said he wished I would make up my mind once and for all. But the thing was still not settled. I was coming to the conclusion that I would not go, when it turned out that all the others had already (probably) left. At this point I found myself in the Chapter room, where there was a line of barber chairs and the monks were getting shaves and haircuts in grand style. Then the bell rang and ended the dream.

February 22, 1950. Ash Wednesday

Grey skies. It rained in the night. The lights all went out at ten to two and we said Matins and the Office of the Dead and Lauds and Prime with many candles. The flu has not left me and my head is full of glue and I can't breathe and I am worried that my neighbors in choir may finally become completely exasperated at my snorting. And yet Ash Wednesday is full of joy. In a minute we will sing None and go barefoot to get ashes on our head to remember, with great relief, that we are dust. God is all our joy and in Him our dust can become splendor. The great sorrow of mankind is turned to joy by the love of Christ, and the secret of happiness is no longer to see any sorrow except in the light of Christ's victory over sorrow. And then all sorrow contributes somehow to our happiness. Thus I sit here in the corner of the upstairs Scriptorium and look out the window at the bare trees in the *preáu* and the grey guest house wall and at my own little happy corner of the sky.

February 23, 1950

I came out of choir yesterday morning after the distribution of the ashes and put on our shoes and socks in the cloister and walked off to work with a keen desire to read some very obscure, very disciplined poetry – something like William Empson. Of course I was much too busy. But this unexpected hunger still strikes me as having been clean and even somehow appropriate to Lent. Only at the end of work did I get a minute, and I came away from the archives with *Four Quartets* and read the magnificent opening to "Little Gidding" which, though not obscure, exactly suited my mood.

February 25, 1950

The wind buffets the side of the building bringing perhaps more rain and more influenza. I had a second dose of influenza after Ash Wednesday. As a professor I take the frustulum along with my students. I had to find another Lenten penance, so after the frustulum I am studying moral theology for a few minutes every day. It is four years since I had my course in Moral. I have forgotten everything that Caius and Titius did. I no longer know the ins and outs of Bertha's marriages. And I never learned the comic rhyme that helps the young confessor to call to mind the ecclesiastical censures he cannot absolve unless he gets around them by mean of Canon 2254.

February 27, 1950. Monday of the First Week in Lent

The song of my Beloved beside the stream. The birds descanting in their clerestories. His skies have sanctified my eyes, His woods are clearer than the King's palace. But the air and I will never tell our secret.

The first Sunday of Lent, as I now know, is a great feast. Christ has sanctified the desert and in the desert I discovered it. The woods have all become young in the discipline of spring, but it is the discipline of expectancy only. Which one cut more keenly? The February sunlight, or the air? There are no buds. Buds are not guessed or even thought of this early in Lent. But the wilderness shines with promise. The land is first in simplicity and strength. Everything foretells the coming of the holy spring. I had never before spoken freely or so intimately with woods, hills, buds, water and sky. On this great day, however, they understood their position and they remained mute in the presence of the Beloved. Only His light was obvious and eloquent. My brother and sister, the light and the water. The stump and the stone. The tables of rock. The blue, naked sky. Tractor tracks, a little waterfall. And Mediterranean solitude. I thought of Italy after my Beloved had spoken and was gone.

The difference between the moral life and the mystical life is discovered in the presence of contradiction. When we move ourselves as men, morally, *humano modo* [in the human way] we end up by choosing one horn of the dilemma and hoping for the best. But when we are moved by God, mystically, we seem to solve the dilemma in ease and mystery by choosing at the same time both horns of the dilemma and no horn at all, and always being perfectly right. For instance in choir: orders are to keep up the pitch and make a pause of two beats at the mediant of the psalm verse, but the cantors drop the pitch and rush through the mediant at one beat. Moral activity: either a) follow the cantor with a pure intention, or, b) shut up and concentrate on praying, also with a pure intention. Mystical activity – the dilemma suddenly ceases to matter. You both follow the cantor and pray and find God and suddenly, if God wills, the contradiction disappears, and some attempt begins to be made to keep the rules.

March 1, 1950

I enter into this gay, windy month with my mind full of the Book of Josue. Its battle scenes are like the Bayeaux tapestry. The books of the Old Testament become to us as signs of the zodiac and Josue (somewhere near the spring equinox) stands at the opposite side of heaven from Job (when all the sky is sailing down to darkness). Here is a book for spring. The sap is rising in the trees and the children of God are winning all their battles. And it is Lent, when Josue (our Christ) calls the five captive kings cowering from their cave and makes his officers put their feet upon their necks. Then the five kings go to the gibbet. That is what Jesus makes us do to the five senses in Lent. Josue is a conqueror and even a poet. He lifted up his head in the heat of battle and sang a two-line poem to the sun and moon and they both stood still. For the sun did not go down towards Gabaon nor the moon to the valley of Ajalon. Even so, Christ has delayed the day of Judgment, giving us time to do penance, until the number of the elect be filled and His enemies be all cast down into the lake of fire.

So Josue is my favorite epic. I like it better than *The Iliad*, infinitely better than Virgil or the *Song of Roland*. It is a clean book, full of asceticism. The field is swept clean of all enemies. Only one small band of them remains: the Gabaonites with their old shoes and their mended wineskins and their dry bread, who pretended to have come from a distant land to make a treaty, knowing the children of God had been told to clear the Promised Land of all its natives. And all the while their town was just over the hill.

God leans over Canaan and spreads His hand over the mountain and sends forth His armies to work His work, to plant the seed of His promise and blessings in a safe land overflowing with plenty. And the enemies of Israel fight with their long swords in their hands and their football noseguards over their faces and their eyes questioning the brilliant and cloudless heavens. (Look, outside the window the sky is beginning to be very blue and the sun is dazzling on the white side of the Church! I love this corner of the upstairs Scriptorium, where God has prepared me a bower under the iron mezzanine, face to face with sermons which no one ever reads.)

God is delighted with the victories of Josue because they are victories of obedience and, therefore, this is a Benedictine book. But the whole Pentateuch is Benedictine.

St. Bernard (who entered Cîteaux with a whole family of Josues) says that God cannot truly take pleasure in our acts unless He is their cause. And if He is their cause, He must also be their end. *Insipida namque Deo et insulsa quodammodo nostra obedientia seu etiam patientia est nisi omnium quae vel agimus vel patimur ipse sit causa.* [Our obedience and even our patience are tasteless and without savor to God unless He be the cause of all our actions and all our suffering.] We know if He is the cause of our actions when we know the end for which we perform them. And the purer the love with which we seek His glory, the more completely does He live and act in us. This purity is the sign of His action. By our bright armed virginity that suffers no compromise with idols, we glorify Him by the victories of Josue and march into the mountains of contemplation, our Promised Land.

March 3, 1950

The Christian life – and especially the contemplative life – is a continual discovery of Christ in new and unexpected places. And these discoveries are sometimes most profitable when you find Him in something you had tended to overlook and even despise. Then the awakening is purer and its effect more keen, because He was so close at hand, and you neglected Him. I am ashamed that it has taken me so long to discover Him in moral theology. I thought moral theology was just a set of rules by which one learned to keep imperfect Christians and sinners from getting mad at the Church and walking out altogether – as if they needed to know how much they could get away with and still remain Christians. That may perhaps be the way moral is applied in practice sometimes, but my attitude had something a little impious about it. In assuming that moral theology was almost necessarily an apparatus devised for pharisees, I myself have been a pharisee, and more than that, a fool as well. St. Theresa had much more sense because she had much more humility. Because we are all sinners, moral theology applies to us all, not as a system of sanctions and restrictions, but as a means to finding Christ in God's commandments and in His sacraments.

What would be the use of ascetical and mystical theology for a priest who was slovenly and careless and unintelligent in the reception and administration of the sacraments? I am studying the Sacrament of Penance and find to my shame that I have had far too little appreciation of it, precisely because I looked at it only from an ascetic point of view without a real foundation in moral.

March 5, 1950

My Lent is all influenza and chant and moral theology. Got rid of the flu last Sunday and received it back again last Friday. It is going in waves through the community. In choir and in Chapter we are swept by periodic storms of nose blowing that drown all words and all thought. And I am trying to teach the novices to desire mystical prayer and the mystical life, and they write me notes saying, "We do not understand, but it is not your fault. What books should we read?"

Chant. Professor Lefèvre came from Paris to teach us chant. He made his debut on my birthday, January 31st. On that day he gave a lecture in the chapter room full of illuminating remarks about the relations of Gregorian chant to Gnostic, Hebrew, and Greek music. Ever since then we have been practicing furiously every day: voice training in Chapter every morning for fifteen minutes or more after Lauds and Prime. Special classes in the interval after dinner. Schola practice at the beginning of the afternoon work. No more time for anything. The choir as a whole improves a little. Professor Lefèvre fills the air with lamentations, declaring that we think only of quantity and know nothing of quality, and it is true: the old business of solving all problems by energy. Hard work and good will are not enough: taste and intelligence and a certain sensitiveness to musical _values_ are what we lack most of all. Without them we are more or less wasting our time, and all our earnest labor. The professor is probably going to have a nervous breakdown as a result of all this, but he is not as unhappy as he pretends to be and has moments of real elation when, by accident, we do not sing like iron machines.

He directs the _Salve_ standing on a little stool near the presbytery step, while one of the brother oblates points a flash-light at him. This throws a dim target of light on his stomach, which is a distraction to everybody. The _Salve_ is a little less heavy and perhaps even a little less harsh.

Two and three and four years ago, when I complained bitterly that there was no time in my life for contemplation, all these demands on our time and energy would probably have upset me considerably. For now it is actually a fact and not a fancy that we get very little time to ourselves. But it no longer upsets me, and I find that I am not tempted to waste time in complaining. That shows that I must have learned something since ordination.

So now the time I would have lost in fretting and beefing is spent in something more like union with God.

March 7, 1950. St. Thomas Aquinas

The feast of the Angelic Doctor falls this year on the Tuesday of the Second Week in Lent. So there is a very striking coincidence in the liturgy: the Gospel of the feast speaks of the true Teachers, the salt of the earth, who "do and teach" and whose *works* shine before men, and the Gospel of the feria speaks of the false teachers who have sat in the chair of Moses and have not done the works of Moses, that is, they have not kept the laws they talked about. Yet they have done works that have been dazzling in the eyes of men and have done them *in order to shine* before men, to have the first places in the synagogues and to be called Rabbi. The theme of both the feast and the feria is summed up in the line, *Unus est Magister vester, Christus* [Only one is your Teacher, Christ]. It is Jesus who teaches us in and through St. Thomas Aquinas and in St. Bonaventure and St. Augustine and in all the other doctors of the Church. We have no other Father and no other Doctor than Christ. It is Jesus whose works shine in the lives of the saints. It is Jesus Who manifests Himself to us through the words of the Fathers and the theologians. The false doctors preach their own sanctity and Christ is not seen or heard in them. But the true preach the sanctity of Christ, and He shines through them. He it is whose Truth has made them holy.

March 8, 1950

There are lovely things in the little new *Kyriale* that has come over from France. Since I haven't yet had time to read the *monitum* [prefatory note], I do not know where this *Kyriale* comes from or what it is all about. All I know is that the Carmelite nuns in Cherbourg are responsible for the peculiar lettering. The *Kyriale* itself, of course, is ours. I am sure this Celtic sounding *Kyrie* we sang yesterday for the first time, on St. Thomas' day, was never in our old books. The same Mass has a haunting *Sanctus* and the *Agnus Dei* is very poignant. This morning we were practicing a *Kyrie* for Paschal time which is one of the freshest and most beautiful things I have ever seen. I could easily believe that it was dictated by the angels (as so many of St. Dunstan's antiphons are supposed to have been. I believe it, too, of the sixth tone *Gaudent in coelis* which we sang for Sts. John and Paul – John Paul's feast day). This Easter *Kyrie* has all the cleanness not only of spring but the new leaven of Christ's rising. It has the pure savor of another life, the savor of heaven, of the Risen Savior walking the earth with men in His new Kingdom. My whole being longs for Easter, to drink this wine new with Christ in His Father's Kingdom, and to know that Christ our Pasch is slain and that our life is in heaven and [I] hear the Spirit crying out in my heart (as He cried out at Mass this morning) that we are the Sons of God and God is our Father.

March 9, 1950

Before dawn. Red Mars hangs like a tiny artificial fruit from the topmost branch of a bare tree in our *préau*.

Today: commemoration of the forty martyrs who were left naked on the ice to freeze to death in Armenia. They helped me once at St. Bonaventure, in tribulation. It is cold here, too. Fingers numb, during Mass at Our Lady of Lourdes altar, in the back sacristy, at the extreme end of the heat line, where the steam does not quite come.

Yesterday, out in the beginning of a snowstorm, dipped into the spiritual notes of Charles de Foucauld and was moved by their intensity. He speaks to God in a clear and vibrant voice, simple words, sentences of fire. This voice rings in the ear of your heart after you have put the book away and turned to others less saintly, even though they may be religious voices, too. M. Lefèvre saw I had the book and told me how, some twenty-five years ago, it had made him weep and had driven him to the seminary. From which, as he said, by the grace of God, he eventually emerged again into the world. I forget whether he has ten children or twelve.

March 10, 1950

God gives Himself to those who give themselves to Him. The way does not matter much, as long as it is the way He has chosen for us. I find that I can get just as close to God in studying the dry problems of moral theology as by reading the more burning pages of the mystics. For it is God's will that I, as a priest, should know my moral theology. Duty does not have to be dull. Love can make it beautiful and fill it with life. As long as we show lines of division between duty and pleasure in the world of the spirit, we will remain far from God and from His joy.

March 12, 1950. Third Sunday in Lent

On this grey morning when the birds sing in the rain, I proclaim that there is a sad note to our spring. We lift our eyes to you in heaven, O God of eternity, wishing we were poorer men, more silent men, more mortified.

Lord, give us liberty from all the things that are in this world, from the preoccupations of earth and of time, that we may be called to cleanness, where the saints are, the gold and silver saints before your throne.

March 14, 1950

Dawn. I looked out the window again and this time Mars is much lower down in the branches of the tree. In ten days the planet will hide behind the Church. Yesterday, St. Gregory's day, was in some ways terrible. All our time went west. Not one decent interval, barely ten minutes here and there to read or to pray. We learned an Ambrosian *Gloria* and *Sanctus* for the feast. Special schola work in the afternoon. No time to prepare classes, let alone write. Got some letters, but didn't have time to find out if they were important. No Lenten reading. The dentist, Dr. Simons, came from Cincinnati and I spent three quarters of an hour in the chair watching the buzzards circling in the grey sky over the old sheep barn while he drilled a wisdom tooth. At night my head was full of chant and my mouth tasted of silver nitrate and the tooth was sore and for some time I did not sleep.

March 15, 1950

In the Mass, in which all prayer is perfect, we talk to everybody. Sometimes we speak to the Blessed Trinity *(Suscipe Sancta Trinitas)*, sometimes to the Father *(Elevatis oculis ad Te Deum Patrem . . .)*, sometimes to Jesus the Word, sometimes to the Holy Ghost *(Veni Sanctificator)*, sometimes to the saints in heaven and sometimes to the people around us and sometimes even to ourselves, musing the presence of God – *Quid retribuam Domino? . . . calicem salutaris accipiam.* [What shall I render to the Lord? . . . I will take the chalice of salvation (Psalms 115:12–13).] If we don't talk to the angels (until the prayers after Mass), at least we talk to God about the angels who are present as His ministers and play an active part in the Sacrifice. And we talk to Him of the saints and of the holy souls in Purgatory and of the Pope and the Bishop and of all our friends. Nothing could be less private than the Mass. And yet it is also a perfect solitude.

March 16, 1950. Mid-Lent

This morning I directed the Schola and the whole choir at the Conventual Mass. It was the first time I had ever tried anything like cheironomy and at first I was scared. But it went well enough. Cheironomy is not difficult as long as you don't bother to follow any set rule. I shall never forget this

Mass as long as I live. For three nights I have sung it in my sleep. *"Salus populi ego sum dicit Dominus."* ["I am the Salvation of my people, says the Lord."] The movements of my hand might or might not have had something to do with the neums in the book. Anyway, my right arm was active. I hoped that what I was doing was also artistic. But I do not have the presumption to imagine that it was Gregorian. Yesterday at practice Professor Lefèvre said, "If the monks of Solesmes saw you, they would have a fit." Secretly, however, I am very pleased, and sometimes, when I am by myself, I direct some snatch of chant I know by heart, trying to make my hand tumble like a seagull in the wind, following the imagined music like a leaf in November, sailing earthward through the branches of the trees.

My helpers in the Schola were Frater Francis de Sales and Frater Thomas, who was a radio operator and secret service man in the navy, and Frater Martin de Porres who is colored, all three of them novices, and the other was Fr. Benedict, the Cantor of Our Lady of the Holy Ghost, who used to be a Benedictine and who is here to follow the instructions in chant.

I was in the Cellarer's new office. It is very pleasant with venetian blinds and two small rooms paneled with cedar, which smells overpowering. There is a nook for the Farm boss, and a door leads into a fair-sized warehouse, then there is a small garage to hide the Jeep in, and a larger place where trucks can drive in and unload the riches of Araby and Ophir.

Having once directed the Schola, I have been dispensed from any more special practice, and have returned to the rank and file in order to have time to prepare my classes and get something done on those four books I am supposed to be writing. In the last two weeks I have hardly been able to do any work at all, and *Orate Fratres* is waiting for an article.

But my chief joy was to escape to the attic of the garden house and the little broken window that looks out over the valley. There in the silence I love the green grass. The tortured gestures of the apple trees have become part of my prayer. I look at the shining water under the willows and listen to the sweet songs of all the living things that are in our woods and fields. So much do I love this solitude that, when I walk out along the road to the old barns that stand alone, far from the new buildings, delight begins to overpower me from head to foot and peace smiles even in the marrow of my bones.

March 17, 1950

The people of Israel were afraid to come too close to God. They wanted Moses to protect them and stand between them and God, lest God come down too close to them, and lest His fire consume them. They wanted men to reign over them, rather than God. But Gideon said to them: "I shall not rule you, neither shall my sons, but the Lord God shall rule you" (Judges VIII: 23). And when Samuel was old and the people demanded a king, God said to them, "It is not you they have rejected, but me" [1 Kings 8:7]. For a king would make treaties with other kings, and treaties meant compromise with the gods of other kings. But our God is God with whom no idol can enter into contract because there is no communion between light and darkness, between the temple of God and idols, between Pure Being and the fictions of men. For Israel, unlike all other people, was made to have no ruler and no king but God. In the end, on Good Friday, the Rulers of Israel cried out, "We have no king but Caesar."

It is St. Patrick's day. Fr. Mark, the monastery electrician, has hung up a green streamer and a picture of St. Patrick in the library doorway: and yet, he is not Irish, but Dutch. The sun is out and, during the procession, reciting the Penitential Psalms, I was praying for two nineteen-year old boys who are being electrocuted as murderers somewhere today. Word came in asking us to pray for them. *Percussus sum ut faenum et aruit cor meum* . . . [I am smitten as grass, and my heart is withered . . . (Psalms 101:5).] We are praying for another one, who is in prison for life.

March 18, 1950

This morning at Mass, read the long history of Susanna and came out of it at the end half-carried away with exultation at the triumph of Daniel for "innocent blood was spared in that day." But at Tierce and Sext – from which we have just come – I was haunted by the mercy of Jesus to the woman taken in adultery. That is the day's Gospel and the counterpart to Susanna in the Old Testament Lesson.

My soul is trying to awaken and discover again the beauty of penance. I am ashamed of having made so many confessions of my faults in the monastery with so little sorrow and so feeble a hope of doing better. I want to say, over and over again, that I am sorry. I do not know how I can go on living unless I convince You, Jesus, that I am really sorry. The psalms say this better than I ever could. I am sorry that it has taken me so long to begin to discover the psalms. I am sorry that I have not lived in them.

Their words are full of the living waters of those true tears with which You taught the Samaritan your mercy. She did not weep with her eyes, or, if she did, the Gospel does not tell us, but her simplicity and frankness won her compunction. Her penance was above all a matter of admiration: "I have found a man who told me everything I have ever done. Can He be the Christ? [John 4:29]" (Her penance misled, but it was none the less rich in compunction.)

I am sorry for having let myself become so stupid and so torpid, thinking more of myself than of what I owe to Your Love – and I owe You everything. Forgive me for paying so little attention. Without compunction and deep sorrow, contemplation is likely to be nothing more than a kind of idolatry. How can I love You if I do not know who I am and who You are? And how can I know this without sorrow. Jesus, I no longer want to have anything to do with love that forgets that it was born in sorrow, and therefore forgets to be grateful. Otherwise I will only go on lying to You, and I want to be done with all insincerity for ever and for ever.

Every day I mean to pray, especially in choir, for all the priests in the world who hear confessions and for all their penitents. I ask that everywhere this Sacrament may be administered and received in truth and justice and prudence and mercy and sorrow, and that priests and penitents may better know what they are doing and that they be filled with a great love and reverence for what they do. I ask that everywhere men may discover in themselves a great admiration for this Sacrament and may love it with their whole being, giving themselves entirely with contrite hearts to the mercy and truth of God, that His love may re-make them in His own likeness – that is, that He may make them true.

The Pharisees accused the woman taken in adultery and, when Jesus bent down to write with His finger in the dust, perhaps he meant to show them by this mystery that the judgments of men are words written in the dust, and that only God's judgments are true and just. *Judicia Domini recta, justificata in semetipsa. Rectum judicium praedicate* . . . [The judgments of the Lord are true, justified in themselves. Proclaim a right judgment . . . (Psalms 18:10).] They judged according to appearances. And because they did so, they tried to judge the Uncreated Truth by the light of their own principles. For Christ is the Truth, and they had accused the adulteress, not out of love for truth, but out of hatred for Truth. His is Justice, and they were trying to judge and destroy Him by a subversion of that technical justice which ceases to be just as soon as it ceased to express the will of

Him in Whom Justice and Mercy are one. Daniel delivered Susanna by a judgment inspired by the Holy Spirit, and Christ came down to the Temple from the Mount of Olives to deliver the adulteress with the grace of counsel. The Mount of Olives is the mount of chrism, of anointing, of inspiration and counsel and the gifts of the Holy Spirit. But the most striking thing of all about the Gospel is that, in saving the adulteress, Jesus was also saving Himself. Defending and delivering a sinner from the injustice of the legally "just," He was saving the Truth from defilement by the unholiness of the holy. For these ascetics were so holy that they hated Mercy and thus their holiness was a sin. The test of their sin was this: when Truth came to them as a Person, not as an abstraction, they rejected Him. The abstraction they clung to was then no more than a fiction because it had in it nothing of Him Whom they had decided to kill.

March 21, 1950. Feast of St. Benedict

Contemplative prayer is the recognition that we are the Sons of God, an experience of Who He is, and of His love for us, flowing from the operation of that love in us. Contemplative prayer is the voice of the Spirit crying out in us, "Abba, Pater." In all valid prayer it is the Holy Ghost who prays in us, but in the graces of contemplation He makes us *realize*, at least obscurely, that it is He who is praying in us with a love too deep and too secret for us to comprehend. We exult in the union of our voice with His voice, and our soul springs up to the Father, through the Son, having become one flame with the Flame of their Spirit. The Holy Ghost is the soul of the Church and it is to His presence in us that is attributed the sanctity of each one of the elect. He prays in us now as the Soul of the Church and now as the life of our own soul – but the distinction is only real in the external order of things. Interiorly, whether our prayer be private or public, it is the same Spirit praying in us: He is really touching different strings of the same instrument.

Down there in the wooded hollow full of cedars I hear a great outcry of bluejays, and yonder is one of the snipes that are always flying and ducking around St. Joseph's hill. In all this I am reassured by the sweet, constant melody of my cardinals, who sing their less worldly tunes with no regard for any other sound on earth. And now the jays have stopped. Their tribulation rarely lasts very long.

A third plague of flu has hit in the community. This time it is a bad one. The choir is half empty. There were so few in their stalls on the Abbot's side this night, at Vigils, that the psalms of the second nocturn were being given out by scholastics in simple vows. Sunday morning, Feast of St. Joseph, during Lauds of the Little Office towards one-thirty, Fr. Bernard collapsed on our side and was carried off to bed. He came back for Chapter and was up for a day and is now back in bed. There are too many ill for the infirmary. They lie and cough in the dormitories. Food is brought to them. They cannot touch it, for the most part. And Father Abbot this morning was forced to lift the fast. We are dispensed. There was mixt this morning after Chapter.

We have just finished High Mass. The sacristan being ill, there were not enough hosts for the communions of the novice and brothers. Fr. Urban went to get the Blessed Sacrament from the novitiate and the infirmary. Then the sanctuary is all torn up, ready to be rebuilt, according to the Ritual, with the *gradus altaris* [altar step] in the proper place. The carpenters began work yesterday. I find, by the grace of God, that carpenters no longer disturb me when I pray in Church. But now I am under the sky. The birds are all silent now except for some quiet bluebirds. But the frogs have begun singing their pleasure in all the waters and in the warm, green places where the sunshine is wonderful. Praise Christ, all you living creatures. For Him you and I were created. With every breath we love Him. My psalms fulfill your dim, unconscious song, O brothers in this wood.

I am sitting on a pile of lumber by the ruins of the old horse-barn. There is a beautiful blue haze in the sky beyond the enclosure wall, eastward and over the brow of the hill. There is going to be a new orchard there, and I see the furrows Fr. Albert has been plowing with the John Deere tractor. I guess I will stop and read Origen.

March 22, 1950

Toward the fall of night the ghosts in the community come down and stagger through the cloister on some vague business before returning to their cells. We, who are nearly as badly off as they, make them signs to ask if they are well and they reply with haggard smiles that they are better. But I have the flu again myself. I do not have it badly enough to be in bed. I am sick enough to fall asleep over a very good Lenten book (St. Theresa – Volume II) and I cannot breathe in choir and I rated a shot of penicillin this morning and I have that same old pain in my chest.

This morning in Chapter Reverend Father told us that the Abbey of Our Lady of the Valley burned down last night. The monks all escaped and no one was hurt, but the whole monastery, except for the Novitiate, was destroyed with all their books and everything. The fire started about ten-thirty last night (on the Feast of St. Benedict) in that old fire-trap of a guest-house. The monks and novices are scattered around in various religious communities in the neighboring towns.

March 25, 1950. The Annunciation

Yesterday evening I went down with a slight fever. The infirmary is full. In the dormitory there is a lot of noise to which I contribute by my unsuccessful efforts to breathe. In spite of an atomizer and whatnot, every breath demands a concentrated intensity of purpose, a firm act of will, then a snort and a gasp, followed by the earnest wish that I were dead. Fr. Vincent dug up an army cot and we put it up in St. Gabriel's room and there I sweated and slept, full of penicillin, next to the guest-house kitchen. You can tell the time, roughly, by the noise in the kitchen.

St. Gabriel's is where I am temporarily working. The vault is torn up. New book shelves are to be put in and (I secretly hope) a new floor. But St. Gabriel's room appalls me. Designed for visiting Abbots, salesmen, etc., it has its own bath and toilet. Thank heaven the splendid bed with the inner spring mattress was taken out before I fell sick. Someone left scented soap in the bathroom. When you walk into the place, you smell soap and steam heat, and you would think for all the world that you were in a hotel room in Cincinnati, and therefore the place appalls me. I have the windows wide open to let out the bourgeois smells. If it were not for the straw mattress I brought down from the dormitory, I would die of shame. I am still hoping the community will not find out where I am. However, I shaved in the private bathroom and made faces in the mirror, sang a little, and prayed God to forgive me. Am I gradually sinking once again to the Perry Street level of my existence? I said Mass at 4:20, went back to bed shivering, listened to Fr. Stephen read a very long sermon over the public address system, from Chapter, to the Brothers in the guest-house kitchen. But after mixt (in the Community refectory) I felt better. The best part of the morning was when I went to choir to sing Our Lady's Mass, but I have not been there for any of the Offices. It is distracting to say Office in the choir of the infirmary. The best Office today was None, which I said sitting in the sun in a broken down carriage behind the garden house, looking at the woods and hills, in a world of light and warmth and singing cardinals.

The terrible thing about sickness is that you tend to think you are sick. Your thoughts are narrowed down to your own poor little bitch of a body.

And you take care of her. My God, forgive me. I take care of myself too well to be a good Cistercian. True, Fr. Vincent is glad. He doesn't have to worry about me much. He came in this morning and I said I had been out in the sun. He was satisfied and went away. Yet Reverend Father encourages me to love the sun behind the garden house, where I am alone. There I sat this morning in that Bermuda carriage. (A carriage fits my most decent ideas of comfort. I feel human in a modest carriage with beautiful wheels. I forget the cursed bathroom and its scented soap.) And there, bewildered, with Fr. François de St. Marie's book about the Rule of Carmel in my hand, I wondered if I ought to try to begin my Cistercian life over again from the beginning. O my God, what does it mean to love You? What does it mean to believe in You? What does it mean that You have brought us all here? Is it after all good for me to be sitting in a carriage? Yes. I think it is good for me to sit there and bad for me to think about my sitting there rather than thinking about God. It is good to go to the Minor Mass, where I am now going, to pray for love which is the health of the soul, wherefore my soul also is sick for lack of love.

March 26, 1950. Passion Sunday

I forgot to write about how many of the monks collapsed and fell down in public places during the epidemics. One of them was old Father Alphonsus who staggered into Church on Wednesday morning, supported by Frs. Walter and [indecipherable], rang his bell and proceeded to vest for Mass at St. Thérèse's altar, where I had just finished Mass myself. In the middle of my thanksgiving I heard a commotion over there. I looked and saw them depositing Fr. Alphonsus on a bench where he sat mute and shivering, with his head bowed, pallor and sweat on his forehead. We took him to the infirmary which was already full. They put him in the bed of Fr. Sebastian, who was then saying Mass, and was more or less well enough to sleep elsewhere. Then on Tuesday afternoon, the feast, teaching an orientation class in the singing room and not feeling too well myself, we heard someone collapse in the dormitory upstairs. I never found out who it was. Fr. Prior collapsed while he was saying Mass and Fr. Edward got up to get a drink of water and passed out with the glass in his hand. They found him lying in a pool of water.

The Liturgy of Passion Sunday has never impressed me so much before. I have been talking to the orientation classes about attention and vigilance in the life of prayer, and so for the first time I noticed how important is this theme of vigilance in the Passion Liturgy. *Hodie si vocem ejus audieritis* ... [Today if you shall hear His voice, harden not your hearts (Psalms 94:8).] And that terrifying Gospel: "Everyone that is of God hears the words of God ..." [John 8:47]. The Pharisees had so hardened their hearts that, when the Messiah came, they accused Him of "having a devil." They who were the custodians of the Law and the interpreters of the word of God crucified the Word of God in the name of His own Law. It was the ones who had most thoroughly searched the Scriptures who were unable to recognize Him whom the Scriptures promised. And it happened that the twenty-eighth chapter of Deuteronomy was read in the refectory today. I wonder when I ever heard anything so moving as those curses, in the light of today's Office. "But if you dost refuse to listen to Him ..." *Hodie si vocem ejus audieritis!* And yet the Scribes and Pharisees and the Doctors of the Law thought they were listening. Perhaps the one thing that made it impossible for them to hear the voice of God when He spoke to them was their conviction that they were the only ones capable of hearing it! "Thou hast hidden these things from the wise and prudent and revealed them to little ones [Luke 10:21]." So to listen to God means, first of all, to recognize our helplessness, our stupidity, our blindness and ignorance. How can we ever hear Him if we think of ourselves as experts in religion?

March 28, 1950

This is a most peculiar disease. It pretends to leave you, but it only pretends. Actually it is only drawing back to take a good spring at you and claw you all over again. I thought at first that I was doing very well. The day after going to bed I was back in choir. I offered to sing on the Schola to replace Fr. Thomas, who was beginning to be ill, and then, after two days, I found myself worse off than before. This afternoon I finally stayed in bed for good. Why should it be a penance to stay in bed? I scarcely know. It is quiet and pleasant, and you can pray. Yet it almost takes ropes to keep me there. For instance, I am not there now. But I shall take up the breviary and say Matins and reflect with sorrow that it is hard to become a saint by taking care of your health, but that there just doesn't seem any point in dragging this thing out indefinitely either. So in the end the best thing is to do what the infirmarian wants me to do, and get ready, by God's grace, to get back entirely into the community life.

April 2, 1950. Palm Sunday

On Wednesday I picked up our bedding and moved back to the dormitory. By Saturday I was knocked out again and moved back to St. Gabriel's room. Several others who were up are all back in bed again, although most of the community seems to have recovered. I got as far as getting up at 2:45 for two days. In St. Gabriel's I sleep until 3:30 – the infirmary schedule. Fr. Vincent plied me with penicillin from every angle. I even have Penicillin chewing gum, which I chewed this morning while washing dishes, as it was my Sunday to be in the kitchen after mixt. With the new sanctuary half-finished, Palm Sunday was beautiful. But after dinner I went to bed and stayed there. I still have a cough that tries to turn me inside out.

After Vespers (I said Vespers sitting up on the cot), I at last rediscovered a moment of true solitude in the midst of the false, dead solitude of sickness in which silence is poured away in sleep or wasted in the soul's immersion in its own dead flesh.

Still, I have a new outlook on this business of being sick in bed. So much of my anxiety to be up and doing is born of human respect. Here I have a chance to be a Carthusian and I am ashamed to take it. Part of the shame comes from conscience, but part comes from vanity. And now I burn with a desire to forget all the complex stupidities that my own mind can place between me and God. If only I could somehow awaken and live in God. If only I could somehow find in myself the perfect sincerity that goes directly to Him because it is never diverted by vain reflection on things that have no substance. *Longe a salute mea verba delictorum meorum.* [Far from my salvation are the words of my sins (Psalms 21:2).] This sincerity is found in silence, because it must evade the words with which we try to give reality to the illusions of selfishness. *(Verba delictorum.)* [The words of (my) crimes.] Yet I am grateful for the solitaries who have spoken and written of themselves even though they might not have spoken or written entirely well.

April 5, 1950. Good Friday

Yesterday, Holy Thursday, it was not altogether easy to get up at two o'clock. Half the night the carpenters had been hammering the Church, trying to finish the new sanctuary before Holy Thursday, and I lay and listened to the echoing hammers and to the coughing of my neighbors in the dormitory. (I moved back to the dormitory on Tuesday.) Also, I had the sorest throat I can remember ever having had. I tied a clean handkerchief around my neck because warmth is vaguely helpful. And I lay there praying and smelling of Vapo-Rub with a green lozenge dissolving in my mouth without doing anything for the throat.

So, when the bell rang – by the time the bell rang I had actually had a few hours of what could truthfully be called sleep – I lay and debated within myself, wondering if I ought to stay in bed. But I got up and peeled off the sweaty clothes I had been sleeping in and got into something dry and staggered off to choir, and, when the Office began, instead of feeling worse, I began to feel better. I was Deacon at the High Mass, and when we were vesting and the Choir was chanting None, I felt pretty tired, but it was nice in the clean new sanctuary. The spaciousness of it is rather calming. I could hardly produce a sound while singing the Gospel, but I sang it slowly with no desire to be appreciated by anyone but Our Lord. And perhaps He was the only One who heard me. After that I was very happy. It was the first time I had stood at the clean, new marble altar in any capacity and I now know that the whole sanctuary, which is now built according to our ancient usages, is exactly what it ought to be, except the step immediately leading to the altar makes it rather difficult to give Communion. We were crowded and I thought I might tumble off the step with the paten in my hand.

Today I was back again by the garden house and in the mute solitude that is indifferent to verbal communication. The sun was warm and all the living creatures sang.

April 8, 1950. Holy Saturday

The darkness is thinning and expects the sun. Birds begin to sing. No Mass. Everything is waiting for the Resurrection.

At the end of the Night Office, when the whole choir sank into the darkness of death and chanted without the faintest light, I thought of the darkness as a luxury, simplifying and unifying everything, hiding all the accidents that make one monk different from another monk and submerging all distractions in plain obscurity. Thus we are all one in the death of Christ. The darkness that descends upon us at the end of Lauds hears us sing the *Benedictus*, the canticle of thanksgiving for the Light who is to be sent. Now He is sent. He has come. He has descended into the far end of night, gathered our Fathers, the Patriarchs and Prophets, to Himself in Limbo. Now we will all be manifest. We will see one another with white garments, with palm branches in our hands. The darkness is like a font from which we shall ascend washed and illumined, to see one another, now no longer separate, but one in the Risen Christ.

For we must see one another. Christ must be manifest in glory. His soul is now charged with the glory of victory, demanding a Body, and not only His own physical Body, but the whole Mystical Body of the elect. Jesus, how can You be so patient? How can You deny the desire of Your soul for all those centuries? His soul has desired us in the night of death in which

He has sought us and found us and united us to Himself. All history has become like the Blessed Mother, in whose womb is formed the Mystical Christ, and the last day will be Christmas and Easter and the Ascension; all Liturgy will be explained and enacted in one word; Liturgy will be the world's judgment.

Louis Bouyer has a marvelous chapter on the connection between the Resurrection and the founding of the Church. Now that the Humanity of Christ is fully divinized, a mysterious spiritual gravitation draws all humanity to Him as to its natural center (*Myst. Pasch.*, p. 372). Then, too, by His risen Humanity, the Savior communicates Himself to all men and feeds them with His Body in order that they might all grow up into the fullness of His Mystical humanity, into a perfect man (Eph. 4:13). Our destiny is to be deified by the vision of the divinity in the Risen Christ. Through His Soul and in His risen Body He reveals and communicates to us the Godhead, Essential Light. The means He has chosen for this is the Sacraments, that we may be transformed from glory to glory by the Spirit of the Lord.

April 9, 1950. Easter Sunday

The grace of Easter is a great silence, an immense tranquility and a clean taste in your soul. It is the taste of heaven, but not the heaven of some wild exaltation. The Easter vision is not riot and drunkenness of spirit, but a discovery of order above all order – a discovery of God and of all things in Him. This is a wine without intoxication, a joy that has no poison in it. It is life without death. Tasting it for a moment, we are briefly able to see and love all things according to their truth, to possess them in their substance hidden in God, beyond all sense. For desire clings to the vesture and accident of things, but charity possesses them in the simple depths of God.

If Mass could only be, every morning, what it is on Easter morning! If the prayers could always be so clear, if the Risen Christ would always shine in my heart and all around me and before me in His Easter simplicity! For His simplicity is our feast. This is the unleavened bread which is manna and the bread of heaven, this Easter cleanness, this freedom, this sincerity. O my God, what can I do to convince You that I long for Your Truth and Your simplicity, to share in Your infinite sincerity which is the mirror of Your True Being, and is Your Second Person! Only the little ones can see Him. He is too simple for any created intelligence to fathom. Sometimes we taste some reflection splashed from the clean Light that is the Life of all things: First Mass, Baptism, Easter Morning. Give us always this bread of heaven. Slake us always with this water that we might not thirst forever!

This is the life that pours down into us from the Risen Christ, this is the breath of his Spirit, this is the love that quickens His Mystical Body.

April 12, 1950. Easter Wednesday

This afternoon we were out planting trees in the woods. There is no work I can think of that would be more capable of pleasing me than this. The woods have been sadly cut. There is no real timber left there since Dom Frederic sold all our white oak to the distillery. And yet there are many trees still lying on the ground, rotting where they were cut. When the brothers bought that chain saw three or four years ago, they went off on an orgy of cutting, and felled trees on steep hillsides and in gullies without stopping to consider where a horse and wagon could get close enough to haul them away. So now we spent the afternoon putting slips of pine into the ground. Most of the monks were working south of the lake, but the Cellarer got me and we went off into that deep valley behind the lake, which is the quietest and most isolated corner of our forest, planted on a shoulder of hill where the trees were very thin and where, several Sundays ago, I entertained for five minutes the dream of building a hermitage.

For the first time I have come to understand why all the Graduals sung in the Masses of Easter week are basically the same. Easter week is the extension of the Christian eighth day, the Lord's day which is a Sabbath beyond and above our Sabbaths, because it really belongs outside time. Sunday is less the first day of the week than the eighth day in a seven-day week, which is to say that Sunday is the "day" of eternity. And so this octave signifies the eternal "day" of heaven and every day hears the return of the same melody and phrases from the same psalms of the Hallel which Jesus and His disciples sang at the Last Supper, at His passage out of the world, just as all the Jews chanted them in memory of the passage of the Chosen People through the Red Sea and out of Egypt – just as we will chant them in eternity. *Confitemini Domino, quoniam bonus, quoniam in saeculum misericordia ejus. Dicat nunc Israel quoniam bonus* . . . [Give praise to the Lord, for he is good; for his mercy endureth forever (Psalms 105:1). Let Israel now say that he is good . . . (Psalms 106:1).] because this is the NOW of heaven.

April 14, 1950

The mystery of speech and silence is resolved in the Acts of the Apostles. Pentecost is the solution. The problem of language is the problem of sin. The problem of silence is also a problem of love. How can a man really know whether to write or not, whether to speak or not, whether his words and his silence are for good or for evil, for life or for death, unless he understands the two divisions of tongues – the division of Babel, when men were scattered in their speech because of pride, and the division of Pentecost, when the Holy Ghost sent out men of one dialect to speak all the languages of the earth and bring all men to unity: that they may be one, Father, Thou in Me and I in them, that they may be one in us.

The Acts of the Apostles is a book full of speech. It begins with tongues of fire. The Apostles and disciples come downstairs and out into the street like an avalanche, talking in every language. And the world thought they were drunk. But before the sun had set, they had baptized three thousand souls out of Babel into the One Body of Christ. At Pentecost we sing of Whom they spoke. The antiphon _Loquebantur_ even now displays its sunlit cadences in my heart. The false Jerusalem, the old one that was a figure and had died, could not prohibit them from speaking (Acts 4). But the more they loved one another and loved God, the more they declared His word. And He manifested Himself through them. That is the only possible reason for speaking – it justified speaking without end, as long as the speech formed is from silence and brings your soul again to silence.

April 16, 1950. Saturday in Albis

No time to put down notes on the tremendous liturgy of the week. I never really began to know what Easter meant before the priesthood. Now I _know_ that the Mass is the Easter mystery, and our Redemption.

All week I have been thinking of the inestimable greatness and dignity of faith. Faith is higher and more perfect than all knowledge that is accessible to us on earth. The only really valuable mystical experience is a deepening and intensification of faith by love and the gifts of the Holy Ghost – an intensification that only simplifies our faith and makes it more clear by purifying it of every created image and species. So that the purest experience of all begins with the realization of how far faith transcends experience. So that all that can be thought of and desired as an experience, this side of the simplicity of faith, is worthless compared with faith. And the greater it seems to be, the more worthless it is. Our only true greatness is in the humility of living faith. The simpler and purer our faith is, the closer it brings us to God, Who is infinitely great. That is why everyone who humbles himself shall be exalted, and everyone who exalts himself, in the appetite for great lights and extraordinary experiences and feelings and mystical consolations, shall be humbled. Because the richer he desires to be in these things, the poorer he will be in the sight of God, in Whose eyes greatness is nothing.

Penance does not end with Lent. On Easter day they began reading *What Are These Wounds?* in the refectory. It is the book I wrote about St. Lutgarde five years ago, when I was just beginning theology and thought I knew everything. It is really atrocious. I have to sit and listen to myself uttering those self-complacent judgments.

April 18, 1950

The task of a priest is to spiritualize the world. He raises his consecrated hands and the grace of Christ's resurrection goes out from him to enlighten the souls of the elect and of them that sit in darkness and in the shadow of death. Through his blessing material creation is raised up and sanctified and dedicated to the glory of God. The priest prepares the coming of Christ by shedding upon the whole world the invisible light that enlightens every man that comes into the world. Through the priest the glory of Christ seeps out into creation until all things are saturated in prayer.

April 24, 1950. Monday

I write in a new setting. Was I in St. Gabriel's room for a month or two months or more? I cannot remember. It seemed like a very long time. And I never liked it there. The place got dirtier and dirtier because I kept thinking I would move out in two days and then I would sweep and arrange everything. Meantime, books came from France, letters and magazines from everywhere, and I threw them all on the bare cot that was left over from my three weeks of flu. And even last week I was still a little knocked out.

Last Friday Fr. Anselm finished the new black tile floor in the vault and I got a helper at the distribution of the work and moved back in, sweeping, arranging books in the new shelves and, at last, after the bell, standing and rejoicing wearily in the silence and spaciousness of the room. And after it was all over it suddenly occurred to me to wonder how the vault got that way. The whole project dates back to the morning of some feast day when I met the Cellarer in the hall and, on an impulse, made him a sign about changing everything and getting the closets full of vestments out of there. After that, things just happened, almost without my thinking of them at all, and now I am in a new wonderful room full of ancient books on one side and brand new books on the other. Even when you move about, all things are silent. Yet the traxcavator is roaring beyond the wall where they are building a new guest-wing – another happy dream. Now the guests will be out of our cloister. They should be as happy as we for they will have a clean new building and plenty of showerbaths and, when they want to talk together, they can sit in a comfortable lounge, just like every other hotel in the universe, and we will no longer hear their voices in our dormitory.

One of the things I am starting to do in the new vault is this: I have made a list of seventeen novices who do not seem to object to the notion of being urged to read the Fathers of the Church and especially the twelfth century Cistercians. What are we all going to do in the vault? I am not yet sure. But they will see the old manuscripts and I will try to tell them what to look for when they are reading St. Bernard, and they will learn the names of writers they have not yet heard of and in whom, perhaps, they will discover ways to God they had not conceived. I don't know.

This afternoon I tried to work on the pamphlet, *What Is Contemplation?* It is to be reprinted in England. I thought it would need to be changed, but now that I look at it, I am almost afraid it will have to be rewritten. I spent most of the afternoon with my head in my hands, scarcely able to think or move. Everything I have written makes me intensely unhappy. The Lutgarde book goes on and on in the refectory. The novice who is reading this week reads well. But he started by accidentally skipping the only pages I was still fond of – the ones about the Office of St. Agnes. Almost everything else in the book upsets me except what I wrote about the Liturgy and about Christ being the center of contemplation and perhaps some of the stuff about love and the Cistercian Fathers. It makes me afraid to go ahead with the work on St. Ailred. And, in any case, for that I must wait upon the publication of new sermons of his in England and for the *De Anima* and for other publications – the complete edition of Walter Daniel's *Vita* by Maurice Powicke who, as I discover, has now been knighted.

April 27, 1950

Fr. Hilary, who certainly ought to know, made me a sign that there are now one hundred four novices and postulants in the community. Two more came in today – both entered the Lay-brother's novitiate.

If I revise the Contemplation pamphlet, I will start out with the Rite of Baptism. Nothing could state more clearly or more simply the place of contemplation in the Christian life. However, Bob Giroux wrote the other day, asking for this *Journal* in a hurry. He thinks it is all typed and edited, and speaks of having it in proof in a few weeks and in circulation by this fall. Meanwhile, a wire from Naomi tells me to keep quiet and answer nothing until hearing from her. There is no hurry – and, anyway, I have to pick out what ought to be printed and type it up. I am only as far as December, 1947, with my typing. And incidentally, going over the events of that month, I am impressed with the big influence my two conversations with Dom Marie-Joseph have had in my life. He would not have had such an effect if everything he said had been completely new. But he brought out a score of ideas that I was prepared for and needed and which I might almost have expressed for myself, if I had not been so intent on a way of spirituality that made such a thing almost impossible. I simply did not have the freedom of spirit to do so. But his words and the example of his own particular kind of integrity did something to wake me up. The course I am now trying to give to the novices, the spiritual "orientation," which they seem to need and like, all began with that impulsion. It is the fruit of his words and his visit.

The Lutgarde book, on the other hand, is a good example of the wrong path I was following so conscientiously – as if it were my duty to be stale and dull! Now they are reading the last chapter and I like it, not because it is good, but because it is the last.

Yesterday we were planting pine trees again. This time I managed to find myself working alone.[53]

October 9, 1950

Two colored bricklayers from South Carolina are working on the guest house building with the rest of Mr. Ray's secular crew. The Laybrothers are on their novitiate. The two colored bricklayers from South Carolina are the two best dressed bricklayers I ever saw. Especially one of them, who works in a soft felt hat and what appears to be a gabardine suit. The other is more informal, but wears a baseball cap and windbreaker. They are very high priced bricklayers.

[53] No extant journal exists from April 28, 1950, through October 8, 1950. The first two journals of "The Whale and the Ivy" were bound notebooks. The third journal, which begins on October 9, 1950, is a three-hole punch, fastener-type folder in which loose pages were fastened. Thus, from April 28, 1950, through July 5, 1952, Merton could have edited his journal entries by tearing out pages without any means of detection by a future editor.

Today they came in from work with newspapers and sat down out of the rain on some potato sacks under the cellar entry by the secular kitchen. As they opened their papers, I thought I will never again be mad at people for reading the newspapers.

The mystical body of those who read the newspapers.

For half a second I wondered if I were missing something, not because of the news, but because of the calm of the two bricklayers sitting on the potato sacks.

October 10, 1950

There are times when ten pages of some book fall under your eye just at the moment when your very life, it seems, depends on your reading those ten pages. You recognize in them immediately the answer to all your most pressing questions. They open a new road. The first ten pages of Pierre Emmanuel's *Qui est cet homme?* [ou Le Singulier Universel. Paris, 1947] (Chapter I) are that for me. They tell me clearly what I was trying to get obscurely last month out of *Ecclesiastes*. His is the message of *Ecclesiastes*. He is the enemy of my angelism. He has given me the word *discontinuity*, and has reminded me of what I already found out about isolation being different from solitude.[54]

Discontinuity = chaos = animality, even though you pretend to think like a pure spirit. page 18 – like St. Bernard

October 21, 1950

When I was in the hospital, Benediction, rosary, litanies in chapel with the Sisters and nurses, made a big impression on me: sense of the religious vitality in these devotions which are frowned on as "unliturgical." Felt that the Holy Spirit was really there – sense that this was the Church at prayer, even though not liturgy – official public prayer. Seemed to me that something of Catholicism was lacking at Gethsemani on this account – yet we can't have all these things. They are not for us – except in private. I would never do without the Rosary.

Ideas of authority and freedom in *Mediator Dei*:

> Mass – it is stressed – is "unconstrained and voluntary homage to God."

---

[54] Emmanuel's text begins with an epigraph from Thomas Hardy, *The Dynasts*: "He who is with himself dissatisfied/ though all the world find satisfaction in him/ is like a rainbow coloured bird gone blind,/ That gives delight it shares not."

Jesus the deliverer – first paragraph.

Later – quote from St. Ambrose on the Psalms

The Psalms – voice of Christ – confession of faith "signifying deep attachment to authority – the joy of freedom."

The Church (Christ) is our liberator. Submission to her authority is *freedom.*

Catholicity is freedom – *no* limitation on the spirit. Authority prohibits what limits and restricts the spirit of men. Hence, errors condemned in *Mediator Dei:* narrowness of exaggerated archaism in liturgy. Protects freedom of spirit in devotions – protects mental prayer, etc. Holy Spirit must be permitted to "breathe where He will" in spiritual exercises and retreats. (#179 translation). Churches not to be locked up outside time of public liturgical services. Freedom protected by protection of unity in spiritual life – error of those who had begun to create a division between public and private prayer, "morality and contemplation."

Must not interpret *Mediator Dei* as a defense of mere individualism. Individualism not freedom. *Sentire cum Ecclesia* [To think with the Church] is freedom. Catholicity. Individualism also limitation – false freedom, separation from Christ.

November 3, 1950. Feast of St. Malachy

I am in the hospital for a nose operation.

Yesterday morning, All Soul's Day, at Gethsemani, during my three Masses: I was at the consecration of the third Mass and the choir was chanting *Lauds.* I paused just before pronouncing the words of consecration over the Host and these words of Psalm 87 came clearly to me from the choir: *Sicut vulnerati dormientes in sepulchris quorum non es memor amplius* . . . [Like the slain sleeping in the sepulchers, whom Thou rememberest no more . . . (Psalms 87:6).]

Darkness and depth of purgatory. Mercy of God seen in contradiction He has "forgotten" them, and yet, if He had not remembered them, He would not be there at my Mass; He would not have us saying three Masses for the Poor Souls. Happiness, simplicity in this paradox. Because His "memory" of the dead is infinitely deep, it is necessary that we accuse Him, as if we were Job, of having forgotten. They sleep in the bosom of His forgetfulness which is deep mercy, as He bides His time, doing all things well. The day will come when they will be born. Meanwhile his punishment is like a womb. The poverty of Christ has bought them.

In the hospital – this time I am on the first floor in the priest's corridor which is a wild, amusing section of the world. I believe many more men have died in the bed I sleep in than in the one I had on third west. We are five Trappists: Fr. Joachim with his last shreds of stomach, Brother Leo, deaf, hernia, and his knee out (I hear furious bell-ringing – that is Fr. Joachim), Fr. Bernard, whose stomach is to be operated on, Bro. Canisius with ulcers, and me with my nose and my spastic colitis. (Ding-ding-ding. Maybe it is Bro. Leo, but he *is* usually in the chapel.)

A moment ago, Fr. Joachim's voice booming all down the corridor as he roars at Bro. Leo (next door): "Do what Sister tells you! *Obey!* [underlined twice] OBEY!!"

Fr. Howard is a novice priest who was at the Angelicum at Rome, but did not know Father Paul Philippe. He assures me Garrigou-Lagrange is *not* [underlined twice] dead.

A Passionist scholastic stopped me yesterday in the corridor and we had a long discussion of various points in *Seeds of Contemplation*, and he took me up to see a Passionist priest who was in a head-on collision and is lying upstairs in an apparatus evidently designed by Salvador Dali.

The loudspeakers are calling for Doctor Vajaro, who, as I know, is a Hindu, but I haven't seen him. And, before I left home, Brother Charles was making me signs which I could only interpret as follows: on the feast of St. Charles Borromeo (tomorrow) his brother is to marry the little Hindu nurse here who runs around taking blood out of everybody's arm.

November 5, 1950

It is Day of Recollection in the hospital.

First time in my life I have said Mass without a proper server. Brother Camillus, who was serving me, went home yesterday. Sister Imelda knelt behind a pillar and answered the prayers while I wondered what to do with the cruets.

Over the public address system they seemed to be paging "Sister Tenacious! Sister Tenacious!"

Bright sun, trees nearly bare. Behind the hospital, that line of low houses with sycamores and willows, the iron fence, the wooden garages. The field, the blue sky, would have interested Manet. At first it appeared to me drab, but since I used to walk up and down saying the Little Office there, it has become for me the prettiest scene in Louisville.

November 6, 1950

Behind the hospital: the willows were like silver this morning. Beautiful sky. Then came a junk wagon along the little road behind the wire fence at the far side of the field. First I heard its bells ringing. The wagon seemed to be all bells, like a Chinese temple. Then I saw the mule, the wagon of the negro driver. The mule was flashing with brass disks. Brass and bells all over his harness. And then the wagon: the two front wheels seemed to be of different sizes. Yet the wagon was majestic. The two rear wheels were greater than the front. I think there was a wooden bucket suspended from the tail end of the wagon. It was not piled high with junk. I was trying to think what kind of boat the wagon resembled. I am sorry for the ambiguity, but it had something of the lines of a Chinese junk. How can I explain the green, aged boards that made up this delicate cart? On top of it all sat the driver with his dog. Both were immobile. They sailed forward amid their bells. The dog pointed his nose straight forward like an arrow. The negro captain sat immersed in a grey coat. He did not look to right or left, and I would have approached, with great respect, what seemed to be solid mysticism. But I stood a hundred yards off, enchanted by the light on the mule's harness, enchanted by the temple bells.

November 12, 1950

I was going to write something on November 10th, but I ran out of ink, and now suddenly it is November 12th, Sunday. Quiet and bright. The planes swim low over the hospital, making for the airport.

Wednesday, when it was neither quiet nor bright, Doctor Roser cut some three inches of bone and cartilage out of my nose. Since it did not hurt, I was unnecessarily jocose. Sister Helen Elizabeth stood by saying the Rosary. A student nurse got sick. I sweated mightily. Sister Helen Elizabeth put cold towels around my neck and on my forehead. Doctor Roser sweated, but less mightily, and got no cold towels from anybody.

Impressions on arriving for a nose operation: it is nothing like the movies. You find you are going to be operated on in a very small room – a sort of closet that the architect forgot about and which has a window. This small room is full of people scrubbed and dressed in white. In this respect, it is like the movies. Uniforms. Everything is sterile. I think the most interesting thing about it all is that you are surrounded by people, mostly women, in white gauze masks and caps. This is delightful. I was waiting for the time when the masks would all come off. Perhaps Doctor Roser would clap his hands twice and cry, "It is finished!" And they would all unmask, some smiling, some solemn, some tired. What actually happened was that the nurse went away and got sick and Doctor Roser said, "Don't go tell another nurse to get scrubbed up. He's got blood all over everything anyway, so we might as well break technique." This turned out to be nicer after all. It made me feel very informal – and that the end was in sight. A delightful sense of liberty came over me, as if somehow "technique" had been a restriction on my own self-expression. It was then that I began to talk to Sister Helen Elizabeth about Elizabeth of the Trinity. It was the day before Elizabeth's "feast." Sister Helen Elizabeth declared that she claimed no part in Elizabeth of the Trinity who was "too interior." I discussed the point briefly while Doctor Roser was chopping the last few bits of bone out of my left nostril. I did not commit the indignity of crossing my legs, or waving my arms in the air with grand gestures. However, I was capable of anything at that time. I even descended so low as to say, "Tell the nurse I will be praying for her." After this astonishing piece of pharisaism, I was wheeled off to the elevator reclining on my left elbow like a guest at a Roman banquet.

However, in the afternoon, the dope wore off and they insisted on giving me hypos. These upset me – at least they throw me into a brief turmoil before knocking me out. In one of the crises, I had just begun to vomit up the cocaine and dead blood that filled my stomach, when Reverend Father walked in, and I guess he must have thought I was pretty sick.

Meanwhile, most of the Trappist patients had gone home. Brother Leo was leaving with Reverend Father. He came in and told me so triumphantly, when I was absolutely at my worst.

Yesterday I was here all alone.

They are still trying to figure out my colitis, and I had a slightly bad chest X-ray which the Doctor thinks calls for rest and penicillin. My own theory is this: the Doctor is overworked and would like to have a vacation, but, since he cannot, he is satisfying his instincts by making sure that *I* have one.

I have to go down town to his clinic for treatments on the nose.

Louisville: miles and miles of one-story homes.

For years after I entered the monastery, I had cherished the notion that Louisville was somehow a glamorous city. The glamour was all borrowed from Gethsemani. Louisville had registered in my memory as "wonderful" because it was the last outpost before the wilderness of the monastery. Now I know why Father Placid thinks the place is dead. He thinks he can say that of Louisville because he himself comes from St. Louis.

I feel, very dutifully, that Louisville is my city. Why? Well, it is the place to go to when I say, "I am going to town." The fact that I practically never leave the monastery to go "in town" makes no difference whatsoever. Louisville (not Chicago, Cincinnati, Boston, Atlanta, or even Bardstown) is *town*.

There is no reason why a monk should not have a definite attitude toward the place which, in relation to his monastery, is "town." I do not think that being a monk means living on the moon.

November 19, 1950. Sunday
  The Necessity of Silence
    1) Exterior Silence – Its special necessity in our world – in which there is so much noise and inane speech.
    As *protest* and *reparation* against the "sin" of noise.
    Babel. Silence not a virtue, noise not a sin. True. But the turmoil and confusion and constant noise of modern society are the expression of the ambiance of its greatest sins – its godlessness, its despair. A world of propaganda, of endless argument, vituperation, criticism, or simply of chatter, is a world of atheism.
    Advertising – radio, television, etc.
    Catholics who associate themselves with that kind of noise, who enter into the Babel of tongues, become to some extent exiles from the City of God.
    Mass – racket and confusion. Tension – babble.
    All prayer becomes exterior and interior noise –
    Soul-less and hasty repetition of rosary . . .
    Carmel . . .
    Hence, though it is true that we must know how to bear with noise, to have interior life, by *exception* here and there (St. Thomas' principles for activity), yet to resign oneself to a situation in which contemplative community is *constantly* overwhelmed with activity, noise of machines, etc., is an abuse.
    What to do: Catholics inside and outside of cloister – form *casas* [houses] of silence – homes – peace – etc.
    1. Get rid of sources of noise – radio, etc. Let them find people who can be silent. Provide people with places where they can go to be quiet – relax minds and hearts in presence of God – reading rooms, chapels, etc. For many a great renunciation is giving up movies.
    2. The end – Interior silence – of judgments, passions, desires. Saint Gregory the Great. Elizabeth of the Trinity.
    Conclusion: When you gain this interior silence you can carry it around with you in the world, and pray everywhere. But just as interior asceticism

cannot be acquired without concrete and exterior mortification, so it is absurd to talk about interior silence where there is no exterior silence.

I remain interminably in this hospital, although I am well. Doctor Roser will not let me out of the range of his clinic yet, as my nose must still be poked at. Doctor Bizot came in this afternoon imagining that perhaps I could give him some magic answer by which he could cure all those who come to him with psychosomatic complaints.

I am surprised to find how much of the artist there is in doctors, for medicine is an art as well as a science, and therefore its techniques demand a certain skill that is not abstract, but born of a connatural intuition. And doctors adapt themselves to situations pretty much like poets or actors, although they would probably be incensed to hear me say so. They live their way into somebody else's symptoms and search for their secrets as much by the vital sympathy of art as by scientific intelligence. And, in any case, diseases do not exist all by themselves: they only present themselves in patients. The physician's art is respectable because the physician treats not merely diseases but human beings.

The Louisville Carmel is in such a grand mansion that, although I went looking for it, I missed it. I knew the high wall of the garden was undoubtedly something to do with the convent, but this fine brick house, I thought, was a neighbor who overlooked the enclosure. Wondering what the millionaires would think of the nuns, and the nuns of the millionaires, I went looking for the convent around the corner on Sixth Street, and found nothing. When I came back on Park Avenue, I saw the big white cross on top of the mansion. I went up the porch steps. You walk right in the front door and there, at the left, is the outer chapel – small and quiet, in a converted drawing room with a blocked-up fire-place. The dark iron grille behind the altar on the Gospel side entranced me and I knelt tasting the silence that came forth from the whole house, feeling that it was all Tabernacle, as if God were in the *Shekinah* behind the grille and not only in the little gold box on the tiny altar.

Presently a bell rang inside the house somewhere. It signaled the ending of all joy, for there was a lady visitor in the chapel. She evidently had been waiting for this bell. She got up and went to the turn, which was right next to the chapel. She rang, and called up the tunnel to a Sister who came pattering on the floor above our heads. It was the beginning of an interminable conversation – or rather, of a soliloquy of this inexhaustible woman who stood with her head in the turn, reciting in a nasal voice the history of all her physical ills and those of her kin and of her friends, particularly of "Miss Mary" (whom Sister evidently knew), who was caught in a department store in the Christmas rush and hated it, and whose message was, "If ever I needed prayers, I need them now."

The Sisters [at the hospital] eat dinner in a place on this ground floor of their wing that looks like the dining room of an English seaside hotel. I saw them this evening through the curtains as I went out walking, beyond the parking lot, in a dark interval between rainstorms.

November 29, 1950. Vigil of St. Andrew

I came home last Saturday, which was the feast of St. Catherine. We were nearly killed driving to the monastery from the station. Coming down St. Joseph's hill, just before turning in to the monastery, we pulled over on the curve to make room for a yellow truck coming the other way. As we pulled over we skidded on the ice. The car went spinning across the middle of the road like something you pay a dime to ride in at Coney Island. It looked as if the truck were going to hit us broadside on, but we had turned around before it reached us. We ended up in the ditch, but, since we had spun completely around, we were facing in the right direction. I had been praying the rosary all the way from the station, praying that the truck wouldn't hit us, praying to get out of the ditch. We got home, hastened across the snowy garden, and there was a colored retreatant standing by Our Lady's statue. He looked at me and said, "Father Merton?" but I made him a sign that I couldn't talk.

Talking was what exhausted me most in the hospital. I tried to do as little of it as possible. I spent a lot of time hiding in Room 122, a conference room, which is never used for anything. It has a big table and a few chairs in it, and there, with Father Osbourn's typewriter, I added something like twenty-five pages to _Bread in the Wilderness_. I had wired to Laughlin in New York for the manuscript.

Feast of the Presentation:[55]

That morning was when I finished work on _Bread in the Wilderness_. I called up Gethsemani and asked Reverend Father if I could go to Carmel to say the Proper Mass of St. John of the Cross, on St. John's feast. So then

[55] In the following text, Merton records events of November 21, Feast of the Presentation; of November 23, Thanksgiving Day in 1950; and of November 24, the Feast of St. John of the Cross.

I went to Carmel to get Reverend Mother's permission, too. I rang the bell at the turn and said I came from Gethsemani and wanted to see Reverend Mother. The Sister, whose excitement I could not see, exclaimed in a faint, breathless voice, "O Father! Please give me your blessing!" Then I talked with Reverend Mother in what they call the Speak-room. I suppose the term is better than "parlor." The place is nothing like what anyone would think of as a "parlor." (In the South were parlors, great salons where you could see everything reflected in the floor. Or did they have vast deep carpets? I would say the Good Shepherd Sisters on Bank Street really had a parlor. I have never forgotten the August day when I went there with Dom Gabriel.)

On Thanksgiving Day I said the Community Mass at the hospital and gave them all Communion and in the evening I gave the Holy Hour in place of Father Osborne who went home to get a turkey dinner. For my own part, I was so scared I could hardly eat supper.

On the 24th, the feast of St. John of the Cross, it suddenly got very cold. It had been snowing that night and there was snow on the ground. The streets were icy, and the parking lot was full of frozen cars. One of these was the car of the technician in the X-ray department who had arranged to drive me down to Carmel when he went off night duty.

A taxi, ordered by someone else who had already left, showed up at the hospital just when I needed it.

Everything was beautifully quiet. Only two ladies – lay people – were there, and were in on what was going on. They were the ones who told me where to find the vestments in the sacristy, who lit the candles, put them out, gave me breakfast. All the rest of the world was kept away by angels. Silence and sunlight everywhere outside. Bright snow on the slopes, among the sycamores in the park. Silence everywhere inside the convent. It was like saying Mass in a hermitage on top of a mountain.

The nuns behind the grille and behind the wall behind the altar were so silent I once wondered if they were there at all: I felt like Cassian at the Night Office of the desert fathers. No one even sneezed. The Carmelites are not like Trappists. We have great boots and shoes as heavy as gunboats. They are silent in slippers or sandals. No one was coughing, though the house was cold. I would not have been completely happy saying that beautiful Mass in an overheated room. One nun answered the prayers, behind the grille. She had a nice calm voice, and took her time, and spoke the Latin words well.

To wash your hands in the sacristy there was a basin of warm water with a towel, in the turn. I thought of something in Saint Theresa about rose-water. There was a faint scent somewhere – but maybe it came from the soap I did not need to use. And the Mass. _Anima mea desideravit te in nocte! Conversatio nostra est in coelis_ . . . [My soul hath desired thee in the night (Isaiah 26:9)! Our converse is in heaven . . . (Philippians 3:20)] transformed from brightness to brightness as by the Spirit of the Lord!

December 3, 1950. On Retreat

Rain. It is cold. Everyone is getting colds, including Father Ignatius Smith, O.P., who is preaching to us. I bet his brother is a cop. All retreats do me good. And this one, too. Conferences simple, hard-boiled, and sometimes very loud. If his brother is not a cop, I'll settle for a football coach. But he does me good.

After having doctors and Sisters telling me for three weeks to rest and take care of myself, it is a relief to have someone roar at me about idleness and timidity. "If you are worn out," he says, "you are just getting off to a good start."

Thursday, before the beginning of the retreat, got off to a false start. (Had to go to Louisville to the clinic to get my nose "fixed." This afternoon Father Ignatius Smith, O.P., whose brother is at the very least a fire chief, told us that "the Eye-Ear-Nose and Throat business is the biggest racket of 1950.") I went into St. Martin's Church, which might have been in Würzburg, but for the street outside, though the guardian angel in the sooty yard looked more like Dublin. Churches in cities are the most wonderful solitudes. No one was there. Much quieter than Gethsemani. Emptiness, awful stained glass windows, rows and rows of empty pews. The place seemed enormously wide. There I sat facing a brigade of large and small statues, all of them quite tame. And the Tabernacle. And the silence. Big votive lights in front of Saint Anthony like ice-cream sodas. It must cost a dollar and a half to burn one. I began thinking about the Rule of Saint Benedict, solitude, poverty, starting a new order, twelve men in log cabins wearing the overalls of the country. That was what I referred to as the false start of my annual retreat.

I am haunted by the _Cautelas_ of St. John of the Cross. Especially the second, against the flesh, against solicitude for material things.

The hospital did me good in some ways, harm in others. I am back here where the flesh receives only rudimentary attention, and find that I have to struggle to get back to the state in which I think little or not at all about the needs of the body. I am under doctor's order to take care of this body and to rest it. Easy enough to make special arrangements. No more thought is required. And yet I think of emergencies that have not arisen. I have lost the spirit of poverty – if I ever had it. And in exchange I have learned the names of many new medicines. I am aware of the physiology of my head. It is, says Roser, undergoing a change. It shall suffer a sea-change into something rich and strange. "Those are pearls that were his eyes." "Thy nose shall be as a tower of ivory." I am aware of the physiology of my chest. I have heard of the things that might have to be done to my chest. To my shame I find myself – not even subconsciously – consciously wanting them done, although the emergency has not arisen, nor is likely to arise.

And when I am in choir I am aware how out of breath I am.

There are too many books in the place where I write books.

It is after first bell for Vespers, and through the window I cannot see the Church, nor the rain, nor the storm, for my steam. Praise be Jesus forever! Amen.

December 4, 1950

Domus Jacob, venite, et ambulemus in lumine Domini. [O house of Jacob, come ye, and let us walk in the light of the Lord (Isaiah 2:5).]

Moments of beauty in this day. Reading that line of Isaias was another. The cover of the new French translation of St. John of the Cross. Sunlight and clear sky and wet grass behind the old wagon shed. Three young bulls in a pen where the chickens were, near that spring at the south end of the vegetable garden. Of the bulls I was afraid. But, to return to beauty – looking at the crucifix in the infirmary refectory. The crucifix on the yellow wall.

Domus Jacob, venite, et ambulemus in lumine Domini.

December 6, 1950

After those beautiful pages on morning and on being awake, Thoreau writes in his *Walden:*

"I went to the woods because I wished *to live deliberately, to front only the essential facts of life, and see if I could not learn what it had to teach and not, when I came to die, discover that I had not lived.*" (p. 89)

He adds mysteriously, "nor did I wish to practice resignation unless it was quite necessary." I suppose he means he did not intend to be resigned to anything like a compromise with life, unless it could not be avoided.

December 8, 1950

Compare the basic asceticism in *Walden* with that of St. John of the Cross –
agreement on the fundamental idea – not, of course, on the means or technique, except to some extent. Ascesis of solitude. Simplification of life. The
separation of reality from illusion.

"If we respected only what is inevitable, and has a right to be, music and
poetry would resound along the streets." (p. 94).

The retreat is over. The retreat master confessed at last that he had been a
football coach and a boxing coach into the bargain. And a coach of something else besides, which I have forgotten. He is gone and we miss him – we
always get attached to whomever it is preaches to us for these eight days!

And he told us of Mike McCauliffe, the New York policeman, who was
shot on First Avenue by an eighteen-year-old kid who was hopped up on
heroin. And he told us of the old rakes in the veterans' hospital and of the
governor who walked about the grounds reading Greek poetry. He told us
a lot of things. He told us to pray for the world. When I went to speak to
him, he told me that the Dominicans were allowed and even encouraged to
accumulate "books without number," so that I did not need to feel so bad
about all the books in the vault.

Yesterday there was snow again and wind froze ribs on top of the drifts
along the hillsides; sun shone through the copper grass that grew above the
snow on St. Joseph's hill, and it looked as if the snow were all on fire. And
there were jewels all over the junk the brothers dumped out there where
the old horse barn used to be. A bunch of window-screens were lying about
and they shone in the sun like crystal.

December 13, 1950. Feast of St. Lucy

Nine years at Gethsemani, daffy with joy although my guts are broken and
give forth blood. Crude liver shots with a long needle. Fr. Vincent de Paul
was an army doctor and was here infirmarian until his temporary vows ex-
pired and he left. I sympathize with the concern felt by the Philistines in the
book of Kings, over their piles. When I have pain, I cheer interiorly, like the
passengers on the Titanic when she went down. Diarrhea all the time. So
happy, so happy. Walking in the snow. All the world is white and grey.

The junk wagon I saw in Louisville comes back to me like the memory of
something very precious once seen in the Orient. I saw it several times, and

once I heard the bells on the mule without seeing anything. Once the driver had on a green sweater, and the dog was running behind the wagon. That was on a nice day. Then, on a bad day, in a storm of rain, the driver was riding bundled up in many old coats, under a huge, grey canvas umbrella. There was no dog at all. The dog stayed home. Now, having seen all this and remembered it, I dreamt last night that I saw the wagon again. The bells of the mules were ringing. The brass discs glittered in the sun. The green boards held themselves together by miracle in their marvelous disorder. And the junk man's wife was driving, and the junk man walked behind.

About Gray Street, Louisville.

A black carnival mask with broken elastic lying in the dirty snow in front of one of those ancient ornate houses. Gray Street must look nice in spring when the sun comes shining through the sycamores. If I were there in spring, I would think of getting back as fast as I could to Gethsemani, where spring is nicer.

In front of another house: a mounting block or step, or whatever you call those stone steps fashionable people used to get up on to mount a horse, or climb into a carriage. And on this step was written, as it were recently, by an amateur, *"Vive la France!"*

You can tell at once that Grace Church is Protestant by the way the word "Mass" jumps out at you from its signboard – and they announce it especially for Sundays, as if they had caught some rare creature and had it in a cage for men to come and view. The Church is dignified and has character and there is not a single thing about it that would lend one remotely to suspect that it knew the meaning of a word like "Mass." Gothic though it pretend to be, it is a meeting house and not a Church – by Church I mean the house of God, not the house of a congregation.

I passed two men on Fourth Street where the shops were gay for Christmas, and one man was saying to the other, ". . . so he drops his damn gun and reaches for a club." I would put down the long story about the shooting up the road at Smith's corner, two miles from Gethsemani, but I haven't time.

There is much to say on this day about what I long to do and be.

In one mist of melting snow, which overhangs Gethsemani and Louisville alike, I see the whole world like smoke and I am not part of it. There is nothing on this earth that does not give me diarrhea. Conversation in town, ambition in the cloister: I mean even the ambition to do great things for God. That ambition is too much like the ambitions of the town.

And I am aware of silence all around me in the country as of a world that is closed to men. They live in it and yet its door is closed to them. This silence, it is everywhere. It is the room Jesus told us to enter into when we pray.

December 15, 1950. Saturday

Curious experience – practicing the Christmas chant, on a dark winter morning before dawn, and singing the Responsories that also come in the summer Office of _Corpus Christi. Verbum caro factum est_ [The Word was made flesh (John 1:14)] – flowers on the cloister pavement and the abbey full of sun and the song of birds – the baldachin with nodding plumes – and the procession, where you sing to Christ with ineffable pleasure – weary, with hot wax running down your candle and across the back of your hand . . . No! Now it is winter! But as I write, it is beautiful winter – with bright sun on the bare trees and on the white walls of our building.

Scripture – communion with God. But be careful. Geoffrey of Auxerre's ideas that St. Bernard's interpretations were guided by the same Spirit that inspired the prophets must be handled with care. It sounds a lot like Luther. The modern Popes are wiser. I read the controversy in _Dieu Vivant._ Claudel vs. Steinman. Daniélou's summary gives the correct doctrine as far as I can see. But the problem worries me. Everything inside me revolts against an interpretation of the Old Testament that makes it seem as if God never spoke to anyone but the Jews. Are not the words of Isaias for me? Did his prophecies run out, and did their message end when all the Jews came back from Babylon?

Ne timeas, quia ego tecum sum; ne declines, quia ego Deus tuus; confortavi te, et auxiliatus sum tibi, et suscepit te dextera Justi mei. [Fear not, for I am with thee; turn not aside for I am thy God; I have strengthened thee and have helped thee, and the right hand of my just One hath upheld thee (Isaiah 41:10).]

Who is God talking to? Israel. Who is Israel? Christ. I live, now not I, but Christ liveth in me. Who is God talking to? To me, to this monk in Gethsemani.

February 21, 1951. Feast of St. Peter's Chair at Antioch

Today is the ninth anniversary of my reception of the habit of novice, and it occurred to me that I should go on writing this notebook which I had deliberately stopped again. There is nothing against it, since it is not a "spiritual Journal."

This morning at Prime – (at once I write something professionally and tediously spiritual) – this morning at Prime I was struck by the title the Trappist printer invented for Psalm 14, _De Via ducente ad beatitudinem_ [Of the road leading to blessedness]. In the light of that light suddenly the whole psalm becomes full of light. It was as if I had never understood it before, though in fact I wrote something about it in _Bread in the Wilderness_, saying "there is more to this Psalm than you might think."

The line that struck me most was _qui loquitur veritatem in corde suo_ [he that speaketh truth in his heart (Psalms 14:3)]. It could mean: the man who is completely true to the Word God utters within him, who is, by his simplicity, in perfect harmony with truth. That is our vocation – mine. I have to think about it more, but not on paper.

Someone sent a book with an excerpt in it from Gertrude Stein's _Toklas_, which I had never read. But from the excerpt it seems to be one of the few sensible books written in our time. Perhaps I think that only because it is very well written.

I would have been more glad than I was to break rock with a sledge hammer yesterday if it had not upset me, but precisely for that reason I ought to be enough of a Trappist to be very glad. After nine years I am at last getting around to an appreciation of penance, not in so far as it is "the spirit of an Order," but because it is pleasing to God and enables Him to take undisturbed possession of the soul. How secret penance has to be, with the left hand not knowing what the right hand is doing, and the "Spiritual Journal" receiving no busy resolutions. It is the impurity of immature penance that brings distress, but deep and hidden suffering is joy. Part of this depth and hiddenness comes from the fact that such suffering really _diminishes_ you, reduces you to nothing, places you in darkness, and tells you you are nothing and that, as the _Imitation_ says, and a thousand other guys might also have said, "The old man is not dead." And yet, love can easily get rid of him, though not so much our love as Christ's, which becomes ours.

February 28, 1951

Studying the baby-talk citizenship text-book that is given out to help us aliens prepare for our naturalization. Suddenly realized that this business of citizenship raises an important moral question. Impossible to take it as a mere formality. Either it means something or it doesn't. There is more to this than a problem in semantics. It is a question of justice and of charity. Why do half the people in America seem to think it is a moral weakness to admit that they owe America something – and perhaps everything? And that the country is worth loving. And that it is full of very good people – and that we owe it to one another to try to keep the place from getting like Russia or anywhere else in Europe that I can think of.

March 3, 1951

March is St. Benedict's month. Clearing thorn trees from the rocky shoulder over the middle bottom, where the new road is being made, I got to be good friends with his relic yesterday. How weary I am of being a writer. How necessary it is for monks to work in the fields, in the rain, in the sun, in the mud, in the clay, in the wind: these are our spiritual directors and our novice masters. They form our contemplation. They instill into us virtue. They make us as stable as the land we live in. You do not get that out of a typewriter. *Tunc vere monachi sunt si de labore manuum suarum vivunt sicut et Patres nostri et Apostoli.* [For then are they truly monks when they live by the labour of their hands, as our Fathers and the Apostles did (RB 48:8).]

The sanity of St. Benedict has something to do with the mystery of a monk becoming an American citizen. Yesterday I looked closely for the first time in ten years at the ms. of the *Journal of My Escape from the Nazis*,[56] which I wrote ten years ago at St. Bonaventure's at the beginning of the war.

There is some fair writing in the book. But it reflected great moral disintegration in my own life: more than I ever suspected! I revealed more of myself than I meant to in those pages that are by no means as cryptic as I thought, but I did not think of hiding anything. In being obscure, I was only trying to discover something of myself. And I could not see what was so plain.

It was a very inhibited book, in spite of all the uninhibited explosives of an invented language which I still like. The action can never progress forwards. In fact, there is no action. A situation presents itself and the stream of the book – which after all has a stream – stops and forms a lake. It is sometimes quite a bright lake. But I can do nothing with it.

[56] Published in 1968 as *My Argument with the Gestapo*.

Sitting in the garden house I viewed the pale glare of sunlight on the roof of the distillery a mile away against the dark hills, and I thought about the whole business. And, although my thinking was a little incoherent – *motus orbicularis*, circling the subject with a laziness appropriate to the hour, which was 1:15 P.M. – nevertheless I came out of it more healthy than I went in, and descended the ladders more in one piece than I had climbed them.

One of the problems of the book was my personal relation to the world and to the war. When I wrote it, I thought I had a very supernatural solution. After nine years in a monastery I see that this was no solution at all. The false solution was this: the whole world, of which the war is a characteristic expression, is evil. It has, therefore, to be first ridiculed, then spat upon, and at last formally cursed.

Actually, I have come to the monastery to find my place in the world, and if I fail to find this place, I will be wasting my time in the monastery.

It would be a grave sin for me to be on my knees in this monastery, flagellated, penanced, though not now as thin as I ought to be, and spend my time cursing the world without distinguishing what is good in it from what is bad.

Wars are evil, but the people involved in them are good, and I can do nothing whatever for my own salvation or for the glory of God if I merely withdraw from the mess people are in and make an exhibition of myself and write a big book saying, "Look! I am different!" To do this is to die. Because any man who pretends to be either an angel or a statue must die the death. The immobility of that *Journal of My Escape* was a confession of my own nonentity, and this was the result of a psychological withdrawal.

On the other hand, if you let yourself be washed away with all the dirt on the surface of the stream, you pile up somewhere in another kind of immobility, with the rest of the jetsam in the universe.

Coming to the monastery has been, for me, exactly the right kind of withdrawal. It has given me perspective. It has taught me how to live. And now I owe everyone else in the world a share in that life. My first duty is to start, for the first time, to live as a member of a human race which is no more (and no less) ridiculous than I am myself. And my first human act is the recognition of how much I owe to everybody else. There is a world which Christ would not pray for. (Father Raymond reminded me of the distinction when some lady, who came to Frater Joachim's solemn profession, said she was mad because I hadn't made it.) But the world also was made by God and is good, and, unless that world is our mother, we cannot be saints, because we cannot be saints unless we are first of all human.

—

Thus God has brought me to Kentucky where the people are, for the most part, singularly without inhibitions. This is the precise place He has chosen for my sanctification. Here I must revise all my own absurd plans, and take myself as I am, Gethsemani as it is, and America as it is – atomic bomb and all. It is utterly peculiar, but none the less true that, after all, one's nationality should come to have a meaning in the light of eternity. I have lived for thirty-six years without one. Nine years ago I was proud of the fact. I thought that, to be a citizen of heaven, all you had to do was throw away your earthly passport. But now I have discovered a mystery: that the ladies in the Office of the Deputy Clerk of the Louisville District are perhaps in some accidental way empowered to see that I am definitely admitted to the Kingdom of Heaven forever.

For now I am beginning to believe that perhaps the only, or at least the quickest way, I shall become a saint is by virtue of the desires of many good people in America that I should become one. Last night I dreamt I was telling several other monks, "I shall be a saint," and they did not seem to question me. Furthermore, I believed it myself. If I do – (I shall) – it will be because of the prayers of other people who, though they are better than I am, still want me to pray for them.

March 4, 1951. Day of Recollection

If I am to become a saint, does it mean cleaning up the vault very soon? Tomorrow?

Yes, Tomorrow or Tuesday, if possible. Yet at the heart of this confusion God is still found.

Shall I go on thinking about the *Journal of My Escape from the Nazis?* It distracted me yesterday: rediscovery of my old self in a cleaner light than I expected, and the discovery of some pleasant writing. I speak as one less wise. Got Frater Thomas to type out that one little bit about B. Then put the rest aside until Naomi says something for or against. Didn't I make a resolution to do no more writing in Lent than was necessary to finish *The Ascent to Truth?* Well, I spent half of Lent on that, and there is still a little to be done, but I'll go out to the fields a lot anyway.

Shall I re-read the bits in *The Ascent of Mount Carmel* about the memory? They seem to do me so much good – always. Year after year, returning to them. In what sense do they make a difference in my life?

This *Journal* [underlined twice]. I mean this one I am writing right now. Apparently I have not yet written enough of it to become completely solitary and to be able to do without it. It is useless to drop the thing and say I am solitary just because I am not writing a *Journal*, when, in fact, the writing could help me find my way to where I am supposed to be traveling.

So I read about forgetting and write down all I remember. And somehow there is no contradiction here. It is simply a somewhat particular way of becoming a saint. I by no means insist that it is sanctity. All I say is that I must do what the situation seems to demand, and sanctity will appear when out of all this Christ, in His own good time, appears and manifests His own glory.

March 10, 1951. Saturday before Passion Sunday

Tenderness of the Epistle, austerity of the Gospel in this morning's Mass. Last night, before Compline, out by the horsebarn, looking at the orchard and thinking about what St. John of the Cross said about having in your heart the image of Christ crucified.

Confusion and fog pile up in your life, and then, by the power of the Cross, things once again are clear, and you know more about your wretchedness and you are grateful for another miracle.

These words get in between me and the naked truth.

The Archbishop is here in a sleek new monster of a Buick – a streamlined Vatican on wheels. In about five minutes we will go to None and, after that, Frater Hilary will be ordained deacon.

March 10, 1951[57]

Now, here are things to be done.

I have not yet cleaned out the vault – not properly, although at least I swept it.

It is good that I have been out to the common work more often, even though I nearly set the whole forest on fire yesterday burning brush out by St. Gertrude's field on the slope nearest the lake.

Wind ... flames springing up in the leaves across the creek like the spread of attachments in an unmortified soul!

So, *confortetur cor tuum et viriliter age! [(viriliter agite et confortetur cor vestrum)* do ye manfully, and let your heart be strengthened (Psalms 30:25)]: Here are the things to be done:

Many lights are burning that ought to be put out.

Kindle no new fires. Live in the warmth of the sun.

[57] Merton repeats date of March 10th.

There are books to be discarded. The house must be made clean. Drawings to be thrown away.

April 6, 1951

Jean Cayrol has written a book about the dreams men had in the concentration camps. When first arrested, they dreamt they had not been arrested but had escaped. Then, resigned to their arrest, they dreamt they were allowed to go home from time to time. This in prison, before the camp itself. In the concentration camp magnificent dreams of landscapes, of baroque architecture.

Color in their dreams. (And I thought of Doctor Morris Thompson in Louisville who was telling everybody about his visions of color. Doctor Henry thought he was going crazy!) Blue dreams, green dreams, red dreams of salvation. A sailor who saw a diamond cross rising out of the sea.

Dreams which tell us something about our own immediate future! Things the body already knows before the soul has found them out. Jung, I think, holds something to this effect. This worked out in those salvation dreams.

I have walked alone on the road to the barns, looking at the high clouds and thinking, "In war and in battle men look up sometimes and see such clouds as these." Cayrol tells of the Appel [roll-call] at Mauthausen, men being beaten up in the presence of a magnificent sunset on the Austrian Alps.

The ones who were completely *incommunicado* were called *Nacht und Nebel* [Night and Mist], which might conceivably be the name of a perfume.

And I thought of St. John of the Cross. His *Spiritual Canticle* was born of the imprisonment at Toledo! Confirmation of Cayrol's thesis in these two studies.

Elles (ces études) ont tenté d'expliquer comment naissent dans un univers voué à l'echec et à la négation toutes les défenses surnaturelles de l'homme, comment elles se développent clandestinement et comment elles survivent dans des prolongements multiples, difficilement séparables. [They (these studies) have tried to explain how all of man's supernatural defenses are born in a universe headed for failure and negation, how such defenses develop clandestinely and how they survive in multiple extensions, hardly separable from them.]

April 11, 1951

Feast of St. Leo the Great. Preparing the Scripture course. Finished Leo XIII's *Providentissimus Deus* this morning. Keep dipping into St. Thomas.

Quiet, contemplative work. First time I have really made use of the opportunities the vault offers. For two years I have been a hermit and have not
appreciated the fact, or lived as one. *Nunc coepi.* [Now I begin.] Father
Barnabas Mary wrote me about Father Charbel who lived as a hermit in
Syria. He was a Maronite. Everyone forgot about him. He died. Fifty years
later his body was discovered incorrupt and in a short time he worked over
six hundred miracles. He is my new companion. My road has taken a new
turning. It seems to me that I have been asleep for nine years – and that before that I was dead. I have never been a monk or a solitary. *Take up thy bed
and walk!* Great help from the prayers of the Carmelites, the relics of St.
John of the Cross, St. Theresa, and St. Thomas Aquinas.

April 22, 1951

O April, we are coming to your end.

You, Father Charbel, hidden from men in glory, because of you, perhaps
this Journal is coming to an end.

Because I will not tell them about the moon, about the cold hour beyond
Prime, the mist in the early valley, the sun I did not know was rising behind
me, or the sweet smelling earth.

This morning was like the morning of that first poem, the retreat in the
guesthouse, ten years ago. The barn – that is, the garden-house, which
from my room seemed to be beautiful and mysterious – had become the
very mystery in which I was hidden. It was the same hour. Perhaps the
years are no more. The tired man is on his tower among the little boxes.
There was a quilt for covering plants in a garden. It smelled of rats. Also
the chicken houses had been moved. The outward orchard is all down.
The trees are gone. The earth is sown with new grass. When I carried the
sacks of apples on my shoulders, the summer when I was sick, I did not
think I would get to the house. Fr. Ignatius, whose last name was Bartik, he
helped me. I wonder where he went to?

Famous but unknown, tired and powerful, a man without virtue and
without prayer, impotent, hungry, at peace, unable to speak, looking at the
valley: *Who is like unto God!*

God, my God, here is a traitor who loves You beyond speech! And yet I
have no love. I have no moon, I have no valley.

I sat by the orchard heaters until I smelled all over of it and flame. I saw
the moon through the flame. Without heart, without brain, the senseless
man has prayed for fire and apparently received none. Everywhere is
beauty. Where are You, O my God? I was ashamed of singing on the road
to the barn, but what else could I have done?

Alive and dead I climb the glorious barn. The mud of my feet going up is the mud of my hands going down. I will go down more wretched than I went up because more glorious. This barn cannot be known. It is Mount Lebanon, where Father Charbel saw the sun and moon.

I leaned my chin upon the window-sill and prayed to You, my Lover, in the following terms:

> "When the pie was opened
> The birds began to sing.
> Was this not a dainty dish
> To set before the King?"

My God, Who is like You? How can I compare the visits of your children with the silence that dwells on the hills? Yet I have made their hearts suffer by loving them. I have defiled many lives with my impertinence. We have all gone away and have begun over and over to pray, and I believe conversation is a punishment for false mysticism. How can we help ourselves? But I am once again made clean by frost and morning air, here in the presence of the moon.

As long as I do not pretend I suffer, as long as I do not trade in false coin, nor camp too much upon flowers, nor claim that I have disappeared, my brothers' prayers can always mend me. The windows are open. Let the psalms fly in. Prime each morning makes me safe and free. The Day Hours sustain me with their economy, by night I am buried in Christ. At three A.M. I wear the old white vestments and say the Mass *de Beata* [of the Blessed Virgin]. Through the gaps in my own prayer come the psalms of the Night Office that I discovered in the woods yesterday afternoon.

There, there is the crooked tree, the moss with my secrets, those pines upon that cliff of shake, the valley living with the tunes of diesel trains. Nobody knows the exact place I speak of and why should I tell them? For every man is his own Jacob, wakes up at the foot of his own ladder, sees the angels going up and down, with God at the top of the ladder. And thus he wakes up in his own unrecognizable house, his gate of heaven.

What happens after that? Do you put down, "The rest is silence," and close the book, and sell it to the public?

That would be a lie. For Jacob afterward married. His first wife, the fertile one, was ugly. He served fourteen years. He bred sheep. He fled from Rachel's father. His flocks drank from the well where Jesus later sat and spoke with my elder sister.

We, too, have all married over and over again, and yet we have no husband, but thank God for the hill, the sky, the morning sun, the manna on the ground which every morning renews our lives and makes us forever virgins.

May 7, 1951

Since Easter was early we are already on the threshold of Pentecost. Yesterday, in bright, blazing sun, we planted cabbage seedlings in the garden, and, over the wall, I could hear them mowing hay in Saint Joseph's field where probably tomorrow we will all be loading wagons.

Last week was the week of the Visitation and the busiest I had ever spent in my life. Dom Louis [Pennuen], our Father Immediate, the new Abbot of New Melleray, is young and likes work and does not know enough English to do without an interpreter. I was working on most days from seven in the morning to six at night with time out only for dinner and the meridienne. Later on in the week, when the interviews were over, I was able to slip away for part of the Conventual Mass. He left the night before last (Sunday) after inviting me to dinner up in the guest house with Father Abbot and Father Prior.

One of the things that happened during the visitation was that Dom Louis decided that he did not want me going off into the woods by myself any more for fear that it might introduce a kind of "Carthusian spirit" into the house.

Every time I have been in the woods to pray I have loved them more. Perhaps I have not written of the wonderful day, two or three weeks ago, when the Feast of Saint Benedict was transferred, and I was out there all afternoon. I had even written to the Abbot General to sound him out about getting permission to stay out there all day . . .

Yet I was surprised how little it cost me to accept Dom Louis' decision – almost nothing at all!

Only twenty-four hours later did I realize the implications of this easy acceptance. I was sitting in the refectory at mixt, looking out the window at the sun on the water tower, when I was suddenly overwhelmed with the conviction that, if I had given up the woods so easily, it must be because I love God.

At once I remembered all the afternoons I had been out there, the dark afternoons in the gullies along the creeks and the rainy afternoons on top of the knobs and the day I sang the *Pater Noster* on one knob and then on another; the day I found the daffodils in an unexpected place, and the other day when I picked them in a place where I knew they would be; and the immense silence of last Good Friday when I sat on a rotten log in a sheltered corner by a stream with a relic of the Holy Cross . . . and then I knew that all the time I had truly gone out there for the love of God and not for the love of scenery or even of solitude. It set the seal on the silences in which I had found Him without seeming to find anything, and I knew (as I had always guessed) that I had every time come home with something tremendous although my hands were always empty.

Thus I neither regretted the loss of those hours of solitude nor the enjoyment of them, for it was as if I still possessed them, as if they were something that had become mine forever and that I could never conceivably lose. As for the pleasure of going out again, I can only think of being dizzy with happiness that there is one big pleasure left for me to sacrifice to God.

All this makes me feel wise and serene about the imperfections that I do not seem to be able to get rid of, because I am more than ever convinced that they will vanish in God's own good time. Meanwhile I am happy to suffer them and to shoulder their burden and carry it as well as I can, happy that a creature as low as I am is able to please a God so great that no man has ever seen Him and lived.

June 13, 1951

It is sometime in June. At a rough guess, I think it is June 13 which may or may not be the feast of Saint Anthony of Padua. In any case every day is the same for me because I have become very different from what I used to be. The man who began this journal is dead, just as the man who finished *The Seven Storey Mountain* when this journal began was also dead, and what is more the man who was the central figure in *The Seven Storey Mountain* was dead over and over. And now that all these men are dead, it is sufficient for me to say so on paper and I think I will have ended up by forgetting them. Because writing down what *The Seven Storey Mountain* was about was sufficient to get it off my mind for good. Last week I corrected the proofs of the French translation of the book and it seemed completely alien. I might as well have been a proofreader working for a publisher and going over the galleys of somebody else's book. Consequently, *The Seven Storey Mountain* is the work of a man I never even heard of. And this journal is getting to be the production of somebody to whom I have never had the dishonor of an introduction.

Ecce nova facio omnia! [Behold I make all things new (Revelation 21:5)!]

On Trinity Sunday I was named Master of the Scholastics. Dom Louis had asked for the formation of a regular scholasticate. Some of our large monasteries have them. They are absolutely necessary when the young professed are too numerous to remain for a long time in the novitiate. And they need a Spiritual Director as well as some sort of family life of their own. The problems of the young professed turn out to be perhaps the most crucial thing in their Cistercian formation.

The fact that I have suddenly ended up in this position clarifies all the foolish pages of the journal I have written about my own problems as a scholastic. For now I know that the reason why I had to resist the temptation to become a Carthusian was in order to learn how to help all the other ones who would be one way or another tempted to leave the monastery. And when I read such a lot of Duns Scotus, it was in order to learn, after all, the importance of keeping to the straight line of Thomism and of keeping scholastics out of difficulties which are too great for a Cistercian to solve. Our life is not designed for theological controversy and Scotus is more than the Cistercian head can bear – at least until somebody distills his essence and gives it to us second-hand.

And now, finally, about the vault and the woods: I am appalled by the number of useless books that have piled up in the vault. As long as I was a writer I thought of them as possibly coming in handy for the compilation of a book. But now that I am a spiritual director I have to live beyond my own borders in the souls of those whom God has placed in my charge. And it is immediately evident that very few of these books will ever help me to help them. On the contrary, most of the stuff on those shelves would only encourage me to disturb them. I am embarrassed at having walked with eyes wide open into such an obvious sin.

As for the woods, on Whitmonday (just before we cut down the last grove of cedars where one could still hide inside the enclosure) I explored a wooded bluff outside the east wall which is sufficiently fenced-in to be considered an extension of the enclosure. With the full approval of Dom Louis, Reverend Father has given me this wood as a refuge for my scholastics. It is a pleasant place, and one can more quickly find solitude there than in the forest, which is further away. And so I find that now I spend more time praying and less time walking; and, since the solitude is theirs rather than mine, I have less time for self-admiration. My prayer is more confusing and more obscure. I disappear and know nothing (except a confused awareness that I and the woods exist, but that I have a center which is outside the sphere of this existence). Two hours are the same as five minutes, and the bell rings and I am too often late for Vespers. Meanwhile in the vault, I bless my children and talk to them one by one and it is much more interesting than writing a book, besides being less fatiguing. Furthermore, since I am obliged to live the Rule in order to talk about it with any degree of authority, I go out to work as often as I can, and I now have blisters again the way I had them in the novitiate and I come home full of dirt and sweat and bathe and change and sit down under a tree behind the church where you can really pray.

Thus I sit on the threshold of a new existence. The one who is going to be most fully formed by the new scholasticate is the Master of the Scholastics. It is as if I were beginning all over again to be a Cistercian: but this time I am doing it without asking myself the abstract questions which are the luxury and the torment of one's monastic adolescence. For now I am a grown-up monk and have no time for anything but the essentials. The only essential is not an idea or an ideal: it is God Himself, Who cannot be found by weighing the present against the future or the past, but only by sinking into the heart of the present as it is.

June 23, 1951

Yesterday morning, after saying a Votive Mass of the Seven Dolors and trying to make a thanksgiving in the back sacristy in the short interval that was left before Prime, I slipped out and shaved and got into a black suit and a Roman collar to go to Louisville and become an American citizen.

All week long I had been trying to think about it, but in the end I have come to the conclusion that I can't kid myself that it is as important a step as religious profession or taking the habit of novice and it is useless to try to act as if it were. However, I prayed over it, and Thursday evening, after supper, I was sitting out in the small calf pasture, on the north side of the vineyard, watching the blazing hot sunset over the wooded knobs, and it seemed to me that all that triumphant fire out there served as a sort of anticipated celebration. Within twenty-four hours there would be a sense in which I could definitely speak of all this as "my country." It was a bit disturbing to find that I was suddenly discovering America in 1951 when it was supposed to have been discovered for me by Christopher Columbus in 1492. And to think that I had lived in Kentucky all this time without ever questioning the fact that I belonged to the place and that it belonged to me! Perhaps that only proves that, after all, papers do not make a man a citizen of any country, earth or heaven.

Anyway, I drove to town with two family brothers. By the time we left the sun was glaring through an angry haze and everybody knew it was going to be hot, including the men in undershirts and dungarees who were coming out with their mules to cultivate their plots of tobacco in all parts of Nelson County.

The ditches along the road were full of cornflowers and hollyhocks, and there were tiger lilies everywhere. Wild roses were climbing over the fences of the farms and were in bloom, and the trumpet vines were putting fourth their dull red soundless horns. After I said the *Itinerarium* [prayers for travelers] and Tierce and Sext, I sat back to memorize some of the things a citizen is supposed to know. I got them all out of a textbook that comes from the University of Kentucky and which we keep around here because almost every year now someone becomes a citizen. Last year it was Father Michael, who came over from Ireland, and maybe in a year or two it will be Father Sebastian who also came over from Ireland.

I thought we were going to be late at the Federal Building, and according to the notification, I was late indeed, but there was still plenty of time before the Court Session. The corridors were full of people, one of whom turned out to be a reporter. This is a peculiar world, in which the only man in a big crowd who has to worry about the reporters is a Trappist monk who has left the world.

My first sensation on entering the Court Room was one of spiritual discomfort at being in a place that was big enough to be a church but manifestly had no tabernacle. I had to stop myself from making a moderate bow to an imaginary crucifix, as if I were walking into the Chapter Room of a monastery. This bow would have seemed very mysterious to the bystanders, I am sure. The three big armchairs behind the Judge's bench failed, I fear, to remind me that all authority comes from God. The thought only occurred to me now, not yesterday, when it should have done so.

I looked for a chair in an out of the way place, but almost immediately they lined us up in some kind of official order, and I found myself sitting with the aisle on one side and a little red-haired lady on the other. When the Judge came in, the procedure began to be a lot of fun, because almost at once the examiner made each one stand up and say where he came from and what he did. It was very amusing to sit there and find so much about so many strangers – their names, their ages, the countries they came from, and when they came from them, and why. It seems to me that most of them were German girls who had married soldiers now stationed at Fort

Knox. But there were several Russians and there was a man with a fruit and vegetable business who came from Mount Lebanon, which is what they now call Syria, and there was a man from Finland and a little man called Romeo who was from Italy and sold insurance and there was a girl from Iceland and a tall red-haired man from Ontario who turned out to be married to a relative of one of the doctors in Saint Joseph's Infirmary. So when the atmosphere became more intimate, I had to stand up and explain why I had once belonged to the National Students League. While I did so, a lot of eminently respectable ladies, who were quite obviously not immigrants, turned around and gave me the once-over. It was then that I realized that these were members of the D.A.R. and my surmise turned out to be quite correct, for when it was all over – our naturalization, I mean – they stood up and started to make speeches and they gave us American flags.

November 29, 1951

John the Baptist sends Andrew to Jesus, and Andrew gets Peter and Peter tells Philip and Philip speaks to Nathaniel, who does not think that anything good can come out of Nazareth. But Jesus says that Nathaniel's suspicions are without guile. He speaks to Nathaniel about the fig tree. All at once the Kingdom of God is formed in the world – *regnum Dei intra vos est* [the kingdom of God is in the midst of you]. The angels are ascending and descending upon the Church, the Mystical Body of the Son of Man. Before Advent gets a chance to start (at least this year's Advent), Christ appears among us – *Parousia*. He cometh. He is already formed before our eyes in His saints, even before the Church can begin to start from the beginning, and draw Him forth from the types and mysteries of the Old Testament. Before the cycle has begun, it has already ended. The Vigil of Saint Andrew is a prelude to Pentecost, it contains Pentecost. The Body that is to be vivified with the Breath of God is already being formed from the slime of the earth.

Elias was a man like unto us. Andrew, Peter, James and John were men like unto us. And like them we bring our infirmities to Christ in order that His strength may be glorified in the transformation of our weakness. Day after day the outward man crumbles and breaks down and the inward man, the Man of Heaven, is born and grows in wisdom and knowledge before the eyes of men – who cannot recognize him. Neither can we recognize ourselves in the image of Him which is formed in us because we do not yet have the eyes with which to see Him. And yet we suspect His presence in the mystery which is not revealed to the wise and prudent. We feel His eyes upon us as we sit under the fig tree and our souls momentarily spring to life at the touch of His hidden finger. This flash of fire is our solitude; but it binds us to our brethren. It is the fire that has quickened the Mystical Body since Pentecost so that every Christian is, at the same time, a hermit and the whole Church, and we are all members one of another. It remains for us to recognize the mystery that your heart is my hermitage and that the only way I can enter into the desert is by bearing your burden and leaving you my own.

It is now six months since I have been Master of the Scholastics and have looked into their hearts and taken up their burdens upon me. I have not always seen clearly and I have not carried their burdens too well and I have stumbled around a lot, and on many days we have gone around in circles and fallen into ditches because the blind was leading the blind.

I do not know if they have discovered anything new, or if they are able to love God more, or if I have helped them in any way to find themselves, which is to say: to lose themselves. But I know what I have discovered: the kind of work I once feared because I thought it would interfere with "solitude" is, in fact, the only true path to solitude. One must be in some sense a hermit before the care of souls can serve to lead one further into the desert. But once God has called you to solitude, everything you touch leads you further into solitude. Everything that affects you builds you into a hermit, as long as you do not insist on doing the work yourself and building your own kind of hermitage.

What is my new desert? The name of it is *compassion*. There is no wilderness so terrible, so beautiful, so arid and so fruitful as the wilderness of compassion. It is the only desert that shall truly flourish like the lily. It shall become a pool, it shall bud forth and blossom and rejoice with joy. It is the desert of compassion that the thirsty land turns into springs of water, that the poor possess all things. There are no bounds to contain the inhabitants of this solitude in which I live alone, as isolated as the Host on the altar, the food of all men, belonging to all and belonging to none, for God is with me, and He sits in the ruins of my heart, preaching His Gospel to the poor.

Do you suppose I have a spiritual life? I have none, I am indigence, I am silence, I am poverty, I am solitude, for I have renounced spirituality to find God, and He it is Who preaches loud in the depths of my indigence, saying: "I will pour out my spirit upon thy children and they shall spring up among the herbs as willows beside the running waters" (Isaias 44:3–4). "The children of thy barrenness shall say in thy ears: The place is too strait for me, make me room to dwell in" (Isaias 49:20). I die of love for you, Compassion: I take you for my Lady, as Francis married poverty, I marry you, the Queen of hermits and the Mother of the poor.

There came from France a tiny, ancient leaflet, printed somewhere in the Auvergne at least half a century ago. It is about Our Lady of the Olive Trees, at Murat. Had I heard of her? I must have. I stood in the shadow of her church. She knew me when I was under the fig tree. Or under her olives – in the mountain where no olives grow.

January 10, 1952

The sun comes out, and so does the typewriter. All week I have been knocking myself out trying to prepare conferences and Scripture classes and give spiritual direction. Half my spiritual children have colds and some of them are depressed, and one just changed over to the laybrothers, which was a good thing, while two of them are trying to kill themselves with over-work, being cantors and directing the choir even during the psalmody of the little hours. I understand their anguish which, five years ago, was my own anguish. But I do not approve of their exhaustion. The choir now is different beyond all belief from what is was when I was a student and a sub-cantor.

All week I have been deacon, because last week I sang the High Mass. So this week I sing the Epiphany Gospel, and, as I sing it, the trees of the woods come before me, because, when I was working alone in the woods all week, I sang over to myself some of the phrases of the Gospel. The questions of the Magi and the plot of Herod. *Ubi est qui natus est rex Judae-orum?* [Where is he that is born King of the Jews (Matthew 2:2)?] I know where He is. He and I live in the trees. And yet I am more of a family man than I ever was in my life – and for that precise reason I have now become, as I think, a mature hermit. (Mature: today as we marched back into the sacristy after the High Mass, I thought to myself that in a few days I would be thirty-seven and that a graceless middle age was descending upon me.)

Thanks to my job in the woods, the curve below my chest has flattened out again. I had feared I was in for a corpulent middle age like any other writer.

The job in the woods is this: since October I have been the timber marker. I suddenly found out all about the trees. Next spring I shall presumably be in charge of planting ten thousand seedlings to replace what has been cut down. I started out with my pot of paint in October. The work began on the northeast flank of the lake knob, behind Donohue's place. After that we worked north. I am generally a couple of days' work ahead of the brothers who are after me with chain-saws and axes and that orange army truck and old jeep. The old jeep is distinguished from the flashy red jeep which some brother postulant brought from Kansas, but this "new" jeep is reserved for the novices.

Right now we are in a deep valley I never knew about before. It is between two knobs which do not have names, but one of which has become for me Mount Carmel. I have marked the trees in many different colors. Sometimes white, sometimes slate-blue. I began the year nineteen fifty-two with canary yellow. So all the west side of the smallest knob we see at the east end of our line of knobs is splashed with canary yellow, and it was there, too, that I sang the Epiphany Gospel to the silent glens. *Videntes autem stellam gavisi sunt gaudio magno valde!* [Seeing the star, they rejoiced with exceedingly great joy (Matthew 2:10)!]

On the whole, the best paint was that casein paint I used on the beech trees and the blighted elms and on the twisted tan oaks along that slope outside the valley, where Frater Caleb brought the novices a couple of times. Frater Caleb, the undermaster is one of my scholastics. That was also the place where, just after a lot of timber had been cut down and stacked for loading, and a lot of brush was lying around, a forest fire broke out in November, on the feast of the Dedication of the Church. Brother Gelgan got the jeep in the afternoon and I went out with him and three other brothers and we put out the fire with Indian pumps strapped on our backs. These are very effective – much more so than flapping at the flames with a cedar branch, or scuffing them with pitchforks.

On the feast of the Holy Innocents I took four of the scholastics out on this knob which I secretly call Mount Carmel. It is the finest of all the knobs. It runs north and south behind the lake knob and from the top, which is fairly clear of trees, you can see all over this part of Kentucky – miles of woods over to the northwest, and in the direction of Hanekamp's house and New Haven. Out there, somewhere a few miles on, lies the place where Lincoln was born.

So we took a truck as far as Donohue's. After that we got out and walked to the last cornerstone of our property at the end of the valley, and then climbed the knob. There was a high wind blowing and it was cold but wonderful. And I looked down into the big wide bowl of woods which is McGinty's hollow because somebody called McGinty once had a log cabin there or something. But it is all woods now, and I got lost there exactly a year before, on the feast of the Holy Innocents in 1950.

It is a strange thing, now that I have twenty-five scholastics to look after, I am more alone that I ever was before. When I am alone, I really am alone. When I am with them, I am also with God, which is the same as solitude – a deep and rich solitude. The more I get to know my scholastics the more reverence I have for their individuality and the more I meet them in my own solitude. The best of them, and the ones to whom I feel closest, are also the most solitary and at the same time the most charitable. All this experience replaces my theories of solitude. I do not need a hermitage, because I have found one where I least expected it. It was when I knew my brothers less well that my thoughts were more involved in them. Now that I know them better, I can see something of the depths of solitude which are in every human person, but which most men do not know how to lay open either to themselves or to others or to God.

The young ones, I admit, do not have half the problems I used to have when I was a scholastic. Their calmness will finally silence all that remains of my own turbulence. They come to me with intelligent questions, or sometimes with an even more intelligent absence of questions. They refresh me with their simplicity. Very spontaneously, they come to share my love of anything I may have discovered, around here, that is simple. But they ignore my persistent interest in theological complications. This is to me both a confusion and an education – to see that they can mostly get along quite well without what I used to think I needed, even though, when I was sane, I realized I did not need it at all.

I say theological complications, not theology. For I constantly preach to them from the encyclicals that they must know theology. Myself, in the afternoons after dinner, I read and love Saint Thomas on a pile of logs beyond the horse-pasture where the neighbors come on Sunday afternoons to hunt with shotguns. And there I have discovered that, after all, what the monks most need is not conferences on mysticism, but more light about the ordinary virtues, whether they be faith or prudence, charity or temperance, hope or justice or fortitude. And above all what they need and what they desire is to penetrate the Mystery of Christ and to know Him in His Gospels and in the whole Bible (some of them seem to read nothing else but the Bible).

Thus it is that I live in the trees. I mark them with paint, and the woods cultivate me with their silences, and all day long even in choir and at Mass I seem to be in the forest: but my children themselves are like trees, and they flourish all around me like the things that grow in the Bible.

February 26, 1952. Shrove Tuesday

The blue elm tree near at hand and the light blue hills in the distance: the red bare clay where I am supposed to plant some shade trees: these are before me as I sit in the sun for a free half hour between direction and work. Tomorrow is Ash Wednesday and today, as I sit in the sun, big blue and purple fish swim past me in the darkness of my empty mind, this sea which opens within me as soon as I close my eyes. Delightful darkness, delightful sun, shining on a world which, for all I care, has already ended.

It does not occur to me to wonder whether we will ever transplant the young maples from the wood, yonder, to this bare leveled patch – the place where the old horsebarn once stood. It does not occur to me to wonder how everything here came to be transformed. I sit on a cedar log half chewed by some novice's blunt axe, and do not reflect on the plans I have made for this place of prayer, because they do not matter. They will happen when they happen.

The hills are as pure as jade in the distance. God is in His transparent world, but He is too sacred to be mentioned, too holy to be observed. I sit in silence. The big deep fish are purple in my sea.

Different levels of depth.

First, there is the slightly troubled surface of the sea. Here there is action. I make plans. They toss in the wake of other men's traffic: passing liners. I speak to the scholastics. I make resolutions to speak less wildly, to say fewer of the things that surprise myself and them. Where do they spring from?

Second, there is the darkness that comes when I close my eyes. Here is where the big blue, purple, green, and gray fish swim by. Most beautiful and peaceful darkness: is it the cave of my own inner being? In this water-cavern I easily live, whenever I wish. Dull rumors only of the world reach me. Sometimes a drowned barrel floats into the room. Big gray-green fish, with silver under their purple scales. Are these the things the blind men see all day? I close my eyes to the sun, and live on the second level, a natural prayer, peace. When I am tired, it is almost slumber. There is no sound. Soon even the fish are gone. Night, night. Nothing is happening. If you make a theory about it, you end up in quietism. All I say about it is that it is comfortable. It is a rest. I half-open my eyes to the sun, praising the Lord of glory. Lo, thus I have returned from the blank abyss, re-entering the shale cities of Genesis. Ferns and fish return. Lovely dark green things. In the depth of the waters, peace, peace, peace. Such is the second level of waters under the sun. We pray therein, slightly waving among the fish.

Words, as I think, do not spring from this second level. They are only meant to drown there.

The question of socialization does not concern these waters. They are nobody's property. Animality. Game preserve. Paradise. No questions whatever perturb their holy botany. Neutral territory. No man's sea.

I think God intended me to write about this second level, however, rather than the first. I abandon all problems to their own unsatisfactory solutions, including the problem of "monastic spirituality." I will not even answer, as I answer the scholastics, that the Desert Fathers talked not about monastic spirituality but about purity of heart and obedience and solitude, and about God. And the wiser of them talked very little about anything. But the divine life, which is the life of the soul, as the soul is the life of the body: this [divine life] is a pure and concrete thing and not to be measured by your ascetic theory, and God in you is not to be weighed in the scales of my doctrine. Indeed, He is not to be weighed at all.

Third level. Here there is positive life swimming in the rich darkness which is no longer thick like water but pure, like air. Starlight, and you do not know where it is coming from. Moonlight is in this prayer, stillness, waiting for the Redeemer. Walls watching horizons in the middle of the night. *[Et fuit illis] in velamento diei et in luce stellarum nocte.* [And Wisdom was to them for a cover by day and for the light of stars by night (Wisdom 10:17).] Everything is charged with intelligence, though all is night. There is no speculation here. There is vigilance; life itself has turned to purity in its own refined depths. Everything is spirit. Here God is adored, His coming is recognized, He is received as soon as He is expected, and because He is expected, He is received, but He has passed by sooner than He arrived. He has gone before He came. He returned forever. He never yet passed by and already He had disappeared for all eternity. He is and He is not. Everything and Nothing. Not light, not dark, not high not low, not this side not that side. Forever and forever. In the wind of His passing the angels cry, "Thy Holy One is gone." Therefore I lie dead in the air of their wings. Life and night, day and darkness, between life and death. This is the holy cellar of my mortal existence, which opens into the sky.

It is a strange awakening to find the sky inside you and beneath you and above you and all around you so that your spirit is one with the sky, and all is positive night.

Here is where love burns with an innocent flame, the clean desire for death: death without sweetness, without sickness, without commentary, without reference and without shame. Clean death by the sword of the spirit in which is intelligence. And everything in order. Emergence and deliverance. I think this also is the meaning of Ash Wednesday: mourn, man, because you are not yet dust. Receive your ashes and rejoice.

Receive, O monk, the holy truth concerning this thing called death. Know that there is in each man a deep will, potentially committed to freedom or captivity, ready to consent to life, born consenting to death, turned inside out, swallowed by its own self, prisoner of itself like Jonas in the whale.

This is the truth of death which, printed in the heart of every man, leads him to look for the sign of Jonas the prophet. But many have gone into hell crying out that they had expected the resurrection of the dead. Others, in turn, were baptized and delivered: but their powers remained asleep in the dark and in the bosom of the depths.

Many of the men baptized in Christ have risen from the depths without troubling to find out the difference between Jonas and the whale.

It is the whale we cherish. Jonas swims abandoned in the heart of the sea. But it is the whale that must die. Jonas is immortal. If we do not remember to distinguish between them, and if we prefer the whale and do not take Jonas out of the ocean, the inevitable will come to pass. The whale and the prophet will soon come around and meet again in their wanderings, and once again the whale will swallow the prophet. Life will be swallowed again in death and its last state will be worse than the first.

We must get Jonas out of the whale and the whale must die at a time when Jonas is in the clear, busy with his orisons, clothed and in his right mind, free, holy and walking on the shore. Such is the meaning of the desire for death that comes in the sane night, the peace that finds us for a moment in clarity, walking by the light of the stars, raised to God's connatural shore, dry-shod in the heavenly country, in a rare moment of intelligence.

But even if we are not always intelligent, we must inevitably die.

I pursue this thought no further. It came to me because Frater John of God got a lot of kids' pictures from a sister in a school somewhere in Milwaukee. The pictures were supposed to be by backward children. Backward nothing. Most of them were of Jonas in or near the whale. They are the only real works of art I have seen in ten years, since entering Gethsemani. But it occurred to me that these wise children were drawing pictures of their own lives. They knew what was in their own depths. They were putting it all down on paper before they had a chance to grow up and forget. They were proving better than any apologist that there is something in the very nature of man that expects a Redeemer and resurrection from the dead. The sign of Jonas is written in our being. No wonder that this should be so when all creation is a vestige of the Creator, but also contains, written everywhere, in symbols, the economy of our Redemption.

March 17, 1952

The Communion antiphon sounded like bugles at the end of the Conventual Mass. This was because it is in the fifth tone and the fifth tone is full of melodies that echo in the new Jerusalem the silver trumpets that sounded in the temple of old. The sun is bright, and the spring is upon us, though the winds are cold. There are daffodils coming out by the door of the secular kitchen and in the beds outside this window. The Traxcavator roars merrily where they are trying to haul beams that weigh three tons up to the top floor of the new brothers' novitiate. And for my own part, I came out of Mass thinking about the trench where Frater John of God and I made haste to heel six thousand seedlings for the forest on Saturday afternoon. Today I hope to take about twenty novices out to the section of the woods behind Donohue's and start planting these seedlings in the places we logged most heavily last winter. The seedlings are yellow poplar, and short leaf pine, and loblolly pine. The latter have the most curious name and the most interesting smell and I like the red and purple tinge on the end of their needles. Yesterday, when I was coming in for Vespers, I saw a fire out there in the knobs in the section where we hope to start planting. The second fire in that spot since last November. I hope it will be the last for a long time, but I also hope the brothers will dig us a firebreak out there with one of their cats.

If the weather is nice, maybe I can take some of the scholastics out to plant on the feasts of Saint Joseph and Saint Benedict. And now I think of last year's feast of Saint Benedict, when I was walking around out there in those same woods, praying that the Abbot General would give me permission to spend a day each month alone and praying in the woods. The permission to go out merely for the sake of prayer was denied: and now I find that, instead of going out there once a month to pray, I have been out, day after day, to work: and the work I do does not interfere with prayer, but even in some sense makes it better, because, when you do something with an exceptional permission, you tend to be hampered by the latent consciousness that you are indulging in some unusual behavior of your own choosing and it makes the prayer less pure. On the other hand, when you are doing some work (and believe me nothing is more usual in a monastery than work) which is assigned by obedience, then you are paradoxically much more free to pray, providing the work is not the kind of work that takes up all your mind – or all your time!

So in the end I realize that Saint Benedict answered my prayer in a much wiser way than I myself had asked or hoped for it to be answered, and, as is usual in the Kingdom of Heaven, by giving up what I wanted I ended up having more than I had thought of wanting.

When your tongue is silent, you can rest in the silence of the forest. When your imagination is silent, the forest speaks to you, tells you of its unreality and of the Reality of God. But when your mind is silent, then the forest suddenly becomes magnificently real and blazes transparently with the Reality of God. For now I know that the Creation, which first seems to reveal Him in concepts, then seems to hide Him by the same concepts, finally *is revealed in Him,* in the Holy Spirit. And we who are in God find ourselves united in Him with all that springs from Him. This is prayer, and this is glory!

jhs

for EPILOGUE Sign of Jonas.[58]

June. Octave of Corpus Christi

It is June. On Pentecost Sunday it is my turn again to take my week as hebdomadary and sing the Conventual Mass. Then I am deacon the next week, when Corpus Christi comes. Once again, the cloister is paved with flowers, the sanctuary white hot under the floodlights concealed behind the pillars, high in the ceiling: and you look up at the monstrance through a cloud of hot, sweet smoke from the censer, and the sweat runs down into your eyes! I feel as though I had never been anywhere in the world except Gethsemani – as if there were no other place in the world where I had ever really lived. I do not say I love Gethsemani in spite of the heat, or because of the heat. I love Gethsemani: that means burning days and nights in summer, with the sun beating down on the metal roof and the psalms pulsing exultantly through the airless choir, while, row upon row of us, a hundred and forty singers, we sway forward and bow down. And the clouds of smoke go up to God in the sanctuary, and the novices get thin and go home forever.

On two sides of us the new buildings are complete. Half factory and half a Venetian palace, the new "garden house" with the cheese factory in the

---

[58] The remainder of this journal was composed on the typewriter.

cellar and the brothers' novitiate on the roof rises enormous over the cabbages in the garden. Then on the other side, half-veiled behind the trees, the slick new yellow guest house is full of priests from Evansville who have been coming here on retreat, in shifts week by week, all June. And I looked at their name-cards where they vested in the sacristy and wondered who these Fathers were: old Fathers and young Fathers, Father Hut, Father Mattingly, Father Pfau. And right at the place where our Father Raymond is vesting for the Mass *pro defunctis* [for the dead], this week, they have a card for a Father Flanagan, of the Evansville retreat. Now this is very funny, but of course you, reader, do not understand why it is funny because you do not know that Father Raymond's last name is also Flanagan.

Meanwhile there is supposed to be *another* new building. This time it will have to be an infirmary and a place where we can take a few more showerbaths than we are actually taking. And when Dom Gabriel Sortais came back again last month and made another visitation (he is our new Abbot General) he told us to make rooms opening on the infirmary chapel so that the partition can be rolled back and the very sick monks, the dying monks, can hear Mass from their beds. I do not stop to ask myself if I shall die in such a bed, or in any bed at all. It means another year of cement mixers and air-compressors in the yard outside this window, where I no longer have time to write books and where my spiritual children come to talk about God.

This week I am the third hebdomadary, which means it is my turn to say the brothers' Communion Mass, Our Lady's Mass. It is always a votive Mass of the Blessed Virgin, always the same. I like it that way. In the summer time, this Mass is said at three o'clock in the morning. So I leave the choir after morning meditation to go and say it while the rest of the monks recite Matins and Lauds. I generally finish the Brothers' communions by the end of the second nocturn, and then go off into the back sacristy and kneel in the dark behind the relic case next to St. Malachy's altar, while the sky grows pale outside over the forest, and a little cool air seeps in through the slats of the broken shutters. And the birds sing, and the crickets sing, and I am silent with God.

As soon as the morning angelus rings, I go out into the new day, my own new private dawn, which belongs to me alone. The priests are saying their Masses. The novices and scholastics are getting ready for Communion, and the brothers are peeling potatoes in the work room or slinging milk cans around the tile floor of the new dairy.

One of the best things that happens to a priest at Gethsemani is to be the hebdomadary of the Mass *de Beata*.

You walk out afterwards and have the day to yourself. You have almost two hours to pray or read or think by yourself and make up the night office. You are all alone in the cool world of morning. You are all alone with the birds and the blue hill and the herd that lows across the fields in our neighbor's pasture, and the rooster that sings sol-do in the coop behind the apple trees, and Aidan Nally growling at a team of mules on the side of his hill over yonder.

Already I am hoping that it will be somewhat the same one day next week, on the feast of Saint John the Baptist, when I will say Mass late, and consequently have this same long interval to myself, in the blue, wide-open, lonely morning. On that day Frater Caleb's family is coming from St. Louis and he wants me to say Mass for them, and thus I will give communion to his little sister Mary Ann who just made her first communion and who thinks she wants to be either a policewoman or a Carmelite when she grows up.

How lovely are thy tabernacles, O Lord of hosts! The sparrow hath found herself a house and the turtle dove a nest for herself where she may lay her little ones [Psalms 83:2, 4]!

This is the land where you have given me roots in eternity, O God of heaven and earth. This is the burning promised land, the house of God, the gate of heaven, the place of peace, the place of silence, the place of wrestling with the angel. Each tomato patch is named after a saint. And the tomatoes called *"St. Benedict, ora pro nobis"* are under the care of Rod Mudge whom Dan Walsh rescued from some sort of quandary at Columbia. He came down with Dan to my ordination. A year later he came back as a novice and soon expects to make profession.

Blessed are they who dwell in thy house, O Lord! They shall praise thee for ever and ever [Psalms 83:5].

The roof is peeling off the old garden house, which has become a rejected building. One of the pillars of the old wagon shed has been knocked down by a tractor. There will be a new metal hangar for all the machines. This corner of the farm, where the old horsebarn used to be, is the desert that has been given to me for the planting of shade trees, that it may some day be a place of contemplation. *Altaria tua, Domine virtutum!* [Your altars, O God of hosts (Psalms 83:4)!]

Down there, the young bulls sleep behind the single strand of their electric fence.

It is four o'clock in the morning.

———

The Lord God is present where the new day shines in the moisture on the young grasses. The Lord God is present where the small wildflowers are known to Him alone. The Lord God passes suddenly, in the wind, at the moment when night ebbs into the ground. He Who is infinitely great has given to His children a share in His own innocence. His alone is the greatest of loves: whose pure flame respects all things.

God, Who owns all things, leaves them all to themselves. He never takes them for His own, the way we take them for our own and destroy them. He leaves them to themselves. He keeps giving to them, giving them all that they are, asking no thanks of them save that they should receive from Him and be loved and nurtured by Him, and that they should increase and multiply. He saw that all things were good, and He did not enjoy them. He saw that all things were beautiful and He did not want them. His love is not like ours. His love is unpossessive. His love is pure because it needs nothing. *If I should be hungry I would not tell thee* [Psalms 50:12]. But in Him there is no hunger. He is unknown to those who need delight. Those who are thirsty have never heard of Him Who thirsts for nothing.

All things belong to Him precisely because He possesses nothing. They owe Him everything, and they can repay Him nothing. They exist in Him with an uncreated existence which is nevertheless not their own existence but His existence, holy and pure, infinitely above them.

Lord, what is the secret of this world that does not own itself and is not owned by you, as by a user, by a proprietor?

The most wonderful thing about the world is that it is nobody's property, not even God's! We who are ruined by our own indigence to the point of thinking that we can possess something worship a false god, a god of possession, that is, a god of destruction. God is the God of the living.

We who have been destroyed by our own vain hunger, and who destroy and deaden everything that we touch with our desire, we think the whole world is impure, whereas it is we who are impure. God is pure, and because He is pure He does not need to keep the birds in cages. God is great, and because He is great He can let the grasses grow where they will, and the weeds go rambling over our fallen buildings (for the day will come when all our buildings will have fallen down, because they were somebody's possession). We, who rule all things with iron laws, describe the universe as if God also laid down laws. God is His own law and the law of all things is in His freedom. Therefore the stars serve Him freely and the sun rises with a song of joy and the moon, the clean gentle speechless moon goes down to her bed without protest. Every wave of the sea is free. Every river on earth proclaims its own liberty. The independent trees own nothing and are owned by no one and they lift up their leafy heads in freedom. Never were two of them alike. Never were two leaves of the same tree identical. Never were two cells of the same leaf exactly the same. Because the trees grow the way they like: and all things do the things they do for the pleasure of God, as if He could be pleased with them! But we use the word pleasure, and we say He is pleased, because in all these things it is *His freedom* [in which He] takes His pleasure. Pleased, not because it is His, but because it is theirs. For He has given it to them.

God, without being touched by them, without being mixed in with His creatures, without descending Himself to the level of their joy, shares with them His Secret, His innocence, His being, His freedom, His mystery. That is what we mean by glory. That is what His creatures have to give Him: glory. But what is glory? God's glory is God in them without possessing them. God in them without touching them. God in them without being touched by them. God giving them everything and retaining His own infinite separation. God being their Father without being related to them. They are related to Him, but never come near Him Who is within them. God's glory and God's shyness are one. His glory is to give them everything and to be in the midst of them as unknown.

O children of men! Don't you know that God refuses to be seen? If you only could see how unlike our glory is His glory, you would die for love of Him. But how can we believe who seek glory from one another [John 5:44]?[59] If we only knew that God never seeks glory except by *giving glory*. He does not ask us to give Him any glory we have not received from Him. . . . And where can we find Him to give Him back what we have received from Him? The moment we have found Him, He is already gone!

To love God perfectly we have to share His infinite innocence. But this innocence is a love too perfect to be shared, that is, too perfect to be divided. It can only be completely given. The giving never ends, the Giver is never completely received. Yet, if He is not completely received, is He received at all?

We speak of possessing Him. Ultimately, this notion of possession has to be renounced, except as an abstract term. We do not find Him Who is without possession until the precise moment when He lets us love, as He loves, without possession. This is what it means to be in heaven. Ultimately there is no greater disinterestedness than to receive all from Him. For

[59] Merton has cited this text three times in these journals.

when we have received everything from Him, we have still received nothing, since we have not received Him.

No matter how much He gives us, in the order of nature or of grace, there is still an infinite distance from what He has given to what He IS. Shall we still stretch out our hands for what He is? Shall we crave His being as our *possession?*

That was the sin of Adam and the sin of the fallen angels. The desire to possess divinity, to possess God's being, to own that to which no one has any right. And God Himself does not possess Himself. He does not even claim Himself by right! He does not put a fence around His Divine Nature and say: this is my property, no trespasser shall enter this land!

It is those who want to possess God who remain far from Him because they think He is far from them. Actually, they can possess all that God has given them, and receive it with gratitude, and glorify Him, and have all things without possession. But there remains one thing more to be done. Not to seek Him as a possession, but to love Him and know Him and see Him as unseen and unknown and unpossessed. This is to have God beyond possession. This alone is the life of the children of God. This alone is the sharing of the divine nature which has been given us to share with Him. To be perfectly disinterested, our love must not refuse to accept anything from Him. It must receive *all* from Him. But, beyond this, it must go out to Him Who is beyond all that we can ever receive, without the hope of possessing His limitless being. For possession would set a limit to His being, and therefore He does not even possess Himself: possession would make Him something less than infinite.

We love Him perfectly, who is perfectly free, when we are content to leave Him His freedom.

We cannot respect His freedom unless we let Him give us all that He desires to give us.

His desires for us, His generosity to us, is next to limitless.

In order to love Him disinterestedly we must receive all things, and almost the infinite, from Him.

But beyond what we can receive lies the Infinite. Beyond His gifts there remains His freedom. If we love Him, we cannot desire to capture His freedom. If, having received all from Him, we still desire to capture Him, we lose all things that we have received and fall back into the depths of poverty, that is to say into the prison of our own possession in which we crave all good things with passion and fear all evil with a mortal terror, and are never able to have what we crave or escape the evil that we fear.

In order to love God perfectly, then, we must let Him love us perfectly. We must let Him give us all things, and we must hold on to none of them as if they were our own. In this way we imitate Him Who does not claim them as His own, even though He has made them.

At the summit of perfection we come upon this paradox: that we cannot love God perfectly except by perfectly loving ourselves.

We love ourselves perfectly when we love His love for us. We love ourselves perfectly when we love ourselves as He loves Us. For in loving ourselves as He loves us, we love Him as He loves us. This is what it means to say that perfect love reestablishes in us the true likeness of God, in whose image we were created. Our souls, by pure love, are made perfect and spotless mirrors of His freedom, His perfection.

Thus we receive all things and hold on to nothing. We own all things in Him and possess nothing. We touch all things and defile nothing. We are in all things and are not mixed up with them. We retain our integrity and they retain their integrity and God retains His integrity. Things are everlastingly themselves and we are everlastingly ourselves and God is God forever. There is no absorption of personalities, there is no confusion of substances, there is perfection of love. Pure freedom is vindicated by this perfection.

Thus, when we love ourselves perfectly, we disappear.

For God, by loving all things perfectly, is never clearly seen in them. If He possessed them, if He sealed them with the brand of appropriation, we would be able to see Him directly in them and we would catch Him at last. Who is uncatchable.

All He has left in things is his invisible vestige.

All that we know of Him in them is His own inviolable freedom.

July 5th, 1952

Custos, quid de nocte! [Watchman, what of the night (Isaiah 21:11)!]

The night, O my Lord, is a time of freedom.

You have seen the morning and the night, and the night was better. In the night all things began, and in the night the end of all things has come before me.

In the night I have spoken to you on the roof of the house that shall one day perish.

Baptized in the rivers of night, Gethsemani has recovered her innocence. The night is a time of freedom. It is the time when the evil become the prisoners of evil and the good are liberated from the boundaries of their own history. Darkness brings a semblance of order before all things disappear. With the clock slung over my shoulder, in the silence of the fourth of July, it is my time to be the night watchman, in the house that will one day perish.

Here is the way it is when you go on the fire watch.

Before eight o'clock the monks are packed in the belly of the great heat, singing to the Mother of God like exiles traveling to their slavery, hoping for glory. The night angelus unlocks the place and sets them free. The holy monster which is "the community" divides itself into segments and disperses through airless cloisters where yellow lamps do not attract the bugs.

The watchman's clock, together with the watchman's sneakers, are kept in a box, together with a flashlight and the keys to various places, at the foot of the infirmary stairs.

Rumors behind me and above me and around me signalize the Fathers going severally to bed in different dormitories. Where there is cold water some stay to take salt tablets. Thus we fight the heat. I take the heavy clock and sling it on its strap over my shoulder. I walk to the nearest window on my silent feet. I recite the second nocturn of Saturday, sitting by the window, and the house begins to be silent.

One late Father, with a change of dry clothes slung over his shoulder, stops to look out the window and pretends to be frightened when he sees me sitting around the corner in the dark, holding the breviary in the yellow light, saying the Psalms of Saturday.

It is ten or fifteen minutes before there are no more feet echoing along the cloisters, shuffling up the stairs. (When you go late to the dormitories, you have to take off your shoes and make your way to bed in socks, as if the others were already sleeping in this weather!)

At eight-fifteen I sit in darkness. I sit in human silence. Then I begin to hear the eloquent night, the night of wet trees, with moonlight sliding over the shoulder of the Church in a haze of dampness and subsiding heat. The world of this night resounds from heaven to hell with animal eloquence, with the savage innocence of a million unknown creatures. While the earth eases and cools off like a huge living thing, the enormous vitality of their music pounds and rings and throbs and echoes until it gets into everything, drums in everything, and swamps the whole world in its neutral madness which never becomes an orgy because all things are innocent, all things are pure. Nor would I have mentioned the possibility of evil, except that I remember how the heat and the wild music of living things drive people crazy, when they are not in monasteries, and make them do things which the world has forgotten how to lament.

That is why some people act as if the night and the forest and the heat and the animals had in them something of contagion, whereas the heat is holy and the animals are the children of God and the night was never made to hide sin, but only to open infinite distances to charity and send our souls to play beyond the stars.

Eight-thirty. I begin my round in the cellar of the south wing. The place is full of naked wires and stinks of the hides of slaughtered calves. Your feet are walking on a floor of earth, down a long catacomb, at the end of which there is a brand new locked door in the guest wing that was only finished the other day. So you punch your clock for the first time in the catacomb, you turn your back on the new wing, and the fire watch is on.

Around one corner is a hole in the wall with a vat where they stew fruit. Under this vat Dom Frederic told me to burn all the letters that were in the pigeon holes of the room where he had been prior. Around another corner is an old furnace where I burned the rest of the papers that he told me to burn, that were in the same room. In this musty silence which no longer smells of wine (because the winery is in another building now) the flashlight creates a little dizzy tennis ball upon the walls and floor. Concrete begins under the watchman's catfeet and moonlight reaches through the windows into a dark place with jars of prunes and applesauce on all the shelves. There is a thin grey smell of dishwater in the room where half a dozen tin cups and supper plates are swimming in the tank where they were dropped by late eaters.

Then suddenly, after the old dirt floor of the catacomb over yonder, you hit something dizzy and new: the kitchen, which the brother novices painted up, each wall in a different color, tile under the shining vats and scripture close to the ceiling: "Little children, love one another!" Some of the monks complained of the different walls, but a watchman has no opinions.

There are blue benches in the scullery, and the room is cool. Sometimes, when you go up the stairs without making any noise, a brother comes in late from the barns through the kitchen door and runs into you by surprise in the darkness and is blinded by the flashlight and (if he is a novice) is probably scared to death.

For a few feet, the way is familiar. You are in the little cloister which is the monastery's main stem. It goes from the places where the monks live to the places where they pray. But now it is empty and, like everything else, it is a lot nicer when there is nobody there. The steps down to the tailor shop have a different sound. They drum under your rubber soles. You run into the smell of duck and cotton, mixed with the smell of bread. There is light in the bakery, and someone is working late, around the corner, behind the oven. This is where you punch your clock, it is the second station.

The third station is the hottest one: the furnace room. This time the stairs don't drum, they ring: they are iron. You fight your way through a jungle of wet clothes, drying in the heat, and go down by the flanks of the boiler to the third station which is there up against the bricks, beneath an engraving of the Holy Face.

After that, you are in the choir novitiate. Here, too, it is hot. The place is swept and recently painted and there are notice boards at every turn in the little crooked passageways where each blue door is named after a saint. Long lists of appointments for the novices' confession and direction. Sentences from the liturgy. Fragments of severe and necessary information. But the walls of the building have their own stuffy smell and I am suddenly haunted by my first days in religion, the freezing, tough winter when I first received the habit and always had a cold, the smell of frozen straw in the dormitory under the chapel, and the deep unexpected ecstasy of Christmas – that first Christmas when you have nothing left in the world but God!

It is when you hit the novitiate that the night watch begins in earnest. Alone, silent, wandering on your appointed rounds through the corridors of a huge, sleeping monastery, you come around the corner and find yourself face to face with your monastic past and with the mystery of your vocation.

The fire watch is an examination of conscience in which your task as watchman suddenly appears in its true light: a pretext devised by God to isolate you and to search your soul with lamps and questions, in the heart of darkness.

God, my God, God whom I meet in darkness, with You it is always the same thing! Always the same question that nobody knows how to answer!

I have prayed to you in the daytime with thoughts and reasons, and in the night time you have confronted me, scattering thought and reason. I have come to you in the morning light and with desire, and you have descended upon me, with great gentleness, with most forbearing silence, in this inexplicable night, dispersing light, defeating all desire. I have explained to you a hundred times my motives for entering the monastery and you have listened and said nothing, and I have turned away and wept with shame.

Is it true that all my motives have meant nothing? Is it true that all my desires were an illusion?

While I am asking questions which You do not answer, you ask me a question which is so simple that I cannot answer. I do not even understand the question.

This night, and every night, it is the same question.

There is a special, living resonance in these steep hollow stairs to the novitiate chapel, where You are all alone, the windows closed upon You, shutting you up with the heat of the afternoon.

Here, when it was winter, I used to come after dinner, heavy with sleep and with potatoes, and kneel all the time because that was the only period in which we were allowed to do what we liked. Nothing ever happened, but that was what I liked.

Here, on Sunday mornings, a crowd of us would try to make the Way of the Cross, jostling one another among the benches, and, on days of recollection in summer, we would kneel there all afternoon with the sweat running down our ribs, while candles burned all around the tabernacle and the veiled ciborium stood shyly in the doorway, peeping out at us between the curtains.

And here, now, by night, with this huge clock ticking on my right hip and the flashlight in my hand and sneakers on my feet, I feel as if everything had been unreal. It is as if the past had never existed. The things I thought were so important – because of the effort I put into them – have turned out to be of small value. And the things I never thought about, the things I was never either able to measure or to expect, they were the things that mattered.

(There used to be a man who walked down the back road singing on summer mornings, right in the middle of our thanksgiving after Communion: singing his own private song, every day the same. It was the sort of song you would expect to hear out in the country, in Kentucky.)

But in this darkness I would not be able to say, for certain, what it was that mattered. That, perhaps, is part of Your unanswerable question! Only I remember the heat in the beanfield the first June I was here, and I get the same sense of mysterious, unsuspected value that struck me after Father Alberic's funeral.

This is a different city, with a different set of associations. The ceramic studio is something relatively new. Behind the door (where they burnt out one kiln and bought a new one) little Fr. John of God suddenly made a good crucifix, just a week ago. And he is one of my scholastics. And I think of the clay Christ that came out of his heart. I think of the beauty and the simplicity and the pathos that were sleeping there, waiting to become an image. I think of this simple and mysterious child, and of all my other children. What is waiting to be born in all their hearts? Suffering? Deception? Heroism? Defeat? Peace? Betrayal? Sanctity? Death?

On all sides I am confronted by questions that I cannot answer, because the time for answering them has not yet come. Between the silence of God and the silence of my own soul, stands the silence of the souls entrusted to me. Immersed in these three silences, I realize that the questions I ask myself about them are perhaps not actual because they are not yet answerable.

And perhaps the most urgent and practical renunciation is the renunciation of all questions.

The most poignant thing about the fire watch is that you go through Gethsemani not only in length and height, but also in depth. You hit strange caverns in the monastery's history, layers set down by the years, geological strata: you feel like an archaeologist suddenly unearthing ancient civilization. But the terrible things is that you yourself have lived through those ancient civilizations. The house has changed so much that ten years have as many different meanings as ten Egyptian dynasties. The meanings are hidden in the walls. They mumble in the floor under the watchman's rubber feet. The lowest layer is at once in the catacomb under the south wing and in the church tower. Every other level of history is found in between.

The Church.

In spite of the stillness, the huge place seems alive. Shadows move everywhere, around the small uncertain area of light which the sanctuary light casts on the Gospel side of the altar. And there are faint sounds in the darkness, empty choirstalls creak and hidden boards mysteriously sigh.

The silence of the sacristy has its own sound. I shoot the beam of light down to Saint Malachy's altar and the relic cases. Vestments are laid out for my Mass tomorrow, at Our Lady of Victories altar. Keys rattle again in the door and the rattle echoes all over the church. When I was first on for the fire watch I thought the church was full of people praying in the dark. But no. The night is filled with unutterable murmurs, the walls with traveling noises which seem to wake up and come back, hours after something has happened, to gibber at the places where it happened.

This nearness to You in the darkness is too simple and too close for excitement. It is commonplace for all things to live an unexpected life in the night: but their life is illusory and unreal. The illusion of sound only intensifies the infinite substance of Your silence.

Here, in this place where I made my vows, where I have had my hands anointed for the Holy Sacrifice, where I have had Your priesthood seal the depth and intimate summit of my being, a word, a thought, would defile the quiet of Your inexplicable love.

Your Love, O God, speaks to my life as to an intimate, in the midst of a crowd of strangers: I mean these walls, this roof, these arches, this (overhead) ridiculously large and unsubstantial tower. Lord, God, the whole world tonight seems to be made out of paper. The most substantial things are ready to crumble or tear apart and blow away.

How much more so this monastery which everybody believes in and which has perhaps already ceased to exist?

O God, my God, the night has values that day has never dreamed of. All things stir by night, waking or sleeping, conscious of the nearness of their ruin. Man only makes himself illuminations he conceives to be solid and eternal. But while we ask our questions and come to our decisions, God blows our decisions out, the roofs of our houses cave in upon us, the towers are undermined by ants, the walls crack and cave in and the holiest buildings burn to ashes while the watchman is composing a theory of duration.

Now is the time to get up and go to the tower. Now is the time to meet You, God, where the night is wonderful, where the roof is almost without substance under my feet, where all the mysterious junk in the belfry scorns the proximate coming of three new bells, where the forest opens out under the moon and the living things sing terribly that only the present is eternal and that all things having a past and a future are doomed to pass away.

This, then, is the way from the floor of the Church to the platform on the tower.

First I must make a full round of the house on the second floor. Then I must go to the third-floor dormitories. After that, the tower.

Cloister. Soft feet, total darkness. The brothers have torn up the tent in the cloister garden, where the novices were sleeping two winters ago, and where some of them got pneumonia.

Just yesterday they put a new door on Father Abbot's room, while he was away with Dom Gabriel, visiting the foundations.

I am in the corridor under the old guest house. In the middle of the hallway a long table is set with knives and forks and spoons and bowls for the breakfast of the postulants and family brothers. Three times a day they eat in the corridor. For two years there has been no other place to put them.

The high, light door into the old guest wing swings back and I am on the stairs.

I had forgotten that the upper floors were empty. The silence astonishes me. The last time I was on the fire watch there was a retreat party of fifty lined up on the second floor, signing their names in the guest register in the middle of the night. They had just arrived in a bus from Notre Dame. Now the place is absolutely empty. All the notices are off the walls. The bookshelf has vanished from the hall. The population of holy statues has been diminished. All the windows are wide open. Moonlight falls on the cool linoleum floor. The doors of some of the rooms are open and I see that they are empty. I can feel the emptiness of all the rest.

I would like to stop and stand here for an hour, just to feel the difference. The house is like a sick person who has recovered. This is the Gethsemani that I entered, and whose existence I had almost forgotten. It was this silence, this darkness, this emptiness that I walked into with Brother Matthew eleven years ago this spring. This is the house that seemed to have been built to be remote from everything, to have forgotten all cities, to be absorbed in the eternal years. But this recovered innocence has nothing reassuring about it. The very silence is a reproach. The emptiness itself is my most terrible question.

If I have broken this silence, and if I have been to blame for talking so much about this emptiness that it came to be filled with people, who am I to praise the silence anymore? Who am I to publicize this emptiness? Who am I to remark on the presence of so many visitors, so many retreatants, so many postulants, so many tourists? Or have the men of our age acquired a Midas touch of their own, so that as soon as they succeed, everything they touch becomes crowded with people?

In this age of crowds in which I have determined to be solitary, perhaps the greatest sin would be to lament the presence of people on the threshold of my solitude. Can I be so blind as to ignore that solitude itself is their greatest need? And yet if they rush in upon the desert in thousands, how shall they be alone? What went they out into the desert to see? Whom did I myself come here to find but You, O Christ, Who have compassion on the multitudes?

Nevertheless, Your compassion singles out and separates the one on whom Your mercy falls, and sets him apart from the multitudes even though You leave him in the midst of the multitudes. . . .

With my feet on the floor I waxed when I was a postulant, I ask these useless questions. With my hand on the key by the door to the tribune, where I first heard the monks chanting the psalms, I do not wait for an answer, because I have begun to realize You never answer when I expect.

The third room of the library is called hell. It is divided up by wallboard partitions into four small sections full of condemned books. The partitions are hung with American flags and pictures of Dom Edmond Obrecht. I thread my way through this unbelievable maze to the second room of the library, where the retreatants used to sit and mop their brows and listen to sermons. I do not have to look at the corner where the books about the Carthusians once sang to me their siren song as I sail past with clock ticking and light swinging and keys on my hand to unlock the door into the first room of the library. Here the scholastics have their desks. This is the upper Scriptorium. The theology books are all around the walls. Yonder is the broken cuckoo clock which Father Willibrod winds up each morning with a gesture of defiance, just before he flings open the windows.

Perhaps the dormitory of the choir monks is the longest room in Kentucky. Long lines of cubicles, with thin partitions a little over six feet high, shirts and robes and scapulars hang over the partitions trying to dry in the night air. Extra cells have been jammed along the walls between the windows. In each one lies a monk on a straw mattress. One pale bulb burns in the middle of the room. The ends are shrouded in shadows. I make my way softly past cell after cell. I know which cells have snorers in them. But no one seems to be asleep in this extraordinary tenement. I walk as softly as I can down to the far west end, where Frater Caleb sleeps in the bell-ringer's corner. I find my station inside the door of the organ loft, and punch the clock, and start off again on soft feet along the other side of the dormitory.

There is a door hidden between two cells. It leads into the infirmary annex, where the snoring is already in full swing. Beyond that, steep stairs to the third floor.

One more assignment before I can climb them. The infirmary, with its hot square little chapel, the room that contains the retreats I made before all the dates in my monastic life: clothing, professions, ordinations. I cannot pass it without something unutterable coming up out of the depths of my being. It is the silence which will lift me on to the tower.

Meanwhile I punch the clock at the next station, at the dentist's office, where next week I am to lose another molar.

Now the business is done. Now I shall ascend to the top of this religious city, leaving its modern history behind. These stairs climb back beyond the civil war. I make no account of the long laybrothers' dormitory where a blue light burns. I hasten to the corridor by the wardrobe. I look out the low windows and know that I am already higher than the trees. Down at the end is the doorway to the attic and the tower.

The padlock always makes a great noise. The door swings back on swearing hinges and the night wind, hot and gusty, comes swirling down out of the loft with a smell of ancient rafters and old, hidden, dusty things. You have to watch the third step or your feet go through the boards. From here on the building has no substance left, but you have to mind your head and bow beneath the beams on which you can see the marks of axes with which our French Fathers used to hew them out a hundred years ago . . .

And now the hollowness that rings under my feet measures some sixty feet to the floor of the church. I am over the transept crossing. If I climb around the corner of the dome, I can find a hole once opened by the photographers and peer down into the abyss, and flash the light far down upon my stall in choir.

I climb the trembling, twisted stair into the belfry. The darkness stirs with a flurry of wings high above me in the gloomy engineering that holds the steeple together. Nearer at hand the old clock ticks in the tower. I flash the light into the mystery which keeps it going, and gaze upon the ancient bells.

I have seen the fuse box. I have looked in the corners where I think there is some wiring. I am satisfied that there is no fire in this tower which would flare like a great torch and take the whole abbey up with it in twenty minutes . . .

And now my whole being breathes the wind which blows through the belfry, and my hand is on the door through which I see the heavens. The door swings out upon a vast sea of darkness and of prayer. Will it come like this, the moment of my death? Will You open a door upon the great forest and set my feet upon a ladder under the moon, and take me out among the stars?

The roof glistens under my feet, this long metal roof facing the forest and the hills, where I stand higher than the treetops and walk upon shining air.

Mists of damp heat rise up out of the field around the sleeping abbey. The whole valley is flooded with moonlight and I can count the southern hills beyond the watertank and almost number the trees of the forest to the north. Now the huge chorus of living beings rises up out of the world beneath my feet: life singing in the watercourses, throbbing in the creeks and the fields and the trees, choirs of millions and millions of jumping and flying and creeping things. And far above me the cool sky opens upon the frozen distance of the stars.

I lay the clock upon the belfry ledge and pray cross-legged with my back against the tower, and face the same unanswered question.

Lord God of this great night: do You see the woods? Do You hear the rumor of their loneliness? Do You behold their secrecy? Do You remember their solitudes? Do You see that my soul is beginning to dissolve like wax within me?

[Deus meus] clamabo per diem, et non exaudies; et nocte, et non ad insipientiam mihi! [O my God, I shall cry by day, and thou wilt not hear: and by night, and it shall not be reputed as folly in me (Psalms 22:3)!] Do you remember the place by the stream? Do You remember the top of the Vineyard Knob that time in autumn, when the train was in the valley? Do you remember McGinty's hollow? Do You remember the thinly wooded hillside behind Hanekamp's place? Do You remember the time of the forest fire? Do You know what has become of the little poplars we planted in the spring? Do You observe the valley where I marked the trees?

There is no leaf that is not in Your care. There is no cry that was not heard by You before it was uttered. There is no water in the shales that was not hidden there by Your wisdom. There is no concealed spring that was not concealed by You. There is no glen for a lone house that was not planned by You for a lone house. There is no man for that acre of woods that was not made by You for that acre of woods.

But there is greater comfort in the substance of silence than in the answer to a question. Eternity is in the present. Eternity is in the palm of the hand. Eternity is a seed of fire, whose sudden roots break barriers that keep my heart from being an abyss.

The things of Time are in connivance with eternity. The shadows serve You. The beasts sing to You before they pass away. The solid hills shall vanish like a worn out garment. All things change and die and disappear. Questions arrive, assume their actuality, and also disappear. In this hour I shall cease to ask them, and silence shall be my answer. The world that Your love created and that the heat has distorted and that my mind is always misinterpreting shall cease to interfere with our voices.

Minds which are separated pretend to blend in one another's language. The marriage of souls in concepts is mostly an illusion. Thoughts which travel outward bring back reports from You from outward things: but a dialogue with You, uttered through the world, always ends by being a dialogue with my own reflection in the stream of time. With You there is no dialogue unless You choose a mountain and circle it with cloud and print your words in fire upon the mind of Moses. What was delivered to Moses on tablets of stone, as the fruit of lightning and thunder, is now more thoroughly born in our souls as quietly as the breath of our own being.

You, Who sleep in my breast, are not met with words, but in the emergence of life within life and of wisdom within wisdom. With You there is no longer any dialogue, any contest, any opposition. You are found in communion! Thou in me and I in Thee and Thou in them and they in me: dispossession within dispossession, dispassion within dispassion, emptiness within emptiness, freedom within freedom. I am alone. Thou art alone. The Father and I are One.

The hand lies open. The heart is dumb. The soul that held my substance together, like a hard gem in the hollow of my own power, will one day give in. Meanwhile I have beheld the light of the moon made prisoner in the heart of this gem, but I no longer believe the moon to be my own. Although I see the stars, I no longer pretend to know them. Although I have walked in these woods, how can I claim to love them? One by one I shall forget the names of individual things.

The Voice of God is heard in Paradise:

"What was vile has become precious. What is now precious was never vile. I have always known the vile as precious: for what is vile I know not at all.

What was cruel has become merciful. What is now merciful was never cruel. I have always overshadowed Jonas with my mercy, and cruelty I know not at all. Have you had sight of Me, Jonas, my child? Mercy within mercy within mercy. I have forgiven the universe without end, because I have never known sin.

What was poor has become infinite. What is infinite was never poor. I have always known poverty as infinite: riches I love not at all. Prisons within prisons within prisons. Do not lay up for yourselves ecstasies upon earth, where time and space corrupt, where the minutes break in and steal. No more lay hold on time, Jonas, my son, lest the rivers bear you away.

What was fragile has become powerful. I loved what was most frail. I looked upon what was nothing. I touched what was without substance, and within what was not, I am."

There are drops of dew that show like sapphires in the grass as soon as the morning sun appears, and leaves stir behind the hushed flight of an escaping dove.

The Daily Schedule at Gethsemani During the 1940s

Winter A.M.		Summer A.M.	
2:00	Rise, go to choir, recite Matins and Lauds of Our Lady's Office	2:00	As in winter
2:30	Meditation	2:30	As in winter
3:00	Night Office (Canonical Matins and Lauds)	3:00	As in winter
4:00	Priests say private Masses Others receive Communion Reading or private prayer	4:00	As in winter
5:30	Prime, followed by Chapter; then *frustulum* for those not fasting until dinner	5:30	As in winter
6:30	Reading, study, or private prayer	6:30	Mixt
7:45	Tierce, High Mass, Sext	6:45	Work (students study)
9:00	Work (students study)	9:00	Reading, private prayer
10:45	Reading or prayer	9:30	Tierce, High Mass, Sext
11:07	None	11:00	Dinner
11:30	Dinner		

Winter P.M.		Summer P.M.	
12:15	Reading, private prayer	12:00	Meridienne [siesta]
1:30	Work	1:30	Reading, private prayer
3:30	Reading, private prayer	2:00	Work
4:30	Vespers	4:30	Reading, private prayer
5:15	Meditation	5:15	Vespers, meditation
5:30	Collation	6:00	Supper
5:40	Reading, prayer	6:30	Reading, prayer
6:10	Compline, *Salve Regina* Examination of Conscience	7:10	Compline, *Salve Regina* Examen
7:00	All Retire	8:00	All Retire

A Glossary of Monastic Terms

Black Fast: An ascetic practice in which the monk totally abstains from food and liquids, even water.

Cellarer: The monk who organizes the work of a monastery and is responsible for the abbey's material needs.

Chapter: The meeting of the entire monastic community in a designated Chapter Room.

Chapter of Faults: A meeting in the Chapter Room for the purpose of having the monks "proclaim" themselves or each other for violations of their community's rule or customs.

Cistercian Order: The Order of Cistercians of the Strict Observance (O.C.S.O.), also known as the Order of Reformed Cistercians (O.C.R.), nicknamed Trappists after the reform initiated by Armand-Jean de Rancé at the Monastery of La Trappe in France. It is distinguished from the Sacred Order of Cistercians (S.O.C.), whose monks engage in active apostolates. Merton signed his monastic name M. Louis, O.C.S.O. or M. Louis, O.C.R. The M. stood for "Mary," an honorific initial in each Cistercian's name for the Mother of God, the patroness of all Cistercians.

Collation: A light refreshment in place of an evening meal on fast days: bread, fruit, and a hot drink.

Conventual Mass: A daily Solemn High Mass attended and chanted by the choir monks of the monastic community.

Enclosure: The limit defining the separation between the monastic areas (the cloister) from other places accessible to visitors.

Frustulum: A minimal breakfast taken after Chapter (around 6 A.M.) on fast days by those who were relieved from fasting until Dinner (about 11:30 A.M.).

General Chapter: The meeting every two years of all abbots and superiors of monasteries in the Cistercian Order.

Hebdomadary: A monk appointed as principal celebrant of the Conventual Mass on a weekly basis.

Incunabula: Early printed books, usually printed before the sixteenth century.

Indulgence: A supplementary portion served at every meal for the ill or young. Called the "relief" at Gethsemani.

Lay Brother: A layperson (nonclerical) who has canonical religious status in simple and solemn vows. Lay brothers devoted more time to manual labor than the choir monks and were exempt from chanting the Office.

Lectio Divina: Literally, "sacred reading," the monastic practice of slowly and meditatively reading sacred scripture.

Major Orders: The three progressive phases in the ordination of a choir monk into the priesthood. Merton was ordained a sub-deacon on December 21, 1948; ordained a deacon on March 19, 1949; and ordained a priest on May 26, 1949.

Master of Novices: The monk who supervises the formation of those aspirants in the monastery who have not yet made simple vows. Merton served as Master of Novices from September 1955 until August 20, 1965.

Master of Scholastics: The monk who supervises the formation of junior monks in temporary vows. Merton held this position from May 20, 1951, until September, 1955.

Matutinal Mass: The Low Mass (without chanting) celebrated after the office of Prime on Feasts of Sermon and Sundays.

Minor Orders: The minor orders of porter, acolyte, exorcist, and lector were conferred by an Abbot upon clerical students in the final stages of their studies.

Mixt: A light breakfast after Chapter on non-fast days.

Oblates and Family Brothers: Oblates, who wore the habit of novices, were laypersons officially recognized as living within the monastery without formal vows. Family brothers were laypersons attached to the monastery who assisted the monks in various service occupations.

Postulant: An aspirant who lives in the guest house until the Abbot receives him into the novitiate as a novice. Merton arrived at the guest house on December 10, 1941, and was officially accepted as a postulant on December 13, 1941. He became a novice on February 22, 1942; made his simple profession on March 19, 1944, and his solemn profession of vows on March 19, 1947. He was ordained a priest on May 26, 1949.

Prior: The second superior of an abbey who assumes authority when the Abbot is absent.

Refectory Reading: The monks ate their meals in silence, sitting on one side of tables set in rows facing one another. During meals a lector read from a book not always of a religious nature.

Scriptorium: A room where monks had use of common desks for study and writing.

Seniors/Seniority: Each monk's seniority at Gethsemani was an important determinant of status, e.g., his place in choir and processions. The monk longest in community life is the "most senior" and not necessarily the eldest monk.

Sign Language: Silence is a Cistercian custom, not a vow. The monks remained in recollected silence throughout the day and most particularly throughout the night hours, the Great Silence. The Cistercians adapted a monastic sign language of long usage for communicating without "sounding."

Tonsure: The custom of shaving all or part of the hair of the head as a symbol of clerical status.

Usages: Monastic regulations which governed all aspects of communal life in minute detail.

Visitation: An official annual visit of a filiation by the abbot of its founding monastery, the Father Immediate. The visitor has private appointments with each community member (the scrutiny). The visitor finally executes written recommendations, the Visitation Card.

Vows of Cistercians: Cistercians take three vows: stability within the monastery of profession; obedience to the Abbot and lawful superiors; and a third vow of conversion of manners in the monastic state, which includes poverty (common ownership of goods and a simple life) and chastity.

Index